THEORY OF COMPUTATION

A M Natarajan
Principal
Kongu Engineering College
Perundurai, Tamil Nadu

A Tamilarasi
Professor
Department of CSE
Kongu Engineering College
Perundurai, Tamil Nadu

P Balasubramani
Professor
Department of CSE
Kongu Engineering College
Perundurai, Tamil Nadu

Publishing Globally

NEW AGE INTERNATIONAL (P) LIMITED, PUBLISHERS
LONDON • NEW DELHI • NAIROBI
Bangalore • Chennai • Cochin • Guwahati • Hyderabad • Kolkata • Lucknow • Mumbai
Visit us at **www.newagepublishers.com**

Published by New Age International (P) Ltd., Publishers
First Edition: 2003
Reprint: 2020

GLOBAL OFFICES

- **New Delhi** **NEW AGE INTERNATIONAL (P) LIMITED, PUBLISHERS**
7/30 A, Daryaganj, New Delhi-110002, (INDIA)
Tel.: (011) 23253771, 23253472, **Telefax:** 23267437, 43551305
E-mail: contactus@newagepublishers.com • Visit us at www.newagepublishers.com
- **London** **NEW AGE INTERNATIONAL (UK) LTD.**
27 Old Gloucester Street, London, WC1N 3AX, UK
E-mail: info@newacademicscience.co.uk • Visit us at www.newacademicscience.co.uk
- **Nairobi** **NEW AGE GOLDEN (EAST AFRICA) LTD.**
Ground Floor, Westlands Arcade, Chiromo Road (Next to Naivas Supermarket)
Westlands, Nairobi, KENYA, **Tel.:** 00-254-713848772, 00-254-725700286
E-mail: kenya@newagepublishers.com

BRANCHES

- **Bangalore** 37/10, 8th Cross (Near Hanuman Temple), Azad Nagar, Chamarajpet, Bangalore- 560 018
Tel.: (080) 26756823, **Telefax:** 26756820, **E-mail: bangalore@newagepublishers.com**
- **Chennai** 26, Damodaran Street, T. Nagar, Chennai-600 017, **Tel.:** (044) 24353401, **Telefax:** 24351463
E-mail: chennai@newagepublishers.com
- **Cochin** CC-39/1016, Carrier Station Road, Ernakulam South, Cochin-682 016
Tel.: (0484) 2377303, **Telefax:** 4051304, **E-mail: cochin@newagepublishers.com**
- **Guwahati** Hemsen Complex, Mohd. Shah Road, Paltan Bazar, Near Starline Hotel, Guwahati-781 008
Tel.: (0361) 2513881, **Telefax:** 2543669
E-mail: guwahati@newagepublishers.com
- **Hyderabad** 105, 1st Floor, Madhiray Kaveri Tower, 3-2-19, Azam Jahi Road, Near Kumar Theater, Nimboliadda Kachiguda, Hyderabad-500 027, **Tel.:** (040) 24652456, **Telefax:** 24652457
E-mail: hyderabad@newagepublishers.com
- **Kolkata** RDB Chambers (Formerly Lotus Cinema) 106A, 1st Floor, S N Banerjee Road, Kolkata-700 014, **Tel.:** (033) 22273773, **Telefax:** 22275247
E-mail: kolkata@newagepublishers.com
- **Lucknow** 16-A, Jopling Road, Lucknow-226 001, **Tel.:** (0522) 2209578, 4045297, **Telefax:** 2204098
E-mail: lucknow@newagepublishers.com
- **Mumbai** 142C, Victor House, Ground Floor, N.M. Joshi Marg, Lower Parel, Mumbai-400 013
Tel.: (022) 24927869, **Telefax:** 24915415, **E-mail: mumbai@newagepublishers.com**
- **New Delhi** 22, Golden House, Daryaganj, New Delhi-110 002, **Tel.:** (011) 23262368, 23262370
Telefax: 43551305, **E-mail: sales@newagepublishers.com**

ISBN: 978-81-224-1473-8
C-20-01-12374

Printed in India at R.K Printers, Delhi.

NEW AGE INTERNATIONAL (P) LIMITED, PUBLISHERS
7/30 A, Daryaganj, New Delhi-110002
Visit us at **www.newagepublishers.com**
(CIN: U74899DL1966PTC004618)

Preface

Theory of Computation is an introduction to the classical contemporary theory of computation. The topics covered are: theory of automata and regular languages, pushdown automata and context free languages, computability by turing machines and recursive functions and undecidability. The treatment is mathematical but the viewpoint is that of computer science.

What is a computation? It consists of executing an algorithm; starting with some input followed by step-by-step procedure that will produce an output. In other words, computation is simply a sequence of steps that can be performed by a computer. The computers under study are not actual; they are abstract machines. This text deals with several abstract machines of models of computation which will be defined mathematically. Some of the machines are as powerful in principle as real computers (turing machines), while the simple ones are less powerful (finite state automata). *Theory of Computation* has range of applications in compiler design robotics, Artificial Intelligence (AI) and knowledge engineering.

In chapter 1 we take up several restricted model of an actual computer, called finite automation. It shares with a real computer the fact that its central processor is of fixed finite capacity, depending on its original design. However, beyond this fixed capacity to handle information, a finite automaton has no auxiliary memory at all. It receives its input as a string; the input string is delivered to it on an input tape. It delivers no output at all except an indication of whether the input is considered acceptable.

Another reason for studying finite automata is their applicability to the design of several common types of computer algorithms and programs. For example, lexical analysis phase of a compiler is often based on the simulation of finite automaton. The problem of finding an occurrence of one string with another (for example, a particular word within a large text file) can also be solved efficiently by methods originating from the theory of finite automata.

The most obvious limitation of a finite automaton is that, except for being able to keep track of its current state, such a machine can recognize only simple languages. Context free languages allow richer syntax than regular languages. They can be generated using context free grammars and can be recognized by computing devices called pushdown automata (a pushdown automata is a finite automata with an auxiliary memory in the form of a stock). Context free grammars are important in computer science because they can describe much of the syntax of high level programming languages and other related formal languages. The corresponding machine PDA, provides a natural way to approach the problem of parsing a statement in a high-level programming language: determining the syntax of the statement by reconstructing the sequence of roles by which it is derived in the context free grammar. These ideas are dealt with in chapter 2 and chapter 3. Pushdown automata are briefly discussed as an extension of finite automaton in chapter 3.

The determination pushdown automata (DPDA's) accept a family of languages, the deteministic context free languages, (DCFL's) that lies between regular sets and the context free languages. The syntax of many progamming languages can be described by means of DCFL's. LR (O) grammar generates a DCFL and for every DCFL with the prefix property there is an LR (O) grammar. These concepts are dealt in chapter 3.

The generalization of a PDA is a Turing Machine (TM) which is discussed elaborately in chapter 4. TM can be designed to accept quite complicated languages and to calculate the volumes of nontrivial arithmetical functions. A brief discussion of Church's thesis is also included in chapter 4.

A decision problem is a problem for which every specific instance can be answered in the form of 'yes' or 'no' response. Chapter 5 deals with undecidability.

In chapter 6, the closure properties of regular sets and CFL are discussed.

The explanations are given in clear and lucid way so that an average student can understand the subject easily. Numerous examples have been provided to illustrate the basic concepts.

We express our sincere gratitude to our correspondent Mr. M.N. Ramasamy and our secretary Mr. D. Venkateshwaran B.E., M.S. (USA) and all members of the KVIT trust for their constant inspiration and encouragement. Also we thank our colleagues and our students for their timely help and enthusiasm in preparing this book.

We hope that this book will be received enthusiastically and that it will be useful to students and teachers handling Theory of Computation.

Suggestions for improvement of this book are most welcome.

Authors

Contents

CHAPTER 1

Regular Languages and Finite Automata

The basic building block of programming and natural languages are the strings, a string is a sequence of symbols taken from a set of characters. In computer languages, the sequence of characters are taken from the set of ASCII characters. In any language, some strings are part of the languages and others are not. There are many ways to describe how the strings belong to a language. One way is to describe how the strings are generated from simpler strings using string operations. Another way is to specify an algorithmic procedure for *recognizing* whether a given string is in the language. Regular languages are the simplest one that are generated from one element languages by using standard operations a finite number of times. A kind of device that acts like a computer executing a program, called *finite automaton* recognizes a regular language.

Finite Automata (FA) is the first mathematical model of how a computer functions while running a program. It is used to compile a regular expression into a recognizer. A compiler is a program for translating programs written in a high-level programming language into machine language.

A compiler operates in three phases and the first phase is lexical analysis. The main task of lexical analyser is to read the input character and produce as output a sequence of tokens analysed by the parsen. The lexical analysis is based on the simulation of FA. The lex compiler constructs a transition table for a FA from the regular expression patterns in the lex specification. The lexical analyser itself consists of a finite automaton simulator that uses the transition table to look for the regular expression patterns in the input buffer.

This chapter studies the process of recognizing whether strings belong to a given language, but the later chapters study in detail the various ways of defining languages. It begins with the study of strings, languages and some other mathematical concepts. It also discusses the notions like deterministic FA, non-deterministic FA and regular expressions. Further, it provides a powerful tool, called the *pumping lemma* to show certain languages are not regular. As a highlight the last section of this chapter deals with solved problems to understand the theory well.

1.1. PRELIMINARIES

In this section the concepts like graphs, trees, sets and relations, strings, abstract languages and mathematical induction are given.

1.1.1. Alphabet

An *alphabet* is a finite set of symbols denoted by Σ.

Examples:

(*i*) $\Sigma = \{0, 1\}$, (*ii*) $\Sigma = \{a, b, c, ...\}$

(*iii*) $\Sigma = \{0, 1, a, b, ...\}$.

1.1.2. String

A *string* or *word* over an alphabet Σ is a finite ordered list of symbols chosen from the set Σ.

Examples:

(*i*) 00110, 01, 1, 0 are all strings over an alphabet $\Sigma = \{0, 1\}$

(*ii*) *abab*, *aabb*, *ab*, *ba*, *a*, are all strings over an alphabet $\Sigma = \{a, b\}$.

Note that the lower case letters like x, y, z, u, v, w denote the strings.

1.1.3. Length of a String

Let u be a string. Then the *length of the string* u is denoted by $|u|$ and defined as "the number of symbols in the string".

Examples:

(*i*) If $u = 000111$, then $|u| = 6$

(*ii*) If $u = abab$, then $|u| = 4$.

1.1.4. Empty or Null String

The string having no symbol is called the empty (or null) string. In other words, "if the length of a string is zero", then it is called *empty string* or *null string*. It is denoted by ε or λ. Hence $|\varepsilon| = |\lambda| = 0$.

1.1.5. Reverse of a String

It is obtained by writing symbols in reverse order. If u is a string, then u^R is the reverse or reflection of u.

For example, if $u = abc$, then $u^R = cba$. Let Σ be the alphabet. Then Σ^m is the set of all strings of length m with symbols from Σ.

Let $\Sigma = \{a, b\}$. Then

(*i*) $\Sigma^0 = \{\varepsilon\}$, empty string is the only string of length 0

(*ii*) $\Sigma^1 = \{a, b\}$, set of all strings over $\Sigma = \{a, b\}$ of length one

(*iii*) $\Sigma^2 = \{ab, ba, aa, bb\}$, set of all strings of length 2.

(*iv*) $\Sigma^3 = \{aaa, aab, aba, baa, abb, bab, bba, bbb\}$ and so on.

1.1.6. The Kleene Star (Closure)

Let Σ be the alphabet set. The *Kleene star* Σ^* denotes the set of all strings (including ε, the empty string) over the alphabet set Σ and $\Sigma^+ = \Sigma^* - \{\varepsilon\}$.

For Example:

(*i*) If $\Sigma = \{0\}$, then $\Sigma^* = \{\varepsilon, 0, 00, 000, ...\}$

(*ii*) If $\Sigma = \{a, b\}$, then $\Sigma^* = \{\varepsilon, a, b, aa, ab, ba, bb, aaa, ...\}$

(*iii*) If $\Sigma = \phi$ (empty set), then $\Sigma^* = \{\varepsilon\}$

Hence we write

$$\Sigma^* = \Sigma^0 \cup \Sigma^1 \cup \Sigma^2 \cup ...$$

If $\Sigma = \{x\}$, then $\Sigma^* = \{\varepsilon, x, xx, xxx, ...\}$ and

$$\Sigma^+ = \{x, xx, xxx, ...\}$$

1.1.7. Definition Substring

A string u if it appears within another string w then u is called a *substring* of w.

For example, let $w = ab\ ba\ ba$ be a string over an alphabet set $\Sigma = \{a, b\}$, then $a, ab, abb, ...$ are all substrings of w.

1.1.8. Definition Concatenation

Let u and v be any two strings of alphabet Σ. The *concatenation* of u and v denoted by uv is a new string obtained by u followed by v.

Let $u = a_1a_2 \ldots a_i$ and $v = b_1b_2 \ldots b_j$, then $uv = a_1a_2 \ldots a_i\, b_1b_2 \ldots b_j$.

Since the length of u is i and the length of v is j, then the length of uv is $i + j$. Concatenation with empty string does not change the string. That is, ε is called the *identity for concatenation* as $u\varepsilon = u = \varepsilon u$.

If $w = uv$, then u is called *prefix* of w and v is called the *suffix* of w. Generally, if $w = uv$, then u and v are substrings of w. Also $u\varepsilon = u = \varepsilon u$, therefore every string is a substring of itself, is a prefix of itself and is a suffix of itself.

If $w = 0111$, then the

$$\text{set of prefixes} = \{\varepsilon, 0, 01, 011, 0111\}$$

$$\text{set of suffixes} = \{\varepsilon, 1, 11, 111, 0111\}.$$

1.1.9. Definition Palindrome

A *palindrome* is a string which is the same whether written forward or backward.

Example. Malayalam

If the length of palindrome is even then it can be obtained by the concatenation of string and its reverse.

Example. If $u = ab$, then $u^R = ba$, and the even palindrome is *abba*.

1.1.10. Properties

(1) Concatenation on a set Σ^* is associative since for each u, v, w in Σ^*,

$$u(vw) = (uv)w$$

(2) Σ^* has left and right cancellation. For $u, v, w \in \Sigma^*$,

$$wu = wv \Rightarrow u = v \qquad \text{(left cancellation)}$$

$$uw = vw \Rightarrow u = v \qquad \text{(right cancellation)}$$

(3) For $u, v \in \Sigma^*$, we have

$$| uv | = | u | + | v |.$$

1.1.11. Languages

Let Σ be an alphabet and Σ^* be the set of all strings over Σ. Consider a subset of Σ^*. This subset is called *language* over Σ and denoted by L. *i.e.*, $L \subseteq \Sigma^*$.

If a language consists of only empty string, then $L = \{\varepsilon\}$ and it is a language over any alphabet.

Note. One must not confuse with ϕ and $\{\varepsilon]$. ϕ has no string whereas $\{\varepsilon\}$ is a language having one string namely ε.

1.1.12. Example:

(1) If $\Sigma = \{a, b]$, then $\Sigma^* = \{\varepsilon, a, b, aa, ab, ba, bb, ... \}$. Then the set $\{ab, abab, aabb\}$ is a language over Σ. Since its length is finite, it is a finite language.

(2) $L = \{a^n b^n : n \geq 0\}$ is an infinite language, because it contains an infinite string.

From the definition of languages, it is clear that it is a set. So all the operations like union, intersection and differences as in the case of sets hold true for languages also.

The *complement* of L is denoted by $\bar{L}$. Therefore

$$= \Sigma^* - L$$

The *inverse* of L is denoted by L^{-1}. Therefore

$$L^{-1} = \{w^R : w \in L\}$$

The concatenation of L_1 and L_2 is

$$L_1 L_2 = \{uv : u \in L_1 \text{ and } v \in L_2\}$$

The union of L_1 and L_2 denoted by $L_1 \cup L_2$ is

$$L_1 \cup L_2 = \{w : w \in L_1 \text{ or } w \in L_2\}.$$

The intersection of L_1 and L_2 is

$$L_1 \wedge L_2 = \{w : w \in L_1 \text{ and } w \in L_2\}.$$

1.1.13. Definition Graphs and Trees

A *graph*, denoted $G = (V, E)$ consists of a finite set of *vertices* (or nodes) V and a set E of pairs of vertices called *edges* E. An example of a graph is shown below.

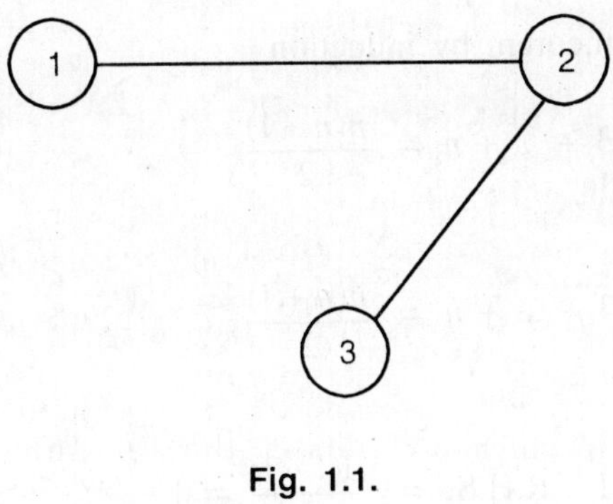

Fig. 1.1.

A *path* in a graph is a sequence of vertices $v_1, v_2, \ldots v_k$, $k \geq 1$ such that there is an edge $(v_i, v_i + 1)$ for each i, $1 \leq i < k$. The length of the path is $k - 1$. For example 1, 2, 3 is a path in graph of Fig. 1.1. If, $v_1 = v_k$ in a path, then the path is said to be *cycle*. That is a path staring and ending at a same vertex is called as a cycle.

A *Directed Graph (or Digraph)*

A directed graph is a graph with each edge directed. Example (Refer Fig. 1.2)

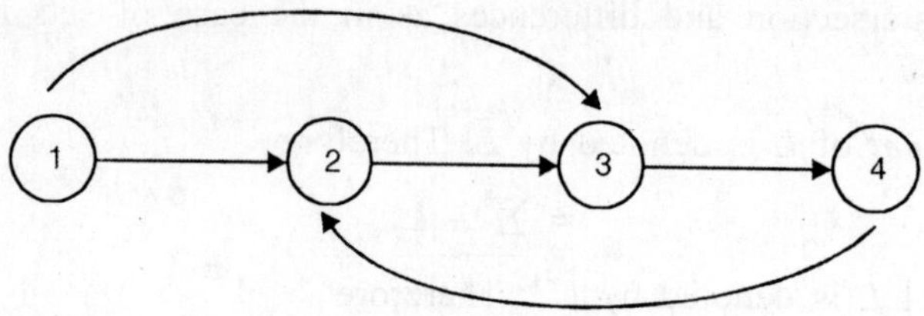

Fig. 1.2.

A *tree* is a connected graph without cycle.

1.1.14. Mathematical Induction

Many theorems in this book are proved by using mathematical induction.

Let $P(n)$ be a statement about a non negative integer n. Then the principle of mathematical induction is that $P(n)$ follows from

(*i*) $P(1)$, and

(*ii*) $P(n-1)$ implies $P(n)$ for all $n \geq 1$.

Condition (*i*) is called the *basis step* and condition (*ii*) is called the *inductive step*. $P(n-1)$ is called the *induction hypothesis.*

1.1.15. Example:

Prove the following theorem by induction

$$1 + 2 + 3 + \ldots + n = \frac{n(n+1)}{2}$$

Solution:

Let $P(n) : 1 + 2 + 3 + \ldots + n = \frac{n(n+1)}{2}$

Basis step

For $n = 1$, L.H.S. = 1, R.H.S. $= \frac{1(1+1)}{2} = 1$

Inductive step

Assume the result for $n = k$. That is, let

$$1 + 2 + 3 + \ldots + k = \frac{k(k+1)}{2}$$

We prove the result for $n = k + 1$. Now

$$1 + 2 + 3 + \ldots + k + (k + 1) = \left(\frac{k(k+1)}{2}\right) + (k+1)$$

$$= (k+1)\left[\frac{k}{2}+1\right]$$

$$= \frac{(k+1)(k+2)}{2}$$

Hence the result is true for $n = k + 1$. By induction the result is true for all n.

1.1.16. Sets

Set is a collection of objects without repetition. The elements of a set are called *members or objects.* The sets are usually denoted by capital letters like A, B, ... , X, Y... . The elements are denoted by small letters a, b, ... , x, y, ...

We denote set by set builder notation as

$$\{x \in A : P(x)].$$

That is, the set of all elements in A such that $P(x)$ is true, where $P(x)$ is some statement about objects x.

If every A is a member of B, then we write $A \subseteq B$ and say A is *contained* in B. Two sets A and B are said to be *equal* if they have the same mumbers. That is, $A = B$ if and only if $A \subseteq B$ and $B \subseteq A$.

Set Operations.

(*i*) $A \cup B$, the *union* of A and B is

$\{x : x$ is in A or x is in $B\}$

(*ii*) $A \cap B$, the *intersection* of A and B is

$\{x : x$ is in A and x is in $B\}$

(*iii*) $A - B$, the *difference* of A and B, is

$\{x : x$ is in A and x is not in $B\}$

(*iv*) $A \times B$, the *cartesian product* of A and B, is

$\{(x, y) : x \in A$ and $y \in B\}$

(*v*) The power set of A, denoted by 2^A, is the set of all subsets of A.

Example. Let $A = \{1, 2]$, $B = \{2, 3\}$. Then

$$A \cup B = \{1, 2, 3\};\ A \cap B = \{2\},\ A - B = \{1\},$$

$$A \times B = \{(1, 2), (1, 3), (2, 2), (2, 3)\}$$

and $$2^A = \{\phi, \{1\}, \{2\}, \{1, 2\}\}$$

The number of elements in a set A is said to be cardinality of A and is denoted by $|A|$ or $n(A)$ or A set having finite number of elements is called a *finite set.* Otherwise, it is called as an *infinite set.*

A binary relation R from a set A into another set B, is a subset of $A \times B$. That is, R is said to be a *relation* iff $R \subseteq A \times B$. If R is a relation, and $(a, b) \in R$, then we often write aRb.

Properties of Relations: Let R be a relation on a set S. Then R is said to be a *reflexive relation* if aRa for all $a \in S$. R is said to be a *symmetric relation* if aRb implies bRa. The relation R is said to be *transitive* if aRb, bRc implies aRc. A relation which is reflexive, symmetric and transitive is said to be an *equivalence relation.* A relation R is said to be *antisymmetric* if aRb, bRa implies $a = b$. The relation R which is reflexive, antisymmetric, transitive is said to be *partial order relation.*

Let R be an equivalence relation on S. Let $a \in R$. The equivalence class of a denoted by $[a]$ is

$$[a] = \{b \in S : aRb\}.$$

Note the R partition S into disjoint non-empty equivalence classes such that

$$[a] \cap [b] = \phi \text{ for } a \neq b$$

$$\bigcup_{a \in S} = S.$$

Example: Let a, b be any two integers and n be a non-negative integer. Define $a \equiv_n b$ or $a \equiv b(\text{mod } n) \Leftrightarrow a - b$ is divisible by n. Then $\equiv_n$ is an equivalence relation. That is

(*i*) $a \equiv_n a$, as $a - a = 0$ is divisible by n.

(*ii*) If $a \equiv_n b$, then $a - b$ is divisible by n. That is $(a - b) = nk$ for some integer k. So, $b - a = -(a - b) = -nk = n(-k)$.
Hence $b \equiv_n a$ which implies $\equiv_n$ is a symmetric relation.

(*iii*) If $a \equiv_n b$, $b \equiv_n c$, then $a - b = nk$, $b - c = nl$, for some integers k and l. Now

$$a - c = (a - b) + (b - c) = nk + nl = n(k + l)$$

As $k + l$ is an integer, n divides $a - c$ which implies $\equiv_n$ is transitive and hence $\equiv_n$ is an equivalence relation. The equivalence classes are n in number which are:

$$\{\ldots., -n, 0, n, 2n, \ldots.\}$$

$$\{\ldots., -(n - 1), 1, n + 1, 2n + 1, \ldots.\}$$

$$\{\ldots., -1, n - 1, 2n - 1, 3n - 1, \ldots.\}$$

Closure of relations

Let $\wp$ be either reflexive, symmetric or transitive relation. Then the $\wp$-closure of a relation R is the smallest relation that contains R as a subset and possesses the properties reflexive (or) symmetric (or) transitive in $\wp$. For example, the transitive closure of R, denoted by R^+ is the relation which contains R as subset and it is the smallest transitive relation.

$$R^+ = R \cup R^2 \cup R^3 \cup \ldots$$

For example, let $R = \{(1, 2), (2, 3), (3, 4)]$ be a relation on the set $\{1, 2, 3, 4]$.

Then $\quad R^+ = R \cup R^2 \cup R^3$

where $\quad R^2 = \{(1, 3), (2, 4)\}$

$$R^3 = \{(1, 4)\}$$

$$R^4 = \phi = R^5 = \ldots.$$

Hence $\quad R^+ = \{(1, 2), (2, 3), (3, 4), (1, 3), (2, 4), (1, 4)\}.$

1.17. Functions

A *function* or a map from a set X in to a set Y is a rule which assigns to every element x in X a unique element in Y which is denoted by $f(x)$. The element $f(x)$ is called the *image* of x under f. The function is denoted by $f : X \to Y$.

Example: $f : Z \to Z$, where Z is the set of integers, defined by $f(x) = x + 3$ is a function.

A function $f : X \to Y$ is said to be *one-to-one* (*or injective*) if different elements in X have different images. That is,

$$f(x_1) = f(x_2) \Rightarrow x_1 = x_2.$$

A function $f : X \to Y$ is said to be *onto* (*surjective*) if for every element y in Y there exists an element $x \in X$ such that $f(x) = y$.

A function which is both one-to-one and onto is said to be a *bijection* or in *one-to-one* correspondence.

Example:

(*i*) $f : Z \to Z$ given by $f(x) = 2x$ is *one-to-one* but not *onto*.

(*ii*) The function $f : R \to R - \{1]$, where R is the set of real numbers, defined by

$$f(x) = \frac{x+1}{x-1} \text{ is } onto.$$

(*iii*) The function $f : Z \rightarrow 2Z$ defined by $f(x) = 2x$ is both *one-to-one* and *onto*.

1.1.18. Pigeon Hole Principle

Let D and R be finite sets. If $| D | > | R |$, then for any fuction $f : D \rightarrow R$, there exist $d_1, d_2 \in D$ such that $f(d_1) = f(d_2)$.

1.2. FINITE STATE SYSTEMS

The finite automaton is a mathematical model of a system with discrete inputs, discrete outputs and a finite number of memory configurations called as '*states*'.

The state of a system summarizes the information concerning past inputs that is needed to determine the behaviour of the system on subsequent inputs.

1.2.1. Example

A switching circuit is a finite state system where the states of a switching network with n gates is any one of the 2^n assignments of 0 or 1 to the various gates. Although the voltage on each gate can assume any of an infinite set of values, the electronic circuitary is so designed that only the two voltages corresponding to 0 and 1 are stable and other voltages will almost instantaneously adjust themselves to one of these voltages.

1.2.2. Example

Computer itself can be viewed as a finite state system. Theoretically the state of the system is a central processor, main memory, and auxiliary storage at any time is one of a very large but finite number of states. One cannot extend the memory indefinitely.

1.2.3. Example

Human brain can be viewed as a finite state system. The states are the brain cells or neurons which are estimated as 2^{35}.

A special class of finite state system, is a *finite state automata,* which is the simplest model of the workings of a computer program. Finite automatons are used to model processes which involve the determination of whether a particular string is acceptable for a specific purpose.

Basic Definition

A *Finite Automaton* (FA) or *Finite State Automaton* (FSA) consists of a finite set of states and a set of transitions from state to state that occur on input symbols chosen from an alphabet Σ. For the same input symbol there may be zero, one or more transition from each state. One state usually denoted by q_0 is the *initial state* in which the automaton starts. Some states are designated as *final* or *accepting states*. For each input symbol, if there is exactly one transition from each state, then the FA is said to be *Deterministic Finite State Automaton* (DFA); otherwise the finite state automaton is called *Non Deterministic Finite State Automaton* (NFA).

A finite automaton provides a function from Σ^* into {Yes, No] in the following way:

Given a string in Σ^* with first symbol x, first the value of $\delta(q_0, x) = q_1$ is evaluated. Suppose the next input symbol is y, then the value of $\delta(q_1, y)$ is evaluated, until the last symbol in the input string is reached. If the final evaluation of δ leads to a accepting state, then the string is said to be *accepted* or *recognized* by the automaton, and regarded the automaton as having returned a value of yes. If the final evaluation of δ does not leads to accepting state, then the string in question is said to be *rejected*, and the automaton is regarded as returned to a value of No.

Before proceeding further, a formal definition of DFA is given and then describe a way to represent FA as directed graphs.

1.2.4. Deterministic Finite State Automaton (DFA)

A deterministic finite state automaton is specified by a 5-tuple $(Q, \Sigma, \delta, q_0, F)$ where

Q = a finite set of states

Σ = a finite set of input alphabet

q_0 = the initial state

F = the set of final states and $F \subseteq Q$

δ = $Q \times \Sigma \rightarrow Q$, the transition function such that $\delta(q, a)$ is a state for each state q and for each input symbol a.

Finite Control

It is main part of a finite automata, also called *black box* and contains all the transition states either deterministic or non determinisitic.

DFA has an input tape of cells, a reading head and finite control. (See Fig. 1.3.)

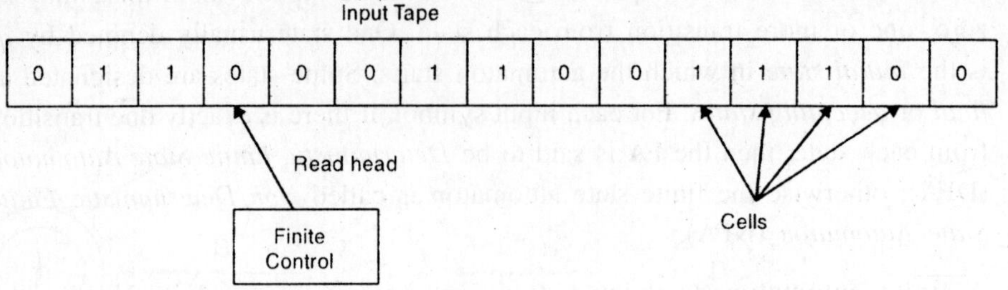

Fig. 1.3.

In one move, the FSA in state q and scanning the symbol 'a' enters state $\delta(q, a)$ and moves its head one symbol to the right. If $\delta(q, a)$ is an accepting state, then FSA is said to have accepted the string on its input tape.

Note:

The transition function $\delta : Q \times \Sigma \rightarrow Q$ can be extended to the function $\hat{\delta} : Q \times \Sigma^* \rightarrow Q$. That is $\hat{\delta}(q, w)$ is the unique state p such that there is a path in the transition diagram from q to p labeled w. We define

(*i*) $\hat{\delta}(q, \varepsilon) = q$

(*ii*) $\hat{\delta}(q, wa) = \delta(\hat{\delta}(q, w), a)$

for all strings $w \in \Sigma^*$ and input symbols a.

(*i*) says that if the input is an empty string, then the automata does not change its state.

(*ii*) tells how to find the state after reading a non-empty input string wa. Since $\hat{\delta}(q, a) = \delta(\hat{\delta}(q, \varepsilon), a) = \delta(q, a)$ (substituting $w = \varepsilon$ in (*ii*)) we can consider δ instead of $\hat{\delta}$ hereafter.

Often directed graph is used to represent the action of a finite automaton, which is defined as follows.

1.2.5. Definition

A *transition diagram* associated with DFA is a directed graph whose vertices are the states of DFA. The edges of the graph are the transitions from one state to another state.

1.2.6. Example

The transition diagram of a DFA $M = (Q = \{q_0, q_1, q_2\}, \Sigma = \{a, b\}, q_0, \delta,$

$F = \{q_2\})$, where δ is defined as

$\delta(q_0, a) = q_1$; $\delta(q_1, a) = q_2$; $\delta(q_2, b) = q_1$, is illustrated in Fig. 1.4.

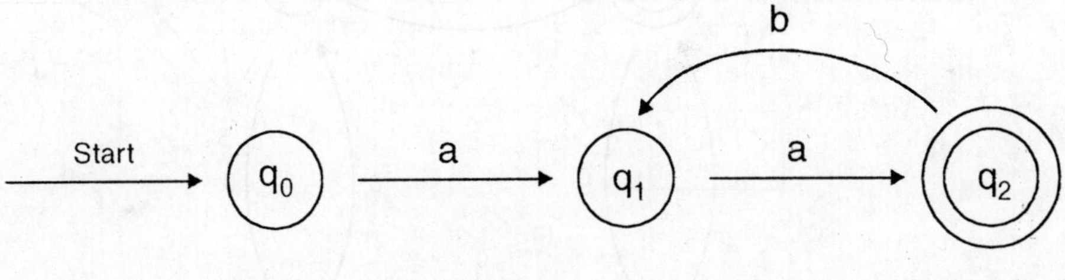

Fig. 1.4.

The initial state q_0 is indicated by the arrow labeled "start". There is one final state q_2 indicated by double circle.

1.2.7. Definition

A string x is said to be *accepted* by a finite state automata $M = (Q, \Sigma, \delta, q_0, F)$ if $\delta(q_0, x) = p$ for some $p \in F$. The language accepted by M denoted by $L(M)$ is the set $\{x : \delta(q_0, x) \in F\}$. A language is said to be a *regular set* or *regular language* if it is accepted by some FSA.

Let $M = (Q, \Sigma, \delta, q_0, F)$ be a DFA. A word qx is said to be a *configuration* of M, where $q \in Q$, $x \in \Sigma^*$. It represent the current state of M and the remaining unread input of M. Initially, M is in configuration $q_0\, x$, where x is the input word. Finally, when M has read all its input, then M is in configuration p for some p. If px and qy are any two configurations of M, then we write

$$px \vdash qy$$

if $x = ay$ for some a $\in \Sigma$ and $\delta(p, a) = q$.

$$px \vdash^{k} qy$$

means k steps of M on px.

1.2.8. Definition

The table which represent the list of transition rules (functions) of a finite automaton is called *transition table*. With the help of transition table one can easily observe the different transitions of FSA.

1.2.9. Example

Find the language accepted by the given DFA as in Fig. 1.5.

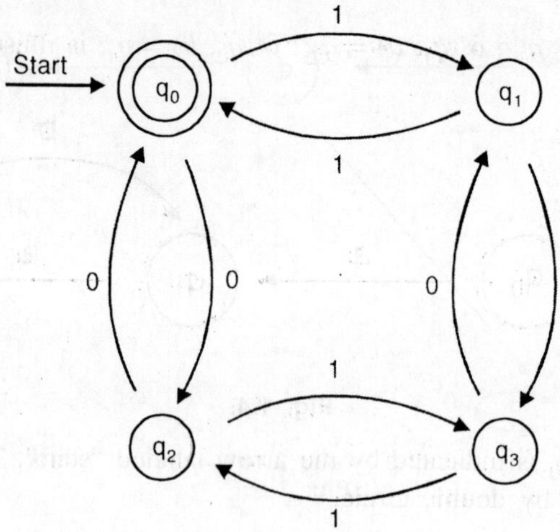

Fig. 1.5.

Solution

Let $M = (Q, \Sigma, q_0, \delta, F)$ be the DFA with $Q = \{q_0, q_1, q_2, q_3\}$, $\Sigma = \{0, 1\}$, $F = \{q_0\}$ and δ is given by the table 1.1.

Table 1.1.

States	Inputs	
	0	*1*
q_0	q_2	q_1
q_1	q_3	q_0
q_2	q_0	q_3
q_3	q_1	q_2

$$\delta(q_0, 11) = \delta(\delta(q_0, 1), 1) = \delta(q_1, 1) = q_0$$

Hence $11 \in L(M)$. similarly we find

$$\delta(q_0, 1010) = q_0, \ \delta(q_0, 110101) = q_0.$$

Thus $1010 \in L(M)$, $110101 \in L(M)$. So $L(M)$ is the set of all strings with an ever number of 0's and even number of 1's.

1.2.10. Example

Describe the language accepted by DFA M whose transition diagram is given in Fig. 1.6.

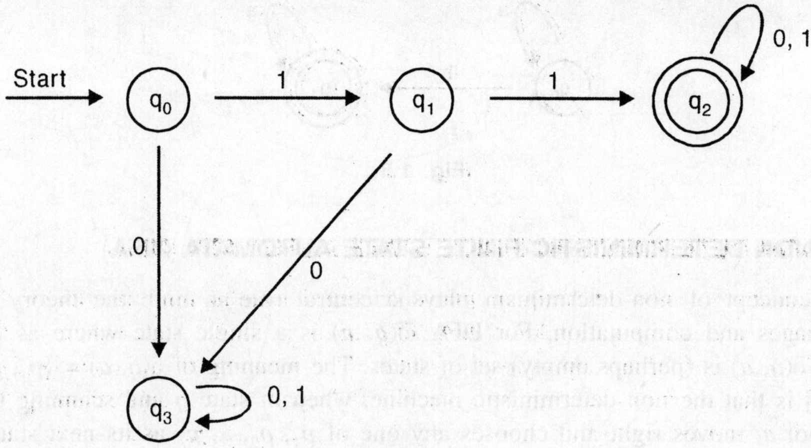

Fig. 1.6.

Solution

$$\delta(q_0,\ 0) = q_3, \text{ non accepting state}$$
$$\delta(q_0,\ 10) = \delta(q_1,\ 0) = q_3, \text{ non accepting state}$$
$$\delta(q_0,\ 11) = q_2, \text{ accepting state}$$
$$\delta(q_0,\ 110^*) = q_2, \text{ accepting state}$$
$$\delta(q_0,\ 110^*\ 1^*) = q_2, \text{ accepting state.}$$

Hence the strings of 0 and 1 that begins with two 1's is accepted by M.

1.2.11. Example

Design a DFA that accepts the strings having (*i*) even number of a's (*ii*) exactly one b over the input set $\{a, b]$.

Solution

(*i*) Let $Q = \{q_0, q_1\}$, $\Sigma = \{a, b\}$, $F = \{q_0\}$ and the transition diagram is

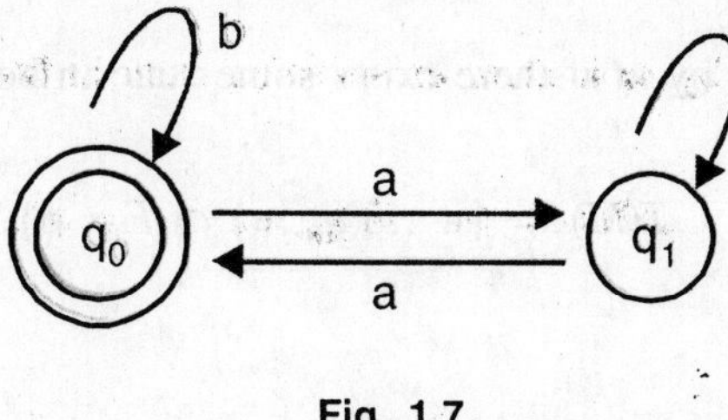

Fig. 1.7.

(*ii*) Let $Q = \{q_0, q_1\}$, $\Sigma = \{a, b\}$, $F = \{q_1\}$ and the transition diagram is

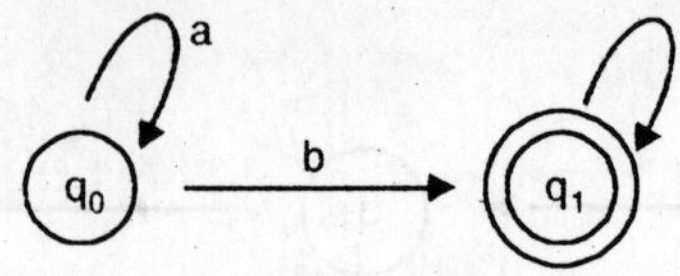

Fig. 1.8.

1.3. NON DETERMINISTIC FINITE STATE AUTOMATA (NFA)

The concept of non-determinism plays a central role in both the theory of languages and computation. For DFA, $\delta(q, a)$ is a single state where as for NFA $\delta(q, a)$ is (perhaps empty) set of states. The meaning of $\delta(q, a) = \{p_1, p_2, \ldots p_n]$ is that the non deterministic machine, when in state q and scanning the symbol a, moves right and chooses any one of $p_1, p_2, \ldots p_n$ as its next state.

1.3.1. Definition

A *non deterministic finite state automaton* M is a 5-tuple $(Q, \Sigma, q_0, \delta, F)$, where Q is a finite set of states, Σ is a finite set of input symbols, $q_0 \in Q$ is the initial state, δ is a mapping of $Q \times \Sigma$ into 2^Q, the set of all subsets of Q, and $F \subseteq Q$ is the set of final states.

The function δ can be extended to a function $\hat{\delta}$ mapping $Q \times \Sigma^*$ to 2^Q such that

$$\hat{\delta}(q, \varepsilon) = \{q\}$$

$$\hat{\delta}(q, wa) = \bigcup_{p \in \hat{\delta}(q, w)} \delta(p, a) \text{ for each } w \in \Sigma^*, a \in \Sigma.$$

Since $\hat{\delta}(q, a) = \delta(q, a)$ for an input symbol 'a' we may use δ in place of n. Also

$$\delta(\{p_1, p_2, \ldots p_n\}, x) = \bigcup_{i=1}^{n} \delta(p_i, x).$$

1.3.2. Definition

A language is **accepted** by M if there exists some state in both F and $\delta(q_0, w)$. That is

$$T(M) = \{w : \delta(q_0, w) \cap F \neq \phi\}.$$

1.3.3. Example

Construct a machine that accepts the set of all strings in $\{a, b, c]^*$ such that the last symbol in the input string also appears earlier in the string. That is a string of the form $bacb \in T(M)$, but $cbbca \notin T(M)$.

Solution

Let $M = (\{a, b, c\}, \{q_0, q_1, q_2, q_3, q_4\}, q_0, \delta, \{q_4\})$ and δ is defined by the Table 1.2.

Table 1.2.

States	*Inputs*		
	a	*b*	*c*
q_0	$\{q_0, q_1\}$	$\{q_0, q_2\}$	$\{q_0, q_3\}$
q_1	$\{q_1, q_4\}$	$\{q_1\}$	$\{q_1\}$
q_2	$\{q_2\}$	$\{q_2, q_4\}$	$\{q_2\}$
q_3	$\{q_3\}$	$\{q_3\}$	$\{q_3, q_4\}$
q_4	ϕ	ϕ	ϕ

The transition diagram is given by Fig. 1.9.

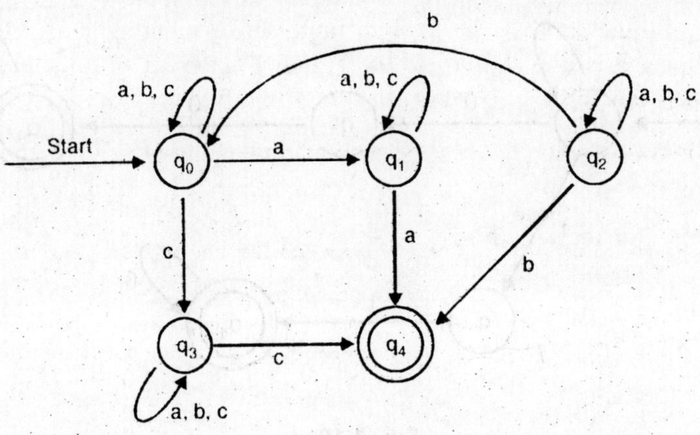

Fig. 1.9.

If $w = a\ c\ a$, then

$$\delta(q_0, aca) = \delta(\delta\ (q_0, a), ca)$$

$$= \delta(\{q_0, q_1\}, ca)$$

$$= \delta(q_0, ca) \cup \delta\ (q_1, ca)$$

$$\delta(q_0, ca) = \delta(\delta(q_0, c), a)$$

$$= \delta(\{q_0, q_3\}, a)$$

$$= \delta(q_0, a) \cup \delta(q_3, a)$$

$$\delta(q_0, a) = \{q_0, q_1\}$$

$$\delta(q_3, a) = \{q_3\}$$

$$\delta(q_1, ca) = \delta(\delta(q_1, c), a) = \delta(q_1, a) = \{q_1, q_4\}$$

Hence $$\delta(q_0, aca) = \delta(q_0, ca) \cup \delta(q_1, ca)$$

$$= \{q_0, q_1, q_3\} \cup \{q_1, q_4\}$$

$$= \{q_0, q_1, q_3, q_4\}$$

and since $\delta(q_0, aca) \cap \{q_4\} \neq \phi$, the string *aca* is accepted by the machine.

1.3.4. Example

Consider the NFA given in Fig. 1.10.

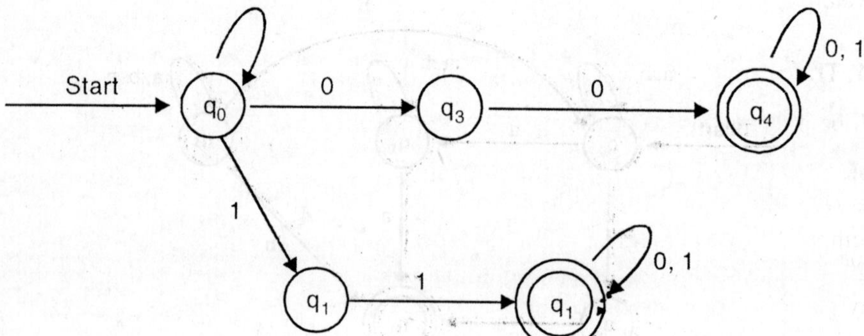

Fig. 1.10.

The transition table is given by

States	*Inputs*	
	0	*1*
q_0	$\{q_0, q_3\}$	$\{q_0, q_1\}$
q_1	–	$\{q_2\}$
q_2	$\{q_2\}$	$\{q_2\}$
q_3	$\{q_4\}$	–
q_4	$\{q_4\}$	$\{q_4\}$

Let the input string be 01001. Then

$$\delta(q_0, 0) = \{q_0, q_3\}$$

$$\begin{aligned}\delta(q_0, 01) &= \delta(\delta(q_0, 0), 1)\\ &= \delta(\{q_0, q_3\}, 1)\\ &= \delta(q_0, 1) \cup \delta(q_3, 1)\\ &= \{q_0, q_1\}\end{aligned}$$

similarly we compute

$$\delta(q_0, 010) = \{q_0, q_3\},\ \delta(q_0, 0100) = \{q_0, q_3, q_4\}$$

and $$\delta(q_0, 01001) = \{q_0, q_1, q_4\}.$$

1.4. EQUIVALENCE OF DFA AND NFA

As every DFA is an NFA, the class of languages accepted by NFA's includes the class languages accepted by DFA's. For every NFA we can construct an equivalent DFA.

1.4.1. Theorem

Let L be a language accepted by a NFA. Then there exists a DFA that accepts L.

Proof. Let $M = (Q, \Sigma, \delta, q_0, F)$ be an NFA accepting L. Define a DFA $M^1 = (Q^1, \Sigma^1, \delta^1, q_0^1, F^1)$ as follows. The states of M^1 are all the possible non-empty subsets of the set of states for M. If M has n states (say), then M^1 has $2^n - 1$ states which permit it to simulate all the states in which M could be at any particular point in time. The state symbols in Q^1 will be denoted by $[q_0]$, $[q_1]$, ..., $[q_{n-1}]$, $[q_0, q_1]$, $[q_0, q_2]$, ... $[q_0, q_{n-1}]$, $[q_1, q_2]$, ... $[q_1, q_{n-1}]$... $[q_{n-2}, q_{n-1}]$, ... $[q_0, q_1, q_2]$, ... $[q_0, q_1, ... q_{n-1}]$. Also $\delta^1(q_0^1, x) \in F^1$ exactly when $\delta(q_0, x) \cap F \neq \phi$. Both machines have the same alphabet and $q_0^1 = [q_0]$.

Define δ^1 as follows.

$$\delta^1([q_1, q_2, ..., q_i], a) = [p_1, p_2, ..., p_j]$$

if and only if

$$\delta(\{q_1, q_2, ..., q_i\}, a) = \{p_1, p_2, ..., p_j\}$$

That is, if we apply δ to each of $q_1, q_2, ... q_i$ and taking the union, we get some new set of states $p_1, p_2, ...p_j$. This new set of states has representative $[p_1, p_2, ... p_j] \in Q^1$ and that the element is the value of $\delta^1([q_1, q_2, ..., q_i], a)$. By construction it is clear that M^1 is deterministic.

We must now show that $T(M^1) = T(M)$. We prove by induction on the length of the input string x that $\delta^1(q_0^1, x) = [p_1, p_2, ...p_j] \Leftrightarrow \delta(q_0, x) = \{p_1, p_2, ...,p_j\}$.

Basis step. If w is of length zero, *i.e.* w in an empty stringe ε, then δ^1 ($[q_0]$, $\varepsilon = [q_0]$) and $\delta(q_0, w)$ if and only if $\delta(q_0, \varepsilon) = q_0$.

Induction step. Suppose that the result is true for inputs of length n or less. Now we prove the results for string of length $n + 1$. Let $w = xa$ be a string with x having length n and $a \in \Sigma$. Then by induction assumption,

$$\begin{aligned} \delta^1(q_0{}^1, xa) &= \delta^1(\delta^1(q_0{}^1, x), a) \\ &= \delta^1([p_1, p_2, \ldots p_j], a) \\ &= [r_1, r_2, \ldots, r_k] \end{aligned}$$

if and only if

$$\delta(\{p_1, p_2, \ldots p_j\}, a) = \{r_1, r_2, \ldots r_k\}.$$

Thus, $\delta^1(q_0{}^1, xa) = [r_1, r_2, \ldots r_k]$.

if and only if $\delta(q_0, xa) = \{r_1, r_2, \ldots r_k\}$.

Hence the result is true for a string of length $n + 1$. By induction hypothesis the result is true for all n. Thus M and M^1 both accept the same string w if and only if δ^1 $(q_0{}^1, x)$ or $\delta(q_0, x)$ respectively contains a state in F^1. Therefore $T(M) = T(M^1)$.

Note. As DFA and NFA accept the same sets, we shall not distinguish between them unless it becomes necessary and we refer both as finite automata.

1.4.2. Example

Construct a DFA equivalent to the NFA

$M = (\{q_0, q_1\}, \{0, 1\}, \delta, q_0, \{q_1\})$ where δ is given by the Table 1.4.

Table 1.4.

States	*Inputs*	
	0	*1*
q_0	$\{q_0, q_1\}$	q_1
q_1	–	$\{q_0, q_1\}$

Solution

Construct a DFA $M^1 = (Q^1, \{0, 1\}, \delta^1, \{q_0\}, F^1)$ accepting $L(M)$ as follows :

$$\begin{aligned} Q^1 &= \text{set of all subsets of } \{q_0, q_1\} \text{ (except the empty set)} \\ &= \{[q_0], [q_1], [q_0, q_1]\} \end{aligned}$$

Since $\delta(q_0, 0) = \{q_0, q_1\}$, $\delta^1([q_0], 0) = [q_0, q_1]$. Similarly we have

$$\delta^1([q_0], 1) = [q_1], \text{ since } \delta(q_0, 1) = \{q_1\}$$

$$\delta^1([q_0], 0) = [q_0, q_1], \text{ since } \delta(q_0, 0) = \{q_0, q_1\}$$

$$\delta^1([q_0, q_1], 0) = [q_0, q_1], \text{ since } \delta(\{q_0, q_1,\}, 0) = \delta\{q_0, 0\} \cup \delta\{q_1, 0\} = \{q_0, q_1\}$$

$$\delta^1([q], 1) = [q_0, q_1], \text{ since } \delta\{q_1, 1\} = \{q_0, q_1\}$$

$$\delta^1([q_0, q_1], 1) = [q_0, q_1], \text{ since}$$

$$\delta(\{q_0, q_1\}, 1) = \delta\{q_0, 1\} \cup \delta\{q_1, 1\} = \{q_1\} \cup \{q_0, q_1\} = \{q_0, q_1\}.$$

The transition table for DFA is :

Table 1.5.

States	*Inputs*	
	0	*1*
$[q_0]$	$[q_0, q_1]$	$[q_1]$
$[q_1]$	–	$[q_0, q_1]$
$[q_0, q_1]$	$[q_0, q_1]$	$[q_0, q_1]$

The set of final states of $M^1 = ([q_1], [q_0, q_1])$.

1.4.3. Example

Let $M = (\{q_0, q_1, q_2\}, \{a, b\}, q_0, \delta, \{q_2\})$ be a non deterministic finite state automaton, where δ is given as follows.

$$\delta(q_0, a) = \{q_0, q_1\}; \quad \delta\{q_0, b\} = \{q_2\};$$

$$\delta\{q_1, a\} = \{q_1\}; \quad \delta\{q_1, b] = \{q_0\};$$

$$\delta\{q_2, a\} = \{q_0\}; \quad \delta\{q_2, b\} = \{q_1, q_2\}.$$

Construct an equivalent DFA.

Solution

We construct $M^1 = (Q^1, \{a, b\}, [q_0], \delta^1, F^1)$ an equivalent DFA which accepts T(M) as follows :

Q^1 contains all subsets of $\{q_0, q_1, q_2\}$ (except the empty set); that is

$$Q^1 = \{[q_0], [q_1], [q_2], [q_0, q_1], [q_0, q_2], [q_1, q_2], [q_0, q_1, q_2]\}$$

Since $\delta\{q_0, a\} = \{q_0, q_1\}$, $\delta^1([q_0], a) = [q_0, q_1]$.

Similarly,

$$\delta^1([q_0], b) = [q_2]; \quad \delta^1([q_1], a) = [q_1]$$

$$\delta^1([q_2], a) = [q_0]; \quad \delta^1([q_2], b) = [q_1, q_2]$$

$$\delta^1([q_1], b) = [q_0];$$

and $\delta^1([q_0, q_1], a) = [q_0, q_1]$

since $\delta([q_0, q_1], a) = \delta[q_0, a] \cup \delta[q_1, a] = [q_0, q_1] \cup [q_1] = [q_0, q_1]$.

Also, since $\delta(\{q_0, q_1\}, b) = \delta\{q_0, b\} \cup \delta\{q_1, b\} = \{q_0, q_2\}$,

$$\delta^1([q_0, q_1], b) = [q_0, q_2].$$

Similarly we prove

$$\delta^1([q_0, q_2], a) = [q_0, q_1]; \quad \delta^1([q_0, q_2], b) = [q_1, q_2]$$

$$\delta^1([q_1, q_2], a) = [q_0, q_1]; \quad \delta^1([q_1, q_2], b) = [q_0, q_1, q_2]$$

$$\delta^1([q_0, q_1, q_2], a) = [q_0, q_1]; \quad \delta^1([q_0, q_1, q_2], b) = [q_0, q_1, q_2]$$

The transition table is given as :

Table 1.6.

States	Inputs	
	a	b
$[q_0]$	$[q_0, q_1]$	$[q_2]$
$[q_1]$	$[q_1]$	$[q_0]$
$[q_2]$	$[q_0]$	$[q_1, q_2]$
$[q_0, q_2]$	$[q_0, q_1]$	$[q_0, q_2]$
$[q_0, q_2]$	$[q_0, q_1]$	$[q_1, q_2]$
$[q_1, q_2]$	$[q_0, q_1]$	$[q_0, q_1, q_2]$
$[q_0, q_1, q_2]$	$[q_0, q_1]$	$[q_0, q_1, q_2]$

The set of final states of F^1 is given by

$$F^1 = \{[q_2], [q_0, q_2], [q_1, q_2], [q_0, q_1, q_2]\}.$$

1.5. FINITE AUTOMATON WITH ε-MOVES

We may extend the NFA to include transitions on the empty input ε. Usually, an NFA accepts a string w if there is some path labeled ε from the initial state to a final state. Of course, edges labeled ε may be included in the path, although ε's do not appear explicity in w. For example, the word 012 is accepted by the NFA of Fig. 1.11 by the path $q_0\ q_0\ q_1\ q_1\ q_2\ q_2$ with arcs labeled 0 ε 1 ε 2.

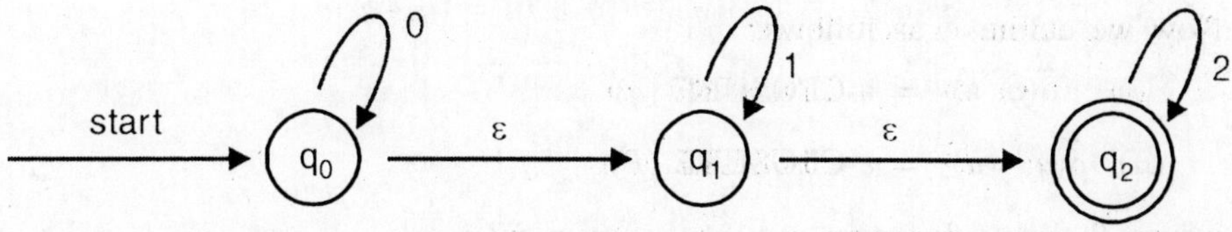

Fig. 1.11.

1.5.1. Definition

The quintuple $(Q, \Sigma, \delta, q_0, F)$ with all components as before but δ the transition function maps $Q \times (\Sigma \times \{\varepsilon\})$ to 2^Q is said to be *non deterministic finite automata with ε-moves.*

Note that $\delta(q, a)$ will consist of all states p such that there is a transition labeled 'a' from q to p, where 'a' is either ε or any symbol in Σ.

We extend the transition function δ to a function $\hat{\delta} : Q \times \Sigma^* \rightarrow 2^Q$ such that $\hat{\delta}(q, w)$ will be all states p such that we go from q to p along a path labeled w, also including edges labeled ε. In constructing $\hat{\delta}$ it will be important to compute the set of states reachable from a given state q using ε transitions only. We use ε-CLOSURE (q) to denote the set of all vertices p such that there is a path from q to p labeled ε. A path of length zero has no arcs, and therefore trivially all its arcs are labeled ε.

1.5.2. Example

The transition function for NFA of Fig. 1.11. is Table 1.7.

Table 1.7.

States	*Inputs*			
	0	*1*	2	ε
q_0	$\{q_0\}$	–	–	$\{q_1\}$
q_1	–	$\{q_1\}$	–	$\{q_2\}$
q_2	–	–	$\{q_2\}$	–

The ε-CLOSURE $(q_0) = \{q_0, q_1, q_2\}$. That is the path consisting of q_0 alone (there are no arcs on the path), is a path from q_0 to q_0 with all arcs labeled ε. Path from q_0 to q_1 labeled ε shows that $q_1 \in$ ε-CLOSURE (q_0) and path q_0, q_1, q_2 shows that $q_2 \in$ ε-CLOSURE (q_0).

1.5.3. Definition

Let P be a set of states. Then ε-CLOSURE $(P) = \bigcup_{q \in P} \varepsilon-\text{CLOSURE}\,(q)$

Now we define $\hat{\delta}$ as follows:

(*i*) $\hat{\delta}(q, \varepsilon) = \varepsilon\text{-CLOSURE}\,(q)$

(*ii*) $\hat{\delta}(q, wa) = \varepsilon\text{-CLOSURE}\,(P)$,

where $P = \{p : \text{for some } r \in \hat{\delta}(q, w)\ p \in \delta\,(r, a)\}$.

$w \in \Sigma^*, a \in \Sigma.$

(*iii*) $\delta(R, a) = \bigcup_{q \in R} \delta(q, a)$

(*iv*) $\hat{\delta}(R, w) = \bigcup_{q \in R} \hat{\delta}(q, w)$

for set of states R.

Note. $\hat{\delta}(q, a)$ is not necessarily equal to $\delta(q, a)$, since $\hat{\delta}(q, a)$ includes all states reachable from q by paths labeled a (including paths labeled ε), while $\delta(q, a)$ includes only those states reachable from q by arc labeled a. Similarly is not necessarily equal to $\delta(q, \varepsilon)$. So there is a distinction between δ and $\hat{\delta}(q, \varepsilon)$ for NFA with ε-transitions.

We define T(M) the langulage accepted by $M = (Q, \Sigma, \delta, q_0, F)$ to be

$$T(M) = \{w : \hat{\delta}(q_0, w) \text{ contains a state in } F\}$$

1.5.4. Example

Consider the NFA with ε-moves

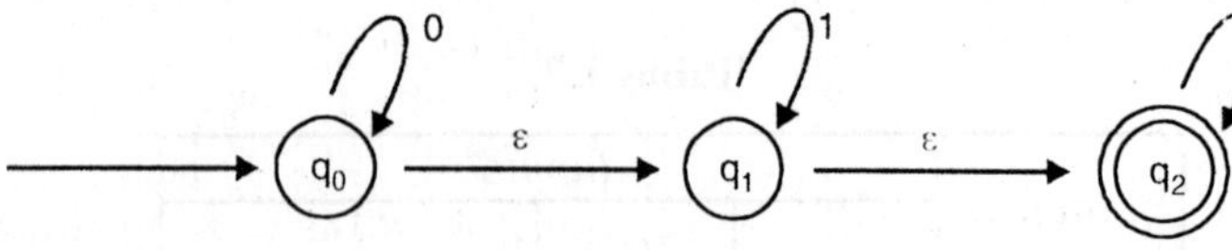

Fig. 1.12.

$$\begin{aligned}
\hat{\delta}(q_0, \varepsilon) &= \varepsilon\text{-CLOSURE}\,(q_0) = \{q_0, q_1, q_2\} \\
\hat{\delta}(q_0, 0) &= \varepsilon\text{-CLOSURE}\,(\delta\,(\hat{\delta}\{q_0, \varepsilon\}, 0) \\
&= \varepsilon\text{-CLOSURE}\,(\delta\{q_0, q_1, q_2\}, 0) \\
&= \varepsilon\text{-CLOSURE}\,(\delta\{q_0, 0\} \cup \delta\{q_1, 0\} \cup \delta\{q_2, 0\}) \\
&= \varepsilon\text{-CLOSURE}\,(\{q_0\} \cup \phi) \\
&= \varepsilon\text{-CLOSURE}\,(\{q_0\}).
\end{aligned}$$

$$\begin{aligned}
\hat{\delta}(q_0, 1) &= \varepsilon\text{-CLOSURE } \delta(\hat{\delta}(q_0, \varepsilon), 1) \\
&= \varepsilon\text{-CLOSURE } (\delta(\{q_0, q_1, q_2\}, 1)) \\
&= \varepsilon\text{-CLOSURE } (q_1) \\
&= \{q_1, q_2\}. \\
\hat{\delta}(q_0, 01) &= \varepsilon\text{-CLOSURE } \{\delta(\hat{\delta}(q_0, 0), 1)\} \\
&= \varepsilon\text{-CLOSURE } (\delta\{q_0, q_1, q_2\}, 1) \\
&= \varepsilon\text{-CLOSURE } (\delta(q_0, 1) \cup \delta(q_1, 1) \cup \delta(q_2, 1)) \\
&= \varepsilon\text{-CLOSURE } (\phi \cup q_1) \\
&= \varepsilon\text{-CLOSURE } \{q_1\} \\
&= \{q_1, q_2\}. \\
\hat{\delta}(q_0, 2) &= \varepsilon\text{-CLOSURE } (q_2) = \{q_2\} \\
\hat{\delta}(q_0, 0) &= \varepsilon\text{-CLOSURE } (\delta(\hat{\delta}(q_1, \varepsilon), 0) \\
&= \varepsilon\text{-CLOSURE } (\{q_1, q_2\}, 0) \\
&= \phi.
\end{aligned}$$

1.6. EQUIVALENCE OF NFA'S WITH AND WITHOUT ε-MOVES

1.6.1. Theorem

If L is accepted by a NFA with ε-transitions, then L is accepted by an NFA without ε-transitions.

Proof. Let $M = (Q, \Sigma, \delta, q_0, F)$ be an NFA with ε-transition. Let $M^1 = (Q, \Sigma, \delta^1, q_0, F^1)$ where

$$F^1 = \begin{cases} F \cup \{q_0\} & \text{if } \varepsilon\text{-CLOSURE } (q_0) \text{ contains a state in } F \\ F & \text{otherwise.} \end{cases}$$

$$\delta^1(q, a) = \hat{\delta}(q, a),\ q \in \alpha,\ a \in \Sigma.$$

Then M^1 has no ε-transitions. Note that δ^1 and are $\hat{\delta}^1$ same but δ and $\hat{\delta}$ are not same.

We show by induction that $\delta^1\{q_0, w\} = \hat{\delta}(q_0, w)$ for any string w. Note that for $w = \varepsilon$, $\delta^1(q_0, \varepsilon) = \{q_0\}$ and $\hat{\delta}\{q_0, \varepsilon\} = \varepsilon$-CLOSURE $\{q_0\}$. So $\delta^1(q_0, \varepsilon) \neq \hat{\delta}(q_0, \varepsilon)$. So the induction is not true for the string having length 0. We start our induction for the string having length 1.

Basis step. Let a be a string of length one. That is, $a \in \Sigma$. $\delta^1\{q_0, a\} = \hat{\delta}(q_0, a)$ by definition of δ^1.

Induction. Assume that $\delta^1(q_0, x) = \hat{\delta}(q_0, x)$ for any string x of length $\leq n$. Assume w is a string of length $n + 1$. Let $w = xa$ for some symbol $a \in \Sigma$. Then

$$\begin{aligned}\delta^1(q_0, w) &= \delta^1(q_0, xa) \\ &= \delta^1(\delta^1\{q_0, x), a) \\ &= \delta^1(\hat{\delta}(q_0, x), a) \\ &= \delta^1(P, a)\end{aligned}$$

where $P = \hat{\delta}(q_0, x)$ (say)

We must show that $\delta^1(P, a) = \hat{\delta}(q_0, xa)$.

But
$$\begin{aligned}\delta^1(P, a) &= \bigcup_{q \in P} \delta'(q, a) = \bigcup_{q \in P} \hat{\delta}(q, a) \\ &= \text{(by (4) of Definition 1.4.3)} \\ &= \hat{\delta}\left(\hat{\delta}(q_0, x), a\right) \\ &= \hat{\delta}(q_0, xa) \\ &= \hat{\delta}(q_0, w)\end{aligned}$$

Hence
$$\delta^1(q_0, w) = \hat{\delta}(q_0, w)$$

Lastly, we show that $\delta^1(q_0, w)$ contains a state of F^1 if $\hat{\delta}(q_0, w)$ and only if contains a state of F. Let $\delta^1(q_0, w)$ contains a state of F^1. If $w = \varepsilon$, then

$$\delta^1\{q_0, \varepsilon\} = \{q_0\} = \hat{\delta}(q_0, \varepsilon) = \varepsilon\text{-CLOSURE } \{q_0\}.$$

Note that ε-CLOSURE $\{q_0\}$ contains a state (possibly q_0) in F. Hence $\hat{\delta}(q_0, \varepsilon)$ contains a state in F. Converse is clear from the definition of F^1.

If $w \neq \varepsilon$, then $w = xa$ for some symbol a. If $\hat{\delta}(q_0, w)$ contains a state of F, then surely $\delta^1(q_0, w)$ contains the same state in F^1. Conversely, if $\delta^1(q_0, w)$ contains a state in F^1 other than q_0, then $\hat{\delta}(q_0, w)$ contains a state in F. If $\delta^1(q_0, w)$ contains q_0, $q_0 \notin F$, then $=$ ε-CLOSURE $(\delta(\hat{\delta}(q_0, x), a)$ the state in ε-CLOSURE (q_0) and in F must be in .

1.6.2. Example

Consider the NFA with ε-moves

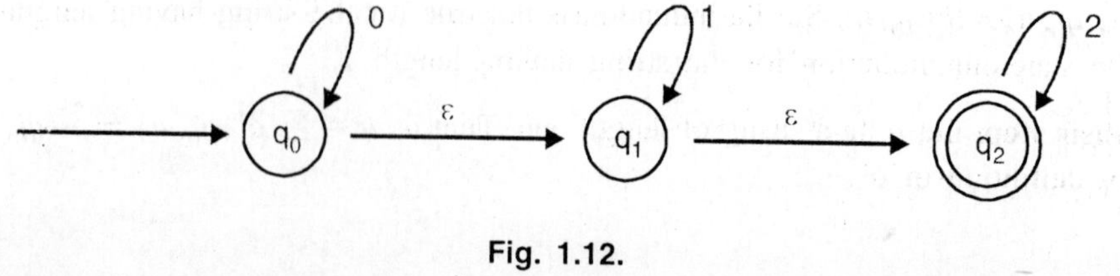

Fig. 1.12.

Find an equivalent NFA without ε-moves.

Solution. Let $M = (Q, \Sigma, \delta, q_0, F)$ be the given NFA with ε-transitions, where $Q = \{q_0, q_1, q_2\}$, $\Sigma = \{0, 1, 2, \varepsilon\}$, q_0 is the starting state,

$F = \{q_2\}$ and the transition diagram is given in Fig. 1.12. Define $M^1 = (Q, \Sigma^1, \delta^1, q_0, F^1)$ the NFA without ε-transitions as follows.

$Q = \{q_0, q_1, q_2\}$, $\Sigma^1 = \{0, 1, 2\}$ the transition function δ^1 of M^1 is given by Table 1.8.

Table 1.8.

States	*Inputs*		
	0	*1*	*2*
q_0	$\{q_0, q_1, q_2\}$	$\{q_1, q_2\}$	$\{q_2\}$
q_1	–	$\{q_1, q_2\}$	$\{q_2\}$
q_2	–	–	$\{q_2\}$

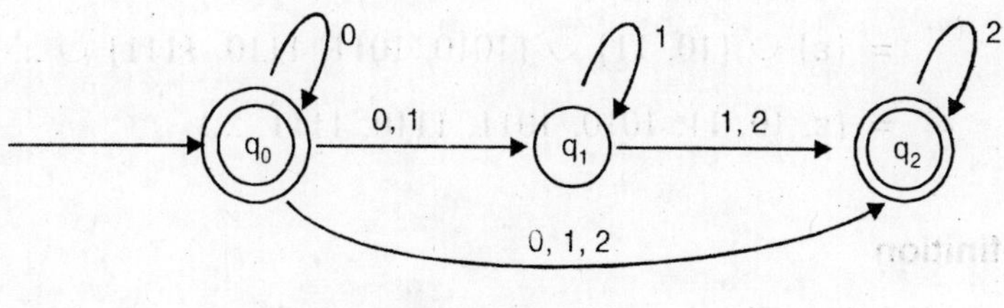

Fig. 1.13. NFA without ε-transitions.

The set of final states of $M^1 = F \cup \{q_0\} = \{q_0, q_2\}$ since ε-CLOSURE $\{q_0\} = \{q_0, q_1, q_2\}$.

1.7. REGULAR EXPRESSIONS AND ITS MANIPULATION

The language accepted by finite automata are called regular expressions. In this section we prove the languages accepted by finite automata is precisely the class of languages described by regular expressions.

1.7.1. Definition

Let Σ be a finite set of symbols. Let L_1, L_2 be set of strings in Σ^*. The concatenation of L_1 and L_2 denoted by $L_1 L_2$ is the set of all strings of the form xy, where $x \in L_1$, and $y \in L_2$.

Let $L^0 = \{\varepsilon\}$ and $L^i = LL^{i-1}$ for $i \geq 1$.

The *kleene closure or closure* of L, denoted by L^* is the set

$$L^* = \bigcup_{i=0}^{\infty} L^i$$

and the positive closure of L_1 denoted by L^+ is the set

$$L^+ = \bigcup_{i=0}^{\infty} L^i = L^* - \mathrm{L}^0 = L^* - \{\varepsilon\}.$$

L^+ contains ε if and only if L does.

1.7.2. Example

Let $L_1 = \{01, 10\}$, $L_2 = \{11, 00\}$. Then

$L_1 L_2 = \{0111, 0100, 1011, 1000\}$. Let $L = \{10, 11\}$

Then $L^* = L^0 \cup L^1 \cup L^2 \cup ...$

$= \{\varepsilon\} \cup \{10, 11\} \cup \{1010, 1011, 1110, 1111\} \cup ...$

$= \{\varepsilon, 10, 11, 1010, 1011, 1110, 1111, ...\}$

1.7.3. Definition

Let Σ be an alphabet. The regular expressions over Σ and the sets that they denote are defined recursively as follows.

(*i*) ϕ is a regular expression and denotes the empty set.

(*ii*) ε is a regular expression and denotes the set {ε}.

(*iii*) For each $a \in \Sigma$, 'a' is a regular expression and denotes the set $\{a\}$.

If ***r*** and ***s*** are regular expressions denoting the languages R and S respectively, then $(\boldsymbol{r} + \boldsymbol{s})$, $(\boldsymbol{r}, \boldsymbol{s})$ $(\boldsymbol{r})^*$ are regular expressions that denotes the sets ***R∪S, RS*** and R^* respectively.

1.7.4. Example

00 is a regular expression representing {00}. The expression $(0 + 1)^*$ denotes all string of 0's and 1's. Also $(0 + 1)^*$ 00 $(0 + 1)^*$ denotes all strings of 0's and 1's with atleast two consecutive 0's.

1.7.5. Theorem (Conversion of regular expression to FSA)

For every regular expression r there exists a NFA with ε-transitions that accepts $L(r)$.

Proof. We prove by induction on the number of operators in the regular expression r that there is an NFA M with ε-transitions, having one final state and no transitions out of this final state such that $T(M) = L(r)$.

Basis Step. Suppose r is ε, φ or a for some $a \in \Sigma$. Then NFA's in Fig. 1.14 (*a*), (*b*), (*c*) clearly satisfy the conditions.

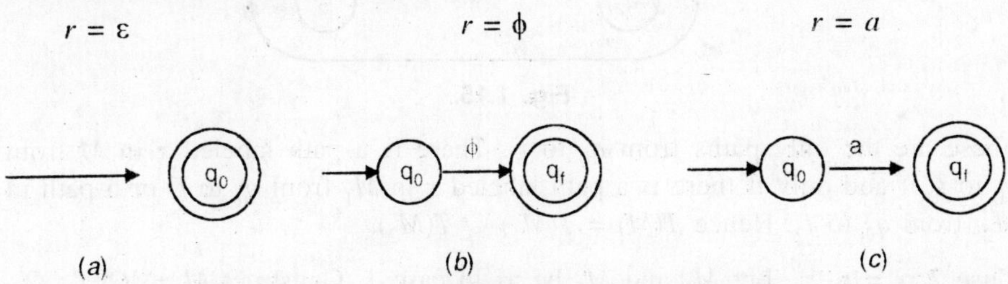

Fig. 1.14.

Induction Step. Assume the theorem is true for r having fewer than i operators, $i \geq 1$. Let r have i operators. We discuss three cases depending on the form of r.

Case 1. Let $r = r_1 + r_2$. Both r_1 and r_2 must have fewer than i operators. Thus there are NFA's $M_1 = (Q_1, \Sigma_1, \delta_1, q_1, \{f_1\})$ and $M_2 = (Q_2, \Sigma_2, \delta_2, q_2, \{f_2\})$ with $T(M_1) = L(r_1)$ and $T(M_2) = L(r_2)$. Assume Q_1 and Q_2 are disjoint. Let q_0 be a new initial state and f_0 a new final state construct.

$$M = (Q_1 \cup Q_2 \cup \{q_0, f_0\}, \Sigma_1 \cup \Sigma_2, \delta, q_0, \{f_0\})$$

where δ is defined by

(*i*) $\delta\{q_0, \varepsilon\} = \{q_1, q_2\}$

(*ii*) $\delta\{q, a\} = \delta_1\{q, a\}$ if $q \in Q_1 - \{f_1\}, a \in \Sigma_1 \cup \{\varepsilon\}$

$= \delta_2\{q, a\}$ if $q \in Q_2 - \{f_2\}, a \in \Sigma_2 \cup \{\varepsilon\}$

(*iii*) $\delta_1(f_1, \varepsilon) = \delta_2(f_2, \varepsilon) = \{f_0\}$.

All the moves of M_1 and M_2 are present in M. The construction of M is depicted in Fig. 1.15. Any path in the transition diagram of M from q_0 to f_0 must be going to either q_1, or q_2 on ε and follow any path in M_1 or in M_2 corresponding by and reaches f_0 along the path ε.

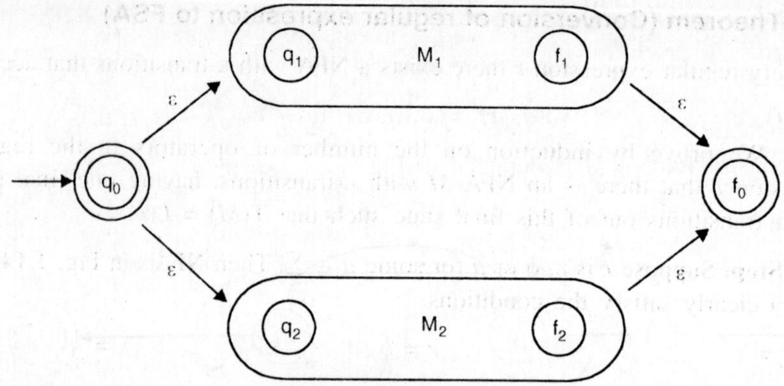

Fig. 1.15.

These are the only paths from q_0 to f_0. There is a path labeled x in M from q_0 to f_0 if and only if there is a path labeled x in M_1 from q_1 to f_1 or a path in M_2, from q_2 to f_2. Hence $T(M) = T(M_1) \cup T(M_2)$.

Case 2. $r = r_1\, r_2$. Let M_1 and M_2 be as in case 1. Construct $M = (Q_1 \cup Q_2, \Sigma_1 \cup \Sigma_2, \delta, \{q_1], \{f_2\})$ where δ is given by

(*i*) $\delta(q, a) = \delta_1\,(q, a)$ for $q \in Q_1 - \{f_1\}, a \in \Sigma_1 - \{\varepsilon\}$

(*ii*) $\delta(f_1, \varepsilon) = \{q_2\}$

(*iii*) $\delta(q, a) = \delta_2(q, a), q \in Q_2, a \in \Sigma_2 \cup (\varepsilon)$.

The construction of M is depicted in Fig. 1.16.

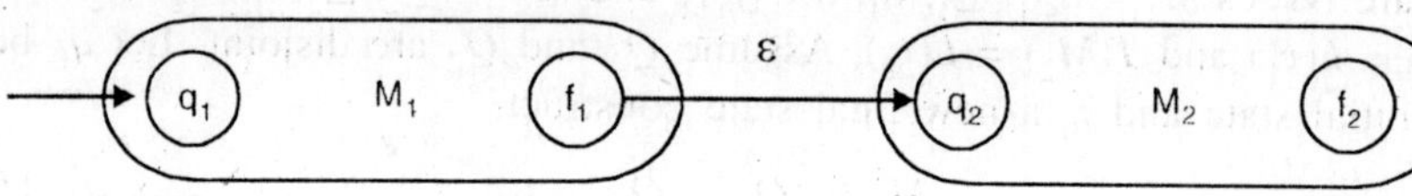

Fig. 1.16.

E very path in M from q_1 to f_2 is a path labeled by some string x from q_1 to f_1 followed by the edge from f_1 to q_2 labeled ε, followed by a path labeled by some string y from q_2 to f_2. Thus

$$T(M) = \{xy : x \in T(M_1),\ y \in T(M_2)\}$$

and hence

$$T(M) = T(M_1)\ T(M_2).$$

Case 3. $r = (r_1)^*$. Let $M_1 = (Q_1, \Sigma_1, \delta_1, q_1, \{f_1\})$

and $T(M_1) = r_1$. Construct

$$M = (Q_1 \cup \{q_0, f_0\}, \Sigma, \delta, q_0, \{f_0\})$$

where δ is given by

(*i*) $\delta(q_0, \varepsilon) = \delta(f_1, \varepsilon) = \{q_1, f_0\}$

(*ii*) $\delta(q, a) = \delta_1(q, a)$ for $q \in Q_1 - \{f_1\}$, $a \in \Sigma_1 \cup \{\varepsilon\}$.

The construction of M is depicted in Fig. 1.17.

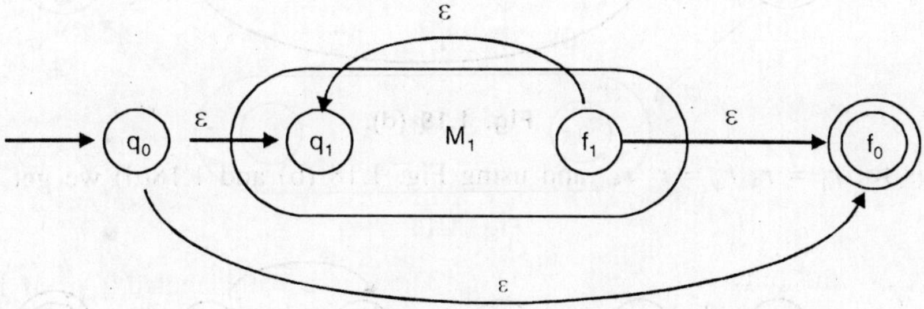

Fig. 1.17.

Any path from q_0 to f_0 consists either of a path from q_0 to f_0 on ε or a path from q_0 to q_1 on ε followed by some number of paths from q_1 to f_1, then back to q_1 on ε. There is a path in M from q_0 to f_0 labeled x if and only if we write $x = x_1x_2 \ldots x_j$ for some $j \geq 0$ such that each $x_i \in T(M_1)$. Hence $T(M) = T(M_1)^*$.

1.7.6. Example

Construct a NFA for the regular expression $01^* + 1$.

Solution. $01^* + 1$ is of the form $r_1 + r_2$ where $r_1 = 01^*$ and $r_2 = 1$. The automaton for r_2 is

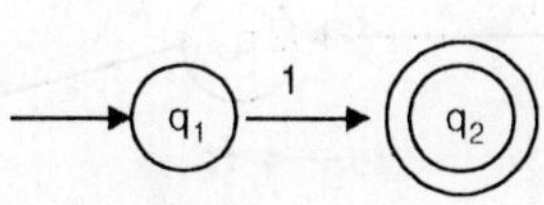

Fig. 1.18. (a).

we express $r_1 = 01^* = r_3\, r_4$ where $r_3 = 0$, $r_4 = 1^*$. The automaton for r_3 is

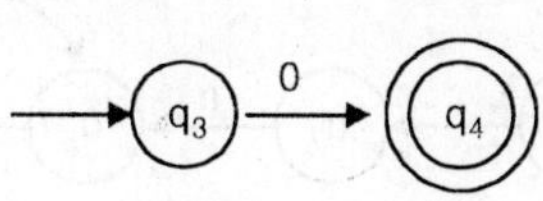

Fig. 1.18. (b).

Now $r_4 = 1^* = r_5^*$ where $r_5 = 1$. The automata for r_5 is

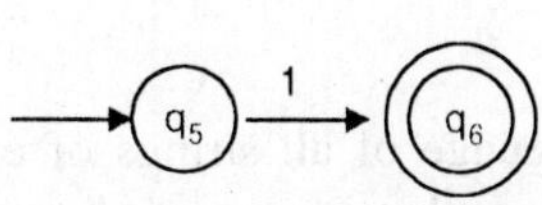

Fig. 1.18 (c).

Now we construct NFA for $r_4 = r_5^*$ as in case of Theorem 1.7.5.

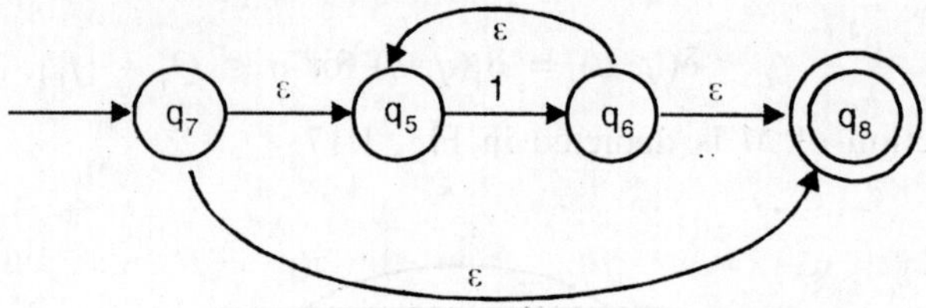

Fig. 1.18 (d).

Thus for $r_1 = r_3\ r_4 = r_3\ r_5^*$ and using Fig. 1.18 (b) and 1.18(d) we get

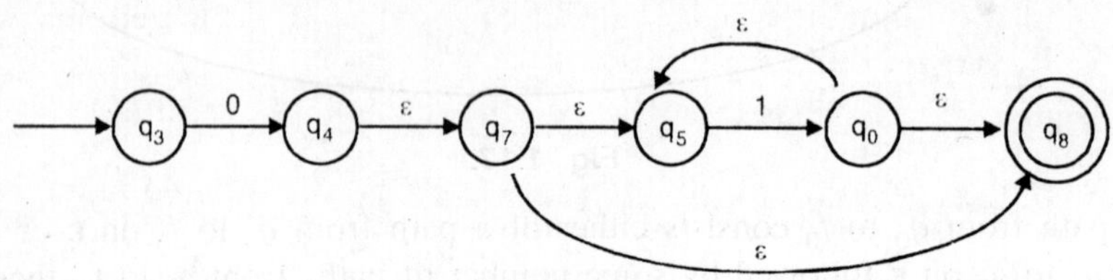

Fig. 1.18 (e).

Finally, use the construction of Fig. 1.15 to find the NFA for $r = r_1 + r_2$. Two states q_9 and q_{10} are created to fill the roles of q_0 and f_0 in that construction and the transition diagram is depicted in Fig. 1.18 (f).

$$r = 01^* + 1.$$

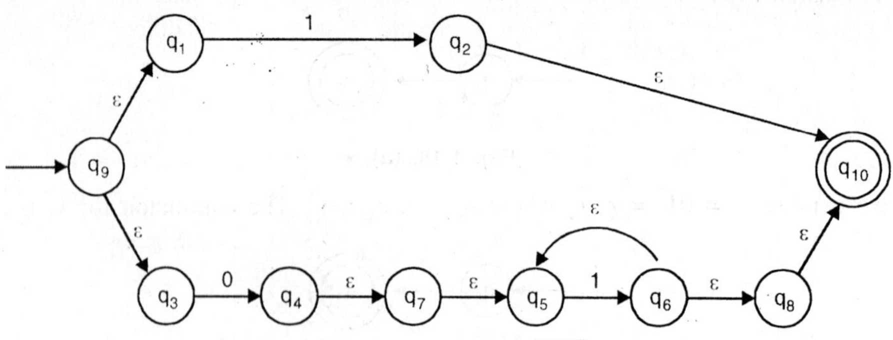

Fig. 1.18 (f).

1.7.7. Example

Let $L \subseteq \{0, 1\}^*$ be the language of all strings of even length (since 0 is even, $\varepsilon \in L$). Is L regular? If it is, what is a regular expression corresponding to it?

Solution. Any string of even length can be obtained by concatenating zero or more strings of length 2. Conversely, any such concatenation has even length. It follows that $L = \{00, 01, 10, 11\}^*$ so that one regular expression corresponding to L is $(00 + 01 + 10 + 11)^*$ and another is $((0 + 1)(0 + 1))^*$.

1.7.8. Example

Describe in words the strings in each of the following regular sets

(*a*) 10^* (*b*) $(10)^*$ (*c*) $1^*0\ (0)^*$ (d) $(0)^*1$

Solution.

(*a*) 1 followed by any number of 0's (including no zero).

(*b*) Any number of copies of (10) (including null string).

(*c*) Any number of 1's followed by one or more 0's.

(*d*) Any string of 0's ending with 1.

Regular expressions from DFA

1.7.9. Theorem

If L is accepted by a DFA then L is denoted by a regular expression.

Proof. Let L be the set accepted by the DFA $M = (Q, \Sigma, \delta, q_1, F)$, where $Q = \{q_1, q_2, ..., q_n\}$. Let R_{ij}^k be the set of strings that takes M from state q_i to state q_j without entering and leaving through any state numered higher than k. That is if $x \in R_{ij}^k$ then.

$\delta(q_i, x) = q_j$ and if $\delta(q_j, y) = q_l$

for any y which is of the form $x = y\ x_i \ldots x_n$, then $l \leq k$. (or) $y = \varepsilon$ and $l = i$ (or) $x = y$ and $j = l$.

Note that R_{ij}^n denotes all strings that take q_i to q_j as there is no state numbered greater than n.

We can define R_{ij}^k recursively as follows. When the input string is given, M moves from q_i to q_j without passing through a state higher than q_k are either

(*i*) in R_{ij}^{k-1} (that is, they never pass through a state as high as q_k).

(*ii*) Composed of a string in R_{ik}^{k-1} (which takes M to q_k first time) followed by zero or more strings in R_{kk}^{k-1} (which take M from q_k back to q_k without passing through q_k or a higher-numbered state) followed by a string in R_{kj}^{k-1} (which takes M from state q_k to q_j). That is

$$R_{ij}^{k-1} = R_{ij}^{k} \cup R_{ik2}^{k-1} (R_{kk}^{k-1})^* R_{kj}^{k-1} \qquad (1.1)$$

$$R_{ij}^{0} = \begin{cases} a : \delta(q_i, a) = q_j] \text{ if } i \neq j \\ a : \delta(q_i, a) = qj] \cup \{\varepsilon\} \text{ if } i = j \end{cases}$$

We show for each i, j, k there exists a regular expression r_{ij}^{k} denoting the language R_{ij}^{k}. We proceed by induction on k.

Basis step. When $k = 0$, $R_{ij}^{0} = \{a\}$ or ε. Thus r_{ij}^{0} can be written as $a_1 + a_2 + ... + a_p$ if $i \neq j$ or $a_1 + a_2 + ... + a_p + \varepsilon$ if $i = j$ where $\{a_1, a_2, ... a_p\}$ is the set of symbols 'a' such that $\delta(q_i, a) = q_j$. If there are no such 'a's then ϕ or (ε in the case $i = j$) is r_{ij}^{0}.

Induction step. Assume by induction that, for each l and m, there exists a regular expression r_{lm}^{k-1} such that $L(r_{lm}^{k-1}) = R_{lm}^{k-1}$ Hence by (1.1) there exists a regular expression r_{ij}^{k} such that

$$r_{ij}^{k} = r_{ik}^{k-1} \cdot (r_{kk}^{k-1})^* \, r_{kj}^{k-1} + r_{ij}^{k-1}.$$

This completes the induction as the recursive formula for R_{ij}^{k} involves only the regular expression operators union, concatenation and closure.

To complete the proof we observe that

$$T(M) = \bigcup_{q_j \in F} R_{ij}^{n}$$

Since R_{ij}^{n} denotes the set of all strings that take q_1 to q_j. T(M) is denoted by the regular expression

$$r_{ij_1}^{n} + r_{ij_2}^{n} + ... + r_{ij_p}^{n}$$

where $F = \{q_{j_1}, q_{j_2}, ... , q_{j_p}\}$. Hence the proof.

1.7.10. Example

Let $M = (Q, \Sigma, q, \delta, F)$ be an NFA with $Q = \{q_1, q_2, q_3\}$, $\Sigma = \{0, 1\}$, $F = \{q_2, q_3\}$ and the transition diagram is Fig. 1.19.

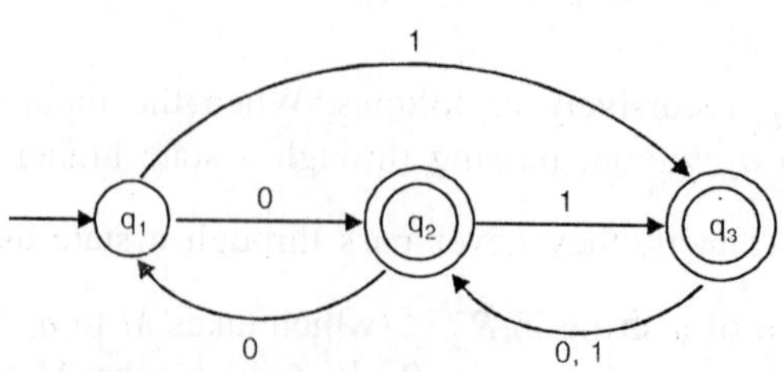

Fig. 1.19.

In required regular expression is $r_{12}^{3} + r_{13}^{3}$.

In Order to simplify the expressions we may use the equivalences like

$$(r + s)t = rt + st, (\varepsilon + r)^* = r^*$$

so on. Note that $r_{11}^{0} = \varepsilon$, $r_{11}^{1} = r_{11}^{0} + r_{11}^{0}(r_{11}^{0})^* r_{11}^{0}$

$= \varepsilon(\varepsilon)^* \varepsilon + \varepsilon = \varepsilon$; $r_{12}^{0} = 0$ since $\delta(q_1, 0) = q_2$.

$$r_{12}^{1} = r_{11}^{0} (r_{11}^{0})^* r_{12}^{0} + r_{12}^{0} = \varepsilon(\varepsilon)^* 0 + 0 = 0$$

$$r_{11}^{2} = r_{12}^{1} (r_{22}^{1})^* r_{21}^{1} + r_{11}^{1} = 0(\varepsilon + 00)^* 0 + \varepsilon = (00)^*$$

where $r_{22}^{1} = r_{21}^{0} (r_{11}^{0})^* r_{12}^{0} + r_{22}^{0} = 0\varepsilon^* 0 + \varepsilon = 00 + \varepsilon.$

$$r_{13}^{2} = r_{12}^{1} (r_{22}^{1})^* r_{23}^{1} + r_{13}^{1}$$

$$= 0(00 + \varepsilon)^* (1 + 01) + 1,$$

$$r_{23}^{1} = r_{21}^{0} (r_{11}^{0})^* r_{13}^{0} + r_{23}^{0} = 0(\varepsilon)^* 1 + 1 = 01 + 1.$$

$$r_{12}^{2} = r_{12}^{1} (r_{22}^{1})^* (r_{22}^{1}) + r_{12}^{1} = 0\ (00 + \varepsilon)^* (00 + \varepsilon) + 0$$

$$= 0\ (00 + \varepsilon)^* + 0 = 0\ (00)^*.$$

observe that $(00 + \varepsilon)^* = (00)^*$ and that $1 + 01$ is equivalent to $(\varepsilon + 0)1$, we have

$$r_{13}^{2} = 0(00)^* (\varepsilon + 0)\ 1 + 1 = (00)^* 1 + 1 = 0^* 1.$$

$$r_{12}^{3} = r_{13}^{2} (r_{33}^{2})^* r_{32}^{2} + r_{12}^{21}$$

where $r_{33}^{2} = r_{32}^{1} (r_{22}^{1})^* r_{23}^{1} + r_{33}^{1}$

$$r_{32}^{1} = r_{31}^{0} (r_{11}^{0})^* r_{12}^{0} + r_{32}^{0}$$

$$= \varepsilon(\varepsilon)^* 0 + 0 + 1 = 0 + 1$$

$$r_{33}^{1} = r_{31}^{0} (r_{11}^{0})^* r_{13}^{0} + r_{33}^{0}$$

$$= \varepsilon(\varepsilon)^* 1 + \varepsilon = 1 + \varepsilon$$

$$r_{33}^{2} = r_{32}^{1} (r_{22}^{1})^* r_{23}^{1} + r_{33}^{1}$$

$$= (0 + 1)\ (00 + \varepsilon)^* (01 + 1) + (1 + \varepsilon)$$

$$= (0 + 1)\ (00)^* (01 + 1) + (1 + \varepsilon)$$

$$= (0 + 1)\ (00)^* (0 + \varepsilon)\ 1 + (1 + \varepsilon)$$

$$= (0 + 1)\ 0^* 1 + 1 + \varepsilon$$

$$= ((0 + 1)\ 0^* + \varepsilon)\ 1 + \varepsilon$$

$$= (0 + 1)\ 0^* 1 + \varepsilon$$

$$r_{32}^{2} = r_{32}^{1} (r_{22}^{1})^{*} r_{22}^{1} + r_{32}^{1}$$

$$= (0 + 1) (00 + \varepsilon)^{*} (00 + \varepsilon) + (0 + 1)$$

$$= (0 + 1) (00)^{*} (00) + (0 + 1)$$

$$= (0 + 1) (00)^{*} + (0 + 1)$$

$$= (0 + 1) [(00)^{*} + \varepsilon]$$

$$= (0 + 1) (00)^{*}$$

Hence $\quad r_{12}^{3} = r_{13}^{2} (r_{33}^{2})^{*} r_{32}^{2} + r_{12}^{2}$

$$= 0^{*}1 ((0 + 1) 0^{*} 1 + \varepsilon)^{*} (0 + 1) (00)^{*} + 0 (00)^{*}$$

$$= 0^{*}1 ((0 + 1) 0^{*} 1)^{*} (0 + 1) (00)^{*} + 0 (00)^{*}.$$

$$r_{12}^{3} = 0^{*}1 (0 + 1) 0^{*} 1)^{*} (0 + 1) (00)^{*} + 0 (00)^{*}$$

$$r_{13}^{3} = r_{13}^{2} (r_{33}^{2})^{*} r_{33}^{2} + r_{13}^{2}$$

$$= 01^{*} [\varepsilon + (0 + 1) 0^{*}1)^{*} (\varepsilon + (0 + 1) 0^{*} 1] + 0^{*} 1$$

$$= 0^{*}1 [(0 + 1) 0^{*} 1]^{*}$$

Hence

$$r_{12}^{3} + r_{13}^{3} = 0^{*}1(0 + 1) 0^{*} 1)^{*} [\varepsilon + (0 + 1) (00)^{*} + 0(00)^{*}]$$

A method using Arden's Theorem to find regular expression for a given FSA

(*i*) The FA does not have ε-moves.

(*ii*) It has only one initial state, say q_1.

(*iii*) Its states are $q_1, q_2, ..., q_n$.

(*iv*) q_i is the regular expression representing the set of string accepted by the FA even though q_i is a final state.

(*v*) α_{ij} denotes the regular expression representing the set of labels of edges from q_i to q_j. When there is no such edge $\alpha_{ij} = \phi$. Consequently, we can get the following set of equations in $q_1, q_2, ... q_n$.

$$q_1 = q_1 \alpha_{11} + q_2 \alpha_{21} + ... + q_n \alpha_{n1} + \varepsilon$$

$$q_2 = q_1 \alpha_{12} + q_2 \alpha_{22} + ... + q_n \alpha_{n2}$$

....

$$q_n = q_1 \alpha_{1n} + q_2 \alpha_{2n} + ... + q_n \alpha_{nn}$$

By repeatedly applying substitutions and Arden's Theorem we can express q_i in terms of α_{ij}'s. To get the set of strings recognized by FSA we have to take the union of all q_i's corresponding to final states.

Identities for regular expressions.

$$I_1 = \phi + R = R$$
$$I_2 = \phi R = R\phi = \phi$$
$$I_3 = \Lambda R = R\Lambda = R$$
$$I_4 = \Lambda^* = \Lambda \text{ and } \phi^* = \Lambda$$
$$I_5 = R + R = R$$
$$I_6 = R^* R^* = R^*$$
$$I_7 = RR^* = R^*R$$
$$I_8 = (R^*)^* = R^*$$
$$I_9 = \Lambda + RR^* = R^* = \Lambda + R^*R$$
$$I_{10} = (PQ)^*P = P(QP)^*$$
$$I_{11} = (P + Q)^* = (P^*Q^*)^* = (P^* + Q^*)^*$$
$$I_{12} = (P + Q)\,R = PR + QR \text{ and}$$
$$R(P + Q) = RP + RQ.$$

1.7.12. Example.

Construct a regular expression corresponding to the transition diagram given in Fig. 1.20.

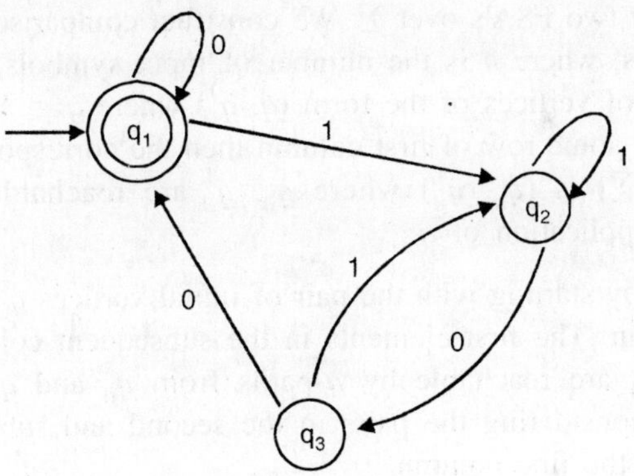

Fig. 1.20.

Solution. There is only one initial state. Also there are no ε-moves. The equations are

$$q_1 = q_1 0 + q_3 0 + \varepsilon$$
$$q_2 = q_2 1 + q_3 1 + q_1 1$$
$$q_3 = q_2 0$$

Now $\quad q_2 = q_2 1 + q_2 0\ 1 + q_1 1 = q_1\ 1 + q_2(1 + 01)$

By applying Arden's Theorem we get

$$q_2 = q_1 1\ (1 + 01)^*$$

Also
$$\begin{aligned} q_1 &= q_1 0 + q_2 00 + \varepsilon, \text{ since } q_3 = q_2 0 \\ &= q_1 0 + q_1 1(1 + 01)^*\ 00 + \varepsilon \\ &= q_1\ (0 + 1\ (1 + 01)^*\ 00) + \varepsilon \end{aligned}$$

Once again applying Arden's Theorem, we get

$$\begin{aligned} q_1 &= \varepsilon(0 + 1\ (1 + 01)^*\ 00)^* \\ &= (0 + 1\ (1 + 01)^*\ 00)^*. \end{aligned}$$

As q_1 is the only final state, the regular expression corresponding to the given FSA is $(0 + 1\ (1 + 01)^*\ 00)^*$.

1.7.13. Definition

Two regular expressions r and s are equivalent if and only if the corresponding DFA's are equivalent.

1.7.14. Definition

Two FSA's are *equivalent* over Σ if they accept the same set of strings over Σ.

There is a method called *comparison method* to test the equivalence of two FSA's over Σ.

1.7.15. Comparison Method

Let M and M^1 be two FSA's over Σ. We construct comparison table consisting of $n + 1$ columns, where n is the number of input symbols. The first column consists of pairs of vertices of the form (q, q^1) where $q \in M$ and $q^1 \in M^1$. If (q, q^1) appears in some row of first column then the corresponding entry in the a-column $(a \in \Sigma)$ is (q_a, q_a^1) where q_a, q_a^1 are reachable from q and q^1 respectively on application of a.

It is constructed by starting with the pair of initial vertices q_0, q_0^1 of M and M^1 in the first column. The first elements in the subsequent columns are (q_a, q_a^1) where q_a and q_a^1 are reachable by a-paths from q_0 and q_0^1. We repeat the construction by considering the pairs in the second and subsequent columns which are not in the first column.

The row wise construction is repeated. There are two cases:

Case 1. If we reach a pair (q_f, q_g^1) such that q_f is a final state of M, and q_g^1 is a non final state of M^1 or vice versa, then we terminate the construction and conclude that M and M^1 are not equivalent.

Case 2. Here the construction is terminated when no new element appears in the second and subsequent columns which are not in the first column.

In this case we conclude that M and M^1 are equivalent.

1.7.16. Example. Show that M and M^1 given in Fig. 1.21 (*a*), (*b*) are equivalent.

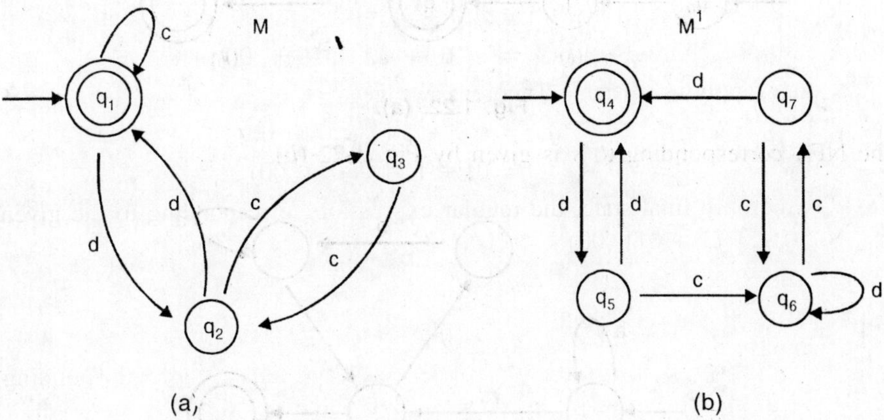

Fig. 1.21.

Solution. The initial states in M and M^1 are q_1 and q_4 respecitively. Hence the first element of the first column in the comparison table must be (q_1, q_4). The first element in the second column is (q_1, q_4) since both q_1 and q_4 are ε-reachable from the respective initial states. The complete table is (Table 1.9).

Table 1.9.

(q, q^1)	(q_c, q_c^1)	(q_d, q_d^1)
(q_1, q_4)	(q_1, q_4)	(q_2, q_5)
(q_2, q_5)	(q_3, q_6)	(q_1, q_4)
(q_3, q_6)	(q_2, q_7)	(q_3, q_6)
(q_2, q_7)	(q_3, q_6)	(q_1, q_4)

As we do not get a pair (q, q^1) where q is a final state and q^1 is a non final state (or vice-versa) at every row, we proceed until all the elements in the second and third columns are also in the first column. Therefore M and M^1 are equivalent.

1.7.17. Example

Prove $(a + b)^* = a^* (ba^*)^*$.

Solution. Let r and s denote $(a + b)^*$ and $a^* (ba^*)^*$ respectively. Using Theorem 1.7.5, the NFA corresponding to r is given in Fig. 1.22 (*a*)

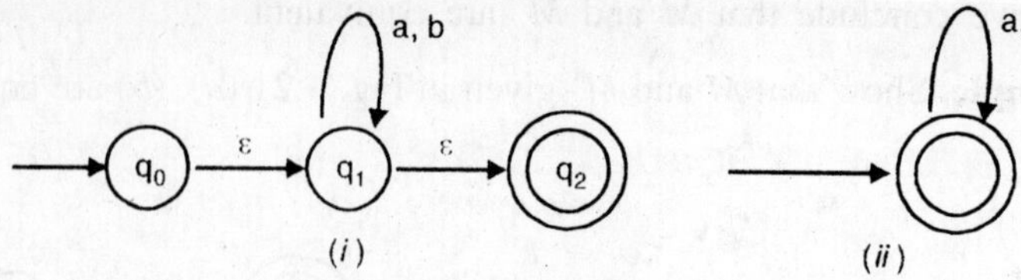

Fig. 1.22. (a).

The NFA corresponding to s is given by Fig. 1.22 (b).

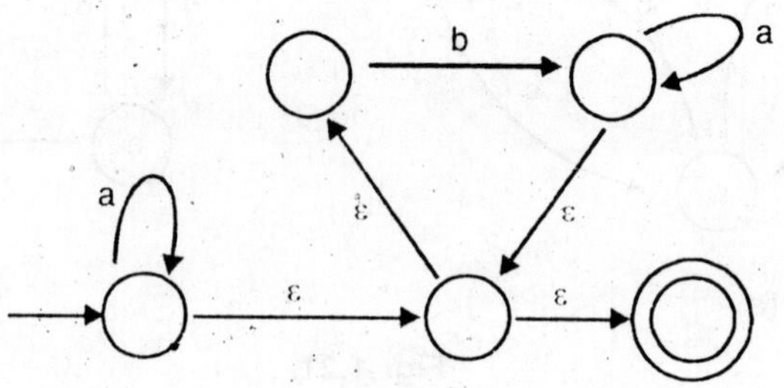

Fig. 1.22. (b).

Eliminating ε-moves we get

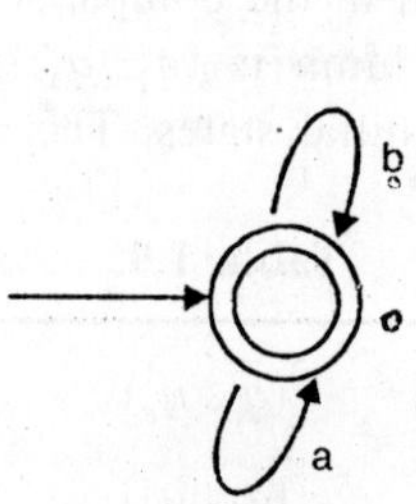

Fig. 1.22 (c).

Fig. 1.22 (a) (ii) and 1.22 (c) are obtained after eliminating ε-moves. As these two NFA's are the same. We conclude that $r = s$.

1.7.15. Theorem (Kleen's Theorem)

The class of regular sets over Σ is the smallest class R containing $\{a\}$ for every $a \in \Sigma$ and closed under union, concatenation and closure.

Proof. The set $\{a\}$ is represented by the regular expression a. So $\{a\}$ is regular for every $a \in \Sigma$. As the class of regular sets is closed under union, concatenation, and closure, $\mathfrak{R}$ is contained in the class of regular sets.

Let L be a regular set. Then $L = T(M)$ for some DFA, $M = (\{q_1, q_2, ..., q_k\}, \Sigma, \delta, q_0, F)$.

By Theorem 1.7.9, $L = \bigcup_{j=1}^{n} R^k_{1f_j}$, where $F = \{q_{f_1}, q_{f_2}, ..., q_{f_n}\}$ and $R^k_{1f_j}$ is obtained by applying union, concatenation and closure to singletons in Σ. Thus L is in $\mathfrak{R}$.

1.8. PUMPING LEMMA FOR REGULAR SETS

It is a tool for proving certain languages that are not regular. Also it is useful to check whether the language accepted by a given finite automaton is finite or infinite. 'Pumping' means repeated as many times as we like, and the resulting string will be accepted by the finite automaton.

1.8.1. Lemma

Let L be a regular set. Then there is a constant n (the number of states of the smallest automaton that accepts L) such that if z is any word in L, $|z| \geq n$, we write $z = u\ v\ w$ such that $|uv| \leq n$, $|v| \geq 1$ and for all $i \geq 0$, $u\ v^i\ w \in L$.

Proof. Let L be a regular language suppose $M = (Q, \Sigma, \delta, q_0, F)$ be a finite state automaton recognizing L having 'n' number of states. Consider an input of n or more symbols $a_1\ a_2 \ldots a_m$, $m \geq n$ and for $i = 1, 2, \ldots, m$, let

$$\delta(q_0, a_1 a_2 \ldots a_i) = q_i.$$

Since there are n different states, it is not possible for each of the $n + 1$ states $q_0, q_1, \ldots, q_n$ to be distinct. That is there exists two integers j and k, $0 \leq j < k \leq n$ such that $q_j = q_k$. Since $j < k$, the string $a_{j+1} \ldots a_k$ is of length atleast 1, and since $k \leq n$, its length is no more than n. Let $u = a_1 a_2 \ldots a_j$, $v = a_{j+1} \ldots a_k$, $w = a_{k+1} \ldots a_m$. Now

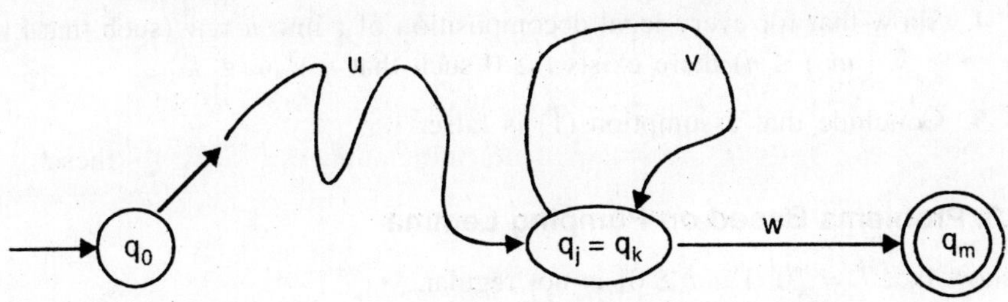

Fig. 1.23.

$$\delta(q_0, a_1 a_2 \ldots a_j) = q_j \Rightarrow \delta(q_0, u) = q_j$$

$$\delta(q_j, a_{j+1} a_{j+2} \ldots a_k) = q_j = q_k \Rightarrow \delta(q_j, v) = q_j$$

$$\delta(q_j, a_{k+1} a_{k+2} \ldots a_m) = q_m \Rightarrow \delta(q_j, w) = q_m.$$

If $q_m \in F$, i.e. $a_1\ a_2 \ldots a_m \in T(M)$, then $a_1\ a_2 \ldots a_j\ a_{k+1} \ldots a_m$ is also in $T(M)$, since there is a path from q_0 to q_m that goes through q_j but not around the loop labeled v. Now

$$\delta(q_0, u\ v^0\ w) = \delta(q_0, a_1 a_2 \ldots a_j\ a_{k+1} \ldots a_m)$$

$$= \delta(\delta(q_0, a_1a_2 \ldots a_j), a_{k+1} \ldots a_m)$$
$$= \delta(q_j, a_{k+1} \ldots a_m)$$
$$= q_m$$

since $\delta(q_j, v) = q_j$, we have $\delta(q_j, v^i) = q_j$ for every $i \geq 0$ and it follows that

$$\delta(q_0, u\, v^i\, w) = \delta(q_0, (a_1a_2 \ldots a_j)\,(a_{j+1} \ldots a_k)^i\, a_{k+1} \ldots a_m)$$
$$= \delta((q_0, a_1a_2 \ldots a_j), (a_{j+1} \ldots a_k)^i\, a_{k+1} \ldots a_m)$$
$$= \delta((q_j, (a_{j+1} \ldots a_k)^i), a_{k+1} \ldots a_m)$$
$$= \delta(q_j, a_{k+1} \ldots a_m)$$
$$= q_m.$$

Hence $u\, v^i\, w \in T(M)$.

In order to use the pumping lemma to show the language L is not regular we must show that L fails to have the property described in the lemma. We do this by assuming that the property is satisfied and deriving a contradiction.

1.8.2. Steps to Prove That *L* is not Regular

1. Assume that the language is regular.
2. Let n be some constant of the pumping lemma.
3. Pick a suitable string z with $|z| \geq n$.
4. Show that for every legal decomposition of z into $u\, v\, w$ (such that $|v| \geq 1$, $|uv| \leq n$) there exists $i \geq 0$ such that $u\, v^i\, w \notin L$.
5. Conclude that assumption (1) is false.

1.8.3. Problems Based on Pumping Lemma

1. Show that $L = \{0^i\, 1^i : i \geq 0\}$ is not regular.

Solution. Suppose L is regular and let n be the integer in the pumping lemma. Let $z = 0^n\, 1^n$. By the pumping lemma $0^n\, 1^n$ may be written as $z = u\, v\, w$ for some u, v, w such that $0 < |v|$, $|u\, v| \leq n$, $u\, v^m\, w \in L$ for all m.

We have three possibilities to consider:

(*i*) $uv = 0^k$ for some k and $v = 0^j$ for some j such that $j \leq k$, $w = 1^k$.

(*ii*) $u = 0^{k-i}$, $v = 0^i\, 1^j$, $w = 1^{k-j}$.

(*iii*) $u = 0^k$, $v = 1^j$, $w = 1^{k-j}$.

In each case, looking at $m = 2$ is enough to obtain a contradiction. For case (*i*)

$$uv^2w = uvvw = 0^k\, 0^j\, k = 0^{k+j}\, 1^k.$$

The string uv^2w contains j extra 0's in the first part and cannot be in L as $j > 0$.

For case (*ii*)

$$uv^2w = 0^{k-i}\,(0^i,\, 1^j)\,(0^i\, 1^j)\, 1^{k-j}$$
$$= 0^k\,(1^j\, 0^i) 1^k.$$

The string uv^2w contains the substring $1^j\, 0^i$ and is therefore not in L as $i, j > 0$.

For case (*iii*)

$$uv^2w = 0^k\, 1^j\, 1^j\, 1^{k-j} = 0^k\, 1^{k+j} \notin L \text{ as } j > 0.$$

This contradiction allows us to conclude that L cannot be regular.

2. Show that the set $L = \{a^{i2} : i \geq 1\}$ is not regular.

Solution. Let L be regular and let n be the number of states in FSA accepting L.

Let $z = a^{n2}$. Then $|z| = n^2 > n$. By pumping lemma we write $z = uvw$ with $|uv| \leq n$, $|v| > 0$. Consider uv^2w. Now

$$|uv^2w| = |u| + 2|v| + |w| > |u| + |v| + |w| \text{ as } |v| > 0$$

$$\Rightarrow \quad n^2 = |uvw| = |u| + |v| + |w| < |uv^2w|$$

as $\quad |uv| \leq n$, $|v| \leq n$. Therefore

$$n^2 < |uv^2w| = |u| + 2|v| + |w| \leq n^2 + n < n^2 + n + n + 1.$$

Hence $|uv^2w|$ strictly lies between n^2 and $(n + 1)^2$ but is not equal to any one of them. Hence $|uv^2w|$ is not a perfect square and so $uv^2w \notin L$. Hence there is a contradiction so L is not regular.

3. Show that $L = \{a^p : p \text{ is a prime}\}$ is not regular.

Solution. Suppose L is regular and let n be the number of states in FSA accepting L. Let p be a prime number greater than n. Let $z = a^p$. By pumping lemma we write $z = uvw$ with $|uv| \leq n$, $|v| > 0$. Let $v = a^m$ for some m such that $1 \leq m \leq n$.

Let $\quad i = p + 1$. Then

$$|u\, v^i\, w| = |u\, v\, w| + |v^{i-1}|$$
$$= p + (i - 1)m$$
$$= p + pm$$
$$= p\,(1 + m)$$

but $p\,(1 + m)$ is not a prime. Hence $u\, v^i\, w \notin L$. So L is not regular.

4. Show that $L = \{ww : w \in \{a, b\}^*\}$ is not regular.

Solution. Suppose L is regular and let n be the number of states in the automaton accepting L. Let us consider $ww = a^n\ b\ a^n\ b \in L$.

$$|\ ww\ | = 2(n + 1) > n.$$

By pumping lemma we write $ww = uvz$ with $|\ v\ | > 0$, $|\ uv\ | \leq n$.

The string v has no b's. Since if v has one b then $|\ uv\ | \geq n + 1$. This is not possible. Also if v has 2 b's then $|\ uv\ | = n + 2 > n$. This is also not possible. Take $i = 0$, $uv^0z = uz = (a^m b)\ (a^m b)$, $m = n - k < n$.

We cannot write uz in the form uu with $u \in \{a, b\}^*$ and so $u\ z \notin L$.

1.8.4. Theorem Weak Form of Pumping Lemma

Suppose L is an infinite regular language. Then there are strings u, v and w so that $|\ v\ | > 0$, $uv^m\ w \in L$ for every $m \geq 0$.

Proof. This follows immediately from Lemma 1.8.1. No matter how big the integer n in the statement of that theorem is, L must contain a string atleast that long because L has infinitely many elements.

1.8.5. Another Weaker Form of Pumping Lemma

Suppose L is an infinite regular language. There are integers p and q with $q > 0$, so that every $m \geq 0$, L contains a string of length $p + mq$. In other words the set of integers

$$\text{Lengths } (L) = \{|\ u\ | : u \in L\}.$$

contains the arithmetic progression of all integers $p + mq$ (where $m \geq 0$).

Proof. The proof follows from Theorem 1.7.4. by taking $p = |\ u\ | + |\ w\ |$, $q = |\ v\ |$.

1.9. MINIMISATION OF FSA

A DFA can recognize a unique language, but the converse does not hold. So for a given language there exists more than one DFA that accepts it. All these DFAs are called equivalent automaton. Two or more equivalent automata will differ only in the number of possible states. Two states p and q of a DFA are equivalent if both $\delta\ (p, w)$ and $\delta\ (q, w)$ are final states or both are non-final states for all $w \in \Sigma^*$. As Σ^* contains infinite number of strings, it is difficult to construct $\delta(p, w)$ or $\delta(q, w)$ for all $w \in \Sigma^*$. Two states p and q are n-equivalent denoted by $\equiv n\ (n \geq 0)$ if both $\delta\ (p, w)$ and $\delta\ (q, w)$ are either final states or both non final states for all w such that $|\ w\ | \leq n$.

The relation ≡ n is an equivalence relation on the set of states Q. It defines a partition on Q, and the members of the partition are the disjoint equivalence classes. Let S and S_n be the partitions of Q, here the elements of S_n are n-equivalent classes p and q are said to be equivalent if p and q are n-equivalent; that is, $p \equiv q$. Further if p and q are $(n + 1)$ – equivalent, then they are n-equivalent n. Continuing in this way for some n, $S_n = S_{n+1}$.

1.9.1. Procedure For Minimization Of DFA

Step 1. Construct the set of all final states of given DFA. Let it be Q^0_1. Set $Q^0_2 = Q - Q^0_1$, where Q is the set of all states. Finally the 0-equivalence S_0 is given by $S_0 = \{Q^0_1, Q^0_2\}$.

Step 2. Consider any subset $Q^n t$ of S_n, let q_1, q_2 are in $Q^n t$. q_1 and q_2 will be $(n + 1)$-equivalent if $\delta(q_1, b)$ and $\delta(q_2, b)$ are in the same equivalence class in S_n for all $b \in \Sigma$. Then divide $Q^n t$ again into $(n + 1)$-equivalence classes. Continuing this procedure for every $Q^n t$ in S_n we get all the element of S_{n+1}.

Repeat this procedure of construction of S_n for $n = 1, 2, ...$ unitl $S_n = S_{n+1}$.

At last we get the automaton with minimum number of states in which the states are the equivalence classes. That is, the elements of S_n and whose transition table is obtained by replacing the state by its corresponding equivalence class.

1.9.2. Example. Construct a minimum state automaton equivalent to a given automaton A, whose transition graph is given by the Fig. 1.24.

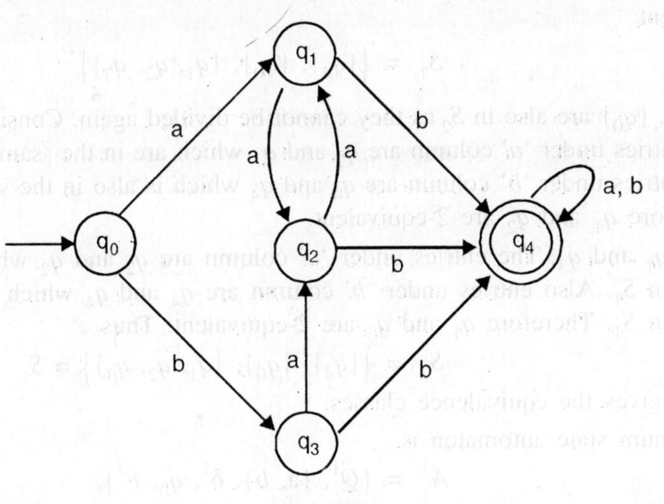

Fig. 1.24.

Solution. The transition table for the above figure is

Table 1.10.

States	Inputs	
	a	b
q_0	q_1	q_3
q_1	q_2	q_4
q_2	q_1	q_4
q_3	q_2	q_4
q_4	q_4	q_4

By step 1, we have $Q^0_1 = F = \{q_4\}$

$$Q^0_2 = Q - Q^0_1 = \{q_0, q_1, q_2, q_3\}$$

Therefore, $S_0 = \{Q^0_1, Q^0_2\} = \{\{q_4\}, \{q_0, q_1, q_2, q_3\}\}$.

Since $\{q_4\}$ has only one element so it can not be divided again. So $Q_1' = \{q_4\}$.

Consider $q_0, q_1 \in Q^0_2$. From table it is easy to see that under 'a' column, the entries corresponding to q_0 and q_1 are q_1 and q_2 which are in Q^0_2 and under 'b' column the entries are q_3 and q_4. Since $q_3 \in Q^0_2$ and $q_4 \in Q^0_1$, therefore q_0 and q_1 are not 1-equivalent. Similarly q_0 is not 1-equivalent to q_2 and q_3.

Next consider q_1 and q_2 and observe the entries under 'a' column. The corresponding entries are q_2, q_1 both are in Q^0_2. Similarly the entries under 'b' column are $q_4, q_4 \in Q^0_1$, hence q_1 and q_2 are 1-equivalent. Similarly q_1, q_3 are 1-equivalent.

Hence $S_1 = \{\{q_4\}, \{q_0\}, \{q_1, q_2, q_3\}\}$

Now $\{q_4\}, \{q_0\}$ are also in S_2 as they cannot be divided again. Consider q_1 and q_2. The entries under 'a' column are q_2 and q_1 which are in the same set in S_1 and the entries under 'b' column are q_4 and q_4 which is also in the same set in S_1. Therefore q_1 and q_2 are 2-equivalent.

Consider q_1 and q_3. The entries under 'a' column are q_2 and q_2 which are in same set in S_1. Also entries under 'b' column are q_4 and q_4 which are in the same set in S_1. Therefore q_1 and q_3 are 2-equivalent. Thus

$$S_2 = \{\{q_4\}, \{q_0\}, \{q_1, q_2, q_3\}\} = S_1$$

Hence S_1 gives the equivalence classes.

The minimum state automaton is

$$A^1 = \{Q^1, \{a, b\}, \delta^1, q_0, F^1\},$$

where

$$Q^1 = \{[q_4], [q_0], [q_1, q_2, q_3]\}$$

$$q^1_0 = [q_0]$$

$$F^1 = [q_4]$$

and δ^1 is given by the Table 1.11.

Table 1.11

States	*Inputs*	
	a	*b*
$[q_0]$	$[q_1, q_2, q_3]$	$[q_1, q_2, q_3]$
$[q_4]$	$[q_4]$	$[q_4]$
$[q_1, q_2, q_3]$	$[q_1, q_2, q_3]$	$[q_4]$

The transition graph for minimum state automaton is given by the diagram

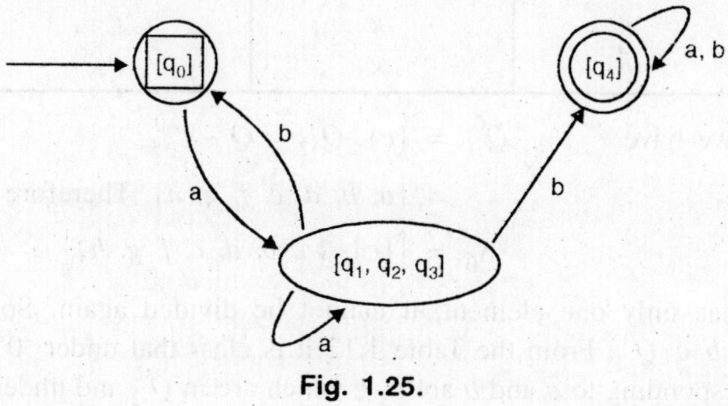

Fig. 1.25.

1.9.3. Example

Let M be a finite automaton of figure 1.26. Construct a minimum state automaton equivalent to M.

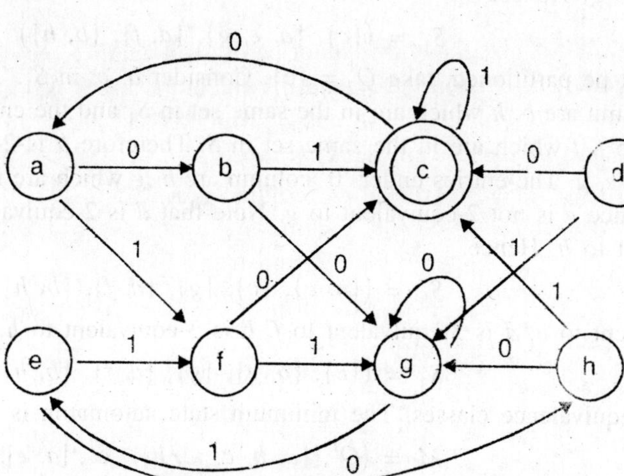

Fig. 1.26.

Solution. The transition Table 1.12. is given by:

Table 1.12.

States	Inputs	
	0	*1*
a	*b*	*f*
b	*g*	*c*
ⓒ	*a*	*c*
d	*c*	*g*
e	*h*	*f*
f	*c*	*g*
g	*g*	*e*
h	*g*	*c*

By step 1, we have $Q^0_1 = \{c\}, Q^0_2 = Q - Q^0_1$

$= \{a, b, d, e, f, g, h\}$. Therefore

$$S_0 = \{\{c\}, \{a, b, d, e, f, g, h\}\}.$$

Since $\{c\}$ has only one element, it cannot be divided again. So $Q_1{}^1 = \{c\}$. Consider $a, b \in Q^0{}_2$. From the Table 1.12 it is clear that under '0' column the entries corresponding to a and b are b, g which are in $Q^0{}_2$ and under 'b' column the entries are f, c, where $f \in Q^0{}_2$, $c \in Q^0{}_1$. Hence a, b are not 1-equivalent. Similarly b, d ; a, d; a, f; b, f; g, f; g, d; h, f; h, d; d, e; f, e are all not 1-equivalent. Again by looking at the Table 1.12, we conclude that a is 1-equivalent to e, g and d is 1-equivalent to f, b is 1-equivalent to h, e is 1-equivalent to g. Hence.

$$S_1 = (\{c\}, \{a, e, g\}, \{d, f\}, \{b, h\})$$

As $\{c\}$ cannot be partitioned, take $Q^1_2 = \{c\}$. Consider a, e, in S_1. The entries under '0' column are b, h which are in the same set in S_1 and the entries under '1' column are f, f which are in the same set in S. Therefore a is 2-equivalent to e. Consider e, g. The entries under '0' column are h, g which are in different sets in S_1. Hence e is not 2-equivalent to g. Note that d is 2-equivalent to f, b is 2-equivalent to h. Hence.

$$S_2 = (\{a, e\}, \{c\}, \{g\}, \{d, f\}, \{b, h\}) \neq S_1.$$

a is 3-equivalent to e, d is 3-equivalent to f, b is 3-equivalent to h,

$$S_3 = (\{c\}, \{a, e\}, \{g\}, \{d, f\}, \{b, h\})$$

S_3 gives the equivalence classes. The minimum state automaton is

$$M = (Q^1, \{a, b, c, ..., h\}, \delta^1, [a, e], F^1)$$

where $Q^1 = ([c], [a, e], [g], [d, f], [b, h])$

$$F^1 = [c]$$

and δ^1 is given by the Table 1.13.

Table 1.13

States	*Inputs*	
	0	*1*
$[a, e]$	$[b, h]$	$[f]$
$[c]$	$[a, e]$	$[c]$
$[d, f]$	$[c]$	$[g]$
$[g]$	$[g]$	$[e]$
$[b, h]$	$[g]$	$[c]$

and the transition diagram is given in Fig. 1.27.

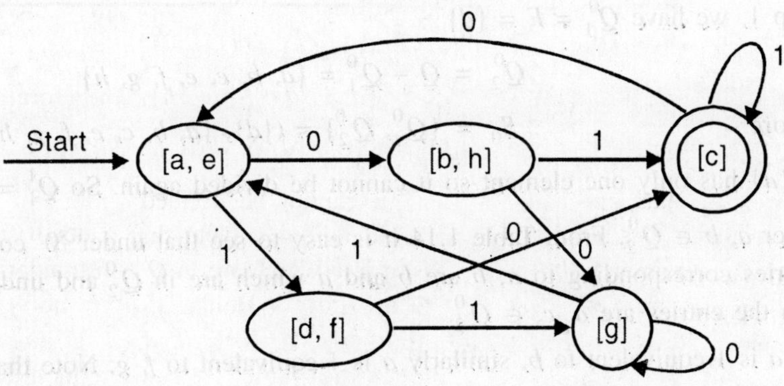

Fig. 1.27.

1.9.4. Example. Find the minimum-state finite automaton equivalent to the transition diagram of the fig. 1.28.

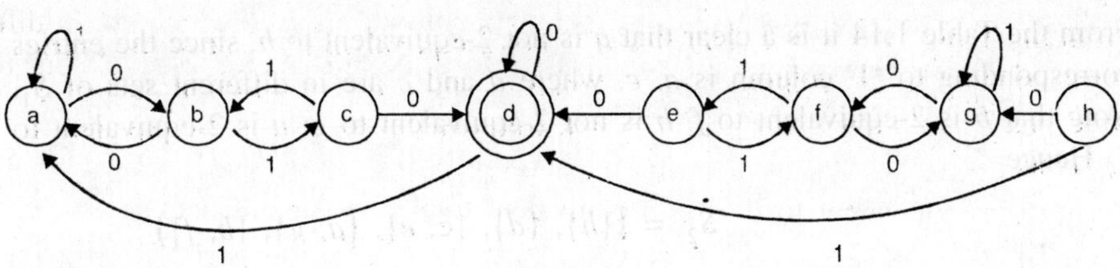

Fig. 1.28.

Solution. The transition table 1.14 corresponding to the diagram is

Table 1.14

States	Inputs	
	0	*1*
a	*b*	*a*
b	*a*	*c*
c	*d*	*b*
(*d*)	*d*	*a*
e	*d*	*f*
f	*g*	*e*
g	*f*	*g*
h	*g*	*d*

By step 1, we have $Q_1^0 = F = \{d\}$

$$Q_2^0 = Q - Q_1^0 = \{a, b, c, e, f, g, h\}$$

Therefore $\qquad S_0 = \{Q_1^0, Q_2^0\} = (\{d\}, \{a, b, c, e, f, g, h\})$

Since $\{d\}$ has only one element so it cannot be divided again. So $Q_1^1 = \{d\}$.

Consider $a, b \in Q_2^0$. From Table 1.14 it is easy to see that under '0' column, the entries corresponding to a, b are b and a which are in Q_2^0 and under '1' column the entries are $a, c, \in Q_2^0$.

Hence a is 1-equivalent to b, similarly a is 1-equivalent to f, g. Note that c is 1-equivalent to e. Also note that g and h are not 1-equivalent, e and f not 1-equivalent, c and f are not 1-equivalent, a and c are not 1-equivalent, f and h are not 1- equivalent. Hence

$$S_1 = (\{d\}, \{c, e\}, \{a, b, f, g\}, \{h\})$$

Since $\{d\}$, $\{h\}$ has only one element so it cannot be divided again so $Q_2^1 = \{d\}$, $Q_2^2 = \{h\}$.

From the Table 1.14 it is a clear that a is not 2-equivalent to b, since the entries corresponding to '1' column is a, c, where a and c are in different sets of S_1. Note that b is 2-equivalent to f. b is not 2-equivalent to g; a is 2-equivalent to g. Hence

$$S_2 = (\{h\}, \{d\}, \{c, e\}, \{a, g\}, \{b, f\})$$

As c and e are 3-equivalent, a is 3-equivalent to g,

$$S_3 = (\{h\}, \{c, e\}, \{d\}, \{a, g\}, \{b, f\}) = S_2.$$

Hence S_3 gives the equivalence classes. The minimum state automaton is

$$M = (Q^1, \{a, b, c, ..., h\}, \delta^1, [a, g], F^1)$$

where $\quad Q^1 = ([h], [c, e], [d], [a, g], [b, f])$

$$F^1 = [d]$$

and δ' is defined by the Table 1.15 as :

Table 1.15

States	*Inputs*	
	0	*1*
$[a, g]$	$[b, f]$	$[a, g]$
$[c, e]$	$[d]$	$[b, f]$
$[d]$	$[d]$	$[a, g]$
$[b, f]$	$[a, g]$	$[c, e]$
$[h]$	$[a, g]$	$[d]$

The transition diagram is given in Fig. 1.29.

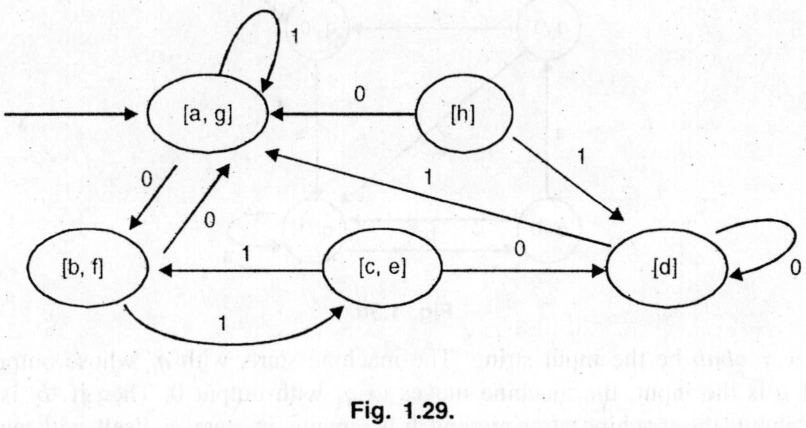

Fig. 1.29.

1.10. MOORE AND MEALY MACHINES

So far we have considered the finite automaton with the property that either they accept the string or reject the string. Now consider the automaton in which the output is choosen from some other alphabet. If the output function depends only on the present state, the automaton is called *Moore Machine* and if the output function depends on both present state and present input then the automaton is called *Mealy Machine.*

1.10.1. Moore Machine

A Moore machine $M = (Q, \Sigma, O, f, \delta, q_0)$ where Q represent the finite set of states, Σ is the input alphabet, O is the output alphabet, $\delta : Q \times \Sigma \rightarrow Q$ is the transition function, f is the output function mapping a state into output alphabet *i.e.*, $f : Q \rightarrow O. q_0$ is the initial state.

1.10.2. Example. Consider the machine defined by the Table 1.16.

Table 1.16

Present States	*Next States*		*Output*
	After input a	*After input b*	
q_0	q_1	q_3	1
q_1	q_3	q_1	0
q_2	q_0	q_3	0
q_3	q_3	q_2	1

The transition graph of this machine is given in Fig. 1.30.

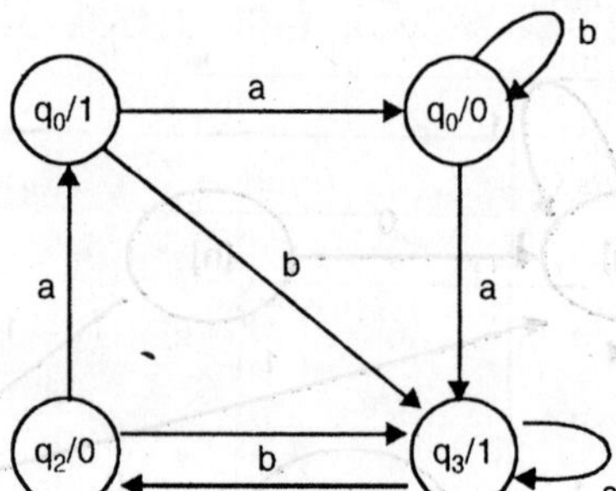

Fig. 1.30.

Let $w = abab$ be the input string. The machine starts with q_0 whose output is 1. If a is the input, the machine moves to q_1 with output 0. Then if 'b' is the next input, the machine after reading b it remains in state q_1 itself with output 0. Now if a is an input, the machine reads 'a' and moves to q_3 producing an output as 1. Next input is b, then after reading b, it moves to q_2 and the output is 0 and processing ends here. Therefore the output sequence is 10010.

1.10.3. Mealy Machine

A Mealy machine $M = (Q, \Sigma, O, \delta, f, q_0)$, where all the symbols except f have the same meaning as in the Moore machine. Here f is the output function mapping $\Sigma \times Q$ into O.

1.10.4. Example

A transition graph of a Mealy machine is given in Fig. 1.31.

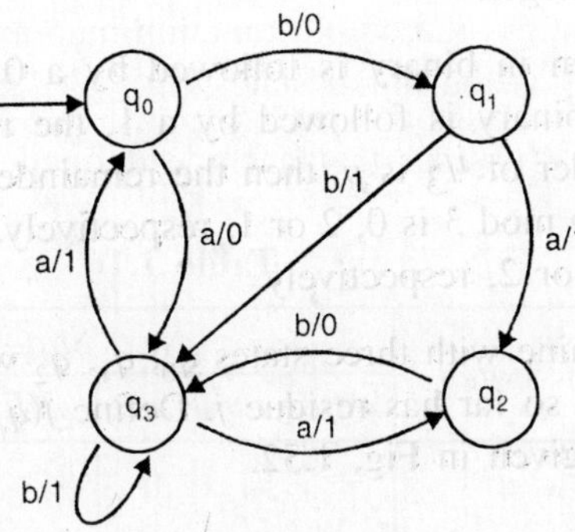

Fig. 1.31

From the figure each edge is lablelled $i/_0$ where i is an input symbol '0' is the output symbol. The transition table for the mealy machine for the figure 1.31 is given in Table 1.17.

Table 1.17

Present States	*Next States*			
	Input a		*Input b*	
	State	*Output*	*State*	*Output*
q_0	q_3	0	q_1	0
q_1	q_2	1	q_3	1
q_2	q_3	1	q_3	0
q_3	q_0	1	q_3	1

Let the input string be *bbbaa*. The machine starts with q_0 and if '*b*' is the input symbol, the machine reads '*b*' and moves to state q_1 with output 0. If one other input '*b*' is given, the machine in state q_1, after reading *b* moves to q_3 with output 1. If third input symbol '*b*' is given, the machine after reading '*b*' moves to the state q_3 itself producing output 1. If '*a*' is an input to the machine, the machines moves to q_0 producing an output 1. Lastly reading the input '*a*' the machine in q_0, moves to q_3 with output 0. Hence the output string is 01110.

Note. (*i*) In a Mealy machine the number of characters in output string is same to the number of letters in input string. But in Moore machine the length of output string is one more than the length of input strings.

(*ii*) As Moore and Mealy machines do not accept or reject an input string, therefore they do not define a language of accepted words, hence they have no final states.

1.10.5. Example

Design a Moore machine to determine the residue mod 3 for each binary string treated as a binary integer.

Note that if 'i' written in binary is followed by a 0, the resulting string has value $2i$ and if i in binary is followed by a 1, the resulting string has value $2i + 1$. If the remainder of $i/3$ is p, then the remainder of $2i/3$ is $2p$ mod 3. If $p = 0$, 1, or 2, then $2p$ mod 3 is 0, 2 or 1, respectively. Similarly, the remainder of $(2i + 1)/3$ is 1, 0, or 2, respectively.

Design a Moore machine with three states q_0, q_1, q_2 where q_j is entered if and only if the input seen so far has residue j. Define $f(q_j) = j$ or $j = 0, 1, 2$. The transition diagram is given in Fig. 1.32.

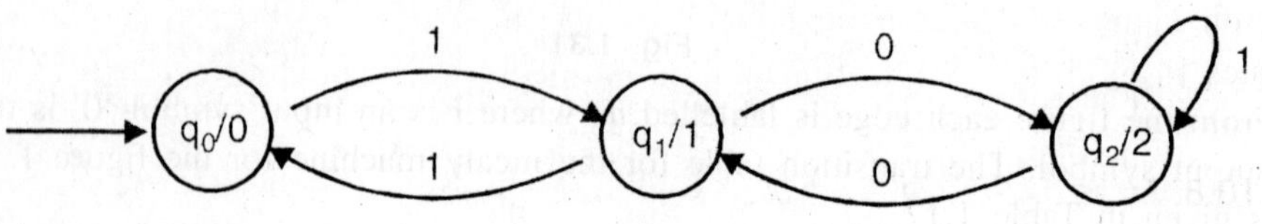

Fig. 1.32.

On input 1010 the sequence of states entered is q_0, q_1, q_2, q_2, q_1, giving output sequence 01221.

Equivalence of Moore And Mealy Machines

Let M be a Mealy or Moore machine. Define $T_M(w)$ for input string w, to be the output produced by M on input w. There can never be exact identity between the functions T_M and T_{M^1} if M is a Mealy machine and M^1 a Moore machine because $|T_M(w)|$ is one less than $|T_{M^1}(w)|$ for each w. However neglecting the response of a Moore machine to input ε, Mealy machine M is said to be *equivalent* to Moore machine M^1 for all inputs w, $b\, T_M(w) = T_{M^1}(w)$, where b is the output of M^1 for its initial state.

1.10.6. Theorem

If $M_1 = (Q, \Sigma, O, \delta, f, q_0)$ is Moore machine, then there is a Mealy machine M_2 equivalent to M_1.

Proof. Let $M_2 = (Q, \Sigma, O, \delta, f^1, q_0)$ and define $f^1(q, a) = f(\delta(q, a))$ for all states q and input symbols a.

Then M_1 and M_2 enter the same sequence of states on the same input, and with each transition M_2 emits the output that M_1 associates with the states entered.

1.10.7. Theorem

Let $M_1 = (Q, \Sigma, O, \delta, f, q_0)$ be a Mealy machine. Then there is a Moore machine M_2 equivalent to M_1.

Proof. Let $M_2 = (Q \times O, \Sigma, O, \delta^1, f^1, [q_0, b_0])$, where b_0 is an arbitrarily selected member of O. That is, the states of M_2 are pairs $[q, b]$ consisting of a state of M_1 and an output symbol. Define

$$\delta^1([q, b], a) = [\delta[q, a], f(q, a)] \text{ and}$$
$$f^1([q, a]) = b.$$

The second component of state $[q, b]$ of M_2 is the output made by M_1 on some transition into state q only the first components of M_2s state determine the moves made by M_2. An induction on n shows that if M_1 enters states $q_0, q_1, \ldots q_n$ on input $a_1, a_2, \ldots, a_n$ and produces outputs $b_1, b_2, \ldots, b_n$ then M_2 enters states $[q_0, b_0], [q_1, b_1], \ldots. [q_n, b_n]$ and produces outputs $b_0, b_1, \ldots, bn$.

1.10.8. Example

Construct a Mealy machine equivalent to the Moore machine given below.

Table 1.18

Present states	Next states		Output
	0	1	
q_0	q_1	q_2	1
q_1	q_3	q_2	0
q_2	q_2	q_1	1
q_3	q_0	q_3	1

Solution. For each input symbol in a Moore machine construct the pair of next state and its corresponding output.

Table 1.19

Present states	Next states			
	0		1	
	State	Output	State	Output
q_0	q_1	0	q_2	1
q_1	q_3	1	q_2	1
q_2	q_2	1	q_1	0
q_3	q_0	1	q_3	1

which is the Mealy machine for given Moore machine.

1.10.9. Example

Construct a Moore machine equivalent to a Mealy machine given in Table 1.20.

Table 1.20

Present states	*Next state*			
	0		*1*	
	States	*Outputs*	*States*	*Outputs*
q_1	q_1	1	q_2	0
q_2	q_4	1	q_4	1
q_3	q_2	1	q_3	1
q_4	q_3	0	q_1	1

Solution. Let M_1 be the Mealy machine of Fig. 1.33.

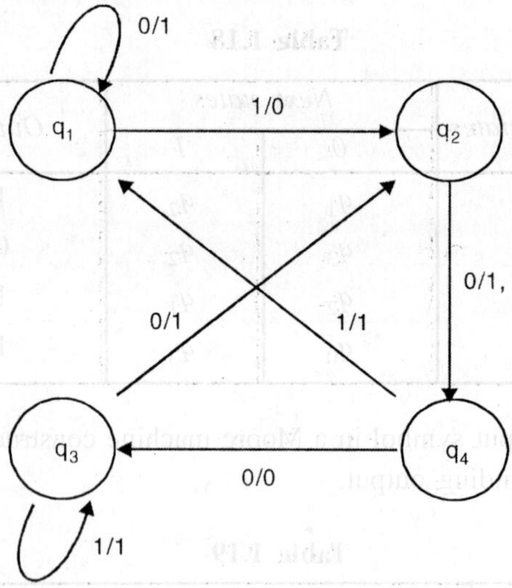

Fig. 1.33.

Now the states of the Moore machine M_2 are $[q_1, 1]$, $[q_1, 0]$, $[q_2, 1]$, $[q_2, 0]$, $[q_3, 1]$ $[q_3, 0]$, $[q_4, 1]$, $[q_4, 0]$. Choose $[q_1, 1]$ as start state. Define $\delta^1([q_1, 1], 0) = [\delta(q_1, 0), f(q_1, 0)] = [q_1, 1]$, $f^1([q_1, q] = 1$. Similarly other transition follows from the diagram

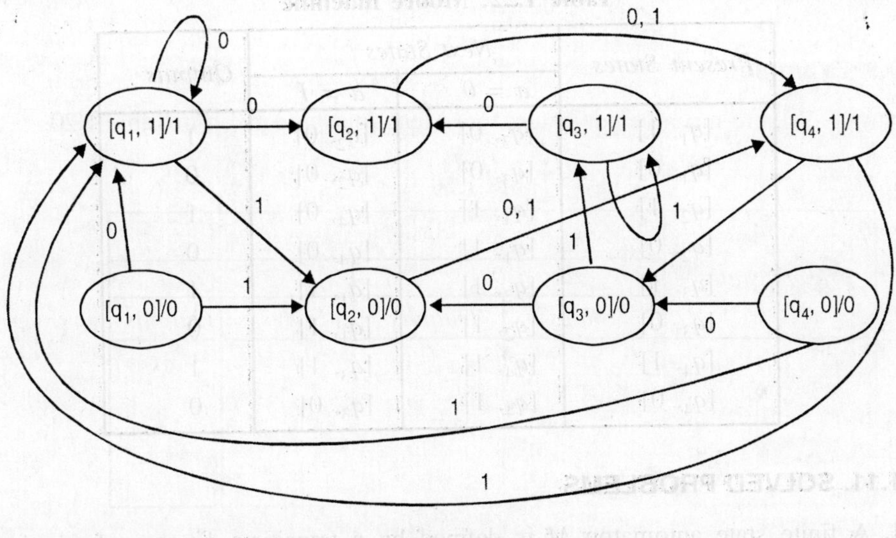

Fig. 1.34.

1.10.10 Example

Consider the Mealy machine described by the transition table given in Table 1.21 construct a Moore machine which is equivalent to the Mealy machine.

Table 1.21: Mealy machine

Present States	*Input a = 0*		*Input a = 1*	
	States	*Outputs*	*States*	*Outputs*
q_1	q_3	0	q_2	0
q_2	q_1	1	q_4	0
q_3	q_2	1	q_1	1
q_4	q_4	1	q_3	0

The states of the Moore machine M_2 are:

$[q_1, 1]$ $[q_1, 0]$, $[q_2, 1]$, $[q_2, 0]$ $[q_3, 1]$, $[q_3, .0]$ $[q_4, 1]$ $[q_4, 0]$

Moore machine of Example 1.10.10 is

Table 1.22: Moore machine

Present States	*Next States*		*Outputs*
	a = 0	*a = 1*	
$[q_1, 1]$	$[q_3, 0]$	$[q_2, 0]$	1
$[q_1, 0]$	$[q_3, 0]$	$[q_2, 0]$	0
$[q_2, 1]$	$[q_1, 1]$	$[q_4, 0]$	1
$[q_2, 0]$	$[q_1, 1]$	$[q_4, 0]$	0
$[q_3, 1]$	$[q_2, 1]$	$[q_1, 1]$	1
$[q_3, 0]$	$[q_2, 1]$	$[q_1, 1]$	0
$[q_4, 1]$	$[q_4, 1]$	$[q_3, 1]$	1
$[q_4, 0]$	$[q_4, 1]$	$[q_3, 0]$	0

1.11. SOLVED PROBLEMS

1. A finite state automaton M is defined by a transition diagram shown in Fig. 1.35.

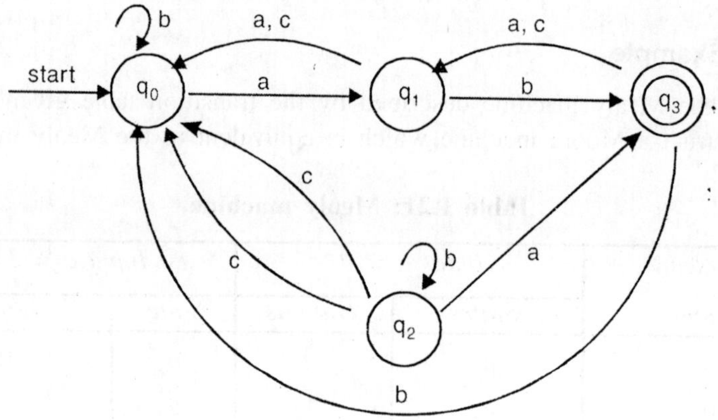

Fig. 1.35.

(*a*) Find its states

(*b*) Find its input symbols

(*c*) Find the initial state

(*d*) Find its accepting states

(*e*) Find $\delta(q_0, c)$

(*f*) Write its transition table.

Solution.

(a) States of $M = \{q_0, q_1, q_2, q_3\}$
(b) Input set of $M = \{a, b, c\}$
(c) Initial state is : q_0
(d) Accepting state is : q_3
(e) $\delta(q_0, c) = q_2$.

Table 1.23.

States	*Inputs*		
	a	b	c
q_0	q_1	q_0	q_2
q_1	q_0	q_3	q_0
q_2	q_3	q_2	q_0
q_3	q_1	q_0	q_1

2. Let $\Sigma = \{a, b\}$. Draw the transition diagram of a finite state automaton M that accepts the given set of strings having odd number of a's.

Solution. Let M be a required DFA which contains two distinct states q_0, q_1 as shown in Fig. 1.36.

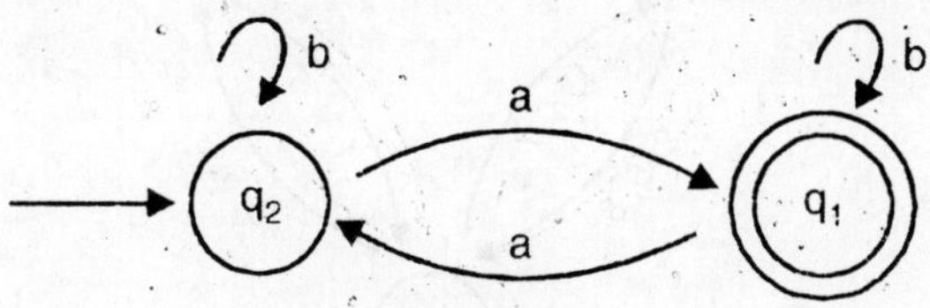

Fig. 1.36.

This machine accepts only input strings having odd numbers of a's.

3. Describe the languge accepted by the NFA whose transition diagram is shown in Fig. 1.37.

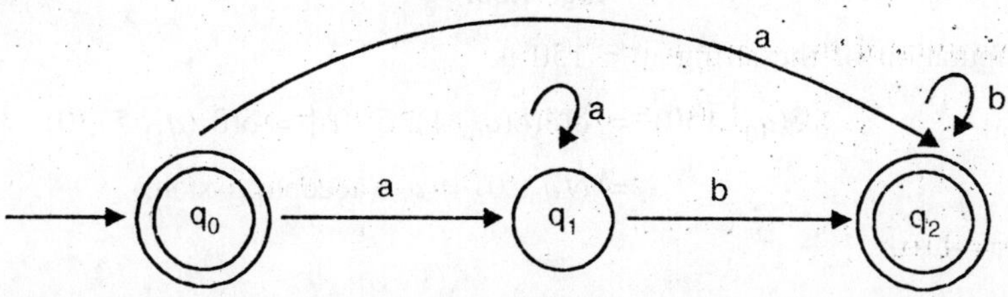

Fig. 1.37.

Solution. Here the initial state q_0 and the state q_2 both are accepting states. Since initial as well as accepting state is q_0, ε is also the language recoginized by M. There are two ways to reach the state q_2, one from q_0 to q_2 via the label a and the other is from q_0 to q_1, then to q_2. Hence the language accepted by M is

$$L(M) = \{\varepsilon, a\} \bigcup \{a^m b^n : m, n \geq 1\}.$$

4. Construct a finite state automata that accept the set of natural numbers x which are divisible by 3.

Solution. Let $M = (Q, \Sigma, q_0, \delta, F)$ be a machine with $Q = \{q_0, q_1, q_2\}$, $\Sigma = \{0, 1, 2, 3, 4, 5, 6, 7, 8, 9\}$ $F= \{q_0\}$, and δ is defined as

$$\delta\{q_0, a\} = q_0;\ \delta(q_1, a) = q_1\ ;\ \delta(q_2, a) = q_2 \text{ for } a \in \{0, 3, 6, 9\}$$

$$\delta(q_0, b) = q_1\ ;\ \delta(q_1, b) = q_2,\ \delta(q_2, b) = q_0 \text{ for } b \in \{1, 4, 7\}$$

$$\delta(q_0, c) = q_2\ ;\ \delta(q_1, c) = q_0,\ \delta(q_2, c) = q_1 \text{ for } c \in \{2, 5, 8\}$$

The transition diagram for this machine is given in Fig. 1.38.

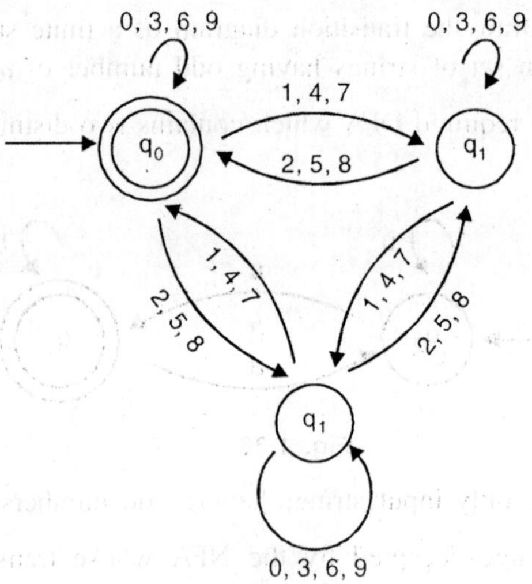

Fig. 1.38.

The computation of the string w = 150 is

$$\delta(q_0, 150) = \delta[\delta(\delta(q_0, 1), 5, 0)] = \delta(\delta\ (q_1, 5), 0)$$

$$= \delta(q_0, 0) = q_0 \text{ (accepting state)}$$

and for w = 116,

$$\delta(q_0, 116) = \delta[\delta(\delta(q_0, 1), 1), 6)]$$

$$= \delta(\delta(q_1, 1), 6)$$

$$= \delta(q_2, 6)$$

$$= q_2 \qquad \text{(non accepting state)}$$

5. Let $\Sigma = \{a, b\}$ construct an automaton M which will accept precisely those strings from Σ which end in two b's.

Solution. Since bb is accepted, but not ε or b, we need three states q_0, the initial state, and q_1 and q_2 with an arrow labeled b going from q_0 to q_1 and one from q_1 to q_2. Also q_2 is an accepting state, but not q_0 and q_1 as in Fig. 1.39. If there is an a, then we want to go back to q_0, and if we are in q_2 and there is a b then we stay back in q_2.

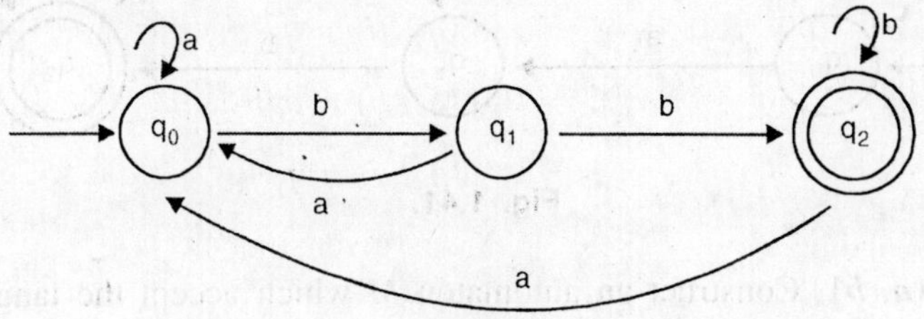

Fig. 1.39.

6. Let $\Sigma = \{a, b\}$. Construct an automaton M which will accept those strings from Σ where the number of b's is divisible by three.

Solution. We need three states q_0 the initial state, q_1 and q_2. We need arrows labeled b going from q_0 to q_1, from q_1 to q_2, and from q_2 back to q_0. The states count the number of b's modulo, 3, so q_0 is an accepting state but not q_1 or q_2. The arrows labeled 'a' does not change the state. The required automaton is given in Fig. 1.40.

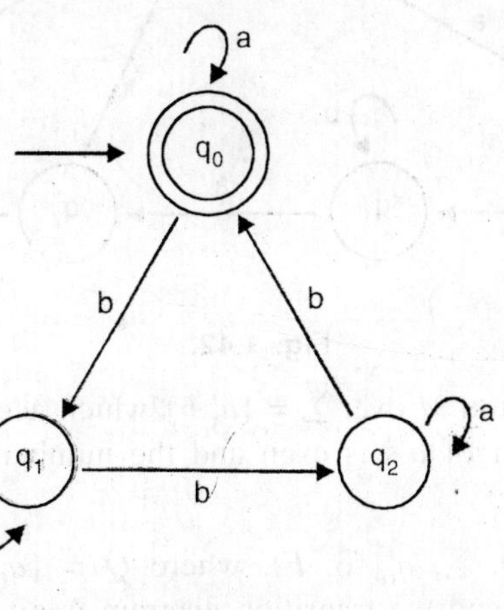

Fig. 1.40.

7. Let $\Sigma = \{a, b\}$. Construct an automaton M that will accept the language $L = \{a^m b^n : m \text{ and } n \text{ positive}\}$.

Solution. Let $M = \{Q, \Sigma, q_0, \delta, f\}$ where $Q = \{q_0, q_1, q_2, q_3\}$, $\Sigma = \{a, b\}$, and $F = \{q_2\}$, the transition diagram is given in Fig.1.41.

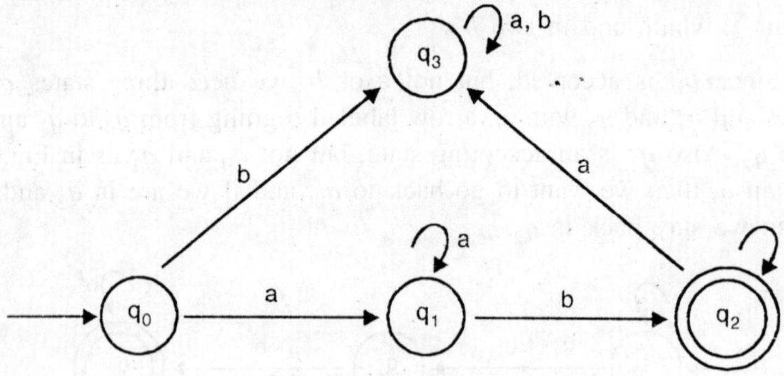

Fig. 1.41.

8. Let $\Sigma = \{a, b\}$. Construct an automaton M which accept the language

$$L = \{b^m ab^n : m \text{ and } n \text{ positive}\}.$$

Solution. Let $M = \{Q, \Sigma, q_0, \delta, F\}$ where $Q = \{q_0, q_1, q_2, q_3, q_4\}$, $\Sigma = \{a, b\}$, $F = \{q_3\}$ and the transition diagram is given in Fig. 1.42.

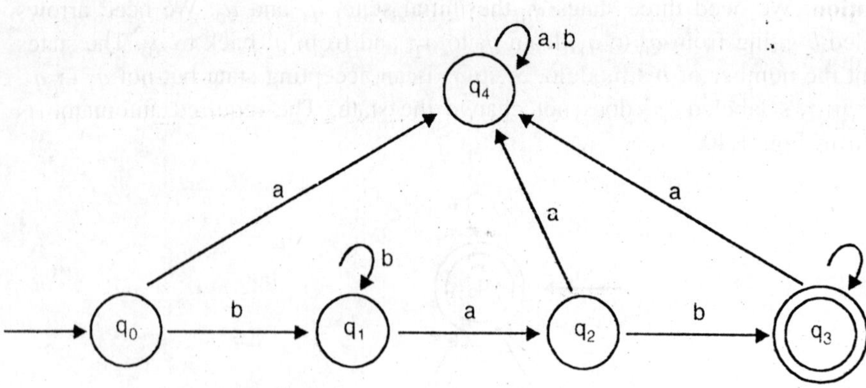

Fig. 1.42.

9. Construct an automaton M over $\Sigma = \{a, b\}$ which accepts those words from Σ such that the number of a's is even and the number of b's is divisible by three.

Solution. Let $M = (Q, \Sigma, q_0, \delta, F)$, where $Q = \{q_0, q_1, q_2, q_3, q_4, q_5\}$, $\Sigma = \{a, b\}$, $F = \{q_0\}$, and the transition diagram is given in Fig. 1.43.

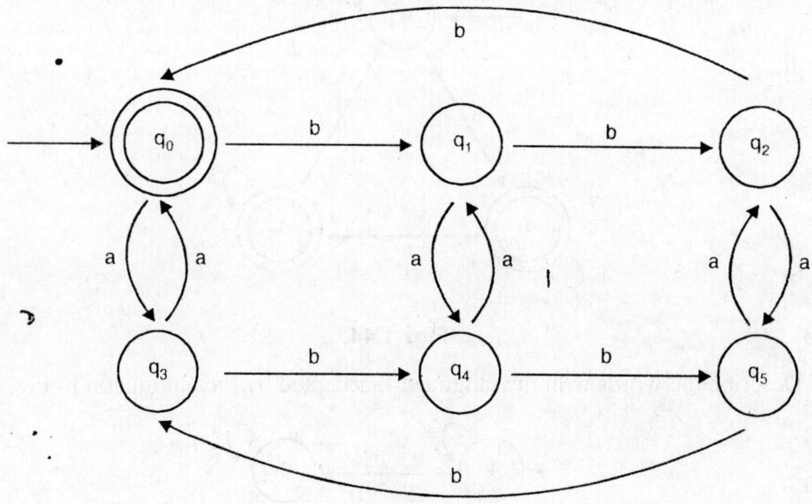

Fig. 1.43.

10. Let $M = \{Q, \Sigma, q_0, \delta, F\}$ and $M^1 = \{Q^1, \Sigma, q_0^{\,1}, \delta^1\ F^1\}$ be automatons over the same alphabet Σ which accept the language $L(M)$ and $L(M^1)$ over Σ, respectively

(*i*) Contstruct an automaton N over Σ which accepts precisely $L(M) \cap L(M^1)$.

(*ii*) Construct an automaton N over Σ which accepts precisely $L(M) \cup L(M^1)$.

Solution.

(*i*) Let $Q \times Q^1$ be the set of states of N. Let (q, q^1) be an accepting state of N, if q, q^1 are accepting states in M and M^1 respectively; and let$(q_0, q_0^{\,1})$ be the initial state of N. The next state function of N is $\Delta : (Q \times Q^1) \times \Sigma \rightarrow Q \times Q^1$ defined by

$$\Delta(\{q, q^1\}, a) = (\delta(q, \text{a}), \delta^1(q^1, a))$$

Then N will accept precisely those words in $L(M) \cap L(M^1)$.

(*ii*) Let $Q \times Q^1$ be the set of states of N and let $(q_0, q_0^{\,1})$ be the initial state of N. Let $(Q \times F^1) \cup (F \times Q^1)$ be the accepting states in N. The transition function Δ is again defined by

$$\Delta((q, q^1), a) = (\delta(q, q), \delta^1(q^1, a)).$$

Then N will accept precisely those words in $L(M) \cup L(M^1)$.

11. Construct an automaton M over $\Sigma = \{a, b]$ which will accept those words over Σ where the number of b's is not divisible by three.

Solution. The required FSA is given in Fig. 1.44.

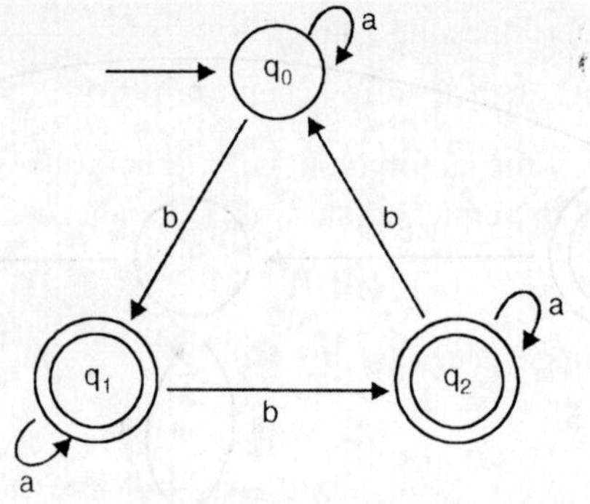

Fig. 1.44.

12. Describe the words *w* in the language *L* accepted by the automaton in Fig. 1.45.

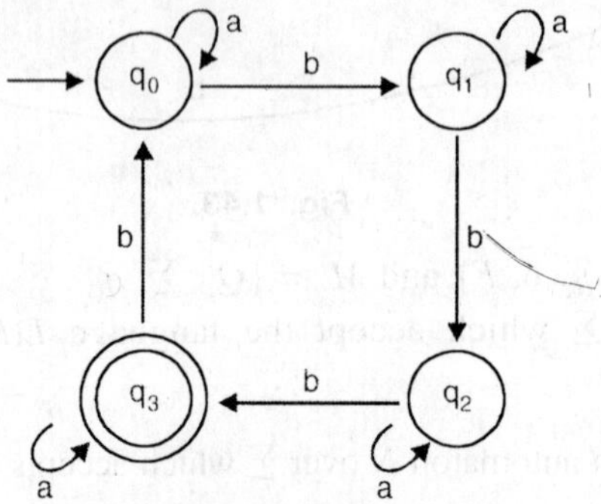

Fig. 1.45.

Solution. Each *a* in *w* does not change the state of the system, whereas each *b* in *w* changes the state of the system from q_i to q_{i+1} (modulo 4). Thus *w* is accepted by *M* if the number *n* of *b*'s in *w* is congruent to 3 modulo 4 *i.e.* when $n = 3, 7, 11, \ldots$

13. Consider the automaton given in Fig. 1.46. Check whether the strings aba bba, baab are accepted by *M* or not.

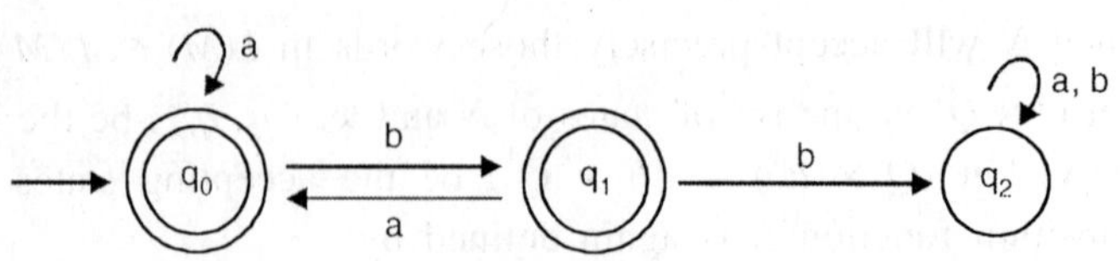

Fig. 1.46.

Solution.

We obtain the path as $q_0 \xrightarrow{a} q_0 \xrightarrow{b} q_1 \xrightarrow{a} q_0 \xrightarrow{b} q_1 \xrightarrow{b} q_2 \xrightarrow{a} q_2$, where q_2 is non-accepting state. Hence the string aba bba is not accepted by *M*.

The word w = baab determines the path $q_0 \xrightarrow{b} q_1 \xrightarrow{a} q_0 \xrightarrow{a} q_0 \xrightarrow{b} q_1$.

Here q_1 is a final state, hence w is accepted by M.

14. To what state does the automaton go when the symbols of the following strings are input to it in sequence starting from the initial state?

(*i*) 0010 (*ii*) 10101 (*iii*) 010100.

(*b*) What is the language accepted by M?

Solution.

(*a*) (*i*) $q_0 \xrightarrow{0} q_1 \xrightarrow{0} q_2 \xrightarrow{1} q_0 \xrightarrow{0} q_1$

(*ii*) $q_0 \xrightarrow{1} q_0 \xrightarrow{0} q_1 \xrightarrow{1} q_0 \xrightarrow{0} q_1 \xrightarrow{1} q_0$

(*iii*) $q_0 \xrightarrow{0} q_1 \xrightarrow{1} q_0 \xrightarrow{0} q_1 \xrightarrow{1} q_0 \xrightarrow{0} q_1 \xrightarrow{0} q_2$.

(*b*) We note that if x is any string that ends in 00, then x is accepted by M. In general, any strings of 0's and 1's that ends in 00 is accepted by M.

15. Consider the NFA given in Fig. 1.47.

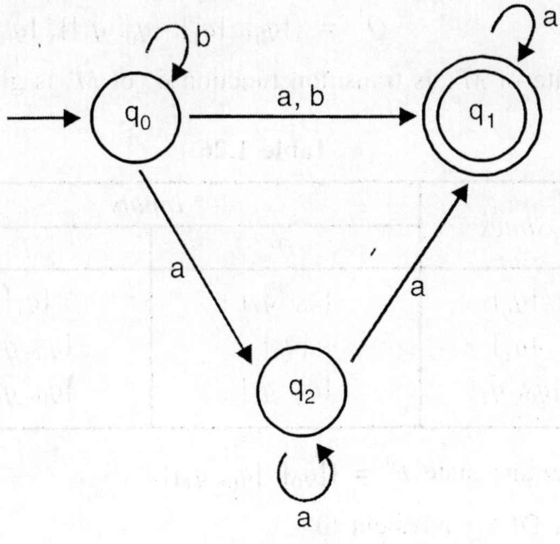

Fig. 1.47.

$Q = \{q_0, q_1, q_2\}$, $\Sigma = \{a, b\}$, q_0 is the initial state. q_1 is the final state and δ is given by the Table 1.24.

Table 1.24.

States	Inputs	
	a	b
q_0	q_1, q_2	q_0, q_1
q_1	q_1	—
q_2	q_1, q_2	—

16. Construct a DFA equivalent to

$M = (Q, \Sigma, \delta, q_0, F)$ where

$Q = \{q_0, q_1\}, \Sigma = \{0, 1\}, F = \{q_0\}$, δ is given by the Table 1.25.

Table 1.25.

States	Inputs	
	0	*1*
q_0	q_0, q_1	q_1
q_1	q_0	q_0, q_1

Solution. We construct a DFA $M^1 = (Q^1, \Sigma, \delta^1, q_0^{\ 1}, F^1)$ accepting $L(M)$ as follows.

$$Q^1 = \{[q_0], [q_1], [q_0, q_1]\}, [q_0]$$

is the initial state of M^1, is transition function δ^1 of M^1 is given in Table 1.26.

Table 1.26.

States	Inputs	
	0	*1*
$[q_0]$	$[q_0, q_1]$	$[q_1]$
$[q_1]$	$[q_0]$	$[q_0, q_1]$
$[q_0, q_1]$	$[q_0, q_1]$	$[q_0, q_1]$

The set of accepting state $F^1 = \{[q_0], [q_0, q_1]\}$.

17. Construct a DFA equivalent to

$$M = (\{q_0, q_1\}, \{0, 1\}, \delta, q_0, \{q_0\})$$

where δ is given by Table 1.27.

Table 1.27

States	Inputs	
	0	*1*
q_0	q_0	q_1
q_1	q_1	q_0, q_1

Solution. Let $M^1 = (Q^1, \{0, 1\}, \delta^1, [q_0], F^1)$ be the required DFA where

$$Q^1 = \{[q_0], [q_1], [q_0, q_1]\}, \delta^1 \text{ is defined by the Table 1.28.}$$

Table 1.28.

States	Inputs	
	0	*1*
$[q_0]$	$[q_0]$	$[q_1]$
$[q_1]$	$[q_1]$	$[q_0, q_1]$
$[q_0, q_1]$	$[q_0, q_1]$	$[q_0, q_1]$

$$F^1 = \{[q_0], [q_0, q_1]\}.$$

18. Find a DFA equivalent to

$$M = (\{q_0, q_1, q_2\}, \{a, b\}, \delta, q_0, \{q_2\})$$

where δ is given by Table 1.29.

Table 1.29.

States	Inputs	
	a	*b*
q_0	q_0, q_1	q_2
q_1	q_0	q_1
q_2	–	$q_0\ q_1$

Solution. The DFA equivalent to M is defined as follows :

$$Q^1 = \{[q_0], [q_1], [q_2], [q_0, q_1], [q_0, q_2], [q_1, q_2], [q_0, q_1, q_2]\}$$

$$\Sigma = \{a\ b\}, [q_0] \text{ is the initial state}$$

$$F^1 = \{[q_0, q_2], [q_1, q_2], [q_2], [q_0, q_1, q_2]\}$$

and δ^1 is defined by Table 1.30.

Table 1.30.

States	Inputs	
	a	b
$[q_0]$	$[q_0, q_1]$	$[q_2]$
$[q_1]$	$[q_0]$	$[q_1]$
$[q_2]$	–	$[q_0, q_1]$
$[q_0, q_1]$	$[q_0, q_1]$	$[q_1, q_2]$
$[q_1, q_2]$	$[q_0]$	$[q_0, q_1]$
$[q_0, q_2]$	$[q_0, q_1]$	$[q_0, q_1, q_2]$
$[q_0, q_1, q_2]$	$[q_0, q_1]$	$[q_0, q_1, q_2]$

19. Describe the following sets by regular expressions

(*a*) {01, 10}, (*b*) {101]}, (*c*) {λ, 1, 1, 11, 111, ...}, (*d*) {1, 11, 111, ...}.

Solution.

(*a*) As {01, 10] is the union of {01] and {10], hence {01, 01] is represented by $01 \cup 10$.

(*b*) 101 is the concatenation of 1, 0 and 1. Hence {101] is represented by 101.

(*c*) {λ, l, 1, 11, ...] is represented by $(1)^*$.

(*d*) Any element in {1, 11, 111, ...] can be obtained by concatenating 1 and any element of $(1)^*$. Hence {1, 11, 111, ...] is represented by $1(1)^*$.

20. Express each of the following sets using a regular expression.

(*a*) The set of strings of one or more 0's followed by a '1'.

(*b*) The set of all strings of 0's and 1's ending in 00.

Solution.

(*a*) The set of one or more 0's is represented by $0(0)^*$. The set of one or more 0's follwed by 1 is obtained by concatenation of $0(0)^*$ and 1 and hence is represented by $0(0)^*\ 1$.

(*b*) The set {0, 1] is represent by $(0 \cup 1)$. The set of all strings of 0's and 1's is represented by $(0 \cup 1)^*$. The set of all strings of 0's and 1's ending in 00 is obtained by concatenation of $(0 \cup 1)^*$ and 00 and hence represented by $(0 \cup 1)^*\ 00$.

21. Let A = {a, b, c]. Describe the language $L(r)$ for each of the regular expression.

(*a*) $r = a^* b^* c^*$ (*b*) $a^* \cup b^* \cup c^*$

Solution.

(*a*) Here $L(r) = L(a)\ (L(b))^*\ (L(c))^*$. This language contains all words in *a*, *b*, *c*, with *a* as a first letter.

(*b*) Here $L(r) = (L(a))^* \cup (L(b))^* \cup (L(c))^*$. This language contains ε, and all words only in '*a*', or only in '*b*' or only in '*c*'.

22. Let $\Sigma = \{a, b]$ be an alphabet. Show that

(*a*) $a^*\ (a \cup b)^*$ (*b*) $aa^*\ (a \cup b)^*\ a$

(*c*) $(a \cup b)^*\ (a \cup \phi)$

are regular expressions over Σ.

Solution.

(*a*) Since $a, b \in \Sigma$, *a* and therefore a^* are regular expression over Σ. Also $a \cup b$ and therefore $(a \cup b)^*$ are regular expressions on Σ. Hence by concatenation of two regular expressions, $a^*\ (a \cup b)^*$ is a regular expression.

(*b*) Here *a* and a^* are regular expressions and hence by concatenation aa^* is a regular expression. Again $(a \cup b)^*$ is a regular expression and therefore by concatenation, $aa^*\ (a \cup b)^*$ is regular expression. This regular expression concatenates with the regular expression *a* produces a regular expression $aa^*\ (a \cup b)^*\ a$ on Σ.

(*c*) Since $a, b \in \Sigma$, ϕ , *a*, *b* are regular expressions. Hence $a \cup \phi$ and therefore $(a \cup \phi)^*$ is a regular expression. Again $(a \cup b)$ and $(a \bullet\cup b)^*$ is a regular expression. By concatenation of two regular expressions $(a \cup b)^*\ (a \cup \phi)$ is a regular expression over Σ. Note that ϕ represents the empty set, that is , the set with no strings.

23. Construct a DFA with reduced state equivalent to the regular expression $10 + (0 + 11)\ 0^*\ 1$. (*U.P. Tech, M.C.A. 2001*)

Solution. First we construct a transition system of the given, regular expression. The construction is given below.

The automaton for 10:

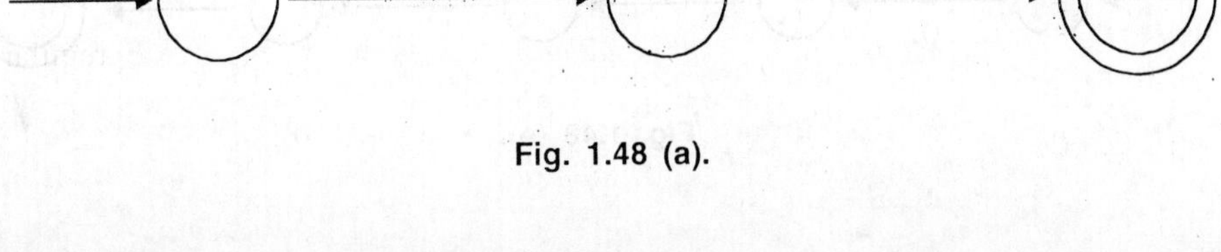

Fig. 1.48 (a).

The automaton for 0 + 11:

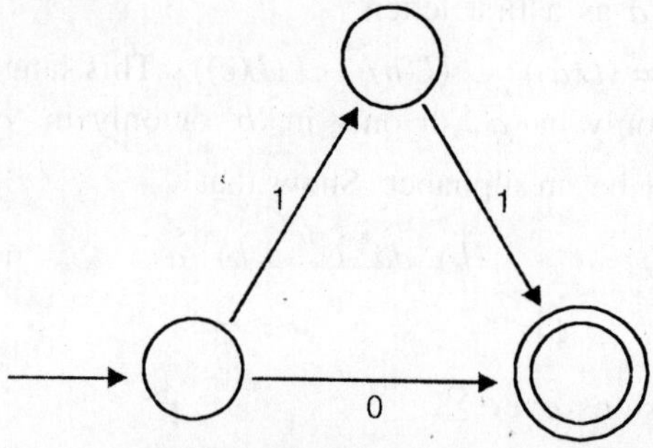

Fig. 1.48 (b).

The automaton for 0^*

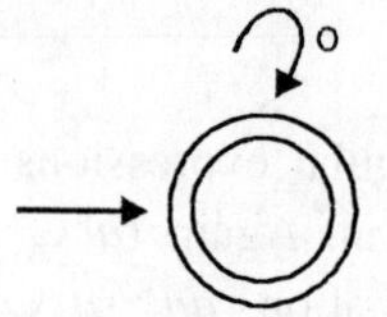

Fig. 1.48 (c).

The automaton for 0^* 1

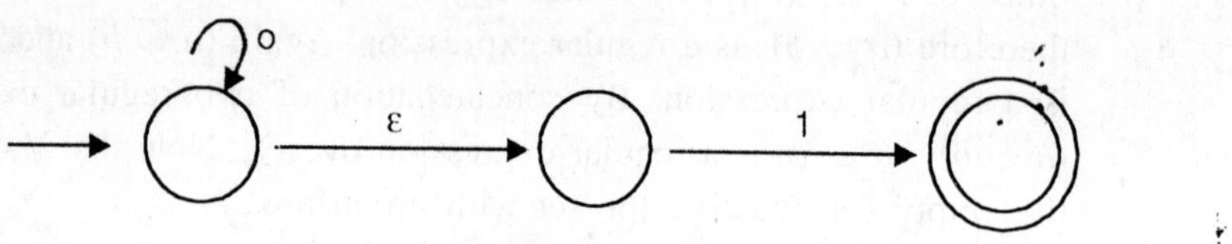

Fig. 1.48 (d).

The automaton for (0 + 11) 0^* 1.

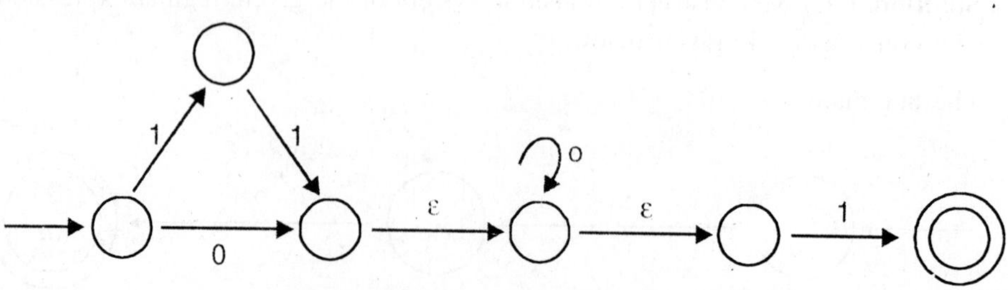

Fig. 1.48 (e).

The automaton for $10 + (0 + 11)\, 0^* 1$.

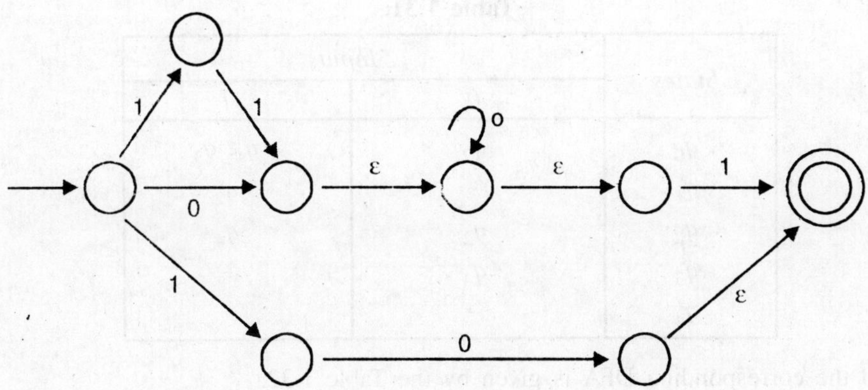

Fig. 1.48 (f).

After removing all ε-moves we get a transition gr: h of the equivalent NFA for the given regular expression as in Fig. 1.48 (g).

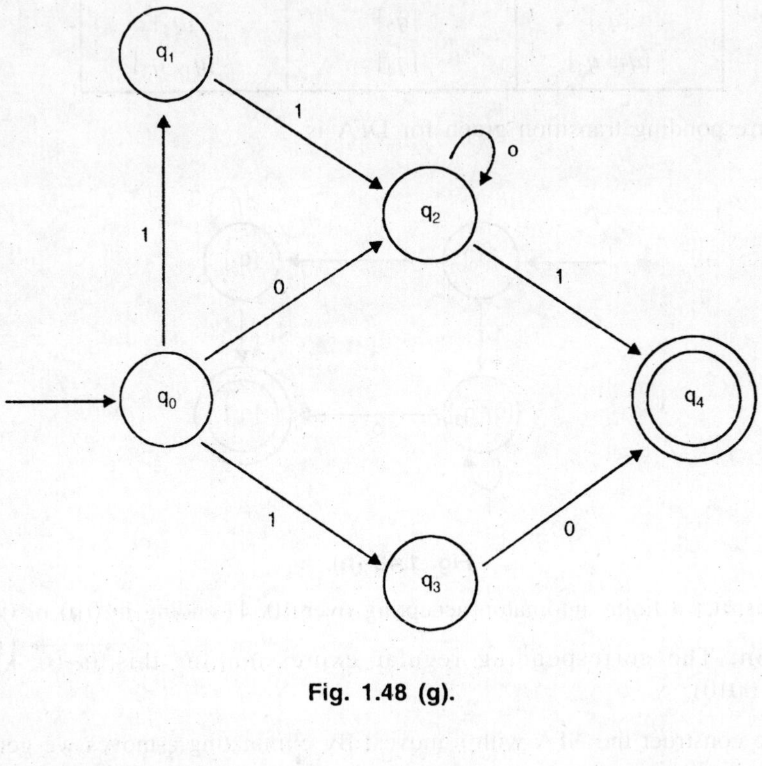

Fig. 1.48 (g).

The corresponding transition Table is 1.31

Table 1.31.

States	*Inputs*	
	0	*1*
q_0	q_2	q_1, q_3
q_1	–	q_2
q_2	q_2	q_4
q_3	q_4	–
q_4	–	–

and the corresponding DFA is given by the Table 1.32.

Table 1.32.

States	*Inputs*	
	0	*1*
$[q_0]$	$[q_2]$	$[q_1, q_3]$
$[q_2]$	$[q_2]$	$[q_4]$
$[q_1, q_3]$	$[q_4]$	$[q_1, q_3]$

The corresponding transition graph for DFA is

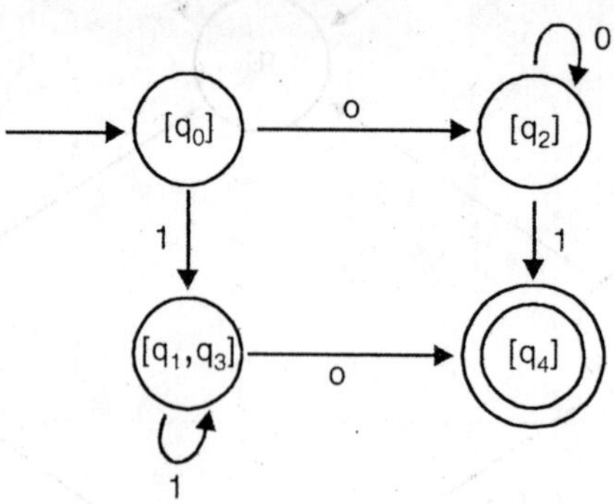

Fig. 1.48 (h).

24. Construct a finite automaton accepting over {0, 1} ending in 010 or 0010.

Solution. The corresponding regular expression for this is $(0 + 1)^*$ $(010 + 0010)$.

First we construct the NFA with ε-moves. By eliminating ε-moves we get the

NFA without ε-moves as in Fig. 1.49.

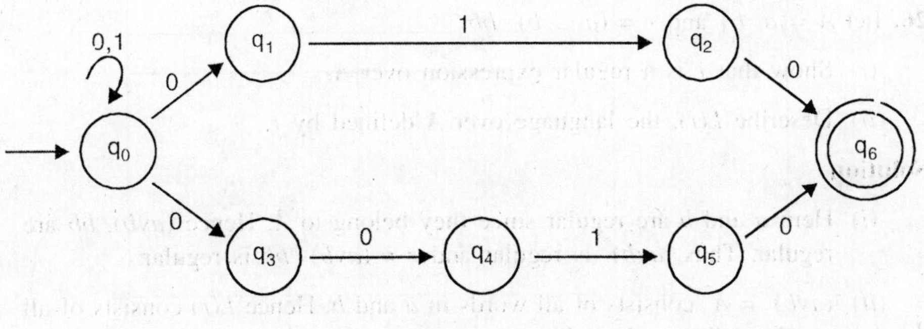

Fig. 1.49.

The equivalent transition table for NFA is Table 1.33.

Table 1.33.

States	*Inputs*	
	0	*1*
q_0	q_0, q_1, q_3	q_0
q_1	–	q_2
q_2	q_6	–
q_3	q_4	–
q_4	–	q_5
q_5	q_6	–
q_6	–	–

The equivalent DFA is given by Table 1.34.

Table 1.34.

States	*Inputs*	
	0	*1*
$[q_0]$	$[q_0, q_1, q_3]$	$[q_0]$
$[q_0, q_1, q_3]$	$[q_0, q_1, q_3, q_4]$	$[q_0, q_2]$
$[q_0, q_2]$	$[q_0, q_1, q_3, q_6]$	$[q_0]$
$[q_0, q_1, q_3, q_4]$	$[q_0, q_1, q_3, q_4]$	$[q_0, q_2, q_5]$
$[q_0, q_1, q_3, q_6]$	$[q_0, q_1, q_3, q_4]$	$[q_0, q_2]$
$[q_0, q_2, q_5]$	$[q_0, q_1, q_3, q_6]$	$[q_0]$

25. Define a regular set or regular language L over an alphabet A.

Solution. L is regular if L is a language defined by a regular expression r over A. That is if there is a regular expression r such that $L = L(r)$.

26. Let $A = \{a, b\}$ and $r = (a \cup b)^* bb$,

(*i*) Show that r is a regular expression over A.

(*ii*) Describe $L(r)$, the language over A defined by r.

Solution.

(*i*) Here a and b are regular since they belong to A. Hence (avb), bb are regular. Thus $(avb)^*$ is regular and $r = (avb)^* bb$ is regular.

(*ii*) $(avb)^* = A^*$ consists of all words in a and b. Hence $L(r)$ consists of all words ending in $b^2 = bb$.

27. Let $A = \{a, b\}$. Determine whether or not each r is a regular expression over A and if it is, describe $L(r)$.

(*a*) $r = a^*$ (*b*) $r = aa^*$.

Solution.

(*a*) $r = a^*$ is a regular expression since $a \in A$ is regular. $L(r)$ consists of all words in a (including the empty word λ).

(*b*) Since a and a^* are regular, $r = aa^*$ is regular. Also $L(r)$ consists of all words in 'a' excluding the empty string.

28. Find a regular expression r over $A = \{a, b\}$ such that $L(r) = \{a^m b^m : m > 0\}$.

Solution. No such r exists. That is, the language is not regular.

29. Find a regular expression r over $A = \{a, b\}$ such that

$$L(r) = \{b^m a b^n : m > 0, n > 0\}.$$

Solution. Note that $L(r)$ consists of those words w whose letters are all 'b' except for one 'a' that is not the first or last letter of w thus $r = bb^* abb^*$ is a solution.

30. Find $L(r)$ for the regular expression $r = b^* ab^* ab^*$ over $A = \{a, b\}$.

Solution. $L(r)$ will consists of all words with exactly two a's.

31. Construct an FSA equivalent to the regular expression.

$(0 + 1)^* (00 + 11) (0 + 1)^*$

Solution. $(0 + 1)^* (00 + 11) (0 + 1)^*$ is of the form rsr, where

$$r = (0 + 1)^*$$

and $$s = 00 + 11.$$

We express $r = (0 + 1)^* = (r_1 + r_2)^*$ where $r_1 = 0$, $r_2 = 1$

and $s = s_1 + s_2$ where $s_1 = 00$ and $s_2 = 11$.

The automaton for $r_1 = 0$ is:

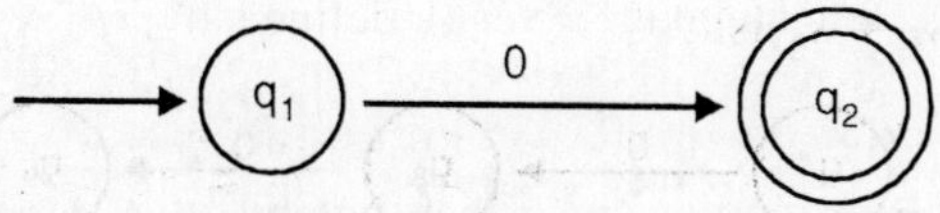

Fig. 1.50 (a)

The automaton for $r_2 = 1$ is:

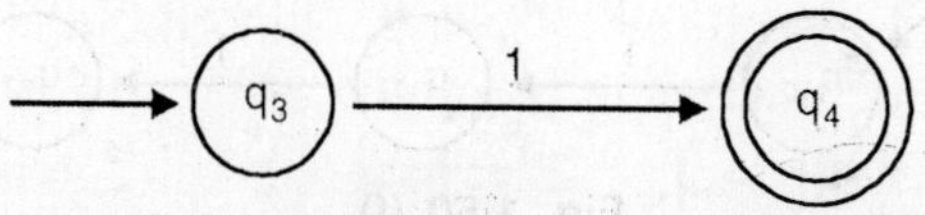

Fig. 1.50 (b).

The construction for $r = (r_1 + r_2)^*$ is:

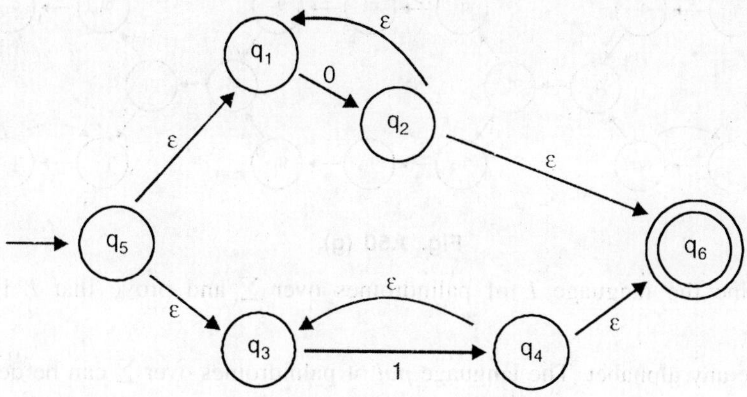

Fig. 1.50 (c).

The automaton for $s_1 = 00$ is:

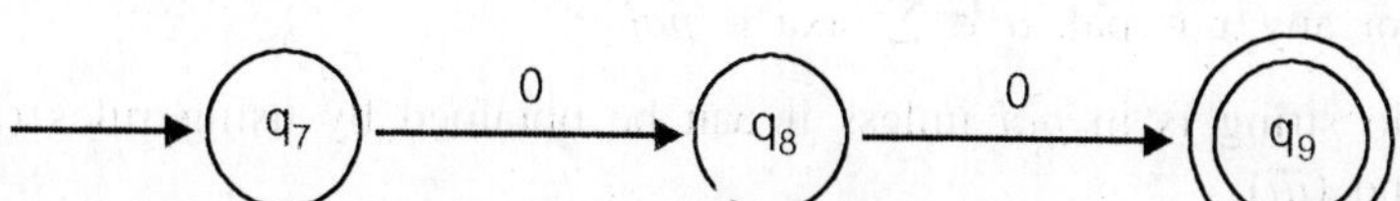

Fig. 1.50 (d).

The automaton for $s_2 = 11$ is:

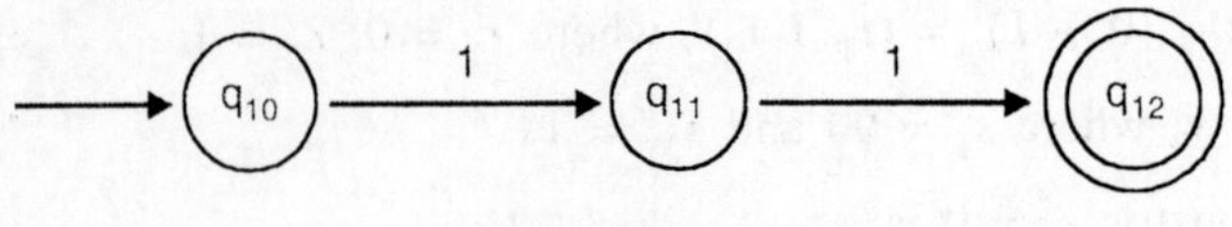

Fig. 1.50 (e).

The automaton for $s_1 + s_2$ is:

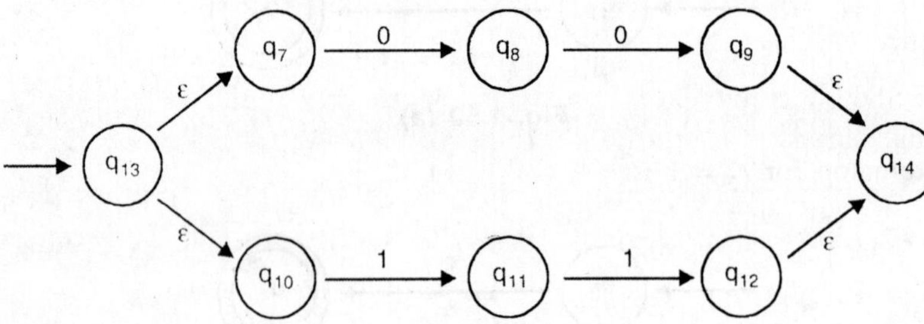

Fig. 1.50 (f).

Hence the automaton for $(r_1 + r_2)^* (s_1 + s_2) (r_1 + r_2)^*$ is :

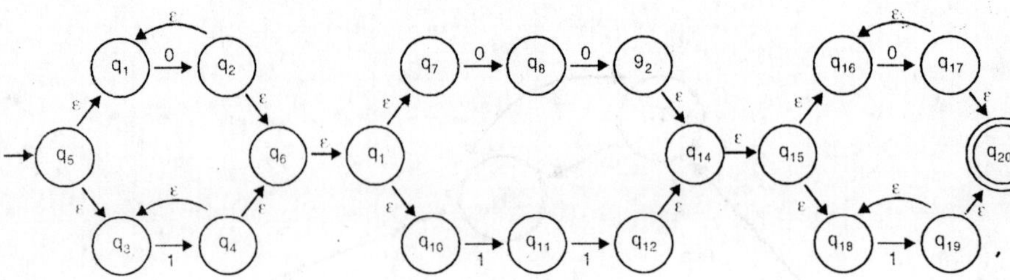

Fig. 1.50 (g).

32. Define the language L of palindromes over Σ and prove that L is not regular.

Let Σ be any alphabet. The language *pal* of palindromes over Σ can be defined as follows.

(*i*) $\varepsilon \in pal$

(*ii*) For any $a \in \Sigma$, $a \in pal$

(*iii*) For any $x \in$ pal, $a \in \Sigma$, axa $\in pal$

(*iv*) No string is in *pal* unless it can be obtained by using rules (*i*), (*ii*), and (*iii*)

Next we prove that L is not regular.

Let $x = 0^n\ 1\ 0^n$. Choose the substring v as 0^j $(j > 0)$, $uv = 0^n$, $w = 1\ 0^n$. We can obtain a contradiction by taking $m = 0$ or $m > 1$.

If $m = 0$, then

$$uv^0\ w\ =\ 0^{n-j}\ 10^n\ \notin L$$

and for $m = 2$

$$uv^2w\ =\ 0^n\ 0^j\ 1\ 0^n = 0^{n+j}\ 1\ 0^n\ \notin L.$$

Hence L cannot be regular.

33. Show that the automaton M_1 and M_2 given in Fig. 1.51. (*a*) and (*b*) are not equivalent.

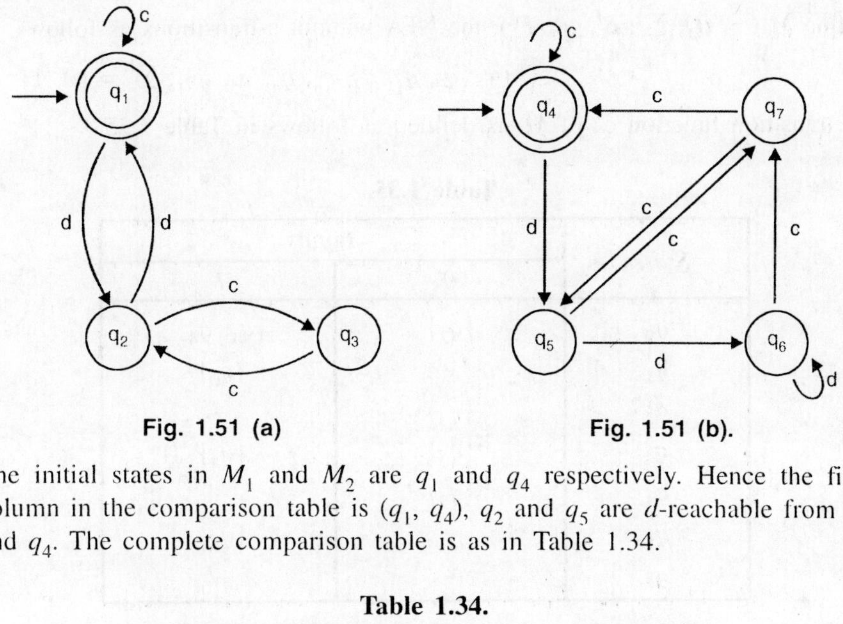

Fig. 1.51 (a) **Fig. 1.51 (b).**

The initial states in M_1 and M_2 are q_1 and q_4 respectively. Hence the first column in the comparison table is (q_1, q_4). q_2 and q_5 are d-reachable from q_1 and q_4. The complete comparison table is as in Table 1.34.

Table 1.34.

$[q, q^1]$	$[q_c, q_c^1]$	$[q_d, q_d^1]$
$[q_1, q_4]$	$[q_1, q_4]$	$[q_2, q_5]$
$[q_2, q_5]$	$[q_3, q_7]$	$[q_1, q_6]$

As q_1 is a final state of M_1 and q_6 is non final state in M_2, M_1 and M_2 are not equivalent.

34. Consider a finite automaton with ε-moves given in Fig. 1.52. Obtain an equivalent automaton without ε-moves.

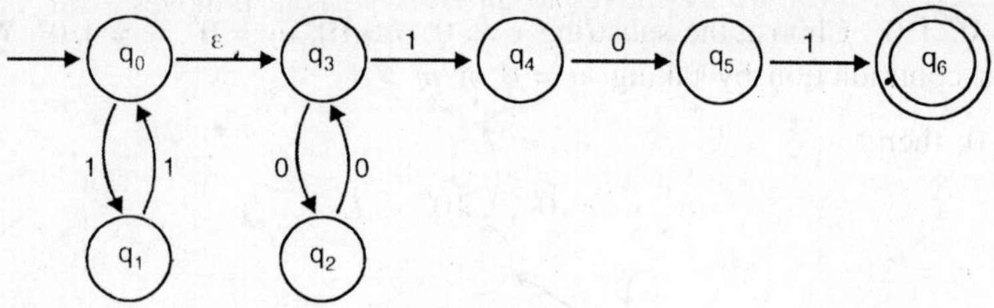

Fig. 1.52.

Solution. Let $M = (Q, \Sigma, \delta, q_0, F)$ be the given NFA with ε-transitions, where $Q = \{q_0, q_1, q_2, q_3, q_4, q_5, q_6\}$, $\Sigma = \{0, 1, \varepsilon\}$, q_0 is the starting state, $F = \{q_6\}$ and the transition diagram is given in Fig. 1.54.

Define $M^1 = (Q, \Sigma^1, \delta^1, q_0, F^1)$, the NFA without ε-transitions as follows.

$$Q = \{q_0, q_1, q_2, q_3, q_4, q_5, q_6\}, \Sigma^1 = \{0, 1\}$$

the transition function δ^1 of M^1 is defined as follows in Table 1.35.

Table 1.35.

States	*Inputs*	
	0	*1*
q_0	$\{q_2\}$	$\{q_1, q_4\}$
q_1	–	$\{q_0\}$
q_2	$\{q_3\}$	–
q_3	$\{q_2\}$	$\{q_4\}$
q_4	$\{q_5\}$	–
q_5	–	$\{q_6\}$
q_6	–	–

The set of final states of $M^1 = F^1 = F = \{q_6\}$ since ε-CLOSURE $\{q_0\} = \{q_3\} \notin F$.

The transition diagram is:

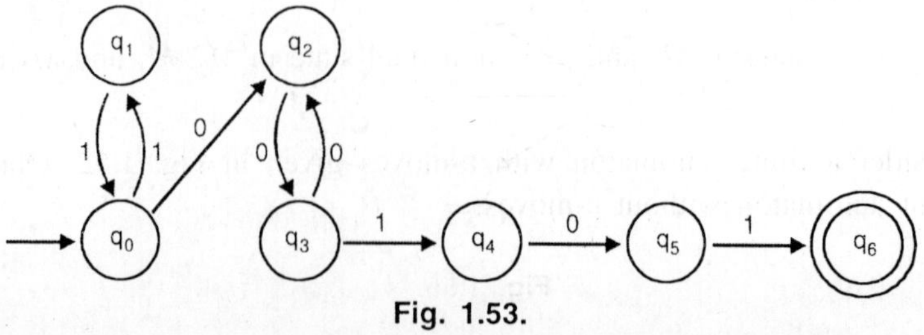

Fig. 1.53.

35. Convert an NFA with ε-moves to an NFA without ε-moves.

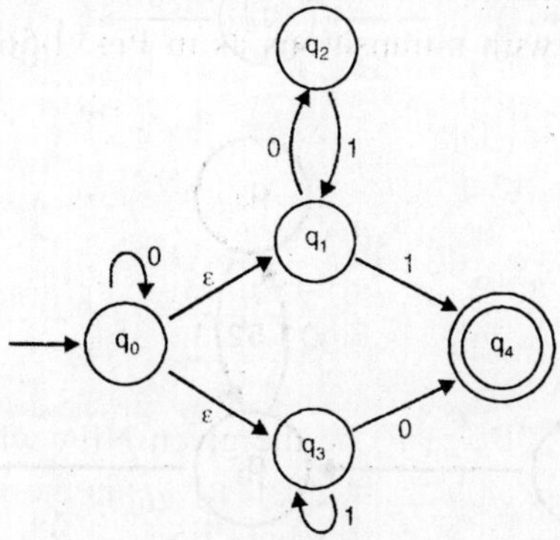

Fig. 1.54.

Solution. Let $M = (Q, \Sigma, \delta, q_0, F)$ be an NFA with ε-moves with $Q = \{q_0, q_1, q_2, q_3, q_4\}$, $\Sigma = \{0, 1, \varepsilon\}$, q_0 is the initial state, $F = \{q_4\}$, the transition diagram is given by Fig. 1.56.

Let $M^1 = (Q, \Sigma^1, \delta^1, q_0, F^1)$ be an NFA with out ε-moves with $Q = \{q_0, q_1, q_2, q_3, q_4\}$, $\Sigma^1 = \{0, 1\}$ and δ^1 is given by the Table 1.36.

Table 1.35.

States	Inputs	
	0	1
q_0	$\{q_0, q_1, q_2, q_3, q_4\}$	$\{q_4, q_3\}$
q_1	$\{q_2\}$	$\{q_4\}$
q_2	–	$\{q_1\}$
q_3	$\{q_4\}$	$\{q_3\}$
q_4	–	–

The transition diagram is in Fig. 1.55.

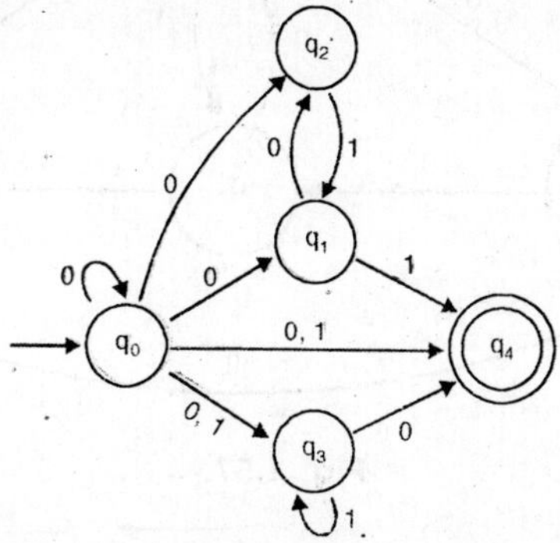

Fig. 1.55.

Note that the initial state q_0 is not an accepting state, since in the original device an accepting state cannot be reached with only ε-transitions.

37. Let M be the NFA with ε-transitions as in Fig. 1.56. Convert into an NFA without ε-transitions.

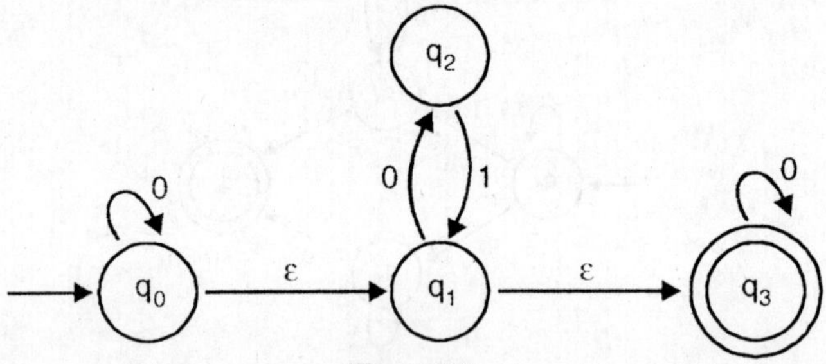

Fig. 1.56.

Solution. We show in Table 1.37 the values of the transition function for the resulting NFA without ε-transitions

Table 1.37.

States	*Inputs*	
	0	*1*
q_0	$\{q_0, q_1, q_2, q_3\}$	–
q_1	$\{q_2, q_3\}$	–
q_2	–	$\{q_1, q_3\}$
q_3	$\{q_3\}$	–

The transition diagram is as follows:

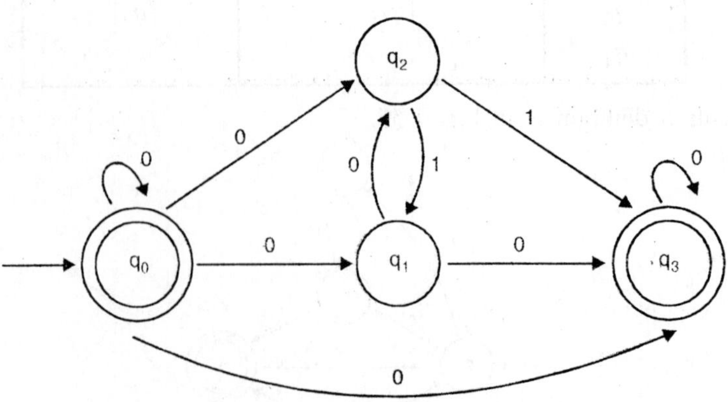

Fig. 1.57.

37. Construct on NFA with ε-transition for $(00 + 1)^* (10)^*$.

Solution. The automaton for 00 is depicted in Fig. 1.58 (*a*).

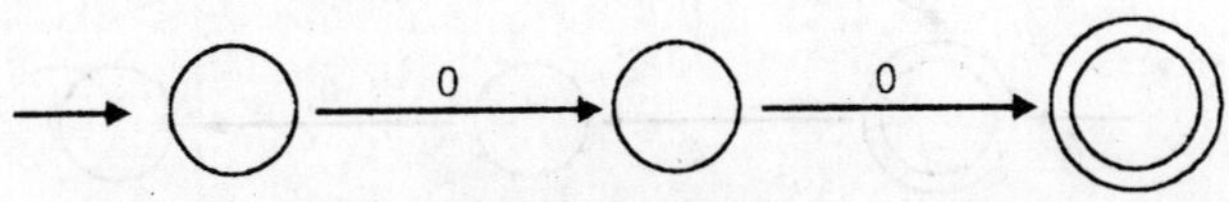

Fig. 1.58 (a).

The automaton for 10 is depicted in Fig. 1.58 (b).

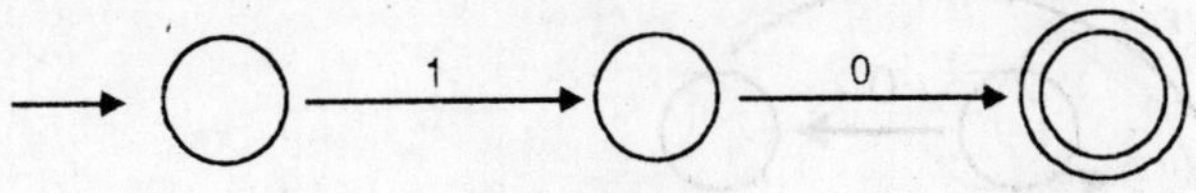

Fig. 1.58 (b).

The automaton for 00 + 1 is depicted in Fig. 1.58 (c).

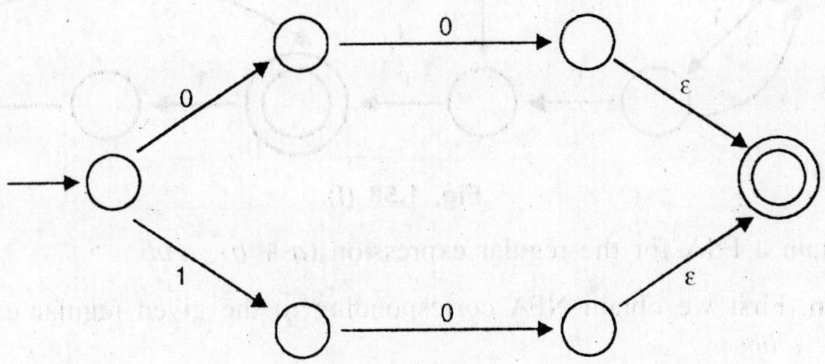

Fig. 1.58 (c).

The automaton for $(00 + 1)^*$ is depicted in Fig. 1.58 (d).

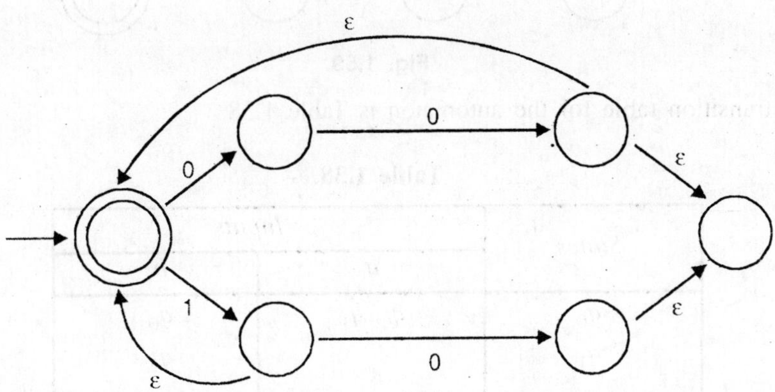

Fig. 1.58 (d).

The automaton $(10)^*$ is depicted in Fig. 1.58 (e).

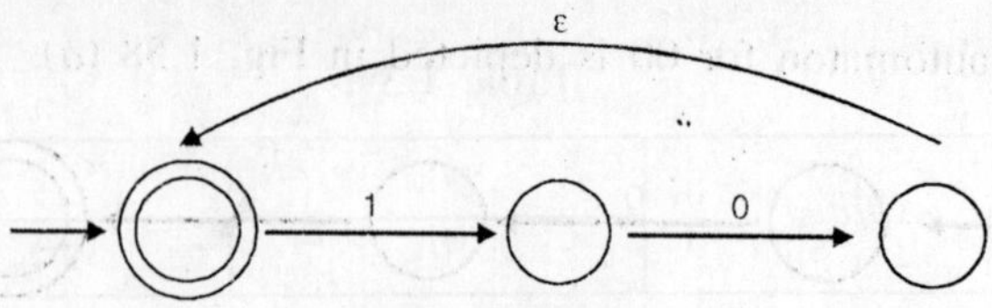

Fig. 1.58 (e).

The automaton for $(00+1)^*\ (10)^*$ is depicted in Fig. 1.58 (f).

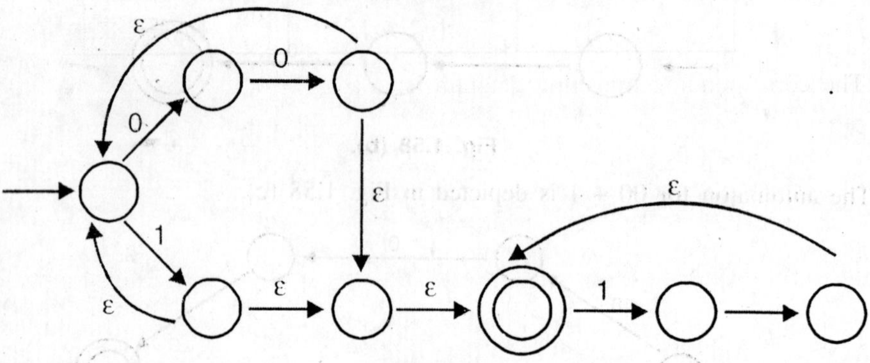

Fig. 1.58 (f).

38. Obtain a FSA for the regular expression $(a + b)^*\ a\ bb$.

Solution. First we obtain NFA corresponding to the given regular expression $(a + b)^*\ a\ bb$.

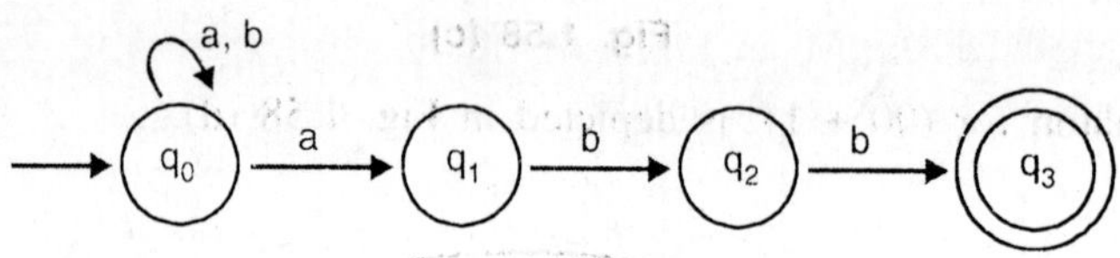

Fig. 1.59.

The transition table for the automaton is Table 1.38.

Table 1.38.

States	Inputs	
	a	b
q_0	q_0, q_1	q_0
q_1	–	q_2
q_2	–	q_3
q_3	–	–

The corresponding DFA is given by the Table 1.39.

Table 1.39.

States	Inputs	
	a	b
$[q_0]$	$[q_0, q_1]$	$[q_0]$
$[q_0, q_1]$	$[q_0, q_1]$	$[q_0, q_2]$
$[q_0, q_2]$	$[q_0, q_1]$	$[q_0, q_3]$
$[q_0, q_3]$	$[q_0, q_1]$	$[q_0]$

The corresponding transition diagram is:

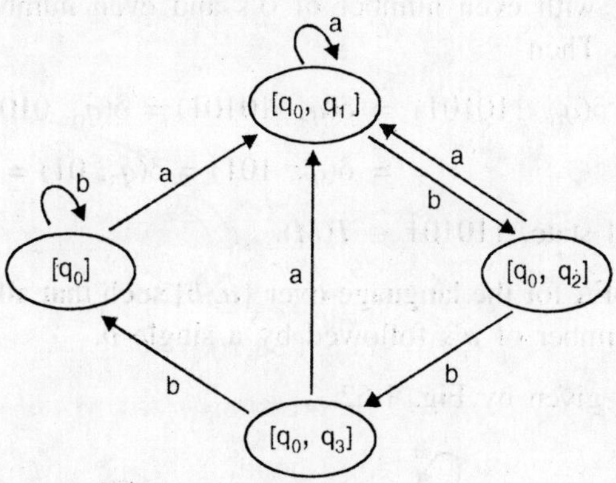

Fig. 1.60.

39. Consider the FSA 'M' in Fig. 1.61. Show that there exist a string having even number of 0's and even number of 1's in $L(M)$.

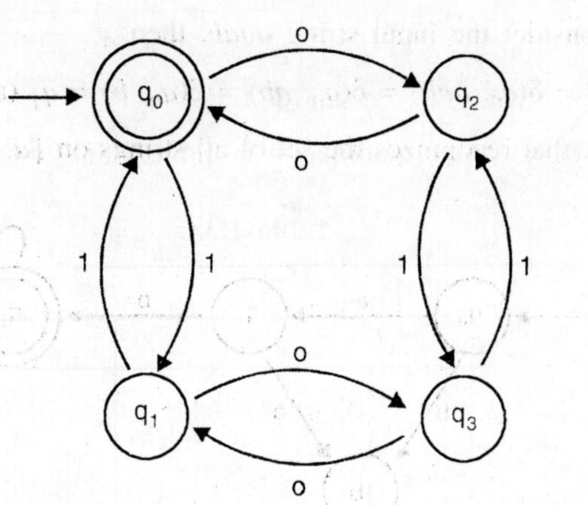

Fig. 1.61.

Solution. Let $M = (Q, \Sigma, q_0, \delta, F)$ be the FSA with $Q = \{q_0, q_1, q_2, q_3\}$, $\Sigma = \{0, 1\}$, $F = \{q_0\}$, and the transition for δ in given by Table 1.40.

Table 1.40.

States	*Inputs*	
	0	*1*
q_0	q_2	q_1
q_1	q_3	q_0
q_2	q_0	q_3
q_3	q_1	q_2

Consider a string with even number of 0's and even number of 1's. Let the string be 110101. Then

$$\delta(q_0, 110101) = \delta(q_1, 10101) = \delta(q_0, 0101)$$
$$= \delta(q_2, 101) = \delta(q_3, 01) = \delta(q_1, 1) = q_0$$

since q_0 is a final state, $110101 \in T(M)$.

40. Construct a DFA for the language over $\{a, b]$ such that all strings consisting of an arbitrary number of a's followed by a single b.

Solution. DFA is given by Fig. 1.62.

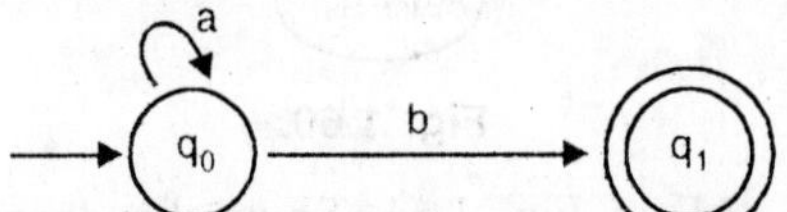

Fig. 1.62.

For example consider the input string *aaab*. then

$$\delta(q_0, aaab) = \delta(q_0, aab) = \delta(q_0, ab) = \delta(q_0, b) = q_1 \text{ (accepting state).}$$

41. Find a DFA that recognizes the set of all strings on $\{a, b]$ starting with *ab*.

Solution.

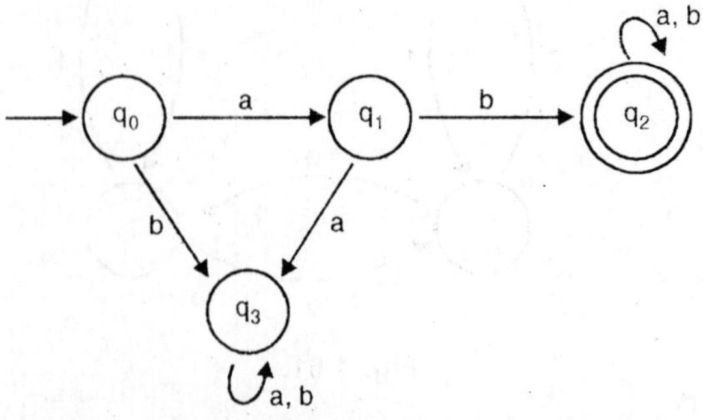

Fig. 1.63.

For this type of DFA we need four states: an initial state, two states for recognizing 'ab' ending in a final state, and one non-final state. Hence q_0 is initial state, q_2 is a final state and q_1, q_3 are its not final states. If a string starts with '*a*' and the second symbol is '*b*' the automaton goes to final state q_2 and the remaining part of the string does not matter. On the other hand if first symbol is not '*a*' and the second one is not '*b*' then the transition goes to non-final state q_3.

42. Design a DFA that accepts the language

$L = \{w : w \in \{0, 1\}^*\}$ and w does not contain three consecutive 1's}.

Solution. Let $M = \{Q, \Sigma\ \delta, q_0, F\}$ be a DFA with $Q = \{q_0, q_1, q_2, q_3\}$, $\Sigma = \{0, 1\}$, $F = \{q_0, q_1, q_2\}$ and δ is given by the Table 1.41.

Table 1.41

States	*Inputs*	
	0	*1*
q_0	q_0	q_1
q_1	q_0	q_2
q_2	q_0	q_3
q_3	q_3	q_3

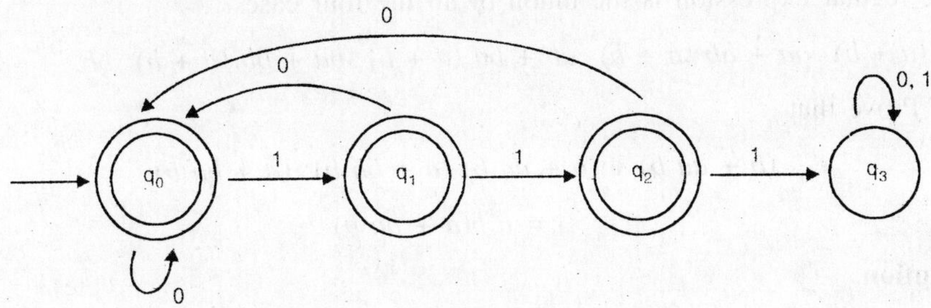

Fig. 1.64.

Whenever '0' is read and M is in state q_0, q_1, q_2, M returns to its initial state q_0. Since q_0, q_1, q_2 are all final states, so any input string not containing three consecutive 1's will be accepted. If a string containing three consecutive 1's then M will be in state q_3, a non-accepting state.

43. Give a regular expression for the set of all strings on $\{a, b]$ end by either an '*a*' or '*bb*'.

Solution.

The first part of this example is the set of all strings on $\{a, b\}$ which is $(a + b)^*$. The second part gives the union of a and bb. That is $(a + bb)$. The final result is the concatenation of $(a + b)^*$ $(a + bb)$.

44. Give the regular expression for the set of strings with an even number of 'a's followed by an odd number of b's.

Solution. The regular expression for even number of 'a's is given by $(aa)^*$, while the odd number of b's is $(bb)^* b$. Therefore the regular expression is the concatenation of $(aa)^*$ and $(bb)^* b$. That is $(aa)^* (bb)^* b$.

45. Find a regular expression for

$$L = \{uvu : u, v \in \{a, b\}^*, | u | = 2\}.$$

Solution. We have the following cases for $| u | = 2$.

(i) If $u = aa$, $v = (a + b)^*$, then $uvu = aa(a + b)^* aa$

(ii) If $u = ab$, $v = (a + b)^*$, then $uvu = ab (a + b)^* ab$

(iii) If $u = ba$, $v = (a + b)^*$, then $uvu = ba (a + b)^* ba$

(iv) If $u = bb$, $v = (a + b)^*$, then $uvu = bb(a + b)^* bb$.

The regular expression is the union of all the four cases.

$$aa (a + b)^* aa + ab (a + b)^* ab + ba (a + b)^* ba + bb (a + b)^* bb.$$

46. Prove that

$$(b + aa^* b) + (b + aa^* b) (a + ba^* b)^* (a + ba^* b) = a^* b(a + ba^* b)^*.$$

Solution.

$$\begin{aligned} \text{L.H.S.} &= (b + aa^* b) + (b + aa^* b) (a + ba^* b)^* (a + ba^* b) \\ &= (b + aa^* b) [\varepsilon + (a + ba^* b)^* (a + ba^* b)] \\ &= (b + aa^* b) (a + ba^* b)^* && \text{by Theorem 1.7.11.} \\ &= (\varepsilon + aa^*) b(a + ba^* b)^* \\ &= a^* b (a + ba^* b)^* && \text{by Theorem 1.7.11.} \end{aligned}$$

47. Construct a NFA with ε-moves for the regular expression $(a + b)^*$ over $\Sigma = \{a, b\}$.

Solution. Ler $r = (a + b)^*$ be a regular expression over $\{a, b\}$. The NFA with ε-moves is given by Fig. 1.65.

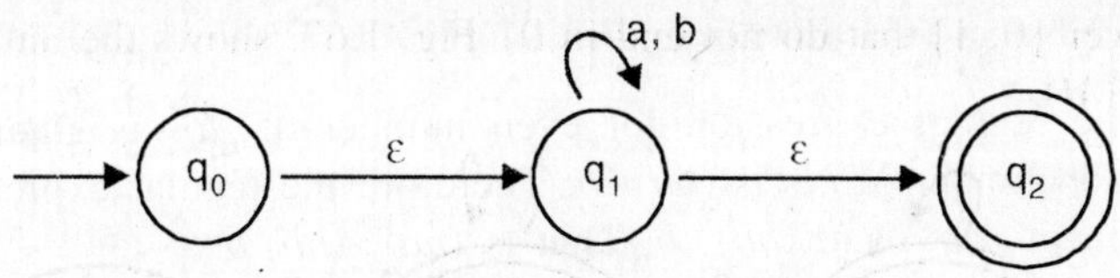

Fig. 1.65.

48. Show that $L = \{a^i\, b^j\, c^k : 0 \le i < j < k]$ is not regular.

Solution. Assume that L is regular. Let n be the constant. By using pumping lemma, let $w = a^n\, b^{n+1}\, c^{n+2} = u\, v\, w$ with $|\, u\, v\, | \le n$, and $|\, v\, | > 0$. Then $u\, v$ is a string of a's, so that the string $uv^2\, w = a^{n+|v|}\, b^{n+1}\, c^{n+2}$. Since $|\, v\, | > 0$, the number of a's is now at least equal to the number of b's so that $uv^2 w \notin L$. Hence L is not regular.

49. Prove that, if L_1 and L_2 are regular languages, then $L_1 \cup L_2$, L_1L_2, L_1^* are also regular languages.

Solution. We prove the result using regular expression. Let r_1 and r_2 be the regular expression such that $L_1 = L(r_1)$ and $L_2 = L(r_2)$. By the definition of regular expressions $r_1 + r_2$, r_1r_2, r_1^* are also regular expressions denoted by the languages $L_1 \cup L_2$, L_1L_2, L_1^* respectively. Hence they are closed under union, concatenation and kleene star.

50. If L is a regular language over Σ. Then the complement $\bar{L} = \Sigma^* - L$ is also a regular language.

Solution. Let $L = T(M)$ for some DFA $M = (Q, \Sigma, \delta, q_0, F)$, then $\bar{L} = T(M_1)$ is the language recognized by $M_1 = (Q, \Sigma, \delta, q_0, Q - F)$. That is M_1 is exactly matching with M, but the final states of M are non final states of M_1 and vice versa. There fore a string.

$w \in \mathrm{T}(M_1) \Leftrightarrow \delta\,(q_0, w) \in Q - F \Leftrightarrow w \notin T(M).$

51. Let M be the FSA given in Fig. 1.66.

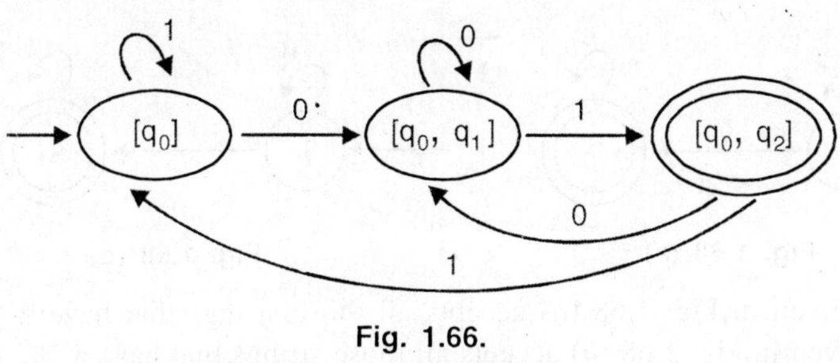

Fig. 1.66.

DFA accepting the language $(0 + 1)^*\, 01$.

From Fig. 1.68, we see that M accepts all strings over $\{0, 1]$ which end in 01. The regular expression is $(0 + 1)^*\, 01$ and the complement of $T(M)$ is the set of all strings over {0, 1} that do not end in 01 Fig. 1.67. shows the automaton for $\{0, 1\}^* - T(M)$.

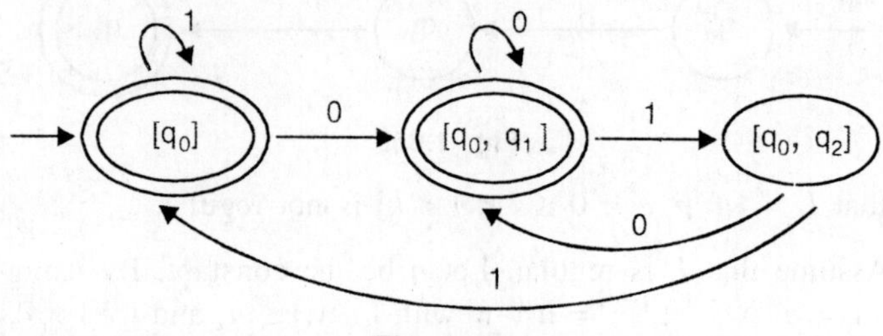

Fig. 1.67.

DFA accepting the completement of the language $(0 + 1)^*$ 01.

52. If L_1 and L_2 are regular languages, then show that the intersection of L_1 and L_2 is also regular.

Solution. Let $M_1 = (Q_1, \Sigma, \delta_1, q_1, F_1)$ and $M_2 = (Q_2, \Sigma, \delta_2, q_2, F_2)$ represents the automaton for L_1 and L_2 respectively over Σ. If the alphabets for L_1 and L_2 are different, then Σ will be union of those alphabets.

For $L_1 \cap L_2$ we construct an automaton M that simulates both M_1 and M_2. The states of M are in pairs (q_i, q_j), where $q_i \in Q_1$, $q_j \in Q_2$. The initial state of M is (q_1, q_2), where q_1 is the initial state of M_1 and q_2 is the initial state of M_2. Also the final states of M are all those pairs (p_1, p_2) such that p_1 is a final state of M_1 and p_2 is a final state of M_2. Hence

$$M = (Q_1 \times Q_2, \Sigma, \delta, (q, q_2), F_1 \times F_2),$$

where $$\delta((q_i, q_j), b) = (\delta_1(q_i, b), \delta_2(q_j, b))$$

Let w be an input string. Then M accepts w iff $\delta((q_1, q_2), w) \in F$. That is δ_1; $(q_1, w) \in F_1$ and $\delta_2 (q_2, w) \in F_2$.

53. Consider two FSA given in Fig. 1.68 (*a*) and (*b*)

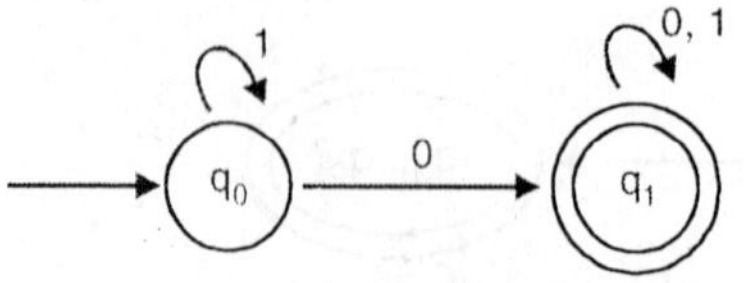

Fig. 1.68 (a).

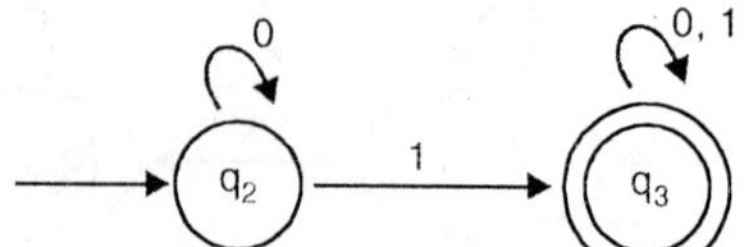

Fig. 1.68 (b).

The FSA given in Fig. 1.68 (*a*) accepts all those strings that have a '0' while the FSA given in Fig. 1.68 (*b*) accepts all those strings that have a '1'. Fig. 1.68 (*c*) shows the product of these two automata. Its states are labeled by the pairs of states of the automaton in Fig. 1.68 (*a*) and (*b*)

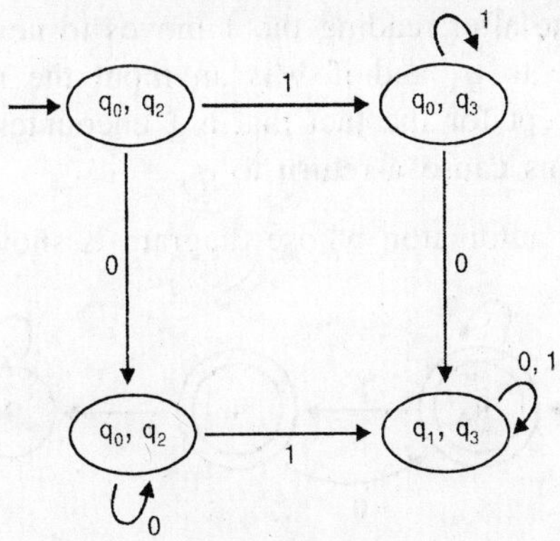

Fig. 1.68 (c).

From Fig. 1.68 (c) it is easy to see that, this automaton accepts the intersection of first two languages given in Fig. 1.68 (a) and Fig. 1.68 (b).

54. Design a finite automaton to test a string to determine whether the string 1101 occurs as a substring.

Solution. Let $M = (Q, \Sigma, \delta, q_0, F)$ be a FSA with

$$Q = \{q_0, q_1, q_2, q_3, q_4\}, \Sigma = \{0, 1\}, F = \{q_4\}$$

and δ is given by Table 1.42

Table 1.42

States	*Inputs*	
	0	*1*
q_0	q_0	q_1
q_1	q_0	q_2
q_2	q_3	q_2
q_3	q_0	q_4
q_4	q_4	q_4

The state diagram of M is Fig. 1.69.

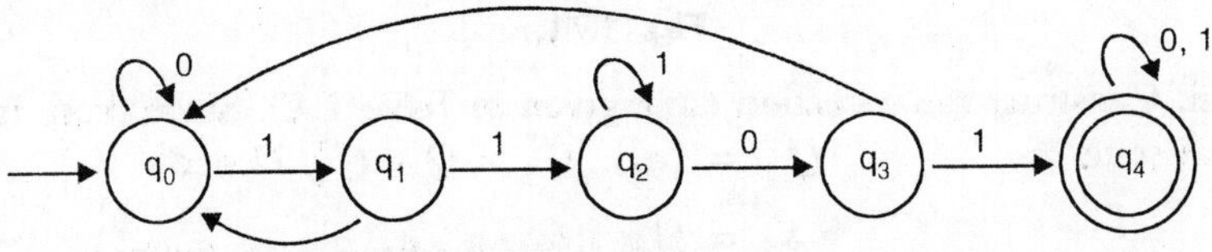

Fig. 1.69.

Starting with q_0, after encountering 1, the machine moves to q_1. If one more 1 is an input, the machine after reading the 1 moves to next state q_2. When 0 is an input, then it move to q_3 and if 1 is an input the machine move to the accepting state q_4. Except for the fact that a 1 encountered in q_2 leaves in q_2 itself, all other situations cause a return to q_0.

55. Consider the finite automaton whose diagram is shown in Fig. 1.70.

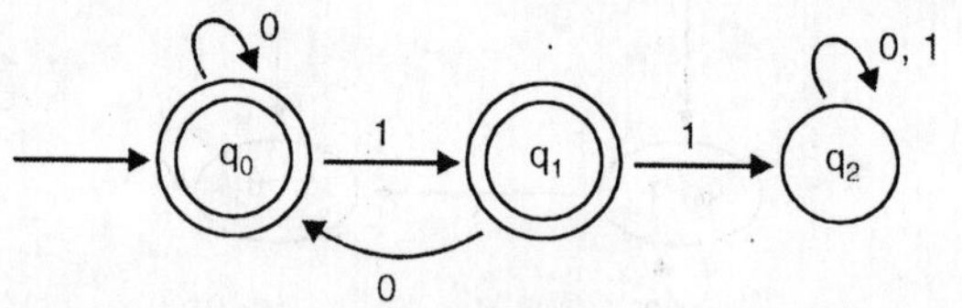

Fig. 1.70.

What kinds of strings are accepted by this machine ?

Solution. The only rejecting state is q_2, since once q_2 is entered there is no way for a computation to leave that state. Any string of the form $y11x$, where y ends in a 0 or y is ε, and x is a string ending 0 or 1, will not be accepted by the machine. In any case, all strings with two consecutive 1s will be rejected, and hence only strings with two consecutive 1s will be rejected.

56. Construct the minimum state automaton equivalent to the transition diagram given in Fig. 1.71.

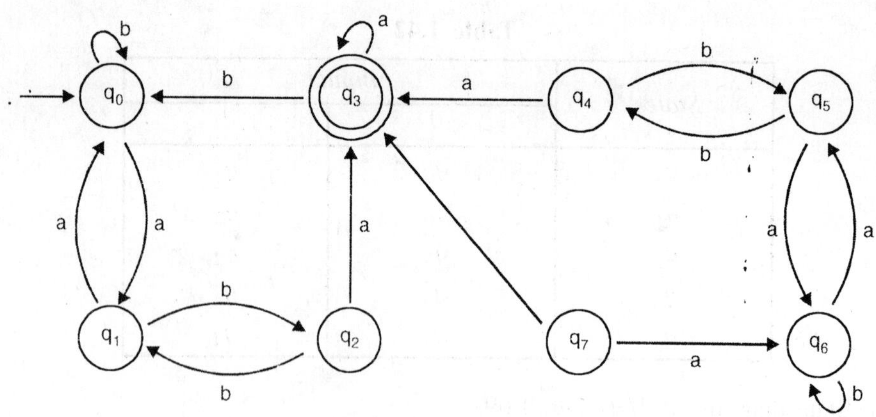

Fig. 1.71.

Solution. Construct the transition table given in Table 1.43. Since there is only one final state q_3, $Q_1^0 = \{q_3\}$, $Q_2^0 = Q - Q_1^0$. Hence

$$S_0 = \{\{q_3\}, \{q_0, q_1, q_2, q_4, q_5, q_6, q_7\}\}.$$

As $\{q_3\}$ cannot be divided again, $Q_1^1 = \{q_3\}$.

Now q_0 is 1-equivalent to q_1, q_5, q_6, but not to q_2, q_4, q_7 and so

$$Q_2^1 = \{q_0, q_1, q_5, q_6\}.$$

q_2 is 1-equivalent to q_4. Hence $Q_3^1 = \{q_2, q_4\}$.

The only element left out in Q_2^0 is q_7. Therefore $Q_4^1 = \{q_7\}$. Thus

$$S_1 = \{\{q_3\}, \{q_0, q_1, q_5, q_6\}, \{q_2, q_4\}, \{q_7\}\}$$

q_0 is 2-equivalent to q_6 but not to q_1 or q_5. So,

$Q_2^2 = \{q_0, q_6\}$, As q_1 is 2-equivalent to q_5,

$Q_3^2 = \{q_1, q_5\}$. As q_2 is 2-equivalent to q_4,

$Q_4^2 = \{q_2, q_4\}$, $Q_5^2 = \{q_7\}$. Thus

$$S_2 = \{\{q_3\}, \{q_0, q_6\}, \{q_1, q_5\}, \{q_2, q_4\}, \{q_7\}\}$$

$$Q_1^3 = \{q_3\}.$$

As q_0 is 3-equivalent to q_6, q_1 is 3-equivalent to q_5, q_2 is 3-equivalent to q_4.

$Q_2^3 = \{q_0, q_6\}$, $Q_3^3 = \{q_1, q_5\}$,

$Q_4^3 = \{q_2, q_4\}$, $Q_5^3 = \{q_7\}$. Therefore

$$S_3 = \{[q_3], [q_0, q_6], [q_1, q_5], [q_2, q_4], [q_7]\}$$
$$= S_2,$$

S_3 gives the equivalence classes, the minimum state automaton is

$$M^1 = (Q^1, \{a, b\}, \delta^1, q_0^1, F^1)$$

where $Q^1 = \{[q_3], [q_0, q_6], [q_1, q_5], [q_2, q_4], [q_7]\}$.

$$q_0^1 = [q_0, q_6], F^1 = [q_3]$$

δ^1 is given by Table 1.43.

Table 1.43.

States	*Inputs*	
	a	*b*
$[q_0, q_6]$	$[q_1, q_5]$	$[q_0, q_6]$
$[q_1, q_5]$	$[q_0, q_6]$	$[q_2, q_4]$
$[q_2, q_4]$	$[q_3]$	$[q_1, q_5]$
$[q_3]$	$[q_3]$	$[q_0, q_6]$
$[q_7]$	$[q_0, q_6]$	$[q_3]$

The transition diagram for M^1 is given in Fig. 1.72.

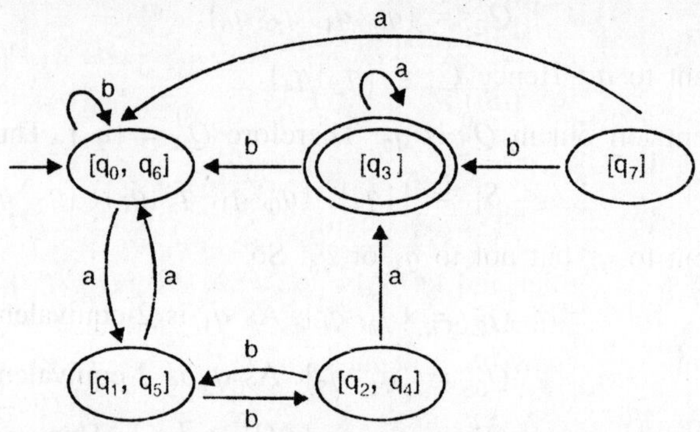

Fig. 1.72.

57. Prove that $L = \{ww^R : w \in \{a, b\}^*\}$ is not regular.

Solution: Suppose L is regular and let $M = (Q, \delta, q_0, F)$ be the *FSA* accepting L. Let n be the number in the pumping lemma.

Let $z = a^n b^n b^n a^n$. Then $|z| = 4n > n$. Then by pumping lemma we can write $z = uvw$ such that $|uv| \leq n$ and $|v| > 0$. Since $|uv| \leq n$ it follows that v cannot contain b's.

Hence $uv = a^n$, $w = b^n b^n a^n$

Take $i = 0$

Then $uv^0w = a^k b^n b^n a^n$ with $k < n$ and so $uv^0w \notin L$ and so L is not regular.

58. Prove that the language $L = \{(ab)^n a^k : n > k, k \geq 0\}$ is not regular.

Solution: Suppose L is regular and let $M = (Q, \Sigma, \delta, q_0, F)$ be the *FSA* accepting L. Let n be the number in the pumping Lemma.

Let $z = (ab)^{n+1} a^n$. Then $z \in L$ and $|z| = 2n + 1 > n$. Hence we can write $z = uvw$ with $|uv| \leq n$ and $|v| > 0$. Since $|uv| \leq n$, both u and v must be in the part of the string made up of ab's.

Case (i) v contain a only

Case (ii) v contain ab's

Case (iii) v contain b only

Case *(i)* Let $i = 0$

Then $uv^0w = (ab)^n a^0 b a^n \notin L$

Case *(ii)* Let $i = 0$

Then $uv^0v = (ab)^n (ab)^0 a^n \notin L \quad [\because n = n]$

Case *(iii)* Let $i = 0$

Then $uv^0w = (ab)^n a(b)^0 a^n$

$= (ab)^n a^{n+1} \notin L \quad [\because n \ngtr n+1]$

Hence L is not regular

59. Show that $L = \{a^{n!} : n \geq 0\}$ is not regular.

Solution: Suppose L is regular and let m be the FSA accepting L. Let n be the number of the pumping Lemma. Let $z = a^{n!}$ then $z \in L$ and $|z| = n! > n$. Hence by pumping Lemma we can write $z = uvw$ with $|uv| \leq n$ and $|v| > 0$.

Let v be such that $|v| = k \leq n$.

Then when $i = 0$, $uv^0w = uw$ has length $n! - k$. This sting is in L only if there exists a j such that $n! - k = j!$. But this is impossible, since for $n > 2$ and $k \leq n$ we have

$$n! - k > (n-1)!$$

Hence $uv^0w \notin L$ and so L is not regular.

EXERCISES

1. Represent the following sets by regular expression

   (i) The set of all strings over $\{0, 1\}$ which has atmost two 0's.

   (ii) $\{a^n : n$ is divisible by 2 or 3 or $n = 5\}$.

   (iii) The set of all strings over $\{a, b\}$ beginning and ending with 'a'.

   (iv) $\{1^{2n+1} : n > 0\}$.

2. Give the regular expressions for the following languages.

   (i) $L = \{a^n b^m : n \geq 4, m \geq 3\}$

   (ii) $L = \{a^n b^m : n \geq 1, m \geq 1 \text{ nm} \geq 3\}$.

3. Describe in English languages, the sets represented by the following regular expressions.

   (i) $a(a + b)^* ab$.

   (ii) $a^* b + b^* a$.

   (iii) $a^* + (ab + a)^*$.

   (iv) $(11 + 0)^* (00 + 1)^*$.

   (v) $((00 + 11) + (01 + 10)(00 + 11)^* (01 + 10))^*$.

4. Write regular expressions for the following languages over $\{0, 1\}$

(*i*) All strings ending in 01.

(*ii*) All strings not ending in 01.

(*iii*) All strings containing an even number of 0's.

(*iv*) All string having at least two occurrence of the substring 00.

5. Construct finite automata equivalent to the following regular expression.

   (*i*) $10 + (0 + 11)\,0^*\,1$.

   (*ii*) $01\,(1\,(10)^* + 111)^* + 0)^*\,1$.

   (*iii*) $((0 + 1)\,(0 + 1))^* + ((0 + 1)\,(0 + 1)\,(0 + 1))^*$.

6. Find an NFA that accepts the languages

   (*i*) $aa^* + aba^*\,b^*$

   (*ii*) $(a + b)^*\,b\,(a + bb)^*$

7. Construct *a* NFA corresponding to the regular expression

   (*i*) $(ab + c^*)^*\,b$

   (*ii*) $a + bb + ba\,b^*a$

   (*iii*) $a\,(a + b)^*\,ab$

   (*iv*) $a^*\,b + b^*\,a$.

8. Construct a finite automaton for the following regular expression.

   (*i*) 01^*

   (*ii*) $(0 + 1)^*\,01$

   (*iii*) $00\,(0 + 1)^*$.

9. Find the regular expression corresponding to the automaton given in Fig. 1.73.

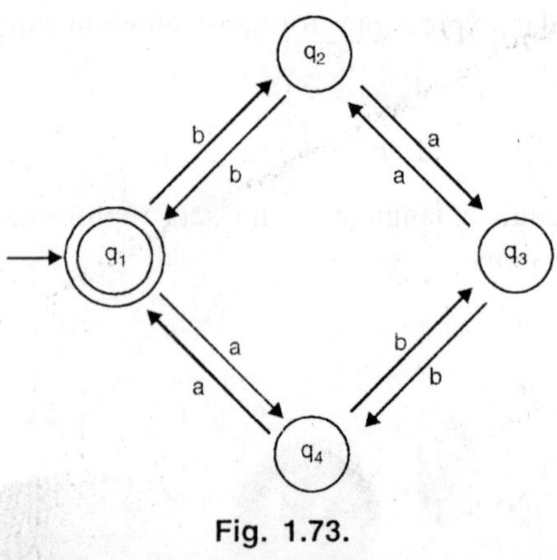

Fig. 1.73.

10. Construct a regular expression corresponding to the transition diagram given in Fig. 1.74.

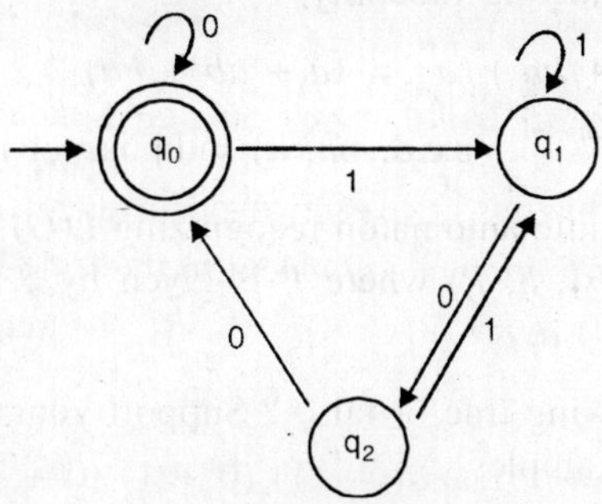

Fig. 1.74.

11. Show that $L = \{a^n\, b^{2n} : n > 0\}$ is not regular.
12. Show that $L = \{a^{n!} : n \geq 0\}$ is not regular.
13. Show that $L = \{a^n\, b^l\, a^k : n, l, k \geq 0\}$ is not regular.
14. Prove or dis prove the following for regular expressions r, s.

    (i) $$(r + s)^* = r^* + s^*$$

    (ii) $$(rs + r)^* r = r\,(sr + r)^*.$$

15. Construct DFA's equivalent to the NFA's

    (a) $(\{p, q, r, s\}, \{0, 1\}, \delta_1, p, \{s\})$

    (b) $(\{p, q, r, s\}, \{0, 1\}, \delta_2, p, \{q, s\})$

    where δ_1 and δ_2 are given in Table 1.44 and Table 1.45.

Table 1.44

States	*Inputs*	
	0	*1*
p	*p, q*	*p*
q	*r*	*r*
r	*s*	–
s	*s*	*s*

Table 1.45.

States	*Inputs*	
	0	*1*
p	*q, s*	*q*
q	*r*	*q, r*
r	*s*	*p*
s	–	*p*

16. Prove the following indentity:

$$(a^* ab + ba^*)^* a^* = (a + ab + ba)^*$$

17. Show that $\{0^m 1^n : \text{g.c.d.}\ (m, n) = 1\}$ is not regular.

18. Construct a finite automaton recognizing $L(G)$ where G is the grammar $(\{S, A\}, \{a, b\}, S, P)$ where P is given by $S \to aS \mid bA \mid b$, $A \to aA \mid bS \mid a$.

19. Are the following true or false ? Support your answer by giving proofs or counter examples

(*a*) If L^* regular, then L is regular

(*b*) If $L_1 L_2$ is regular and L_1 is regular, then L_2 is regular.

(*c*) IF $L_1 \cup L_2$ is regular and L_1 is regular, then L_2 is regular.

20. Show that $\{a^n b^n : n > 0]$ is not a regular set without using pumping Lemma.

ANSWERS

1. Here we have three cases :

(*i*) w contains no 0; one 0 or two 0's.

The required regular expression is

$1^* + 1^* 01^* + 1^* 01^* 01^*$.

(*ii*) $(aa)^* + (aaa)^* + (aaaaa)^*$.

(*iii*) $a (a + b)^* a$

(*iv*) $1 (11)^*$.

3. (*i*) The set of all strings starting with a and ending in ab.

(*ii*) The strings are either strings of a's followed by a single 'b' or strings of b's followed by a single 'a'.

(*iii*) The strings are either strings of a's are strings of $ab + a$.

4. (*i*) $(0 + 1)^* 01$

(*ii*) $0 (0 + 1)^* 0 + 1(0 + 1)^* 0 + 1 (0 + 1)^* 1$.

(*iii*) $(00) (0 + 1)^* (00)$.

5. (*i*)

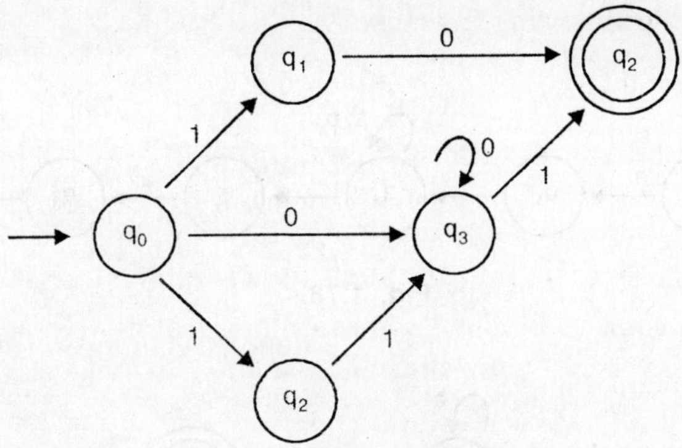

Fig. 1.75.

7. (*i*)

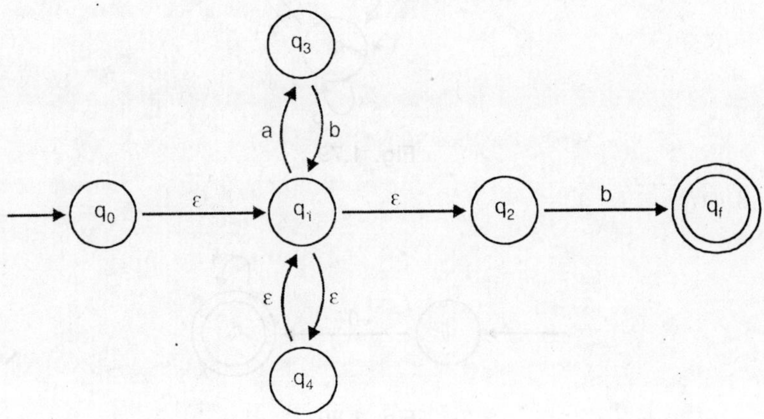

Fig. 1.76.

(*ii*)

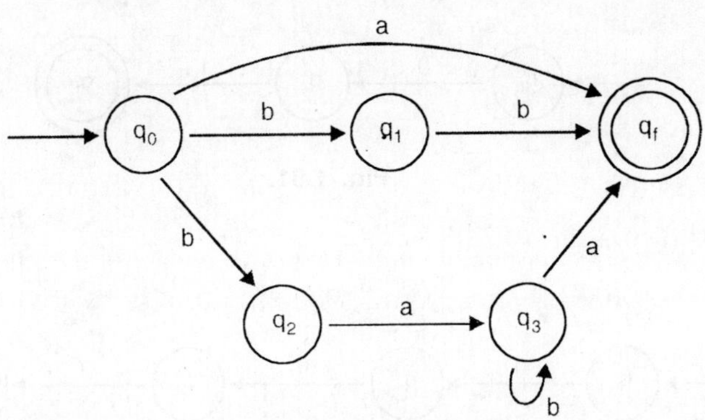

Fig. 1.77.

(*iii*)

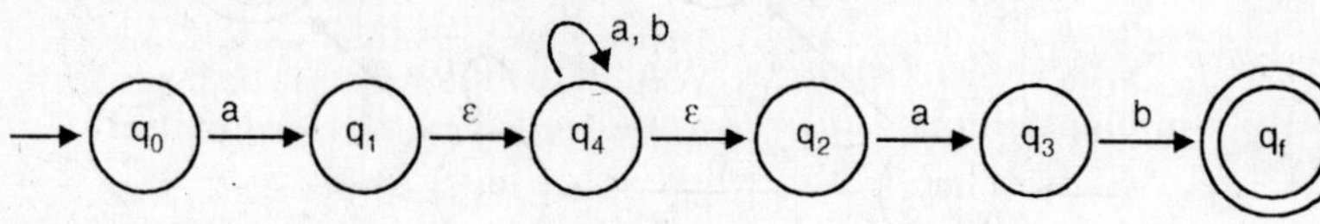

Fig. 1.78.

(*iv*)

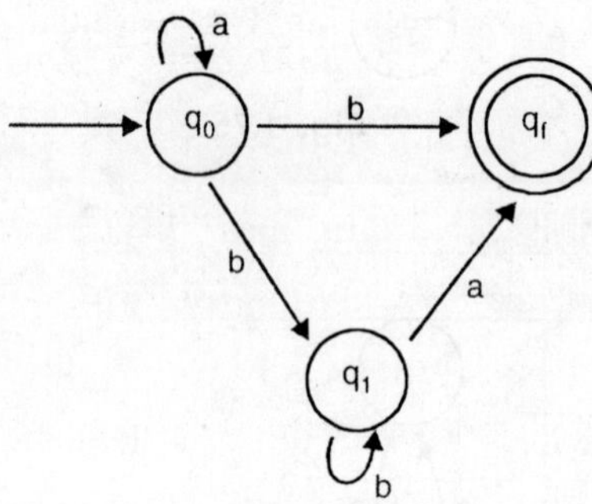

Fig. 1.79.

8. (*i*)

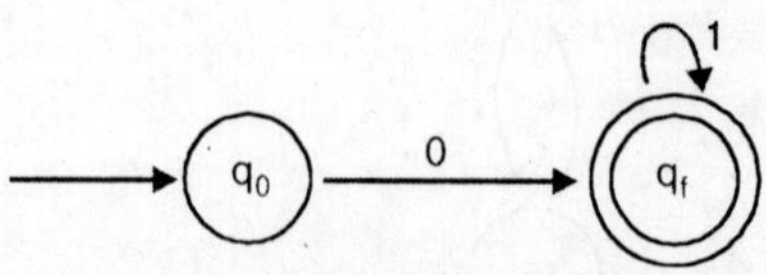

Fig. 1.80.

(*ii*)

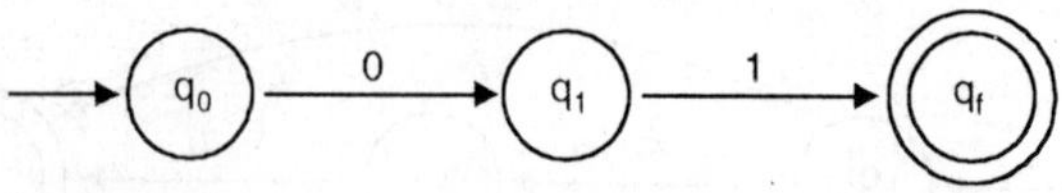

Fig. 1.81.

(*iii*)

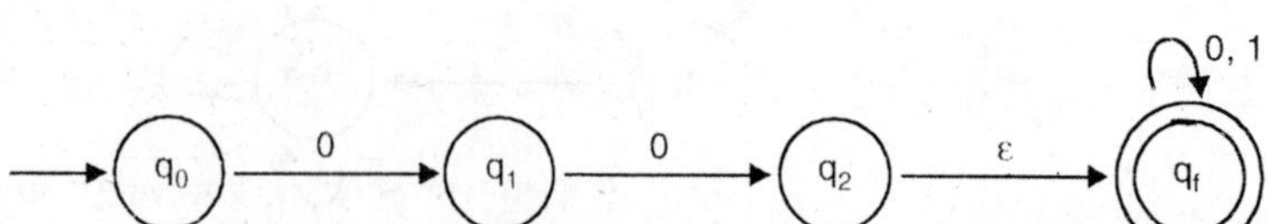

Fig. 1.82.

10. $(0 + 1\ (1 + 01)^*\ 00)^*$

11. Let $L = \{a^n\ b^{2n} : n > 0]$. We prove L is not regular by contradiction.

    Let L be regular. Let n be the number of states. Let $w = a^n\ b^{2n}$. By pumping lemma $z = uvw$ with $|\ uv\ | \leq n$, $|\ v\ | > 0$ and $uw \in L$. As $|\ uv\ | \leq n$, $uv = a^m$, $v = a^l$ where $0 < l \leq n$. So $uw = a^{n-1}\ b^{2n} \in L$, a contradiction, since $n - 1 \neq n$. Thus L is not regular.

18. Let $M = (\{q_0, q_1, q_f\}, \{a, b\}, \delta, q_0, \{q_1\})$ where q_0 and q_1 correspond to S and A respectively. Then the NFA accepting $L(G)$ is given by Table 1.46.

Table 1.46.

States	*Inputs*	
	a	*b*
q_0	q_0	q_1, q_f
q_1	q_1, q_f	q_0

CHAPTER 2

Context Free Languages

You can recognize a legal English sentence when you hear one. You can immediately tell when reading such sentences whether they formed according to generally accepted rules for sentence structure. In this respect you are acting as a language recognizer : a device that accepts valid strings. The finite automata of the last chapter are formalized types of language recognizers.

You also however are capable of producing legal English sentences. Again why you would want to do so and how you manage to do it are not our concern; but the fact is that you occasionally speak or write sentences, and in general they are syntactically correct (even when they are lies). In this respect you are acting as a language generator. In this chapter we study certain types of formal generators. Such a device begins, when given some sort of start signal to construct a string. Its operation not completely determined from the beggining but is nevertheless limited by a set of rules. Finally this process halts and the device outputs a completed string. The language defined by the device is the set of all string that it can produce.

Neither a recognizer nor a generator for the English language is at all easy to produce; indeed from a formal standpoint these tasks may be impossible. Nevertheless the idea of a language generator has some explanatory force in attempts to discuss human language. More important for us, however is the theory of generators of formal artificial languages such as the regular languages and the important class of context free langulages. The context free languages, like the regular sets, are of great practical importance, notably in defining programming languages in formalizing the notion of parsing simplifying translation of programming languages, and in other string processing applications. As an example context free grammars are useful for describing arithmetic expressions, with arbitrary resting of balanced parenthesis, and block structure in programming languages can be represented by regular expressions. Regular expressions serve as language generators in such a way that the strings in the language can be produced from left to right, that is, we can imagine each symbol of the generated string to be output as it is determined. But context free grammars are more complex sorts of language generators, which are based on a more complex understanding of the structure of the strings belonging to the language.

While linguists were studying context free grammers computer scientists began to describe programming languages by a notation called Backus-Naur Form (BNF) which is the context free grammar Notation with minor changes in format and some shorthand. This use of context free grammars has greatly simplified the definition of progamming languages and the construction of compilers. The reason for this success is undoubtedly due in part to the natural way in which most programming language construct are described by grammars.

In this chapter we study context free grammars and context free languages. We define derivation trees and study the ambiguity of the language. The two normal forms Chomsky Normal Form (CNF) and Greibech Normal Form (GNF) are dealt with.

2.1. CONTEXT FREE GRAMMARS

2.1.1. Definition

A grammar $G = (N, T, S, P)$, where N is a finite nonempty set of non-terminals, T, a finite nonempty set of terminal ($N \cap T = \phi$), $S \in N$ is called as a starting symbol and P set of production rules of the form $A \to \alpha$ (L.H.S. is a single non-terminal) and $\alpha \in (N \cup T)^*$ is called as a *Context Free Grammar* (CFG).

In otherwords a grammar G is said to be a CFG if in every production $A \to \alpha$, the L.H.S. is *a* single non-terminal.

2.1.2. Example

Consider the grammar G given by $G = (N, T, S, P)$ where $N = \{S\}$, $T = \{a, b, c\}$, S-starting symbol and $P = \{S \to aSa, S \to bSb, S \to c, S \to a, S \to b, S \to \lambda\}$. We observe that G is a context free grammar since in every production L.H.S. is a single non-terminal.

Note. G can also represented as

$$G = (\{S\}, \{a, b, c\}, S, \{S \to aSa, S \to bSb, S \to c, S \to a, S \to b, S \to \lambda\})$$

2.1.3. Example

Consider the grammar G, given by $G_1 = (N, T, P, S)$ where $N = \{S\}$, $T = \{a, b\}$, S- starting symbol and $P = \{S \to aSb, S \to ab\}$. We observe that G_1, is a CFG.

2.1.4. Definition

If G is a context free grammar. $L(G)$ is the set of all strings that can be obtained by starting with S and applying the production rules a finite number of times until no non-terminal chracters remain. $L(G)$ is known as the language generated by ((or) derived) by G.

2.1.5. Definition

A popular alternate form of defining the production rules in a grammar is BNF (Backus-Naur-Form). If the production rules $A \to B_1$, $A \to B_2$, $A \to B_3$, ... $A \to B_n$ are part of a grammar, they would be written in BNF as

$$A ::= B_1/B_2/B_3 \ldots, B_n.$$

The production symbol $\to$ is replaced by the symbol $::=$, and / is used to separate different right hand side of productions corresponding to the same left hand side. The symbol $::=$ is read as "is defined as" and/as "or".

2.1.6. Example

The production given in Example 2.1.2 can be represented as

$$S ::= aSa/bSb/c/a/b/\lambda.$$

The production given in example 2.1.3 can be represented as

$$S ::= aSb/ab.$$

2.2. DERIVATIONS AND LANGUAGES

2.2.1. Definition

Let $G = (N, T, S, P)$ be a grammar (not necessarily context free). If $\alpha \to \beta$ is a production and $x, y \in (N \cup T)^*$, we say that $x\,\beta\,y$ is *a direct derivation* of $x\,\alpha\,y$ or $x\,\beta\,y$ is *directly derivable* from $x\,\alpha\,y$ (or) $x\,\alpha\,y$ directly derives $x\,\beta\,y$ in G and write $x\,\alpha\,y \Rightarrow x\,\beta\,y$. Two strings are related by $\Rightarrow$ exactly when the second is obtained from the first by one application of some production.

If $\alpha_i \in (N \cup T)^*$ and $\alpha_i \Rightarrow \alpha_{i+1}$ for $i = 1, \ldots, r-1$, we say that α_i derives α_r in G and write

$$\alpha_1 \Rightarrow \alpha_2 \Rightarrow \alpha_3 \Rightarrow \ldots \Rightarrow \alpha_{r-1} \Rightarrow \alpha_r \qquad \ldots(2.1)$$

Thus, α_1 derives α_r in G, if α_r is predictable from α_1, by employing a finite number of productions from G. An expression of the form (2.1) is called a *derivation* in G and can be abbreviated into the expression $\alpha_1 \overset{*}{\Rightarrow} \alpha_r$.

2.2.2. Definition

A *sentential form* is any derivative of the unique non-terminal symbol S. The language L generated by a grammar G is the set of all sentential forms whose symbols are terminals.

$$\text{i.e. } L(G) = \left\{\sigma / S \overset{*}{\Rightarrow} \sigma \text{ and } \sigma \in T^*\right\}$$

A language L is a *Context Free Language* (CFL), if there is a CFG G such that $L = L(G)$.

2.2.3. Example

Consider the context free grammar $G = (N, T, S, P)$ where $T = \{a, b\}$, $N = \{S\}$, S-starting symbol and $P = \{S \to aSbb,\ S \to abb\}$.

$$S \Rightarrow abb \qquad \text{[derivation of } abb = a^1\, b^2]$$

$$S \Rightarrow a\underline{S}bb \Rightarrow aa\underline{S}\ bbbb \Rightarrow aaabbbbbb \Rightarrow a^3\ b^6$$

$$\text{i.e. } S \overset{*}{\Rightarrow} a^3\ b^6.$$

Hence G generates sentential forms of the form $a^i\ b^{2i}$

$\therefore\ L = L(G) = \{a^i\ b^{2i} / i \geq i\}$ is the CFL generated by G.

2.2.4. Remark

Every regular grammar is context free, so a regular language is also a context free one. Hence the family of regular languages is a proper subset of the family of context free languages.

Context free grammars derive their name from the fact that the substitution of the variable on the left of the production can be made any time such a variable appears in a sentential form. It does not depend on the symbols in the rest of the sentential form (the context).

OPERATIONS ON LANGUAGES

2.2.5. Definition

If L_1 and L_2 are two languages, then the *union* of L_1 and L_2 is

$$L_1 \cup {'}_2 = \{w / w \text{ is in } L_1 \text{ or in } L_2\}.$$

2.2.6. Definition

If L_1 and L_2 are two languages, the *product* or *concatenation* (or catenation) of L_1 and L_2, written $L_1 \circ L_2$ is

$$L_1 \circ L_2 = \{w/w = xy,\ x \in L_1,\ y \in L_2\}$$

we usually write $L_1 L_2$ instead of $L_1 \circ L_2$.

2.2.7. Definition

Let L be a language, we define

$$L^2 = L \circ L$$

$$L^3 = L^2 \circ L$$

....

$$L^n = L^{n-1} \circ L$$

and
$$L^+ = \bigcup_{i=1}^{\infty} L^n \quad (L^1 = L)$$

The star or Kleene closure of L is defined as

$$L^* = L^+ \cup \{\epsilon\}.$$

2.2.8. Theorem

If L_1 and L_2 are context free languages then the languages $L_1 \cup L_2$, $L_1 L_2$ and $L_1{}^*$ are also CFL's.

Proof. Starting with CFG's $G_1 = (N_1\ T_1,\ S_1,\ P_1)$ and

$G_2 = (N_2, T_2, S_2, P_2)$ generating L_1 and L_2 respectively, we show how to construct a new CFG for each of the three cases.

A grammer $G = (N, T, S, P)$ generating $L_1 \cup L_2$. First we rename the elements of N_2 if necessary so that $N_1 \cap N_2 = \phi$, and we define $N = N_1 \cup N_2 \cup S$ where S is a new symbol not in N_1 or N_2. Then we let

$$P = P_1 \cup P_2 \cup \{S \to S_1/S_2\}.$$

On the one hand, if x is in either L_1 or L_2, then $S \overset{*}{\Rightarrow} x$ in the grammar G, because we can start a derivation with either $S \to S_1$ or $S \to S_2$ and continue with the derivation of x in G_1 or G_2. Therefore $L_1 \cup L_2 \subseteq L\ (G)$.

On the other hand, if x is derivable from S in G, the first step in any derivation must be $S \Rightarrow S_1$ or $S \Rightarrow S_2$. In the first case, all subsequent productions used must be productions in G_1, because no variables in N_2 are involved, and thus $x \in L_1$. In the second case, $x \in L_2$. Therefore $L(G) \subseteq L_1 \cup L_2$. Hence $L(G) = L_1 \cup L_2$. Thus $L_1 \cup L_2$ is a CFL.

A grammar $G^1 = (N^1, T^1, S^1, P^1)$ generating L_1 o L_2. Again we relebel relabel if necessary so that $N_1 \cap N_2 = \phi$ and define $N^1 = N_1 \cup N_2 \cup \{S^1\}$. This time we let $P^1 = P_1 \cup P_2 \cup \{S^1 \rightarrow S_1\ S_2\}$. If $x \in L_1\ L_2$, then $x = x_1\ x_2$ where $x_i \in L_i$ for each i. We may then derive x in G^1 as follows.

$$S^1 \Rightarrow S_1\ S_2 \overset{*}{\Rightarrow} x_1 S_2 \overset{*}{\Rightarrow} x_1 x_2 = x.$$

where the second step is the derivation of x_1 in G_1 and the third step is the derivation of x_2 in G_2. Conversely, if x can be derived from S', then since the first step in the derivation must be $S^1 \Rightarrow S_1\ S_2$, x must be derivable from $S_1\ S_2$. Therefore $x = x_1 x_2$ where for each i, x_i can be derived from S_i in G^1. Since $N_1 \cap N_2 = \phi$, being derivable S_i in G^1 means being derivable from S_i in G_i, anc so $x \in L_1\ L_2$.

A grammar $G^* = (N'', T'', S'', P')$ generating L_1^*. Let $N'' = N_1 \cup \{S\}$ where $S \notin N_1$. The language L^* contains strings of the form $x = x_1 x_2 ... x_k$ where each $x_i \in L_1$. Since each x_i can be derived from S_1, then to derive x from S it is enough to be able to derive a string of k $S_1^{'s}$. We can accomplish this by including the productions.

$$S'' \rightarrow SS'/\lambda \text{ in } P.$$

Therefore, let $P'' = P_1 \cup \{S'' \rightarrow S_1\ S/\lambda\}$

The proof that $L_1^* \subseteq L(G^*)$ is straight forward. If $x \in L(G^*)$, on the other hand, then either $x = \lambda$ or x can be derived from some string of the form S_1^k in G^*. In the second case, since the only productions in G^* beginning with S_1 are those in G_1, we may conclude that $x \in L(G_1)^k \subseteq L(G_1)^*$.

Note. The above theorem provides a way of obtaining new CFL's from languages that are known to be context free.

2.2.9. Corollary

Every regular language is a CFL.

Proof. It is observed that regular languages over T are the languages obtained from ϕ, $\{\lambda\}$ and $\{a\}$ $(a \in T)$ by using the operations of union, concatenation and kleenestar. Each of the primitive languages ϕ, $\{\lambda\}$ and $\{a\}$ is a CFL. (In the first case we can use the trivial grammar with no productions and in the other two cases one production is sufficient). The corollary therefore follows from Theorem 2.2.8., using the principle of induction.

2.2.10. Example

Consider the language

$$L = \{x \in \{0, 1\}^* \mid n_0(x) \neq n_1(x)\}.$$

We can express L as the union of the languages L_0 and L_1, where

$$L_0 = (x \in \{0, 1\}^* \mid n_0(x) > n_1(x)\}$$

$$L_1 = \{x \in \{0, 1\}^* \mid n_1(x) > n_0(x)\}$$

$n_i(x)$ is the number of i's in x. We observe that $G_0 = (N_0, T_0, S_0, P_0)$ where $N_0 = \{S_0\}$

$$T_0 = \{0, 1\} \text{ and } P_0 = \{S \rightarrow O/SoloS\}$$

is the grammar generating L_0 and thus we concentrate on finding a CFG G_0 generating the language L_0. Clearly $0 \in L_0$, and for any $x \in L_0$, both $x0$ and $0x$ are in L_0. This gives the productions $S \rightarrow o/Solo S$.

We also need to be able to add 1's to our strings. We cannot expect that adding a 1 to an element of L_0 will always produce an element of L_0; however if we have two strings in L_0, concatenating them produces a string with atleast two more 0's than 1's and then adding a single 1 will still yield an element of L_0. We could add it at the left, at the right, or between the two.

The corresponding productions are

$$S \rightarrow 1SS/SS1/S1S.$$

It is not hard to see that any string derived by using the productions $S \rightarrow 0/S0/0S/1SS/SS1/S1S$ is an element of L_0. In the converse direction we can do even a little better : if G_0 is the grammar with prodcutions

$$S \rightarrow 0/0S/1SS/SS1/S1S$$

every string in L_0 can be derived in G_0.

The proof is by induction on the length of the string. Let $d(x) = n_0(x) - n_1(x)$. The basis step, for a string in L_0 of length 1, is straight forward. Suppose that $k \geq 1$ and that for any x for which $|x| \leq k$ and $d(x) > 0$ can be derived in G_0; and consider a string x for which $|x| = k + 1$ and $d(x) > 0$.

We consider the case in which $x = 0y0$ for some string y. If x contains only 0's it can be derived from using the productions $S \rightarrow 0/0S$; we assume, therefore, that x contains at least one 1. Our goal is to show that x has the form.

$x = w_1z$ for some w and z with $d(w) > 0$ and $d(z) > 0$. Once we have done this, the induction hypothesis will tell us that both w and z can be derived from S, so that we will be able to derive x by starting with the production $S \rightarrow S1S$.

To show that x has this form, suppose x contains n 1's where $n \geq 1$. For each i, with $1 \leq i \leq n$, let w_i be the prefix of x upto but not including the ith 1, and z_i be the suffix of x that follows this 1. In otherwords, for each i,

$$x = w_i 1 z_i$$

where the 1 is the ith 1 in x. If $d(w_n) > 0$, then we may let $w = w_n$ and $z = z_n$. The string z_n is 0^j for some $j > 0$ because x ends with 0, and we have the result we want. Otherwise $d(w_n) \leq 0$. In this case we select the first i with $d(w_i) \leq 0$, say $i = m$. Now since x begins with 0, $d(w_1)$ must be > 0, which implies that $m \geq 2$. At this point, we can say that $d(w_{m-1}) > 0$ and $d(w_m) \leq 0$. Because w_m has only one more 1 than w_{m-1}, $d(w_{m-1})$ can be no more than 1. Therefore, $d(w_{m-1}) = 1$. Since $x = w_{m-1}\ 1\ z_{m-1}$ and $d(x) > 0$, it follows that $d(z_{m-1}) > 0$. This means that we get the result we want by letting $w = w_{m-1}$ and $z = z_{m-1}$. The proof in this case is complete.

For the other two cases, the one in which x starts with 1 and the one in which x ends with 1.

Now it is easy enough to obtain a context free grammar G generating L. We use S as our start symbol. A as the start symbol of the grammar we have just derived generating L_0, and B as the start symbol for the corresponding grammar generating L_i. The grammar G then has the productions.

$$S \to A/B$$

$$A \to 0/0A/1AA/AA1/A1A$$

$$B \to 1/1B/0BB/BB0/B0B.$$

2.2.11 Example

Let $L = \{0^i\ 1^j\ 0^k / j > i + k\}$. We try to express L as the concatenation of CFL's although it may seen at first that it is an obvious approach. Writing L as a conceteration $L_1L_2L_3$, where these three languages contain strings of 0's, strings of 1's and strings of 0's respectively is doomed to failure. L contains both $0^1\ 1^3\ 0^1$ and $0^1\ 1^4\ 0^1$, but if we allowed L_1 to contain 0^1, L_2 to contain 1^3, and L_3 to contain 0^2, then $L_1L_2L_3$ would also contain $0^1\ 1^3\ 0^2$, and this string is not an element of L. Observe that $0^i\ 1^{i+k}\ 0^k = 0^i\ 1^i\ 1^i\ 0^k$.

The only difference between this and a string x in L is that x has at least one extra 1 in the middle.

$$x = 0^i\ 1^i\ 1^m\ 1^k\ 0^k \text{ (for some } m > 0)$$

A correct formula for L is therefore $L = L_1\ L_2\ L_3$,

where $\qquad L_1 = \{0^i\ 1^i\ /i \geq 0\}$

$$L_2 = \{1^m / m > 0\}$$
$$L_3 = \{1^k 0^k / k \geq 0\}$$

The second part of Theorem 2.2.8, applied twice, reduces the problem to finding CFG's for these three languages. The final CFG $G = (N, T, S, P)$ incorporating these pieces is shown below.

$$N = \{S, A, B, C\}, \quad T = \{0, 1\} \text{ and}$$
$$P = \{S \to ABC, A \to 0A1/\lambda, B \to 1B/1, C \to 1C0/\lambda\}$$

A derivation of $01^4 0^2 = (01)\,(1)\,(1^2 0^2)$, for example is

$S \Rightarrow ABC \Rightarrow 0A1BC \Rightarrow 0\lambda 1BC \Rightarrow 011C \Rightarrow$

$0111C0 \Rightarrow 01111\ C\ 00 \Rightarrow 01111\lambda 00 \Rightarrow 0111100.$

2.2.12. Construction of CFG equivalent to a regular expression

Construct a CFG equivalent to the regular expression $(011 + 1)^* (01)^*$.

Solution. The productions $A \to 011/1$ generate the language $\{011, 1\}$. Following the third part of Theorem 2.2.8, we can use the productions

$$B \to AB/\lambda$$
$$A \to 011/1$$

with B as the start symbol to generate the language $\{011, 1\}^*$. Similarly, we can use

$$C \to DC/\lambda$$
$$D \to 01$$

to derive $\{01\}^*$ from the start symbol C. Finally we generate the concatenation of the two languages by adding the production $S \to BC$. The final grammar has start symbol S, auxillary variables A, B, C, D and productions

$$S \to BC$$
$$B \to AB/\lambda$$
$$A \to 011/1$$
$$C \to DC/\lambda$$
$$D \to 01.$$

Remark

Starting with any regular expression, we can obtain an equivalent CFG using he techniques illustrated in the above example.

2.2.13. Definition

Let $w = a_1 \ldots a_n$ be a string. Then the reversal or reflection of w is $w^R = a_n \ldots a_1$. If L is a language, then the reflection of L is $L^R = \{w^R / w \text{ is in } L\}$.

2.2.14. Theorem

The family of CFL is closed under reflection.

Proof. Let L be a CFL generated by $G = (N, T, S, P)$. Consider the CFG, $G_1 = (N_1, T_1, S_1, P_1)$ where $N_1 = N$, $T_1 = T$, $S_1 = S$ and P_1 consists of the productions of the form $\alpha^R \to \beta^R$ if $\alpha \to \beta$ is a rule in P (Note that $\alpha^R = \alpha$). Then G_1 generates L^R. Hence L^R is a CFL.

2.2.15. Definition

If L_1 and L_2 are languages, the intersection of L_1 and L_2 is

$$L_1 \cap L_2 = \{w/w \text{ is in } L_1 \text{ and in } L_2\}$$

.2.16. Theorem

The family of CFL is not closed under intersection.

Proof. We have to prove that, if L_1 and L_2 are CFL's $L_1 \cap L_2$ need not be a CFL. Let

$$L_1 = \{a^i\, b^j\, c^j \,/\, i, j \geq 1\}.$$

L is generated by the CFG.

$$G_1 = (\{S\}, \{a, b, c\}, S, \{S \to aS, S \to bSc, S \to bc\}.$$

Hence L_1 is a CFL. Similarly, $L_2 = \{a^i\, b^i\, c^j \,/\, i, j \geq 1\}$ is also a CFL. But $L_1 \cap L_2 = \{a^n\, b^n\, c^n \,/\, n \geq 1\}$, which is not a CFL. Hence the family of CFL is not closed under intersection.

2.3. RELATIONSHIP BETWEEN DERIVATION AND DERIVATION TREES

It is possible to represent the derivation process by means of a tree (*A* connected graph without circuits).

2.3.1. Definition

Let $G = (N, T, S, P)$ be a CFG. A tree is a *derivation* (*or parse generation*) *tree* for G if

1. Every vertex has a label, which is a symbol of $N \cup T \cup (\in)$.
2. The label of the root is S.

3. If a vertex is interior and has a label A, then A must be in V.

4. If n has label A and vertices $n_1, n_2, ..., n_k$ are sons of the vertex n, in order from the left, with labels $X_1, X_2, ... X_k$, respectively, then $A \to X_1, X_2 ... X_k$ mus be a production in P.

5. If vertex n has label ε, then n is a leaf and is the only son of its father.

2.3.2. Example

Consider a context free grammar generating the CFL, $L = \{a^n\ b^n\ /\ n \geq 1\}$. We know that

$$G = (\{S\}, \{a, b\}, S, \{S \to aSb, S \to ab\}) \text{ generates } L.$$

Now consider the derivations of the strings

$$ab \quad (n = 1)$$

$$a^2\ b^2 \quad (n = 2)$$

$$a^3\ b^3 \quad (n = 3)$$

For ab, the derivation is: $\quad S \Rightarrow ab$

The corresponding derivation tree is

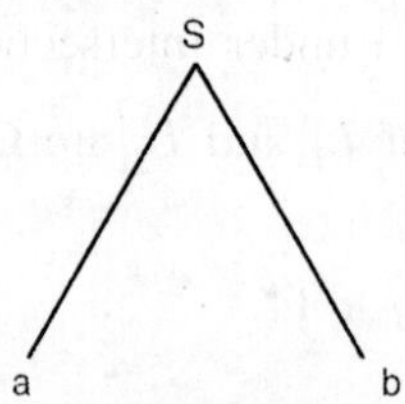

Fig. 2.1

For ab, the derivation is : $\quad S \Rightarrow a\ \underline{S}b \Rightarrow aabb = a^2\ b^2$.

The corresponding derivation tree is

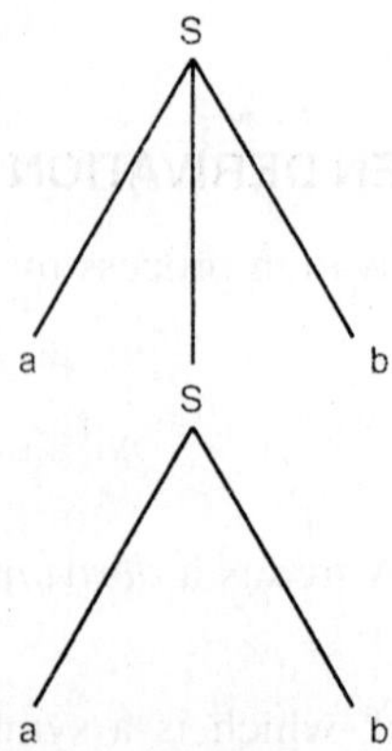

Fig. 2.2.

For a^3b^3 the derivation is: $a \Rightarrow a\,\underline{S}b \Rightarrow aa\underline{S}\;bb \Rightarrow aaabbb = a^3\;b^3$.

The corresponding derivation tree is

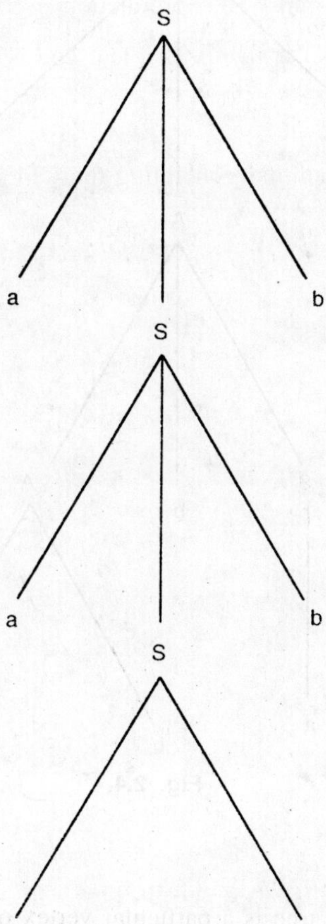

Fig. 2.3.

We observe that if we read from left to right we get a string. The string is known as the yield of the derivation tree. Yield of the derivation tree 2.1 is ab; yield of the derivation tree 2.2. is $a^2\;b^2$; yield of the derivation tree 2.3 is $a^3\;b^3$.

2.3.3. Example

Consider the CFG, $G = (N, T, S, P)$ where $N = \{S, A\}$, $T = \{a, b\}$, S and $P = \{S \rightarrow aAS,\ S \rightarrow a,\ A \rightarrow SbA,\ A \rightarrow SS,\ A \rightarrow ba\}$. For the string $aabbaa$, the derivation is

$S \Rightarrow a\underline{A}S \Rightarrow a\underline{S}bAS \Rightarrow aab\underline{A}S \Rightarrow aabbaS \Rightarrow aabbaa.$ $\quad \left(i.e., S \overset{*}{\Rightarrow} aabbaa\right)$

The corresponding derivation tree is

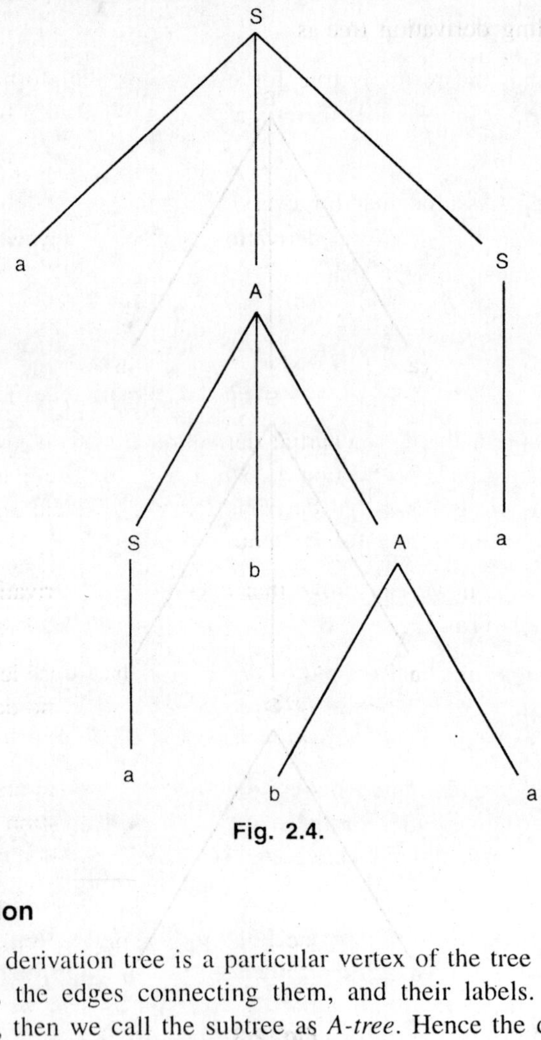

Fig. 2.4.

2.3.4. Definition

A *subtree* of a derivation tree is a particular vertex of the tree together with all its decendants, the edges connecting them, and their labels. If a variable A labels the root, then we call the subtree as *A-tree*. Hence the derivation tree is known as *S-tree* since *S* is the root.

The following theorem establishes the relationship between a derivation and a derivation tree.

Theorem 2.3.5.

Let $G = (N, T, S, P)$ be a context free grammar. Then for every $w \in L(G)$, there exists a derivation tree of *G* whose yield is *w*. Conversely the yield of any deviation tree is in $L(G)$. Also, if t_G is any partial derivation tree for *G* whose root is labelled *S*, then the yield of t_G is a sentential form of *G*.

Proof. First we show that for every sentential form of $L(G)$ there is a corresponding partial derivation tree. The proof is by induction on the number of steps in the derivation.

Basis. Note that the result is true for every sentential form derivable in one step. Since $S \Rightarrow u$ implies that there is a production $S \rightarrow u$ by the definition of derivation tree.

Induction step. Assume that for every sentential form derivable in 'n' steps there is a corresponding partial derivation tree. Now any word w derivable in $(n + 1)$ steps must be such that

$$S \overset{*}{\Rightarrow} xAy,\ x,\ y, \in (N \cup T)^*,\ A \in N \text{ in } n \text{ steps}$$

and $$xAy \Rightarrow xa_1a_2...a_my = w,\ a_i \in N \cup T.$$

By our assumption there is a partial derivation tree with yield xAy, and since the grammar must have production $A \rightarrow a_1a_2...a_m$, we see that by expanding the leaf labeled A, we get a partial derivation tree with yield $xa_1a_2...a_my = w$. By induction the restult is true for all sentential forms.

In a similar fashion we can prove that every partial derivation tree represents some sentential form.

Since a derivation tree is also a partial derivation tree whose leaves are terminals, it follows that every sentence in $L(G)$ is the yield of some derivation tree of G and that the yield of every derivation tree is in $L(G)$.

Note. Derivation trees show which productions are used in obtaining a sentence, but do not give the order of their application. Derivation trees are able to represent any derivation, reflecting the fact that this order is irrelevant.

In context free grammars that are not linear (A linear grammar is one which at most one variable can occur on the RHS of any production), a derivation may involve sentential forms with more than one variable. In such cases, we have a choice in the order in which variables are replaced. So we often require that the variabels be replaced in a specific order.

2.3.6. Definition

Given a grammar $G = (N, T, S, P)$. If at each step in the derivations a production is applied to the left most non-terminal symbol, then the derivation is said to be a *leftmost derivation* or *top down parsing*.

2.3.7. Definition

A derivation in which the rightmost non-terminal symbol is replaced at each step is said to be *right most derivation* (or) *bottom up parsing*.

Note. A sentential form (string or word) has several leftmost or rightmost derivation.

2.3.8. Example

Consider the grammar $G = (N, T, S, P)$ where $N = \{A, B, C, S\}$, $T = \{a, b, c\}$, S-starting symbol and $P = \{S \to AB, A \to Ca, B \to Ba, B \to Cb, B \to b, C \to Cb, C \to b\}$.

The leftmost derivation of the string *Cbab* is

$S \Rightarrow \underline{A}B \Rightarrow \underline{C}aB \Rightarrow Cba\underline{B} \Rightarrow Cbab.$

The rightmost derivation of the string *Cbab* is

$S \Rightarrow A\underline{B} \Rightarrow Ab \Rightarrow \underline{C}ab \Rightarrow Cbab.$

PARSING AND AMBIGUITY

The term parsing describes finding a sequence of productions by which $a\ w \in L(G)$ is derived. Given a string w in $L(G)$, we can parse it in a rather obvious fasion : we systematically construct all possible (say, leftmost) derivations and see whether any of them match w. Specifically, we start at round one by looking at all productions of the form $S \to x$ finding all x that can be derived from S in one step. If none of these result in a match with w, we go to the next round, in which we apply all applicable productions to the leftmost variable of every x. This gives us a set of sentential forms, some of them possibly leading to w. On each subsequent round, we again take all leftmost variables and apply all possible productions. It may be that some of these sentential forms can be rejected on the grounds that w can never be derived from them, but in general, we will have on each round a set of possible sentential forms. After the first round, we have sentential forms that can be derived by applying a single production, after the second round we have the sentential forms that can be derived in two steps, and so on. If $w \in L(G)$, then it must have a leftmost derivation of finite length. This method will eventually give a leftmost derivation of w.

Any word $w \in L(G)$ will produce a derivation tree for w. We say "*a*" derivation tree rather than "the" derivation tree because of the possibility that a number of different derivation trees may exist. This situation is referred to as ambiguity.

2.3.9. Definition

A grammar G is said to be *ambiguous* if there is some word in $L(G)$ generated by more than one leftmost derivation or rightmost derivation. In other words a grammar G is said be ambiguous if there is some word in $L(G)$ has atleast two derivation trees.

A grammar which is not ambiguous is said to be *unambiguous*. (or) A grammar is said to be unambiguous if every word generated by it has a unique derivation tree.

2.3.10. Definition

A language is said to be unambiguous if there is atleast one unambiguous grammar generating it and inherently ambiguous if there is no unambiguous grammar generating it.

2.3.11. Example

Let $G = (N, T, S, P)$ where $N = \{S, A\}$

$T = \{a, b\}$ and $P = \{S \to aAb, S \to abSb, S \to a$

$A \to bS, A \to aAAb\}$.

The two leftmost derivations of the word *abab* are

$$S \Rightarrow abSB \Rightarrow abab$$

$$S \Rightarrow aAb \Rightarrow abSb \Rightarrow abab$$

Thus the word *abab* is ambiguously derivable in G. Hence G is ambiguous.

2.3.12. Example

Let $G = (N, T, S, P)$, where $N = \{S, A\}$

$T = \{a, b, c\}$ and $P = \{S \to a^2 Sa, S \to aSa, S \to aS, S \to \lambda\}$.

The two leftmost derivation of the word $aaa = a^3$ is

$$S \Rightarrow a^2Sa \Rightarrow a^2a = aaa = a^3 \text{ and}$$

$$S \Rightarrow aSa \Rightarrow aaSa \Rightarrow aaa = a^3$$

Thus G is ambiguous.

2.3.13. Example

Prove that the language

$$L = \{a^n b^n \mid n \geq 1\} \text{ is unambiguous.}$$

Solution. Consider the grammar $G_1 = (N_1, T_1, S_1, P_1)$

where $N_1 = \{S\}, T_1 = \{a, b\}, P_1 = \{S_1 \to aS_1b, S_1 \to ab\}$

and $G_2 = (N_2, T_2, S_2, P_2)$ where $N_2 = \{S_2, A\}$

$T_2 = \{a, b\}$ and $P_2 = \{S \rightarrow aASb, S \rightarrow aSb, S \rightarrow ab, A \rightarrow \lambda\}$.

Then $L = L(G_1) = L(G_2)$.

The grammar G_1 is unambiguous, since the word $a^n b^n$ $(n \geq 1)$ is obtained by an unique leftmost derivation, namely, $S \overset{*}{\Rightarrow} a^{n-1} S b^{n-1} \Rightarrow a^n b^n$.

But the grammar G_2 is ambiguous since the word *aabb* has two leftmost derivations, namely

$$S \Rightarrow aASb \Rightarrow aSb \Rightarrow aabb \text{ and}$$

$$S \Rightarrow aSb \Rightarrow aabb.$$

since there exists an unambiguous grammar G_1 for the language L, L is unambiguous.

Note. Every regular language (or regular set) is unambiguous. In other words, every regular language has atleast one unambiguous grammar generating it.

There are inherently ambiguous context free languages for which there is no unambiguous grammar. That is every grammar generating it is ambiguous.

2.4. SIMPLIFICATION OF CONTEXT FREE GRAMMARS

In a CFG, G, it may not be neccessary to use all the symbols in $N \cup T$, or all the productions in P for deriving sentences. So when we study a context free languages $L(G)$, we try to eliminate symbols and productions in G which are not useful for derivation of sentences.

Consider the grammar $G = (N, T, S, P)$ where $N = \{S, A, B, C, E\}$, $T = \{a, b, c\}$, $P = \{S \rightarrow AB, A \rightarrow a, B \rightarrow b, B \rightarrow C, E \rightarrow c/\lambda\}$. We observe that $L(G) = \{ab\}$. It should be noted that C does not produce any terminal, $B \rightarrow C$ simply replaces B by C. Also C and E cannot serve any purpose in the derivation of the string. Hence the given grammar can be simplified as $G_1 = (N_1, T_1, S_1, P_1)$ where $N_1 = \{S, A, B\}$, $T_1 = \{a, b\}$, $P_1 = \{S \rightarrow AB, A \rightarrow a, B \rightarrow b\}$. We see that $L(G) = L(G_1)$.

Hence we can eliminate variables not deriving terminal strings, symbols not appearing in any sentential form, null productions and productions of the form $A \rightarrow B$ in a grammar.

2.4.1. Theorem

If G is a CFG such that $L(G) = \phi$, we can find an equivalent grammar G^1 such that each variable in G^1 derives some terminal string.

Proof. Let $G = (N, T, S, P)$. We define $G_1 = (N_1, T_1, S, P_1)$ as follows.

(*a*) Construction of N^1. We define $W_1 \subseteq N$ by recursion. $W_1 = \{A \in N/$ there exists a production $A \to w$ where $w \in T^*\}$. (If $W_1 = \phi$, some variable will remain after the application of any production, and so $L(G) = \phi$).

$$W_{i+1} = W_i \cup \{A \in N/ \text{ there exists some production } A \to \alpha \text{ with } \alpha \in (T \cup W_i)^*\}.$$

By the definition of W_i, $W_i \subseteq W_{i+1}$ for all i. As N has only finite number of variables, $W_k = W_{k+1}$ for some $k \le |N|$. Therefore $W_k = W_{k+j}$ for $j \ge 1$. We define $N^1 = W_k$.

(*b*) Construction of P^1

$$P^1 = \{A \to \alpha/A, \alpha \in \{N^1 \cup T)^*\}.$$

We can define $G^1 = (N^1, T, S, P^1)$, S is in N^1. We can prove that every variable in N^l defines some terminal string. So $S \notin N^1$, $L(G) = \phi$. But $L(G) = \phi$. Now we prove that G^1 is the required grammar.

(*i*) If each $A \in N^1$ then $A \underset{G^1}{\overset{*}{\Rightarrow}} w$ for some $w \in T^*$; conversely, if $A \underset{G^1}{\overset{*}{\Rightarrow}} w$ then $A \in N^1$.

(*ii*) $L(G^1) = L(G)$.

To prove (*i*) we note that $W_{k+1} = W_1 \cup W_2 \cup \ldots \cup W_k$. We prove by induction on i that for $i = 1, 2, \ldots k$, $A \in W_i$ implies $A \underset{G^1}{\overset{*}{\Rightarrow}} w$ for some $W \in T^*$. If $A \in W_1$, then $A \underset{G}{\Rightarrow} w$. So the production $A \to w$ is in P^1. Therefore, $A \underset{G^1}{\overset{*}{\Rightarrow}} w$. Thus there is basis for induction. Let us assume the result for i. Let $A \in W_{i+1}$. Then either $A \in W_i$, in which case, $A \underset{G^1}{\overset{*}{\Rightarrow}} w$ for some $w \in T^*$ by induction hypothesis. Or, there exists a production $A \to \alpha$ with $\alpha \in (T \cup W_i)$. By definition of P^1, $A \to \alpha$ is in P'. We can write $\alpha = X_1 X_2 \ldots X_m$, where $X_j \in T \cup W_i$. If $X_j \in W_i$ by induction hypothesis, $X_j \underset{G^1}{\overset{*}{\Rightarrow}} W_j$ for some $W_j \in T^*$. So $A \underset{G^1}{\overset{*}{\Rightarrow}} W_1 W_2 \ldots W_m \in T^*$ (when X_j is a terminal, $W_j = X_j$). By induction the result is true for $i = 1, 2, \ldots, k$.

The converse part can be proved in a similar way by induction on the number of steps in the derivation $A \underset{G}{\overset{*}{\Rightarrow}} w$. We see immediately that $L(G^1) \subseteq L(G)$ as $N^1 \subseteq N$ and $P^1 \subseteq P$.

To prove $L(G) \subseteq L(G^1)$, we need an auxillary result.

$$A \underset{G^1}{\overset{*}{\Rightarrow}} w \text{ if } A \underset{G}{\overset{*}{\Rightarrow}} w \text{ for some } w \in T^* \qquad \ldots(2.3)$$

We prove by (2.3) in induction on the number of steps in the derivation $A \overset{*}{\underset{G}{\Rightarrow}} w$. If $A \underset{G}{\Rightarrow} w$, then $A \to w$ is in P and $A \in W_1 \subseteq N^1$. As $A \in N^1$ and $w \in T^*$, $A \to w$ is in P^1. So $A \underset{G'}{\Rightarrow} w$, and there is a basis for induction. Assume (2.3) for derivations in atmost k steps. Let $A \overset{K+1}{\underset{G}{\Rightarrow}} w$. We can split this as

$$A \underset{G}{\Rightarrow} X_1 X_2 \dots X_m \overset{K}{\underset{G}{\Rightarrow}} w_1 w_2 \dots w_m \text{ such that } X_j \overset{*}{\underset{G}{\Rightarrow}} w_j.$$

$$\text{If } X_j \in T \text{ then } w_j = x_j. \qquad \dots (2.4)$$

If $X_j \in N$ then by (2.3) above, $X_j \in N^1$. As $X_j \overset{*}{\underset{G}{\Rightarrow}} w_j$ is atmost k steps, $X_j \overset{*}{\underset{G^1}{\Rightarrow}} w_j$. Also, $X_1, X_2, \dots X_m \in (T \cup N^1)^*$ implies $A \to X_1X_2 \dots X_m$ is in P^1. Thus $A \underset{G^1}{\Rightarrow} X_1X_2 \dots X_m \overset{*}{\underset{G^1}{\Rightarrow}} w_1w_2 \dots w_m$. Hence by induction, (2.3) is true for all derivations. In particular, $S \overset{*}{\underset{G}{\Rightarrow}} w$ implies $S \overset{*}{\underset{G^1}{\Rightarrow}} w$. This prove that $L(G) \subseteq L(G^1)$, and (2.4) is completely proved.

2.4.2. Example

Let $G = (N, T, P, S)$ where $N = \{S, A, B, C, E\}$, $T = \{a, b, c\}$ and $P = \{S \to AB, A \to a, B \to b, B \to C, E \to C\}$. Find G^1 such that every variable in G^1 derives some terminal string.

(*a*) **Construction of N^1.** Now $W_1 = \{A, B, E\}$ since $A \to a$, $B \to b$, $E \to c$ are productions with a terminal string on the R.H.S.

$$W_2 = W_1 \cup \{A_1 \in N \mid A_1 \to \alpha \text{ for some } \alpha \in (T \cup \{A, B, E\})^*\}$$

$$= W_1 \cup \{S\} = \{A, B, E, S\}$$

$$W_3 = W_2 \cup \{A_1 \in N \mid A_1 \to \alpha \text{ for some } \alpha \in (T \cup \{S, A, B, E\})^*\}$$

(*b*) **Construction of P^1**

$$P^1 = \{A_1 \to \alpha / A_1, \alpha \in (N^1 \cup T)^*\}$$

$$= \{S \to AB, A \to a, B \to b, E \to C\}$$

Therefore $\quad G^1 = (\{S, A, B, E\}, \{a, b, c\}, S, P^1)$

2.4.3. Theorem

For every CFG $G = (N, T, S, P)$, we can construct an equivalent grammar $G^1 = (N^1, T^1, S, P^1)$, such that every symbol in $N' \cup T'$ appears in some sentential form *i.e.* for every X in $N^1 \cup T^1$ there exists α such that $S \overset{*}{\underset{G^1}{\Rightarrow}} \alpha$ and X is a symbol in the string α).

Proof. We construct $G^1 = (N^1, T^1, S, P^1)$ as follows:

(*a*) Construction of W_i for $i \geq 1$.

(*i*) $W_1 = \{S\}$

(*ii*) $W_{i+1} = W_i \cup \{X \in N \cup T /$there exists *a* production $A \to \alpha$ with $A \in W_i$ and α containing the symbol $X\}$

We may note that $W_i \subset N \cup T$ and $W_i \subseteq W_{i+1}$. As we have only finite number of elements in $N \cup T$, $W_k = W_{k+1}$ for some k. This means that $W_k = W_{k+j}$ for all $j \geq 0$.

(*b*) **Construction of N^1, T^1 and P^1.** We define $N^1 = N \cap W_k$. $T^1 = T \cap W_k$ and $P^1 = \{A \to \alpha / A \in W_k\}$.

To prove that G^1 is the required grammar, we have to show that

(*a*) every symbol in $N^1 \cup T^1$ appears in some sentential form of G^1 and

(*b*) conversely, $L(G^1) = L(G)$.

To prove (*a*), consider $X \in N^1 \cup T^1 = W_k$. By construction $W_{k+1} = W_1 \cup ... \cup W_k$. We prove that $X \in W_i$, $i \leq k$, appears in some sentential form by induction on *i*. When $i = 1$, $X = S$ and $S \overset{*}{\underset{G^1}{\Rightarrow}} S$. Thus there is a basis for induction. Assume the result for all variables in W_i. Let $x \in W_{i+1}$. Then either $X \in W_i$, in which case, X appears in some sentential form by induction hypothesis. Otherwise, there exists a production $A \to \alpha$, where $A \in W_i$ and a contains the symbol X_i. A appears in some sentential form, say $\beta A\gamma$. Therefore

$$S \overset{*}{\underset{G^1}{\Rightarrow}} \beta A \gamma \underset{G^1}{\Rightarrow} \beta \alpha \gamma .$$

This means that $\beta\alpha y$ is some sentential form and X is a symbol in $\beta\alpha y$. Thus by induction the result in true for $X \in W_i$, $i \leq k$.

Conversely, if X appears in some sentential form, say $\beta X y$, then $S \overset{l}{\underset{G}{\Rightarrow}} \beta X \gamma$. This implies $X \in W_l$. If $l \leq k$, then $W_l \subseteq W_k$. If $l > k$, then $W_l = W_k$. Hence X appears in $N^1 \cup T^1$. This proves (*a*).

To prove (*b*), we note $L(G^1) \subseteq L(G)$ as $N^1 \subseteq N$, $T^1 \subseteq T$ and $P^1 \subseteq P$. Let w be in $L(G)$ and

$S = \alpha_1 \Rightarrow \alpha_2 \Rightarrow \alpha_3 = ... \Rightarrow \alpha_{n-1} \underset{G}{\Rightarrow} w$. We prove that every symbol in α_{i+1} is in W_{i+1} and $\alpha_i \underset{G^1}{\Rightarrow} \alpha_{i+1}$ by induction on *i*. $\alpha_1 = S \underset{G}{\Rightarrow} \alpha_2$ implies $S \to \alpha_2$ is a production in P. By construction, every symbol in α_2 is in W_2 and

$S \to \alpha_2$ is in P^1, that is $S \underset{G}{\Rightarrow} \alpha_2$. Thus there is basis for induction. Let us assume the result for i. Consider $\alpha_{i+1} \underset{G}{\Rightarrow} \alpha_{i+2}$. This one step derivation can be written in the form.

$$\beta_{i+1} A \gamma_{i+1} \Rightarrow \beta_{i+1} \alpha\gamma_{i+1}$$

where $A \to \alpha$ is the production we are applying. By induction hypotesis. $A \in W_{i+1}$. By construction of W_{i+2} every symbol in α is in W_{i+2}. As all the symbols in β_{i+1} and γ_{i+1} are also in W_{i+1} by induction hypothesis, every symbol in $\beta_{i+1}\alpha\gamma_{i+1} = \alpha_{i+2}$ is in W_{i+2}. By construction of P^1, $A \to \alpha$ is in P^1. This means that $\alpha_{i+1} \underset{G}{\Rightarrow} \alpha_{i+2}$. Thus the induction procedure is complete. So $S = \alpha_1 \underset{G'}{\Rightarrow} \alpha_2 \underset{G'}{\Rightarrow} \alpha_3 \Rightarrow \ldots \Rightarrow \alpha_{n-1} \underset{G'}{\Rightarrow} W$. Therefore $w \in L(G^1)$. This proves (*b*).

2.4.4. Example

Consider $G = (\{S, A, B, E\}, \{a, b, c\}, S, P)$, where $P = \{S \to AB, A \to a, B \to b, E \to c$.

Now $W_1 = \{S\}$

$W_2 = \{S\} \cup \{X \in N \cup T /$ there exists a production $A \to \alpha$ with $A \to W_1$ and α constaining $X\}$

$= \{S\} \cup \{A, B\}$

$W_3 = \{S, A, B\} \cup \{a, b\}$

$W_4 = W_3$

$N^1 = \{S, A, B\}$ $T^1 = \{a, b\}$

$P^1 = \{S \to AB, A \to a, B \to b\}$

Thus the required grammar is $G^1 = (N^1, T^1, S, P^1)$.

2.4.5. Definition

Let $G = (N, T, S, P)$ be a CFG. G is said to reduce or nonredundant if every symbol in $N \cup T$ appears in the course of the derivation of some terminal string, *i.e.* for every X in $N \cup T$, there exists a derivations $S \overset{*}{\Rightarrow} \alpha X \beta \overset{*}{\Rightarrow} w \in L(G)$. (We can say X is useful in the derivation of terminal strings).

2.4.6. Theorem

For every CFG G there exists a reduced grammar G^1 which is equivalent to G.

Proof. We construct the reduced grammar in two steps.

Step 1. We construct a grammar G_1 equivalent to the given grammar G so that every variable in G_1 derives some terminal string.

Step 2. We construct a grammar $G^1 = (N^1, T^1, S, P^1)$ equivalent to G_1 so that every symbol in G^1 appears in some sentential form of G^1 which is equivalent to G_1 and hence to G. G^1 is the required reduced grammar.

By Step 2 every symbol X in G^1 appears in some sentential form, say $\alpha X \beta$. By step 1 every symbol in $\alpha\ X\ \beta$ derives some terminal string. Therefore $S \overset{*}{\Rightarrow} \alpha X \beta \overset{*}{\Rightarrow} w$ for some w in T^* *i.e.* G^1 is reduced.

Note. To get a reduced grammar, we first apply Theorem 2.4.1 and Theorem 2.4.3. For if we apply Theorem 2.4.3. first and then Theorem 2.4.1, we may not get a reduced grammar.

Problem. Construct a reduced grammar equivalent to the grammar $G = (N, T, S, P)$ where $N = \{S, A, C, D, E\}$, $T = \{a, b\}$, $P = \{S \to a\,Aa, A \to Sb, A \to bCC, A \to DaA, C \to abb, C \to DD, E \to aC, D \to aDA\}$

Solution.

Step 1. $W_1 = \{C\}$ as $C \to abb$ is the only production with a terminal string on the R.H.S.

$$W_2 = \{C\} \cup \{E, A\}$$

as $E \to aC$ and $A \to bCC$ are prodcutions with R.H.S. in $(T \cup \{C\})^*$

$$W_3 = \{C, E, A\} \cup \{S\} \text{ as } S \to aAa \text{ and } aAa \text{ is in } (T \cup W_2)^*.$$

$$W_4 = W_3 \cup \phi$$

Hence $N^1 = W_3 = \{S, A, C, E\}$

$$P^1 = \{A_1 \to \alpha \,/\, \alpha \in (N^1 \cup T)^*\}$$

$$= \{S \to aAa, A \to Sb, A \to bCC, C \to abb, E \to aC\}$$

$$G_1 = (N_1, \{a, b\}, S, P_1\}.$$

Step 2. We have to apply Theorem 2.4.3. to G_1. We start with $W_1 = \{S\}$

As we have $S \to aAa$,

$$W_2 = \{S\} \cup \{A, a\}$$

As $A \to Sb$, $A \to bCC$,

$$W_3 = \{S, A, a\} \cup \{S, b, C\}$$
$$= \{S, A, C, a, b\}$$

As we have $C \to abb$, $W_4 = W_3 \cup \{a, b\} = W_3$.

Hence $P'' = \{A_1 \to \alpha \,/ A_1 \in W_3) = \{S \to aAa, A \to Sb, A \to bCC, C \to abb\}$

$\therefore$ $G_1 = (\{S, A, C\}, \{a, b\}, P'', S)$ is the required grammar.

Elimination of Null Productions

A context free grammar may have productions of the form $A \to \lambda$. The production $A \to \lambda$ is just used to erase A. So a production of the form $A \to \lambda$, where A is a variable is called a *null production*.

As an example, consider G whose productions are $S \to aS$, $S \to aA$, $S \to \lambda$, $A \to \lambda$. We have two null productions $S \to \lambda$ and $A \to \lambda$. We can delete $A \to \lambda$ provided we erase A whenever it occurs in the course of a derivation of a terminal string. So we can replace $S \to aA$ by $S \to a$. If G_1 denotes the grammar whose productions are $S \to aS$, $S \to a$, $S \to \lambda$, then $L(G_1) = L(G) = \{a^n \,/\, n \geq 0\}$. Thus it is possible to eliminate the null production $A \to \lambda$. If we elimiante $S \to \lambda$, We cannot generate λ in $L(G)$. But we can generate $L(G) - \{\lambda\}$ even if we eliminate $S \to \lambda$.

2.4.7. Definition

A variable A in a context free grammar is *nullable* if $A \overset{*}{\Rightarrow} \lambda$.

2.4.8. Theorem

If $G = (N, T, S, P)$ is a context free grammar, then we can find a context free grammar G_1 having no null productions such that $L(G_1) = L(G) - \{\lambda\}$.

Proof. We construct $G_1 = (N, T, P^1, S)$ as follows.

Step 1. Construction of the set of nullable variables : We find the nullable variable recursively.

(*i*) $W_1 = \{A \in N \mid A \to \lambda \text{ is in } P\}$

(*ii*) $W_{i+1} = W_i \cup \{A \in N \mid \text{there exists a production } A \to \alpha \text{ with } \alpha \in W_i^*\}$.

By definition of W_i, $W_i \subseteq W_{i+1}$ for all i. As N is finite $W_{k+1} = W_k$ for some $k \leq |N|$. So $W_{k+j} = W_k$ for all j. Let $W = W_k$. W is the set of all nullable variables.

Step 2.

(*a*) Construction of P^1 : Any production whose R.H.*S*. does not have any nullable variable is included in P^1.

(*b*) If $A \rightarrow X_1X_2...X_k$ is in P, the productions of the form $A \rightarrow \alpha_1\alpha_2 \ldots \alpha_k$ are included in P^1, where $\alpha_i = X_i$ if $X_i \notin W$. $\alpha_i = X_i$ or λ if $X_i \in$ W and $\alpha_1\,\alpha_2 \ldots \alpha_k \neq \lambda$. Actually (b) gives several production in P^1. The productions are obtained either by not eresing any nullable variable on the R.H.*S*. of $A \rightarrow X_1X_2...X_k$ or by erasing some or all nullable variables provided some symbol appears on the R.H.*S*. after erasing.

Let $G_1 = (N, T, P^1, S)$. G_1 has no null productions. Now we prove that G_1 is the required grammar.

Step 3. $L(G_1) = L(G) - \{\lambda\}$. To prove that $L(G_1) = L(G) - \lambda$, we prove an auxillary result given by the following relation : For all $A \in N$ and $w \in T^*$.

$$A \overset{*}{\underset{G^1}{\Rightarrow}} w \text{ if and only if } A \overset{*}{\underset{G}{\Rightarrow}} w \text{ and } w \neq A \qquad ...(2.5)$$

we prove "if" part first. Let $A \overset{*}{\underset{G}{\Rightarrow}} w$ and $w \neq \lambda$. We prove that $A \overset{*}{\underset{G^1}{\Rightarrow}} w$ by induction on the number of steps in the derivation $A \overset{*}{\underset{G}{\Rightarrow}} w$. If $A \underset{G}{\Rightarrow} w$ and $w \neq \lambda$, $A \rightarrow w$ is a production in P^1 and so $A \underset{G^1}{\Rightarrow} w$. Thus there is basis for induction. Assume the result for derivations in atmost i steps. Let $A \overset{i+1}{\underset{G}{\Rightarrow}} w$ and $w \neq \lambda$. We can split the derivation as $A \underset{G}{\Rightarrow} X_1\, X_2 \ldots X_k \overset{i}{\underset{G}{\Rightarrow}} w_1\, w_2 \ldots w_k$, where $w = w_1w_2...w_k$ and $A_j \overset{*}{\underset{G}{\Rightarrow}} w_j$. As $w \neq \lambda$, not all w_j's are λ. If $w_j \neq \lambda$, then by induction hypothesis, $x_j \overset{*}{\underset{G_1}{\Rightarrow}} w_j$. If $w_j = \lambda$ then $x_j \in w$. So using the production $A \rightarrow A_1\, A_2 \ldots A_k$ in P, we construct $A \rightarrow \alpha_1, \alpha_2 \ldots \alpha_k$ in P^1, where $\alpha_j = X_j$ if $w_j \neq \lambda$ and $\alpha_j = \lambda$ if $w_j = \lambda$ (*i.e.* $X_j \in w$). Therefore, $A \underset{G_1}{\Rightarrow} \alpha_1\, \alpha_2 \ldots \alpha_k$ $\overset{*}{\underset{G_1}{\Rightarrow}} w_1\, \alpha_2 \ldots \alpha_k \overset{*}{\underset{G_1}{\Rightarrow}} \ldots \Rightarrow w_1\, w_2 \ldots w_k = w$. By the principle of induction, 'if' part of (2.5) is proved.

We prove the only if part by induction on the number of steps in the derivation of $A \overset{*}{\underset{G_1}{\Rightarrow}} w$. If $A \underset{G_1}{\Rightarrow} w$, then $A \rightarrow w$ is in P_1. By construction of P^1, $A \rightarrow w$ is obtained from some production $A \to X_1 X_2 \dots X_n$ in P by erasing some (or none of) nullable variables. Hence $A \underset{G}{\Rightarrow} X_1 X_2 \dots X_n \overset{*}{\underset{G}{\Rightarrow}} w$. So there is a basis for induction Assume the result for derivation in atmost j steps.

Let $A \overset{j+1}{\underset{G_1}{\Rightarrow}} w$. This can be split as $A \Rightarrow X_1 X_2 \dots X_k \overset{j}{\underset{G_1}{\Rightarrow}} w_1 w_2 \dots w_k$, where $X_i \overset{*}{\underset{G_1}{\Rightarrow}} w_i$. The first production $A \to X_1 X_2 \dots X_k$ in P' is obtained from some production $A \to \alpha$ in P by erasing some (or none of) nullable variables in α. So $A \underset{G}{\Rightarrow} \alpha \overset{*}{\underset{G}{\Rightarrow}} X_1 X_2 \dots X_k$. If $X_i \in T$ then $X_i \overset{0}{\underset{G}{\Rightarrow}} X_i = w_i$. If $X_i \in N$ then by induction hypothesis, $X_i \overset{*}{\underset{G}{\Rightarrow}} w_i$. So we get $A \overset{*}{\underset{G}{\Rightarrow}} X_1 X_2 \dots X_k \overset{*}{\underset{G}{\Rightarrow}} w_1 w_2 \dots w_k$. Hence by the principle of induction whenever $A \overset{*}{\underset{G_1}{\Rightarrow}} w$, we have $A \overset{*}{\underset{G}{\Rightarrow}} w$ and $w \neq \lambda$. Thus (2.5) is completely proved.

By applying (2.5) to S, we have $w \in L(G_1)$ if and only if $w \in L(G)$ and $w \neq \lambda$. This implies $L(G_1) = L(G) - \{\lambda\}$.

2.4.9. Example

Consider the grammar $G = (N, T, S, P)$ where $N = \{S, A, B, D\}$, $T = \{a, b\}$, $P = \{S \to aS/ AB, A \to \lambda, B \to \lambda, D \to b\}$.

Now we construct a grammar G_1 without null productions generating $L(G) - \{\lambda\}$.

Step 1. Construction of the set W of all null variables

$$W_1 = \{A_1 \in N/A_1 \to \lambda \text{ is a production in } G\}$$
$$= \{A, B\}$$
$$W_2 = \{A, B\} \cup \{S\} \text{ as } S \to AB \text{ is a production with } AB \in W_1^*.$$
$$= \{S, A, B\}$$
$$W_3 = W_2 \cup \phi = W_2.$$

Thus, $W = W_2 = \{S, A, B\}$

Step 2. Construction of P^1.

(*i*) $D \to b$ is included in P^1.

(*ii*) $S \to aS$ gives rise to $S \to aS$ and $S \to a$.

(*iii*) $S \to AB$ gives rise to $S \to A$ and $S \to B$.

We cannot erase both the nullable variables A and B in $S \to AB$ as we will get $S \to \lambda$ in that case. Hence the required grammar without null productions is

$$G_1 = (\{S, A, B, D\}, \{a, b\}, S, P^1\} \text{ where } P^1 \text{ consists of}$$

$$D \to b,\ S \to aS,\ S \to AB,\ S \to a,\ S \to A,\ S \to B.$$

2.4.10. Corollary

There exists an algorithm to decide whether $\lambda \in L(G)$ for a given context free grammar G.

Proof. $\lambda \in L(G)$ if and only if $S \in W$, *i.e.*, S is nullable. The construction given in Theorem 2.4.8 is recursive and terminates in a finite number of steps (actually in atmost $| N |$ steps). So the required algorithm is as follows

(*i*) Construct W;

(*ii*) Test whether $S \in W$.

2.4.11. Corollary

If $G = (N, T, S, P)$ is a context free grammar we can find an equivalent context free grammar $G_1 = (N^1, T, S_1, P)$ without null production except $S_1 \to \lambda$ when λ is in $L(G)$. If $S_1 \to \lambda$ is in P_1, S_1 does not appear on the R.H.S. of any production in P_1.

Proof. By corollary 2.4.10, we can decides whether λ is in $L(G)$.

Case 1. If λ is not in $L(G)$, G_1 obtained by using Theorem 2.4.8 is the required equivalent grammar.

Case 2. If λ is in $L(G)$, construct $G^1 = (N, T, P^1, S)$ using Theorem 2.4.8. $L(G^1) = L(G) - \{\lambda\}$. Define $G_1 = \{N \cup \{S\}, T, P_1, S_1)$, where $P_1 = P^1 \cup \{S_1 \to S, S_1 \to \lambda\}$. S_1 does not appear on the R.H.S. of any production in P_1, and so G_1 is the required grammar with $L(G_1) = L(G)$.

Elimination of unit productions

A context free grammar may have productions of the form $A \to B$, $A, B \in N$.

Consider a grammar G with productions $P = \{S \to A, A \to B, B \to C, C \to a\}$. It is easy to see that $L(G) = \{a\}$. The productions $S \to A$, $A \to B$, $B \to C$ are useful just to replace S by C. To get a terminal string, we need $C \to a$. If G_1 is $S \to a$, then $L(G_1) = L(G)$.

The next construction eliminates productions of the form $A \to B$.

2.4.12. Definition

A unit production (or a chain rule in a context free grammar G is a production of the form $A \to B$, where A and B are variables in G.

2.4.13. Theorem

If G is a context free grammar, we can find a context free grammar G_1 which has no null productions such that $L(G') = L(G)$. Let A be any variable in N.

Step 1. *Construction of the set of variables derivable from A.* Define W_i (A) recursively as follows :

$$W_0(A) = \{A\}$$

$$W_{i+1}(A) = W_i(A) \cup \{B \in N\} / C \to B \text{ is in } P \text{ with } C \in W_i(A)\}.$$

By definition of $W_i(A)$, $W_i(A) \subseteq W_{i+1}(A)$. As N is finite, $W_{k+1}(A) = W_k(A)$ for some $k \le | N |$. So $W_{k+j}(A) = W_k(A)$ for all $j \ge 0$. Let $W(A) = W_k(A)$. Then $W(A)$ is the set of all variables derivable from A.

Step 2. *Construction of A-productions in* G_1. The A-productions in G_1 are either (a) the nonunit production in G' or (b) $A \to \alpha$ whenever $B \to \alpha$ is in G with $B \in W(A)$ and $\alpha \notin N$ (Actually, (b) covers (a) as $A \in W(A)$. Now we define $G_1 = (N, T, S, P_1)$ where P_1 is constructed using step 2 for any $A \in N$.

Now we prove that G_1 is the required grammar.

Step 3. $L(G^1) = L(G)$. If $A \to \alpha$ is in $P_1 - P$, then it is induced by $B \to \alpha$ in P with $B \in W(A)$, $\alpha \notin N$, $B \in W(A)$ implies $A \overset{*}{\underset{G^1}{\Rightarrow}} B$. Hence $A \overset{*}{\underset{G^1}{\Rightarrow}} B \underset{G^1}{\Rightarrow} \alpha$. So if $A \underset{G_1}{\Rightarrow} \alpha$, then $A \overset{*}{\underset{G^1}{\Rightarrow}} \alpha$. This proves $L(G_1) \subseteq L(G^1)$.

To prove the reverse *inclusion*, we start with a leftmost derivation $S \underset{G}{\Rightarrow} \alpha_1 \underset{G}{\Rightarrow} \alpha_2 \dots \underset{G}{\Rightarrow} \alpha_n = w$ in G^1. Let i be the smallest index such that $\alpha_i \underset{G^1}{\Rightarrow} \alpha_{i+1}$ is obtained by a unit production and j be the smallest index greater than i such that $\alpha_j \underset{G}{\Rightarrow} \alpha_{i+1}$ is obtained by a nonunit production. So, $S \underset{G_1}{\Rightarrow} \alpha_i$, and $\alpha_i \overset{*}{\underset{G^1}{\Rightarrow}} \alpha_{j+1}$ can be written as

$$\alpha_i = w_i A_i \beta_i \Rightarrow w_i A_{i+1} \beta_i \Rightarrow \dots \Rightarrow w_i A_j \beta_i \Rightarrow w_i \gamma \beta_i = \alpha_{j+1}.$$

$A_j \in W(A_i)$ and $A_j \to \gamma$ is a nonunit production. Therefore $A_i \to \gamma$ is a production in P_1. Hence, $\alpha_i \overset{*}{\underset{G_1}{\Rightarrow}} \alpha_{j+1}$. Thus we have $S \overset{*}{\underset{G_1}{\Rightarrow}} \alpha_{j+1}$.

Repeating the argument whenever some unit production occurs in the remaing part of the derivation, we can prove that $S \overset{*}{\underset{G_1}{\Rightarrow}} \alpha_n = w$. This proves

$$L(G') \subseteq L(G).$$

2.4.14. Example

Let G be $S \to AB$, $A \to a$, $B \to C$, $B \to b$, $C \to D$, $D \to E$ and $E \to a$. Eliminate unit productions and get an equivalent grammar.

Step 1. $W_0(S) = \{S\}$, $W_1(S) = W_0(S) \cup \phi$

Hence $W(S) = \{S\}$. Similarly, $W(A) = \{A\}$, $W(E) = \{E\}$

$W_0(B) = \{B\}$, $W_1(B) = \{B\} \cup \{C\} = \{B, C\}$

$W_2(B) = \{B, C\} \cup \{D\}$, $W_3(B) = \{B, C, D\} \cup \{E\}$,

$W_4(B) = W_3(B)$.

Therefore, $W(B) = \{B, C, D, E\}$.

Similarly, $W_0(C) = \{C\}$, $W_1\{C\} = \{C, D\}$,

$W_2(C) = \{C, D, E\} = W_3(C)$.

Therefore $W(C) = \{C, D, E\}$, $W_0(D) = \{D\}$.

Hence $W_1(D) = \{D, E\} = W_2(D)$

Thus $W(D) = \{D, E\}$

Step 2. The production in G_1 are

$S \to AB$, $A \to a$, $E \to a$, $B \to b$, $B \to a$, $C \to a$, $D \to a$. By construction G_1 has no unit productions.

2.4.15. Corollary

If G is a context free grammar, we can construct an equivalent grammar G^1 which is reduced and has no null productions or unit productions.

Proof. We construct G_1 in the following way.

Step 1. Eliminate null productions to get G_1.

Step 2. Eliminate unit productions in G_1 to get G_2.

Step 3. Construct a reduced grammar G^1 equivalent to G_2.

G^1 is the required grammar equivalent to G.

Note. We have to apply the constructions only in the order given in corollary 2.4.10 of Theorem 2.4.8 to simplify grammars. If we change the order we may not get the grammar in the most simplified form.

2.5. NORMAL FORMS FOR CONTEXT FREE GRAMMARS

In a context free grammar, the R.H.S. of a production can be any string of variables and terminals. When the productions in G satisfy certain restrictions, then G is said to be in a '*normal form*'. Among several 'normal forms' study of them—the Chomsky Normal Form (CNF) and Greibach Normal Form (GNF) in this section.

2.5.1. Definition

A context free grammar G is in *Chomsky Normal Form* if every production is of the form $A \to a$ or $A \to$ BC and $S \to \lambda$ is in G if $\lambda \in L(G)$. When λ is in $L(G)$, we assume that S does not appear on the R.H.S. of any production.

For example, consider G whose productions are $S \to$ AB, $S \to \lambda$, $A \to a$, $B \to b$. Then G is in CNF.

Note 1. For a grammar in CNF, the derivation tree has the following property. Every node has atmost two descendants either two internal vertices or a single leaf.

2.5.2. Theorem

For every context free grammar, there is an equivalent grammar in Chomsky Normal Form.

Proof.

Step 1. Elimination of null productions. We apply Theorem 2.4.8 to eliminate null productions. We then apply Theorem 2.4.13. to the resulting grammar to eliminate chain productions. Let the grammar thus obtained be $G = (N, T, S, P)$.

Step 2. Elimination of terminals on R.H.S. We define $G_1 = (N^1, T, S, P_1)$ where P_1 and N^1 are constructed as follows.

(*i*) All the productions in P of the form $A \to a$ or $A \to BC$ are included in P_1. All the variables in N are included in N^1.

(*ii*) Consider $A \to X_1 X_2 \ldots X_n$ with some terminal on R.H.S. If X_i is a terminal, say a_i add, a new variable C_{a_i} to N^1 and $C_{a_i} \to a_i$ to P_1. In production $A \to X_1 X_2 \ldots X_n$, every terminal on R.H.S. is replaced by the corresponding new variable and the variables on the R.H.S. are retained. The resulting production is added to P_1. Thus we get $G_1 = (N^1, T, P_1, S)$.

Step 3. Restricting the number of variables on R.H.S. For any production in P_1, the R.H.S. consists of either a single terminal (or λ in $S \to \lambda$) or two or more variables. We define $G_2 = (N'', T, P_2, S)$ as follows.

(*i*) All productions in P_1 are added to P_2 if they are in the required form. All the variables in N^1 are added to N''.

(*ii*) Consider $A \rightarrow A_1 A_2 \ldots A_m$, where $m \geq 3$. We introduce new productions $A \rightarrow A_1C_1$, $C_1 \rightarrow A_2 C_2$, ..., $C_{m-2} \rightarrow A_{m-1} A_m$, and new variables $C_1, C_2, \ldots, C_{m-2}$. These are added to P'' and N'' respectively.

Thus we get G_2 in Chomsky Normal Form.

Step 4. To complete the proof we have to show that $L(G) = L(G_1) = L(G_2)$.

To show that $L(G) \subseteq L(G_1)$, we start with $w \in L(G)$. If $A \rightarrow X_1X_2 \ldots X_n$ is used in the derivation of *w*, the same effect can be achieved by using the corresponding prodcution in P_1 and the productions involving the new variables. Hence $A \overset{*}{\Rightarrow} X_1 X_2 \ldots X_n$. Thus $L(G) \subseteq L(G_1)$.

Let $w \in L(G_1)$. To show that $w \in L(G)$, it is enough to prove the following

$$A \underset{G}{\overset{*}{\Rightarrow}} w \text{ if } A \in N,\ A \underset{G_1}{\overset{*}{\Rightarrow}} w \qquad \ldots(2.6)$$

We prove (2.6) by induction on the number of steps in $A \underset{G_1}{\overset{*}{\Rightarrow}} w$.

If $A \underset{G_1}{\Rightarrow} \omega$. then $A \rightarrow w$ is a production in P_1. By construction of P_1, *w* is a single terminal. So $A \rightarrow w$ is in *P i.e.*, $A \underset{G}{\Rightarrow} w$. Thus is basis for induction.

Let us assume (2.6) for derivations in atmost *k* steps. Let $A \underset{G_1}{\overset{k+1}{\Rightarrow}} w$. We can split this derivation as $A \underset{G_1}{\Rightarrow} A_1 A_2 \ldots A_m \underset{G_1}{\overset{k}{\Rightarrow}} w_1 . w_m = w$ such that $A_i \underset{G_1}{\overset{*}{\Rightarrow}} w_i$. Each A_i is either in *N* or a new variable, say Ca_i. When $A_i \in N$, $A_i \underset{G_1}{\overset{*}{\Rightarrow}} w_i$ is a derivation in atmost *k* steps, and so by induction hypothesis, $A_i \underset{G}{\overset{*}{\Rightarrow}} w_i$. Thus (2.6) is true for all derivations. Therefore $L(G) = L(G_1)$.

The effect of applying $A \rightarrow A_1 A_2 \ldots A_m$ in a derivation for $w \in L(G_1)$ can be acheived by applying the production $A \rightarrow A_1C_1$, $C_1 \rightarrow A_2 C_2$, ... $C_{m-2} \rightarrow A_{m-1} A_m$ in P_2. Hence it is easy to see that $L(G_1) \subseteq L(G_2)$.

To prove $L(G_2) \subseteq L(G_1)$, we can prove an auxillary result.

$$A \underset{G_1}{\overset{*}{\Rightarrow}} w \text{ if } A \in N^1,\ A \underset{G2}{\overset{*}{\Rightarrow}} w \qquad \ldots(2.7$$

Condition (2.7) can be proved by induction on the number of steps $A \overset{*}{\underset{G_2}{\Rightarrow}} w$.

Applying (2.6) to S, we get $L(G_2) \subseteq L(G_1)$.

Thus $L(G) = L(G_1) = L(G_2)$.

Problem 1. Find a grammar in CNF equivalent to

$$S \to aAbB,\ A \to aA/a,\ B \to bB/b.$$

Solution. As there are no unit productions or null productions, we need not carryout step 1. We proceed to step 2.

Step 2. Let $G_1 = (N^1, \{a, b\}, S, P_1\}$ where P_1 and N^1 are constructed as follows.

(*i*) $A \to a$, $B \to b$ are added to P_1.

(*ii*) $S \to aAbB$, $A \to aA$, $B \to bB$ yield

$S \to C_aAC_bB$, $A \to CaA$, $B \to C_bB$,

$C_a \to a$, $C_b \to b$.

$N^1 = \{S, A, B, C_a, C_b\}$.

Step 3. P_1 consists of $S \to C_aA\ C_b\ B$, $A \to C_aA$, $B \to C_bB$, $C_a \to a$, $C_b \to b$, $A \to a$, $B \to b$.

$S \to C_a A\ C_b\ B$ is replaced by $S \to C_aC_1$, $C_1 \to AC_2$, $C_2 \to C_bB$. The remaining production in P_1 are added to P_2. Let

$$G_2 = (\{S, A, B, C_a, C_b, C_1, C_2\}, \{a, b\}, P_2, S),$$

where P_2 consists of $S \to C_a\ C_1$, $C \to AC_2$, $C_2 \to C_bB$.

The remaining productions in P_1 are added to P_2. Let

$$G_2 = (\{S, A, B, C_a, C_b, C_1, C_2\}, \{a, b\}, P_2, S)$$

where P_2 consists of $S \to C_a\ C_1$, $C_1 \to AC_2$, $C_2 \to C_bB$, $A \to C_aA$, $B \to C_bB$, $C_a \to a$, $C_b \to b$, $A \to a$ and $B \to b$.

G_2 is in CNF and equivalent to the given grammar.

Problem 2. Find a grammar in CNF form for the grammar $G = (N, T, S, P)$ where $N = \{S\}$, $T = \{a, b\}$ and $P = \{S \to aSb,\ S \to ab\}$ of the language $L = \{a^n\ b^n\ /\ n \geq 1\}$.

Solution.

Step 1. Replace all the terminals a, b by new non-terminals C_1, C_2. Then we obtain.

$$P_1 = \{S \rightarrow C_1\, S\, C_2,\ S \rightarrow C_1C_2,\ C_1 \rightarrow a,\ C_2 \rightarrow b\}$$

Step 2. Introduce the new non-terminal D_1 and replace the rule $S \rightarrow C_1\, S\, C_2$ by the rules $S \rightarrow C_1\, D_1$, $D_1 \rightarrow SC_2$. The other rules are already in normal form.

Step 3. It can be verified that the grammar $G^1 = (N^1, T, P^1\ S)$ where $N^1 = \{S, C_1, C_2, D_1\}$ and $P^1 = \{S \rightarrow C_1D_1, D_1 \rightarrow SC_2, S \rightarrow C_1\, C_2, C_1 \rightarrow a, C_2 \rightarrow b\}$ is in CNF and generates L.

Greibach Normal Form

Greibach Normal Form (GNF) is another normal form quite useful in some proofs and constructions. A context free grammar generating the set accepted by a pushdown automaton in Greibach Normal Form.

2.5.3. Definition

A context free grammar is in *Greibach normal form* if every production is of the form $A \rightarrow a\alpha$ where $\alpha \in N^*$ and $a \in T$ (α may be λ) and $S \rightarrow \lambda$ is in G if $\lambda \in L(G)$. When $\lambda \in L(G)$, we assume that S does not appear on the R.H.S. of any production. For example, G given by $S \rightarrow aAB/\lambda$, $A \rightarrow bC$, $B \rightarrow b$, $C \rightarrow c$ is in GNF.

2.5.4. Lemma

Let $G = (N, T, S, P)$ be *a* CFG. Let $A \rightarrow \beta\gamma$ be an A-production in P. Let the B-production be $B \rightarrow \beta_1 / \beta_2 / \ldots / \beta_s$. Define.

$$P_1 = (P - \{A \rightarrow \beta\gamma\}) \cup \{A \rightarrow \beta_i\, \gamma\, / \lambda_I \leq i \leq s\}.$$

Then $G_1 = (N, T, S, P)$ is a CFG equivalent to G.

Proof. If we apply $A \rightarrow \beta\gamma$ in some derivation for $w \in L(G)$, we have to apply $B \rightarrow \beta_i$ for some i at a latter step. So $A \overset{*}{\underset{G}{\Rightarrow}} \beta_i\, \gamma$. The effect of applying $A \rightarrow \beta\gamma$ and eliminating B in garammar G is the same as applying $A \rightarrow \beta_i\, \gamma$ for some i in grammar G_1. Hence $w \in L(G_1)$ *i.e.*, $L(G) \subseteq L(G_1)$. Similary, instead of applying $A \rightarrow \beta i\, \gamma$, we can apply $A \rightarrow B\gamma$ and $B \rightarrow \beta_i$ to get $A \overset{*}{\underset{G}{\Rightarrow}} \beta_i\, \gamma$. This proves that $L(G_1) \subseteq L(G)$.

Note. Lemma 2.5.4. is useful for deleting a variable B appearing as the first symbol on the R.H.S. of some A-production provided no B-production has B as the first symbol on R.H.S.

The construction given in Lemma 2.5.4 is simple. To eliminate B in $A \rightarrow \beta\gamma$, we simply replace B by the right hand side of every B-production.

For example, using lemma 2.5.4., we can replace $A \to Bab$ by $A \to aAab$, $A \to bBab$, $A \to aaab$, $A \to ABab$ when the B-productions are $B \to aA/bB/aa/AB$. The lemma is useful to eliminate A from the R.H.S. of $A \to \alpha$.

2.5.5. Lemma

Let $G = (N, T, S, P)$ be a CFG. Let the set of A-productions be $A \to A\alpha_1$ / ... $A\alpha_r$ / β_1 / ... / β_s (β_i's do not start with A). Let z be a new variable. Let $G_1 = (N \cup \{z\}, T, P_1, S)$ where P_1 is defined as follows.

(*i*) The set of A-productions in P_1 are

$$A \to \beta_1 / \beta_2 / \ldots / \beta_s,\ A \to \beta_1 z / \beta_2 z / \ldots / \beta_s z$$

(*ii*) The set of z-productions in P_1 are

$$z \to \alpha_1 / \alpha_2 / \ldots / \alpha_r$$

$$z \to \alpha_1 z / \alpha_2 z / \ldots / \alpha_r z.$$

(*iii*) The productions for other variables are as in P.

Then G_1 is a CFG and equivalent to G.

Proof. To prove $L(G) \subseteq L(G_1)$, consider a leftmost derivation of w in G. The only productions in $P - P_1$ are $A \to A\alpha_1$/ $A\ \alpha_2$ ... / $A\alpha_r$. If $A \to A\alpha_{i1}$, $A \to A\alpha_{i2}$, ... $A \to A\alpha_{ik}$ *ar* used , then $A \to \beta_j$ should be used at a later state (to elimiate A). So we have $A \overset{*}{\underset{G}{\Rightarrow}} \beta_j\ A\alpha_{i1} \ldots \alpha_{ik}$ while deriving w in G. However

$$A \underset{G_1}{\Rightarrow} \beta_j z \underset{G_1}{\Rightarrow} \beta_j\ \alpha_{i1}\ z \ldots \underset{G_1}{\Rightarrow} \beta_j\ \alpha_{i1}\ \alpha_{i2} \ldots \alpha_{ik}$$

i.e.,

$$A \overset{*}{\underset{G_1}{\Rightarrow}} \beta_j A \alpha_{i1} \ldots \alpha_{ik}$$

Thus, A can be eliminated by using productions in G_1. Therefore, $w \in L(G_1)$.

To prove $L(G_1) \subseteq L(G)$, consider a leftmost derivation of w in G_1. The only productions $P_1 - P$ are

$$A \to \beta_1 z / \beta_2 z / \ldots / \beta_s z,\ z \to \alpha_1 / \ldots / \alpha_r,$$

$z \to \alpha_1 z$ / $\alpha_2 z$ / .../ $\alpha_r z$. If the new variable z appears in the course of the derivation of w, it is because of the application of $A \to \beta_{jz}$ in some earlier step. Also, z can eliminated only by a production of the form $z \to \alpha_i$ or $z \to \alpha_{jz}$ for some i and j in a later step. So we get $A \overset{*}{\Rightarrow} \beta_j\ \alpha_{i1}\ \alpha_{i2} \ldots \alpha_{ik}$ in the course of the derivation of w. But we know that $A \underset{G}{\overset{*}{\Rightarrow}} \beta_j \alpha_{i1} \alpha_{i2} \ldots \alpha_{ik}$. Therefore. $w \in L(G)$.

2.5.6. Theorem

Every context free language L can be generated by a context free grammar G in GNF.

Proof. We prove the theorem when $\lambda \notin L$ and then extend the construction to L having λ.

Case 1. Construction of G (when $\lambda \notin L$):

Step 1. We eliminate null productions and then construct a grammar in G in CNF generating L. We rename the variables as $A_1, A_2, \ldots A_n$ with $S = A_1$. We write G as $(\{A_1, A_2, \ldots A_n\}, T, P, A_1)$.

Step 2. To get the productions in the form $A_i \to av$ or $A_i \to A_j v$, where $j > i$, convert the A_i-productions ($i = 1, 2, \ldots, n - 1$) to the from $A_i \to A_j \gamma$ such that $j > i$. Prove that such modifications is possible by induction on i.

Consider A_1-production. If we have some A_1-productions of the form $A_1 \to A_1\gamma$, then we can apply lemma 2.5.5. to get rid of such productions. We get a new variable, say z_1, and A_1-production of the form $A_1 \to a$ or $A_1 \to A_j \gamma'$, where $j > 1$. Thus there is a basis for induction.

Assume we have modified A_1-productions, A_2-productions, ... A_i-productions. Consider A_{i+1}-productions. Productions of the form $A_{i+1} \to \alpha v$ required no modification. Consider the first symbol (this will be a variable) on the R.H.S. of the remaining A_{i+1}-productions. Let t be the smallest index among the indices of such symbols (variables). If $t > i + 1$, there is nothing to prove. Otherwise, apply induction hypothesis, to A_i-productions for $t \le i$. So any A_t production is of the form $A_t \to A_j r$, where $j >$ t or $A_t \to a\gamma^1$. Now we can apply lemma 2.5.4 to A_{i+1}-production whose R.H.S. starts with A_t. The resulting A_{i+1}-productions are of the form $A_{i+1} \to A_j \gamma$, where $j > t$ (or $A_{i+1} \to \alpha\gamma^1$).

We repeat the above constructions by finding t for the new set of A_{i+1} productions. Ultimately, the A_{i+1}-productions are converted to the form $A_{i+1} \to A_i \gamma$, where $j \ge i + 1$ or $A_{i+1} \to a\gamma^1$. Productions of the form $A_{i+1} \to A_{i+1} \gamma$ can be modified by using lemma 2.5.5. Thus we have converted A_{i+1}-productions to the required form. By the principle of induction, the constructions can be carried out for $i = 1, 2, \ldots, n$. Thus for $i = 1, 2, \ldots, n - 1$, any A_i-production is of the form $A_i \to A_j \gamma$, where $j > i$ or $A_i \to a\gamma^1$. Any. A_n-production is of the form $A_n \to A_n\gamma$ or $A_n \to a\gamma^1$.

Step 3. Convert A_n-productions to the form $A_n \to \alpha\gamma$. Here productions of the form $A_n \to A_n \gamma$ are eliminated using lemma 2.5.5. The resulting An-productions are of the form $A_n \to \alpha\gamma$.

Step 4. Modify A_i- productions to the form $A_i \to av$ for $i = 1, 2, \ldots n - 1$. At the end of step 3, the A_n-productions are of the form $A_n \to \alpha\gamma$. The A_{n-1}-productions are of the form $A_{n-1} \to \alpha\gamma^1$ or $A_{n-1} \to A_n\gamma$. By lemma 2.5.4, we eliminate productions of the form $A_{n-1} \to A_n\gamma$.

The resulting A_{n-1}-productions are in the required form. We repeat the construction by considering $A_{n-2}, A_{n-3}, \ldots, A_1$.

Step 5. Modify Z_i-productions. Every time we apply lemma 2.5.5. we get new variable. (We take it as Z_i when we apply the lemma for A_i-productions). The Z_i productions are of the form $Z_i \to \alpha z_i$ or $z \to \alpha$ (where α is obtained from $A_i \to A_i\alpha$) and hence of the form $Z_i \to \alpha\gamma$ or $Z_i \to A_k\gamma$ for some k. At the end of step 4, the R.H.S of any A_k-productions starts with a terminal. So we can apply lemma 2.5.4. to eliminate $z_i \to A_k v$. Thus at the end of step 5, we get an equivalent grammar G_1 in GNF.

It is easy to see that G_1 is in GNF. We start with G in CNF. In G any production is of the form $A \to a$ or $A \to AB$ or $A \to CD$. When we apply lemma 2.5.4. and lemma 2.5.5. in step 2, we get new productions of the form $A \to a$ or $A \to \beta$, where $\alpha \in N^*$ and $\beta \in N^+$ and $a \in T$. In step 3 to 5, the productions are modified to the form $A \to a\alpha$ or $z \to a^1\alpha^1$ where $a, a^1 \in T$ and $a, a^1 \in N^*$

Case 2. (Construction of G when $\alpha \in L$). By the previous construction we get $G^1 = (N^1, \Sigma, P_1, S)$ in GNF such that $L(G^1) = L - \{\lambda\}$. Define a new grammar G_1 as

$$G_1 = (N^1 \cup \{S\}, T, P_1 \cup \{S^1 \to S, S^1 \to \lambda\}, S^1)$$

$S^1 \to S$ can be eliminated by using theorem 2.4.13. As S-production are in the required form, S^1-production are also in the required form so $L(G) = L(G_1)$ and G_1 is GNF.

2.5.7. Remark

Although we convert the given grammar to CNF in the first step, it is not necessary to convert all the productions to the form required for CNF. In step 2–5, we do not disturb productions of the form $A \to a\alpha$, $a \in T$ and $\alpha \in N^*$. So such productions can be allowed in G (in step 1). If we apply lemma 2.5.4. or lemma 2.5.5 as in step 2–5 to productions of the form $A \to \alpha$, where $\alpha \in N^*$ and $|\alpha| \geq 2$, the resulting productions at the end of step 5 are in the required form (for GNF). Hence we can allow productions of the form $A \to \alpha$, where $\alpha \in N^*$ and $|\alpha| \geq 2$.

Thus we can apply steps 2–5 to a grammar whose productions are either $A \to a\alpha$, where $\alpha \in N^*$ or

$A \to \alpha \in N^*$, where $|\alpha| \geq 2$. To reduce productions of the form $A \to \alpha \in N^*$, where $|\alpha| \geq 2$, we can apply step 2 of theorem 2.5.2.

2.6. PROBLEMS RELATED TO CNF AND GNF

Problem 1. Construct a grammar in CNF of the language

$$L = \{wcw^R \,/\, w \in (a, b)^*\}.$$

Solution. We know that the grammar $G = (N, T, S, P)$ where $N = \{S\}$, $T = \{a, b, c\}$ and $P = \{S \to aSa, S \to bSb, S \to c\}$ generates L.

Step 1. Replace the terminals a, b by new non-terminals C_1, C_2. Then we get, $P_1 = \{S \to C_1SC_1, S \to C_2\, S\, C_2, S \to C, C_1 \to a, C_2 \to b\}$.

Step 2. Introduce new non-terminals D_1, D_2 to reduce the first two rules to binary form *i.e.*, $S \to C_1SC_1$ is replaced by $S_1 \to C_1D_1$, $D_1 \to SC_1$ and $S \to C_2SC_2$ is replaced by $S \to C_2D_2$, $D_2 \to SC_2$.

Step 3. Thus $G^1 = (N^1, T^1, S, P^1)$ where $N^1 = \{S, C_1, C_2, D_1, D_2\}$ and $P^1 = \{S \to C_1\, D_1, D_1 \to SC_1, S \to C_2\, D_2, D_2 \to SC_2, S \to C, C_1 \to a\,, C_2 \to b\}$ is in CNF and generates L.

Problem 2. Construct a grammar in CNF for the langulage

$$L = \{a^n\, b^m\, a^n / \, n \geq 0, m \geq 1\}$$

Solution. We know that $G = (N, T, S, P)$ where $N = \{S, A\}$

$T = \{a, b\}$, and $P = \{S \to aSa, S \to bA, A \to bA. S \to b, A \to b\}$ generates L.

Step 1. In the non-terminal rule which is not in binary standard form is $S \to C_1\, S\, C_1$. Introduce new non-terminal D_1 to convert the rule into binary form is $S \to C_1\, S\, C_1$ is replaced by $S \to C_1\, D_1$, $D_1 \to SC_1$.

Step 3. Let $G^1 = (N^1, T^1, S, P^1)$ where $N^1 = \{S, C_1, C_2, D_1\}$ and $P = \{S \to C_1 D_1, D_1 \to SC_1, D_1 \to SC_1, S \to C_2A, A \to C_2A, S \to b, A \to b, C_1 \to a, C_2 \to b\}$. G^1 is in CNF and generates L.

Problem 3. Construct a grammar in GNF to generate the CFL, $L = \{ww^R / \, w \in (a, b)^+\}$.

Solution. We know that $G = (N, T, S, P)$ where $N = \{S\}$, $T = \{a, b\}$ and $P = \{S \to aSa, S \to bSb, S \to aa, S \to bb\}$ generates L.

Step 1. Let $G_1 = (N_1, T, S, P_1)$ where $N_1 = \{S, A, B\}$ and

$$P_1 = \{S \to ASA, S \to BSB, S \to AA, S \to BB, A \to a, B \to b\}.$$

Then $$L(G_1) = L(G).$$

Step 2. Renaming the non-terminals, G_1 is rewritten as

$$G_2 = (N_2, T, P_2, A_1) \text{ where } N_2 = (A_1, A_2, A_3\},$$
$$T = \{a, b\} \text{ and } P_2 = \{A_1 \to A_2 A_1 A_2, A_1 \to A_3 A_1 A_3, A_1 \to A_2 A_2, A_1 \to A_3 A_3, A_2 \to a, A_3 \to b\}.$$

Here again, the rules are in the form required at the end of step 3. So we proceed straight to step 4.

Step 4. It is easy to see that

$$G_3 = (N_3, T, P_3, A_1)$$

where $N_3 = \{A_1, A_2, A_3\}$, $T = \{a, b\}$ and

$$P_3 = \{A_1 \to aA_1A_2, A_1 \to aA_2, A_1 \to bA_1 A_3, A_1 \to bA_3, A_2 \to a, A_3 \to b\} \text{ is in GNF.}$$

2.7. SOLVED PROBLEMS

1. Give context free grammars generating the following sets.

(*a*) The set of palindromes over alphabet $\{a, b\}$ (strings that read the same forward as backward).

(*b*) The set of all string over alphabet $\{a, b\}$ with exactly twice as many a's as b's.

(*c*) The set of all strings over alphabet $\{a, b\}$ not of the form ww for some string w.

(*d*) $\{a^{2n}bc \mid n \geq 0\}$.

(*e*) $\{aaaa, aabb, bbaa, bbbb\}$.

Solution.

(*a*) Consider the grammar $G = (N, T, S, P)$ where $N = \{S\}$, $T = \{a, b\}$, $P : \{S \to aSa, S \to bSb, S \to a, S \to b, S \to \lambda\}$. Observe that the language generated by G is the set of all palindromes over $\{a, b\}$. [Apply $S \to aSa$ any number of times and then apply $S \to bSb$ any number of times. Finally apply $\{S \to a$ or $S \to b$ or $S \to \lambda\}$.

(*b*) L = {The set of all strings over alphabat $\{a, b\}$ with exactly twice as many a's as b's}.

Construct a grammar $G = (N, T, S, P)$ where $N = \{S\}$,

$T = \{a, b\}$ and $P = \{S \to SaSb\ SaS, S \to SaSaSbS, S \to SbSaSaS, S \to \lambda\}$.

Since all the three production rules (other than $S \to \lambda$) involve on the right side $2a$'s and one b, the effect of applying each one of them at any point of the derivation is to provide twice as many a's as b's and to get terminal strings. We have to finally apply $S \rightarrow \lambda$ certain number of times. Hence G generates L.

(*c*) L = {set of all strings over alphabat $\{a, b\}$ not of the form ww for some string w.}

Construct the grammar $G = \{N, T, S, P)$ where

$N = \{S, A, B\}$, $T = \{a, b\}$ and $P = \{S \rightarrow abA, A \rightarrow bA, A \rightarrow b, A \rightarrow \lambda, S \rightarrow baB, B \rightarrow aB, B \rightarrow a, B \rightarrow \lambda, S \rightarrow aS, S \rightarrow bS, S \rightarrow \lambda\}$

It is easily observe that $L = L(G)$.

(*d*) $L = \{a^{2n} \text{ bc} / n \geq 0\}$

Construct a grammar $G = (N, T, S, P)$ where $N = \{S\}$,

$T = \{a, b\}$ and $P = \{S \rightarrow a_2 S, S \rightarrow bc|\}$

Derivation : $S \Rightarrow bc$

$S \Rightarrow a^2S \Rightarrow a^2bc$

$S \Rightarrow a^2S \Rightarrow a^4S \Rightarrow a^4bc$

....

$S \overset{*}{\Rightarrow} a^{2n}\ bc$

$\therefore$ $L = L(G) = \{a^{2n}\ bc\ /\ n \geq 0\}$.

(*e*) $L = \{aaaa, aabb, bbaa, bbbb\}$

Since L has a finite number of string, we can list all strings in the language. Hence the required context free grammmar is $G = (N, T, P, S)$ where $N = \{S\}$ $T = \{a, b\}$ and P consists of the productions $S \rightarrow aaaa$, $S \rightarrow aabb$, $S \rightarrow bbaa$, $S \rightarrow bbbb$.

2. Find the language $L(G)$ generated by the grammar G with variables S, A, B terminals a, b, and productions $S \rightarrow aB, B \rightarrow b, B \rightarrow bA, A \rightarrow aB$.

Solution. Observe that we can only use the first production once since the start symbol S does not appear anywhere else. Also we can only obtain a terminal word by finally using the second production. Otherwise we alternatively add a's and b's using the third and fourth productions. In otherwords $L(G) = \{(ab)^n = abab \ldots ab : n \in N\}$

3. Let L be the set of all words in a and b with an even number of a's. Find a grammar G which will generate L.

Solution. Construct a grammar $G = (N, T, S, P)$ where $N = \{S, A, B\}$, $T = \{a$

$b\}$ and $P = \{S \to aA, S \to bB, B \to bB, B \to aA, A \to aB, A \to bA, A \to a, B \to b\}$. Observe that the sum of the a's and A's in any word a either remains the same or increased by 2 when any production is applied to α. Thus any word w in the terminals a and b which is derived from S must contain the even number of a's. In otherwords $L(G) \subseteq L$. On the otherhand, it is clear which productions should be used to print any word w in L; that is we use $S \to aA$ or $S \to bB$ according as v begin with a or b and we use $A \to aB$ or $B \to aA$ if any subsequent letter is an a and we use $A \to bA$ or $B \to bB$ if any subsequent letter is a b. For the last letter of v we use $A \to a$ or $B \to b$. Thus $L(G) = L$.

4. Describle the language generated by the context free grammar G with productions $S \to aA, A \to bbA, A \to c$.

Solution. Observe that the production $S \to aA$ generates one a and that can be applied only once. Hence all the words in the languge starts with a. Also at any stage of the derivation the number of A is one. If we apply the production $A \to c$ once the process stop. Hence all the words in the language ends with c. The production $A \to bbA$ produce 2 b's at each application. Hence the number of b's in any word is always an even number. Hence $L = L(G) = \{ab^{2n}c\}/\ n \geq 0\}$

5. Construct a context free grammar for the language

$$L = \{a^n\ b^m\ a^m\ b^n\ /\ m, n \geq 1\}$$

Solution. A context free grammar generating L is $G = (N, T, S, P)$ where $N = \{S, A\}$, $T = \{a, b\}$ and

$$P = \{S \to aSa,\ S \to aAb,\ A \to bAa,\ A \to ba\}$$

when $n > 1$, $m > 1$,

$$S \overset{*}{\Rightarrow} a^{n-1}\ S\ b^{n-1} \quad \text{(Applying } S \to aSb\ (n-1) \text{ time)}$$

$$\Rightarrow a^n\ A\ b^n \quad \text{(Applying } A \to bAa \text{ one time)}$$

$$\Rightarrow a^n\ b^{m-1}\ Aa^{m-1}\ b^n \quad \text{(Applying } A \to bAa(m-1) \text{ time)}$$

$$\Rightarrow a^n b^m\ a^m b^n \quad \text{(Applying } A \to ba \text{ one time)}$$

when $n = 1$, $m > 1$

$$S \Rightarrow aAb$$

$$\overset{*}{\Rightarrow} ab^{m-1}\ Aa^{m-1}\ b \quad \text{(Applying } A \to bAa(m-1) \text{ times)}$$

$$\Rightarrow a^n b^m a^m b \quad \text{(Applying } A \to ba \text{ one time)}$$

Similarly, the strings $a^n bab^n$ and $abab$ are also generated.

6. Construct a context free grammars for the language

$$L = \{a^n b^n / n \geq 1\}.$$

Solution. $L = \{a^n b^n / n \geq 1\}$. Construct a grammar $G = (N, T, S, P)$ where $N = \{S\}$, $T = \{a, b\}$ and $P = \{S \rightarrow aSb, S \rightarrow ab\}$

Derivation : $S \stackrel{*}{\Rightarrow} a^{n-1} S b^{n-1}$ (Applying $S \rightarrow aSb(n-1)$ times)

$\Rightarrow a^n b^n$ (Applying $S \rightarrow ab$ one time)

$\therefore \quad L = L(G) = \{a^n b^n / n \geq 1\}$.

Observe that $G_1 = (N_1, T_1, S_1, P_1)$ where $N_1 = \{S_1, A\}$, $T_1 = \{a, b\}$ and $P_1 = \{S_1 \rightarrow aAb, A \rightarrow aAb, A \rightarrow \lambda\}$ is another context free grammar generating L.

For $n > 1$, $\quad S_1 \Rightarrow aAb$

$\stackrel{*}{\Rightarrow} a^n A b^n$ (Applying $A \rightarrow aAb$ $(n-1)$ times)

$\Rightarrow a^n b^n$ (Applying $A \rightarrow \lambda$ once)

when $n = 1$ $\quad S \Rightarrow aAb$

$\Rightarrow ab$

7. Construct a context free grammar for the language $L = \{w/w$ in $\{a, b\}^+$ consists of an equal number of a's and b's$\}$

Solution. A CFG generating the language L is given by $G = (N, T, S, P)$ where $N = \{S, A, B\}$, $T = \{a, b\}$ and $P = \{S \rightarrow aB, S \rightarrow bA, A \rightarrow a, A \rightarrow aS, A \rightarrow bAA, B \rightarrow b, B \rightarrow bS, B \rightarrow aBB\}$ we shall prove that $L(G) = L$, by the following inductive hypothesis :

For w in $(a, b)^+$

1. $S \stackrel{*}{\Rightarrow} w$ iff w consists of an equal number of a's and b's.
2. $A \stackrel{*}{\Rightarrow} w$ iff w has one more a than it has b's.
3. $B \stackrel{*}{\Rightarrow} w$ iff w has one more b than it has a's.

Since $A \rightarrow a$, $B \rightarrow b$ are rules in P, $A \Rightarrow a$ and $B \Rightarrow b$. No other terminal string of length one is derivable from A or B. Also S does not generate any terminal string of length one. Thus the hypothesis is true when $|w| = 1$ ($|w|$ is length of the string w).

Assume the inductive hypothesis is true for all w for which $|w| \leq k - 1$. We shall prove that the hypothesis is true for all w with $|w| = k$.

Let $S \overset{*}{\Rightarrow} w$, $| w | = k$. The first step of this derivation should be either $S \Rightarrow aB$ or $S \Rightarrow bA$, as $S \rightarrow aB$ and $S \rightarrow$ bA are the only rules in P with S on the left side. If $S \Rightarrow aB \overset{*}{\Rightarrow} w$, then $w = aw_1$ where $B \overset{*}{\Rightarrow} w_1$ and $| w_1 | = k - 1$. The hypothesis being true for strings of length $\leq k - 1$, w_1 has one more b than it has a's by 3. Hence $w = aw_1$ has equal number of a's and b's. If $S \Rightarrow bA$ is the first step of the derivation $S \overset{*}{\Rightarrow} w$, we have a similar argument. Conversely if, w has an equal number of a's and b's, so that $| w | = k$, then the first symbol of w is a or b. Suppose $w = aw_1$. Then $| w_1 | = k - 1$ and w_1 has one more b that it has a's. By hypothesis 3, $B \overset{*}{\Rightarrow} w_1$. Thus $S \Rightarrow aB \overset{*}{\Rightarrow} aw_1 = w$ or $S \overset{*}{\Rightarrow} w$. If $w = bw_2$, we have a similar argument. Thus the hypothesis 1 is true for strings w, $| w | = k$.

Similarly, the hypothesis 2 and 3 are proved for strings of length k. Hence, $L(G)$ is the set of all words in T^+ consisting of an equal number of a's and b's.

8. Construct a CFG for the language $L = \{a^i b^j / j > i\}$.

Solution. Construct a grammar $G = (N, T, S, P)$ where $N = \{S, A\}$, $T = \{a, b\}$ and $P = \{S \rightarrow aSb, S \rightarrow aAb, A \rightarrow bA, A \rightarrow b\}$.

Derivation.

$$
\begin{aligned}
S &\overset{*}{\Rightarrow} a^{i-1} S b^{i-1} && \text{(Applying } S \rightarrow aSb \;\; i - 1 \text{ times)} \\
&\Rightarrow a^i A b^i && \text{(Applying } S \rightarrow aAb \text{ one time)} \\
&\overset{*}{\Rightarrow} a^i b^{k-1} A b^i && \text{(Applying } A \rightarrow bA \; (k - 1) \text{ times)} \\
&\Rightarrow a^i b^{k+i} = a^i b^j && \text{(Applying } A \rightarrow b \text{ one time)}
\end{aligned}
$$

where $\quad j = k + i > i$

Hence $\quad L = L(G)$.

9. Construct a CFG for the language

$$L = \{x \in \{0, 1\}^* / n_0(x) = n_1(x)\} \text{ where}$$

$n_i(x)$ is the number of i's on the string x.

Solution. $\quad L = \{x \in \{0, 1\}^* / n_0(x) = n_1(x)\}$

Construct a CFG $G = (N, T, S, P)$ where $N = \{S\}$,

$$T = \{0, 1\} \text{ and } P = \{S \rightarrow \lambda/0S1/1S0/SS\}$$

Derivations. The rule $S \rightarrow \lambda$, produce the string l in which number of zeros in zero and number of 1's is also zero. Application of $S \rightarrow SS$ produce two S's and the application of $S \rightarrow 0S1$ or $S \rightarrow 1S0$ produces equal number of 0's and 1's. Hence $L = L(G)$.

10. In each case, say what language is generated by the CFG with indicated productions.

(*a*) $S \rightarrow aSa/bSb/\lambda$

(*b*) $S \rightarrow aSa/bSb/a/b$

(*c*) $S \rightarrow aSb/bSa/\lambda$

(*d*) $S \rightarrow aS/bS/a$.

Solution. (*a*) The productions are $S \rightarrow aSa$, $S \rightarrow bSb$, $S \rightarrow \lambda$.

Hence, L = {set of all palindromes over $\{a, b\}$}

[Refer problem 1 (*a*)]

(*b*) The productions are $S \rightarrow aSa$, $S \rightarrow bSb$, $S \rightarrow a$, $S \rightarrow b$.

L = {set of all palindromes over (a, b)}

[Refer problem 1(*a*)]

(*c*) The productions are $S \rightarrow aSb$, $S \rightarrow bSa$, $S \rightarrow \lambda$. The application of the rules $S \rightarrow aSb$ and $S \rightarrow \lambda$ produce the language $L_1 = \{a^n b^n / n \geq 1\}$. The applications of the rules $S \rightarrow bSa$ and $S \rightarrow \lambda$ generate the language $L_2 = \{b^n a^n / \ n \geq 1\}$. Application of all the three rules $S \rightarrow aSb$, $S \rightarrow bSa$, $S \rightarrow \lambda$ produce language of the form $L_3 = \{a^n \ b^m \ a^m \ b^n \ / \ m, n \geq 1\}$. Thus the required language $L = L_1 \cup L_2 \cup L_3$.

(*d*) The productions are $S \rightarrow aS/bS/a$.

The application of the rule $S \rightarrow aS$ $(n - 1)$ times and $S \rightarrow a$ one time will produce strings of the form $L_1 = \{a^n / \ n \geq 1\}$. The application of the rule $S \rightarrow bS$ n times and $S \rightarrow a$ produces strings of the form $L_2 = \{b^n \ a / n \geq 0\}$. Also application of all the three rules many times produce the language $L_3 = \{w / w \in \{a, b\}^*\}$ and w terminates with a. Thus the required language $L = L_1 \cup L_2 \cup L_3$.

11. Let G be the grammar $S \rightarrow aS/aSbS/\lambda$ prove that $L(G)$ = {x/each of prefix of x has atleast as many a's as b's}

{**Hint.** For the word *aabab* the prefixes are λ, *a* , *aa*, *aab*, *aaba* and *aabab*}.

Solution. The production rules are $P_1 : S \rightarrow aS$, $P_2 : S \rightarrow aSbS$ and $P_3 : S \rightarrow \lambda$. Since P_1 contains one '*a*' and *no* '*b*' and P_2 contains one '*a*' and one '*b*' the effect of applying each one then at any number of times produce strings with number of '*a*' greater than or equal to number of *b*'s. Finally we have to apply P_3 required number of times. Also both P_1 and P_2 contains '*a*' as a leading symbol. So by the application of P_1 and P_2 in any order we can get words such that each prefix of it contains atleast as many a's as b's.

12. Consider the CFG with productions

$S \rightarrow aSbScS/aScSbS/bSaScS/bScSaS/cSaSbS/cSbSaS/\lambda.$

Does this generate the language $\{x \in \{a, b, c\}^* / n_a(x) = n_b(x) = n_c(a)\}$.

$[n_a(x) \;=\; \text{no of } a\text{'s in } x \text{ etc.}]$

Solution. Yes, the given CFG produce the language

$$L = \{x \in \{a, b, c\}^* / n_a(x) = n_b(x) = n_c(x)\}$$

For all the production rules involve on the right equal number of a's, b's and c's. Hence the application of each one of the production rules generates strings x for which $n_a(x) = n_b(x) = n_c(x)$. Hence $L(G) = L$.

13. Find context free grammar generating the language

(a) $\{a^i\, b^j \,/\, i \leq 2j\}$

(b) $\{a^i\, b^j \,/ i \leq j \leq 2i\}$

Solution.

(a) Construct a CFG $G = (N, T, S, P)$

where $N = \{S, A\}$, $T = \{a, b,\}$ and

$P = \{S \rightarrow aS,\; S \rightarrow b^2A,\; A \rightarrow bA,\; A \rightarrow \lambda\}$

we observe that $L(G) = \{a^i\, b^j \,/ i \leq 2j)$.

(b) Construct a CFG $G = (N, T, S, P)$ where

$N = \{S\}$, $T = \{a, b\}$, $P = S \rightarrow aSb,\; S \rightarrow ab,$

$S \rightarrow SbSaSbS,\; S \rightarrow SbSbSaS,$

$S \rightarrow SbSaSaS,\; S \rightarrow \lambda\}$

We can easily observe that $L(G) = \{a^i b^j \,/\, i \leq j \leq 2i\}$.

14. A context free grammar G has the following productions

$S \rightarrow 0S0/1S1/A,\; A \rightarrow 2B3,\; B \rightarrow 2B3/3.$

Describe the language generated by the productions.

Solution. $S \rightarrow S0S$, $S \rightarrow 1S1$ and $S \rightarrow A$ give the derivation $S \overset{*}{\Rightarrow} wAw$, where $w \in \{0, 1\}^+$. $A \rightarrow 2B3$ and $B \rightarrow 2B3$ give $A \overset{*}{\Rightarrow} 2^m\, B\, 3^m$. Finally $B \rightarrow 3$

gives $B \Rightarrow 3$. Hence $S \overset{*}{\Rightarrow} w\,A\,w \overset{*}{\Rightarrow} w2^m\,B\,3^m\,w \Rightarrow w2^m\;3^{m+1}\,w$. Thus $L(G) \subseteq \{w^{2m}\;w^{m+1}\;w/\;w \in \{0, 1\}^+ \text{ and } m \geq 1\}$. The reverse inclusive can be proved similarly.

15. Let G be the grammar $S \rightarrow aB/bA$, $A \rightarrow a/aS/bAA$, $B \rightarrow b/bS/aBB$. For the string *aaabbabbba* find a

(*a*) leftmost derivation

(*b*) rightmost derivation and

(*c*) parse tree.

Solution.

(*a*) **Leftmost derivation**

$S \Rightarrow a\underline{B} \Rightarrow aa\underline{B}B \Rightarrow aaa\underline{B}BB \Rightarrow aaab\underline{S}BB \Rightarrow aaabb\underline{A}BB \Rightarrow aaabba\underline{B}B \Rightarrow aaabbab\underline{B} \Rightarrow aaabbaabb\underline{S} \Rightarrow aaabbabbb\underline{A} \Rightarrow aaabbabbba$

(*b*) **Rightmost derivation**

$S \Rightarrow a\underline{B} \Rightarrow aaB\underline{B} \Rightarrow aaBbS \Rightarrow aaBbb\underline{A} \Rightarrow aa\underline{B}bba \Rightarrow aaB\underline{B}bba \Rightarrow aaaBb\underline{S}bba \Rightarrow aaaBbaBbba \Rightarrow aaa\underline{B}babbba \Rightarrow aaabbabbba$.

(*c*) **Parse tree**

(corresponding to leftmost derivation)

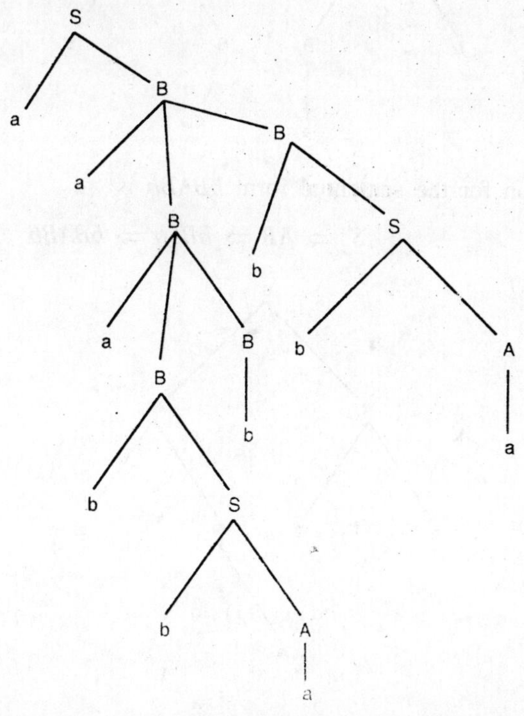

The yield of the tree is *aaabbabbba*.

16. For the grammar G defined by $S \to AB$, $B \to a$, $A \to Aa$, $A \to bB$, $B \to Sb$.

Give derivation trees for the following sentential forms.

(*a*) *baSb*

(*b*) *bBABb*

(*c*) *baabaab.*

Solution.

(*a*) The derivation for the sentential form

baSb is $S \Rightarrow \underline{A}B \Rightarrow b\underline{B}B \Rightarrow ba\underline{B} \Rightarrow baSb$.

The corresponding derivation tree is

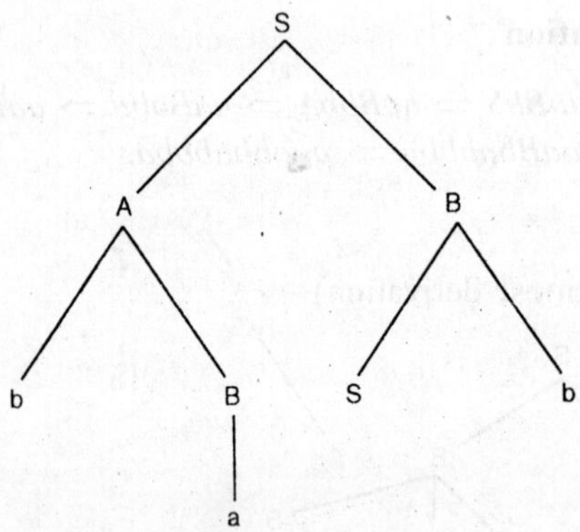

(*b*) The derivation for the sentential form *bBABb* is

$$S \Rightarrow \underline{A}B \Rightarrow bB\underline{S}b \Rightarrow bBABb$$

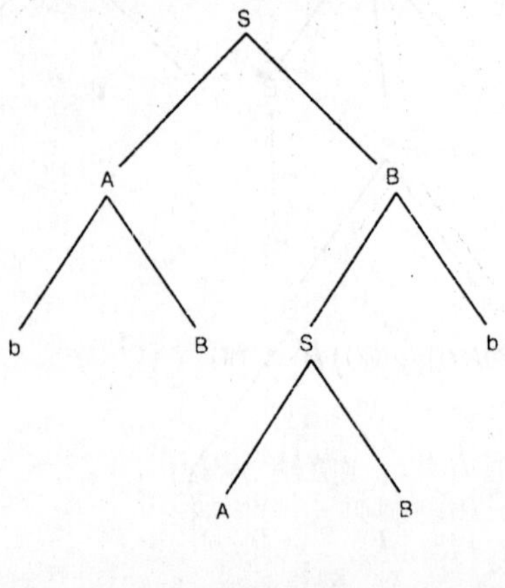

(*c*) The derivation for the sentential form *baabaab* is

$S \Rightarrow \underline{A}B \Rightarrow \underline{A}aB \Rightarrow b\underline{B}aB \Rightarrow baa\underline{B} \Rightarrow baa\underline{S}b \Rightarrow baa\underline{A}Bb \Rightarrow baab\underline{B}Bb \Rightarrow baaba\underline{B}b \Rightarrow baabaab.$

The corresponding derivation tree is

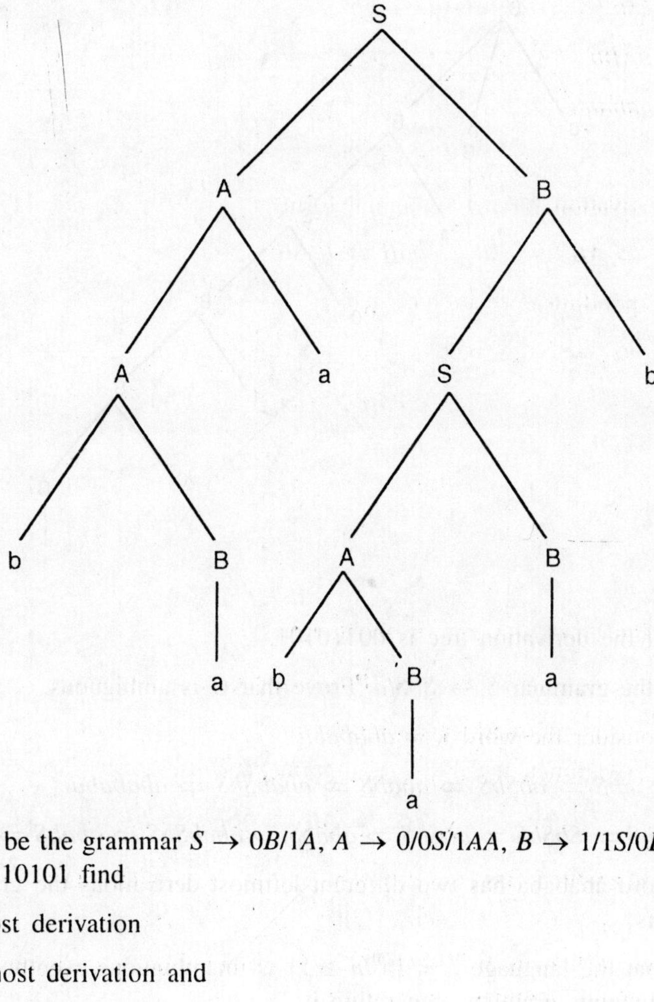

17. Let G be the grammar $S \rightarrow 0B/1A$, $A \rightarrow 0/0S/1AA$, $B \rightarrow 1/1S/0BB$. For the string 00110101 find

(*a*) leftmost derivation

(*b*) rightmost derivation and

(*c*) dervation tree.

Solution.

(*a*) $S \Rightarrow 0\underline{B} \Rightarrow 00\underline{B}B \Rightarrow 001\underline{B} \Rightarrow 0011\underline{S} \Rightarrow 0^21^20\underline{B} \Rightarrow 0^21^201\underline{S} \Rightarrow 0^21^2010\underline{B} \Rightarrow 0^21^20101.$

(*b*) $S \Rightarrow 0B \Rightarrow 00BB \Rightarrow 00B1S \Rightarrow 00B100B \Rightarrow 0^2B101S \Rightarrow 0^2B1010B \Rightarrow 0^2B10101 \Rightarrow 0^2110101.$

(*c*) The corresponding derivation tree is

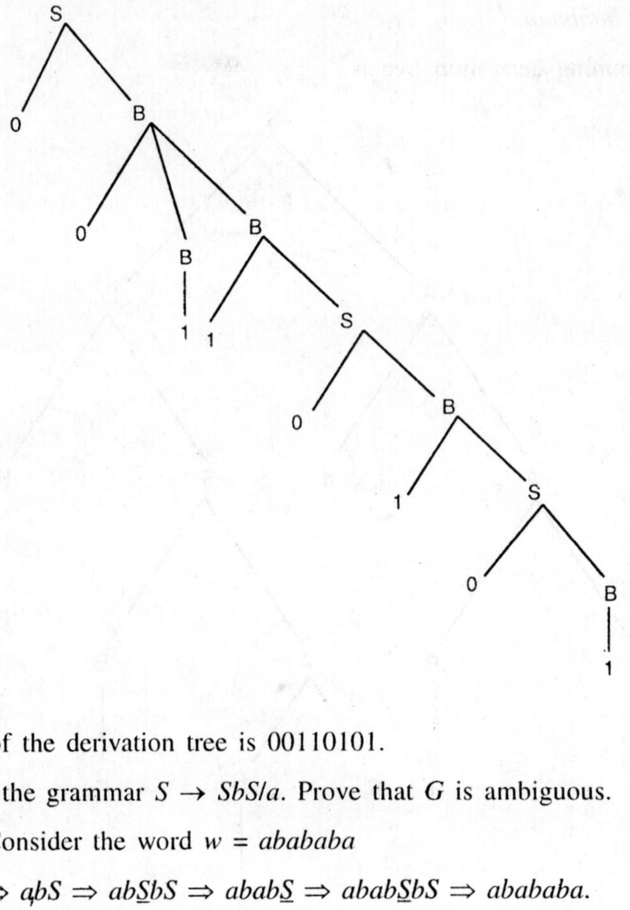

The yield of the derivation tree is 00110101.

18. If G is the grammar $S \to SbS/a$. Prove that G is ambiguous.

Solution. Consider the word $w = abababa$

$S \Rightarrow SbS \Rightarrow abS \Rightarrow ab\underline{S}bS \Rightarrow abab\underline{S} \Rightarrow abab\underline{S}bS \Rightarrow abababa.$

Also $S \Rightarrow SbS \Rightarrow SbSbS \Rightarrow ab\underline{S}bS \Rightarrow abab\underline{S} \Rightarrow abab\underline{S}bS \Rightarrow ababS \Rightarrow abababa$

since the word abababa has two different leftmost derivations the grammar G is ambiguous.

19. Prove that the language $L = \{a^n/n \geq 1\}$ is unambiguous eventhough there exists a ambiguous grammar generating it.

Solution. Let $G_1 = (\{S\}, \{a\}, P_1, S)$ where

$$P_1 = \{S \to SS, S \to a\}$$

We observe that $L(G_1) = \{a^n/\ n \geq 1\}$. Consider the word $a^3 \in L\ (G_1)$. Now

$S \Rightarrow \underline{S}S \Rightarrow \underline{S}SS \Rightarrow \underline{a}SS \Rightarrow aa\underline{S} \Rightarrow aaa = a^3$

$S \Rightarrow \underline{S}S \Rightarrow a\underline{S} \Rightarrow a\underline{S}S \Rightarrow aa\underline{S} \Rightarrow aaa = a^3.$

Thus a^3 has 2 different leftmost derivations G_1 is ambiguous. Thus there exists an ambiguous grammar generating $\{a^n \mid n \geq 1\}$.

Consider the grammar $G_2 = (\{S\}, \{a\}, S, P_2)$ where $P_2 = \{S \to aS, S \to a\}$

$$S \overset{*}{\Rightarrow} a^{n-1}S \qquad \text{(Applying } S \to aS^{(n-1) \text{ times}}\text{)}$$

$$\Rightarrow a^{n-1}a = a^n \qquad \text{(Applying } S \to a \text{ one time)}$$

Thus $L(G_2) = \{a^n / n \geq 1\}$ and a^n has a unique leftmost derivation for all $n \geq 1$. Since there exists an unambiguous grammar generating $\{a^n \mid n \geq 1\}$, the language is unambiguous.

20. Show that the grammar $S \to aB/ab$, $A \to aAB/a$, $B \to ABb/b$ is ambiguous.

Solution. Consider the word ab

The two leftmost derivation of G are

$$S \Rightarrow ab$$

$$S \Rightarrow aB \Rightarrow ab$$

Thus ab is ambiguously derivable by the grammar and so the grammar is ambiguous.

21. Show that the CFG with productions

$S \to a/Sa/bSS/SSb/SbS$ is ambiguous.

Solution. Consider the word $babaa$.

The word $babaa$ has two leftmost derivations as follows .

$$S \Rightarrow b\underline{SS} \Rightarrow b\underline{S}bSS \Rightarrow bab\underline{SS} \Rightarrow babaS \Rightarrow babaa$$

$$S \Rightarrow b\underline{SS} \Rightarrow baS \Rightarrow babSS \Rightarrow babaS \Rightarrow babaa.$$

22. Reduce the following grammar to Chomsky Normal Form. $(\{S, A, B\}, \{a, b\}, P, S\})$ where

$$P = \{S \to bA/aB, A \to bAA/aS/a, B \to aBB/bS/b\}.$$

Solution. The only productions already in proper form are $A \to a$ and $B \to b$. There are no unit productions so we may begin by replacing terminals on the right by variables, except in the case of the productions $A \to a$ and $B \to b$. $S \to bA$ is replaced by $S \to C_bA$ and $C_b \to b$. Similarly, $A \to aS$ is replaced by $A \to C_aS$ and $C_a \to a$, $A \to bAA$ is replaced by $A \to C_bAA$; $S \to aB$ is replaced by $S \to C_aB$, $B \to bS$ is replaced by $B \to C_bS$, and $B \to aBB$ is replaced by $B \to C_aBB$.

The production $A \to C_bAA$ is replaced by $A \to C_bD_1$ and $D_1 \to AA$, and the $B \to C_aBB$ is replaced by $B \to C_a D_2$ and $D_2 \to BB$.

The productions for the grammar in CNF are shown below.

$S \rightarrow C_aA / C_aB \qquad D_1 \rightarrow AA$

$A \rightarrow C_aS / C_b D_1/a \qquad D_2 \rightarrow BB$

$B \rightarrow C_bS/C_aD_2/b \qquad C_a \rightarrow a$

$C_b \rightarrow b.$

23. Obtain a grammar in CNF for the language $L = \{a^nb^n \mid n \geq 1\}$.

Solution. We know that $G = (\{S\}, \{a, b\}, S, \{S \rightarrow aSb, S \rightarrow ab\})$ generates L.

Step 1. Replace the terminals a, b, by new non-terminals C_1, C_2. Then we obtain $P_1 = \{S \rightarrow C_1SC_2, S \rightarrow C_1 C_2, C_1 \rightarrow a, C_2 \rightarrow b\}$.

Step 2. Introduce the new non-terminal D_1 and replace the rule $S \rightarrow C_1SC_2$ by the rules $S \rightarrow C_1D_1$, $D_1 \rightarrow SC_2$. The other rules are already in normal form.

Step 3. It can be verified that the grammar $G^1 = (N^1, T, S\ P^1)$ where $N^1 = \{S, C_1, C_2, D_1\}$ and $P^1\ \{S \rightarrow C_1 D_1, D_1 \rightarrow SC_2, S \rightarrow C_1 C_2, C_1 \rightarrow a, C_2 \rightarrow b\}$ is in Chomsky normal form and generates L.

24. Construct a CFG in GNF to generate the CFL $L = \{a^nb^n / n \geq 1\}$

Solution. We know that $G = (N, T, P, S)$ where

$N = \{S\}$, $T = \{a, b\}$ and $P = \{S \rightarrow aSb, S \rightarrow ab\}$ generates L.

Step 1. Let $G_1 = (N_1, T, P_1, S)$ where $N_1 = \{S, A, B\}$ and $P_1 = \{S \rightarrow ASB, S \rightarrow AB, A \rightarrow a, B \rightarrow b\}$. Then $L(G_1) = L(G)$.

Step 2. Rename the non-terminals as A_1, A_2, A_3 by putting $S = A_1$, $A = A_2$, $B = A_3$. Then G_1 is rewritten as $G_2 = (N_2, T, P_2, A_1)$ where $N_2 = \{A_1, A_2, A_3\}$

$T = \{a, b\}$ and $P_2 = \{A_1 \rightarrow A_2 A_1 A_3, A_1 \rightarrow A_2 A_3, A_2 \rightarrow a, A_3 \rightarrow b\}$.

Step 3. For A_3 and A_2, the rules $A_3 \rightarrow b$ and $A_2 \rightarrow a$ are in normal form. Hence we have only to replace the A_1-rules. The rule $A_1 \rightarrow A_2 A_1 A_3$ is replaced by $A_1 \rightarrow aA_1 A_3$ and the rule $A_1 \rightarrow A_2 A_3$ is replaced by $A_1 \rightarrow aA_3$.

Thus the grammar $G_3 = (N_3, T, P_3, A_1)$ where $P_3 = \{A_1 \rightarrow aA_1A_3, A_1 \rightarrow aA_3, A_3 \rightarrow b\}$ is in GNF.

25. Construct a CFG in CNF to generate the CFL, $L = \{a^n\ b^m \mid n \neq m\}$.

Solution. $L = \{a^n\ b^m \mid n \neq m\}$. We know that $G = (N, T, S, P)$ where $N = \{S, A, B\}$, $T = \{a, b\}$ and $P = \{S \rightarrow aSb, S \rightarrow aA, A \rightarrow aA. A \rightarrow a, S \rightarrow a, S \rightarrow bB, B \rightarrow b, S \rightarrow b\}$ generates L.

Step 1. Replacing a by C_1 and b by C_2 in the non-terminal rules, we get $P_1 = \{S \to C_1SC_2, S \to C_1A, A \to C_1A, A \to a, S \to a, S \to C_2B, B \to C_2B, B \to b, S \to b, C_1 \to a, C_2 \to b\}$.

Step 2. The only non-terminal rule in P_1 which is not in binary standard form is $S \to C_1SC_2$. Introduce new non-terminal D_1 and replace this rule by $S \to C_1D_1, D_1 \to SC_2$.

Step 3. Let $G^1 = (N^1, T, P^1, S)$ where $N^1 = \{S, A, B, C_1, C_2, D_1\}$ and $P^1 = \{S \to C_1\, D_1, D_1 \to SC_2, S \to C_1A, A \to C_1A, A \to a, S \to a, S \to C_2B, B \to C_2B\ B \to b, S \to b, C_1 \to a, C_2 \to b\}$. Then G^1 is in CNF and generates L.

27. Construct a grammar in CNF to generate the language L = {the set of all string over $\{a, b\}$ consisting of equal number of a's and b's}.

Solution. L = {the set of all string over $\{a, b\}$ consisting of equal number of a's and b's}. We know that $G= \{N, T, S, P\}$ where $N = \{S, A, B\}$, $T = \{a, b\}$ and $P = \{S \to bA/\ aB, B \to aBB/b/bS, A \to a/aS/bAA\}$ generates L.

Step 2. The productions obtained in this step are

$$S \to B_1A,\ B_1 \to b,\ S \to A_1B,\ A_1 \to a,\ A \to B_1AA,\ A \to A_1S,\ A \to a,\ B \to A_1BB,\ B \to B_1S,\ \ B \to b.$$

Step 3. The equivalent grammar in CNF is given by

$$G_2 = (N'', \{a, b\}, P_2, S\} \text{ where } P_2 \text{ consists of}$$

(*i*) $S \to B_1A,\ B_1 \to b,\ S \to A_1B\ ,\ A_1 \to a,\ A \to A_1S,\ A \to a,\ B \to B_1S,\ B \to b.$

(*ii*) $A \to B_1C_1,\ C_1 \to AA,\ B \to A_1\, C_2,\ C_2 \to BB.$

corresponding to $A \to B_1AA$ and $B \to A_1\ BB$.

28. Reduce the following grammar to GNF.

$$S \to SS,\ S \to 0S1101.$$

Solution. Rename S as A_1. By remark 2.5.7, it is enough to replace terminals by new variables to get an equivalent grammar G_1. G_1 is defined as

$$G_1 = (\{A_1, A_2, A_3\}, \{0, 1\}, P_1, A_1\}$$

where P_1 consists of

$$A_1 \to A_1A_1/A_2A_1A_3/A_2A_3,\ A_2 \to 0 \text{ and } A_3 \to 1.$$

This complets step 1.

Step 2. All productions of G_1 except $A_1 \to A_1\, A_1$ are in proper form. Applying lemma 2.5.5. to $A_1 \to A_1A_1$, we get a new variable Z_1 and new productions $A_1 \rightarrow A_2 A_1 A_3 Z_1 A_2 A_3 Z_1, Z_1 \rightarrow A_1, Z_1 \rightarrow A_1 Z_1$. The new grammar is

$$G_2 = (\{A_1, A_2, A_3, Z_1\}, \{a, b\}, P_2, A_1)$$

where P_2 consists of

$$A_1 \rightarrow A_2 A_1 A_3/A_2 A_3/A_2 A_1 A_3 Z_1/A_2 A_3 Z_1$$

$$Z_1 \rightarrow A_1 Z_1, Z_1 \rightarrow A_1, A_2 \rightarrow 0 \text{ and } A_3 \rightarrow 1.$$

Step 3. As A_3- productions and A_2-productions are in proper form we have to modify only A_1-productions using lemma 2.5.4. so the modified productions are

$$A_1 \rightarrow 0A_1 A_3/0A_3/ 0A_1 A_3 Z_1/ 0A_3 Z_1.$$

Step 4. The productions $Z_1 \rightarrow A_1$ and $Z_1 \rightarrow A_1 Z_1$ are modified using lemma 2.5.4. They are:

$Z_1 \rightarrow (\{A_1, A_2, A_3, Z_1\}, \{0, 1\}, P_3, A_1)$, where P_3 consists of

$A_1 \rightarrow 0A_1 A_3 / 0A_3/ 0A_1 A_3 Z_1/ 0A_3 Z_1$

$A_2 \rightarrow 0, A_3 \rightarrow 1$

$Z_1 \rightarrow 0A_1A_3/ 0A_3/ 0A_1A_3Z_1/ 0A_3Z_1$

$Z_1 \rightarrow 0A_1A_3 Z_1/ 0A_3 Z_1/ 0A_1 A_3 Z_1Z_1/ 0A_3 Z_1 Z_1.$

29. Reduce the following grammar to GNF.

$S \rightarrow AB, A \rightarrow BSB, A \rightarrow BB, B \rightarrow aAb, B \rightarrow a, A \rightarrow b.$

Solution.

Step 1. Replace $B \rightarrow aSb$ by $B \rightarrow aSc$ and $C \rightarrow b$. Rename S, A, B and C by A_1, A_2, A_3 and A_4. The resulting grammar is

$$G_1 = (\{A_1, A_2, A_3, A_4\}, \{a, b\}, P_1, A_1\} \text{ where}$$

P_1 consists of $A_1 \rightarrow A_2 A_3, A_2 \rightarrow A_3 A_3,$

$A_2 \rightarrow A_3 A_1 A_3, A_2 \rightarrow b, A_3 \rightarrow a A_2 A_4, A_3 \rightarrow a$ and $A_4 \rightarrow b.$

Step 2, 3, 4: Step 2. Construction is not necessary for G_1. The only A_4-production, $A_4 \rightarrow b$ is in proper form. So we go to step 4. The modified A_2-productions are $A_2 \rightarrow aA_2A_4A_3/aA_3/aA_2A_4A_1A_3/aA_1A_3/b$.

The modified A_1-productions are

$A_1 \rightarrow aA_2A_4A_3A_3/aA_3A_3/aA_2A_4A_1A_3A_3/aA_1A_3A_3/bA_3.$

Step 5. is not necessary since there is no new variable in the form is Z_i. So an equivalent grammar in GNF is

$$G_2 = (\{A_1, A_2, A_3, A_4\}, \{a, b\}, P_2, A_1\})$$

where P_2 consists of

$$A_1 \rightarrow aA_2A_4A_3A_3/aA_3A_3/aA_2A_4A_1A_3A_3/aA_1A_3A_3/bA_3$$

$$A_2 \rightarrow aA_2A_4A_3/aA_3/aA_2A_4A_1A_3/aA_1A_3/b$$

$$A_3 \rightarrow aA_2A_4/a,\ A_4 \rightarrow b.$$

30. Find the language generated by the CFG given by the productions

$$S \rightarrow abB,$$

$$A \rightarrow aaBb,$$

$$B \rightarrow bbAa$$

$$A \rightarrow \lambda$$

$$S \Rightarrow abB$$

Solution. We can apply the production $S \rightarrow abB$ only once to produce the sentential form abB. Then we have to apply $B \rightarrow bbAa$ once to produce the sentential form $aabbbAa$. If we apply $A \rightarrow \lambda$ we get the string $ab\ bba$. Otherwise if we apply $A \rightarrow aaBb$ we get the sentential form $abbbaaBb$. Then we apply $B \rightarrow bbAa$ and then $A \rightarrow \lambda$. Hence we get the string $abbbaa\ bba = ab\ (bbaa)^1\ bba$. Proceeding similary, we get.

$L(G) = \{ab\ (bbaa)^n\ bba\ (ba)^n: n \geq 0\}$.

$$\Rightarrow abbbbAa$$

$$\Rightarrow abbba = ab(bbaa)^0\ bba(ba)^0$$

$$S \Rightarrow abB$$

$$\Rightarrow abbbAa$$

$$\Rightarrow abbbaaBba$$

$$\Rightarrow abbbaabbAaba$$

$$\Rightarrow abbbaabbaba = ab(bbaa)^1 bba(ba)^1$$

proceeding in this manner we see that

$$L(G) = \{ab(bbaa)^n\ bba(ba)^n : n \geq 0\}$$

31. Find the language generated by the context free grammar $G = (N, T, S, P)$ where $N = \{S\}$ $T = \{a\}$, and $P = \{S \rightarrow SS\}$.

Solution. Since the only production $S \rightarrow SS$ in G has no terminal on the right hand side, it follows that $L(G) = \phi$.

32. Find the language $L(G)$ generated by the CFG $G = (N, T, S, P)$ where $N = \{S, A\}$

$$T = \{0, 1\} \text{ and}$$

$$P = \{S \rightarrow 0A0, A \rightarrow 0A0, A \rightarrow 1\}.$$

Solution. $S \Rightarrow 0A0 \Rightarrow 010$. S0 $010 \in L(G)$

$$S \Rightarrow 0A0 \text{ (by applying } S \rightarrow 0A0 \text{ one line)}$$

$$\overset{*}{\Rightarrow} 0^n\, A\, 0^n \text{ (by applying } A \rightarrow 0A0\ (n-1) \text{ lines)}$$

$$\Rightarrow 0^n\, 1\, 0^n \text{ (by applying } A \rightarrow 1 \text{ one line)}$$

So, $0^n\ 1\ 0^n \in L(G)$, where $n \geq 1$.

Therefore $\{0^n\ 10^n\ /\ n \geq 1\} \subseteq L(G)$

As the only S-production is $S \rightarrow 0A0$, this is the first production we have to apply in the derivation of any terminal string. If we apply $A \rightarrow 1$, we get 010. Otherwise we have to apply $A \rightarrow 0A0$, either once or several times, so we get $0^n\ A\ 0^n$ with a single variable A. To get a terminal string we have to replace A by 1, by applying $A \rightarrow 1$. So any derivation is of the form

$$S \overset{*}{\Rightarrow} 0^n\ 10^n \text{ with } n \geq 1$$

Therefore

$$L(G) \subseteq \{0^n\ 1\ 0^n\ /\ n \geq 1\}$$

Thus $\qquad L(G) = \{0^n\ 10^n\ /\ n \geq 1\}$.

33. Find the language $L(G)$ generated by the CFG $G = (\{S\}, \{a, b\}, S, \{S \rightarrow$ as/bS/a/$b\})$.

Solution. We show that $L(G) = \{a, b)^+$. As we have only two terminals a, b we have $L(G) \subseteq \{a, b\}^*$. All productions are S-productions, and so λ can be in $L(G)$ only when $S \rightarrow \lambda$ is *a* production in the grammar G. Thus

$$L(G) \subseteq \{a, b\}^* - \{\lambda\} = \{a, b\}^+.$$

To show that $\{a, b\}^+ \subseteq L(G)$, consider any string $a_1\ a_2, \ldots\ a_n$, where each a_i is either a or b. The first production in the derivation of $a_1, a_2, \ldots\ a_n$ is $S \rightarrow aS$ or $S \rightarrow sB$ according as $a_1 = a$ or $a_1, = b$. The subsequent productions are obtained in a similar way. The last production is $S \rightarrow a$ or $S \rightarrow b$ according as $a_n = a$ or $a_n = b$. So $a_1\ a_2 \ldots a_n \in L(G)$.

Thus we we have $L(G) = \{a, b\}^+$.

34. Find the language generated by the context free grammar $G = (N, T, S, P)$ where $N = \{S\}$, $T = \{a\}$ and $P = \{S \rightarrow aS/a\}$.

Solution. We show that $L(G) = \{a\}^+$. As we have only one terminal a, we have $L(G) \subseteq \{a\}^*$. All productions are S-productions, and so λ can be in $L(G)$ only when $S \rightarrow \lambda$ is a production in the grammar G. Thus

$$L(G) \subseteq \{a\}^* - \{\lambda\} = \{a\}^+$$

As $S \to a$ is a prduction, $S \Rightarrow a$. so $a \in L(G)$.

Also for $n \geq 1$,

$$S \overset{*}{\Rightarrow} a^{n-1} S \text{ (applying } S \to aS \text{ } ^{(n-1)} \text{ times)}$$

$$\Rightarrow a^n \text{ (applying } S \to a \text{ one time)}$$

Therefore $\{a\}^+ \subseteq L(G)$. Thus $L(G) = \{a\}^+$.

35. Find a CFG generating $L = \{a^n b^n c^i / n \geq 1, i \geq 0\}$.

Solution. Let $L = L_1 \cup L_2$

$$L_1 = \{a^n b^n / n \geq 1\}$$

$$L_2 = \{a^n b^n c^i / i \geq 1\}$$

We construct L_1 by recursion and L_2 by concatenating elements of L_1 and C_i, $i \geq 1$. We define P as the set of the following productions

$S \to A$, $A \to ab$, $A \to aAb$, $S \to Sc$

Let $\quad G = (N, T, S, P)$, $N = \{S\}$, $T = \{a, b, c\}$

$\quad P = \{S \to A, A \to ab, A \to aA\}$. For $n \geq 1$, $i \geq 0$, we have

$$S \overset{*}{\Rightarrow} Sc^i \Rightarrow Ac^i \overset{*}{\Rightarrow} a^{n-1} Ab^{n-1} c^i \Rightarrow a^{n-1} abb^{n-1} c^i = a^n b^n c^i$$

Thus, $\{a^n b^n c^i / n \geq 1, i \geq 0\} \subseteq L(G)$.

To prove the reverse inclusion, we note that the only S-productions are $S \to Sc$ and $S \to A$. If we start with $S \to A$, we have to apply $A \Rightarrow a^{n-1} Ab^{n-1} \overset{*}{\Rightarrow} a_n b^n$, and so $a^n b^n c^0 \in L(G)$. If we start with $S \to Sc$, we have to apply $S \to Sc$ repeatedly to get Sc^i. But to get a terminal string, we have to apply $S \to A$.

As $A \overset{*}{\Rightarrow} a^n b^n$, the resulting terminal strings is $a^n b^n c^i$. Thus we have shown that

$$L(G) \subseteq \{a^n b^n c^i / n \geq 0, i \geq 0\}$$

$$L(G) = \{a^n b^n c^i / n \geq 1, i \geq 0\}.$$

36. Construct a grammar G so that

$$L(G) = \{a^n b a^m / n, m \geq 1\}.$$

Solution. When $n = m = 1$

$S \Rightarrow aA \Rightarrow abB \Rightarrow aba$. S0 $aba \in L(G)$.

When $n > m > 1$ (or) $m > n > 1$

$$S \Rightarrow aA \overset{*}{\Rightarrow} a^n\ A \text{ (applying } A \to aA^{\ (n-1)} \text{ times)}$$

$$\Rightarrow a^n\ b\ B \text{ (applying } A \to bB \text{ one time)}$$

$$\Rightarrow a^n\ ba\ B \text{ (applying } B \to aB \text{ one time)}$$

$$\overset{*}{\Rightarrow} a^n\ b\ an^{m-1}\ B \text{ (applying } B \to aB^{\ (n-2)} \text{ times)}$$

$$\Rightarrow a^n\ ba^n \text{ (applying } B \to a \text{ one time)}$$

Thus $a^n\ b\ a^m \in L(G)$.

Therefore $\{a^n\ b\ a^m\ /\ n, m \geq 1\} \subseteq L(G)$.

As the only S-production is $S \to aA$, this is the first production we have to apply in the derivation of any terminal string. Then we can apply $A \to aA$ one or more time. So we get $a^n\ A$. Then we apply $B \to aB$ required number of times. Finally we have to apply $B \to a$ one time. So any derivation is of the form

Therefore $\quad S \overset{*}{\Rightarrow} a^n\ b\ a^m$ with $m, n \geq 1$.

$$L(G) \subseteq \{a^n\ b\ a^m\ /\ m, n \geq 1\}$$

Thus $\quad L(G) = \{a^n\ b\ a^m\ /\ m, n \geq 1\}$.

37. Find a CFG generating $\{a, b^n\ c^n\ /\ n \geq 1, j \geq 0\}$.

Solution. Let $\quad L = L_1 \cup L_2$

where $\quad L_1 = \{b^n\ c^n\ /\ n \geq 1\}$

$$L_2 = \{a^j\ b^n\ c^n\ /\ n \geq i, j \geq 0\}$$

We construct L_1 by recursion and L_2 by concatenating a^j, $j \geq 0$ and elements of L_2. We define P as the set of the following productions

$$S \to aS,\ S \to A,\ A \to bAc/\ bc.$$

Let $\quad G = (N, T, S, P)$

where $\quad N = \{S, A\},\ T = \{a, b, c\}$

and P is defined as above.

For $n \geq 1, j \geq 0$, we have

$$S \overset{*}{\Rightarrow} ajS \text{ (applying } S \to aS\ j \text{ times)}$$

$$\Rightarrow \quad a^j\ b^{n-1}\ A\ c^{n-1} \text{ (applying } A \to bAc\ (n-1 \text{ times)}$$

$$\Rightarrow \quad a_j\, b^n\, c^n \text{ (applying } A \to bc \text{ one time)}$$

Thus $\{a^j\, b^n\, c^n \;/\; n \geq 1, j \geq 0\} \subseteq L(G)$

To prove the reverse inclusion, we note that the only S-production are $S \to aS$, $S \to A$. If we start with $S \to A$, we have to apply $A \overset{*}{\Rightarrow} b^{n-1}\, Ac^{n-1} \Rightarrow b^n\, c^n$, and so $a^o\, b^n\, c^n \in L(G)$. If we start with $S \to aS$, we have to apply $S \to aS$ repeatedly to get $a^j S$. But to get a terminal string, we have to apply $S \to A$. As $A \overset{*}{\Rightarrow} a^n\, b^n$, the resulting terminal string is $a^j\, b^n\, c^n$. Thus we have shown that

$$L(G) \subseteq \{a^j\, b^n\, c^n \;/\; n \geq 1, j \geq 0\}$$

$$L(G) = \{a^n\, b^n\, c^i \;/\; n \geq 1, j \geq 0\}.$$

38. If the CFG G given by the productions $S \to aSa/bSb/aa/bb/\lambda$, show that (a) $L(G)$ has not strings of odd length (b) any string in $L(G)$ is of length $2n$, $n \geq 0$, and (c) the number of strings of length $2n$ is 2^n.

Solution. On application of any production (except $S \to \lambda$), a variable is repeated by two terminal and at the most one variable. So every step in any derivation increases the number of terminal by 2 except that involving $S \to \lambda$. Thus we have proved (a) and (b).

To prove (c) consider any string w of length $2n$. Then it is of the form

$a_1\, a_2\, ...\, a_n\, a_n\, ...\, a_1$ involving n parameters $a_1, a_2, ...\, a_n$. Each a_i can be either a or b. So the number of such strings is 2^n. Thus proves (c).

39. Find the language generated by the following CFGs

(a) $S \to 0S1/0A1,\; A \to 1A/1$

(b) $S \to 0S1/0A1,\; A \to 1A0/10$

(c) $S \to 0S1/0A/0/1B/1,\; A \to 0A/0,\; B \to 1B/1.$

Solution. (a) $S \overset{*}{\Rightarrow} 0^n\; S\; 1^n$(applying $0S1$ n times)

$\overset{*}{\Rightarrow} 0^n\, 0^m\; A\; 1^m\; 1^n$ (applying $S \to 0A1$ m times), $n \geq 0$, $m \geq 1$)

$A \overset{*}{\Rightarrow} 1^k A$ (applying $A \to 1A$ k times)

$\Rightarrow 1^{k+1}$ (applying $A \to 1$, 1 time), $k \geq 0$

Hence $0m$, $1^n \in L(G)$ when $n > m \geq 1$.

$$\text{So } L(G) = \{0^m\; 1^n \;/\; n > m \geq 1\}.$$

(b) When $m, n \geq 1$.

$$S \overset{*}{\Rightarrow} 0^{n-1}\ S\ 1^{n-1} \text{ (applying } S \rightarrow 0S1 \ (n-1) \text{ times)}$$

$$\Rightarrow \ 0^{n-1}\ 0\ A11^{n-1} \text{ (applying } S \rightarrow 0A1 \text{ one time)}$$

$$\overset{*}{\Rightarrow} \ 0^n\ 1^{m-1}\ A\ 0^{m-1}\ 1^n \text{ (applying } A \rightarrow 1A0 \ (n-1) \text{ times)}$$

$$\Rightarrow \ 0^n\ 1^m\ 0^m\ 1^n \text{ (applying } A \rightarrow 10 \text{ one time)}$$

Hence $\{0^n\ 1^m\ 0^m\ 1^m \ / \ m, n \geq 1\} \subseteq L(G)$.

It is easy to prove the reverse inclusion.

$$L(G) = \{0^n\ 1^m\ 0^m\ 1^n \ / \ m, n \geq 1\}.$$

(*c*) $S \Rightarrow 0A \overset{*}{\Rightarrow} 0^{m-1}\ A \Rightarrow 0^m$. Thus $0^m \in L(G)$

where $m \geq 1$.

$S \Rightarrow 1B \overset{*}{\Rightarrow} 1^{n-1}\ B \Rightarrow 1^n$. Thus $1^n \in L(G)$ where $n \geq 1$. For $m > n$.

$S \overset{*}{\Rightarrow} 0^n\ S\ 1^n \Rightarrow 0^n\ 0A\ 1^n \overset{*}{\Rightarrow} 0^n\ 0\ 0^{m-n-1}\ 1^n = 0^m\ 1^n$.

Thus $0^m\ 1^n \in L(G)$.

Hence $L(G) = \{0^m\ 1^n \ / \ m \neq n$ and atleast one of m and $n \geq 1\}$.

40. Construct the CFG, accepting each of the following sets.

(*a*) $\{0^n\ 1^m\ 0^m\ 1^n \ / \ m, n \geq 1\}$

(*b*) $0^n\ 1^{2n} \ / \ n \geq 1\}$

(*c*) $\{0^n\ 1^n \ / \ n \geq 1\} \cup \{1^m\ 0^m \ / \ m \geq 1\}$.

Solution. (*a*) See problem 3a (*b*).

(*b*) Consider the CFG, $G = (N, T, S, P)$

where $N = \{S\}$, $T = \{0, 1\}$, $P = \{S \rightarrow 0S\ 11/\ 011\}$

Here we have only S productions. If we apply $S \Rightarrow 011$. Then also number of 1's is twice the number of 0's. We can apply $S \rightarrow 0S11$ any number of times. But each stdp produces two ones and one zero. Finally we have to apply $S \rightarrow 011$. Thus

$$L(G) = \{0^n\ 1^{2n} \ / \ n \geq 1\}$$

(*c*) $L = \{0^n\ 1^n \ / \ n \geq 1\}$ U $(1^m\ 0^m \ / \ m \geq 1\}$

Consider the CFG $G = (N, T, S, P)$

where $N = \{S, A, B\}$, $T = \{0, 1\}$ and

$P = \{S \to 0A1/\ 1B0,\ A \to 0A1/\ \lambda,\ B \to 1B0/\ 1\}.$

$S \overset{*}{\Rightarrow} 0^n\ A\ 1^n \Rightarrow 0^n\ 1^n$. Thus $0^n\ 1^n \in L(G),\ n \geq 1$

$S \Rightarrow 0\ A\ 1 \Rightarrow 01$ and so $01 \in L(G)$.

$S \overset{*}{\Rightarrow} 1^m\ B0^m \Rightarrow 1^m\ 0^m$. Thus $1^m\ 0^m \in L(G),\ m \geq 1$

and $S \Rightarrow 1B0 \Rightarrow 10$. Thus $10 \in L(G)$.

Hence $L(G) = \{0^n\ 1^n\ /\ n \geq 1\} \cup (1^m\ 0^m\ /\ m \geq 1\}$.

41. Test whether the strings 00110, 001010 and 01010 are in the language generated by the CFG.

$$S \to 0S1\ /\ 0A\ /\ 0\ /\ 1B\ /\ 1,\ A \to 0A/0,\ B \to 1B/1.$$

Solution. The derivation of 00110, 001010 or 01010, the first production cannot be $S \to 0S1$. The other possible productions are $S \to 0A$ and $S \to 1B$. In these cases the resulting terminal strings are 0^n and 1^n. So none of the given strings are in the language generated by the given grammar.

42. Find the language generated by the CFG $S \to AB,\ A \to A1/0,\ B \to 2B/3$.

Solution. Since there is any one S-production first we apply $S \to AB$. Then we can apply $A \to A1$ or $A \to 0$. To remove the nonterminal we have to apply $A \to 0$. Thus all strings start with 0. Also we can apply $A \to A1$ any number of times. This will produce $A1^m$. Then we can apply $B \to 2B$ or $B \to 3$. Here the terminal string will be 3. If we apply $B \to 2B$ by n times, that will produce $2^n\ B$. Finally we have to apply $B \to 3$ once.

Thus $L(G) = \{01^m\ 2^n\ 3/\ m,\ n \geq 1\}$.

43. Construct a CFG which generates all positive even integers upto 998.

Solution. Consider the CFG $G = (N, T, S, P)$

where $N = \{S, A, B, C\},\ T = \{0, 1, 2, ..., 9\}$ and

$P = \{S \to 0/2/4/6/8,\ S \to BA,\ B \to 1/2/\ ...\ /9,$

$A \to 0/2/4/6/8,\ S \to BCA,\ C \to 1/2/\ ...\ /9.\}$

$S \to 0/2/4/6/8$ generate even integers with one digit. $S \to BA$ and B-productions and A-productions generate all even numbers with two digits. The remaining productions can be used to generate all even integers with three digits. Thus L = {set of all even integers upto 998}.

44. Construct context free grammars to generate the following.

(a) $\{0^m\ 1^n\ /\ m \neq n,\ m,\ n \geq 1\}$

(*b*) $\{a^l\, b^m\, c^n \,/\,$ one of l, m, n equals 1 and the remaining two are equal$\}$

(*c*) $\{0^m\, 1^n \,/\, 1 \le m \le n\}$

(d) $\{a^l\, b^m\, c^n \,/\, l + m = n\}$.

Solution. (*a*) Construct the CFG $G = (N, T, P, S)$

where $N = \{S, A, B\}, T = \{0, 1\},$

$P = \{S \to 0S1 \,/\, 0A \,/\, 1B \,/\, 0A,\ A \to 0A/0,\ B \to 1B/1\}$

$$S \overset{*}{\Rightarrow} 0^n\, S\, 1^n \text{(apply } S \to 0S1\ n \text{ times)}$$

$$\Rightarrow 0^n\, 01^n = 0^{n+1}\, 1^n \text{ (if we apply } S \to 0 \text{ one time)}$$

$$= 0^m\, 1^n \text{ where } m = n + 1$$

or

$$S \overset{*}{\Rightarrow} 0^n\, S\, 1^n$$

$$\Rightarrow 0^n\, 11^n = 0^n\, 1^{n+1} = 0^n\, 1^m$$

where $m = n + 1$.

Thus we get $0^m\, 1^n$, where m and n differ by 1. To get more 0's (than 1's) in the string we have to apply $A \to 0A/0$, $S \to 0A$, repeatelly. To get more 1's apply $S \to 1B$, $B \to B \to 1B/\,1$ repeatedly.

(*b*) Construct the CFG $G = (N, T, S, P)$

where $N = \{S, A, B, C\}, T = \{a, b, c\}$ and

$P = \{S \to aA,\ A \to bAc,\ A \to bc,\ S \to aBc,\ B \to aBc,\ B \to b,\ S \to Cc,\ C \to aCb,\ C \to ab\}$.

$S \Rightarrow aA$(applying $S \to aA$ one time)

$\Rightarrow ab^{m-1}\, Ac^{m-1}$(applying $A \to bAc$ $(m-1)$ times)

Also $S \overset{*}{\Rightarrow} a^m\, Bc^m$(applying $S \to aBc$ m times)

$\Rightarrow a^m\, bc^m$(applying $B \to b$ one time)

$S \Rightarrow Cc$(applying $S \to Cc$ one time)

$\overset{*}{\Rightarrow} a^{m-1}\, (b^{m-1}\, c$ (applying $C \to aCb$ $(m-1)$ times)

$\Rightarrow a^m\, b^m\, c$ (applying $C \to ab$ one time)

Thus $L(G) = \{a^l\, b^m\, c^m \,/\,$ one of l, m, n equals one and the remaining two are equal$\}$.

(c) $L = \{0^m, 1^n / 1 \leq m \leq n\}$

Construct the CFG $G = (N, T, S, P)$ where $N = \{S, A\}$, $T = \{0, 1\}$ and

$$P` = \{S \to 0S1, S \to 01, S \to 0A1, A \to 1A, A \to 1\}.$$

By applying first two productions we can get $0^m\ 1^n$ where $m = n$.

When $m = n = 1$, we have $S \Rightarrow 01$. Thus $01 \in L(G)$.

By applying $S \to 0S1$, $S \to 0A1$, $A \to 1A$ and $A \to 1$ we can get string $0^m\ 1^n$ where $m < n$. Thus $L(G) = L$.

(d) Construct the CFG $G = (N, T, S, P)$

where $N = \{S, A\}$, $T = \{a, b, c\}$ and

$$P = \{S \to aSc, S \to ac, S \to bc, S \to bAc, A \to bAc, A \to bc\}.$$

A typical string in the given language can be written in the form $a^l\ b^m\ c^m\ c^l$ where $l, m \geq 0$. $S \to aSc$, $S \to ac$ generate $a^l\ c^l$ for $l \geq 1$.

$S \to bAc$, $A \to bAc$, $A \to bc$ generate $b^m\ c^m$ for $m \geq 1$. For getting $a^l\ b^m, c^m\ c^l$, we have to apply $S \to aSc$, $S \to bc$, $S \to bAc$, $A \to bAc$, and $A \to bc$ are to be applied. For $m = 1$, $S \to bc$ has to be applied. For $m > 1$, we have to apply $S \to bAc$, $A \to bAc$ and $A \to bc$ repeatedly. The terminal c is added whenever the terminal a or b is added in the course of the derivation. This takes care of the condition $l + m = n$. Thus $L = L(G)$.

45. Show that the context free grammars

$$G_1 = (\{S\}, \{a, b\}, \{S \to aSb / ab\}, S) \text{ and}$$

$$G_2 = (\{S, A, B, C\}, \{a, b\}, \{S \to AC, C \to SB, S \to AB, A \to a, B \to b\}\ S)$$

are equivalent.

Solution. In G_1

$$S \overset{*}{\Rightarrow} a^{n-1}\ Sb^{n-1} \to a^n\ b^n$$

Thus $L(G_1) = \{a^n\ b^n / n \geq 1\}$

In G_2 $S \Rightarrow AC \Rightarrow ASB \overset{*}{\Rightarrow} A^{n-1}\ S\ B^{n-1}$

$$\overset{*}{\Rightarrow} a^{n-1}\ S\ b^{n-1} \Rightarrow a^{n-1}\ AB\ b^{n-1}$$

$$\Rightarrow a^{n-1}\ a\ B\ b^{n-1} \Rightarrow a^n\ b^n.$$

Thus $L(G) = \{a^n\ b^n / n \geq 1\}$

Hence G_1 and G_2 are equivalent.

46. If each production in a CFG has some variable on its right hand side, what can you say about $L(G)$.

Solution. At each step of the derivation process we get a variable and so no terminal string results. Hence $L(G) = \phi$.

47. Show that $(abc, bca, cab\}$ can be generated by a CFG whose terminal set is $\{a, b, c\}$.

Solution. Let $L = \{abc, bca, cab\}$. Construct the CFG $G = (N, T, S, P)$ where $N = \{S\}$,

$$T = \{a, b, c\} \text{ and}$$

$$P = \{S \to AB, B \to bc, A \to a, S \to bcC, C \to a, S \to CaD, D \to b\}$$

It is easily seen that $L(G) = L$.

48. Construct a CFG to generate
$\{(ab)^n \mid n \geq 1\} \cup \{(ba)^n \mid n \geq 1\}$.

Solution. Consider the CFG $G = (N, T, S, P)$

where $N = \{S, A, B\}, T = \{a, b\}$ and

$$P = \{S \to A, A \to abA, A \to ab, S \to B, B \to baB, B \to ba\}.$$

$$S \Rightarrow A \overset{*}{\Rightarrow} \text{abA} \overset{*}{\Rightarrow} (ab)^{n-1} A \Rightarrow (ab)^n$$

Thus $(ab)^n \in L(G)$ where $n \geq 1$. Also

$$S \Rightarrow B \overset{*}{\Rightarrow} (ba)^{n-1} B \Rightarrow (ba)^n$$

Thus $(ba)^n \in L(G)$, $n \geq 1$.

Hence the required language is $(ab)^n \mid n \geq 1\} \cup \{ba)^n \mid n \geq 1\}$.

49. Find the CFG generating the language

$$L = \{a\,(a^* \cup b^*)\,b\}.$$

Solution. $\quad L = \{a\,(a^* \cup b^*)\,b\}.$

Note that L consists of strings of form that contains a leading a, followed by a middle part generated by $a^* \cup b^*$, followed by trailing b.

Construct a CFG $G = (N, T, S, P)$

where $\quad N = \{S, A, B, C\}$, $T = \{a, b\}$ and

$P = \{S \to aAb,\ A \to B$ and $A \to C,\ B \to \lambda,\ B \to aB,$
$C \to bC,\ C \to \lambda\}$

It is easily seen that $L(G) = L$.

50. Find the language generated by the context free grammar $G = (N, T, S, P)$ where $N = \{S, A\}$, $P = \{S \to AA, A \to AAA, A \to a, A \to bA, A \to Ab\}$.

Solution. $S \Rightarrow AA$(applying $S \to AA$ once)

$\overset{*}{\Rightarrow} A^{2n}$(applying $A \to AAA$ $(n - 1)$ times)

$\overset{*}{\Rightarrow} b^{m}{}_{1} A^{2n}$(applying $A \to bA$ m_1 times)

$\Rightarrow b^{m}{}_{1}\ a\ A^{2n-1}$(applying $A \to a$ once)

$\overset{*}{\Rightarrow} b^{m}{}_{1}\ ab^{m}{}_{2}\ A^{2n-1}$ (applying $A \to bA$ m_2 times)

$\Rightarrow b^{m}{}_{1}\ ab^{m}{}_{2}\ aA^{2n-2}$ (applying $A \to a$ once)

$\vdots$

$\vdots$

$\Rightarrow b^{m}{}_{1}\ ab^{m}{}_{2} \ldots b^{m}{}_{2n}\ Ab^{m}{}_{2n}{}^{+1}$ (applying $A \to Ab^{m}{}_{2n}{}^{+1}$ times)

$\Rightarrow b^{m}{}_{1}\ ab^{m}{}_{2} \ldots b^{m}{}_{2n}\ a\ b^{m}{}_{2n}{}^{+1}$ (applying $A \to a$ once)

Thus $L(G) = \{$set of strings over $\{a, b\}$ that contains even number of a's$\}$

51. Find the language generated by the CFG

$G = (N, T, S, P)$

where $N = \{S\}$, $T = \{(,)\}$ and

$P = \{S \to \lambda, S \to SS, S \to (S)\}$.

Solution. Two derivations in this grammar are $S \Rightarrow SS \Rightarrow S(S) \Rightarrow S((S)) \Rightarrow$ $S(C) \Rightarrow (S)\ (()) \Rightarrow ()\ (())$.

and

$S \Rightarrow SS\ (S)\ S \Rightarrow ()S \Rightarrow ()\ ((S)) \Rightarrow ()\ (())$.

It is easily seen that

$L(G) = \{(n)n : n \geq 0\}$

$L(G) = \{$set of all strings of balanced left and right parenthesis$\}$.

52. Find the language generated by the CFG

$G = (N, T, S, P)$

where $N = \{S, A, B), T = \{a, b\}$ and

$$P = \{S \to bA,\ S \to aB,\ A \to abaS,\ B \to babS,\ S \to \lambda\}$$

Solution. A derivation in G is

$$S \Rightarrow bA \Rightarrow babaS \Rightarrow babaaB \Rightarrow babaababS \Rightarrow babaabab.$$

Since the only rule with A on the right is $S \to bA$ and the only rule with A on the left is $A \to abaS$, any derivation involving A is of the form

$$...WS \Rightarrow WbA \Rightarrow wbabaS \Rightarrow....$$

Similarly, any part of a derivation involving B is of the form

$$...\ wS \Rightarrow waB \Rightarrow wababS \Rightarrow\ ...$$

It is easily seen that

$$L(G) = (abab \cup baba)^*$$

EXERCISE

1. Give context free grammars generating the following sets.

(*a*) The set of all strings over alphabet $\{a, b\}$ not of the form ww for some string w.

(*b*) $\{a^i\, b^j\, c^k / i \neq j \text{ or } j \neq k\}$.

(*c*) The set of even length strings in $\{a, b\}^*$ with the two middle symbols equal.

(*d*) The set of all odd-length strings in $\{a, b\}^*$ whose first, middle, and the last symbols are the same.

(*e*) $\{a^i\, b^j\, c^k \,/\, i = j + k\}$

(*f*) $\{a^i\, b^j\, c^k \,/\, j = i + k\}$

(*g*) $\{a^i\, b^j \,/\, i < 2j\}$

(*h*) $\{a^i\, b^j\, c^k \,/\, j = i \text{ or } j = k\}$.

2. In each case, say what language is generated by the context free grammar with the indicated productions

(*a*) $S \to SS/bS/a$

(*b*) $S \to aT/bT/\lambda,\ T \to aS/bS$

(*c*) $S \to SaS/b$.

(*d*) $S \to 0A/1S/0/1,\ A \to 1A/1S/1$.

3. Determine whether the following grammar is ambiguous or not

(a) $S \to aSa/bSb/\lambda$

(b) $S \to aSa/bSb/a/b$

(c) $S \to aSb/bSa/\lambda$

(d) $S \to aS/bS/a$.

4. Reduce the following grammars to CNF

(a) $S \to 1A/0B$, $A \to 1AA/0S/0$, $B \to 0BB/1S/1$

(b) $G = (\{S\}, \{a, b, c\}, \{S \to a/b/cSS\}, S)$

(c) $S \to abSb/a/aAb$, $A \to bS/aAAb$.

5. Reduce the following grammars to Greibach Normal Form.

(a) $S \to SS$, $S \to 0S1/01$

(b) $S \to aB$, $A \to BSB$, $A \to BB$, $B \to aAb$,

$D \to a$, $A \to b$.

(c) $S \to A0$, $A \to 0B$, $B \to A0$, $B \to 1$.

5. Construct the grammar in CNF to generate the language

$$L = \{a^n\ b^m\ c^n /\ m, n \geq 1\}.$$

6. If G is a context free grammar in CNF and $x \in L(G)$ with $|x| = k$, how many steps are there in a derivation of x in G.

7. Reduce the following grammars to CNF.

(a) $S \to a/abSb/aAb$, $A \to bS/aAAb$.

(b) $S \to aB/ab$, $A \to aAB/a$, $B \to ABb/b$.

(c) $S \to aAa$, $A \to bBB$, $B \to ab$, $C \to aB$.

(d) $S \to AB$, $A \to a$, $B \to C/b$, $C \to D$, $D \to E$, $E \to a$.

8. Construct a CFG to generate the language $L = \{a^n b^m : n \neq m\}$.

9. Find CFG for the following languages (with $n \geq 0$, $m \geq 0$).

(a) $L = \{a^n b^m : n \leq m + 3\}$

(b) $L = \{a^n b^m : n \neq m - 1\}$

(c) $L = \{a^n b^m : n \neq 2m\}$

(d) $L = \{a^n b^m : 2n \leq m \leq 3n\}$

10. Find context free grammars for the following languages (with $n \geq 0$, $m \geq 0$)

(*a*) $L = \{a^n b^m c^k : n = m \text{ or } m \leq k\}$

(*b*) $L = \{a^n b^m c^k : n = m \text{ or } m \neq k\}$

(*c*) $L = \{a^n b^m c^k : k = n + m\}$

(*d*) $L = \{a^n b^m c^k : n + 2m = k\}$

(*e*) $L = \{a^n b^m c^k : k = (n - m)\}$

11. Find a CFG for $\Sigma = \{a, b\}$ for the language $L = \{a^n w w^R b^n : w \in \Sigma^*, n \geq 1\}$

12. Let $L = \{a^n b^n : n \geq 0\}$

(*a*) Show that L^2 is context free.

(*b*) Show that L^k is context free for any given $k \geq 1$.

(*c*) Show that L and L^* are context free.

13. Show that the following language is context free.

$$L = \{uvwv^R : u, v, w \in \{a, b\}^+, |u| = |w| = 2\}$$

14. Consider the grammar with productions

$$S \to aaB$$

$$A \to bB\ b/\lambda$$

$$B \to Aa$$

Show that the string *aabbabba* is not in the language generated by this grammar.

15. Find a CFG for the set of all regular expressions on the alphabet $\{a, b\}$.

16. Prove that the language

$$L = \{a^n b^n c^m\} \cup \{a^n b^m c^m\} \text{ with } m, n \geq 0$$

is inherently ambiguous context free language.

17. Is it possible for a regular grammar to be ambiguous.

18. show that the two grammars

$$S \to abAB/ba,$$

$$A \to aaa,$$

$$B \to aA/bb$$

and $S \to abAaA/abAbb/ba$

$A \to aaa$

are equivalent.

19. Transform the grammar with productions

$S \to aSaA/A$, $A \to abA/b$ into CNF.

20. Transform the grammar with productions

$S \to abAB$,

$A \to bAB/\lambda$,

$B \to BAa/A/\lambda$,

into CNF.

21. Convert the grammar

$S \to ab/aS/aaS$ into GNF.

22. Convert the grammar

$S \to ABb/a$,

$A \to aaA/B$,

$B \to bAb$, into GNF.

CHAPTER 3

Pushdown Automaton

We have seen that the regular languages are precisely those accepted by finite automata. Not every context free language can be recognized by a finite automaton since some context free languages are not regular. Yet the problem of recognizing context free languages is an important one for both theoretical and practical reasons. What sort of more powerful automaton could be used for recognizing arbitrary context free languges? Or to be more specific, what do we need to add a finite automaton so that the construction can be generalized to apply all context free languages ?

If M is a finite automaton accepting L, it is constructed in such a way that states act as a form of primitive memory. The states remember the variables encountered in the course of derivation of a string. Let us consider $L = \{a^n b^n / n \geq 1\}$. This is a context free language but not regular. A finite automaton cannot accept L, *i.e.*, strings of the form $a^n b^n$ as it has to remember the number of a's in a string and so it will require infinite number of states. This difficulty can be avoided by adding an auxillary memory in the form of a stack. The a's in the given string are added to the stack. When the syumbol b is encountered in the input string an a is removed from the stack. Thus the matching of number of $a's$ and number of $b's$ is accomplished. This type of arrangement where a finite automaton has stack leads to the generation of pushdown automaton.

In this chapter we introduce Pushdown Automaton (PDA). We discuss two types of acceptance of sets by pushdown automata. We prove that the sets accepted by pushdown automata are precisely the class of context free languges. We conclude this chapter after proving pumping lemma and giving some decision algorithms.

3.1. INTRODUCTION

In chapter 1 we have introduced the Finite State Automata (FSA) as a class of machines which accept exactly the regular language (regular sets). In this chapter we introduce a class of machines known as Pushdown Automata (PDA) or (pushdown acceptors) which accept exactly the context free languages. In addition to the components of FSA, like the set of states, finite control, input tape, the PDA has a pushdown tape (or pushdown store) which acts on a first in last out basis. Symbols are added or removed only from the top. When a symbol is added on top, the symbol originally on top becomes the second and so on. On the otherhand, when the symbol on top is removed, the symbol which was originally second becomes the top symbol and so on.

3.1.1 Functioning of PDA

The Pushdown automaton consists of a finite set of states, a finite set of input symbols and a finite set of pushdown symbols. The finite control has control of both the input tape and the pushdown store. Depending on the state of the finite control an input

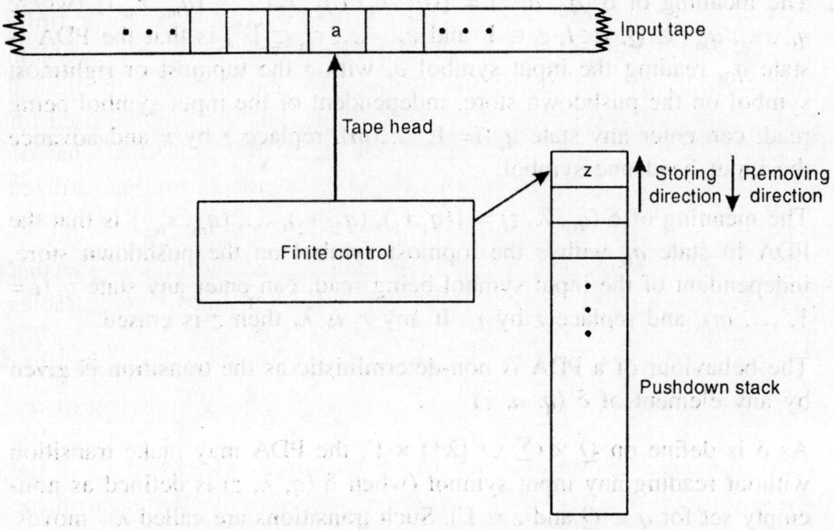

Fig 3.1. Model of pushdown automaton.

Symbol (or λ) just read with a pushdown symbol on the top of the pushdown store, the PDA can (non-deterministically) change state move to the next input symbol to the right (or read the same symbol if it is λ) and replace the top of the pushdown symbol by a string of pushdown symbols or erase it. There is a start state, a start pushdown symbol and a set of final states.

We now give the formal definition of PDA.

3.1.2. Definition

Nordeterministic

A *pushdown automaton* (PDA) is a 7-tuple $M = (Q, \Sigma, \Gamma, q_0\ z_0, \delta, F)$

where Q is a finite set of states, Σ, a finite set of input symbols
Γ, a finite set of pushdown symbols,

q_0, the initial state is an element of Q

z_0 the initial stack symbol (or top most or right most symbol) is an element of Γ

F, the set of accepting (or final) states is a subset of Q

$\delta : Q \times (\Sigma \cup \{\lambda\}) \times \Gamma \rightarrow$ the set of finite subsets of $Q \times \Gamma^*$ (δ is known as transition function or next state function).

3.1.3. Notation and Meaning

1. The meaning of $\delta (q_0, a, z) = \{(q_1, r_1) (q_2, r_2), \ldots, (q_m, r_m)\}$ (where $q_0, \ldots, q_m \in Q$, $a \in I$, $z \in \Gamma$ and $r_1, \ldots, r_m \subseteq \Gamma^*$) is that the PDA is state q_0, reading the input symbol a, with z the topmost or rightmost symbol on the pushdown store, independent of the input symbol being read, can enter any state q_i ($i = 1, \ldots, m$), replace z by r_i and advance the input head one symbol.
2. The meaning of $\delta (q_0, \lambda, z) = \{(q_1, r_1), (q_2, r_2), \ldots, (q_m, r_m)\}$ is that the PDA in state q_0, with z the topmost symbol on the pushdown store, independent of the input symbol being read, can enter any state q_i ($i = 1, \ldots, m$), and replace z by r_i. If any r_i *is* λ, then z is erased.
3. The behaviour of a PDA is non-deterministic as the transition is given by any element of $\delta (q, a, z)$
4. As δ is define on $Q \times (\Sigma \cup \{\lambda\}) \times \Gamma$, the PDA may make transition without reading any input symbol (when $\delta (q, \lambda, z)$ is defined as non-empty set for $q \in Q$ and $z \in \Gamma$). Such transitions are called λ - moves.
5. The PDA cannot make a transition when pushdown store (or stack) (PDS) is empty (we can apply δ only when the PDA reads an input symbol and the topmost pushdown symbol in PDS). In this case the PDA halts.
6. When we write $\alpha = z_m z_{m-1} \cdots z_2 z_2$ in PDS, z_1 is the topmost element, z_2 is below z_1 etc. and z_m is below z_{m-1}

3.1.4. Instantaneous Description (ID)

Let $A = (Q, \Sigma, \Gamma, \delta, q_0, z_0, F)$ be a PDA. An ID is (q, x, α) where $q \in Q$, $x \in \Sigma^*$ and $\alpha \in \Gamma^*$.

For example $(q, a_1 a_2 \cdots a_n, z_m \cdots z_2 z_1)$ is an ID. This describes the PDA when the current state is q, the input string to be processed is $a_1a_2 \cdots a_n$. The PDA will process $a_1 \cdots a_n$ in that order. The PDS has $z_1, z_2 \cdots, z_m$ with z_1 at the top, z_2 the second element from the top etc., and z_m is the lowest element in PDS.

3.1.5. Definition

An initial ID is (q_0, x, z_0). This means intially the PDA is in the intial state q_0, the input string to be processed is x, and the PDS has only one symbol, viz., z_0

Note. In an ID (q, x, α), x may be λ. In this case the PDA makes a λ-move (or ε-move).

3.1.6. Definition

Let A be a PDA, A move relation (denoted by $\vdash$) between ID's is defined as

$(q, a_1\, a_2 \cdots a_n, z_m \cdots z_2z_1) \vdash (q', a_2 \cdots a_n, \beta z_m \cdots z_2)$ if $\delta\,(q, a_1, z_1)$ contains (q', β).

3.1.7. Remark

As $\vdash$ defines a relation in the set of all IDs of a PDA, we can define the reflexive-transitive closure $\overset{*}{\vdash}$ which represents a definite sequence of n moves, where n *is* any non-negative integer.

If $(q, x, \alpha) \overset{*}{\vdash} (q', y, \beta)$ represents n moves, we write

$(q, x, \alpha) \overset{n}{\vdash} (q', y, \beta)$. In particrlar

$(q, x, \alpha) \overset{o}{\vdash} (q, x, \alpha)$. Also $(q, x, \alpha) \overset{*}{\vdash} (q, y, \beta)$ can be split as

$(q, x, \alpha) \vdash (q_1, x_1, \alpha_1) \vdash (q_2, x_2, \alpha_2) \vdash \cdots \vdash (q', y, \beta)$ for some $x_1, x_2, \cdots \in \Sigma^*$, $\alpha_1\, \alpha_2 \cdots \in F^*$.

Note. When we are dealing with more than one PDA, we specify the PDA also while describing the move relation, for example, a move relation in A is denoted by $\overset{A}{\vdash}$

3.1.8. Property

If $$(q_1, x, \alpha) \vdash (q_2, \lambda, \beta) \qquad \ldots(3.1)$$

then for every $y \in \Sigma^*$,

$$(q_1, xy, \alpha) \vdash (q_2, y, \beta) \qquad \ldots(3.2)$$

Conversely if $(q_1, xy, \alpha) \overset{*}{\vdash} (q_2, y, \beta)$ for some $y \in \Sigma^*$, then $(q_1, x, \mu) \overset{*}{\vdash} (q_2, \lambda, \beta)$.

Proof. If the PDA is in state q_1 with α in PDS, and the moves given by (3.1) are effected by processing the string x. the PDA moves to state q_2 with β in

PDS. The same transition is effected by starting with input string xy and processing only x. In this case, y remains to be processed and hence we get (3.2)

In the similar way we can prove (3.2) implies (3.1) Hence the proof.

3.1.9. Property

If $$(q, x, \alpha) \overset{*}{\vdash} (q', \lambda, \nu) \qquad ...(3.3)$$

then for every $\beta \in \Gamma^*$,

$$(q, x, \beta\alpha) \vdash (q', \lambda, \beta\nu) \qquad ...(3.4)$$

Proof. The sequence of moves given by (3.3) can be split as

$$(q, x, \alpha) \vdash (q_i, x_1, \alpha) \vdash (q_2, x_2, \alpha_2) \vdash \cdots \vdash (q', \lambda, \nu)$$

Consider $(q_i, s_i\ \alpha_i) \vdash (q_{i+1}, x_{i+1}, \alpha_{i+1})$. Let $\alpha_i = z_m \cdots z_i$. As a result of this move, z_1, is erased and some string is placed above $z_m \cdots z_2$. So $z_m \cdots z_2$ is not affected. If we have β below $z_m \cdots z_2$, then also $z_m \cdots z_2\beta$ is not affected. so we obtain

$$(q_i, x_i, \beta\alpha_i) \vdash (q_{i+1}, x_{i+1}, \beta\alpha_{i+1})$$

Therefore, we get a sequence of moves

$$(q, x, \beta\alpha) \vdash (q_1, x_1, \beta\alpha_1) \vdash \cdots \vdash (q', \lambda, \beta\nu)$$

i.e., $$(q, x, \beta\alpha) \overset{*}{\vdash} (q', \lambda, \beta\nu)$$

Note. In general (3.4) need not imply (3.3)

3.2 ACCEPTANCE BY PDA

3.2.1. Acceptance by Final State

A word w is accepted (or recognized) by a PDA if starting with the start state in the finite control, the start pushdown symbol on the top the pushdown store, by a sequence of moves, the word w is read from left to right letter by letter and the PDA finally enters a final state (after reading the rightmost symbol). This is called *acceptance by final state*. That is

Let A = $(Q, \Sigma, \Gamma, \delta, q_0, z_0, F)$ be a PDA. The set accepted by PDA by final state is defined by

$T(A) = \{w \in T^*/(q_0, w, z_0) \overset{*}{\vdash} (q_i, \lambda, \alpha)$ for some $q_i \in F$ and $\alpha \in \Gamma^*\}$

3.2.2 Acceptance by empty store (or stack)

A word w may be accepted by emptying the pushdown store also. Here the action of the PDA is similar but instead of entering a final state when the last input letter is read, the PDA accepts the word w if the pushdown store is empty after reading the rightmost input letter. That is

Let $A = (Q, \Sigma, \Gamma, \delta, q_0, z_0, F)$ be a PDA. The set accepted by null store (or empty store) is defined by

$$N(A) = \{w \in \Sigma^* / (q_0, w, z_0) \overset{*}{\vdash} (q, \lambda, \lambda) \text{ for some } q \in Q\}.$$

Note. It can be established that the two kinds of acceptance are equivalent in the sense that if a set of words is accepted by final state by some PDA, it can be accepted by empty store by some other PDA and vice versa.

3.2.3. Theorem

A language L is accepted by a PDA by empty store if and only if L is accepted by a PDA by final state

(or)

If L is $T(M_1)$ for some PDA M_1 if and only if L is $N(M_2)$ for some PDA M_2

Proof. Let $M_1 = (Q, \Sigma, \Gamma, \delta, q_0, z_0, F)$ be a PDA accepting L by final state. That is $L = T(M_1)$ then $M_2 = (Q, \Sigma', \Gamma', \delta', q_0', z_0', F')$ where $F_1 = \{\phi\}$

$$Q' = Q \cup \{q_0', q_e\} \text{ where } q_0', q_e \notin Q.$$
$$\Sigma' = \Sigma$$
$$\Gamma' = \Gamma \cup \{z'_0\}, \text{ where } z_0' \notin \Gamma$$

and δ' is defined as follows.

1. $\delta'(q_0', \lambda, z_0')$ contains $(q_0, z_0' z_0)$
2. $\delta'(q_i, a, z)$ is same as $\delta(q_i, a, z)$ for all $q_1 \in, Q$, $a \in \Sigma \cup \{\lambda\}$ and $z \in \Gamma$.
3. $\delta'(q_i, \lambda, z)$ contains (q_e, λ) for $q_i \in F$ and for all $z \in \Gamma \cup \{z_0'\}$
4. $\delta'(q_e, \lambda, z)$ contains (q_e, λ) for all $z \in \Gamma \cup \{z_0'\}$

It can be easily seen that $T(M_1) = N(M_2)$

[For, 1 causes M_2 to enter the intial configuration of M_1 with z'_0 as the leftmost pushdown symbol. The effect of z is to make M_2 simulate. The behaviour of M_1, thus reading an input word w if M_1 reads w and enters a final state. Once w is read and M_2 enter a final state of M_1, the dffect of 3 and 4 is to empty the pushdown store].

Thus w is in $T(M_1)$ iff

$$(q_0', w, z_0') \overset{*}{\underset{M_1}{\vdash}} (q_i, \lambda, r) \text{ for some } q_i \in F$$

$(q_0', w, z_0') \vdash_{M_2} (q_0, w, z_0' z_0)$ by 1

$\overset{*}{\vdash} (q_i, \lambda, z_0' r)$ by 2 where $q_i, \in F$

$\overset{*}{\vdash} (q_e, \lambda, \lambda)$

by 3 and 4. That is w is in $N(M_2)$. That is L is accepted by empty store by M_2. That is $L = N(M_2)$.

Conversely, let $M_2 = (Q', \Sigma', \Gamma', \delta', q_0', z_0', \phi)$ be a PDA accepting L by empty store is $L = N(M_2)$. Then $M_1 = (Q, \Sigma, \Gamma, \delta, q_0, z_0, F)$ where

$Q = Q^1 \cup \{q_0, q_j\}$ where $q_0, q_i, \notin, Q'$

$\Gamma = \Gamma' \cup \{z_0\}$, where $z_0 \notin \Gamma'$

$F = \{q_j\}$ and δ is defined as follows.

1. $\delta(q_0, \lambda, z_0)$ contains $(q_0', z_0 z_0')$
2. $\delta(q_i, a, z)$ is the same as $\delta'(q_i, a, z)$ for all $q_i \in Q'$, $a \in \Sigma \cup \{\lambda\}$ and $z \in \Gamma'$
3. $\delta(q_i, \lambda, z_0)$ contains (q_j, z_0) for all $q_i \in Q'$.

It can be easily verified that $N(M_2) = T(M_1)$ [For rule 1 causes M_1 to enter the initial configuration of M_2 with the difference that z_0 is the bottom most symbol on the pushdown store. The effect of 2 is to allow M_1 to simulate the behaviour of M_2. When M_2 erases the pushdown store and accepts w, M_1 will erase the entire pushdown store except the bottom symbol z_0. When z_0 is the topmost pushdown symbol, 3 causes M_1 to enter the final state q_j, there by accepting the input w, hence the theorem.]

3.2.4. Problem

1. Construct a PDA to accept a given language L by final state where $L = \{a^n b^n / n \geq 1\}$.

Solution. Let

$$M = (Q, \Sigma, \Gamma, \delta, q_0, z_0, F) \text{ where}$$
$$Q = \{q_0, a_1, q_2\}$$
$$\Sigma = \{a, b\}$$
$$\Gamma = \{z_0, z_1, z_2\}$$
$$F = \{q_2\}$$

and δ is defined as follows

$$\delta(q_0, a, z_0) = \{(q_0, z_1)\}$$
$$\delta(q_0, a, z_1) = \{(q_0, z_1 z_2)\}$$
$$\delta(q_0, b, z_2) = \{(q_0, z_2 z_2)\}$$
$$\delta(q_0, b, z_1) = \{(q_2, z_1)\}$$

$$\delta\ (q_0,\ b,\ z_2)\ =\ \{(q_1,\ \lambda)\}$$
$$\delta\ (q_1,\ b,\ z_2)\ =\ \{(q_1,\ \lambda)\}$$
$$\delta\ (q_1,\ b,\ z_1)\ =\ \{(q_2,\ z_1)\}$$

Then $(q_0, ab, z_0) \vdash (q_0, b, z_1) \vdash (q_2, \lambda, z_1)$ so that $ab \in T(M)$

also for $n > 1$.

$$\begin{aligned}(q_0,\ a^nb^n,\ z_0) &\vdash (q_0,\ a^{n-1}b^n,\ z_1)\\ &\vdash (q_0,\ a^{n-2}b^n,\ z_1z_2)\\ &\vdash (q_0,\ a^{n-3}b^n,\ z_1z_2^{\,2})\\ &\vdash (q_0,\ a^{n-4}b^n,\ z_1z_2^{\,3})\\ &\overset{*}{\vdash} (q_0,\ b^n,\ z_1z_2^{\,n-1})\\ &\vdash (q_1,\ b^{n-1},\ z_1z_2^{\,n-2})\\ &\overset{*}{\vdash} (q_1,\ b,\ z_1z_2^{\,n-n}) = (q_1b, z_1)\\ &\vdash (q_2,\ \lambda,\ z_1)\end{aligned}$$

So that $a^nb^n \in T\ (M)$. Hence the PDA, M accepts L by final state.

Remark. We can also represent the transition function by a table known as transition table.

For example consider the function δ given in problem 1. We can represent it in the form of transition table as follows.

States	*Inputs*	*Stake symbols*	*Move(s)*
q_0	a	z_0	(q_0, z_1)
q_0	a	z_1	(q_0, z_1z_2)
q_0	a	z_2	(q_0, z_2z_2)
q_0	b	z_1	(q_2, z_1)
q_0	b	z_2	(q_1, λ)
q_1	b	z_2	(q_1, λ)
q_1	b	z_1	(q_2, z_1)

2. Construct a PDA to accept a given language L by empty store where $L = \{a^nb^n/n{\geq}1\}$

Solution. Let $L = \{a^nb^n/n \geq 1\}$

Let

$$M^1 = (Q^1\ \Sigma', \Gamma', \delta', q_0'\ z_0', F') \text{ where}$$

$$Q' = \{q_0'\},$$

$$\Sigma' = \{a, b\}$$

$$Z' = \{z_0', z_1', z_2'\}$$

$$F' = \phi \text{ and } \delta' \text{ is defined as follows}$$

$$\delta'(q_0', \lambda, z_0') = \{(q_0', z_2'z_0'z_1')\ (q_0', z_2'\ z_1')\}$$

$$\delta'(q_0', a\ z_1') = \{(q_0', \lambda)\}$$

$$\delta'(q_0', b, z_2') = \{(q_0', \lambda)\}$$

Then

$$(q_0', a^n b^n, z_0') \vdash (q_0', a^n b^n, z_2'\ z_0'\ z_1')$$

$$\vdash (q_0', a^{n-1} b^n, z_2'\ z_0')$$

$$\vdash (q_0', a^{n-1} b^n, z_2'\ z_2'\ z_0'\ z_1')$$

$$\vdash (q_0', a^{n-2} b^n, z_2'\ z_2'\ z_0')$$

$$\vdash (q_0', a^{n-2} b^n, z_2'^3\ z_0' z_1')$$

$$\vdash (q_0', a^{n-3} b^n, z_2'^3\ z_0')$$

$$\overset{*}{\vdash} (q_0', ab^n, z_2'^{(n-1)}\ z_0')$$

$$\vdash (q_0', ab^n, (z_2')^n\ z_1')$$

$$\vdash (q_0', b^n, (z_2')^n)$$

$$\vdash (q_0', b^{n-1}, (z_2')^n)$$

$$\vdash (q_0', b^{n-1}, (z_2')^{n-1})$$

$$\overset{*}{\vdash} (q_0', \lambda, \lambda)$$

so that $a^n b^n \in N(M')$

Hence the PDA, M' accepts L by empty store. That is $N(M') = L$

3. Consturct a PDA to accept the language $L = \{wew^R / w \text{ is in } (a, b)^*\}$ by final state

Solution. Consider a PDA

$$M = (Q, \Sigma, \Gamma, \delta, q_0, z_0, F) \text{ where}$$

$$Q = \{q_0, q_1, q_2\}$$

$$\Sigma = \{a, b, c\}$$

$$Z = \{z_0, z_1, z_2\}$$

$$F = \{q_2\} \text{ and } \delta \text{ is defined as follows.}$$

$$\delta(q_0, a, z_0) = \{q_0, z_0 z_1\}$$
$$\delta(q_0, a, z_1) = \{q_0, z_1 z_1\}$$
$$\delta(q_0, a, z_2) = \{q_0, z_2 z_1\}$$
$$\delta(q_1, a, z_1) = \{(q_1, \lambda)\}$$
$$\delta(q_0, b, z_0) = \{(q_0, z_0 z_2)\}$$
$$\delta(q_0, b, z_1) = \{(q_0, z_0 z_2)\}$$
$$\delta(q_0, b, z_2) = \{(q_0, z_1 z_2)\}$$
$$\delta(q_1, b, z_2) = \{(q_1, \lambda)\}$$
$$\delta(q_0, c, z_0) = \{(q_1, z_0)\}$$
$$\delta(q_0, c, z_1) = \{(q_1, z_1)\}$$
$$\delta(q_0, c, z_2) = \{(q_1, z_2)\}$$
$$\delta(q_1, \lambda, z_0) = \{(q_2, z_0)\}$$

If w is in $(a,b)^*$ then

$$(q_0, wcw^{R}, z_0) \overset{*}{\vdash} (q_0, cw^R, z_0 W)$$
$$\vdash (q_1, w^R, z_0 W)$$
$$\overset{*}{\vdash} (q_1, \lambda, z_0)$$
$$\vdash (q_2, \lambda, z_0)$$

where W is w with a replaced by z_1 and b by z_2. Thus $T(M) = L$.

4. Construct a PDA to accept the language $L = \{wcw^{R}/w \text{ in } (a, b)^*\}$ by empty store.

Solution. $L = \{wcw^R/w \text{ in } (a, b)^*\}$

Let $M' = (Q^1, \Sigma', \Gamma', q'_0, z_0', \delta', F')$

where $Q_0' = \{q_0', q_1'\}$

$$\Sigma' = \{a, b, c\}$$
$$\Gamma' = \{z_0', z_1', z_2'\}$$
$$F' = \phi$$

and δ' is defined as follows

$$\delta'(q_0', a, z_0') = \{(q_0'\ z_0'\ z_1')\}$$
$$\delta'(q_0', a, z_1') = \{(q_0'\ z_1'\ z_1')\}$$

$$\delta'(q_1', a, z_2') = \{(q_0' z_2' z_1')\}$$

$$\delta'(q_1', a, z_1') = \{(q_1', \lambda)\}$$

$$\delta'(q_0', b, z_0') = \{(q_0', z_0' z_2')\}$$

$$\delta'(q_0', b, z_1') = \{(q_0', z_1' z_2')\}$$

$$\delta'(q_0', b, z_2') = \{(q_0', z_2' z_2')\}$$

$$\delta'(q_0', b, z_2') = \{(q_1', \lambda)\}$$

$$\delta'(q_0', c, z_0') = \{(q_1', z_0')\}$$

$$\delta'(q_0', c, z_1') = \{(q_1', z_1')\}$$

$$\delta'(q_0', c, z_2') = \{(q_1', z_2')\}$$

$$\delta'(q_1', \lambda, z_0') = \{(q_1', \lambda')\}$$

we see that if w is in $(a,b)^*$, then

$$(q_0', wcw^R, z_0') \overset{*}{\vdash} (q_0', cw^R, z_0' W)$$

$$\vdash (q_1', w^R, z_0' W)$$

$$\overset{*}{\vdash} (q_1', \lambda, z_0')$$

$$\vdash (q_1', \lambda, \lambda)$$

where W is w where a is replaced by z_1' and b by z_2'. Hence $N(M') = L$.

Now we will see few applications of Theorem 3.2.3.

5. Construct a PDA to accept the language $L = \{wcw^R/w \text{ in } (a, b)^*\}$ by final state.

Solution. Consider the PDA M' given in problem 4. we have proved that M' accepts

$$L = \{wcw^R/w \text{ in } (a, b)^*\} \text{ by empty store.}$$

Now we use Theorem 3.2.3 to construct the required PDA

Let $$M = (Q, \Sigma, \Gamma, q_0, z_0, \delta, F)$$

where $$Q = Q' \cup \{q_0, q_j\} = \{(q_0', q_1', q_0, q_j)\}$$

$$\Gamma = \Gamma' \cup \{z_0\} = \{z_0', z_1', z_2', z_0\}$$

$$F = \{q_j\} \text{ and } \delta \text{ is defined as follows.}$$

$$\delta(q_0, \lambda, z_0) = \{(q_0', z_0 z_0')\}$$

$$\delta(q_0', a, z_0') = \{(q_0', z_0' z_1')\}$$

$$\delta(q_0', a, z_1') = \{(q_0', z_1' z_1')\}$$
$$\delta(q_0', a, z_2') = \{(q_0', z_2' z_1')\}$$
$$\delta(q_1', a, z_1') = \{(q_1', \lambda)\}$$
$$\delta(q_0', b, z_0') = \{(q_0', z_0' z_2')\}$$
$$\delta(q_0', b, z_1') = \{(q_0', z_1' z_2')\}$$
$$\delta(q_0', b, z_2') = \{(q_0', z_2' z_2')\}$$
$$\delta(q_0', b, z_2') = \{(q_0', z_2' z_2')\}$$
$$\delta(q_0', c, z_0') = \{(q_0', z_0')\}$$
$$\delta(q_0', b, z_2') = \{(q_1', \lambda)\}$$
$$\delta(q_0', c, z_1') = \{(q_1', z_1')\}$$
$$\delta(q_0', c, z_2') = \{(q_1', z_2')\}$$
$$\delta(q_1', \lambda, z_0') = \{(q_1', \lambda)\}$$
$$\delta(q_0', \lambda, z_0) = \{(q_j, z_0)\}$$
$$\delta(q_1', \lambda, z_0) = \{(q_j, z_0)\}$$

We can easily seen that $T(M) = L = N(M')$

[For, $(q_0, wcw^R, z_0) \vdash (q_0', wcw^R, z_0 z_0')$

$\overset{*}{\vdash} (q_0', cw^R, z_0 z_0' w)$

$\vdash (q_1', w^R, z_0 z_0' w)$

$\overset{*}{\vdash} (q_1', \lambda, z_0 z_0')$

$\overset{*}{\vdash} (q_1', \lambda, z_0)$

$\vdash (q_j, z_0)$]

6. Construct a PDA to accept the language $L = \{a^n b^n / n \geq 1\}$ by empty store.
Solution. Consider the PDA M given in problem 1. Then M accepts L by final state. We now use Theorem 3.2.3 to construct the required PDA.

Let $M' = (Q', \Sigma', \Gamma', \delta', q_0', z_0', F')$

where $Q' = Q \cup \{q_e, q_0'\}$, q_e and $q_0' \notin Q$

$= \{q_0, q_1, q_2, q_e, q_0'\}$

$\Sigma' = \{a, b\}$

$\Gamma' = \Gamma \cup \{z_0'\}$

$= \{z_0, z_1, z_2, z_0'\}$

$F' = \phi$ and δ' is defined as follows.

$$\delta'(q_0', \lambda, z_0') = \{(q_0, z_0'z_0)\}$$

$$\delta'(q_0, a, z_0) = \{(q_0, z_1)\}$$

$$\delta'(q_0, a, z_1) = \{(q_0, z_1z_2)\}$$

$$\delta'(q_0, a, z_2) = \{(q_0, z_2z_2)\}$$

$$\delta'(q_0, b, z_1) = \{(q_2, z_1)\}$$

$$\delta'(q_0, b, z_2) = \{(q_1, \lambda)\}$$

$$\delta'(q_1, b, z_2) = \{(q_1, \lambda)\}$$

$$\delta'(q_1, b, z_1) = \{(q_2, z_1)\}$$

$$\delta'(q_2, \lambda, z_0) = \{(q_e, \lambda)\}$$

$$\delta'(q_2, \lambda, z_1) = \{(q_e, \lambda)\}$$

$$\delta'(q_2, \lambda, z_2) = \{(q_e, \lambda)\}$$

$$\delta'(q_2, \lambda, z_0) = \{(q_e, \lambda)\}$$

$$\delta'(q_e, \lambda, z_0) = \{(q_e, \lambda)\}$$

$$\delta'(q_e, \lambda, z_1) = \{(q_e, \lambda)\}$$

$$\delta'(q_e, \lambda, z_2) = \{(q_e, \lambda)\}$$

$$\delta'(q_e, \lambda, z_0') = \{(q_e, \lambda)\}$$

It is easily seen that $N(M') = L = T(M)$.

3.3. PUSHDOWN AUTOMATA AND CONTEXT FREE LANGUAGES

3.3.1. Theorem

If L is a context free language, then there exists a PDA M such that $L = N(M)$.

(Procedure to construct a PDA for a given language)

Proof. Let $G = (N, T, S, P)$ be a CFG generating $L(G)$.

Let $M = (\{q_0\}, \Sigma, \Gamma, \delta, q_0, z_0, \phi)$

where $\Sigma = T$

$$\Gamma = N \cup T$$

$$z_0 = S$$

and δ is defined as follows. For each $a \in \Sigma$ and $A \in N$

(*i*) $\delta(q_0, \lambda, A) = \{(q_0, \alpha^R)/A \to \alpha \text{ is in } p\}$

(*ii*) $\delta(q_0, a, a) = \{(q_0, \lambda)\}$

The pushdown symbols in *M* are terminals and non-terminals, if the PDA reads a variable *A* on the top of pushdown store, it match a λ- move by replacing the reverse of R.H.S. of any *A*-production (after erasing *A*). If the PDA read, a terminal '*a*' on PDS and if it matches with the current input symbol, then the PDA erases *a*. In other cases PDA halts.

If $w \in L(G)$ is obtained by a leftmost derivation $S \Rightarrow u_1A_1\alpha_1 \Rightarrow u_1u_2A_2\alpha_2\alpha_1 \Rightarrow \cdots \Rightarrow w$, then A can empty the PDS on application of input string *w*. The first move of *M* is by a λ move corresponding to $S \to u_1A_1\alpha_1$. The PDA erases the symbols in u_1 by processing prefix of *w*. Now the topmost symbol in PDS is A_1. Once again by applying the λ-move corresponding to $A_1 \to u_2A_2\alpha_2$, the PDA erases A_1 and stores $\alpha_2A_2u_2$ above α_1 proceeding in this way, the PDA empties the PDS by processing the entire string *w*.

Now we prove that $L(G) = N(M)$. Let $w \in L(G)$. Then it can be derived by a leftmost derivation. Any sentential form in a leftmost derivation is of the form $u\ A\ \alpha$ where $u \in T^*$, $A \in N$ and $\alpha \in (N \cup T)^*$. We prove the following auxillary result.

If $S \overset{*}{\Rightarrow} uA\alpha$ by a leftmost derivation, then $(q, uv, S) \overset{*}{\vdash} (q, v, \alpha A)$ for every $v \in \Sigma^*$ ...(3.5)

We prove (3.5) by induction on the number of steps in the derivation of $uA\alpha$. If

$S \overset{*}{\Rightarrow} uA$, then $u = \lambda$, $\alpha = \lambda$ and $S = A$.

As $(q, v, S) \overset{*}{\vdash} (q, v, S)$, there is a basis for induction.

Suppose $S \overset{n+1}{\Rightarrow} uA\alpha$ by a leftmost derivation. This derivation can be split as

$S \overset{n}{\vdash} u_1\ A_1\alpha_1 \Rightarrow uA\alpha$. If in the A_1 — production we apply in the last step $A_1 \to u_2A\alpha_2$, then $u = u_1u_2$, $\alpha = \alpha_2\alpha_1$.

As $S \overset{n}{\Rightarrow} u_1A_1\alpha_1$, by induction hypothesis,

$$(q_1, u_1u_2v, S) \overset{*}{\vdash} (q_1, u_2v, \alpha_1A_1) \qquad ...(3.6)$$

As $A_1 \to u_2A\alpha_2$ is a production in *P*, by rule (*i*), we get

$(q, \lambda, A_1) \vdash (q, \lambda, \alpha_2\ Au_2)$. Applying 3.1.8. and 3.1.9, we get

$(q, u_2v, \alpha_1A) \vdash (q, u_2v, \alpha_1\alpha_2\ A\ u_2) \vdash (q, u, A\alpha_2\alpha_1)$ by rule (*ii*)

Hence $(q, u_2v, \alpha_1A_1) \overset{*}{\vdash} (q, v, \alpha_1\alpha_2 A)$ ...(3.7)

But $u_1u_2 = u$ and $\alpha_1\alpha_2 = \alpha$. So from (3.6) and (3.7), we have

$$(q, uv, S) \overset{*}{\vdash} (q, v, \alpha A)$$

Thus (3.5) is true for $S \overset{n+1}{\Rightarrow} uA\alpha$. By the principle of induction, (3.5) is true for any derviation. Now we prove that $L(G) \subseteq N(M)$.

Let $w \in L(G)$. Then w can be obtained from a leftmost derivation.

$$S \overset{*}{\Rightarrow} uAv \Rightarrow uu'v = w$$

From (*i*)

$$(q, uu'v, S) \overset{*}{\vdash} (q, u'v, vA)$$

As $A \rightarrow u'$ is in P,

$$(q, u'v, vA) \overset{*}{\vdash} (q, u'v, vu')$$

By rule (*ii*)

$$(q, u'v, vu') \overset{*}{\vdash} (q, \lambda, \lambda)$$

Therefore,

$w = uu'v \in N(A)$ proving $L(G) \subseteq N(m)$. Next we prove $N(m) \subseteq L(G)$.

Before proving the inclusion, let us prove the following auxillary result.

$$S \overset{*}{\Rightarrow} u\alpha \text{ if } (q, uv, S) \overset{*}{\vdash} (q, v, \alpha) \qquad ...(3.8)$$

we prove (3.8) by the number of moves in $(q, uv, S) \overset{*}{\vdash} (q, v, \alpha)$. If $(q, uv, S) \overset{*}{\vdash} (q, v, \alpha)$, then $u = \lambda$, $S = \alpha$; obviously $S \overset{*}{\Rightarrow} \lambda\alpha$.

Thus there is a basis for induction.

Let us assume (3.8) when the number of moves is n. Assume

$$(q, uv, S) \overset{*}{\vdash} (q, v, \alpha) \qquad ...(3.9)$$

The last move in (3.9) is obtained either from $(q, \lambda, A) \vdash (q, \lambda, \alpha')$ or $(q, a, a) \vdash (q, \lambda, \lambda)$. In the first case (3.9) can be split as

$(q, uv, S) \overset{n}{\vdash} (q, v, \alpha^2 A) \vdash (q, v, \alpha_2\alpha_1) = (q, v, \alpha)$.

By induction hypothesis, $S \overset{*}{\Rightarrow} uA\alpha_2$, and the last move is induced by $A \rightarrow \alpha_1$.

Thus,

$S \overset{*}{\Rightarrow} uA\alpha_2$ implies $\alpha_1\alpha_2 = \alpha$. So $S \overset{*}{\Rightarrow} uA\alpha_2 \Rightarrow u\alpha_1\alpha_2 = u\alpha$.

In the second case (3.9) can be split as

$$(q, uv, S) \overset{n}{\vdash} (q, av, \alpha a) \vdash (q, v, \alpha)$$

Also $u = u'a$ for some $u' \in \Sigma$. So $(q, u'av, S) \overset{n}{\vdash} (q, av, \alpha a)$ implies (by induction hypothesis) $S \overset{*}{\Rightarrow} u'\, a\alpha = u\alpha$. Thus in both cases we have shown that $S \overset{*}{\Rightarrow} u\alpha$. By the principle of induction (3.8) is true.

Now we can prove that if $w \in N(M)$ then

$w \in L(G)$. As $w \in N(A)$,

$(q, w, S) \overset{*}{\vdash} (q, \lambda, \lambda)$. By taking $u = w$, $v = \lambda$, $\alpha = \lambda$ and applying (3.8), we get $S \overset{*}{\Rightarrow} w\lambda = w$ *i.e.* $w \in L(G)$.

Thus $$L(G) = N(M).$$

3.3.2. Example

Consider a context free grammar given by the production rules $S \to aAA$, $A \to aS/bS/a$.

That is $G = (N, T, S, P)$ where $N = \{S, A\}$, $T = \{a, b\}$ and $P = \{S \to aAA, A \to aS, A \to bS, A \to a\}$.

Let $M = (\{q_0\}, \Sigma, \Gamma, \delta, q_0, z_0, F)$ where $\Sigma = T = \{a, b\}$, $\Gamma = N \cup T = \{S, A, a, b\}$, $F = \phi$ and δ is defined as

$$\delta(q_0, \lambda, S) = \{(q_0, AAa)\}$$

$$\delta(q_0, \lambda, A) = \{(q_0, Sa), (q_0, Sb), (q_0, a)\}$$

$$\delta(q_0, a, a) = \{(q_0, \lambda)\}$$

$$\delta(q_0, b, b) = \{(q_0, \lambda)\}$$

It can be easily verified that $L(G) = N(M)$.

3.3.3. Theorem

If $M = (Q, \Sigma, \Gamma, \delta, q_0, z_0, F)$ is a PDA, then there exists a context free grammar G such that $L(G) = N(M)$.

Proof. We first give the construction of G and prove that $N(M) = L(G)$.

We define $G = (N, T, S, P)$ where

$$N = \{[q, z, q'] / q, q' \in Q, Z \in \Gamma\} \cup \{S\}$$

i.e. any element of N is either the new symbol S acting as the start symbol for G or an ordered triple whose first and third elements are states and the second element is a pushdown symbol.

The productions in P are induced by moves of PDA as follows.

(*i*) S-production are given by $S \rightarrow [q_0, z_0, q]$ for every q in Q.

(*ii*) Each move erasing a pushdown symbol given by $(q', \lambda) \in \delta(q, a, z)$ induces the production $[q, z, q'] \rightarrow a$

(*iii*) Each more not erasing a pushdown symbol given by $(q_1, z_m \,....\, z_1) \in \delta(q, a, z)$ induces many productions of the form

$$[q, z, q'] \rightarrow a\,[q_1, z_1, q_2]\,[q_2, z_2, q_3] \,....\, [q_m, z_m, q']$$

where each of the states $q', q_1, q_2, \ldots, q_m$ can be any state in Q. Each move yields many productions because of (*iii*). We now prove that $L(G) = N(M)$.

We know that a variable $[q, z, q^1]$ indicates that for the PDA the current state is q and the topmost symbol in PDA is z. In the course of a derivation, a state q' is chosen in such a way that PDS is emptied ultimately. This corresponds to applying (*ii*).

To prove $N(M) = L(G)$, we need an auxillary result.

$$[q, z, q'] \overset{*}{\underset{G}{\Rightarrow}} w \qquad ...(3.8)$$

if any only if $\quad (q, w, z) \overset{*}{\vdash} (q', \lambda, \lambda) \qquad ...(3.9)$

We prove the if part by induction on the number of steps in (3.9).

If $(q, w, z) \vdash (q', \lambda, \lambda)$, then w is either a in Σ or λ. So we have

$$(q', \lambda) \in \delta(q, w, z).$$

By (3.9) we get a prodcution $[q, z, q'] \rightarrow w$. So, $[q, z\, q'] \underset{G}{\Rightarrow} w$. Thus there is a basis for induction.

Let us assume the result viz., (3.9) implies (3.9) when the former has less than k moves. Consider $(q, w, z) \overset{k}{\vdash} (q', \lambda, \lambda)$. This can be split as

$$(q, aw'\, z) \vdash (q, w', z_m z_2 \ldots z_1) \overset{k-1}{\vdash} (q', \lambda, \lambda) \qquad ...(3.10)$$

where $w = aw$; and $a \in \Sigma$ or $a = \lambda$, depending on the first move.

Consider the second part of (31.0). This means that the PDS has $z_m \ldots z_2 z_1$ initially and on application of w, the PDS is emptied. Each move of PDA can either erase the topmost symbol on the PDS or replace the topmost symbol by some non-empty string. So several moves may be required for getting z_2 on the top of PDS. Let w_1 be the prefix of w such that the PDS has $z_m \dots z_3 z_2$ after the application of w_i. We can note that $z_m \dots z_3 z_2$ are not disturbed while applying w_1. Let w_i be the substring of w such that the PDS has $z_m \dots z_{i+1}$ on application of w_i . $z_m \dots z_{i+1}$ is not disturbed while applying $w_1, w_2, \dots, w_i$.

In terms of ID's we have

$$(q_i, w_i, z_i) \overset{*}{\vdash} (q_{i+1}, \lambda, \lambda) \text{ for } i = 1, 2, \dots, m, \; q_{m+1} = q' \quad \dots (3.11)$$

As each move in (3.11) requires less than k steps, by induction hypothesis we have

$$[q_i, z_i, q_{i+1}] \overset{*}{\Rightarrow} w_i \text{ for } i = 1, \dots, m \quad \dots(3.12)$$

The first proof of (3.10) is given by

$(q_1, z_m z_2 \dots z_1) \in \delta(q, a, z)$. By (3.10) we get a production.

$$[q, z, q'] \rightarrow a [q_1, z_1, q_2] [q_2, z_2, q_3] \dots [q_m, z_m, q'] \quad \dots(3.13)$$

From (3.12) and (3.13) we get

$$[q, z, q'] \overset{*}{\Rightarrow} aw_1 w_2 \dots w_m = w.$$

By the principle of induction (13.9) ⇒ (13.8)

We prove the only if part by induction on the number of steps in the derivation of (3.8). Suppose $[q, z, q'] \Rightarrow q$. Then $[q, z, q'] \rightarrow w$ is a production in P. This production is obtained by 2. So $w = \lambda$ or $w \in \Sigma$ and $(q', \lambda) \in \delta(q, w, z)$. This gives the move $(q, w, z) \vdash (q, \lambda, \lambda)$. Thus there is a basis for inudction.

Assume the result for derivations where the number of steps is less than k. Consider $[q, z, q'] \overset{k}{\vdash} w$. This can be split as

$$[q, z, q'] \Rightarrow a [q, z_m, q_2] [q_2, z_{m-1}, q_3] \dots [q_m, z_1, q'] \overset{k-1}{\vdash} w \quad \dots(3.14)$$

As G is context free we can write $w = aw_1 w_2 \dots w_m$. where

$$[q_i, z_i, q_{i+1}] \underset{G}{\overset{*}{\Rightarrow}} w_i \text{ and } q_{m+1} = q^1$$

By induction hypothesis, we have

$$(q_i, w_i, z_i) \vdash^* (q_{i+1}, \lambda, \lambda) \text{ for}$$
$$i = 1, 2, \dots, m \quad \dots.(3.15)$$

By applying 3.1.8. and 3.1.9., we get

$$(q_i, w_i, z_m \dots z_{i+1} z_i) \overset{*}{\vdash} (q_{i+1}, \lambda, z_m \dots z_{i+1})$$

$$(q_i, w_i w_{i+1} \dots w_m, z_m \dots z_i) \vdash (q_{i+1}, w_{i+1} \dots w_m, z_m \dots z_{i+1}) \quad \dots.(3.16)$$

By combining the moves given by (3.15), we get

$$(q_1, w_1w_2 \ldots w_m, z_m \ldots z_1) \overset{*}{\vdash} (q', \lambda, \lambda) \qquad \ldots(3.17)$$

The first step in (3.13) is induced by

$$(q_1, z_m \ldots z_1) \in \delta\,(q, a, z).$$

The corresponding move is

$$(q, a, z) \vdash (q_1, \lambda, z_m \ldots z_1)$$

By applying property 3.1.8., we get

$$(q, aw_1, \ldots w_m, z) \overset{*}{\vdash} (q_1, w_1 \ldots w_m, z_m \ldots z_1) \qquad \ldots(3.18)$$

From (3.18) and (3.19), we get $(q, w, z) \overset{*}{\vdash} (q', \lambda, \lambda)$. By the principle of induction (3.8) $\Rightarrow$ (3.9).

Thus we have proved the auxillary result. In particular,

$$[q_0, z_0, q'] \overset{*}{\Rightarrow} w \text{ iff } (q_0, w, z_0) \overset{*}{\vdash} (q', \lambda, \lambda) \qquad \ldots(3.19)$$

Now $w \in L\,(G)$ iff $S \overset{*}{\Rightarrow} w$

iff $\quad S \Rightarrow [q_0, z_0, q'] \overset{*}{\Rightarrow} w$ (for some q' by (*i*)

iff $\quad (q_0, w, z_0) \overset{*}{\vdash} (q', \lambda, \lambda)$ by the auxillary result.

iff $\quad w \in N\,(A)$

Thus $\quad N\,(M) = L\,(G)$.

3.3.4. Corrollary

If A is a PDA, then there exists a CFG such that $T\,(A) = L\,(G)$.

Proof. By Theorem 3.2.3. we can find a PDA A' such that $T\,(A) = N\,(A')$. By Theorem 3.3.3. we can construct a grammar G such that $N\,(A') = L\,(G)$. Thus $T\,(A) = L\,(G)$.

3.3.5. Problem

Given a grammar for the language $N\,(M)$ where $M = (\{q_0, q_1\}, \{0, 1\}, \{z_0, X\}, \delta, q_0, z_0\ \phi)$ and δ is given by

$$\delta\,(q_0, 0, z_0) = \{(q_0, xz_0)\}$$

$$\delta\,(q_1, \lambda, X) = \{(q_1, \lambda)\}$$

$$\delta\,(q_0, 1, X) = \{(q_1, \lambda)\}$$

$$\delta(q_0, 1, X) = \{(q_1, \lambda)\}$$

$$\delta(q_0, 0, X) = \{(q_0, XX)\}$$

$$\delta(q_1, \lambda, z_0) = \{(q_1, \lambda)\}$$

Solution. Let $G = (N, T, S, P)$

where $T = \{0, 1\}$

$N = \{[p, A, q] \ / \text{ for all } p, q \in k \text{ and } A \in z\} \cup \{S\}$

$= \{[q_0, z_0, q_1], [q_1, z_0, q_0] \ [q_0, x, q_1], [q_1, x, q_0], [q_0, z_0, q_0], [q_0, x, q_0], [q_1, z_0, q_1], S\}$, S is a new symbol.

P ; $[q_1, X, q_1]$, $S \rightarrow [q_0, z_0, q_0]$,

$S \rightarrow [q_0, z_0, q_1]$.

Next we add productions of the variable $[q_0, z_0, q_0]$.

These are $[q_0, z_0, q_0] \rightarrow 0\ [q_0, X, q_0]\ [q_0, z_0, q_0]$

$[q_0, z_0, q_0] \rightarrow 0\ [q_0, X, q_1\}\ [q_1, z_0, q_0]$

These productions are required by

$$\delta(q_0, 0, z_0) = \{(q_0, X z_0)\}$$

Next the productions for $[q_0, z_0, q_1]$ are

$[q_0, z_0, q_1] \rightarrow 0\ [q_0, X, q_0]\ [q_0, z_0, q_1]$

$[q_0, z_0, q_1] \rightarrow 0\ [q_0, X, q_1]\ [q_1, z_0, q_1]$

These are also required by $\delta(q_0, 0, z_0) = \{(q_0, Xz_0)\}$

The productions for the remaining variable and the relevant moves of the PDA are

1. $[q_0, X, q_0] \rightarrow 0\ [q_0, X, q_0]\ [q_0, X, q_0]$

   $[q_0, X, q_0] \rightarrow 0\ [q_0, X, q_1]\ [q_1, X, q_0]$

   $[q_0, X, q_1] \rightarrow 0\ [q_0, X, q_0]\ [q_0, X, q_1]$

   $[q_0, X, q_1] \rightarrow 0\ [q_0, X, q_1]\ [q_1, X, q_1]$

   since $\delta(q_0, 0, X) = \{(q_0, XX)\}$

2. $[q_0, X, q_1] \rightarrow 1$ since $\delta(q_0, 1, X) = \{(q_1, \lambda)\}$

3. $[q_1, z_0, q_1] \rightarrow \lambda$ since $\delta(q_1, \lambda, z_0) = \{(q_1, \lambda)\}$

4. $[q_1, X, q_1] \rightarrow \lambda$ since $\delta(q_1, \lambda, X) = \{(q_1, \lambda)\}$

5. $[q_1, X, q_1] \rightarrow 1$ since $\delta(q_1, 1, X) = \{(q_1, \lambda)\}$

It should be noted that there are no productions for the variables $[q_1, X, q_0]$ and $[q_1, z_0, q_0]$. As all the productions for $[q_0, X, q_0]$ and $[q_0, z_0, q_0]$ have $[q_1, X, q_0]$ or $[q_1, z_0, q_0]$ on the right, no terminal string can be derived from $[q_0, X, q_0]$ or $[q_0, z_0, q_0]$ either. Deleting all productions involving one of these four variables on either the right or left , we end up with the following productions.

$$S \to [q_0, z_0, q_1]$$

$$[q_0, z_0, q_1] \to 0\,[q_0\, X, q_1]\,[q_1, z_0, q_1]$$

$$[q_1, X, q_1] \to 0\,[q_0, X, q_1]\,[q_1, X, q_1]$$

$$[q_0, X, q_1] \to 1$$

$$[q_1, z_0, q_1] \to \lambda$$

$$[q_1, X, q_1] \to \lambda$$

$$[q_1, X, q_1] \to 1$$

3.4. Pumping Lemma For CFL

The pumping lemma for regular set states that every sufficiently long string in a regular set contains a short substring that can be pumped. That is, inserting as many copies of the substring as we like always yields a string in the regular set.

The pumping lemma for CFL's states that there are always two short substrings close together that can be repeated, both the same number of times as often as we alike. The construction we make use of in proving pumping lemma yields some decision algorithms regarding CFLs.

3.4.1. Lemma

Let G be a context free grammar in CNF and T be a derivation tree in G. If the length of the longest path in T is less than or equal to k, then the yield of T is of length less than or equal to 2^{k-1}.

Proof. We prove the result by induction on k, the length of the longest path for all A-trees (Recall an A-tree is a derivation tree whose root has a label A).

When the longest path in an A-tree is of length 1, the root has only one son whose label is a terminal (when the root has two sons, the labels are variables). So the yield is of length *1*. Thus there is a basis for induction.

Assume the result for $k - 1$ $(k > 1)$. Let T be an A-tree with the longest path of length less than or equal to k. As $k > 1$, the root of T has exactly two sons with labels A_1 and A_2. The two subtrees with the two sons are roots have longest paths of length less than or equal to $k - 1$.

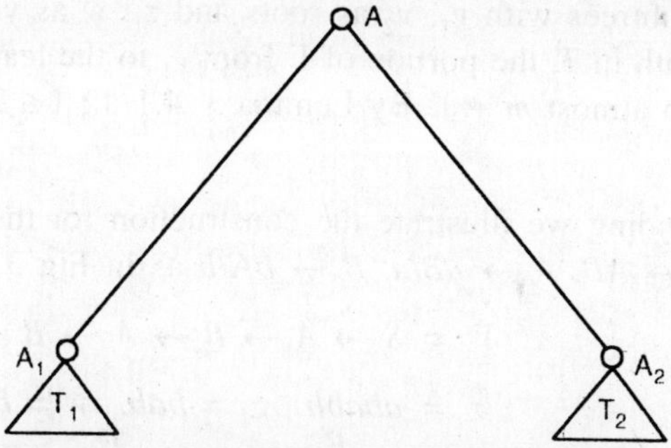

Fig. 3.2. Tree T with subtrees T_1 and T_2.

If w_1 and w_2 are their yields, then by induction hypothesis, $|w| \leq 2^{k-2}$, $|w_2| \leq 2^{k-2}$. So the yield of $T = w_1w_2$, $|w_1w_2| \leq 2^{k-2} + 2^{k-2} = 2^{k-1}$. By the priniciple of induction, the result is true for all A-trees, and hence for all derivation trees.

3.4.2. Theorem

(Pumping lemma for context free languages). Let L be a context free language. Then we can find a natural number n such that

(*i*) every $z \in L$ with $|z| \geq n$ can be written as $uvwxy$ for some strings u, v, w, x, y.

(*ii*) $|vx| \geq 1$.

(*iii*) $|vwx| \leq n$.

(*iv*) $uv^k wx^k y \in L$ for all $k \geq 0$.

Proof. We can decide whether or not $\lambda \in L$. When $\lambda \in L$, we consider $L - \{\lambda\}$ and construct a grammar $G = (N, T, S, P)$ in CNF generating $L - \{\lambda\}$ (when $\lambda \notin L$, we construct G in CNF generating L).

Let $|N| = m$ and $n = 2^m$. To prove that n is the requred number, we start with $z \in L$, $|z| \geq 2^m$, and construct a derivation tree T (parse tree) of z. If the length of a longest path in T is atmost m, by 3.4.1, $|z| \leq 2^{m-1}$ (since z is the yield of T). But $|z| \geq 2^m > 2^{n-1}$. So T has a path say Γ of length greater than or equal to $m + 1$. Γ has atleast $m + 2$ vertices and only the last vertex is a leaf. Thus in Γ all the labels except the last one are variables. As $|N| = m$, some label is repeated.

We choose a repeated label as follows. We start with leaf of Γ and travel along Γ upwards. We stop when some label, say B is reapeated. (Among several repeated labels B is the first). Let v_1 and v_2 be the vertices with label B, v_1 being nearer the root. In Γ, the portion of the path from v_1 to leaf has only one label viz., B, which is repeated, and so its length is atmost $m + 1$.

Let T_1 and T_2 be subtrees with v_1, v_2 as roots and z_1, w as yields respectively. As Γ is a longest path in T, the portion of Γ from v_1 to the leaf is a longest path in T_1 and the length atmost $m + 1$. By Lemma 3. 4.1, $|z_1| \leq 2^m$ (since z_1 is the yield of T_1).

For better understanding we illustrate the construction for the grammar whose productions are $S \to AB$, $A \to aB/a$, $B \to bA/b$ as in Fig 3.2. In the figure

$$\Gamma = S \to A \to B \to A \to B \to b$$

$$z = ababb, \quad z_1 = bab, \quad w = b$$

$$v = ba, \; x = \lambda, \; u = a, \; y = b$$

As z and z_1 are the yields of T and a proper subtree T_1 of T, we can write $z = uz_1y$. As z_1 and w are the yields of T, and a proper subtree T_2 of T_1, we can write $z_1 = vwx$. Also $|vwx| > |w|$. So $|vx| \geq 1$. Thus we have $z = uvwxy$ with $|vwx| \leq n$ and $|vx| \geq 1$. This proves points (*i*)-(*iii*) of the theorem.

As T is an S–tree and T_1, T_2 are B–trees, we get $S \overset{*}{\Rightarrow} u\,By$, $B \overset{*}{\Rightarrow} vBx$ and

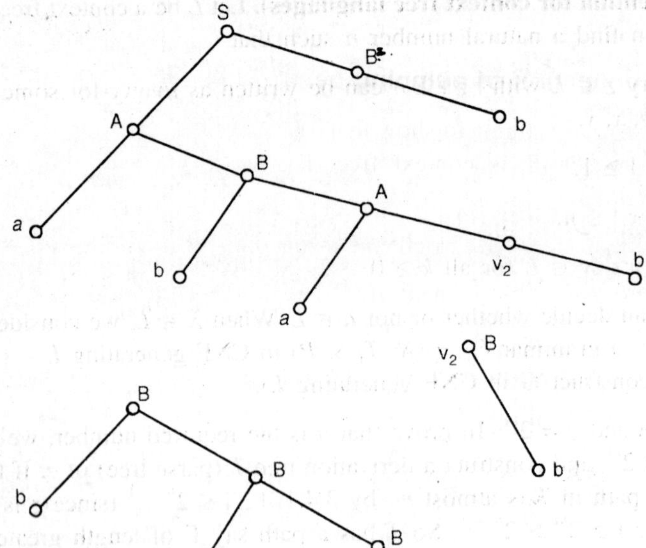

Fig. 3.3.

Tree T and its subtrees T_1 and T_2

$B \overset{*}{\Rightarrow} w$. As $S \overset{*}{\Rightarrow} uBy \Rightarrow Uwy$, $uv^o w\, x^o y \in L$.

For $k \geq 1$,

$S \overset{*}{\Rightarrow} uBy \overset{*}{\Rightarrow} uv^k Bx^k y \overset{*}{\Rightarrow} uv^k wx^k y \in L$. This proves (*iv*) of theorem.

3.4.3. Corollary

Let L be a context free language and n be the natural number obtained by using pumping lemma. Then (*a*) $L \neq \phi$ if and only if there exists $w \in L$ with $|w| < n$, and (*b*) L is infinite if and only if there exists $z \in L$ such that $n \leq |z| < 2n$.

Proof. (*a*) We have to prove the 'only if ' part. If $z \in L$ with $|z| \geq n$, we apply pumping lemma to write $z = uvwxy$, where $1 \leq |vx| \leq n$. Also, $uwy \in L$ and $|uwy| < |z|$. Applying pumping lemma repeatedly we can get $z' \in L$ such that $|z'| < n$. Thus (*a*) is proved.

(*b*) If $z \in L$ such that $n \leq |z| < 2n$, by pumping lemma we can write $z = uvwxy$. Also $uv^k wx^k y \in L$ for all $k \geq 0$. Thus we get infinite number of elements in L. conversely, if L is infinite, we can find $z \in L$ with $|z| \geq n$. If $|z| < 2n$, there is nothing to prove. Otherwise, we can apply pumping lemma to write $z = uvwxy$ and get $uwy \in L$. Every time we apply pumping lemma to get a smaller string and the decrease in length is atmost n (being equal to $|vx|$). So we ultimately get a string z' in L such that $n \leq |z'| < 2n$. This proves (*b*).

3.4.3. Application of pumping Lemma

We use pumping lemma to show that a language L is not a context free language. We assume that L is context free. By Applying pumping lemma we get a contradiction.

The procedure can be carried out using the following steps.

Step 1. Assume L is context free. Let n be the natural number obtained by using the pumping lemma.

Step 2. Choose $z \in L$ so that $|z| \geq n$. Write $z = uvwxy$ using the pumping lemma.

Step 3. Find a suitable k so that $uv^k wx^k y \notin L$. This is a contradiction, and so L is not context free.

Example 1. Show that $L = \{a^n b^n c^n / n \geq 1\}$ is not context free but context sensitive.

Solution. We know that

$G = (\{S, B, C\}, \{a, b, c\}, S, \{S \rightarrow aSBC/aBC, CB \rightarrow BC, aB \rightarrow ab, bB \rightarrow bb, bC \rightarrow bc, cC \rightarrow cc\})$ generates L. We note that in every string of L any symbol appears the same number of times as any other symbol. Also, a cannot appear after b and c cannot appear before b and so on.

Step 1. Assume that L is context free. Let n be the natural number obtained by using pumping Lemma.

Step 2. Let $z = a^n b^n c^n$. Then $| z | = 3n > n$. Write $z = uvwxy$, where $| vx | \geq 1$ *i.e.*, atleast one of v or x is not λ.

Step 3. $uvwxy = a^n b^n c^n$. As $1 \leq | vx | \leq n$, v or x contain all the three symbols a, b, c. So (*i*) v or x of the form $a^i b^j$ (or $b^i c^j$) for some i, j such that $i + j \leq n$ or (*ii*) v or x is a string formed by the repetition of only one symbol among a, b, c.

When v or x is of the form $a^i b^j$, $v^2 = a^i b^j a^i b^j$ (or $x^2 = a^i b^j a^i b^j$).As v^2 is a substring of uv^2wx^2y, uv^2wx^2y cannot be of the form $a^m b^m c^m$ .So $uv^2wx^2y \notin L$. When both v and x are formed by the repetition of a single symbol (*e.g.* $u = a^i$ and $v = b^j$ for some i and j, $i \leq n$, $j \leq n$), the string uwy will contain the remaining symbol, say a_1. Also a_1^n will be a substring of uwy as a_1 does not occur in v or x. The number of occurrences of one of the other two symbols in uwy is less than n. (recall $uvwxy = a^n b^n c^n$), and n is the number of occurrences of a_1. So $uv^0wx^0y = uwy \notin L$.

Thus for any choice of v or x, we get a contradiction. Therefore L is not context free.

Example 2. Prove that $L = \{0^p / p$ is prime$\}$ is not a context free language.

Solution. We use the following property of L. If $w \in L$, the $| w |$ is prime.

Step 1. Suppose $L = L(G)$ is context free. Let n be the natural number obtained by using the pumping lemma.

Step 2. Let p be a prime number greater than n. Then $z = o^p \in L$. we write $z = uvwxy$.

Step 3. By pumping lemma, $uv^0wx^0y = uwy \in L$. so $| uwy |$ is a prime number, say q. Let $| vx | = r$. Then $| uv^qwx^qy| = q + qr$. As $q + qr$ is not a prime, $uv^qwx^qy \notin L$. This is a contradiction. Therefore, L is not context free.

3.4.4. Decision Algorithm for context free language

In this section we give some decision algorithm for context free languages and regular sets.

(*i*) **Algorithm for deciding whether a context free language is empty.** We can apply the construction given in 2.4.1. for getting $N' = w_k$. L is non-empty if and only if $S \in W_k$.

(*ii*) **Algorithm for deciding whether a context free language L is finite.** Construct a non-redundant context free grammar G in CNF generating $L - \{\lambda\}$. We draw a directecd graph whose vertices are variables in Γ.

If $A \to BC$ is a production, there are directed edges from A to B and A to C. L is finite if and only if the directed graph has no cycles.

(*iii*) **Algorithm for deciding whether a regular language L is empty.** Construct a deterministic finite automaton M accepting L. We construct the set of all states reachable from q_0 by applying a single input symbol. These states are arranged as a row under columns corresponding to every input symbol. The construction is repeated for every state appearing in an earlier row. The construction terminates in a finite number of steps. If a final state appears in this tabular column, then L is non-empty. (Actually, we can terminate the construction as soon as some final state is obtained in the tabular column). Otherwise, L is empty.

(*iv*) **Algorithm for deciding whether a regular language L is infinite.** Construct a deterministic finite automaton M accepting L. L is infinite if and only if M has a cycle.

3.4.5. Theorem

The language $L = \{x \in \{a, b\}^* / x = x^r\}$ cannot be accepted by any DPDA.

Proof. Suppose for the sake of contradiction that $M = (Q, \{a, b\}, \Gamma, q_0, z_0, A, \delta)$ is a DPDA accepting L. We can easily modify M if necessary so that every move is either one of the form

$$\delta\,(p, s, X) = (q, \lambda)$$

or one of the form

$$\delta\,(p, s, X) = (q, \alpha, X)$$

where $s \in \{a, b, \lambda\}$ and $\alpha \in \Gamma^*$. The effect of modification is that M can still remove a symbol from the stack or place another symbol on the stack, but if cannot do both in the same move.

We observe next that for any string x, M must eventually read every symbol of x. The string xx^r, for example is a palindrome, and M must read it completely in order to accept it. However becuase M is deterministic, the moves it makes while processing x in the course of accepting xx^r are exactly the moves it must make on input x, whether or not x is followed by anything else.

After M has processed a string x, its stack is in a certain height, depending on how much M needs to remember about x. We may consider how much shorter the stack can ever get as a result of reading subsequent input symbols. For each x, let y_x be a string for which this resulting stack height is as small as possible. (It cannot be 0, because M must still be able to process longer strings with prefix xy_x.) In other words,

$$(q_0, xy_x, z_0) \overset{*}{\vdash} (q_x, \lambda, \alpha_x)$$

for some state q_x and some string $\alpha_x \in \Gamma^*$ with $|\alpha_x| > 0$, and for any string y, any state p, and any string $\beta \in \Gamma^*$,

$$\text{if } (q_0, xy, z_0) \overset{*}{\vdash} (p, \lambda, \beta) \text{ then } |\beta| \geq |\alpha_x|$$

Because of our initial assumption about the moves of M, any move that involves removing a stack symbol decreases the stack height. Therefore, once M reaches the configuration (q_x, λ, α_x), as a result of processing the string xy_x, no symbols of the string α_x will ever be removed from the stack subsequently.

Let A_x be the first symbol of the string α_x. The set S of all strings of the form xy_x is infinite (because we may consider x of any length) and the set of all ordered pairs (q_x, A_x) is finite (because the entire set $Q \times \Gamma$ is finite). Therefore, there must be an infinite subset T of S so that for all the elements xy_x of T, the pairs (q_x, A_x) are equal. In particular, we can choose two different strings $u_1 = xy_x$ and $u_2 = wy_w$ so that

$$(q_0, u_1, z_0) \vdash (q, \lambda, A\beta_1)$$

and $$(q_0, u_2, z_0) \overset{*}{\vdash} (q, \lambda, A\beta_2)$$

for some $q \in Q$, some $A \in \Gamma$, and some strings $\beta_1, \beta_2 \in \Gamma^*$. If we now look at longer strings of the form u_1z and u_2z, we have

$$(q_0, u_1z, z_0) \overset{*}{\vdash} (q, z, A\beta_1)$$

and $$(q_0, u_2z, z_0) \overset{*}{\vdash} (q, z, A\beta_2)$$

and the symbol A is never removed from the stack as a result of processing the string z. The reason this is useful is that although the stack contents may not be the same in the two cases, the machine can never notice the difference. The ultimate result of processing the string u_1z must be exactly the same as that of processing u_2z. Either both strings are acccepted or neither is. Now however, we have the contradiction we are looking for. On the one hand, M treats u_1z and u_2z the same way; on the otherhand, the two strings u_1 and u_2 are distinguishable with respect to L, so that for some z, one of the strings u_1z, u_2z is in L and the other is not. This is impossible if M accepts L.

3.4.6. Theorem

The intersection of a context free language with a regular language is a context free language.

Proof. If L is a context free language and R is a reuglar set, then $L = L(M_1)$ for some $R = L(M_2)$ for some determinisitic finite state automata $M_2 = (Q_2, \Sigma_2, \delta_2, q_2, F_2)$.

The idea is to combine these machines into a single pushdown automaton M

that carries out computations by M_1 and M_2 in parallel and accepts only if both would have accepted.

Specifically, let

$$M = (Q, \Sigma, \Gamma, \delta, q_0, z_0, F)$$

where
$$Q = Q_1 \times Q_2$$
$$\Sigma = \Sigma_1 \cup \Sigma_2$$
$$\Gamma = \Gamma_1$$
$$q_0 = \{q_1, q_2\}$$
$$F = F_1 \times F_2$$
$$Z_0 = Z_1$$

and the transitión function δ is defined by

$$\delta(\{q_1, q_2\}, u, \beta) = \{(\{p_1, p_2\}, v)\} \text{ iff}$$

$$\delta_1(q_1, u, \beta) = \{(p_1, v)\} \qquad \text{...(3.20)}$$

and

$$\delta(q_2, u) \vdash_M^* (p_2, \lambda) \qquad \text{...(3.21)}$$

That is M passes from state (q_1, q_2) to state $\{p_1, p_2\}$ in the same way that M_1, passes from state q_1 to p_1, except that in addition M keeps track of the change in the state of M_2 caused by reading the same input. (3.20) is easy to check, since a deterministic finite automaton reads a single symbol on each move. Thus, in practice , we could construct M by repeatedly choosing a transition $\delta(q_1, u, \beta) = \{(p, \gamma)\}$ of M_1 of a state q_2 and M_2 and simulating M_2 for $|u|$ steps on input u to determine what state p_2 it would reach after reading that input.

3.4.7. Example

Let L consist of all strings of $a's$ and $b's$ with equal numbers of $a's$ and $b's$ but not containing substring $abaa$ or $babb$. Then L is context free, since it is the intersection of the language accepted by pushdown automaton and with the regular language $\{a, b\}^* - \{a, b\}^* \{abaa, babb\} \{a, b\}^*$.

3.5. DETERMINISTIC CONTEXT FREE LANGUAGES (DCFL) AND DETERMINISTIC PUSHDOWN AUTOMATA (DPDA)

3.5.1. Definition

Let $M = (Q, \Sigma, \Gamma, \delta, q_0, Z_0, F)$ be a pushdown automaton. M is deterministic if there is no configuration for which M has a choice of more than one move.

In otherwords, M is deterministic if it statistics both the following conditions

1. For any $q \in Q$, a $\Sigma \cup \{\lambda\}$ and $X \in \Gamma$, the set $\delta\ (q, a, X)$ has atmost one element.

2. For any $q \in Q$ and $X \in \Gamma$, if $\delta\ (q, \lambda, X) \neq \phi$, then $\delta\ (q, a\ X) = \phi$ for every $a \in \Sigma$.

A langu ge L is said to be a *Deterministic Context Free Language* (DCFL) if and only if there is a deterministic PDA (DPDA) such that $L = L(M)$.

3.5.2. Example

Consider a PDA

$M = (Q, \Sigma , \Gamma, \delta, q_0, Z_0, F\ )$

where $Q = \{q_0, q_1\}, \Sigma = \{a, b\}, \Gamma = \{z_0, a, b\}, F = \{q_1\}$

and δ is defined as follows.

$$\begin{aligned}
\delta\ (q_0, a, z_0) &= \{(q_1, z_0)\}\\
\delta\ (q_0, b, z_0) &= \{(q_0, bz_0)\}\\
\delta\ (q_0, a, b) &= \{(q_0, \lambda)\}\\
\delta\ (q_0, b, b) &= \{(q_0, bb)\}\\
\delta\ (q_1, a, z_0) &= \{(q_1, az_0)\}\\
\delta\ (q_1, b, z_0) &= \{(q_0, z_0)\}\\
\delta\ (q_1, a, a) &= \{(q_1, aa)\}\\
\delta\ (q_1, b, a) &= \{(q, \lambda)\}
\end{aligned}$$

Clearly M is a DPDA.

The syntax of many programming languages can be described by means of Deterministic context free languages (DCFL's). A compiler be described by means of a context-free grammar of restricted form, which are nothing but the *LR*-grammars. The *LR*-grammars have the property that they generate exactly the DCFL's.

DPDA's are in *normal form,* is like a PDA's are in normal form, where the only stack operations are to erase the top symbol or to push one symbol.

3.5.3. Lemma

Every DCFL is $L\ (M)$ for a DPDA

$M = (Q, \Sigma, \Gamma, \delta\ , q_0, z_0, F)$ such that if $\delta\ (q, a, X) = (p, v)$ then $|\ v\ | \leq 2$.

Proof. Suppose $\delta\ (q, a, X) = (r, v)$ and $|\ v\ | > 2$. Let $v = X_1\ X_2 ... X_n$, with $n \geq 3$, create new non-accepting state $p_1, p_2, ..., p_{n-2}$ and redefine

$$\delta = (q, a\ X) = (p_1, y_{n-1}\ y_n)$$

$$\delta\ (p_i, \varepsilon, y_{n-i}) = (p_{i+1}, y_{n-i-1}\ y_{n-i})$$

for all $1 \leq i \leq n - 3$, and $\delta\ (p_{n-2}, \varepsilon, y_2) = (r, y_1\ y_2)$.

Now $(q, a, X) \vdash (p_1, \varepsilon, y_{n-1}\ y_n) \vdash (p_2, \varepsilon, y_{n-2} y_{n-1}\ y_n)$

$$\vdash (p_3, \varepsilon, y_{n-3}\ y_{n-2}\ y_{n-1}\ y_n) \overset{*}{\vdash} (p_{n-2}, \varepsilon, y_2\ y_3\ ...\ y_n)$$

$$\vdash (r, \varepsilon, y_1\ y_2\ ...\ y_n).$$

That is, in state q, on input a, with X on top of the stack, the revised DPDA still replaces X by $v = y_1\ y_2\ ...\ y_n$ and enters state r but it takes $(n - 1)$ moves to do so. Hence a contradiction.

The above lemma shows that the DPDA can never push more than one symbol per move.

3.5.4. Lemma

Every DCFL is $L\ (M)$ for a DPDA

$M = (Q, \Sigma, \Gamma, \delta, q_0, z_0, F)$ such that if $\delta\ (q, a, X) = (p, v)$, then v is either ε, (a, pop), X (no stack move), or of the form $Y\ X$ (a push) for some stack symbol y.

Proof. Assume $L = L\ (M')$, where $M' = (Q', \Sigma\ \Gamma', \delta', q_0', x_0, F')$ satisfies Lemma 3.5.3. Construct M simulate M' while keeping the top stack symbol of M' in M's control. Formally, let

$Q = Q' \times \Gamma'$, $q_0 = [q_0', X_0]$, $F = F \times \Gamma'$ and $\Gamma = \Gamma' \cup \{Z_0\}$, where Z_0 is a new symbol not in Γ'. Define δ by:

(*i*) $\delta\ ([q, X], a, y) = ([p, Y], \varepsilon)$, if $\delta'\ (q, a, X) = (p, \varepsilon)$, for all y. That is, if M' pops its stack, M also pops its stack.

(*ii*) $\delta\ ([q, X], a\ Z) = ([p, Y], Z)$, if $\delta'\ (q, a, X) = (p, Y)$, for all Z. That is, of M' changes its top stack symbol, then M records the change in its own control, but does not alter the change.

(*iii*) $\delta\ ([q, X], a, W) = ([p, y], Z\ W)$ if

$$\delta'\ (q, a, X) = (p, y\ W), \text{ for all } W.$$

By induction it can be shown that

$$(q_0', w, X_0) \overset{*}{\underset{M'}{\vdash}} (q, \varepsilon, X_1 X_2 ...\ X_n)$$

if and only if

$$([q_0', X_0)], W, Z_0) \overset{*}{\underset{M}{\vdash}} ([q, X_1], \varepsilon, X_2 ... X_n Z_0).$$

Thus $$L(M) = L(M').$$

3.5.5. Lemma

Let M be a DPDA. There exists an equivalent DPDA M' such that on every input, M' scans the entire input.

Proof. Let $M = (Q, \Sigma, \Gamma, \delta, q_0, Z_0, F)$. Define

$M' = (Q \cup \{q_0', d, f\}, \Sigma, \Gamma \cup \{X_0\}, \delta', q_0', X_0, F \cup \{f\})$ d is a dead state, where no next move is possible. On any input symbol, the only transition from d to d occurs, but no change of stack occurs. The action of δ' is as follows:

(*i*) $\delta'(q_0', \varepsilon, X_0) = (q_0, Z_0 X_0)$.

(*ii*) If $\delta(q, a, Z) = \phi$, $\delta(q, \varepsilon, Z) = \phi$, for some $q \in Q$, $a \in \Sigma$, $Z \in \Gamma$, then $\delta'(q, a\ Z) = (d, Z)$.

Also for all $q \in Q$, $a \in \Sigma$, $\delta'(q, a\ X_0) = (d, X_0)$

(*iii*) $\delta'(d, a, Z) = (d, Z)$, for all $a \in \Sigma$, $Z \in \Gamma \cup \{X_0\}$

(*iv*) If $(q, \varepsilon, Z) \overset{*}{\vdash} (q_i, \varepsilon, v_i)$, then

$$\delta'(q, \varepsilon, z) = (d, z), \text{ provided no } q_i \text{ is final}$$

and $\delta'(q, \varepsilon, z) = (f, z)$, whenever one or more of the q_i's one final.

(*v*) $\delta'(f_1, \varepsilon, z) = (d, z)$ for all $z \in \Gamma \cup \{X_0\}$.

(*vi*) For any $q \in Q$, $a \in \Sigma \cup \{\varepsilon\}$, $z \in \Gamma$, if $\delta'(q, a, z)$ has not been defined by (*ii*) or (*iv*), then define $\delta'(q, a, z) = \delta(q, a, z)$.

Then $L(M) = L(M')$. M' uses all its input. Suppose, some input y is not used. Then we have an ID of the form $(q, y, Z_1, Z_2 .. Z_k X_0)$, such that

$$(q_0', xy, X_0) \overset{*}{\underset{M}{\vdash}} (q, y, Z_1 Z_2, ... Z_k X_0).$$

By (*ii*) it is not possible that M' halts. By (*iv*) it is not possible that M' makes an infinite sequence of ε-moves without erasing z_1. M' erases eventually enter an ID (q', y, X_0).

By rule (*ii*), $(q', y, X_0) \underset{M}{\vdash} (\alpha, y', X_0)$, where $y = ay'$, $a \in \Sigma$.

Hence M' reads all the inputs.

3.5.6. Theorem

The complement of DCFL is a DCFL.

Proof. Let $M = (Q, \Sigma, \Gamma, \delta, q_0, Z_0, F)$ be a DPDA satisfying Lemma 3.5.5. Let $M' = (Q', \Sigma, \Gamma, \delta', q_0, Z_0, F')$ be a DPDA simulating M, where

$$Q' = \{[q, k], q \in Q, k = 1, 2, 3\}$$

$$F' = \{[q, 3] = q \in Q\},$$

$$q_0' = \begin{cases} [q_0, 1] \text{ if } q_0 \in F \\ [q_0, 2] \text{ if } q_0, \notin F \end{cases}.$$

Construct Boolean-valued tables T_1, T_2, T_3 such taht

$T_i\ (q, z, p)$ is true $\Leftrightarrow (q, \varepsilon, z) \overset{*}{\underset{M}{\vdash}} (p, \varepsilon, z)$ for $i = 1, 2, 3$. T_i can be made true by induction.

Basis Step. $T_3\ (q, z, p)$ = true if $\delta\ (q, \varepsilon, z) = (p, yz)$

$$T_1\ (q, z, p) = T_3\ (q, z, p) = \textit{true} \text{ if}$$

$$\delta\ (q, \varepsilon, z) = (p, z),$$

$$T_2\ (q, z, p) = \textit{true} \text{ if } \delta\ (q, \varepsilon, z) = (p, \varepsilon).$$

Induction Step. Whenever $\delta\ (q, \varepsilon, z) = (r, y, yz)$,

then

(*a*) If $T_2\ (r, y, s)$ and $T_2\ (s, z, p)$ are *true*, then set $T_2\ (q, z, p)$ = true.

(*b*) If $T_2\ (r, y, s)$ and $T_1\ (s, z, p)$ are *true.*

set $T_1\ (q, z, p)$ = true.

(*c*) If $[T_2\ (r, y, s)$ and $T_3\ (s, z, p)]$ or $[T_1\ (r, y, s)$ and $T_3\ (s, y, p)]$ are true, set $T_3\ (q, z, p)$ = true.

(*d*) If $T_3\ (r, y, p)$ is true, set $T_3\ (q, z, p)$ = true.

2.Whenever $\delta\ (q, \varepsilon, z) = (r, z)$, then

(*a*) If $T_1\ (r, z, p)$ is true, set $T_1\ (q, z, p)$ = true.

(*b*) If $T_2\ (r, z, p)$ is true, set $T_2\ (q, z, p)$ = true.

(*c*) If $T_3\ (r, z, p)$ is true, set $T_3\ (q, z, p)$ = true.

Here k in $[q, k]$ record between true inputs, whether or not M has entered an accepting state. If M has entered an accepting state since the last true input, then $k = 1$. If M does not enter an accepting state since the last true input, then $k = 2$.

If $k = 1$, when M reads a true input symbol, then M' simulates M and changes k to 1 or 2 depending on the new state of M is in F or not in F. If $k = 2$, M' changes k to 3, and then simulates M and changes k to 1 or 2, depending on the new state of M is in F or not in F. Thus δ' is defined as follows:

(*i*) $\delta'([q, k], \varepsilon, z) = ([p, k'], v)$

if $\delta(q, \varepsilon, z) = (p, v)$, for $k = 1$ or 2, and $k' = 1$ if $k = 1$; $k' = 2$ if $k =$ 2.

(*ii*) $\delta'([q, 2], \varepsilon, z) = \delta'([q, 3], z)$

$$\delta'([q, 1], a, z) = \delta'([q, 3], a, z) = ([p, k], v)$$

if $\delta(q, a, z) = (p, v)$, $a \in \Sigma$, and

$k = 1$ or 2 for $p \in F$ or not in F respectively.

$L(M')$ is the complement of $L(M)$. For, if $a_1 a_2 \ldots a_n \in L(M)$. Then M enters an accepting state after reading a_n. Correspondingly, the second component of the state of M' is 1 before it is possible for M' to use a true input after a_n.

Hence M' does not accept by entering a state whose second component is 3, and a_n was the last true input used.

Suppose $a_1 a_2 \ldots a_n \notin L(M)$. Then by Lemma 3.5.5, M' after reading a_n have no ε-moves and will have to use a true input symbol. At this time, the second component of M' is 2, since $a_1 a_2 \ldots a_n \notin L(M)$. By rule (2), M' will accept before using a true input symbol.

3.5.7. Corollary

Every DCFL is accepted by some DPDA.

Proof. Follows from Theorem 3.5.4.

3.5.8. Example

The language $L = \{0^i 1^j 2^k : i = j \text{ or } j = k\}$

is not DCFL.

Let L be generated by a grammar whose productions are

$S \to AB/CD$, $A \to 0A^1/\varepsilon$, $B \to 2B/\varepsilon$, $C \to 0C/\varepsilon$, $D \to 1D2/\varepsilon$.

Using odgen's Lemma, we can prove $L_1 = \{0^i 1^j 2^k : i \neq j, j \neq k\}$ is not a CFL, hence not a DCFL. Also

$L_1 = \overline{L} \cap 0^* 1^* 2^*$, As L_1 is not DCFL, $\overline{L}$ is not DCFL, and hence L is not DCFL.

3.5.9. Lemma

Let $M = (Q, \Sigma, \Gamma, \delta, q_0, Z_0, F)$ be a DPDA. Let B be any subset of $Q \times \Gamma$. Define $L = \{w \;:\; (q_0, w, Z_0) \overset{*}{\vdash} (q, \varepsilon, Z\, v)$ for some $(q, z)\, \varepsilon B\}$.

Then L is DCFL.

Proof. Define a DPDA M' accepting L as follows:

$$M' = (Q^1, \Sigma, \Gamma, \delta'\, q_0, z_0, F')$$

where

$$Q' = \{q, q', q'' : q \in Q\}$$

$$F' = \{q''\}$$

Define δ' as follows.

(*i*) If $\delta\,(q, a, z) = (p, v)$, then

$$\delta'\,(q, a, z) = (p', v)$$

(*ii*) If $(q, z) \notin B$, then

$$\delta'\,(q', \varepsilon, z) = (q, z).$$

(*iii*) If $(q, z) \in B$

$$\delta'\,(q', \varepsilon, z) = (q'', z) \text{ and}$$

$$\delta'\,(q'', \varepsilon, z) = (q, z).$$

Recall that the quotient of L_1 with respect to L_2, denoted by L_1/L_2 is $\{x :$ there exists w in L_2 such that xw is in $L_1\}$.

3.5.10. Theorem

Let L be a DCFL and R be a regular set. Then L/R is a DCFL.

Proof. Let $L = L\,(M)$ for some DPDA M. Let $R = L\,(A)$ for some finite state automaton A. Suppose $M = (Q_M, \Sigma, \Gamma, \delta_M, q_0, Z_0, F_M)$ and $A = (Q_A, \Sigma, \delta_A, p_0, F_A)$. Then let $M' = \pi\,(M, A) = (Q_M, \Sigma, \Gamma \times \Delta, \delta, q_0, [Z_0, \mu_0], F_M)$ be the predicting machine for M and A, where Δ is set of subset of $Q_M \times Q_A$. If $\pi\,(M, A)$ is in $ID\,(r, x, [z, \mu]\, v)$, the μ consists of exactly those paris (q, p) such that there is a $w \in \Sigma^*$ for which $\delta_A\,(p, w) \in F_A$ and $(q, w, z_\beta) \overset{*}{\underset{M}{\vdash}} (s, \varepsilon, \alpha)$ for some $s \in F_M$, $\alpha, \beta \in \Gamma^*$, where β is the string of first components of v.

Let Mq, z be M with q and z as the starting state and start stack symbol respectively. Let Ap be A with p as the starting state. Let

$$M_0 = \{(q, p) : L\,(Mq, z_0) \cap L\,(Ap) \neq \phi\}$$

Then $$(q_0, x, [z_0\; \mu_0]) \overset{*}{\underset{\pi\,(M, A)}{\vdash}} (r, y, [z_1, \mu_1]\, [z_2, \mu_2] \ldots [z_n, \mu_n$$

if and only if

(*a*) $(q_0, x, z_0) \overset{*}{\underset{M}{\vdash}} (r, y, z_1 z_2, \ldots z_n)$

(*b*) $\mu_i = \{(q, p) :$ for some $w, (q, w, z_i\, z_{i+1} \ldots z_n \overset{*}{\underset{M}{\vdash}} (s, \varepsilon, v)$ for some $s\ \varepsilon$

F_M, $v \in \Gamma^*$, and $\delta_A (p, w) \in F_A\}$ for $1 \le i \le n$.

Now, let B be the subset of $Q_M \times (\Gamma \times \Delta)$ containing all $(q, [z, \mu])$ with (q, p_0) is in μ. Then by Lemma 3.5.9.

$L_1 = \{x : (q_0, x, [z_0, \mu_0] \overset{*}{\underset{M}{\vdash}} (q, \varepsilon, [z, \mu]\ v$ and $(q, p_0) \in \mu\}$ is a DCFL. Also

$L_1 = \{x :$ for some $w \in \Sigma^*, (q_0, x, z_0) \overset{*}{\underset{M}{\vdash}} (q, \varepsilon, Z\ v^1)$

$(q, w, Zv') \overset{*}{\underset{M}{\vdash}} (s, \varepsilon, \beta)\ s \in F_M$, v' is the first component of v; $\delta_A (p_0, w) \in F_A$.

That is, $L_1 = \{x :$ for some $w \in \Sigma^*, x\ w \in L\ (M)$ and $w \in L\ (A)\}$.

Hence $L_1 = L/R$. Thus L_1 is a DCFL.

Now we introduce two operations that preserve DCFL's but not CFL's

MIN(L) = $\{x : x \in L$ and no w in L is a proper prefix of $x\}$

MAX (L) = $\{ x : x \in L$ and x is not a proper prefix of any word in $L\}$.

3.5.11. Theorem

If L is a DCFL, the MIN (L) and MAX (L) are DCFL's.

Proof. Let $M = (Q_M, \Sigma, \Gamma, \delta_M, q_0, Z_0, F_M)$ be a DPDA that accepts L and always scans its entire input. Modify M to make no move in a final state. Then the resulting DPDA M_1, accepts MIN (L). If $w \in$ MIN (L), then let

$$(q_0, w, Z_0) = I_0 \underset{M}{\vdash} I_1 \underset{M}{\vdash} \ldots \underset{M}{\vdash} I_M \ (*\ *)$$

be the sequence of ID's entered by M, where $I\mu = (q, \varepsilon, v)$ for some v, and q is in F_M. Furthermore, since w is in MIN (L), none of $I_0, I_1, \ldots, I_{m-1}$, has an accepting state. Thus (* *) is also a computation of M_1, so w is in L (M).

Conversely if $(q_0, w, Z_0) = I_0 \underset{M_1}{\vdash} I_1 \underset{M_1}{\vdash} I_2 \underset{M_1}{\vdash} \ldots \underset{M_1}{\vdash} I_m$ is an accepting computation of M_1, then none of $I_0, I_1, \ldots, I_{m-1}$ has an accepting state. Thus w is in MIN (L).

To show MAX(L) is a DCFL's. Let $A = (Q_A, \Sigma, \delta_A, p_0, F_A)$ be the simple FSA accepting Σ^+.

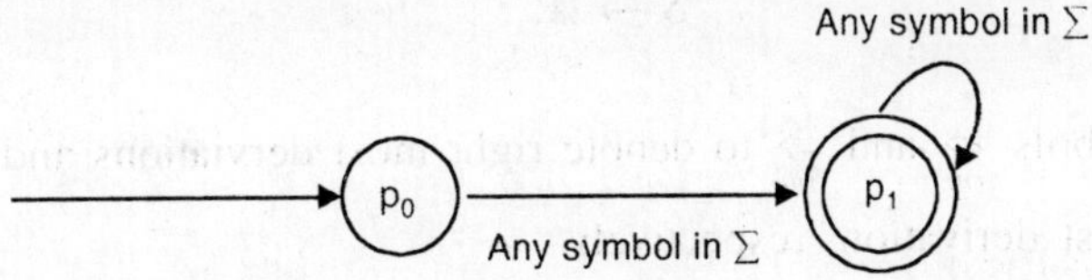

Fig. 3.4.

Let $M = (Q_M, \Sigma, \Gamma \times \Delta, \delta, q_0, [Z_0, \mu_0], F_M)$ be π (M, A). Let $B = \{(q, [z, \mu]) :$ q is in F_M, $(q, p)\mu\}$

Then

$L_1 = \{x : (q_0, z, z_0) \overset{*}{\underset{M}{\vdash}} (q, \varepsilon, v)$ for some q in F_M, and for no $w \neq \varepsilon$ does $(q, w, v) \overset{*}{\vdash} (s, \varepsilon, \beta)$ for s in $F_M\}$ is a DCFL. But L_1 = MAX (L), so MAX (L) is a DCFL.

3.6. LR (0) GRAMMAR

Next we introduce a restricted type of CFG called an *LR (0) grammar*. It stands for "left-to-right scan of the input producing a right most derivation and using 0 symbols of look ahead on the input".

3.6.1 Definition

L is said to have the *prefix property* if whenever w is in L, no proper prefix of w is in L.

3.6.2. Definition

An *item* for a given CFG is a production with a dot anywhere in the right side, including the beginning or end.

In the case of an ε-production, $B \to \varepsilon$, $B \to 0$ is an *item.*

3.6.3. Example

The *items* for grammar with the produciton $S' \to Sc$, $S \to SA/A$, $A \to ab$.

The *items* are,

$$S' \to \cdot\, Sc, \quad S \to \cdot\, SA \quad A \to \cdot ab$$

$$S' \to S\cdot\, c, \quad S \to S.A \quad A \to a\cdot b$$

$$S' \to Sc., \quad S \to SA. \quad A \to ab\cdot$$

$$S \to \cdot A$$

$$S \to A.$$

Use the symbols $\overset{*}{\underset{rm}{\Rightarrow}}$ and $\overset{*}{\underset{rm}{\Rightarrow}}$ to denote right most derviations and single steps in a right most derivation, respectively.

3.6.4. Definiton

A right-sentential form is a sentential form that can be derived by a right most derivation. A *handle* of a right sentential form v for CFG *G* is a substring β, such that

$$S \overset{*}{\underset{rm}{\Rightarrow}} \delta\, Aw \overset{*}{\underset{rm}{\Rightarrow}} \delta\, \beta w$$

and $\delta\, \beta\, w = v$. A *viable prefix* of a *right-sentential form* v is any prefix of v ending no further right than the right end of a *handle* of *u*.

For example, $S' \to SC$, $S \to SA/A$, $A \to aSb/ab$ produces a rightmost derivation.

$$S' \Rightarrow Sc \Rightarrow SA\ c \Rightarrow SaSbc.$$

Thus *SaSbc* is a *right-sentential form*, and its *handle* is *aSb*, ε, *S*, *Sa*, *SaS*.

An *item* $A \to \alpha\ .\ \beta$ is said to be *valid* for a viable prefix v if there is a right most derviation

$$S \overset{*}{\underset{rm}{\Rightarrow}} \delta\, Aw \overset{*}{\underset{rm}{\Rightarrow}} \delta\, \alpha\beta w$$

and $\delta\alpha = v$. An *item* is said to be *complete* if the dot is the right most symbol in the *item*. For example, $A \to \alpha.$ is a *complete item*.

3.6.5. Definition

G is said to be an *LR (0) grammar* if

(*i*) its start symbol does not appear on the right side of any production, and

(*ii*) for every viable prefiex v of *G*, whenever $A \to \alpha\cdot$ is a complete item valid for v, then no other *complete item* nor any item with a terminal to the right of the dot is valid for v.

Now we construct a DPDA from an *LR* (0) *grammar* which differs from the non-deterministic PDA which are constructed from an arbitrary CFL. We introduce a new notation for ID's of a DPDA. Here we use $[q, \alpha, w]$ instead of (q, w, α^R). To simulate right most derivations in an *LR*(0) *grammar* not only do we keep a viable prefix on the stack, but above every symbol we keep a state of the DFA recogninzing viable prefixes. If viable prefix $X_1 X_2 \ldots X_k$ is on the stack, then the complete stack contents will be $s_0 X_1 s_1, \ldots X_k s_k$ where s_i is δ $(q_0, X_1 X_2 \ldots X_i)$ and δ is the transition function of the DFA. The top state s_k provides the valid items for $X_1, X_2 \ldots X_k$.

If s_k contans $A \to \alpha\cdot$, then $A \to \alpha\cdot$ is valid for $X_1 X_2 \ldots X_k$. Thus α is a suffix of α to A by replacing $X_{i+1} X_{i+2} \ldots X_k$ on top of the stack by A. The DPDA will enter a sequence of ID's.

$$[q_1, \text{so } X_1 \ldots s_{k-1} X_k s_k, w] \overset{*}{\vdash} [q, s_0 X_1 \ldots s_{i-1} X_i s_i As, w] \qquad (3\cdot22)$$

where $s = \delta(s_i, A)$. Note that if the grammar is LR (0), s_k contains only $A \to \alpha\cdot$, unless $\alpha = \epsilon$, in which case s_k may contain some incomplete items.

Suppose s_k contains only incomplete items. Then the right sentential form previous to $X_1 X_2 \ldots X_k w$ could not be formed by reducing a suffix of $X_1 X_2 \ldots X_k$ to some variable else there would be a complete item valid for $X_1 X_2, \ldots X_k$. There must be a handle ending to the right of X_k in $X_1 \ldots X_k w$, as $X_1 \ldots X_k$ is a viable prefix. That is,

$$[q, s_0 X_1 \ldots s_{k-1} X_k s_k, ay) \vdash [q, So\ X_i \ldots s_{k-1} X_k s_k \text{ at } y] \qquad \ldots(3.23)$$

where $t = \delta\ (s_k, a)$. If t is not the empty set of items. $X_1 \ldots X_k\ a$ is a viable prefix.

3.6.6. Theorem

If L is L (G) for an $LR(0)$ grammar G, then L is N (M) for a DPDA M.

Proof. Construct from G, the DFA 'A' with transition function δ, that recognizes G's viable prefizes. Let the stack symbols of M be the grammar symbols of G and the states of A. M has starting state q together with some states used by reductions as in (3· *) & (3· **).

If G is LR (0), reductions are the only possible way to get the previous right-sentential form when the state of the DFA on the top of M's stack contains a complete item.

When M starts with w in L (G) on its input and only so on its stack, then it will construct a rightmost derivation for w in reverse order.

When a shift is, as in (3.22), because the top DFA state on M's stack has only incomplete items, then there could not be a handle among the grammar symbols $X_1 X_2, \ldots X_k$ found on the stack at that time. If there were such a handle, then some DFA state on the stack, below the top, would have a complete item.

If the top state on the stack is $\{S \to \alpha\}$ where S is G's start symbol, then G pops its stack, accepting. In this case we have completed the reverse of a rightmost derivation of the original input. Note that as S does not appear on the right of any production, it is impossible that there is an item of the form $A \to$

$S\cdot\alpha$ valid for viable prefix S. Thus there is never a need to shift additional input symbols when S alone appears on the stack. We proved if w is in $L(G)$, M finds a right most derivation of w, reduces w to S, and accepts. Conversely, if M accepts w, the sequence of right sentential forms represented by the ID's of M provides a derivation of w from S. Thus $N(M) = L(G)$.

3.6.7. Lemma

Let $M = (Q, \Sigma, \Gamma, \delta\, q_0, Z_0, \phi)$ be a DPDA. If L is $N(M)$, then L has an LR (0) grammar.

Proof. Let $M = (Q, \Sigma, \Gamma, \delta, q_0, Z_0, \phi)$ be a DPDA. Define grammar $G_M = (V, \Sigma, P, S)$ such that $L(G_M) = N(M)$. V consists of the symbol S, the symbols $[q \times p)$ for q and p in Q and X in Γ, and the symbols A_{qay} for q in Q, a in $\Sigma \cup \{\varepsilon\}$ and Y in Γ.

Symbol A_{qay} indicates that the production is obtained from the move of M in $\delta(q, a, y)$. The productions of G_M are as follows.

(*i*) $S \to [q_0, Z_0\, p]$ for all p in Q

(*ii*) If $\delta(q, a, y) = (p, \varepsilon)$, then there is a production $[q, y\, p] \to A_{qay}$

(*iii*) If $\delta(q, a, y) = (p_1, X_1 X_2 \ldots X_k)$ for $k \geq 1$, then for each sequence of states $p_2, p_3, \ldots, p_{k+1}$, there is a production $[qy\, p_{k+1}] \to A_{qay}\, [p_1 X_1\, p_2] \ldots [p_k\, X_k\, p_{k+1}]$

(*iv*) For all q, a and y, $A_{qay} \to a$.

The right most derivation in G_M starts with $S \Rightarrow [q_0\, z_0\, p]$ for some state p. The only productions for $[q_0\, z_0\, p\,]$ that derive strings beginning with right sides. $Aq_0\, az_0\, [r\, X\, s]\, [s\, y\, t]\, [t\, z\, p]$ for some states s and t. Suppose that the right most derivation finally derives some string w from $[t\, z\, p]$. If $\delta(s, b, y) = (u, Vw)$, then

$$S \underset{rm}{\overset{*}{\Rightarrow}} Aq_0az_0[\,rXs]\,[s\ y\ t]\ w \underset{rm}{\Rightarrow} A\ q_0\ a\ z_0\ [rXs]\ A_{sby}\ [uVv)\ [vWt]w. \tag{3.24}$$

The input corresponding to the above derivation is of the form $ax_1\, bx_2\, x_3\, w$, where $[rXs] \overset{*}{\Rightarrow} x_1$, $[u\ V\ v] \overset{*}{\Rightarrow} x_2$, $[vWt] \overset{*}{\Rightarrow} x_3$. The move is of the form

$$\begin{aligned}(q_0,\ ax_1bx_2x_3w_1Z_0) &\vdash (r,\ x,\ bx_2x_3w,\ XYZ)\\ &\overset{*}{\vdash} (s,\ bx_2\ x_3w,\ YZ)\\ &\vdash (u,\ x_2x_3\ w,\ VWZ)\\ &\vdash (v,\ x_3w,\ WZ)\\ &\vdash (t,\ w,\ Z).\end{aligned}$$

From (3.24) and (3.23) we conclude that given any viable prefix α of G_M, there corresponds ID I of M in which the stack contains all and only the stack symbols that were introduced in a right most derivation of some αw and then replaced by a string of terminals.

3.6.8. Lemma

Let v be a viable prefix of G_M. Then $(q_0, h(v), Z_0) \overset{N(v)}{\vdash} (p, \varepsilon, \beta)$, for some p and β by the sequence of moves $m(v)$.

Proof. As v is a viable prefix, there is some y in Σ^* such that vy is a right sentential form. Then for some state γ, $[q_0, Z_0\ r] \overset{*}{\underset{m}{\Rightarrow}} h(v)\ y$. The last $N(v)$ expansions of A' s in that derivation take place after the right sentential form vy is reached. There is a unique sequence of move $(q_0, h(v)\ y, z_0 \overset{*}{\vdash} (r, \varepsilon, \varepsilon)$, and the first $N(v)$ of these must be $m(v)$.

3.6.9. Lemma

If I is a set of items of G_M, and $B \to \beta.$ is in I, then there is no item $A_{qa}\nu \to \cdot a$ in I.

Proof. Let I be the set of items for viable prefix v.

Case 1. If $B \to \beta$ is a production from rule (i) then $v = \beta$, then v is a single vairbale $[q_0\ z_0\ p]$, since S appears on no right side. If $A_{qay} \to a$ valid for v, then there is a derivation $S \overset{*}{\Rightarrow} \nu\ A_{qay}\ y \underset{rm}{\Rightarrow} vay$. However, no right sentential form begins with a variable $[q_0\ z_0\ p]$ unless it is the first step of a derivation. All subsequent right-sentential forms begin with a subscripted A, until the last, which begins with a terminal. Thus ν could not be followed $A_{qa}\nu$ in a right sentential form.

Case 2. If $B \to \beta$ is introduced by rules (ii) or (iii) then $v'\beta\ A_{qa}\nu$ is a viable prefix, where $v = v'\ \beta$. In any rightmost derivation, when $B \to \beta$ is applied the last symbol of β is immediately expanded by rules (ii), (iii) or (iv), so β could not appear in a right-sentential form followed by $Aqa\nu$.

Case 3. If $B \to \beta$ is $A_{pbz} \to b$ introduced by rule (iv), and $A_{qay} \to \cdot\ a$ is valid for v, then b must be ε, else $v\ A_{qay}$, which is a viable prefix, has a terminal in it. As $A_{p\varepsilon z} \to$ is valid for v, it follows that $\nu A_{p\varepsilon z}$ is a viable-prefix. Thus by previous lemma applied to vA_{qay} and $vA_{p\varepsilon z}$, the first $N(v) + 1$ moves made by M when given input $h(\nu)a$ are both $m(v)\ (p\ \varepsilon\ z)$and in $m(\nu)\ (q\ a\ y)$, contradicting the determinism of M, where m is a homomorphism from v^* to moves defined by $m(A_{qay}) = qay$.

3.6.10 Lemma

If I is a set of items of G_M, and $B \to \beta.$ is in I, then there is no other item $C \to \alpha\cdot$ in I.

Proof. Let v be a viable prefix with set of valid items I.

Case 1. The productions $B \to \beta$, $C \to \alpha$ are not introduced by rule (*iv*). The productions of type (1) are applied only at the first step tell us that as α and β are both suffixes of v, we must have $\beta = \alpha$. If the productions are of type (2) or (3), then $B = C$. But rule (*ii*) requires that $\delta\ (q, a, Y) = (p, \varepsilon)$, so the determinism of M assures that p is unique.

Case 2. $B \to \beta$, $C \to \alpha$ are type (4) productions. Then vB and vC are viable prefixes and by Lemma, M is not deterministic. That is if $\beta = \alpha = \varepsilon$, then the first $N\ (v) + 1$ moves of M on input $h\ (v)$ must be $m\ (vB)$ and $m\ (vC)$. If $\beta = a \neq \varepsilon$, $\alpha = b \neq \varepsilon$, then $a = b$, and the first $N\ (v) + 1$ moves of M on.

input $h\ (v)$ a must be $m\ (vB)$ and $m\ (vC)$. If $\beta = a \neq \varepsilon$, $\alpha = \varepsilon$, then the first $N\ (v) + 1$ moves of M on input $h(v)\ a$ provides a contradiction.

Case 3. $B \to \beta$ is from rule (1) (2), or (3) and $C \to \alpha$ is from rule (4) or vice versa. Then vC is a right-sentential form, and v ends in β.

3.6.11. Theorem

If M is a DPDA, then G_M is an $LR(0)$ grammar.

Proof. Proof follows from Lemma 3.6.9 and 3.6.10.

3.6.12. Theorem

As language L has an LR (0) grammar if and only if L is a DCFL with the prefix property.

Proof. Suppose L is a DCFL with the prefix property. Then L is $L\ (M')$ for some DPDA M' we can make M' accept L by empty stack by putting a bottom-of-stack marker on M' and causing M' to enter a new state that erases the stack whenever it enters a final state. As L has the prefix property, we do not change the language accepted, k and L is accepted by empty stack by the new DPDA M. Hence $L = L\ (G_M)$.

Conversely, if L is $N\ (M)$ for some DPDA, M. Then we know that L is $L\ (M')$ for some DPDA M'. L has the prefix property follows from the fact that a DPDA 'dies' when it empties its stack.

3.6.13. Corollary

$L\ \$$ has $LR\,(0)$ grammar if and only if L is a DCFL, where \$ is not a symbol of L's alphabet.

Proof. $L\ \$$ surely has the prefix property. If $L\ \$$ is a DCFL, then $L = L\ \$/\$$ is a DCFL.

Conversely, if L is a DCFL, then it is easy to construct a DPDA for $L\ \$$.

3.7 PARSING

Parsing becomes important in the case of programming languages. If a statement in a programming language is given, only the derivation of the statement can give the meaning of the statement (semantics). There are two types of parsing.

(*i*) Top-down parsing.

(ii) Bottom-up parsing.

In top down parsing we try to construct the derivation (or the corresponding parse tree) of the input string, starting from the root (with label S) and end in the given input string. This is equivalent to a left most derivation. In bottom-up parsing we try the derivation from the given input string to the top.

3.7.1 Top Down Parsing

The language $L = \{a^n\ b^n : n \geq 0\}$ is generated by the context free grammar

$$G = (\{a, b, S\}, \{a, b\}, R, S,)$$ where R contains

the two rules $S \to aSb$, $S \to \lambda$. This L is accepted by a pushdown automaton.

$$M_1 = (\{p, q\}, \{a, b\}, \{a, b, S\}, \delta_1, p, \{q\}),$$

where

$$\begin{aligned}
\delta_1\,(p, \lambda, \lambda) &= (q, S)\\
\delta_1\,(q, \lambda, S) &= (q, aSb)\\
\delta_1\,(q, \lambda, S) &= (q, \lambda)\\
\delta_1\,(q, a, a) &= (q, \lambda)\\
\delta_1\,(q, b, b) &= (q, \lambda)
\end{aligned}$$

Since M_1 has two different transitions with identical first components, it is not deterministic. That is, since

$$\delta_1\,(q, \lambda, S) = \{(q, \lambda), (q, aSb)\}.$$

M_1 is not deterministic. M_1 can be modified to become a deterministic PDA M_2 that accepts $L\ \$$.

Define $M_2 = (\{p, q, q_a, q_b, q_\$\}, \{a, b, \$\}, \delta_2, p, \{q_\$\}$ where δ_2 is defined as follows.

1. $\delta_2(p, \lambda, \lambda) = (q, S)$
2. $\delta_2(q, a, \lambda) = (qa, \lambda)$
3. $\delta_2(q_a\, \lambda, a) = (q, \lambda)$
4. $\delta_2(q, b, \lambda) = (qb, \lambda)$
5. $\delta_2(q_b, \lambda, b) = (q, \lambda)$
6. $\delta_2(q, \$, \lambda) = (q_\$, \lambda)$
7. $\delta_2(q_a, \lambda, S) =(q_a, aSb)$
8. $\delta_2(q_b, \lambda, S) = (q_b, \lambda)$

From state q, M_2 reads one input symbol and without changing the stack, enters one of the three new states q_a, q_b or $q_\$$. Then uses the information to differentiate the two transitions

$$\delta_2(q, \lambda, S) = (q, aSb)$$

$$\delta_2(q, \lambda, S) = (q, \lambda)$$

The first transition is retained only from state q_a and the second only from state q_b. So M_2 is deterministic. It accepts the input $ab\$$ as follows:

Step	*State*	*Unread Input*	*Stack*	*Transition used*	*Rule of G*
0	p	$ab\$$	λ	–	
1	q	$ab\$$	S	1	
2	q_a	$b\$$	S	2	
3	q_a	$b\$$	aSb	7	$S \to aSb$
4	q	$b\$$	Sb	3	
5	q_b	$\$$	Sb	4	
6	q_b	$\$$	b	8	$S \to \lambda$
7	q	$\$$	λ	5	
8	$q_\$$	λ	λ	6	

δ_0 M_2 is a DPDA accepting $L = \{a^n b^n : n \geq 0\}$.

Devices such as M_2 are called parsers. In particular M_2 is *a* top-down parser because tracing its operation at the steps where nonterminals are replaced on the stack reconstructs a parse tree in a top-down, left-to-right fashion.

Note. By a technique called 'left factoring', we resolve the nondeterminism. It can be summarized as follows.

3.7.2. Theorem

Let G be a consext free grammar having two productions of the from $A \to \alpha\beta$, $A \to \alpha\nu$ with $\alpha \neq \lambda$. Then replace them by the rules $A \to \alpha A^1$, $A^1 \to \beta$, $A^1 \to \nu$, where A^1 is a new non terminal.

Proof. The equivalence can be proved by showing that the effect of applying $A \to \alpha\beta$, $A \to \alpha\nu$ in *a* derivation can be realised by applying $A \to \alpha A^1$, $A^1 \to \beta$, $A^1 \to \nu$ and vice versa.

A variable A is called left recursive if there is production of the form $A \to A\alpha$. Such *a* production can cause a top-down parser into an infinite loop. Techniques for avoiding left recursion are as follows.

3.7.3. Theorem

Let G be a context-free grammar. Let the set of all productions be $\{A \to A\alpha_1, A \to A\alpha_2, \ldots, A \to A\alpha_n, A \to \beta_1, \ldots A \to \beta_m\}$. Then replace these rules by $A \to \beta_1 A^1, \ldots. A \to \beta_m A^1, A^1 \to \alpha_1 A^1, A^1 \to \alpha_2 A^1, \ldots A^1 \to \alpha_n A^1$ and $A^1 \to \lambda$, where A^1 is a new nonterminal.

Proof. A grammar G having the property (by looking ahead for k symbols we derive a given input string in $L(G)$ is called an $LL(k)$ grammar.

Construction of Top down Parser.

(*i*) Eliminate left recursion in G by repeatedly applying Theorem 3.7.3 all left recursive variables.

(*ii*) Apply theorem 3.7.2 to get left factoring whenever necessary.

(*iii*) If the resulting grammar is $LL(k)$ for some natural number k apply top down parsing.

3.7.4. Example

Consider the language consisting of all arthmetic expressions involving + and * and variables x_1 and x_2. This language is generated by a grammar $G = (\{T, F, E\}, \Sigma, P, E)$, where $\Sigma = (x, 1, 2, +, *, (,)\}$ and P consists of

$E \to E + T,$	$F \to (E)$
$E \to T$	$F \to x_1$
$T \to T * F$	$F \to x_2$
$T \to F.$	

We construct a top-down parser for $L(G)$.

Step 1. Since in the rule $E \to E + T$, the nonterminal on the L.H.S is repeated as the first symbol of the right hand side, so we have a left recursion from the rule $E \to E + T$. We simply replace it by the rules $E \to TE'$, $E' \to TE'$, and $E' \to \lambda$ where E' is a new nonterminal.

Similarly $T \to T * F$ and $T \to F$ are replaced by $T \to F T'$, $T' \to * FT'$, $T' \to \lambda$.

The resulting equivalent grammar is

$G' = (\{T, F, E, T', E'\}, \Sigma, P', E)$,

where P' = Consists of

$$E \to TE' \quad T' \to \lambda$$
$$E' \to +TE' \quad F \to (F)$$
$$E' \to \lambda \quad F \to x_1$$
$$T \to FT' \quad F \to x_2$$
$$T' \to *FT'$$

Step 2. Apply theorem 3.7.2 for left factoring $F \to x_1$ and $F \to x_2$ to get new productions $F \to xN$, $N \to 1$ and $N \to 2$.

The resulting equivalent grammar is

$G_2 = (\{T, F, E, T', E'\}, \Sigma, P'', E)$ where P'' consists of

$$P_1 : E \to TE' \qquad P_6 : T' \to \lambda$$
$$P_2 : E' \to +TE' \qquad P_7 : F \to (E)$$
$$P_3 : E' \to \lambda \qquad P_8 : F \to xN$$
$$P_4 : T \to FT' \qquad P_9 : N \to 1$$
$$P_5 : T1 \to *FT' \qquad P_{10} : N \to 2.$$

Step 3. The grammar G_2 obtained in step 2 is an $LL(1)$ grammar. The parsing table is given in Table. The table provides the production to be applied for a given variable with a particular look ahead for one symbol. Let e denote an error. It indicates that the given input string is not in $L(G)$.

	λ	x	1	2	+	*	(	)
E	e	P_1	e	e	e	e	P_1	e
T	e	P_4	e	e	e	e	P_4	e
F	e	P_8	e	e	e	e	P_7	e
T'	P_6	e	e	e	e	P_5	e	P_6
E'	P_3	e	e	e	P_2	e	e	P_3
N	e	e	P_9	P_{10}	e	e	e	e

3.7.5 Bottom up parsing

Reconstruct a parse tree from the leaves to the root, rather than the other way, and this method is called bottom-up.

In bottom-up parsing we have to reverse the production to get S finally. This suggests the following moves for a PDA acting as bottom-up parser.

(*i*) $\delta(p, \lambda, \alpha^R) = \{(p, A) :$ there exists a production $A \to \alpha\}$

(ii) $\delta(p, \sigma, \lambda) = \{(p, \sigma)\}$ for all $\sigma \in \Sigma$.

For acceptability we require some moves when the PDS has S or z_0 on the top.

In bottom-up parsing we follow two types of operations, viz., shifting and reducing. By shifting we mean pushing the input symbol on to the stack. By reducing we mean replacing α^R by A when $A \to \alpha$ is a production in G. (moves given by (*i*)). For (*i*) we use a relation P called a precedence relation. If $(a, b) \in P$, a is the top most symbol on PDS and b is the input symbol then we reduce. Otherwise we shift b onto the stack.

3.7.6. Example

Consider again the grammar for arithmetic expressions analysed in example 3.7.4.

The rules of this grammar G are the following. $E \to E + T$, $E \to T$, $T \to T^* F$, $T \to F$, $F \to (E)$, $F \to x_1$, $F \to x_2$. Using these productions we can construct the precedence relation P. If $(a, b) \in P$, then we have a tick mark ✓ in the (a, b) cell of the table using the table we can decide the moves. For example, if the stack symbol if F, and the next input symbol is *, then we apply reduction. If the stack symbol is E, then any input symbol is pushed auto the stack.

The Precedence Relation

Stack symbol/ Input symbol	x	(	)	1	2	+	*	$
z_0								
x								
(								
)			✓			✓	✓	✓
1			✓			✓	✓	✓
2			✓			✓	✓	✓
+								
*								
E								
T			✓			✓		✓
F			✓			✓	✓	✓

Using the precedence relation and the moves we have defined, it is easy to construct a DPDA.

The DPDA which acts as a bottom up parser is $M' = (Q, \Sigma', \Gamma, \delta, p, z_0, \phi)$, where

$$\Sigma' = \Sigma \cup \{\$\},\ Q = \{p\} \cup \{p_a : a \in \Sigma'\},$$

$$\Gamma = \{E, T, F\} \cup \Sigma \cup \{z_0, \$\}$$

δ is given by the following rules

R_1: $\delta(p, \sigma, \lambda) = (p\sigma, \lambda)$for each $\sigma \in \Sigma'$

R_2 : $\delta(p\sigma, \lambda, a) = (p, \sigma a)$for all $(a, \sigma) \notin P$

R_3 : $\delta(p\sigma, \lambda, T + E) = (p\sigma, E)$for each $\sigma \in \Sigma'$ such that $(T, \sigma) \in P$

R_4 : $\delta(p\sigma, \lambda, Ta) = (p\sigma, Ea)$for each $\sigma \in \Sigma$ such that $(T, \sigma) \in P$ and $a \in G' - \{+\}$

R_5 : $\delta(p_a, \lambda, F^* T) = (p_\sigma, T)$ when $(F, \sigma) \in P$

R_6 : $\delta(p_a, \lambda, Fa) = (p_\sigma, T_a)$ when $(F, \sigma) \in P$ and $a \in \Gamma - \{*\}$.

R_7 : $\delta(p_\sigma, \lambda,)\,E\,(\,) = (p_\sigma, F)$ for each $\sigma \in \Sigma'$ such that ( ), $\sigma) \in P$.

R_8: $\delta(p_\sigma, \lambda, 1x) = (p_\sigma, F)$ for each $\sigma \in \Sigma'$ such that $(1, \sigma) \in P$

R_9 : $\delta(p_\sigma, \lambda, 2x) = (p_\sigma, F)$ for each $\sigma \in \Sigma'$ such that $(2, \sigma) \in P$

R_{10} : $\delta(p_\$, \lambda, E) = (p_\$, \lambda)$

$\delta(p_\$, \lambda, z_0) = (p_\$, \lambda)$. Here M' is deterministic. Further it can accept $L(G)$ \$, and infact it is a bottom-up parser for $L:(G)$ \$. The bottom up parsing for $x_1 + (x_2)$ is given below.

Step	State	Unread Input	Stack	Transition used	Rule of G.
0	p	$x_1 + (x_2)$	z_0	–	
1	p_x	$x_1 + (x_2)$	z_0	–	
2	p_x	$1 + (x_2)$	z_0	R_1	
3	p	$+(x_2)$	xz_0	R_2	
4	p_1	$+(x_2)$	xz_0	R_1	
5	p	(x_2)	$1xz_0$	R_2	
6	p_+	(x_2)	$1x\ z_0$	R_1	
7	p_+	(x_2)	Fz_0	R_8	$F \to x_1$

(Contd.)

Step	State	Unread Input	Stack	Transition used	Rule of G.
8	p_+	(x_2)	Tz_0	R_6	$T \to F$
9	p_+	(x_2)	Ez_0	R_4	$E \to T$
10	p	(x_2)	$+Ez_0$	R_2	
11	$p_($	$x_2)$	$+ Ez_0$	R_1	
12	p	$x_2)$	$(+Ez_0$	R_2	
13	p_x	$2)$	$(+Ez_0$	R_1	
14	p_2	$2)$	$x(+Ez_0$	R_2	
15	p_2	$)$	$x(+ Ez_0$	R_1	
16	$p)$	$)$	$2x (+ Ez_0$	R_2	
17	$p)$	$\$$	$2x (+ Ez_0)$	R_1	
18	$p)$	$\$$	$F (+ Ez_0)$	R_9	$F \to x_2$
19	$p_)$	$\$$	$T (+ E z_0)$	R_6	$T \to F$
20	$p)$	$\$$	$E (+ E z_0)$	R_4	$E \to T$
21	$p_\$$	$\$$	$) E (+ E z_0$	R_2	
22	$p_\$$	λ	$) E (+ E z_0$	R_1	
23	$p_\$$	λ	$F + E z_0$	R_7	$F \to (E)$
24	$p_\$$	λ	$T + E z_0$	R_6	$T \to F$
25	$p_\$$	λ	$E z_0$	R_3	$E \to E + T$
26	$p_\$$	λ	z_0	R_{10}	
27	$p_\$$	λ	λ	R_{11}	

By backtracking we get a right most derivation

$$E \Rightarrow E + T \Rightarrow E + F \Rightarrow E + (E) \Rightarrow E + (T)$$

$$\Rightarrow E + (F) \Rightarrow E + (x_2) \Rightarrow T + (x_2) \Rightarrow F + (x_2) \quad x_1 + x_2).$$

Note. Use of precedence relation to decide whether to shift or reduce, and in some cases reducing the longest possible string do not work in all situations. The grammars for which they do work are called weak precedence grammars; in practice, many grammars can be converted into weak precedure grammars.

3.8. SOLVED PROBLEMS

1. Construct a PDA to accept the language

$$L = \{a^n b^m c^m d^n / m, n \geq 1\} \text{ by final state.}$$

Solution. Let

$$M = (Q, \Sigma, \Gamma, \delta, q_0, Z_0, F) \text{ where}$$

$$Q = \{q_0, q_1, q_2\}, \Sigma = \{a, b, c, d\}, F = \{q_2\}$$

$$\Gamma = \{z_0, z_1, z_2, z_3, z_4, z_5, z_6\}$$

and δ is defined as follows:

$$\delta(q_0, \lambda, z_0) = \{(q_1, z_0 z_5)\}$$

$$\delta(q_1, \lambda, z_5) = \{(q_1, z_4 z_5, z_1), (q_1, z_4 z_6 z_1)\}$$

$$\delta(q_1, \lambda, z_6) = \{(q_1, z_3 z_6 z_2), (q_1, z_3 z_2)\}$$

$$\delta(q_1, a, z_1) = \{(q_1, \lambda)\}$$

$$\delta(q_1, b, z_2) = \{(q_1, \lambda)\}$$

$$\delta(q_1, c, z_3) = \{(q_1, \lambda)\}$$

$$\delta(q_1, d, z_4) = \{(q_1, \lambda)\}$$

$$\delta(q_1, \lambda, z_0) = \{(q_2, z_0)\}.$$

It is easily seen that $T(M) = L$.

2. Construct a PDA to accept the language

$$L = \{a^n b^m a^n / n, m \geq 1\} \text{ by empty store.}$$

Solution. Let $M' = (Q', \Sigma', \Gamma', \delta', q_0', z_0', F)$

where

$$Q' = \{q_0'\}$$

$$\Sigma' = \{a, b\}$$

$$G' = \{z_0', z_1', z_2', z_3'\},$$

$$F = \phi$$

and δ' is defiend as follows

$$\delta'(q_0', \lambda, z_0') = \{(q_0', z_2' z_0' z_2'), (q_0', z_2' z_1' z_2')\}$$

$$\delta'(q_0', \lambda, z_1') = \{(q_0', z_1' z_3'), (q_0', z_3')\}$$

$$\delta'(q_0', a, z_2') = \{(q_0', \lambda)\}$$

$$\delta'(q_0', b, z_3') = \{(q_0', \lambda)\}.$$

We easily see that $N(M') = L$.

3. Construct a PDA to accept the language

$$L = \{ww^R/w \text{ in } (0 + 1)^* \text{ by empty store.}$$

Soltuion. Let $M' = (Q', \Sigma', \Gamma', \delta', q_0', z_0', F')$

where
$$Q' = \{q_0', q_1'\}$$
$$\Sigma' = \{0, 1\}$$
$$\Gamma' = \{z_0', z_1', z_2'\}$$
$$F' = \phi,$$

and δ' is deinfed as follows:

$$\delta' (q_0, 0, z_0') = \{(q_0', z_1' z_0')\}$$
$$\delta' (q_0', 1, z_0') = \{(q_0', z_2' z_0')\}$$
$$\delta' (q_0', 0, z_1') = \{(q_0', z_1' z_1'), (q_1', \lambda)\}$$
$$\delta' (q_0', 0, z_2') = \{(q_0', z_1' z_2')\}$$
$$\delta' (q_0', 1, z_1') = \{(q_0', z_2' z_1')\}$$
$$\delta' (q_0', 1, z_2') = \{(q_0', z_2' z_2'), (q_1', \lambda)\}$$
$$\delta' (q_1', 0, z_1') = \{(q_1', \lambda)\}$$
$$\delta' (q_1', 1, z_2') = \{(q_1', \lambda)\}$$
$$\delta' (q_0', \lambda, z_0') = \{(q_1', \lambda)\}$$
$$\delta' (q_1', \lambda, z_0') = \{(q_1', \lambda)\}.$$

It is easily seen that $L = N (M')$.

4. Construct a PDA to accept the language of palindromes by final state

(or)

Construct a PDA to accept the language $L = \{ww^R/w \text{ in } (a + b^*\}$ by final state.

Solution. Let $M^* = (Q, \Sigma, \Gamma, \delta, q_0, z_0, F)$ where $Q = \{q_0, q_1, q_2),$

$$\Sigma = \{a, b\}$$
$$\Gamma = \{z_0, z_1, z_2\}$$
$$F = \{q_2\}$$

and δ is defined as follows :

$$\delta (q_0, a, z_0) = \{(q_0, z_1 z_0'), (q_1, z_0)\}$$
$$\delta (q_0, b, z_0) = \{(q_0, z_2 z_0), (q_1, z_0)\}$$

$$\delta(q_0, a, z_1) = \{(q_0, z_1z_1), (q_1, z_1)\}$$

$$\delta(q_0, b, z_1) = \{(q_0, z_2z_1), (q_1, z_1)\}$$

$$\delta(q_0, a, z_2) = \{(q_0, z_1z_2), (q_1, z_2)\}$$

$$\delta(q_0, b, z_2) = \{(q_0, z_2z_2), (q_1, z_2)\}$$

$$\delta(q_0, \lambda, z_0) = \{(q_1, z_0)\}$$

$$\delta(q_0, \lambda, z_1) = \{(q_1, z_1)\}$$

$$\delta(q_0, \lambda, z_2) = \{(q_1, z_2)\}$$

$$\delta(q_1, a, z_1) = \{(q_1, \lambda)\}$$

$$\delta(q_1, b, z_2) = \{(q_1, \lambda)\}$$

$$\delta(q_2, \lambda, z_0) = \{(q_2, z_0)\}.$$

It is easily seen that $L = T(M)$.

5. Construct DPDA to accept the language $L = \{x \in \{a, b\}^* / n_a(x) > n_b(x)\}$ by final state.

Solution. Construct a PDA,

$$M = (Q, \Sigma, \Gamma, \delta, q_0, z_0, F) \text{ where}$$

$$Q = \{q_0, q_1\},$$

$$\Sigma = \{a, b\},$$

$$\Gamma = \{z_0, z_1, z_2\}$$

$$F = \{q_1\}$$

and δ is defined as follows :

$$\delta(q_0, a, z_0) = \{(q_1, z_0)\}$$

$$\delta(q_0, b, z_0) = \{(q_0, z_2z_0)\}$$

$$\delta(q_0, a, z_2) = \{(q_0, \lambda)\}$$

$$\delta(q_0, b, z_2) = \{(q_0, z_2z_2)\}$$

$$\delta(q_1, a, z_0) = \{(q_1, z_1z_0)\}$$

$$\delta(q_1, b, z_0) = \{(q_0, z_0)\}$$

$$\delta(q_1, a, z_1) = \{(q_1, z_1z_1)\}$$

$$\delta(q_1, b, z_1) = \{(q_1, \lambda)\}$$

For example for the string *abbabaa* we have

$$(q_0, abbabba, z_0) \vdash (q_1, bbabaa, z_0)$$

$$\vdash (q_0,\ babaa,\ z_0)$$
$$\vdash (q_0,\ abaa,\ z_2z_0)$$
$$\vdash (q_0,\ baa,\ z_0)$$
$$\vdash (q_0,\ aa,\ z_2z_0)$$
$$\vdash (q_0,\ a,\ z_0)$$
$$\vdash (q,\ \lambda,\ z_0).$$

It is easily seen that $L = T(M)$.

6. Construct a PDA accepting the set of all strings over [a, b} with equal number of a's and b's by empty store.

Solution. L = {set of all strings over {a, b} with equal number of a's and b's}.

Construct $\qquad M' = (q', \Sigma', \Gamma', \delta', q_0', z_0', F)$

where $\qquad Q' = \{q_0'\}$

$$\Sigma' = \{a, b\}$$
$$\Gamma' = \{z_0', z_1', z_2'\}$$
$$F' = \phi$$

and δ' is defined as follows :

$$\delta'(q_0', a, z_0') = \{(q_0', z_0'\, z_1')\}$$
$$\delta'(q_0', b, z_0') = \{(q_0', z_0'\, z_2')\}$$
$$\delta'(q_0', a, z_1') = \{(q_0', z_1'\, z_1')\}$$
$$\delta'(q_0', b, z_2') = \{(q_0', z_2'\, z_2')\}$$
$$\delta'(q_0', a, z_2') = (q_0', \lambda)\}$$
$$\delta'(q_0', b, z_1') = \{(q_0', \lambda)\}$$
$$\delta'(q_0', \lambda, z_0') = \{(q_1', \lambda)\}$$

It is easily seen that $L(G) = N(M')$. If w has equal number of a's and b's, then

$$(q_0', w, z_0') \overset{*}{\vdash} (q_0', \lambda, z_0') \vdash (q, \lambda, \lambda).$$

7. Construct a PDA accepting the set of all strings over {a, b} with equal number of a's and b's by final state.

Solution. L = {set of all strings over {a, b}] with equal number of a's and b's}. Consider the PDA M' given in problem 6. We have seen that M' accepts L by empty store. Now we use Theorem 3.2.3 to construct the required PDA.

Construct $M = (Q, \Sigma, \Gamma, \delta, q_0, z_0, F)$

where $Q = Q' \cup \{q_0, q_j\}\ j = \{q_0', q_0, q_j\}$

$\Gamma = \Gamma' \cup \{z_0\}$ where $z_0 \notin \Gamma'$

$= \{z_0', z_1', z_2', z_0\}$

$F = \{q_j\}$ and δ is defined as follows:

$$\delta(q_0, \lambda, z_0) = \{(q_0', z_0 z_0')\}$$
$$\delta(q_0', a, z_0') = \{(q_0', z_0' z_1')\}$$
$$\delta(q_0', b, z_0') = \{(q_0', z_1' z_2')\}$$
$$\delta(q_0', a, z_1') = \{(q_0', z_1' z_1')\}$$
$$\delta(q_0', b, z_2') = \{(q_0', z_2' z_2')\}$$
$$\delta(q_0', a, z_2') = (q_0', \lambda)\}$$
$$\delta(q_0', b, z_1') = \{(q_0', \lambda)\}$$
$$\delta(q_0', \lambda, z_0') = \{(q_0', \lambda)\}$$
$$\delta(q_0', \lambda, z_0') = \{(q_j, z_0)\}.$$

It is easily seen that $L = T(M)$.

8. Construct a PDA accepting $\{a^n b^m a^n / m, n \geq 1\}$ by empty store.

Solution. [For solution 1 see problem 2.]

Construct a PDA $M' = (Q', \Sigma', \Gamma', \delta', q_0', z_0', F')$

where $Q' = \{q_0', q_1'\}$

$\Sigma' = \{a, b\}$

$\Gamma' = \{z_0', z'_1\}$

$F' = \phi$ and δ' is defined as follows:

1. $\delta'(q_0, a, z_0') = \{(q_0', z_0' z_1')\}$
2. $\delta'(q_0', a, z_1') = \{(q_0', z_1' z_1')\}$
3. $\delta'(q_0', b, z_1') = \{(q_1', z_1')\}$
4. $\delta'(q_1', b, z_1') = \{(q_1', z_1')\}$
5. $\delta'(q_1', a, z_1') = \{(q_1', \lambda)\}$
6. $\delta'(q_1', \lambda, z_0') = (q_1', \lambda)\}$.

It is easily seen that $L = N(M')$ [For, we start with the symbol a's until a 'b' occurs (moves 1 and 2). when the current input symbol is b, the state changes, but no change in PDS occurs (move 3). Once all the b's in the input string are exhausted (using move 4), the reaining a's are erased (move 5). Using move 6, z_0 is erased. So

$$(q_0', a^n b^m a^n, z_0') \overset{*}{\vdash} (q_1', \lambda, z_0)$$
$$\vdash (q_1, \lambda, \lambda)].$$

9. Construct a PDA, accepting the language $L = \{a^n b^m a^n / m, n \geq 1\}$ by final state.

Solution. Consider a PDA M' given in problem 8. We have proved that $L = N(M')$. Now we construct a PDA M accepting L by final state using Theorem 3.2.3.

Construct $M = (Q, \Sigma, \Gamma, \delta, q_0, z_0, F)$ where

$$Q = Q' \cup \{q_0, q_j\} = \{q_0', q_1', q_0, q_j\}$$
$$\Sigma = \Sigma' = \{a, b\}$$
$$\Gamma = \Gamma' \cup \{z_0\} = \{z_0', z_1', z_0\}.$$

$F = \{q_j\}$ and δ is defined as follows :

$$\delta(q_0, \lambda, z_0) = \{(q_0', z_0 z_0')\}$$
$$\delta(q_0', a, z_0') = \{(q_0', z_0' z_1')\}$$
$$\delta(q_0', a, z_1') = \{(q_0', z_1' z_1')\}$$
$$\delta(q_0', b, z_1') = \{(q_0', z_1')\}$$
$$\delta(q_1', b, z_1') = \{(q_1', z_1')\}$$
$$\delta(q_1', a, z_1') = \{(q_1', \lambda)\}$$
$$\delta(q_1', \lambda, z_0') = \{(q_1', \lambda)\}$$
$$\delta(q_0', \lambda, z_0) = \{(q_j, z_0)\}$$
$$\delta(q_1', \lambda, z_0) = \{(q_j, z_0)\}$$

It is easily seen that $L = T(M)$.

10. Construct a PDA to accept the language

$$L = [a^n b^{2n} / n \geq 1\} \text{ by empty store.}$$

Solution. Construct a PDA

$$M' = (Q', \Sigma', \Gamma', \delta', q_0', z_0', F')$$
$$Q' = \{q_0', q_1', q_2'\}$$
$$\Sigma' = \{a, b\}$$
$$\Gamma' = \{z_0', z_1'\}$$

$$F = \phi$$

and δ' is defined as follows:

$$\delta' (q_0', a, z_0') = \{(q_1', z_0' z_1')\}$$

$$\delta' (q_1', a, z_1') = \{(q_1', z_1' z_1')\}$$

$$\delta' (q_1', b, z_1') = \{(q_2', z_1')\}$$

$$\delta' (q_2', b, z_1') = \{(q_1'; \lambda)\}$$

$$\delta' (q_1', \lambda, z_0') = \{(q_1', \lambda)\}.$$

It is easily seen that $L = N (M')$.

11. Construct a PDA to accept the language $L = \{a^n b^{2n} / n \geq 1\}$ by final state.

Solution. Consider the PDA M' given in problem 10. We have proved that $L = N (M')$. Now we use 3.2.3. to construct the required PDA.

Construct a PDA $\quad M = (Q, \Sigma, \Gamma, \delta, q_0, z_0, F)$

where

$$Q = Q' \cup \{q_0, q_j\}$$

$$= \{q_0', q_1', q_2', q_0, q_j\}$$

$$\Sigma = \Sigma' = \{a, b\}$$

$$F = \{q_j\}$$

$$\Gamma = \Gamma' \cup \{z_0\}$$

$$= \{z_0, z_0', z_1'\}$$

and δ is defined as follows :

$$\delta (q_0', \lambda, z_0) = \{(q_1', z_0 z_0')\}$$

$$\delta (q_0', a, z_0') = \{(q_0', z_0' z_1')\}$$

$$\delta (q_1', a, z_1') = \{(q_1', z_1' z_1')\}$$

$$\delta (q_1', b, z_1') = \{(q_2', z_1')\}$$

$$\delta (q_2', b, z_1') = \{(q_1', \lambda)\}$$

$$\delta (q_1', \lambda, z_0') = \{(q_1, \lambda)\}$$

$$\delta (q_0', \lambda, z_0) = \{(q_j, z_0)\}$$

$$\delta (q_1', \lambda, z_0) = \{(q_j, z_0)\}$$

$$\delta (q_2', \lambda, z_0) = \{(q_j, z_0)\}$$

It is easily seen that $L = N (M)$.

12. Construct a PDA to accept the language $L = \{a^m b^m c^n / m, n \geq 1\}$ by empty store.

Solution. Construct a PDA $M' = (Q', \Sigma', \Gamma', \delta', q_0', z_0', F']$

where

$$Q' = \{q_0', q_1'\}$$

$$\Sigma' = \{a, b, c\}$$

$$\Gamma' = (z_0', z_1'\}$$

$$F' = \phi$$

and δ' is defined as follows :

$$\delta' (q_0', a, z_0') = \{(q_0', z_0' z_1')\}$$

$$\delta' (q_0', a, z_1') = \{(q_0', z_1' z_1')\}$$

$$\delta' (q_0', b, z_1') = \{(q_1', \lambda)\}$$

$$\delta' (q_1', b, z_1') = \{(q_1', \lambda)\}$$

$$\delta' (q_1', c, z_0') = \{(q_1', z_0')\}$$

$$\delta' (q_1', \lambda, z_0') = \{(q_1', \lambda)\}.$$

It is easily seen that $L = N (M')$.

[For, on reading a, we add z_1' ; on reading b we remove z_1' and the state is changed. If the input is completely read and stack symbol is z_0', then it is removed by a λ-move.]

13. Construct a PDA to accept the language $L = \{a^m b^m c^n / m, n \geq 1\}$ by final state.

Solution. Consider a PDA M' given in problem 12. We have proved that $L = N (M')$. We now construct the required PDA by using M' and Theorem 3.2.3.

Construct $M = (Q, \Sigma, \Gamma, \delta, q_0, z_0, F)$

where $Q = Q' \cup \{q_0, q_j\}$

$$= \{q_0', q_1', q_0, q_j\}$$

$$\Sigma = \Sigma' = \{a, b, c\}$$

$$\Gamma = \Gamma' \cup \{z_0\} = \{z_0', z_1', z_0\}$$

$F = \{q_i\}$ and δ is defined as follows.

$$\delta (q_0', \lambda, z_0) = \{(q_0', z_0 z_0')\}$$

$$\delta (q_0', a, z_0') = \{(q_0', z_0' z_1')\}$$

$$\delta(q_0', a, z_1') = \{(q_0', z_1'z_1')\}$$
$$\delta(q_0', b, z_1') = \{(q_1', \lambda)\}$$
$$\delta(q_1', b, z_1') = \{(q_1', \lambda)\}$$
$$\delta(q_1', c, z_0') = \{(q_1', \lambda)\}$$
$$\delta(q_0', \lambda, z_0) = \{(q_j, z_0)\}$$
$$\delta(q_1', \lambda, z_0) = \{(q_j, z_0)\}$$

It is easily seen that $L = T(M)$.

14. Consider a PDA

$M = (\{q_0, q_1, q_f\}, \{a, b, c\}, \{a, b, z_0\}, \delta, q_0, z_0, \{q_f\})$ where δ is defined as

$$\delta(q_C, a, z_0) = \{(q_0, z_0a)$$
$$\delta(q_0, b, z_0) = \{(q_0, z_0b)\}$$
$$\delta(q_0, a, a) = \{(q_0, aa)\}$$
$$\delta(q_0, b, a) = \{(q_0, ab)\}$$
$$\delta(q_0, a, b) = \{(q_0, ba)\}$$
$$\delta(q_0, b, b) = \{(q_0, bb)\}$$
$$\delta(q_0, c, a) = \{(q_1, a)\}$$
$$\delta(q_0, c, b) = \{(q_1, b)\}$$
$$\delta(q_0, c, z_0) = \{(q_1, z_0)\}$$
$$\delta(q_1, a, a) = \{(q_1, \lambda)\}$$
$$\delta(q_1, b, b) = \{(q_1, \lambda)\}$$
$$\delta(q_1, \lambda, z_0) = \{(q_f, z_0)\}$$

If an initial ID of the PDA *M* is $(q_0, bacab, z_0)$ what is the ID after processing of *bacab* ? If the string is (*i*) *abcba* (*ii*) *abcb* (*iii*) *acba* (*iv*) *abaa* (v) *abab*, will *M* process the entire string. If so what will be the final ID.

Solution. Given that $(q_0, bacab, z_0)$ is the initial ID.

$$\begin{aligned}(q_0, bacab, z_0) &\vdash (q_0, acab, z_0b)\\ &\vdash (q_0, cab, z_0ba)\\ &\vdash (q_1, ab, z_0ba)\\ &\vdash (q_1, b, z_0b)\\ &\vdash (q_1, \lambda, z_0)\end{aligned}$$

$\vdash (q_f, \lambda, z_0)$

(*i*) $(q_0, abcba, z_0) \vdash (q_0, bcba, z_0a)$

$\vdash (q_0, cba, z_0ab)$

$\vdash (q_1, ba, z_0ab)$

$\vdash (q_1, a, z_0a)$

$\vdash (q_1, \lambda, z_0)$

$\vdash (q_f, \lambda, z_0)$.

Yes. The final ID is (q_f, λ, z_0).

(*ii*) $(q_0, abcb, z_0) \vdash (q_0, bcb, z_0a)$

$\vdash (q_0, cb, z_0ab)$

$\vdash (q_1, b, z_0ab)$

$\vdash (q_1, \lambda, z_0a)$.

Yes the final ID is (q_1, λ, z_0a)

(*iii*) $(q_0, acba, z_0) \vdash (q_0, cba, z_0a)$

$\vdash (q_1, ba, z_0a)$.

No, the PDA halts at (q_1, ba, z_0a).

(*iv*) $(q_0, abac, z_0) \vdash (q_0, bac, z_0a)$

$\vdash (q_0, ac, z_0ab)$

$\vdash (q_0, c, z_0aba)$

(q_1, λ, z_0aba).

Yes the final ID is $(q_1, \lambda\ z_0aba)$.

(*v*) $(q_0, abab, z_0) \vdash (q_0, bba, z_0a)$

$\vdash (q_0, ba, z_0ab)$

$\vdash (q_0, a\ z_0abbb)$

$\vdash (q_0, \lambda, z_0abbba)$.

Yes the final ID is (q_0, λ, z_0abba).

15. Let M be a PDA,

$$M = (Q, \Sigma, \Gamma, \delta, q_0, z_0, F) \text{ where}$$

$$Q = \{q_0, q_1, q_f\}$$

$$\Sigma = \{a, b\}$$

$$\Gamma = \{a, z_0\}$$

$$F = \{q_f\}$$

and δ is given by

$$\delta(q_0, a, z_0) = \{(q_0, z_0a)\}$$

$$\delta(q_1, b, a) = \{(q_1, \lambda)\}$$

$$\delta(q_0, a, a) = \{(q_0, aa)\}$$

$$\delta(q_1, \lambda, z_0) = \{(q_1, \lambda)\}$$

$$\delta(q_0, b, a) = \{(q_1, \lambda)\}$$

What is the ID that the PDA M reaches after processing (*i*) a^3b^2 (*ii*) a^2b^3 (*iii*) a^5 (*iv*) b^5 (*v*) b^3a^2 (*vi*) *ababab* if starts with the initial ID.

(*i*)
$$\begin{aligned}(q_0, a^3b^2, z_0) &\vdash (q_0, a^2b^2, z_0a)\\ &\vdash (q_0, ab^2, z_0aa)\\ &\vdash (q_0, b^2, z_0aaa)\\ &\vdash (q_1, z_0aa)\\ &\vdash (q_1, \lambda, z_0a),\end{aligned}$$

Yes the final ID is (q_1, λ, z_0a).

(*ii*)
$$\begin{aligned}(q_0, a^2b^3, z_0) &\vdash (q_0, ab^3, z_0a)\\ &\vdash (q_0, b^3, z_0a)\\ &\vdash (q_0, b, z_0)\end{aligned}$$

No, PDA halts at (q_0, b, z_0).

(*iii*)
$$\begin{aligned}(q_0, a^5, z_0) &\vdash (q_0, a^4, z_0a)\\ &\vdash (q_0, a^3, z_0aa)\\ &\vdash (q_0, a^2, z_0aaa)\\ &\vdash (q_0, a, z_0aaaa)\\ &\vdash (q_0, \lambda, z_0aaaaa).\end{aligned}$$

Yes the final ID is (q_0, λ, z_0a^5).

(*iv*) (q_0, b^5, z_0).

No PDA does not move

(*v*) (q_0, b^3a^2, z_0).

No PDA does not move.

(vi) $(q_0, ababab, z_0) \vdash (q_0, babab, z_0a)$

$\vdash (q_1, abab, b)$.

No PDA halts at $(q_1, abab, z_0)$.

16. Construct a PDA for the following language. The set of all strings over alphabet $\{a, b\}$ that contains exactly twice as many a's as b's.

Solution. Let L = {The set of all strings over alphabet $\{a, b\}$ that contains exactly twice as many a's as b's}. We know that

$$G = (N, T, S, P) \text{ where}$$

$$N = \{S\}$$

$$T = \{a, b\}$$

$$P = \{S \to SaSbSaS, S \to SaSaSbS, S \to SbSaSaS, S \to \lambda\}$$

generates L. Using 3.3.1, Construct a PDA

$$M' = (Q', \Sigma', \Gamma', \delta', q_0', z_0', F^1)$$

where
$$Q_0' = \{q_0'\}$$

$$\Sigma' = T = \{a, b\}$$

$$\Gamma' = N \cup T = \{S, a, b\}$$

$$Z_0' = S,$$

$$F' = \phi$$

and δ' is defined as follows:

$\delta'(q_0', \lambda, S) = \{(q_0', SaSbSaS), (q_0', SbSaSaS), (q_0', SaSaSbS), (q_0', \lambda)\}$

$\delta'(q_0', a, a) = \{(q_0', \lambda)\}$

$\delta'(q_0', b, b) = \{(q_0', \lambda)\}$

It is easily seen that $L = N(M')$.

17. Construct a PDA to accept the language L = {The set of all strings over alphabet $\{a, b\}$ that contains exactly twice as many a's as b's} by final state.

Solution. Consider a PDA M' of problem 16. We have proved that $L = N(M')$. Now we construct a required PDA using Theorem 3.2.3.

$$\text{Construct } M = (Q, \Sigma, \Gamma, \delta, q_0, z_0, F) \text{ where}$$

$$Q = Q' \cup \{q_0, q_j\}$$

$$= \{q_0', q_0, q_j\}$$

$$\Sigma = \{a, b\}$$
$$F = \{q_j\}$$
$$\Gamma = \Gamma' \cup \{z_0\}$$
$$= \{S, a, b, z_0\}$$

and δ is defined as follows:

$$\delta(q_0, \lambda, z_0) = \{(q_0', z_0S)\}$$
$$\delta(q_0', \lambda, S) = \{(q_0', SaSbSaS), (q_0', SbSaSaS),$$
$$(q_0', SaSaSbS), (q_0', \lambda)\}$$
$$\delta(q_0', a, a) = \{(q_0', \lambda)\}$$
$$\delta(q_0', b, b) = \{(q_0', \lambda)\}$$
$$\delta(q_0', \lambda, z_0) = \{(q_j, z_0)\}.$$

It is easily seen that $L = T(M)$.

18. Let $L = \{a^m b^n / n < m\}$. construct (*i*) a context free grammar generating L (*ii*) a PDA accepting L by empty store.

Solution. (*i*) Construct a CFG $G = (N, T, S, P)$

where
$$N = \{S\}$$
$$T = \{a, b\}$$
$$P = \{S \to aSb, S \to aS, S \to a\}.$$

Then
$$L(G) = \{a^m b^n / n < m\}$$

(*ii*) Construct a PDA

$$M' = (Q', \Sigma', \Gamma', \delta', q_0', z'_0, F')$$

where
$$Q' = \{q_0'\}$$
$$\Sigma' = \{a, b\}$$
$$\Gamma' = N \cup T = \{S, a, b\}$$
$$Z_0' = S$$
$$F' = \phi$$

and δ' is defined as follows :

$$\delta'(q_0', \lambda, S) = \{(q_0, bSa), (q_0', Sa), (q_0', a)\}$$
$$\delta'(q_0', a, a) = \{(q_0', \lambda)\}$$

$$\delta' (q_0', b, b) = \{(q_0', \lambda)\}$$

It can be easily seen that $L = N (M')$.

19. Let $L = \{a^m b^n / n < m\}$. Construct a PDA to accept L by final state.

Solution. Consider a PDA M' given in problem 18. we have proved that $L = N (M')$. We construct the required PDA using Theorem 3.2.3.

Construct a PDA

$$M = \{Q, \Sigma, \Gamma, \delta, z_0, F\} \text{ where}$$

$$Q = Q' \cup \{q_0, q_j\}$$

$$= \{q_0', q_0, q_j\}$$

$$\Sigma = \{a, b\}$$

$$\Gamma = \Gamma' \cup \{z_0\}$$

$$= \{S, a, b, z_0\}$$

$$F = \{q_j\}$$

and δ is defined as follows :

$$\delta (q_0, \lambda, z_0) = \{ (q_0', z_0 z_0')\}$$

$$\delta (q_0', \lambda, S) = \{(q_0', bSa), (q_0', Sa), (q_0', a)\}$$

$$\delta (q_0', a, a) = \{(q_0', \lambda)\}$$

$$\delta (q'_0, b, b) = \{(q_0', \lambda)\}$$

$$\delta (q_0', \lambda, z_0) = \{(q_j, \lambda)\}.$$

It is easily seen that $L = T (M)$.

20. Construct a context free grammar generating the following language $L = \{a^n b^n / n \geq 1\} \cup \{a^m b^{2m} / m \geq 1\}$ and hence a PDA accepting L by empty store.

Solution. Construct $G = (N, T, S, P)$ where $N = \{S, A, B\}$, $T = \{a, b\}$, $P = \{S \to A, S \to B, A \to aAb, A \to ab, B \to aBbb, B \to abb\}$.

It is easily seen that $L = L (G)$. Using Theorem 3.3.1 construct a PDA

$$M' = (Q', \Sigma', \Gamma', \delta', q_0', z_0', F')$$

where

$$Q' = \{q_0'\}$$

$$\Sigma' = \{a, b\}$$

$$Z_0' = S$$

$$\Gamma' = N \cup T$$
$$= \{S, A, B, a, b\},$$
$$F' = \phi$$

and δ' is defined as follows:

$$\delta'(q_0', \lambda, S) = \{(q_0', A), (q_0', B)\}$$
$$\delta'(q_0', \lambda, A) = \{(q_0', bAa), (q_0', ba)\}$$
$$\delta'(q_0', \lambda, B) = \{(q_0', bbBa), (q_0', bba)\}$$
$$\delta'(q_0', a, a) = \{(q_0', \lambda)\}$$
$$\delta'(q_0', b, b) = \{(q_0', \lambda)\}.$$

It is easily seen that $L = N(M')$.

21. Construct a PDA to accept the language $L = \{a^n b^n / n \geq 1\} \cup \{a^m b^{2m} / m \geq 1\}$ by final state.

Solution. Consider a PDA M' given in problem 20. We have proved that $L = N(M')$. Now we construct the required PDA by using Theorem 3.2.3.

Construct a PDA

$$M = \{Q, \Sigma, \Gamma, \delta, q_0, z_0, F)$$

where

$$Q = Q' \cup \{q_0, q_j\}$$
$$= \{q_0', q_0, q_j\}$$
$$\Sigma = \{a, b\}$$
$$\Gamma = \Gamma' \cup \{z_0\}$$
$$= \{S, A, B, a, b, z_0\}$$
$$F = \{q_j\}$$

and δ is defined as follows.

$$\delta(q_0, \lambda, z_0) = \{(q_0', z_0S)\}$$
$$\delta(q_0', \lambda, S) = \{(q_0', A), (q_0', B)\}$$
$$\delta(q_0, \lambda, A) = \{(q_0', bAA), (q_0', ba)\}$$
$$\delta(q_0', \lambda, B) = \{(q_0', bbBa), (q_0', bba)\}$$
$$\delta(q_0', a, a) = \{q_0', \lambda)\}$$
$$\delta(q_0', b, b) = \{(q_0', \lambda)\}$$
$$\delta(q_0', \lambda, z_0) = \{(q_j, z_0)\}$$

It is easily seen that $L = T(M)$.

22. Construct a PDA to accept the language $L = \{a^n b^m c^m d^n / m, n \geq 1\}$ by empty store.

Solution. Consider the PDA M, given in problem 1. We have proved that $L = T(M)$. Now we construct a required PDA using Theorem 3.2.3.

Construct a PDA

$$M' = (Q', \Sigma', \Gamma', \delta', q_0', z_0', F')$$

where

$$Q' = Q \cup \{q_e, q_0'\}$$

$$= \{q_0, q_1, q_2\}$$

$$\Gamma' = \Gamma \cup \{z_0'\}$$

$$= \{z_0, z_1, z_2, z_3, z_4, z_5, z_6, z_0'\}$$

$$F' = \phi$$

and δ' is defined as follows.

$$\delta'(q_0', \lambda, z_0') = \{(q_0', z_0' z_0)\}$$

$$\delta'(q_0, \lambda, z_0) = \{(q_1, z_0 z_5)\}$$

$$\delta'(q_1, \lambda, z_5) = \{(q_1, z_4 z_5 z_1), (q_1, z_4, z_6, z_1)\}$$

$$\delta'(q_1, \lambda, z_6) = \{(q_1, z_3 z_6 z_2), (q_1, z_3\ z_2)\}$$

$$\delta'(q_1, a, z_1) = \{(q_1, \lambda)\}$$

$$\delta'(q_1, b, z_2) = \{(q_1, \lambda)\}$$

$$\delta'(q_1, c, z_3) = \{(q_1, \lambda)\}$$

$$\delta'(q_1, d, z_4) = \{(q_2, \lambda)\}$$

$$\delta'(q_1, \lambda, z_0) = \{(q_2, z_0)\}$$

$$\delta'(q_2, \lambda, z_1) = \{(q_e, \lambda)\}$$

$$\delta'(q_2, \lambda, z_2) = \{(q_e, \lambda)\}$$

$$\delta'(q_2, \lambda, z_3) = \{(q_c, \lambda)\}$$

$$\delta'(q_2, \lambda, z_4) = \{(q_e, \lambda)\}$$

$$\delta'(q_2, \lambda, z_5) = \{(q_e, \lambda)\}$$

$$\delta'(q_2, \lambda, z_6) = \{(q_e, \lambda)\}$$

$$\delta'(q_2, \lambda, z_0') = \{(q_e, \lambda)\}$$

$$\delta'(q_2, \lambda, z_0) = \{(q_e, \lambda)\}$$

$$\delta'(q_e, \lambda, z_1) = \{(q_e, \lambda)\}$$

$$\delta'(q_e, \lambda, z_2) = \{(q_e, \lambda)\}$$

$$\delta'(q_e, \lambda, z_3) = \{(q_e, \lambda)\}$$

$$\delta'(q_e, \lambda, z_4) = \{(q_e, \lambda)\}$$

$$\delta'(q_e, \lambda, z_5) = \{(q_e, \lambda)\}$$

$$\delta'(q_e, \lambda, z_6) = \{(q_e, \lambda)\}$$

$$\delta'(q_e, \lambda, z_0') = \{(q_e, \lambda)\}.$$

It is easily seen that $L = N(M')$

23. Construct a CFG which accepts $N(M)$, where $M = (\{q_0, q_1\}, \{a, b\}, \{a, z_0\}, \delta, q_0, z_0, \phi)$ where δ is defined by

1. $\delta(q_0, a, z_0) = \{(q_0, a\ z_0)\}$
2. $\delta(q_0, a, a) = \{(q_0', aa)$
3. $\delta(q_0, b, a) = \{(q_1, a)\}$
4. $\delta(q_1, b, a) = \{(q_1, a)\}$
5. $\delta(q_1, a, a) = \{(q_1, \lambda)\}$
6. $\delta'(q_1, \lambda, z_0) = (q_1, \lambda)\}$

Define $G = (N, T, S, P)$ where N consists of $[q_0, z_0, q_1]$, $[q_1, z_0, q_0]$, $[q_0, a, q_0]$, $[q, a, q_0]$, $[q_0, z_0, q_1]$, $[q_1, z_0, q_1]$, $[q_0, a, q_1]$, $[q_1, a, q_1]$

The productions in P are constructed as follows :

The S — productions are

$$P_1 : S \rightarrow [q_0, z_0, q_0]$$

$$P_2 : S \rightarrow [q_0, z_0, q_1]$$

$\delta(q_0, a, z_0) = \{(q_0, az_o)$ induces

$$P_3 : [q_0, z_0, q_0] \rightarrow a\ [q_0, a, q_0]\ [q_0, z_0, q_0]$$

$$P_4 : [q_0, z_0, q_0] \rightarrow a\ [q_0, a, q_1]\ [q_1, z_0, q_0]$$

$$P_5 : [q_0, z_0, q_1] \rightarrow a\ [q_0, a, q_0]\ [q_0, z_0, q_1]$$

$$P_6 : [q_0, z_0, q_1] \rightarrow a\ [q_0, a, q_1]\ [q_1, z_0, q_1]$$

$\delta(q_0, a, a) = \{(q_0, aa)\}$ yields

$$P_7 : [q_0, a, q_0] \rightarrow a\ [q_0, a, q_0]\ [q_0, a, q_0]$$

$$P_8 : [q_0, a, q_0] \rightarrow a\ [q_0, a, q_1]\ [q_1, a, q_0]$$

$$P_9 : [q_0, a, q_1] \rightarrow a\ [q_0, a, q_0]\ [q_0, a, q_1]$$

$$P_{10} : [q_0, a, q_1] \rightarrow a\ [q_0, a, q_1]\ [q_1, a, q_1]$$

$\delta\ (q_0, b, a) = \{(q_1, a)\}$ gives

$$P_{11} : [q_0, a, q_0] \rightarrow b\ [q_1, a, q_0]$$

$$P_{12} : [q_0, a, q_1] \rightarrow b\ [q_1, a, q_1]$$

$\delta\ (q_1, b, a) = \{(q_1, a)\}$ yields

$$P_{13} : [q_1, a, q_0] \rightarrow b\ [q_1, a, q_0]$$

$$P_{14} : [q_1, a, q_1] \rightarrow b\ [q_1, a, q_1]$$

$\delta\ (q_1, a, a) = \{(q_1, \lambda)\}$ gives

$$P_{15} : [q_1, a, q_1] \rightarrow a$$

$\delta\ (q_1, \lambda, z_0) = \{(q_1, \lambda)\}$ yields

$$P_{16} : [q_1, z_0, q_1] \rightarrow \lambda.$$

24. Construct a PDA A equivalent to the following context free grammar $S \rightarrow OBB$, $B \rightarrow OS/1S/0$. Test whether 010^4 is in $N\ (A)$.

Solution. Using 3.3.1. define PDA

$$M' = (\{q_0'\}, \{0, 1\}, \{S, B, 0, 1\}, \delta', q_0', S, \phi)$$

where δ' is defined as follows:

1. $\delta\ (q_0', \lambda, S) = \{(q_0', BB0)\}$
2. $\delta\ (q_0', \lambda, B) = \{(q_0', S0), (q_0', S1), (q_0'\ 0)\}$
3. $\delta\ (q_0', 0, 0) = \{(q_0', \lambda)\}$
4. $\delta\ (q_0', 1, 1) = \{(q_0', \lambda)\}$

$(q_0', 010^4, S) \vdash (q_0', 010^4, BB0)$ by 1.

$\vdash (q_0', 10^4, BB)$ by 3

$\vdash (q_0', 10^4, BS1)$ by 2

$\vdash (q_0', 0^4, BS)$ by 4

$\vdash (q_0', 0^4, BBB0)$ by 1

$\vdash (q_0', 0^3, BBB)$

$$\overset{*}{\vdash} (q_0', 0^3, 000)$$

$$\overset{*}{\vdash} (q_0', \lambda, \lambda)$$

Thus $010^4 \in N(A)$

25. Show that the set of all strings over $\{a, b, c\}$ in which the number of occurrences of a, b, c is the same is not context free.

Solution. $L = \{x/x \in \{a, b, c\}^* \text{ such that } n_a(x) = n_b(x) = n_c(x)\}$

Take $z = a^n b^n c^n$ in $L(G)$, where $z = uvwxy$, $1 \le |vx| \le n$. So vx cannot contain all the three symbols a, b and c. So uv^2wx^2y contain additional occurrences of two symbols (found in vx) and the number of occurrences of the third symbol remains the same. This means the number of occurrences of the three symbols in uv^2wx^2y are not the same and so $uv^2wxy \notin L$. This is a contradiction. Hence the language is not context free.

26. Show that the language

$L = \{a^m b^m c^n / m \le n \le 2m\}$ is not context free.

Solution. As usual, n is the integer obtained from pumping lemma. Let $z = a^n b^n c^{2n}$. Then $z = uvwxy$, where $1 \le |vx| \le$ n. So vx cannot contain all the three symbols a, b and c. If vx contains only a's and b's then we can choose i such that $uv^i wx^i y$ has more than $2n$ occurrences of a (or b) and exactly $2n$ occurrences of e. This means $uv^i wx^i y \notin L$, a contradiction. In other two cases also we can get a contradiction by proper choice of i. Thus the given language is not context free.

27. Prove that the language

$L = \{x \in \{a, b, c\}^* / n_a(x) < n_b(x) \text{ and } n_a(x) < n_c(x)\}$ is not context free.

Solution. Suppose L is a CFL and let n be the integer obtained from pumping lemma. Let $z = a^n b^{n+1} c^{n+1}$. Then $z = uvwxy$, where $1 \le |vx| \le n$. The string vwx can contain atmost two distinct symbols. This time, two cases are sufficient.

If v or x contains atleast one a, the vx contain any c's. Therefore vu^2wx^2y contains atleast as many a's and c's and cannot be L. If neither v nor x contains an a, then uv^0wx^0y still contains n a's; since vx contains one of the other two symbols, uv^0wx^0y contains fewer occurrences of that symbol then x does and therefore is not in L. We have obtained a contradiction and may conclude that L is not context free.

28. Construct a PDA to accept the language $L = \{a^{2n}bc / n \ge 0\}$ by empty store.

Solution. We know that $G = (N, T, S, P)$

where $N = \{S\}, T = \{a, b\},$

$$P = \{S \to a^2S, S \to bc\} \text{ is the CFL generating } L.$$

Usinbg Theorem 3.3.1 construct a PDA

$$M' = (Q', \Sigma', \Gamma', \delta', q_0', z_0', F')$$

where

$$Q' = \{q_0'\}$$

$$\Sigma' = \{a, b\}$$

$$\Gamma' = N \cup T = \{S, a, b\}$$

$$F' = \phi$$

$$z_0' = S$$

and δ' is defined as follows :

$$\delta' (q_0', \lambda, S) = \{(q_0', Sa^2), (q_0', cb)\}$$

$$\delta' (q_0', a, a) = \{(q_0', \lambda)\}$$

$$\delta' (q_0', b, b) = \{(q_0', b)\}$$

It can be easily seen that $L = N (M')$.

29. Construct a PDA to accept the language $L = \{a^{2n} bc/n \geq 0\}$ by final state.

Solution. Consider the PDA M' given in problem 28. We have proved that $L = N (M')$. We use Theorem 3.2.3. to construct the required PDA. Construct a PDA

$$M = (Q, \Sigma, \Gamma, \delta, q_0, z_0, F)$$

where

$$Q = Q', \cup \{q_0, q_j\}$$

$$= \{q_0', q_0, q_j\}$$

$$\Sigma = \Sigma' = \{a, b\}$$

$$\Gamma = \Gamma' \cup \{z_0\} = \{S, a, b, z_0\}$$

$\Gamma = \{q_j\}$ and δ is defined as follows :

$$\delta (q_0, \lambda, z_0) = \{(q_0', z_0S)\}$$

$$\delta (q_0', \lambda, S) = \{(q_0', Sa^2), (q_0', cb)\}$$

$$\delta (q_0', a, a) = \{(q_0', \lambda)\}$$

$$\delta (q_0', b, b) = \{(q_0', \lambda)\}$$

$$\delta (q_0'; \lambda, z_0) = \{(q_j, z_0)\}$$

It is easily seen that $L = T (M)$.

30. Construct a PDA to accept the language $L = \{(ab)^n / n \geq 1\}$ by empty store.

Solution. $L = \{(ab)^n / n \geq 1\}$. We know that $G = (N, T, S, P)$

where $N = \{S, A, B\}$, $T = \{a, b\}$

and $P = \{S \to aB, B \to b, B \to bA, A \to aB\}$ generates L.

Using Theorem 3.3.1. construct a PDA

$$M' = (Q', \Sigma', \Gamma', \delta', q'_0], z_0', F')$$

where
$$Q' = \{q_0'\}$$
$$\Sigma' = \{a, b\}$$
$$\Gamma' = N \cup T = \{S, A, B, a, b\}$$
$$Z_0' = S$$
$$F' = \phi$$

and δ' is defined as follows.

$$\delta'(q_0', \lambda, S) = \{(q_0', Ba)\}$$
$$\delta'(q_0', \lambda, A) = \{(q_0', Ba)\}$$
$$\delta'(q_0', \lambda, B) = \{(q_0', b), (q_0', Ab)\}$$
$$\delta'(q_0', a, a) = \{(q_0', \lambda)\}$$
$$\delta'(q_0', b, b) = \{(q_0', \lambda)\}$$

It is easily seen that $L = N(M')$.

31. Construct a PDA to accept the language $L = \{(ab)^n / n \geq 1\}$ by final state.

Solution. Consider the PDA M' given in probelm 30. We have proved that $L = N(M')$. Using Theorem 3.2.3. we construct the required PDA as :

$$M = (Q, \Sigma, \Gamma, \delta, q_0, z_0, F) \text{ where}$$
$$Q = Q' \cup \{q_0, q_j\}$$
$$= \{q_0', q_0, q_j\}$$
$$\Sigma = \Sigma' = \{a, b\}$$
$$\Gamma = \Gamma' \cup \{z_0\} = \{S, A, B, a, b, z_0\}$$
$$F = \{q_j\}$$

and δ is defined as follows:

$$\delta(q_0, \lambda, z_0) = \{(q_0', z_0 z_0')\}$$
$$\delta(q_0', \lambda, S) = \{(q_0', Ba)\}$$

$$\delta\ (q_0', \lambda, A) = \{(q_0', Ba)\}$$

$$\delta\ (q_0', \lambda, B) = \{(q_0', b), (q_0', Ab)\}$$

$$\delta\ (q_0', \lambda, z_0) = \{(q_j, z_0)\}.$$

It is easily seen that $L = T\ (M)$.

32. Construct a PDA to accept the language L = {set of all words in a and b with an even number of $a's$} by empty store.

Solution. L = {set of all words in a and b with an even number of $a's$}. We know that $G = (N, T, P, S)$ where $N = \{S, A, B\}$, $T = \{a, b\}$

$P = \{S \to aA, S \to bB, B \to bB, B \to aA, A \to aB, A \to bA, A \to a, B \to b\}$

generates L. We use Theorem 3.3.1. to construct the required PDA. Construct a PDA

$$M' = (Q', \Sigma', \Gamma', \delta', q_0', z_0', F')$$

where

$$Q' = \{q_0'\}$$

$$\Sigma' = \{a, b\}$$

$$\Gamma' = N \cup T = \{S, A, B, a, b\}$$

$$Z_0' = S$$

and δ' is defined as follows :

$$\delta'\ (q_0', \lambda, S) = \{(q_0', Aa)\}$$

$$\delta'\ (q_0', \lambda, A) = \{(q_0', Ba), (q_0', Ab\}, (q_0', a)\}$$

$$\delta'\ (q_0', \lambda, B) = \{(q_0', Bb), (q_0', Aa), (q_0', b)\}$$

$$\delta'\ (q_0', a, a) = \{(q_0', \lambda)\}$$

$$\delta'\ (q_0', b, b) = \{(q_0', \lambda)\}.$$

It is easily seen that $L = N\ (M')$.

33. Construct a PDA to accept the language L = {set of all words in a and b with an even number of $a's$} by final state.

Solution. Consider a PDA M' given in problem 32. We have proved that $L = N\ (M')$. We use Theorem 3.2.3, to construct the required PDA which is :

$$M = (Q, \Sigma, \Gamma, \delta, q_0, z_0, F)$$

where

$$Q = Q' \cup \{q_0, q_j\} = \{q_0', q_0, q_j\}$$

$$\Sigma = \Sigma' = \{a, b\}$$

$$\Gamma = \Gamma' \cup \{z_0\}$$

$$= \{S, A, B, a, b, z_0\}$$

$$F = \{q_j\}$$

and δ is defined as follows

$$\delta\ (q_0, \lambda, z_0) = \{q_0', z_0z_0'\}$$

$$\delta\ (q_0', \lambda, S) = \{(q_0', Aa)\}$$

$$\delta\ (q_0', \lambda, A) = \{(q_0', Ba), (q_0', Ab\}, (q_0', a)\}$$

$$\delta'\ (q_0', \lambda, B) = \{(q_0', Bb), (q_0', Aa), (q_0', b)\}$$

$$\delta'\ (q_0', a, a) = \{(q_0', \lambda)\}$$

$$\delta'\ (q_0', b, b) = \{(q_0', \lambda)\}$$

$$\delta\ (q_0', \lambda, z_0) = \{(q_j, z_0)\}.$$

It is easily seen that $L = T\ (M)$.

34. Construct a PDA to accept the language

$L = \{ab^{2n}c/n \geq 0\}$ by empty store.

Solution. We know that $G = (N, T, S, P)$ where

$$N = \{S, A\}$$

$$T = \{a, b, c\}$$

$$P = \{S \to aA, A \to bbA, A \to c\} \text{ generates } L.$$

We use Theorem 3.3.1 to construct the required PDA.

Construct a PDA

$$M' = (Q', \Sigma', \Gamma', \delta', q_0', z_0', F')$$

where

$$Q' = \{q_0'\}$$

$$\Sigma' = T = \{a, b, c\}$$

$$\Gamma' = N \cup T = \{S, A, a, b, c\}$$

$$Z_0' = S$$

$$F' = \phi$$

and δ′ is defined as follows :

$$\delta'\ (q_0, \lambda, S) = \{(q_0', Aa)\}$$

$$\delta\ (q_0', \lambda, A) = \{(q_0', Abb), (q_0', C)\}$$

$$\delta' (q_0', a, a) = \{(q_0', \lambda)\}$$

$$\delta' (q_0', b, b) = \{(q_0', \lambda)\}$$

$$\delta' (q_0', c, c) = \{(q_0', \lambda)\}.$$

It is easily seen that $L = N (M')$.

35. Construct a PDA to accept the lanaguage $L = \{ab^{2n}c/n \geq 0\}$ by final state.

Solution. $L = \{ab^{2n}c/n \geq 0\}$. We use 3.2.3. to construct the required PDA.

Construct a PDA $M = (Q, \Sigma, \Gamma, \delta, q_0, z_0, F)$

where

$$Q = Q' \cup \{q_0, q_j\}$$

$$\Sigma = \Sigma' = \{a, b, c\}$$

$$\Gamma = \Gamma' \cup \{z_0\} = \{S, A, a, b, c, z_0\}$$

$$F = \{q_j\}$$

and δ is defined as follows :

$$\delta (q_0, \lambda, z_0) = \{(q_0', z_0 z_0')\}$$

$$\delta (q_0', \lambda, S) = \{(q_0', Aa)\}$$

$$\delta (q_0', \lambda, A) = \{(q_0', Abb), (q_0', c)\}$$

$$\delta (q_0', a, a) = \{(q_0', \lambda)\}$$

$$\delta (q_0', b, b) = \{(q_0', \lambda)\}$$

$$\delta (q_0', c, c) = \{(q_0', \lambda)\}$$

$$\delta (q_0', \lambda, z_0) = \{(q_j', z_0)\}$$

It is easily seen that $L = T (M)$.

36. Construct a PDA for the language

$L = \{a^n b^m a^m b^n / m, n \geq 1\}$ by empty store.

Solution. $L = \{a^n b^m a^m b^n / m, n \geq 1\}$. We know that $G = (N, T, S, P)$ where

$$N = \{S, A\}, T = \{a, b\} \text{ and}$$

$$P = \{S \to aSb, S \to aAb, A \to bAa, A \to ba\}$$

generates L. Now we use Theorem 3.3.1 to construct the required PDA.

Construct a PDA

$$M = (Q', \Sigma', \Gamma', \delta', q_0', Z_0', F')$$

where $Q' = \{q_0'\}$

$$\Sigma' = T = \{a, b\}$$

$$\Gamma' = Z \cup T = \{S, A, a, b\}$$

$$z_0' = S$$

and δ' is defined as follows :

$$\delta'(q_0', \lambda, S) = \{(q_0', bSa), (q_0', bAa)\}$$

$$\delta'(q_0', \lambda, A) = \{(q_0', aAb), (q_0', ab)\}$$

$$\delta'(q_0', a, a) = \{(q_0', \lambda)\}$$

$$\delta'(q_0', b, b) = \{(q_0', \lambda)\}.$$

It is easily seen that $L = N(M')$

37. Construct a PDA to accept the language $L = \{a^n b^m a^m b^n / m, n \geq 1\}$ by final state.

Solution. Consider the PDA M' given in problem 36 we have proved that $L = N(M')$. We use Theorem 3.2.3 to construct the required PDA.

Construct a PDA

$$M = (Q, \Sigma, \Gamma, \delta, q_0, z_0, F)$$

where

$$Q = Q' \cup \{q_0, q_j\}$$

$$= \{q_0', q_0, q_j\}$$

$$\Sigma = \Sigma' = \{a, b\}$$

$$\Gamma = \Gamma' \cup \{z_0\}$$

$$= \{S, A, a, b, z_0\}$$

$$F = \{q_j\}$$

and δ is defined as follows :

$$\delta(q_0, \lambda, z_0) = \{(q_0', z_0 z_0')\}$$

$$\delta(q_0', \lambda, S) = \{(q_0', bSa), (q_0', bAa)\}$$

$$\delta(q_0', \lambda, A) = \{(q_0', aAb), (q_0', ab)\}$$

$$\delta(q_0', a, a) = \{(q_0', \lambda)\}$$

$$\delta(q_0', b, b) = \{(q_0', \lambda)\}$$

$$\delta(q_0', \lambda, z_0) = \{(q_j, z_0)\}$$

It is easily seen that $L = T(M)$.

38. Construct a PDA to accept the language $L = \{x \in \{0, 1\}^* / n_0(x) = n_1(x)\}$

by empty store.

Solution. We know that $G = (N, T, S, P)$ where $N = \{S\}$, $T = \{0, 1\}$ and $P = \{S \to \lambda/0S1/1S0/SS\}$ generates L. We use Theorem 3.3.1 to construct a PDA

$$M' = (Q', \Sigma', \Gamma', \delta', q_0', z_0', F')$$

where

$$Q' = \{q_0'\}$$

$$\Sigma' = \{0, 1\}$$

$$\Gamma' = N \cup T = \{S, 0, 1\}$$

$$Z_0' = S$$

and δ' is defined as follows.

$$\delta' (q_0', \lambda, S) = \{(q_0', \lambda), (q_0', 1S0), (q_0', 0S1), (q_0', SS)\}$$

$$\delta' (q_0', 0, 0) = (q_0', \lambda)$$

$$\delta' (q_0', 1, 1) = (q_0', \lambda).$$

It is easily seen that $L = N (M')$.

39. Construct a PDA to accept the language $L = \{x \in \{0, 1\}^*/ n_0 (x) = n_1 (x)\}$ by final state.

Solution. Consider the PDA M' given in problem 38. We have proved that $L = N (M')$. We use Theorem 3.2.3. to construct a PDA

$$M = (Q, \Sigma, \Gamma, \delta, q_0, z_0, F)$$

where

$$Q = Q' \cup \{q_0, q_j\}$$

$$= \{q_0', q_0, q_j\}$$

$$\Sigma = \{0, 1\}$$

$$\Gamma = \Gamma' \cup \{z_0\}$$

$$= \{S, 0, 1, Z_0\}$$

$$F = \{q_j\}$$

and δ is defnied as follows :

$$\delta (q_0, \lambda, z_0) = (q_0', z_0S)$$

$$\delta (q_0', \lambda, S) = \{(q_0', \lambda), (q_0', 1S0), (q_0', 0S1), (q_0', SS)\}$$

$$\delta (q_0', \lambda, z_0) = (q_j, z_0).$$

It is easily seen that $L = T(M)$.

40. Construct a PDA to accept the language $L(G) = \{x/$ each prefix of x has atleast as many a's as b's$\}$ by empty store.

Solution. We know that $G = (N, T, S, P)$ where $N = \{S\}$, $T = \{a, b\}$, $P = \{S \rightarrow aS,\ S \rightarrow aSbS,\ S \rightarrow \lambda)$ generates L. We use Theorem 3.3.1. to construct a PDA

$$M' = (Q', \Sigma', \Gamma', \delta', q_0', z_0', F')$$

where

$$Q' = \{q_0'\}$$

$$\Sigma' = \{a, b\} = T$$

$$\Gamma' = N \cup T = \{S, a, b\}$$

$$z_0' = S$$

and δ' is defined as follows :

$$\delta'(q_0', \lambda, S) = \{(q_0', Sa), (q_0', SbSa), (q_0', \lambda)\}$$

$$\delta'(q_0', a, a) = \{(q_0', \lambda)\}$$

$$\delta'(q_0', b, b) = \{(q_0', \lambda)\}$$

It is easily seen that $L(G) = N(M')$.

41. Construct a PDA to accept the language

$L(G) = \{x/$each prefix of x has atleast as many a's as b's$\}$

by fianl state.

Solution. Consider the PDA M' given in problem in 40. We have proved that $L = N(M')$. By using Theorem 3.2.3 we construct a PDA.

$$M' = (Q, \Sigma, \Gamma, \delta, q_0, z_0, F)$$

where

$$Q = Q' \cup \{q_0, q_j\}$$

$$= \{q_0', q_0, q_j\}$$

$$\Sigma = \Sigma' = \{a, b\}$$

$$\Gamma = \Gamma' \cup \{z_0\} = \{S, a, b, z_0\}$$

$$F = \{q_j)$$

and δ is defined as follows :

$$\delta(q_0, \lambda, z_0) = \{(q_0', z_0S)\}$$

$$\delta(q_0, \lambda, S) = \{(q_0', Sa), (q_0', SbSa), (q_0', \lambda)\}$$

$$\delta(q_0', \lambda\ z_0) = \{(q_j, z_0\}.$$

It is easily seen that $L = T(M)$.

42. Construct a PDA which accepts the language

$$L = \{x \in \{a, b, c\}^* / n_a(x) = n_b(x) = n_c(x)\}.$$

Solution. We know that $G = (N, T, S, P)$ where

$$N = \{S\}$$

$$T = \{a, b, c\}$$

$P = \{S \rightarrow aSbScS/aScSbS/bSaScS/bScSaS/cSaSbS/cSbSaS/\lambda\}$

We use Theorem 3.3.1 to construct a PDA

$$M' = (Q', \Sigma', \Gamma', \delta', q_0', z_0', F')$$

where $Q' = \{q_0'\}$

$$\Sigma' = T = \{a, b, c\}$$

$$\Gamma' = N \cup T = \{S, a, b, c\}$$

$$Z_0' = S$$

$$F' = \phi$$

and δ' as defined as follows :

$$\delta'(q'_0, \lambda, S) = \{(q_0', ScSbSa), (q_0', SbScSa), (q_0', ScSaSb), (q_0', SaScSb), (q_0, SbSaSc), (q_0', SaSbSc), (q_0', \lambda)\}$$

$$\delta'(q_0', a, a) = (q_0', \lambda)$$

$$\delta'(q_0', b, b) = (q_0', \lambda)$$

$$\delta'(q_0', c, c) = (q_0', \lambda).$$

It is easily seen that $L = N(M')$.

43. Construct a PDA which accepts the language

$L = \{x \in \{a, b, c\}^* / n_a^{(x)} = n_b^{(x)} = n_c^{(x)}\}$ by final state.

Solution. Consider the PDA M' given problem 42.We have proved that $L = N(M')$. We use Theorem 3.2.3. to construct the PDA

$$M = (Q, \Sigma, \Gamma, \delta, q_0, z_0, F)$$

where $Q = Q' \cup \{q_0, q_j\} = \{q_0', q_0, q_j\}$

$$\Gamma = \Gamma' \cup \{z_0\} = \{S, a, b, c, z_0\}$$

$$\Sigma = \Sigma' = \{a, b, c\}$$

$$F = \{q_j\}$$

and δ is defined as follows :

$$\delta\,(q_0, \lambda, z_0) = (q_0', z_0S)$$

$$\delta\,(q_0', \lambda, S) = \{(q_0', ScSbSa), (q_0', SbScSa), (q_0', ScSaSb), (q_0', SaScSb), (q_0', SbSaSa), (q_0', SaSbSc), (q_0', \lambda)\}$$

$$\delta\,(q_0', \lambda, z_0) = \{(q_j, z_0)\}$$

$$\delta\,(q_0', \lambda, z_0) = \{(q_j, z_0)\}.$$

It is easily seen that $L = T\,(M)$.

44. Construct a PDA to accept the language $L\ \{a^n/n \geq 1\}$ by empty store.

Solution. We know that $G = (N, T, S, P)$ where $N = \{S\}$, $T = \{a\}$, $P = \{S \rightarrow as/a\}]$ generagtes L. We use Theorem 3.3.1. to construct the PDA.

$$M' = (Q', \Sigma', \Gamma', \delta', q_0', z_0', F')$$

where

$$Q' = \{q_0'\}$$

$$\Sigma' = \{a\}$$

$$\Gamma' = N \cup T = \{S, a\}$$

$$z_0 = S$$

$F = \phi$ and δ' is defined as follows:

$$\delta'\,(q_0', \lambda, S) = \{(q_0', Sa), (q_0', a)\}$$

$$\delta'\,(q_0', a, a) = \{(q_0', \lambda)\}$$

$$(q_0', a^n, S) \vdash (q_0', a^n, Sa)$$

$$\vdash (q_0', a^{n-1}, S)$$

$$\vdash (q_0', a^{n-1}, Sa)$$

$$\vdash (q_0', a^{n-2}, S)$$

$$\overset{*}{\vdash} (q_0', a, a)$$

$$\vdash (q_0', \lambda, \lambda)$$

Therefore, $a^n \in N\,(M')$

That is, $L = N\,(M')$.

45. Construct a PDA to accept the language $L = \{a^n/n \geq 1\}$ by final state.

Solution. Consider the PDA M' given in problem 44. We have proved that $L = N\,(M')$. Using Theorem 3.2.3. construct a PDA

$$M = (Q, \Sigma, \Gamma, \delta, q_0, z_0, F) \text{ where}$$

$$Q = Q' \cup (q_0,\ q_j) = \{q_0', q_0, q_j)$$

$$\Sigma = \Sigma' = \{a\}$$

$$\Gamma = \Gamma' \cup \{z_0\}$$

$$= \{S, a, z_0\}$$

$$F = \{q_j\}$$

and δ is defined as follows:

$$\delta\ (q_0, \lambda, z_0) = \{(q_0', z_0S)\}$$

$$\delta\ (q_0', \lambda, S) = \{(q_0', Sa), (q_0', a)\}$$

$$\delta\ (q_0', a\ , a) = \{(q_0', \lambda)\}$$

$$\delta\ (q_0, \lambda, z_0) = \{(q_j, z_0)\}$$

$$(q_0, q_n, z_0) \vdash (q_0', a_n, z_0S)$$

$$\overset{*}{\vdash} (q_0', \lambda, z_0) \qquad \text{[See prob. 44]}$$

$$\vdash (q_j, \lambda, z_0)$$

Therefore $a^n \in T\ (M)$

Thus $L = \ T\ (M)$.

46. Construct *a* PDA to accept the language $L = \{ww^R/w \in (a, b)^+\}$ by empty store.

Solution. We know that $G = (N, T, S, P)$

where $N = \{S\}, T = \{a, b\}$

$$P = \{S \to aSa, S \to bSb, S \to aa, S \to bb]$$

generates L. Now we use Theorem 3.3.1. to construct a PDA $M' = (Q', \Sigma'. \Gamma', \delta', z_0', q_0', F)$

where $Q' = \{q_0'\}$

$$\Sigma' = \{a, b\} = T$$

$$\Gamma' = \ N \cup T = \{S, a, b\}$$

$$z_0' = S$$

and δ′ is defined as follows :

$$\delta\ '\ (q_0', \lambda, S) = \{(q_0', aSa), (q_0', bSb), (q_0', aa), (q_0', bb)$$

$$\delta'\ (q_0', a, a) = \{(q_0', \lambda)\}$$

$$\delta' (q_0', b, b) = \{(q_0', \lambda)\}$$

It is easily seen that $L = N (M')$.

47. Construct a PDA to accept the language $L = \{ww^R/w \in (a, b)^+\}$ by final state.

Solution. Consider the PDA M' given in problem 46. We have proved that $L = N (M')$. By using Theorem 3.2.3. construct a PDA

$$M = (Q, \Sigma, \Gamma, q_0, z_0, \delta, F)$$

where

$$Q = Q' \cup (q_0, q_j\}$$
$$= \{q_0', q_0, q_j\}$$
$$\Sigma = \{a, b\} = T$$
$$\Gamma = N \cup T = \{S, a, b\}$$
$$F = \{q_j\}$$

and δ is defined as follows :

$$\delta (q_0, \lambda, z_0) = \{(q_0', z_0S)\}$$
$$\delta (q_0', \lambda, S) = \{(q_0', aSa), (q_0', bSb), (q_0', aa) (q_0', bb)\}$$
$$\delta (q_0', a, a) = \{(q_0', \lambda)\}$$
$$\delta (q_0', b, b) = \{(q_0', \lambda)\}$$
$$\delta (q_0', \lambda, z_0) = \{(q_j, z_0)\}.$$

It is easily seen that $L = T (M)$.

48. Prove that the language $\left\{a^{n^2} / n \geq 1\right\}$ is not context free.

Solution. Let n be the natural number got by applying pumping lemma.

Let $z = a^{n^2}$. Write $z = uvwxy$ where $1 \leq | vx | \leq n$ (This is possible since $| vwx | \leq n$ by (*ii*) of pumping lemma). Let $| vx | = m, m \leq n$. By pumping lemma, uv^2wx^2y is in L. As $| uv^2wx^2y | > n^2$, $| uv^2 wx^2y | = k^2$, where $k \geq n + 1$. But $| uv^2wx^2y | = n^2 + m < n^2 + 2n + 1$. So $| uv^2wx^2y |$ strictly lies between n^2 and $(n + 1)^2$ which means $uv^2wx^2y \notin L$, a contradiction. Hence $\left\{a^{n^2} / n \geq 1\right\}$ is not context free.

49. Construct a PDA to accept the language

$L = \{a^ib^j\} \mid i \leq j \leq 2i\}$ by empty store.

Solution. We know that $\quad G = (N, T, S, P)$

where $N = \{S\}, T = \{a, b\}$ and

$P = \{S \to aSb, S \to ab, S \to SbSa\ SbS, S \to SbSbSaS, S \to SbSaSaS, S \to \lambda)\}$

generates L. We use 3.3.1. to construct a PDA.

$$M' = (Q', \Sigma', \Gamma', \delta', q_0', z_0', F')$$

where

$$Q' = \{q_0')$$
$$\Sigma' = T = \{a, b\}$$
$$\Gamma' = N \cup T = \{S, a, b\}$$
$$F' = \phi$$
$$Z_0' = S$$

and δ' is defined as follows :

$$\delta'(q_0', \lambda, S) = \{(q_0', bSa), (q_0', ba), (q_0', SbSaSbS), (q_0', SaSbSbS), (q_0', SaSaSbS), (q_0', \lambda)\}$$

$$\delta', (q_0', a, a) = \{(q_0', \lambda)\}$$

$$\delta'(q_0', b, b) = \{(q_0', \lambda)\}$$

It is easily seen that $L = N(M')$.

50. Construct a PDA to accept the language $L = \{a^i b^j \mid i \le j \le 2i\}$ by final state.

Solution. Considet the PDA M' given in problem 49. We have proved that $L = N(M')$. We use Theorem 3.2.3. to construct a PDA

$$M = (Q, \Sigma, \Gamma, \delta, q_0, z_0, F)$$

where

$$Q = Q' \cup \{q_0, q_j\}$$
$$= \{q_0', q_0, q_j\}$$
$$\Sigma = \Sigma' = \{a, b\}$$
$$\Gamma = \Gamma' \cup \{z_0\}$$
$$= \{S, a, b, z_0\}$$
$$F = \{q_j\}$$

and δ is defined as follows :

$$\delta(q_0, \lambda, z_0) = \{(q_0', z_0S)\}$$

$$\delta(q_0', \lambda, S) = \{(q_0', bSa), (q_0', ba), (q_0', SbSaSbS), (q_0', SaSbSbS), (q_0', SaSaSbS), (q_0', \lambda)\}$$

$$\delta(q_0', a, a) = \{(q_0', \lambda)\}$$

$$\delta(q_0', b, b) = \{(q_0', \lambda)\}$$

$$\delta(q_0', \lambda, z_0) = \{(q_j, z_0)\}.$$

It is easily seen that $L = T(M)$.

51. Construct a Deterministic PDA to accept the language $L = \{a^n b^n : n \geq 0\} \cup \{a\}$.

Solution. Consider an NDPA

$$M = (Q, \Sigma, \Gamma, D, q_0, z_0, F)$$

where
$$Q = \{q_0, q_1, q_2, q_3\}$$

$$\Sigma = \{a, b\}$$

$$\Gamma = \{0, 1\}$$

$$F = \{q_3\}$$

and δ is defined as follows:

$$\delta(q_0, a, 0) = \{(q_1, 10), (q_3, \in)\}$$

$$\delta(q_0, \lambda, 0) = \{(q_3, \varepsilon)\}$$

$$\delta(q_1, a, 1 = \{q_1, 11)\}$$

$$\delta(q_1, b, 1) = \{(q_2, \varepsilon)\}$$

$$\delta(q_2, b, 1) = \{(q_2, \varepsilon)\}$$

$$\delta(q_2, \varepsilon, 0) = \{(q_3, \varepsilon)\}$$

It is easily seen that $L = T(M)$.

52. Construct a PDA to accept the language $L = \{a^n b^n : n \geq 0\} \cup \{a\}$ by empty store.

Solution. Consider a PDA M in problem 51. We have proved that $L = T(M)$. We use 3.2.3. to construct the required PDA.

Construct
$$M' = (Q', \Sigma', \Gamma', \delta', q_0', z_0', F')$$

where
$$Q' = Q \cup \{q_0', q_e\} \text{ where } q_0', q_e \notin Q.$$

$$L = \{q_0, q_1, q_2, q_3, q_0', q_e\}$$

$$\Sigma' = \Sigma = \{a, b\}$$

$$\Gamma' = \Gamma \cup \{z'_0\} = \{0, 1, z'_0\}, z_0' \notin \Gamma$$

and δ' is defined as follows:

$$\delta'(q_0', \varepsilon, z_0') = (q_0, z_0'z_0)$$

$$\delta'(q_0, a, 0) = \{(q, 10, (q_3, \varepsilon)\}$$

$$\delta'(q_0, \varepsilon, 0) = \{(q_3, \varepsilon)\}$$
$$\delta'(q_1, a, 1) = \{(q, 11)\}$$
$$\delta'(q_1, b, 1) = \{(q_2, \varepsilon)\}$$
$$\delta'(q_2, b, 1) = \{(q_2, \varepsilon)\}$$
$$\delta'(q_2, \varepsilon, 1) = \{(q_3, \varepsilon)\}$$
$$\delta'(q_3, \varepsilon, 0) = \{(q_e, \varepsilon)\}$$
$$\delta'(q_3, \varepsilon, 1) = \{(q_e, \varepsilon)\}$$
$$\delta'(q_3, \varepsilon, z_0') = \{(q_e, \varepsilon)\}$$
$$\delta'(q_e, \varepsilon, 0) = \{(q_e, \varepsilon)\}$$
$$\delta'(q_e, \varepsilon, 1) = \{(q_e, \varepsilon)\}$$
$$\delta'(q_e, \varepsilon, z_0') = \{(q_e, \varepsilon)\}$$

It is easily seen that $L = N(M')$.

53. Construct a PDA for the CFG with productions $S \to aSbb/a$,

$$S \to aSA/a,$$
$$A \to bB,$$
$$B \to b.$$

Solution. We use 3.3.1 to construct the required PDA.

Construct $M' = (Q', \Sigma', \Gamma', q_0', \delta', z_0', F')$

where $Q' = \{q_0'\}$

$\Sigma' = T = \{a, b\}$

$\Gamma' = N \cup T = \{a, b, S, A, B\}$

$F' = \phi$ and

δ' is defined as follows:

$$\delta'(q_0', \varepsilon, S) = \{(q_0', bbSa), (q_0', a), (q_0', aSA), (q_0', a)\}$$
$$\delta'(q_0', \varepsilon, A) = \{(q_0', Bb)\}$$
$$\delta'(q_0', \varepsilon, B) = \{(q_0', b)\}$$
$$\delta'(q_0', a, a) = \{(q_0', \varepsilon)\}$$
$$\delta'(q_0', b, b) = \{(q_0', \varepsilon)\}$$

It is easily seen that $L = N(M')$.

54. Construct a PDA for the CFG with productions

$$S \rightarrow aA$$
$$A \rightarrow aABC/bB/a$$
$$B \rightarrow b$$
$$C \rightarrow c$$

Solution. We use 3.3.1. to construct the required PDA

Construct a PDA

$$M' = (Q', \Sigma', \Gamma', \delta', q_0', z_0', F')$$

where
$$Q' = \{q_0'\}$$
$$\Sigma' = \{a, b, c\}$$
$$\Gamma' = N \cup T = \{S, A, B, C, a, b, c\}$$
$$F' = \phi \text{ and}$$

δ' is defined as follows

$$\delta'(q_0', \varepsilon, S) = \{(q_0', Aa)\}$$
$$\delta'(q_0', \varepsilon, A) = \{(q_0', CBAa), (q_0', Bb), (q_0', a)\}$$
$$\delta'(q_0', \varepsilon, B) = \{(q_0', b)\}$$
$$\delta'(q_0', \varepsilon, C) = \{(q_0', c)\}$$
$$\delta'(q_0', a, a) = \{(q_0', \varepsilon)\}$$
$$\delta'(q_0', b, b) = \{(q_0', \varepsilon)\}$$
$$\delta'(q_0', c, c) = \{(q_0', \varepsilon)\}$$

It is easily seen that $L = N(M')$.

55. Prove that the language $L = \{a^n b^n : n \geq 0\}$ is *a* deterministic context free language.

Solution. Consider the PDA

$$M = (Q, \Sigma, \Gamma, \delta, q_0, O, F)$$

where
$$Q = \{q_0, q_1, q_2\}$$
$$\Sigma = \{a, b\}$$
$$\Gamma = \{0, 1\}$$
$$F = \{10\} \text{ and}$$

δ is defined as follows:

$$\delta(q_0, a, 0) = \{(q_1, 10)\}$$

$$\delta\ (q_1, a, 1) = \{(q_1, 11)\}$$

$$\delta\ (q_1, b, 1) = \{(q_2, \varepsilon)\}$$

$$\delta\ (q_2, b, 1) = \{(q_2, \varepsilon)\}$$

$$\delta\ (q_2, \varepsilon, 0) = \{(q_0, \varepsilon)\}$$

It is easily seen that $L = L(M)$

Since M is deterministic, L is *a* DCFL.

56. Give an example of *a* CFL which is not *a* DCFL.

Solution. Let $L_1 = \{a^n b^n : n \geq 0\}$

and $L_2 = \{a^n b^{2n} : n \geq 0\}$

We know that L_1 and L_2 are CFL's. Hence $L_1 \cup L_2$ is also a CFL.

Since the PDA has either to match one b or two against each a, and so has to make an initial choice whether the input is in L_1 or L_2. There is no information available at the beginning of the string by which the choice can be made deterministically. Hence L is a DCFL.

Note. It is observed that {set of all DCFL} $\subset$ {set of all CFL}

57. Prove that the language

$L = \{a^n b^n c^n : n \geq 0\}$ is not context free.

Solution. Let m be the number in the pumping Lemma. Let $z = a^m b^m c^m$. Then $Z \in L$. If V_{xy} to contain only a's then the pumped string will obviously not be in L. If we choose a string containing an equal number of a's and b's then, the pumped string $a^m b^m c^m$ with $k \neq m$ can be generated and gain we have generated a string not in L. If V_y has the same number of a's and b's and c's then $| V_{xy} | \neq m$. Therefore, L is not context free.

58. Prove that the language $L = \{ww : w \in \{a, b\}^*\}$.

Solution. Consider the string $a^m b^m a^m b^m$. There are many choices for the string V_{xy}. If we take the choice as shown in Fig. 3.5.

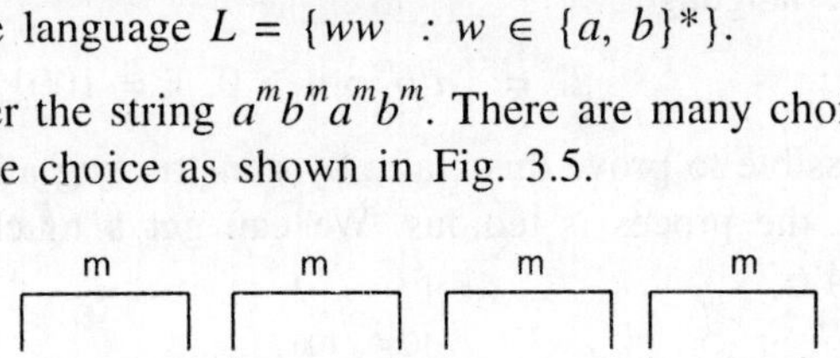

Fig. 3.5.

Take $i = 0$ to get a string of the form

$a^k b^j a^m b^m$, $k < m$ or $j < m$ which is not in L.

Similar arguments can be made for other choices also. We conclude that L is not context free.

59. Show that the language

$$L = \{a^n b^j : n = j^2\} \text{ is not context free.}$$

Solution. Let m be the number in the pumping Lemma. Consider the string $a^{m^2} b^m$. Now we have several choices. The only one that requires much thought is the one given in the following Fig. 3.6.

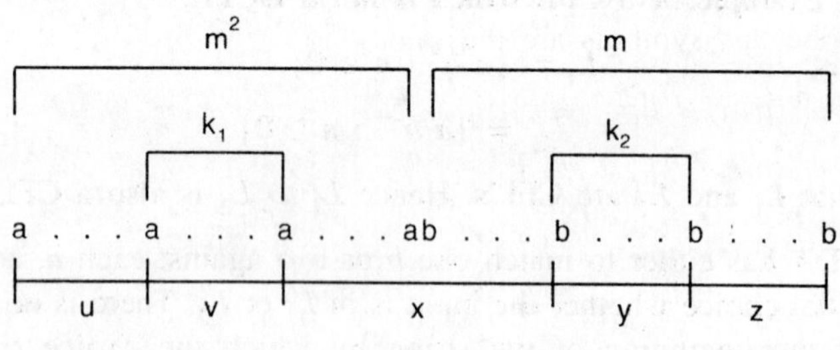

Fig. 3.6.

Pumping i times will yield a new string with $m^2 + (i - 1)\, k$, a's and $m + (i - 1)\, k^2$ b's. If we take $k_1 \neq 0$, $k_2 \neq 0$. We can pick $i = 0$. Since

$$\begin{aligned}(m - k_2)^2 &\leq (m - 1)^2 \\ &= m^2 - 2\,m + 1 \\ &< m^2 - k_1,\end{aligned}$$

the result is not in L. If we take $k_1 = 0$, $k_2 \neq 0$ or $k_1 \neq 0$, $k_2 = 0$, then again with $i = 0$, the pumped string is not in L. Hence we conclude that L is not a context free language.

60. Show that the language

$$L = \{a^n b^n : n \geq 0,\ n \neq 100\} \text{ is context free.}$$

Solution. It is possible to prove this claim by constructing a PDA or a CFG for the language, but the proces is tedious. We can get a much neater argument with Theorem 3.4.6.

Let $$L_1 = \{a^{100}\ b^{100}\}$$

Then, because L_1 is finite, it is regular. Also, it is easy to see that

$$L = \{a^n b^n : n \geq 0\} \cap \overline{L}_1$$

Since the complement of a regular language is regular, $\overline{L}_1$ is also regular. Also $\{a^n b^n : n \geq 0\}$ is a CFL. By Theorem 3.4.6 it follows that L is a CFL.

EXERCISES

1. Give context free grammars generating the following sets:

(*a*) The set of all strings over alphabet $\{a, b\}$ not of the form ww for some string w.

(*b*) $\{a^i\ b^j\ c^k\ /\ i \neq j \text{ or } j \neq k\}$.

(*c*) The set of even length strings in $\{a, b\}^*$ with the two middle symbols equal.

(*d*) The set of all odd length strings in $\{a, b\}^*$ whose first, middle and the last symbols are the same.

(*e*) $\{a^i\ b^j\ c^k\ /\ i = j + k\}$

(*f*) $\{a^i\ b^j\ c^k\ /\ j\ = i + k\}$

(*g*) $\{a^i\ b^j\ /\ i < 2j\}$

(*h*) $\{a^i\ b^j\ c^k\ /\ j = i \text{ or } j = k\}$

(*i*) $\{0^n\ 1^n\ /\ n \geq 0$

[**Hint:** See problem 30 (*j*) $\{0^n\ 1\ 0^n\ /\ n \geq 1\}$]

[**Hint:** See problem 32]

2. Construct a PDA to accept the language $L = \{a^i b^j / j > i\}$ *by* empty store. [See problem 18.]

3. Construct a PDA to accept the language $L = \{a^i b^j / j > i\}$ by final state [See problem 19.]

4. construct a PDA to accept the language $L = \{a^i b^j / i \leq 2_j\}$ by empty store.

5. Construct a PDA to accept the language $L = \{a^i b^j / i \leq 2j\}$ by final state.

6. Construct a PDA equivalent to the following CFG

(*a*) $S \rightarrow 0S0/1S1/A,\ A \rightarrow 2B3,\ B \rightarrow 2B3/3.$

(*b*) $S \rightarrow aB/bA,\ A \rightarrow a/aS/bAA,\ B \rightarrow b/bS/aBB$

(*c*) $S \rightarrow AB,\ B \rightarrow a,\ A \rightarrow Aa,\ A \rightarrow bB,\ B \rightarrow Sb$

(*d*) $S \rightarrow OB/1A,\ A \rightarrow 0/0S/1AA,\ B \rightarrow 1/1S/0BB.$

(*e*) $S \rightarrow SbS/a.$

(*f*) $S \rightarrow aSbb/aab$

7. Show that the following languages are not context free.

(*a*) $L = \{a^m b^n / n = m^2\}$

(*b*) $L = \{ww / w \in \{a, b\}^*\}$

(c) $L = \{a^i b^i a^i b^i / i \geq 0\}$

(d) $L = \{a^i b^i a^i b^i / i, j \geq 0\}$

(e) $L = \{wcw / w \in \{a, b\}^*\}$

(f) $L = \{a^n : n \geq 0\}$

(g) $L = \{a^n b^n : n \geq 0$, n is not a multiple of $5\}$

(h) $L = \{w \in \{a, b\}^* : n^a (w) = n^b (w)$, w does not contain a substring $aab\}$.

8. Construct a context free grammar generating each of the following languages and hence find a PDA accepting them by final state.

(a) $\{a^n b^m a^n / m, n \geq 1\} \cup \}\{a^n c^n / n \geq 1\}$

(b) $\{a^n b^m c^m d^n / m, n \geq 1\}$

9. Construct a PDA accepting by empty store each of the following languages.

(a) $L = \{a^m b^n / m > n \geq 1\}$

(b) $L = \{x \in \{a, b\}^* / n_a (x) < 2n_b (x)\}$

(c) $L = \{a^n b^{n+m} a^m / n, m \geq 0\}$

(d) $L = \{0^n 1^n / n \geq 0\}$

(e) $L = \{0^n 1^n / n \geq 1\}$

(f) $L = \{a, b\}^+$

(g) $L = \{a\}^+$

(h) $L = \{0^m 1^n / m \neq n$ and atleast one of m and $n \geq 1\}$

(i) $L = \{01^m 2^n{}_3 / m, n \geq 1\}$

(j) $L = \{a^n b^n c^i / n \geq 1, i \geq 0\}$

(k) $L = \{a^n b a^m / n, m \geq 1\}$

(l) $L = \{a^j b^n c^n / n \geq 1, j \geq 0\}$

(m) $L = \{0^n 1^n / n \geq 1\} \cup \{1^m 0^m / m \geq 1\}$

(n) $L = \{a^l b^m c^n /$ one of λ, m, n equals 1 and the remaining two are equal.$\}$

(o) $L = \{a^l b^m c^n / l + m = n\}$

(p) $L = \{(ab)^n / n \geq 1\} \cup \{(ba)^n / n \geq 1\}$

(q) $L = \{a^n b^{2n} : n \geq 0\}$

(r) $L = \{a^n b^m c^{n+m} : n \geq 0, m \geq 0\}$

(s) $L = \{a^3 b^n c^n : n \geq 0\}$

(t) $L = \{a^n b^m : n \leq m \leq 3n\}$

(u) $L = \{w : n_a(w) = n_b(w) + 1\}$

(v) $L = \{w : n_a(w) + n_b(w) = n_c(w)\}$

(w) $L = \{w : 2n_a(w) \leq n_b(w) \leq 3n_a(w)\}$

[**Hint:** Construct CFG generating the language then use 3.3.1. to construct the required PDA.]

10. Construct a PDA accepting by final state each of the languages given in problem 8.

[**Hint :** Consider the PDA of problem 8. Then use 3.2.3 to construct the required PDA.].

11. Find an NPDA with atmost two states for the language $L = \{a^n b^{n+1} : n \geq 0\}$.

12. Give reasons why one might conjecture that the following language is not deterministic.

$L = \{a^n b^m c^k : n = m \text{ or } m = k\}$

13. Is the language $\{wcw^R : w \in \{a, b\}^*]$ deterministic.

14. Show that $L = \{w \in \{a, b\}^* : n_a(w) \neq n_b(w)\}$ is a deterministic context free language.

15. Show that every regular language is a deterministic context free language.

16. Show that if L_1 is deterministic context free and L_2 is regular, then the language $L_1 \cup L_2$ is deterministic context free.

17. Show that under the conditions of problem 15, $L_1 \cap L_2$ is a deterministic context free language.

18. Is the following language context free ?

$L = \{a^{nm} : n \text{ and } m \text{ are prime numbers}\}$

19. Prove that the complement of the language

$L = \{a^{n^2} : n \geq 0\}$ is not context free.

20. Give an example of a CFL whose complement is not a CFL.

CHAPTER 4

Turing Machine

The two models of computation we have studied so far involve restrictions on either the amount of memory (an FSA can remember only its current state) or the way the memory is accessed (a PDA can access only the top stack symbol). The machines implementing these models are less powerful then the computers what we are using now.

In this chapter we study the Turing machine, a simple mathematical model of a computer. The machine was introduced by the English mathematician Alan Turing in the year 1936.

Turing began his work by considering a human computer (brain) while solving some problems. Based on this, he assumed that the computer could operate under the following three rules.

1. Examining the symbols written on the paper. The symbols are from some fixed finite set.
2. Each step taken by the computer depends only on the symbol he is currently examining and on his 'state of mind' at the time.
3. Although this state of mind might change as a result of symbols he has seen or computations he has made, only a finite number of distinct states of mind are possible.

A Turing machine will have a finite alphabet set of symbols and a finite set of states, corresponding to the possible 'states of mind' of the human computer. Instead of a sheet of paper, Turing specified a linear 'tape' which has a left end and is infinite to the right. The tape is marked off into squares, each of which can hold one symbol from the alphabet, if a square has no symbol on it, we say that it contains the blank symbol. We may think of the square as being numbered left-to-right, starting from 0.

The reading and writing work being done by a *tape head* which scans one cell of tape at a time. Each cell of the tape may hold exactly one of a finite number of tape symbols. In one move the Turing machine, depending upon the symbol scanned by the tape head and the state of the finite control

(1) Changes state

(2) Prints a symbol on the tape cell scanned replacing what was written there, and

(3) Moves its head left or right one cell.

We can get *final* or *halting* states beyond which the computation need not continue. It is also possible for the computation *not to stop*, and for the Turing machine to continue making moves for ever.

The great advantage of the Turing machine is its simplicity and uniformity. Since there is only one type of instruction, there is no question as to appropriate choices for time and space complexity measures: the time taken by a Turing machine is simply the number of steps taken by the computation and the space used by a Turing machine is simply the total number of distinct tape squares scanned during the computation. The great disadvantage of the Turing machine is that it requires much time to carry out elementary operations that a modern computer can execute in one instruction. Elementary arithmetic, simple tests (e.g., for parity) and especially access to a stored quantity, all require large amount of time on a Turing machine.

4.1. DEFINITIONS AND EXAMPLES

4.1.1. Definition

A Turing machine (TM) is a 5-tuple

$M = (Q, \Sigma, \Gamma, q_0, B, \delta, F)$ where

Q is the finite set of states

Γ is the finite set of allowable tape symbols.

B a symbol of Γ, is the blank.

Σ a subset of Γ not including B, is the set of input symbols.

δ is the next move function, a mapping from $Q \times \Gamma$ to $Q \times \Gamma \times \{L, R, H\}$ (possibly undefined at certain points)

$q_0 \in Q$ is the start state.

$F \subseteq Q$ is the set of final states.

For elements $q, r \in Q$, $X, Y \in \Gamma$ and $D \in \{R, L, H\}$ we interpret the formula

$$\delta(q, X) = \{r, Y, D\}$$

to mean that when M is in state q and the current symbol scanning is X, then the machine replaces X by Y, changes the state q to r and either moves the tape head one cell right or moves it one cell left or halts depending on whether D is R, L or H respectively.

4.1.2. Definition

An *Instantaneous Description* (ID) of the Turing machine M is denoted by $\alpha_1 q \alpha_2$. Here $q \in Q$ is the current state of M; α_1, α_2 is the string in Γ^* that is the contents of the tape up to the rightmost non-blank symbol or the symbol to the left of the head, whichever is rightmost.

We define a *move* of M as follows. Let $X_1 X_2 \ldots X_{i-1} q X_i \ldots X_n$ be an ID. Let $\delta(q_i X_i) = (p, Y, L)$. If $i - 1 = n$, then take X_i as B. If $i = 1$, then there is no next ID, as the tape head is not allowed to fall off the left end of the tape. If $i > 1$, then we write

$$X_1 X_2 \ldots X_{i-1}\, q\, X_i X_{i+1} \ldots X_n \vdash_M X_1 X_2 \ldots X_{i-2}\, p\, X_{i-1} Y X_{i+1} \ldots X_n \qquad \ldots (4.1)$$

Suppose $\delta(q, X_i) = (p, Y, R)$. Then we write

$$X_1 X_2 \ldots X_{i-1}\, q\, X_i X_{i+1} \ldots X_n \vdash_M X_1 X_2 \ldots X_{i-1}\, Y\, p\, X_{i+1} \ldots X_n \qquad \ldots (4.2)$$

If $i - 1 = n$, the string $X_i \ldots X_n$ is empty, and the right side of (4.2) is longer than left side. If one ID results from the another by one move, they are related by the symbol $\vdash_M$.

If one ID results by some finite number of moves, including zero moves, they are related by the symbol $\vdash^*_M$. Some times we drop the subscript M from $\vdash_M$ or $\vdash^*_M$ when no confusion arise.

4.1.3. Definition

The language accepted by M denoted by $L(M)$ is

$\{w : w \in \Sigma^* \text{ and } q_0\, w \vdash^* \alpha_1\, p\, \alpha_2 \text{ for some } p \text{ in } F, \alpha_1, \alpha_2 \in \Gamma^*\}$

When a Turing machine processes an input string x_1, there are three possibilities. The machine can accept the string by entering the accepting state; it can reject the string by entering the non accepting state or it can enter an infinite loop so that it never halts.

4.1.4. Example

Design a TM M to accept the language

$$L = \{0^n 1^n : n \geq 1\}.$$

Solution. The general idea is as follows:

Initially the tape of M contains $0^n\ 1^n$ followed by an infinity of blanks. Repeatedly M replaces the left most 0 by X, moves right to the left most 1 replaces it by Y, moves left to find the right most X, then moves one cell right to the left most 0 and repeats the cycle. While searching for a 1 if M finds a blank, then M halts without accepting. If, after changing *a* 1 to *a* Y, M finds no more 0's then M checks whether there is any other 1's left out, if none, then it accepts.

Let $M = (Q, \Sigma, \Gamma, q_0, B, \delta, F)$ be a TM

where $Q = \{q_0, q_1, q_2, q_3, q_4\}$,

$\Sigma = \{0, 1\}$

$\Gamma = \{0, 1, X, Y, B\}$, q_0 is the starting state,

$F = \{q_4\}$.

q_0 is used immediately prior to each replacement of a left most 0 by an X.

q_1 is used to search right, skipping 0's and Y's until it finds the leftmost 1 and replaces 1 by Y and the machine enters the state q_2.

q_2 is used to search left for an X and if it finds then it enters state q_0, moving right to the leftmost 0, as it changes state.

q_3 is used to scan over Y's and check that no 1's remain. If the Y's are followed by B, then the machine enters the accepting state q_4; otherwise the string is rejected.

The action δ of M is defined as follows :

$\delta(q_0, 0) = (q_1, X, R)$ $\quad\quad$ $\delta(q_2, X) = (q_0, X, R)$

$\delta(q_0, Y) = (q_3, Y, R)$ $\quad\quad$ $\delta(q_2, Y) = (q_2, Y, L)$

$\delta(q_1, 0) = (q_1, 0, R)$ $\quad\quad$ $\delta(q_3, Y) = (q_3, Y, R)$

$\delta(q_1, 1) = (q_2, Y, L)$ $\quad\quad$ $\delta(q_3, B) = (q_4, B, H)$

$\delta(q_1, Y) = (q_1, Y, R)$

$\delta(q_2, 0) = (q_2, 0, L)$

The computation of M on the input string 0011 is as follows:

$$q_0\,0011 \vdash X\,q_1\,011 \vdash X0q_1\,11 \vdash Xq_20Y1$$
$$\vdash q_2\,X\,0Y1 \vdash Xq_0\,0Y1 \vdash XXq_1Y1$$
$$\vdash XXYq_1\,1 \vdash XXq_2YY \vdash Xq_2XYY$$

$$\vdash XXq_0YY \vdash XXYq_3Y \vdash XXYYq_3$$

$$\vdash XXYYBq_4.$$

In most simple examples, it will be helpful once again to draw transition diagram, similar to those of FSA's.

4.1.5. Definition

A *state diagram* or *transition diagram* is a digraph in which each node corresponds to a distinct state of the machine. The label on the edge shows the scanned symbol and the particular action taken. For example, such a state diagram is given in Fig. 4.1. The move

$$\delta(q, X) = (r, Y, D)$$

is represented by

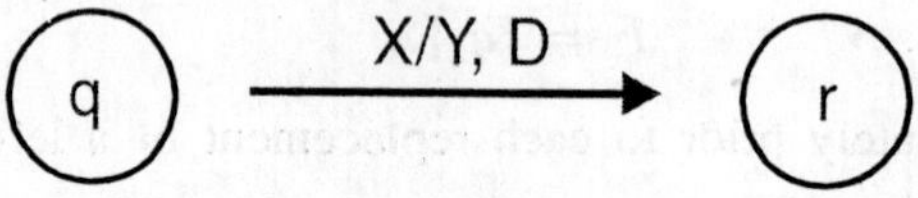

Fig. 4.1.

4.1.6. Definition

Design a TM to accept the language *pal* of palindromes over $\{a, b\}$.

Solution. Let $M = \{Q, \Sigma, \Gamma, q_0, B, \delta, F)$ be a TM, where

$$Q = \{q_0, q_1, q_2, q_3, q_4, q_5, q_6, q_7\}, \Sigma = \{a, b\},$$

$$\Gamma = \{a, b, B\}.$$

We discuss the moves made for three different kinds of input strings.

Non palindrome, even-length palindrome, odd-length palindrome.

The action δ is defined as follows:

$\delta(q_0, B) = (q_1, B, R)$	$\delta(q_2, a) = (q_2, a, R)$
$\delta(q_1, a) = (q_2, B, R)$	$\delta(q_2, b) = (q_2, b, R)$
$\delta(q_1, b) = (q_5, B, R)$	$\delta(q_2, B) = (q_3, B, L)$
$\delta(q_5, B) = (q_6, B, L)$	$\delta(q_3, a) = \{q_4, B, L)$
$\delta(q_5, a) = (q_5, a, R)$	$\delta(q_4, a) = (q_4, a, L)$
$\delta(q_5, b) = (q_5, b, R)$	$\delta(q_4, b) = (q_4, b, L)$
$\delta(q_6, b) = (q_4, B, L)$	$\delta(q_3, B) = (q_7, B, R)$

$\delta(q_6, B) = (q_7, B, R)$ $\delta(q_4, B) = (q_1, B, R)$

$\delta(q_1, B) = (q_7, B, R)$

Diagrammatic form

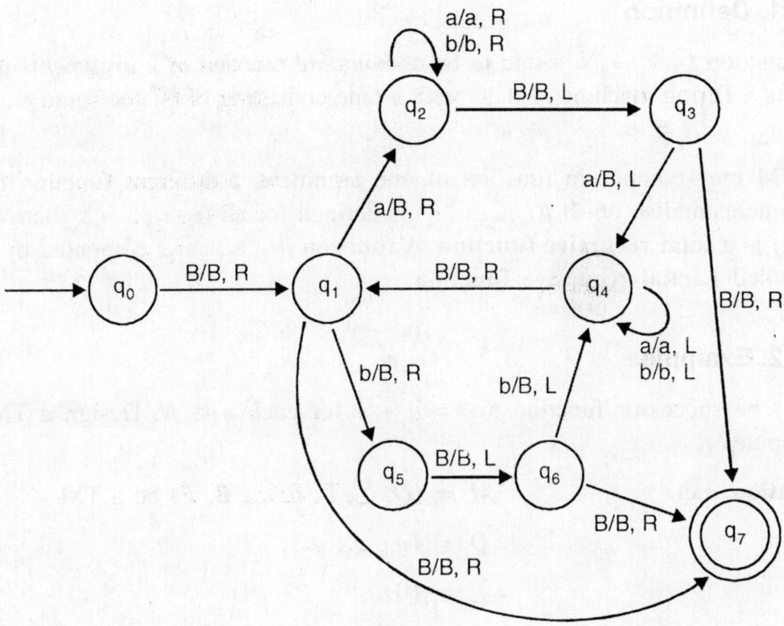

Fig. 4.2.

Even Palindrome

$q_0\ Baa \vdash Bq_1aa \vdash BBq_2\ a \vdash BBaq_2B \vdash BBq_3\ a \vdash Bq_4\ BB \vdash BBq_1B \vdash BBBq_7B$ (accepted)

Odd Palintrome

$q_0Baba \vdash Bq_1aba \vdash BBq_2\ ba \vdash BBbq_2a \vdash BBbaq_2B \vdash BBbq_3a \vdash BBq_4bB \vdash Bq_4Bb \vdash BBq_1b \vdash BBBq_5B \vdash BBq_6B \vdash BBBq_7$ (accepted)

Consider a non palindrome say *abaa*.

$q_0Babaa \vdash Bq_1abaa \vdash BBq_2baa \vdash BBbq_2aa \vdash BBbaq_2a \vdash BBbaaq_2\ B \vdash BBbaq_3a \vdash BBbq_4aB \vdash BBq_4ba \vdash Bq_4Bba \vdash BBq_1ba \vdash BBBq_5a \vdash BBBaq_5B \vdash BBBq_6a$(reject)

4.2. COMPUTABLE LANGUAGES AND FUNCTIONS

The Turing machine may be viewed as a computer of functions from positive integers to positive integers. Each integer will be represented in an unary fashion.

That is, the integer $i \geq 0$ is represented by the string 0^i. If a function has k arguments $i_1, i_2, \ldots i_k$, then these integers are initially placed on the tape separated by B's as $0^{i_1}, 0^{i_2}, \ldots 0^{i_k}$.

4.2.1. Definition

A function $f : N \to N$ is said to be *computable function of k arguments* if there exists a Turing machine M halts with a tape consisting of 0^m for some m, where $f(i_1, i_2, \ldots i_k) = m$.

A TM may compute a function of one argument, a different function of two arguments and so on. If $f(i_1, i_2, \ldots, i_k)$ is defined for all $(i_1, i_2, \ldots i_k)$, then we say that f is a **total recursive function**. A function $f(i_1, i_2, \ldots i_k)$ computed by a TM is called **partial recursive function.**

4.2.2. Example

Let f be successor function $f(n) = n + 1$ for each $n \in N$. Design a TM that computes f.

Solution. Let $M = (Q, \Sigma, \Gamma, \delta, q_0, B, F)$ be a TM

where
$$Q = \{q_0, q_1, q_2\},$$
$$\Sigma = \{0\},$$
$$\Gamma = \{0, B\},$$
$$F = \{q_2\}$$

and δ is as follows:

$$\delta(q_0, 0) = (q_0, 0, R)$$
$$\delta(q_0, B) = (q_1, 0, R)$$
$$\delta(q, B) = (q_2, B, H)$$

For example, the computation of 0^3 is :

$q_0\, 0^3 \vdash 0q_000 \vdash 00q_00 \vdash 000q_0B \vdash 0000q_1B \vdash 0000q_2$ and in general

$$q_00^n \overset{*}{\vdash} 0^{n+1}\, q_2.$$

4.2.3. Example

The function $f(n) = n + 3$ is computable.

Solution. Let $M = (Q, \Sigma, \Gamma, q_1, B, \delta, F)$ be the *TM*

where $Q = \{q_1, q_2, q_3, q_4\},$

$$\Sigma = \{0\},$$
$$\Gamma = \{0, B\},$$
$$F = \{q_4\}$$

and δ is defined as follows:

$$\delta(q_1, 0) = (q_1, 0, L)$$
$$\delta(q_1, B) = (q_2, 0, L)$$
$$\delta(q_2, B) = (q_3, 0, L)$$
$$\delta(q_3, B) = (q_4, 0, H)$$

The computation sequence of the string 0^3 is :

$q_1 0^3 \vdash Bq_1 B0^3 \vdash q_2 B0^4 \vdash q_3 B0^5 \vdash q_4 0^6$.

Note. It is clear that, for any positive integer k, the function $f(n) = n + k$ is computable.

4.2.4. Example

The addition function $f(m, n) = m + n$ is computable.

Solution. Let the input be $w = 0^m\ 0^n$.

Let $M = (Q, \Sigma, \Gamma, q_1, \delta, B, F)$ be the TM with

$$Q = \{q_1, q_2, q_3, q_4\},$$
$$\Sigma = \{0\},$$
$$\Gamma = \{0, 1, B\},$$
$$F = \{q_4\}$$

and δ is defined as follows :

$\delta(q_1, 0) = \{q_2, B, R\}$ $\delta(q_2, 1) = (q_3, 0, R)$

$\delta(q_2, 0) = (q_2, 0, R)$ $\delta(q_3, B) = (q_4, B, H)$

$\delta(q_3, 0) = (q_3, 0, R)$

Consider the string $0^3\ 10^4$. The computation is:

$q_1 0^3 10^4 \vdash Bq_2 0^2 10^4 \overset{*}{\vdash} B00q_2 10^4 \vdash B000q_3 0^4 \overset{*}{\vdash} B0^3 0^4 q_3 B \vdash 0^7 q_4$.

4.2.2. Example

Design a TM that can compute proper subtraction. That is $m - n$

$$m \dot{-} n = \begin{cases} m - n \text{ if } m > n \\ 0 \text{ if } m \le n. \end{cases}$$

Solution. Let $M = (Q, \Sigma, \Gamma, \delta, q_0, B, F)$ be the required TM where

$Q = \{q_0, q_1, q_2, q_3, q_5, q_6\}$

$\Sigma = \{0, 1\}$,

$\Gamma = \{0, 1, B\}$, and the action of M is defined as follows.

Let $w = 0^m/0^n$ be the input string. In order to get the output the machine should halt with 0^{m-n} on its tape. The general idea of construction is as follows:

M repeatedly replaces its leading 0 by B, then searches right for a 1 followed by a 0 and changes the 0 to 1. Next M moves left until it finds a blank and then repeats the cycle. The process comes to an end if;

(*i*) Searching right for a 0, M finds a blank. In that case n 0's in $0^m\ 1\ 0^n$ have all been changed to 1's and $n + 1$ of the m 0's have been changed to B. Then $n + 1$ 1's is changed by a 0 and n B's leaving $m - n$ 0's on its tape.

(*ii*) M cannot find a 0 to change to B, because the first m 0's already have been changed. Then $n \geq m$, so $m - n = 0$. M replaces all remaining 1's and 0's by B.

q_0 is the unitial state.

q_1 is used to search for 1 in the right.

q_2 is used to search for '0' on right. If '0' is found, then changes 0 to 1.

q_3 is used to move left to find a blank and then it enters q_0 to repeat the cycle.

q_4 is used to move left, changing all 1's to B's until encountering a blank B. When q_b is entered, B is changed back to 0 and M halts.

The function δ is described as follows.

States	*Inputs*		
	0	*1*	*B*
q_0	(q_1, B, R)	(q_5, B, R)	–
q_1	$(q_1, 0, R)$	$(q_2, 1, R)$	–
q_2	$(q_3, 1, L)$	$(q_2, 1, R)$	(q_4, B, L)
q_3	$(q_3, 0, L)$	$(q_3, 1, L)$	(q_0, B, R)
q_4	$(q_4, 0, L)$	(q_4, B, L)	$(q_6, 0, R)$
q_5	(q_5, B, R)	(q_5, B, R)	(q_6, B, R)

Let $m = 2$, $n = 1$, then the computation of the string $0^2\ 1\ 0^1$ is as follows:

$q_0\,0010 \vdash Bq_1\,010 \vdash B0q_1 10 \vdash B01q_2 0 \vdash B0q_3 11 \vdash Bq_3\,011 \vdash q_3 B011 \vdash Bq_0 011$

$\vdash BBq_1 11 \vdash BB1q_2 1 \vdash BB11q_2 \vdash BB1q_4 1 \vdash BBq_4 1 \vdash Bq_4 \vdash B0q_6$

(accepting state)

For $m = 1$, $n = 2$, the computation is:

$q_0\ 0100 \vdash Bq_1 100 \vdash B1q_2 00 \vdash Bq_3 110 \vdash q_3 B110 \vdash Bq_0 110 \vdash BBq_5 10 \vdash BBBq_5 0 \vdash BBBBq_5 \vdash BBBBBq_6.$

4.2.5. Theorem

Let $f : N \to N$, $g : N \to N$ be computable functions. Then the composition function $h = g.f$ is computable.

Proof. Suppose M_f and M_g are the Turing machines which compute f and g respectively. Given the input $0^n = \{n\}$, we apply M_f to $\{n\}$ and obtain an expression E with $[E] = f(n)$. We then arrange that E: $\delta(q_0, 0f^{(n)})$. We next add 0 to E to obtain E': $\delta(q_0, 00f^{(n)})$ and apply Mg to E'. This gives $[E''] = g(f(n) = (g \circ f)\ (n)$ as required.

4.2.6. Definition

Let $L \subseteq \Sigma^*$ be a language. A Turing machine M with input alphabet Σ is said to accept L if $L(M) = L$. M recognizes or decides, L if M computes the characteristic function $X_L : \Sigma^* \to \{0, 1\}$. That is M recognizes L if M halts in a state H for every input string $x \in \Sigma^*$ producing output

$$X_L(x) = \begin{cases} 1 \text{ if } x \in L \\ 0 \text{ otherwise.} \end{cases}$$

A language that is accepted by a Turing machine is said to *recursively enumerable*. The class of recursively enumerable languages includes some languages for which we cannot mechanically determine membership. If $L(M)$ is such a language, then any Turing machine recognizing $L(M)$ must fail to halt on some input not in $L(M)$. If w is in $L(M)$, then M eventually halts on input w. However, as long as M is still running on some input, we can never tell whether M will eventually accept if it run forever.

A language L is said to be *recursive* if there exist at least one Turing machine that halts on all inputs (note that halting may or may not be preceded by acceptance).

The partial recursive functions are analogous to the recursively enumerable function, since they are computed by TM that may or may not halt on a given input. The total recursive functions correspond to the recursive languages, since they are computed by TM's that always halt. All common arithmetic functions on integers, such as multiplication, $n!$, $.2^{2^n}$ are total recursive functions.

4.3. TURING MACHINE CONSTRUCTION

In order to describe complicated TM construction we need some higher-level conceptual tools. In this section we discuss the principal tools.

4.3.1. Storage in the finite control.

The finite control can be used to hold only finite amount of information. Consider a TM as in Definition 4.1.1. and instead of taking states of M as a single element, consider it as a pair of elements like $[q_0, a]$. The first component of the state, controls the action while the second component 'stores' a symbol in the finite control.

4.3.2. Example

Design a Turing machine M that looks at the first input symbol, records it in its finite control, and checks that the symbol does not appear elsewhere on its input.

Let $M = [Q, \{0, 1\}, \{0, 1, B\}, \delta, \{q_0, B\}, B, F]$ be a TM with

$Q = \{[q_0, 0], [q_0, 1], [q_0, B], [q_1, 0], [q_1, 1], [q_1, B]\}$ and

$F = \{[q_1, B]\}$.

q_0 is used as the initial state which is the control component of the state, and M moves right. The first component of M's state changed to q_1, and the first symbol is stored in the second component. If M stored 0, then it looks for 1 and continue to move to the right. M enters the final state $[q_1, B]$ if it looks a blank symbol without having encountered a second copy of the first input symbol. If M encounters the tape symbol stored in its state, M halts with out accepting. If M reaches a blank in state $[q_1, 0]$ or $[q_1, 1]$, M accepts.

Define δ as follows:

States	*0*	*1*	*B*
$[q_0, 3]$	$([q_1, 0], 0, R)$	$([q_1, 1], 1, R)$	–
$[q_1, 0]$	–	$([q_1, 0], 1, R)$	$([q_1, B], 0, L)$
$[q_1, 1]$	$([q_1, 1], 0, R)$	–	$([q_1, B], 0, L)$

For state $[q_1, 0]$ and symbol 0 or for state $[q_1, 1]$ and symbol 1, δ is not defined.

For example.

Let w = 110 be the input string then the computation is:

$$[q_0, B]\ 110 \vdash 1[q_1, 1]\ 10 \qquad (\delta \text{ is not defined})$$

since it finds 1 second time, the machine halts.

4.3.3. Multiple tracks

We can image that the tape of the TM is divided into k tracks, for any finite k. The symbols on the tape are considered k-tuples, one component for each track. The finite control have k-components, all but one of which store information.

4.3.4. Example

Design a TM to test whether the input is a prime.

Solution: Consider a TM with a 3 track tape as shown in Fig. 4.4.

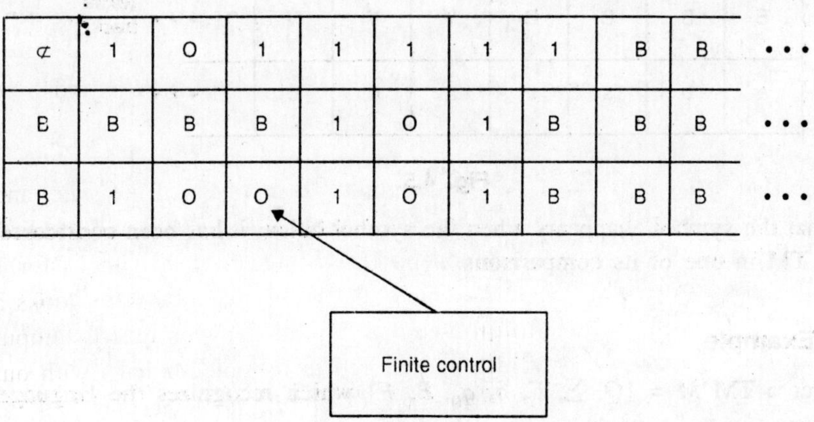

Fig. 4.4.

It takes a binary input greater than 2, written on the first track, and determines whether it is a prime. The input is surrounded by the symbols ¢ and \$ on the first track. Thus the allowable input symbols are [¢, B, B], [0, B, B], [1, B, B] and [\$, B, B]. These symbols can be identified with ¢, 0, 1, & \$ respectively when viewed as input symbols. The blank symbol can be identified with [B, B, B].

To test if the input is a prime, the TM first writes the number 2 in binary on the second track and copies the first track on to the third. Then the second track is subtracted as many times as possible, from the third track effectively dividing the third track by the second and leaving the remainder.

If the remainder is zero, the number on the first track is not a prime. If the remainder is non-zero, the number on the second track is increased by one. If the second track equals the first, the number on the first track is a prime, because it can not be divided by any number lying properly between 1 and itself. If the second is less than first, the whole operation is repeated for the new number on the second track.

4.3.5. Checking off symbols

It is a useful trick for visualizing how a TM recognizes languages defined by repeated strings, such as

$$\{ww : w \in \Sigma^*\} \text{ or } \{ww^R : w \in \Sigma^*\}$$

It is also useful when lengths of substrings must be compared. For example

$$\{a^i b^i : i \geq 1\} \text{ or } \{a^i b^j c^k : i \neq j, \text{ or } j \neq k\}.$$

We introduce an extra track on the tape that holds a blank B or √ as in Fig. 4.5.

B	B	B	B	V	V	V	• • •	(extra track)
a	b	a	c	a	b	c	• • •	

Fig. 4.5.

Note that the symbol √ appears when the symbol below it has been considered by the TM in one of its comparisons.

4.3.6. Example

Consider a TM $M = \{Q, \Sigma, \Gamma, \delta, q_0, B, F\}$ which recognizes the language $L = \{wcw : w \in \{a, b\}^*\}$

Let $Q = \{[q, d] : q = q_1, q_2, \ldots q_9$ and

and $d = a_1\ b, \text{ or } B\}$

$$\Sigma = \{[B, d] : d = a, b \text{ or } c\}$$

$$\Gamma = [\{B, d\} \text{ or } \{\surd, d\} : d = a, b, c, \text{ or } B\}$$

$$q_0 = [q_1, B]$$

$$F = \{[q_9, B]\}$$

Note that $[B, d]$ and d are same. For notational purpose only we are using $[B, d]$. The second component of the state $[q, d]$ is used to store an input symbol in the finite control. Also identify $[B, B]$ with B. That is, think that $[B, B]$ and B are same.

The general idea of computation is as follows.

First M checks the symbol scanned on the tape and stores in the finite control and moves right. It keeps on continuing to look for 'c'. If it finds 'c', then it enters a state with first component q_3. Again M moves right over checked symbols. If M encounters an unchecked symbol, then it checks whether the symbol matches the one stored in the finite control. If the symbols disagree, then M has no next move and it halts without accepting. M also halts if in state q_3 it reaches $[B, B]$ before finding an unchecked symbol. If the unchecked symbol agree with the one in finite control, then M moves to left over checked symbols. Suppose the symbol immediately to the left of c is unchecked, then M proceeds left to find the rightmost checked symbol. If it finds, then it moves right to pick up another symbol for comparison. Then it changes it state with first component q_1.

If a checked symbol appears immediately to the left of c, all symbols to the left of c have been checked. M must test whether all symbols to the right have been checked. If so they must have compared properly with the symbols to the left of c, so M will accept. M moves right, if it finds the blank, it halts and accepts. If M finds an unchecked symbol when its first component of state is q_8, it halts without accepting.

The action of δ is defined as follows:

1. $\delta([q_1, B], [B, a]) = ([q_2, a], [\surd, a], R)$
2. $\delta([q, B], [B, b]) = ([q_2, b], [\surd, b], R)$
3. $\delta([q_2, a] [B, a]) = ([q_2, a], [B, a], R)$
4. $\delta([q_2, a], [B, b]) = ([q_2, a], [B, b], R)$
5. $\delta([q_2, b], [B, a]) = ([q_2, b], [B, a], R)$
6. $\delta([q_2, b], [B, b]) = ([q_2, b], [B, b], R)$
7. $\delta([q_2, a], [B, c]) = ([q_3, a], [B, c], R)$
8. $\delta([q_2, b], [B, c]) = ([q_3, b], [B, c], R)$
9. $\delta([q_3, b], [B, a]) = ([q_4, B], [\surd, a], L)$
10. $\delta([q_3, b], [\surd, b]) = ([q_3, b], [\surd, b], R)$
11. $\delta([q_3, a], [\surd, a]) = ([q_3, a], [\surd, a], R)$
12. $\delta([q_3, a], [B, b]) = ([q_4, B], [\surd, b], L)$
13. $\delta([q_3, a], [B, a]) = ([q_4, B], [\surd, a], L)$

14. $\delta([q_3, b], [B, b]) = ([q_4, B], [\surd, b], L)$

15. $\delta([q_4, B], [\surd, a]) = ([q_4, B], [\surd, a], L)$

16. $\delta([q_4, B], [\surd, b)) = ([q_4, B], [\surd, b], L)$

17. $\delta([q_4, B], [B, c]) = ([q_5, B], [B, c], L)$

18. $\delta([q_5, B], [B, a]) = ([q_6, B], [B, a], L)$

19. $\delta([q_5, B], [B, b]) = ([q_6, B], [B, b], L)$

20. $\delta([q_6, B], [\surd, a]) = ([q_1, B], [\surd, a], R)$

21. $\delta([q_6, B], [\surd, b]) = ([q_1, B], [\surd, b], R)$

22. $\delta([q_5, B], [\surd, a]) = ([q_7, B], [\surd, a], R)$

23. $\delta([q_5, B], [\surd, b]) = ([q_7, B], [\surd, b], R)$

24. $\delta([q_7, B], [B, c]) = ([q_8, B], [B, c], R)$

25. $\delta([q_8, B], [\surd, a]) = ([q_8, B), [\surd, a], R)$

26. $\delta([q_8, B], [\surd, b]) = ([q_8, B], [\surd, b], R)$

27. $\delta([q_8, B], [B, B]) = ([q_9, B], [\surd, B], L)$

Let $w = ab$. Then we check whether the machine accepts the string *abcba* or not. Identify a with $[B, a]$, b with $[B, b]$ c with $[B, c]$.

Then $[q_1, B]$ $[B, a]$ $[B, b]$ $[B, c]$, $[B, b]$, $[B, a]$

$\vdash [\surd, a]\ [q_2, a]\ [B, b]\ [B, c]\ [B, b]\ [B, a]$

$\vdash [\surd, a]\ [B, b]\ [q_2, a]\ [B, c]\ [B, b]\ [B, a]$

$\vdash [\surd, a]\ [B, b]\ [B, c]\ [q_3, a]\ [B, b]\ [B, a]$

$\vdash [\surd, a]\ [B, b]\ [q_4, B]\ [B, c]\ [\surd, b]\ [B, a]$

$\vdash [\surd, a]\ [q_5, B]\ [B, b]\ [B, c]\ [\surd, b]\ [B, a]$

$\vdash [q_6, B]\ [\surd, a]\ [B, b]\ [B, c]\ [\surd, b]\ [B, a]$

$\vdash [\surd, a]\ [q_1, B]\ [B, b\}\ [B, c]\ [\surd, b]\ [B, a]$

$\vdash [\surd, a]\ [\surd, b]\ [q_2, b]\ [B, c]\ [\surd, b]\ [B, a]$

$\vdash [\surd, a]\ [\surd, b]\ [B, c]\ [q_3, b]\ [\surd, b]\ [B, a]$

$\vdash [\surd, a]\ [\surd, b]\ [B, c]\ [\surd, b]\ [q_3, b]\ [B, a]$

$\vdash [\surd, a]\ [\surd, b]\ [B, c]\ [q_4, B]\ [\surd, b]\ [\surd, a]$

$\vdash [\surd, a]\ [\surd, B]\ [q_4, b]\ [B, c]\ [\surd, b]\ [\surd, a]$

$\vdash [\surd, a]\ [q_5, B]\ [\surd, b]\ [B, c]\ [\surd, b]\ [\surd, a]$

$\vdash$ [√, a] [√, b] [q_7, B] [B, c] [√, b] [√, a]

$\vdash$ [√, a] [√, b] [B, c] [q_8, B] [√, b] [√, a]

$\vdash$ [√, a] [√, b] [B, c] [√, b] [q_8, B] [√, a]

$\vdash$ [√, a] [√, b] [B, c] [√, b] [√, a] [q_8, B][B, B]

$\vdash$ [√, a] [√, b] [B, c] [√, b] [q_9, B] [√, a][√, B]

Here [q_9, B] is the accepting state. It checks all the symbols by comparing with the symbols already stored in the finite control.

4.3.7. Shifting over

A Turing machine can make space on its tape by shifting all non-blank symbols to a finite number of cells to the right. For that, the tape head moves to the right, repeatedly storing the symbols read in its finite control and replacing them with symbols read from cells to the left. The TM can then return to the vacated cells and print symbols that have chosen. If space is available, it can push blocks of symbols left in a similar manner.

4.3.8. Example

Construct a TM, $M = (Q, \Sigma, \Gamma, \delta, q_0, B, F)$ that shift non-blank symbols two cells to the right.

Solution. Assume that the tape of M does not contain blanks between non-blanks, so when it reaches a blank it knows to stop the shifting process.

Let Q contain states of the form $[q, A_1, A_2]$ for $q = q_1$ or q_2 and $A_1, A_2 \in \Gamma$. Let X be a special symbol not used by M except in the shifting process. M starts the shifting process in state $[q_1, B, B]$. The function δ are as follows:

(1) $\delta([q_1, B, B], A_1) = [(q_1, B, A_1), X, R]$

for $A_1 \in \Gamma - [B, X]$

M stores the first symbol A_1 read in the third component of its state $[q_1, B, B]$ and X is printed on the cell scanned, and M moves to the right.

(2) $\delta([q_1, B, A_1], A_2) = ([q_1, A_1, A_2], X, R)$ for $A_1, A_2 \in \Gamma - [B, X]$

Now M shifts the symbol A_1 in the third component of the state to second component, stores the symbol being read in the third component, prints an X and moves right.

(3) $\delta([q_1, A_1, A_2], A_3) = ([q_1, A_2, A_3], \text{A}, R)$

for $A_1, A_2, A_3 \in \Gamma - [B, X]$.

Again M reads a symbol A_3 stores it in the third component of state, shifts the symbol previously in the third component, A_2 to the second component, and deposits the second component symbol A_1, on the cell scanned, and moves right. Thus a symbol will be deposited two cells to the right of its original position.

(4) $$\delta([q_1, A_1, A_2], B) = ([q_1, A_2, B], A_1, R)$$
$$A_1, A_2 \in \Gamma - [B, X].$$

When a blank is seen on the tape, the stored symbols are deposited on the tape.

(5) $$\delta([q_1, A_1, B], B) = ([q_2, B, B], A_1, L)$$
$$\delta([q_1, A_2, B], B) = ([q_2, B, B], A_2, L)$$

After all symbols have been deposited, M sets the first component of state to q_2, and moves left to find an X, which marks the right most vacated cell.

(6) $$\delta([q_2, B, B], A) = ([q_2, B, B], A, L)$$
for $$A \in \Gamma - [B, X].$$

M moves left until an X is found. When X is found, M transfers to a state that we have assumed exists in Q and resumes its other functions.

Consider the string A_1A_2. The computation is as follows:

$$[q_1, B, B]\, A_1A_2 \vdash X[q_1, B, A_1]\, A_2$$
$$\vdash XX[q_1, A_1, A_2]\, B$$
$$\vdash XXA_1[q_1, A_2, B]\, B$$
$$\vdash XX[q_2, B, B]\, A_1\, A_2.$$

Hence it shifts two cells to the right.

4.3.9. Subroutines

A subprogram represents a mathematical function that maps each particular set of arguments into a particular set of results. It has the following characteristics :

(*i*) Each subprogram has a single entry point.

(*ii*) The calling program unit is suspended during the execution of the called subprogram which implies that there is only one subprogram in execution at any give time.

(*iii*) Control always returns to the caller when the subprogram execution terminates.

A *subprogram cell* is the explicit request that the subprogram be executed.

There are two distinct categories of subprograms : Procedures (subroutines) and functions.

If a subprogram returns a single result data object explicitly; it is termed as a *function.* If a subprogram returns more than one result or if it modifies its arguments (not returning explicitly), then it is termed as a procedure or *subroutine*. Each subroutine has one entry and one exit, or return.

Procedures can produce results in the calling program unit by two methods. First, if there are variables that are not formal parameters but are still visible in both the procedure and calling program unit, the procedure can change them, Second, if the subprogram has formal parameters that allow the transfer of data to the caller, those parameters can be changed.

Subprograms typically describe computations. There are two ways that a subprogram can gain access to the data that it is to process. Through direct access to non-local variables or through parameter-passing. Latter way is more flexible than the former.

The advanced coding technique-top-down programming is analogous to top-down design. The first code written for a component reflects the highest level of design. The code may contain nothing but conditional statements and call to subroutines. Top-down program encourages modularity. That is each subroutine should be easily replaced by a new module.

As in the case of programs we use subroutines to define elementary processes like ADD, COPY etc. A Turing machine can simulate any type of subroutine including recursive procedures and any of the known parameter passing mechanisms.

Part of a TM program can be written to serve as a subroutine; it have a designated initial state and a designated return state which temporarily has no move and which is used to effect a return to the calling routine. To design a TM that 'calls' the sub routine, a new set of states for the subroutine is made, and a move from the return state is specified.

The call is effected by entering the initial state for the subroutine, and the return is effected by the move from the return state.

4.3.10. Example

Design a TM, M to perform multiplication.

Let M starts with the input $0^m 1 0^n$. The general idea is to place a 1 after 0^m 1 0^n and then copy the block of n 0's on to the right end m times, each time erasing one of the m 0's. The result is 1 0^n 1 0^{mn}. Finally the prefix 10^n 1 is erased leaving 0^{mn}.

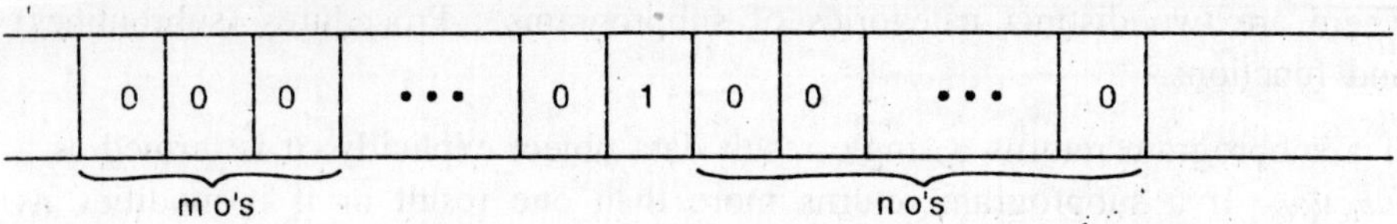

String $0^m 10^n$

Fig. 4.6 (a).

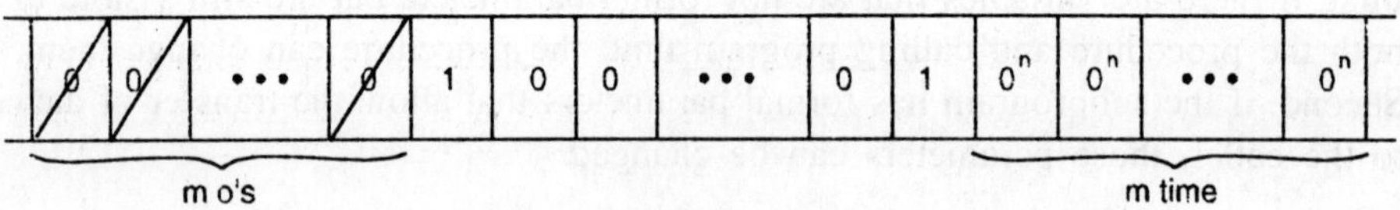

String $10^n 10^{nm}$

Fig. 4.6 (b).

The subroutine copy is defined as follows:

States	0	1	2	*B*
q_1	$(q_2, 2, R)$	$(q_4, 1, L)$		
q_2	$(q_2, 0, R)$	$(q_2, 1, R)$		$(q_3, 0, L)$
q_3	$(q_3, 0, L)$	$(q_3, 1, L)$	$(q_1, 2, R)$	
q_4	–	$(q_5, 1, R)$	$(q_4, 0, L)$	

In state q_1, on seeing *a* 0, *M* changes it to 2 and *M* enters state q_2. In state q_2, *M* moves right to the next blank and deposits 0, and moves left in state q_3. In state q_3, *M* moves left to *a* 2. On reaching *a* 2, state q_1 is entered and the process repeats until the 1 is encountered, signaling that the copying process is complete. State q_4 is used to convert the 2's back to 0's and the subroutine halts in q_5.

To complete the program for multiplication, we add states to convert initial ID $q_0\ 0^m\ 1\ 0^n$ to $B0^{m-1}\ 1\ q_1\ 0^n\ 1$. That is, we need the rules.

$$\delta(q_0, 0) = (q_6, B, R)$$

$$\delta(q_6, 0) = (q_6, 0, R)$$

$$\delta(q_6, 1) = (q_1, 1, R).$$

Additional states are needed to convert an ID $B^i\ 0^{m-i}\ 1q_5\ 0^n\ 1\ 0^{ni}$ to $B^{i+1}\ 0^{m-i-1}\ 1q_1\ 0^n\ 10^{ni}$, which restarts COPY, and to check whether $i = m$, that is all m 0's have been erased. In the case that $i = m$, the leading $10^n\ 1$ is erased and the computation halts in state q_{12}. The additioal moves are shown in Table.

States	0	1	2	B
q_5	$(q_7, 0, L)$	–	–	–
q_7	–	$(q_8, 1, L)$	–	–
q_8	$(q_9, 0, L)$	–	–	(q_{10}, B, R)
q_9	$(q_9, 0, L)$	–	–	(q_0, B, R)
q_{10}	–	(q_{11}, B, R)	–	–
q_{11}	(q_{11}, B, R)	(q_{12}, B, R)	–	–

Note that we could make more than one call to a subroutine if we rewrite the subroutine using a new set of states for each call.

4.3.11. Two way infinite tape

A Turing machine with a two-way infinite tape is denoted by $M = (Q, \Sigma, \Gamma, \delta, q_0, B, F)$, as in the original model. Its tape is infinite to the left as well as to the right and there is an infinity of blank cells both to the left and right of the current non-blank portion of the tape.

The relation $\vdash_M$ which relates two ID's if the ID on the right is obtained from the one on the left by a single move, is defined as in the case of original model together with

(*i*) If $\delta(q, X) = (p, Y, L)$, then

$$q\, X\, \alpha \vdash_M pBY\alpha$$

(*ii*) If $\delta(q, X) = (p, B, R)$, then

$$q\, X\, \alpha \vdash_M p\alpha.$$

The initial ID is q_0w. While there was a left end to the tape in the original model, there is no left end of the tape for the TM to "fall off" so it can be proceed left as far as possible. The relation $\vdash^*_M$ is defined as in the original model.

4.3.12. Theorem

L is recognized by a Turning machine with a two-way infinite tape if and only if it is recognized by a TM with a one way infinite tape.

Proof. Let $M_2 = (Q_2, \Sigma_2, \Gamma_2, \delta_2, q_2, B, F_2)$ be a TM with a two-way infinite tape. We construct a one-tape TM $M_1 = [Q_1, \Sigma_1, \Gamma_1, \delta_1, q_1, B\ F_1)$ capable of simulating the original two-way tape M_2 as follows. M_1 will act like, even look like M_2 as it carries out its moves.

M_1 have two tracks, one to represent the cells of M_2's tape that are on the right of, and including the initial cell scanned. The other track of M_1 contains the cells of M_2's tape that are on the left of the initial cell. Let the initial cell of M_2 be say 0 and the cells to the right are 1, 2, ... and the cells to the left are –1, –2, ... as shown in Fig. 4.7(*a*) and 4.7(*b*).

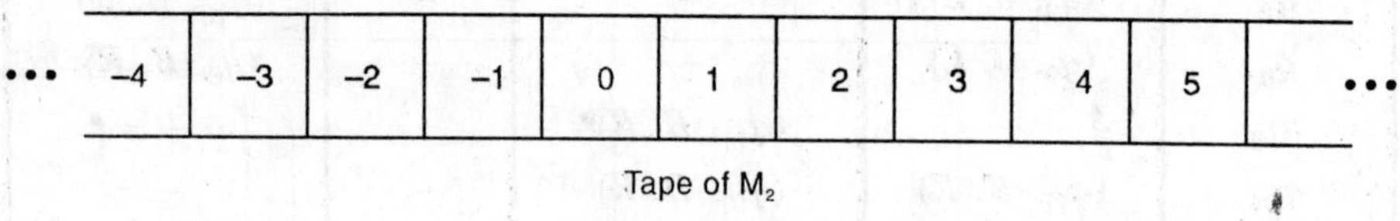

Fig. 4.7 (*a*).

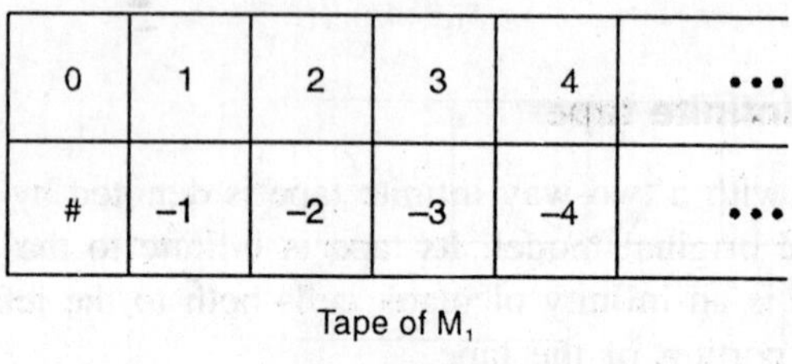

Fig. 4.7 (*b*).

An extra symbol # is inserted initially into the leftmost square, of lower track of M_1 making it easy to find the begining of the tape whenever we want. The finite control of M_1 says whether M_2 is scanning a symbol appearing on the upper or on the lower track of M_1.

The working rule of M_1 is : If M_2 is to the right of the initial position of its input head, then M_1 works on the upper track [see Fig. 4.8(*a*) and (*b*)]. If M_2 is to the left of its initial position of its input head, then M_1 works on its lower track, (See Fig. 4.8.(*c*), (*d*)), moving in the direction opposite to the direction in which M_2 moves.

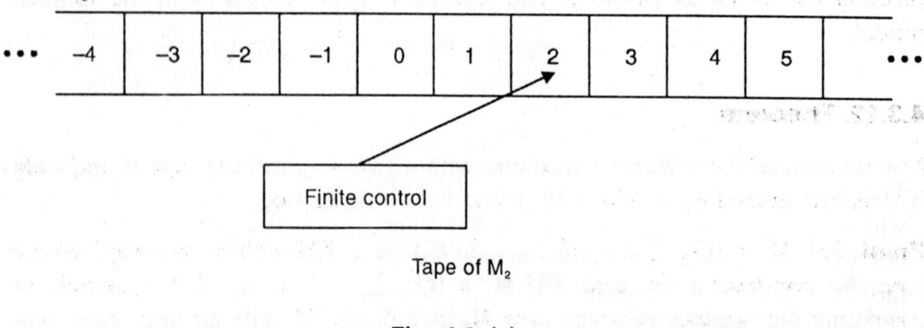

Fig. 4.8 (*a*).

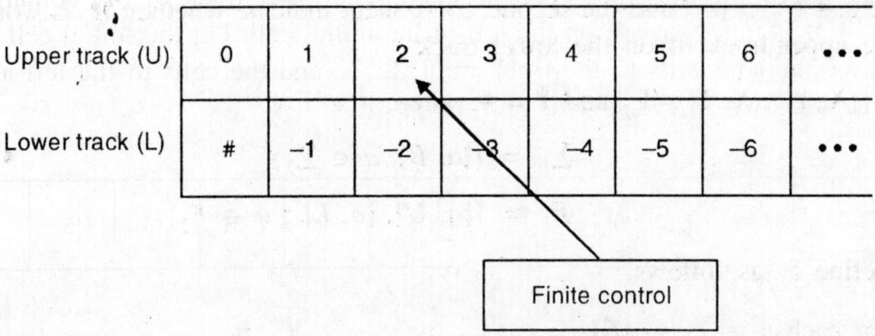

Tape of M_1

Fig. 4.8 (*b*).

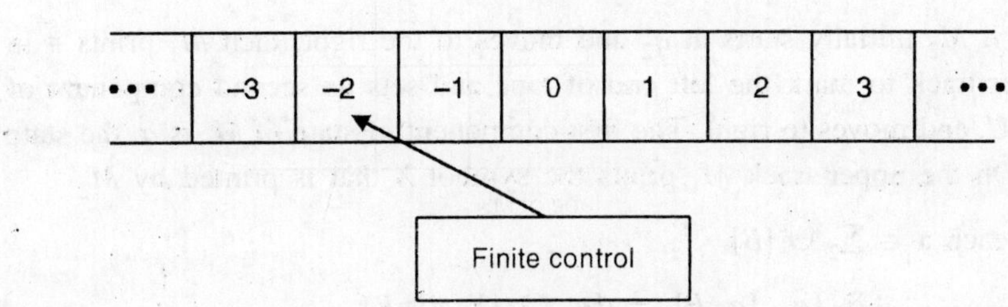

Tape of M_2

Fig. 4.8 (*c*).

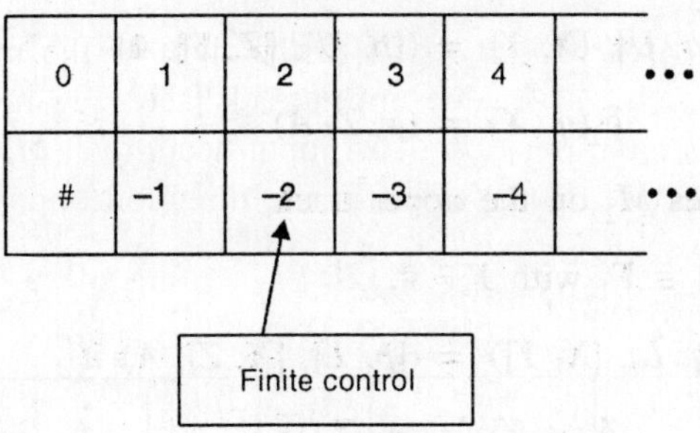

Tape of M_1

Fig. 4.8 (*d*).

The input symbols of M_1 are symbols with a blank on the lower track and while an input symbol of M_2 on the upper track. The elements of two tracks do not exist initially but will be created gradually as M_2 moves its tape head farther and farther the right.

Let us identify B with $[B, B]$. Formally we construct M_1 as follows:

The states Q_1, of M_1 are all objects of the form $[q, U]$ or $[q, L]$, where $q \in Q_2 \cup [q_1]$ and the second component indicate whether M_1 is working on the upper track or on the lower track.

$\Gamma_1 = \{[X, Y] : X, Y \in \Gamma_2$ and $Y = \#$, where $\# \notin \Gamma_2\}$

$$\Sigma_1 = \{[a, B], a \in \Sigma_2\}$$

$$F_1 = \{[q, U], [q, L] : q \in F_2\}.$$

We define δ_1 as follows:

(1) For each a $\in \Sigma_2 \cup [B]$.

$$\delta_1\ (q_1, [a, B]) = ([q, U], [X, \#], R)$$

$$\text{if } \delta_2\ [q_2, a) = (q, X, R)$$

That is, if M_2 initially starts at q_2 and moves to the right, then M_1 prints # in the lower track to mark the left end of tape and sets its second component of state to U, and moves to right. The first component of state of M_1 is q, the state of M_2. On the upper track M_1 prints the symbol X that is printed by M_2.

(2) For each a $\in \Sigma_2 \cup [B]$

$$\delta_1\ (q_1, [a, B] = ([q, L], [X, \#], R)$$

if

$$\delta_2\ (q_2, a) = (q, X, L)$$

(3) For each $[X, Y] \in \Gamma_1$ with $Y \neq \#$, and $A = L$ or R.

$$\delta_1\ ([q, U], [X, Y] = ([p, U], [Z, Y], A)$$

if

$$\delta_2(q, X) = (p, Z, A)$$

That is M_1 simulates M_2 on the upper track

(4) For each $[X, Y] \in \Gamma_1$ with $Y \neq \#$,

$$\delta_1([q, L), [X, Y]) = ([p, L], [X, Z], A) \text{ if}$$

$$\delta_2(q, Y) = (p, Z, \bar{A}).$$

Have A is L if $\bar{A} = R$ and A is R if $\bar{A} = L$. The action above says that M_1 simulates M_2 on the lower track of M_1.

(5) $$\delta_1\ ([q, U], [X, \#]) = \delta_1([q, L], [X, \#])$$

$$= ([p, C], [Y, \#], R)$$

if $\delta_2(q, X) = (p, Y, A)$. Here $C = U$ if $A = R$ and $C = L$ if $A = L$. M_1 next works on the upper or lower track, depending on the direction of moves of M_2. Note that M_1 will always move right in this situation.

4.3.13. Multitape Turing Machines

A multitape TM consists of a finite control with k tape heads and k tapes; each tape is infinite in both directions. On a single move, depending on the state of the finite control and the symbol scanned by each of the tape heads, the machine can

(*i*) Change state;

(*ii*) Print a new symbol on each of the cells scanned by its tape head;

(*iii*) Move each of its tape heads, independently, one cell to the right or left or keep it stationary.

Initially the input appears on the first tape and the other tapes are blank. Tapes 2 through k are used for auxiliary working space, and when the TM halts their contents are ignored. In particular, such a TM computes a function f, if whenever it begins with an input string w in the domain of f, it halts in some configuration $(q_f, B_f(w) \ldots)$ where the contents of tapes 2 through k are arbitrary.

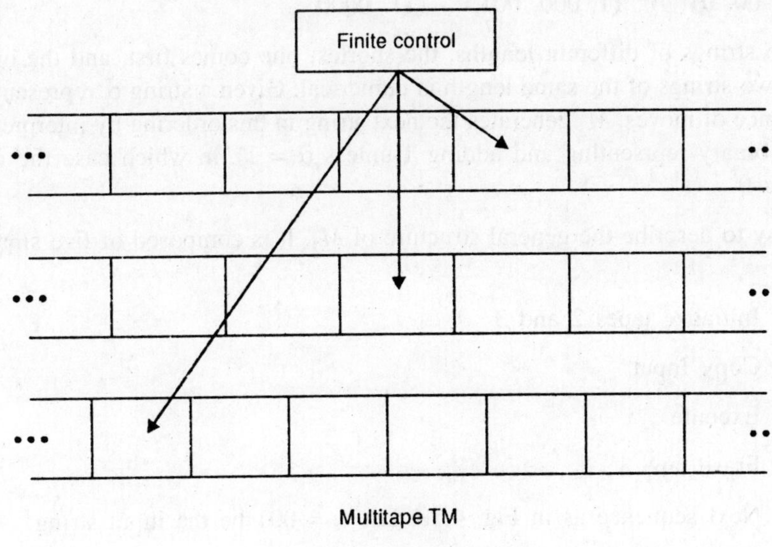

Multitape TM

Fig.4.9. Multitape TM.

4.3.14. Non-deterministic Turing Machines

A Non-deterministic Turing Machine (NTM) $M = (Q, \Sigma, \Gamma, \delta, q_0, B, F)$ is defined exactly the same way as an ordinary TM, except that values of the transition function δ are subsets, rather than single elements, of the set $Q \times \Gamma \times [R, L, H]$. That is, for a given state and an input symbol, the machine has a finite number of choices for the next move. Each choice consists of a new state, a tape symbol to print and the direction. The NTM accepts its input if any sequence of choices of moves leads to an accepting state.

4.3.15. Theorem

If L is accepted by NTM, M_1, then L is accepted by some deterministic TM M_2.

Proof. Let M_2 be a machine having three tapes. The first is used only to save the original input string, and its contents are never changed. The second is used to keep track of the sequence of moves of M_1 that M_2 is currently attempting to execute. The third is the 'working tape' corresponding to M_1's tape, where M_2 actually carries out the steps specified by the current string on tape 2. Every time M_2 begins trying a new sequence the third tape is erased and the input from tape 1 re-copied on it.

A particular sequence of moves will be represented by a string of binary digits. We will use the canonical ordering of [0, 1]*, in which the strings are arranged in the order.

ε, 0, 1, 00, 01, 10, 11, 000, 001, ... 111. 0000, ...

For two strings of different lengths, the shortest one comes first, and the order of the two strings of the same length is numerical. Given a string α representing a sequence of moves, M_2 generates the next string in this ordering by interpreting α as a binary reprsenting and adding 1-unless $\alpha = 1^k$, in which case the next string is 0^{k+1}.

It is easy to describe the general structure of M_2. It is composed of five smaller TM's

(*i*) Initialize tapes 2 and 3

(*ii*) Copy Input

(*iii*) Execute

(*iv*) Erase tape 3.

(*v*) Next sequence as in Fig. 4.10. Let w = 001 be the input string.

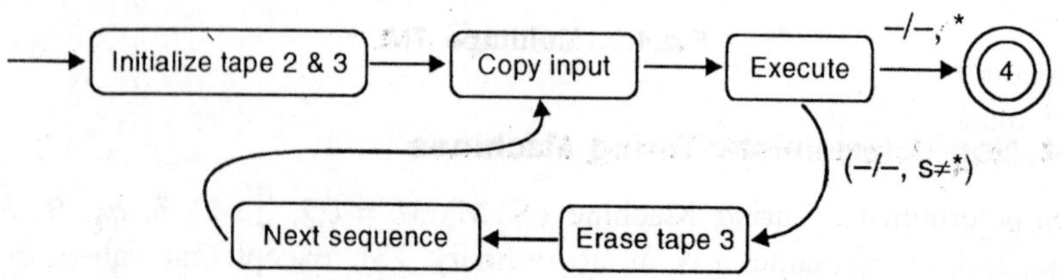

Fig. 4.10.

Simulating M_1, by a three tape TM.

Initialize tape 2 and 3 : Writes the symbol 0 in cell 1 of tape 2 and places the symbol # in cell 0 of tape 3.

Copy Input : Copies the original input string *w* from tape 1 on to tape 3, so that tape 3 has contents # *qBw*.

Execute is the TM that actually simulates the action of M_1 on this input, by executing the sequence of moves currently specified on tape 2. Its crucial feature is that it finishes with a symbol $ in the current cell of tape 3, and s = * if and only if the sequence of moves cause M_1 to accept. In this case M_2 accepts , and otherwise it continues with Erase Tape 3 component.

Erase Tape 3 : restores tape 3 to the configuaration # *q B*. It is able to complete this operation because the length of the string on tape 2 limits how far to the right the rightmost non-blank symbol on tape 3 can be.

Next sequence. It updates the string of digits on tape 2 using the operation similar to adding 1 in binary. It carries out the transformation on the second tape only, ignoring tapes 1 and 3.

The problem of constructing M_2 is reduced to the problem of constructing the component **Execute** which must simulate the sequence of moves of M_1 specified by the string of digits on tape 2.

The move made by **Execute** that simulates the accepting move of M_1 leaves the symbol * in the current position on tape 3 and causes *Execute* to accept.

4.3.16. CHURCH'S THESIS

It says that the collection of functions (or partial functions) which can be computed by an algorithm is the same as the collection of functions which can be computed by a Turing machine.

Computer programs look like algorithms, so church thesis can be interpreted to mean that Turing machines compute exactly the same things that computers compute.

To verify church's thesis is true, we have to show:

(*i*) Every Turing machine can be described as an algorithmic process.

(*ii*) Every algorithmic process can be computed by using a Turing machine.

The second part of church's thesis–that every algorithm can be described as a Turing machine is not so easy to verify and cannot be proved in any formal sense, because we can't offer a precise definition of, an algorithmic process.

The following is one of serveral equivalent statements of church's thesis. It says that any algorithm can be reduced to one written in a very simple language.

CHURCH'S THESIS

Every problem which admits an algorithmic solution can be solved with algorithms which use only the following kinds of instructions.

Let A be a variable and all variables are assumed to be initialized to 0.

(*a*) Add 1 to A and go to the next instruction.

(*b*) If $A \neq 0$, then subtract 1 from A; otherwise, go to statement n.

(*c*) Halt and display the value of A.

Clearly a Turing machine has the capability of performing operations (*a*) to (*c*) and thus this version of church thesis implies the equivalence of Turing machines and algorithms.

Church's thesis is not a theorem, but rather a statement of general principle, since it is a statement about the relationship between two ideas, one of which is well defined [the set of algorithms given by (*a*) to (*c*)] and the other one is not well defined [the set of all processes which can be described by algorithms]. Turing machines themselves be thought of as an algorithm, but it is actually possible to create a kind of Turing machine, known as a *Universal Turing machine* which accepts as an input tape a description of a Turing machine and its input (coded in some suitable form) and then produces the same results as would be produced by using the given data on the described machines.

A Universal Turing machine is really the theoretical equivalence of a progammable computer. In Chapter 5 we discuss some consequences of *Universal Turing Machines.*

4.4. TURING REDUCIBILITY

Language L_1 is *reduced* to L_2 if there exists a function f which is computable by a TM that always halts, such that $f(x)$ is in L_2 if and only x is in L_1. The notion of reducibility is often called *many-one reducibility*. Turing reducibility follows by showing that L_1 is recursive in L_2.

For example consider a Turing machine with oracle A, which is a single tape Turing machine with three special states $q_?$, q_y and q_n. The state $q_?$ is used to ask whether a string is in the set A. When the TM enters state $q_?$, it requests an answer to the question? Is the string of non-blank symbols to the right of the tape head in A? "The answer is : The next move of $q_?$ is one of the states q_y or q_n, depending on whether the answer is yes or no. The computation continues normally unitl the next time $q_?$ is entered when the 'oracle' answer another question.

If A is a recursive set, then the oracle can be simulated by another Turing machine and the set accepted by the TM with oracle A is recursively enumerable. If A is not recursive set, then the TM with oracle A may accept a set that is not recursively enumerable. We denote that TM A with oracle A by M^A. A set L is *recursively enumerable with respect to A* if $L = L(M^A)$ for some TM M. A set L is *recursive with respect to A* if $L = L(M^A)$ for some TM M^A that always halts. Surely $L(M^{L2}) = L_2$, so L_{12}. Turing reduces to L_2. If L_1 is Turing reducible to L_2, if L_1 is undecidable, then so is L_2.

4.5. P AND NP PROBLEMS

Among the decidable problems there are some problems that cannot be solved in full generality on a computer. Such problems, although decidable, requires exponential time to solve. The languages are said to be *tractable* if it can be recognized within reasonable time and space constraints. One normally expects a tractable problem to be solvable in *polynomial* time. The common problems for which no polynomial-time algorithms require exponential run times.

Consider the TM M which has a read only input tape with end markers and k semi-infinite storage tapes. If for every input word of length n, M scans at most $S(n)$ cells on any storage tape, then M is said to be an $S(n)$ *space-bounded TM* or *of space complexity* $S(n)$. THe language recognized by M is also said to be of space complexity $S(n)$. If for every input word of length n, M makes atmost $T(n)$ moves before halting, then M is said to be a $T(n)$ *time-bounded TM* or of *time complexity* $T(n)$. Space complexity $S(n)$ really means max $(1, [S(n)])$ and time complexity function $T(n)$ is atleast $n + 1$ and it means max $(n + 1 [T(n)])$. The concept of time-and space-bounded TM apply also to nondeterministic machines. A non deterministic TM is of time complexity $T(n)$ if no sequence of choices of move causes the machine to make more than $T(n)$ moves. It is of space complexity $S(n)$ if no sequence of choices enables it to scan more than $S(n)$ cells on any storage tape.

4.5.1. Definition

The family of languages of space complexity $S(n)$ is denoted by DSPACE $(S(n))$; the languages of nondeterministic space complexity $S(n)$ are collectively called NSPACE $(S(n))$. The family of language of time complexity $T(n)$ is denoted DTIME $(T(n))$ and that of non deterministic time complexity $T(n)$ is denoted by NTIME $(T(n))$. All these families of languages are called complexity classes. For example if $T(n) = n$, then DTIME $(T(n))$ = max $(n + 1, n) = n + 1$.

If L is in NSPACE $(S(n))$, then L is in NSPACE $(CS(n))$ where c is any constant greater than zero.

If n is the input length, the number of operations for polynomial algorithms is of the form $P(n)$ (P is a polynomial, e.g. n^3); if it is an exponential algorithm, the number of operations is of the form K^n (K is any constant).

4.5.2. Theorem

(*a*) If L is in DTIME ($f(n)$), then L is in DSPACE ($f(n)$).

(*b*) (Savitch Theorem) : If L is in NSPACE ($S(n)$), then L is in DSPACE ($S^2(n)$) provided $S(n)$ is fully space constructible and $S(n) \geq \log_2 n$.

Proof.

(*a*) If TM M makes not more than $f(n)$ moves, it cannot scan more than $f(n) + 1$ cells on the tape. By modifying M to hold two symbols per cell we can lower the storage requirements to $\left\lceil \frac{\{f(n)+1\}}{2} \right\rceil$, which is at most $f(n)$.

(*b*) Let $L = L(M_1)$, where M_1 is an $S(n)$ space- bounded non deterministic TM. For some constant C, there are atmost $C^{S(n)}$ ID's for an input of length n. Let $I_1 \overset{(1)}{\vdash} I_2$ denote that the ID I_2 can be reached from I_1 by a sequence of atmost 2^i moves. The space needed to move from one ID to another is 2^i moves means the space needed to record the ID I' currently being tested plus the space needed to determine if we get from one ID to another in 2^{i-1} moves. Also I_1, I_2, I' are ID's with no more than $S(n)$ cells, we represent each of them in $S(n)$ space. The input head position in binary uses $\log n \leq S(n)$ cells.

The algorithm for testing if w is in $L(M_1)$ may be implemented on a TM M_2 that uses a tape as a stack of activation records for the calls to TEST. The parameter i can be coded in binary using atmost $mS(n)$ cells. Thus each activation record takes space $O(S(n))$. The third parameter decreases by one each time TEST is called, the initial cell has $i = mS(n)$, and no call is made when i reaches zero, the maximum number of activation records on the stack is $O(S(n))$. Thus the total space used is $O(S^2(n))$ and we may redesign M_2 to make the space be exactly $S^2(n)$.

The polynomial algorithms are much most efficient than the exponential algorithms. For example, there are two algorithms say Algorithm 1 and Algorithm 2, for solving a certain problem. Algorithm 1 is of complexity n^2 and Algorithm 2 is of complexity 2^n. Let the computer time availability be 2 hours. The problems are manageable if they are accommodated with in this stipulated time. Let N_2 be the (Longest) input length for Algorithm 2. Then this algorithm would perform 2^{N2} steps in two hours. Let there be another computer which is ten times faster. Then for the given problem with an input of length N'_2 such that

$$2^{N_2^1} = 10.2^{N2} \text{ or}$$

$$N_2^1 = N_2 + \log_2 10.$$

The performance of exponential Algorithm 2 though the second computer is ten times faster shows very little improvement only.

Other hand, if N_1 is the size of input for Algorithm 1, then in the faster computer

$$\left(N_1^1\right)^2 = 10(N_1)^2 \text{ or } N_1^1 = \sqrt{10} \cdot N_1$$

This performance is better. Also if the amount of time taken for an operation is 1 μ sec and then input size $N_1 = N_2 = 50$, Algorithm 1 takes

$$N_1^2 \times 10^{-6} \text{ sec} = .0025 \text{ sec.}$$

whereas Algorithm 2 takes

$$2^{N_2} \times 10^{-6} \text{ sec} = 35 \text{ years}$$

for execution.

Table comparision of polynomial and exponential time algorithms.

Complexity function \ size n	10	20	30	40	50	60
n^2	10^{-4} sec	4×10^{-4} sec	9×10^{-4} sec	16×10^{-4} sec	25×10^{-4} sec	36×10^{-4} sec
n^3	10^{-3} sec	8×10^{-3} sec	27×10^{-3} sec	64×10^{-3} sec	125×10^{-4} sec	216×10^{-3} sec
n^5	10^{-1} sec	3 sec	24 sec	1.7 min	5 min	13 min
2^n	10^{-3} sec	1 sec	18 min	13 days	35 yrs	366 centuries
3^n	6×10^{-2} sec	58 min	6.5 yrs	3855 centuries	2×10^8 centuries	1.3×10^{13} centuries

Hence even improved technology have negligible effects on speeding up the exponential time algorithms. Hence the polynomial time algorithms are most desirable ones. If for some problem, no polynomial time algorithm is known, the problem can then be called *computationally intractable.*

Turing machines classify problems as those for which algorithms can never be written (unsolvable) and those that can be solved and the class solvable problems are subdivided into (*i*) those which can be solved in polynomial time

(*ii*) those for which only exponential time algorithms are known.

The languages recognizable in deterministic polynomial time form a natural and important class, the class $\bigcup_{i \ge 1} \text{DTIME}(n^i)$, denoted by *P*.

There are a number of important problems that do not appear to be in *P* but have efficient non-deterministic algorithms. These problems fall into the class $\bigcup_{i \ge 1} \text{NTIME}(n^i)$ which we denote by NP.

An example is the Hamilton circuit problem. Does a graph have a cycle in which each vertex of the graph appears exactly once? There does not appear a deterministic polynomial time algorithm, but there is a simple non-deterministic algorithm to verify whether in the given graph there is a Hamilton circuit.

The difference between P and NP is analagous to the difference between efficiently finding a proof of a statement and efficiently verifying a proof.

The deterministic polynomial space and non-deterministic polynomial space are defined by:

$$\text{PSPACE} = \bigcup_{i \ge 1} \text{DSPACE}(n^i)$$

$$\text{NSPACE} = \bigcup_{i \ge 1} \text{SPACE}(n^i)$$

By Theorem 4.12.2 (*b*) PSPACE = NSPACE, since NSPACE $(n^i) \subseteq$ DSPACE (n^{2i}). Clearly DSPACE $(\log^k n) \subseteq$ NSPACE $(\log^k n)$, and by Theorem 4.12.2(*b*),

$$\bigcup_{k \ge 1} \text{NSPACE}(\log^k n) = \bigcup_{k \ge 1} \text{DSPACE}(\log^k n)$$

Also $\quad \text{DSPACE}(\log n) \subseteq \text{P} \subseteq \text{NP} \subseteq \text{PSPACE}$

$$\text{DSPACE}(\text{lon } n) \subsetneq \text{DSPACE}(\log^2 n) \subsetneq \text{DSPACE}(\log n) \subsetneq \ldots$$

$$\text{NSPACE}(\log n) \subsetneq \text{NSPACE}(\log^2 n) \subsetneq \text{NSPACE}(\log^3 n) \subsetneq \ldots$$

4.5.3. Definition

A language L' is said to be *polynomial time reducible* to L if there is a polynomial time bounded TM that for each input x produces an output y that is in L if and only if x is in L'.

4.5.4. Lemma

Let L' be polynomial-time reducible to L. Then

(*a*) L' is in NP if L is in NP.

(*b*) L' is in P if L is in P.

Proof.

(*b*) Assume that the reduction is $p_1(n)$ time bounded and that L is recognizable in time $p_2(n)$ where p_1 and p_2 are polynomials. Suppose the input given is of length n, and as the reduction is $p_1(n)$ time bounded, atmost one symbol can be printed per move. Let y be produced using polynomial-time reduction.

Then $|y| \le p_1(n)$. We can test if $y \in L'$ in time $p_2(p_1(n))$. The total time to tell whether x is in L is $p_1(n) + p_2(p_1(n))$ which is polynomial in n. Therefore L is in P.

Similarly we prove if L is in NP then L' is in NP.

4.6. NP-COMPLETE AND NP-HARD PROBLEMS

It is obvious that $P \subseteq NP$. It is not known that whether there exists some language L in NP, which is also accepted by deterministic TM.

4.6.1. Definition

Let L_1 and L_2 be two languages over Σ_1 and Σ_2 respectively, then there is a polynomial time transformation from L_1 to L_2 if

(*i*) There exists a function $f : \Sigma^*_1 \rightarrow \Sigma^*_2$ such that $w \in L_1$ if and only if $f(w) \in L_2$.

(*ii*) f can be computed by a deterministic TM of polynomial-time complexity.

We also say L_1 is polynomial-time reducible to L_2 written $L_1 \le p\ L_2$.

4.6.2. Theorem

1. $\le p$ is transitive : If $L_1 \le p\ L_2$, $L_2 \le p\ L_3$, then $L_1 \le p\ L_3$.
2. If $L_2 \in P$ and $L_1 \le p\ L_2$, then $L_1 \in P$.
3. If $L_2 \in$ NP and $L_1 \le p\ L_2$, then $L_1 \in$ NP.

Proof. Let L_1, L_2, L_3 be three languages over the alphabets Σ_1, Σ_2, and Σ_3 respectively. Let $f : \Sigma^*_1 \rightarrow \Sigma^*_2$, $g : \Sigma_2^* \rightarrow \Sigma^*_3$ be two functions involved in the reductions. Then $g_o f : \Sigma_1^* \rightarrow \Sigma^*_3$, and for every $x \in \Sigma^*_1$, $x \in L_1$ if and only if $(g_o f)(x) \in L_3$. Therefore it is sufficient to show that $g_o f$ is polynomial time computable. M_f and M_g are TM's computing f and g regpectively so that for every n,

$$\tau M_f(n) \leq Cn^j + D$$

$$\tau M_g(n) \leq Cn^k + D$$

for some integers j and k and some constant C and D, τ_M denotes the number of moves made by a TM M while computing a function.

The composition $M = M_f\, M_g$ computes the function gof.

Since composition of polynomials is a polynomial, it follows that M is a polynomial time complexity. Consider the number τ_x of moves made by M_f in computing $f(x)$. If $\tau x \leq |x|$, then M_f cannot change the right most symbol in the input string x and thus $|f(x)| = |x|$. Otherwise $|f(x)| \leq \tau_x$, since a TM needs at least $|f(x)|$ moves to create an output string of length $f(x)$. Note that τ_M is bounded by a polynomial.

(2) Assume that there is a TM M_2 with polynomial time complexity recognizing the language L_2 and there is a function $f : \Sigma^*_1 \rightarrow \Sigma^*_2$ computed by a TM M_f with polynomial time complexity, so that for any $x \in \Sigma^*_1$, $x \in L_1$ if and only if $f(x) \in L_2$. Let $M = M_f\, M_2$. Then M recognizes the language L_1 and also M has polynomial time complexity. Therefore $L_1 \in P$.

(3) The proof follows as in part (2), except that M_2 is an non deterministic TM accepting L_2 in polynomial-time. The composite machine $M = M_f\, M_2$ accepts L_1 and still τ_M is found to be bounded by a polynomial.

4.6.3. Definition

A language L is said to be NP-*hard* if $L_1 \leq p\ L$ for every $L_1 \in$ NP. The language L is NP-complete if $L \in$ NP and L is NP-hard.

4.6.4. Theorem

(1) If L and L_1 are languages for which L is NP-hard and $L \leq p\ L_1$, then L_1 is also NP-hard.

(2) If L is any NP Complete language, then $L \in P$ if and only if P = NP.

Proof. The proof follows immediately from Theorem 4.6.2.

The idea of NP-completeness was introduced by Stephen Cook in 1971. Satisfiability for Boolean expressions is NP-complete.

Boolean expression is an expression composed of variables, parentheses. and the operators $\wedge$ (logical AND), $\vee$ (logical OR) and $\neg$ (negation).

Boolean variables take on values 0 (false) and 1 (true). If E_1, E_2 are Boolean expressions, then the value of $E_1 \wedge E_2$ is 1 if both E_1 and E_2 have value 1 and 0 otherwise. The value of $E_1 \vee E_2$ is 1 if either E_1 or E_2 has value 1, and 0 otherwise. The value of $\neg E_1$ is 1 if E_1 is 0 and $\neg E_1$ is 0 if E_1 is 1.

An expression is *satisfiable* if there is some assignment of 0's and 1's to the variables that gives the expression the value 1.

The satisfiability problem is to determine, given a Boolean expression, whether it is satisfiable.

Let $U = [u_1, u_2, \ldots u_m]$ be a set of Boolean variables. If u is a variable in U, then u and $\bar{u}$ are called *literals* over U. A *clause* over U is a set of literals over $\bar{U}$. For example

$$u_1 \cup \bar{u}_2 \cup u_3 \text{ is a clause.}$$

A Boolean expression is said to be in *Conjunctive Normal Form* (CNF) if it is of the form $E_1 \wedge E_2 \wedge \ldots \wedge E_k$, where each E_i is a clause. The expression is said to be in 2-CNF if each clause has exactly two distinct literals.

4.6.5. Cook's Theorem

The satisfiability problem is NP-complete.

Proof. Represent the satisfiability problem as a language L_{sat}. In order to prove the theorem it is enough to show that every language in NP is reducible to L_{sat}, for each NTM M that is time bounded by a polynomial $p(n)$, we give a log space algorithm that takes as input a string x and produces a Boolean formula E_x that is satisfiable if and only if M accepts x. The Boolean formula E_x is described as follows.

Let # β_0 # β_1 # ... # $\beta_{p(n)}$ be computation of M with β_i.'s as ID consisting of exactly $p(n)$ symbols. If acceptance occurs before the $p(n)$th move accepting ID can be allowed to repeat so that each computation has exactly $p(n) + 1$ ID's. For each symbol that appear in a computation, and for each i, $0 \le i \le (p(n) + 1)^2$, form a Boolean variable C_{iX}, to check whether the ith symbol is in the computation of X. 0th symbol in the computation is the initial #. Construct E_x if and only if C_{iX}'s are true corresponding to a valid computation.

The expression E_x states the following:

(1) The C_{iX} that are true correspond to a string of symbols, in that exactly one C_{iX} is true for each i.

(2) The ID β_0 is an initial ID of M with input x.

(3) The last ID contains a final state.

(4) Each ID follows from the previous one by the move of M that is indicated.

E_x is the logical AND of four formulas.

The first formula gives exactly one C_{iX} is true is

$$\hat{i}\left[\underset{X}{\vee} + C_{i_X} \wedge \rceil\left(\underset{X \neq Y}{\vee}\left(C_{i_X} \wedge C_{i_Y}\right)\right)\right]$$

For a given value of i, the term $\underset{X}{\vee} C_{i_X}$ says atleast one C_{iX} to be true and $\rceil\left(\underset{X \neq Y}{\vee}\left(C_{i_X} \wedge C_{i_Y}\right)\right)$ forces atmost one to be true.

The second formula express β_0 is an initial ID which is the AND of the following four forms.

(*i*) $C_{0\#} \wedge C_{(p(n)+1)\#}$

(*ii*) $C_{1Y1} \vee C_{1Y2} \vee \ldots \vee C_{1YK}$, where $Y_1, Y_2, \ldots, Y_K$

are all the composite symbols that represent tape symbols a_1, the start state q_0, and the moves of M.

(*iii*) $\wedge_{2 \leq i \leq n} C_i a_i$. The 2nd through n symbols of β_0 are correct.

(*iv*) $\wedge_{n < i \leq p(n)} C_{iB}$. The remaining symbols of β_0 are blank.

The third formula says that the last ID has an accepting state.

$$\underset{p(n)(p(n)+1 < i(p(n)+1)^2}{\vee}\left(\underset{X \text{ in } F}{\vee} C_{i_X}\right)$$

where F is the set of composite symbols including final states.

The fourth formula is expressed :

$$\underset{p(n) < j(p(n)+1)^2}{\wedge}\left(\underset{\substack{W, X, Y, Z \text{ such that} \\ f(W, X, Y, Z)}}{\vee} C_{j-p(n)-2, W} \wedge C_{j-p(n)-1, X} \wedge C_{j-p(n), Y} \wedge C_{jZ}\right)$$

where f (W, X, Y, Z) is a predicate that is true if and only if symbol Z appear in position j of some ID given that W, X, Y are symbols in positions $j - 1$, j and $j + 1$ of the previous ID [W is # if $j = 1$, Y is # if $j = p(n)$].

Given an accepting computation of M on x it is easy to find the truth values for the C_{iX}'s that make Ex true. That is C_{iX} is true if and only if the ith symbol of the computation is X. Converse follows from the four formulas.

The formulas composing E_x are of length $O(p^2(n))$ and a log-space TM can generate then given x on its input. The logarithm of a polynomial in n is some constant times log n, TM have $O(\log n)$ storage to count up to $(p(n) + 1)^2$. Hence every language in NP is log-space reducible to L_{sat} proving L_{sat} is NP-complete.

4.6.6. Theorem

3-satisfiable problem is NP-complete.

Proof. Let $\Sigma = [x, \bar{x}, \wedge, 1]$, let $E \subseteq \Sigma^*$ be the set of strings representing expressions in CNF. Let $3E$ be the subset of E corresponding to those expression in which each clause contains no more than the literals. Because a TM can easily determine in polynomial time whether an element of Σ^* is in E, construct a function

$$f : E \rightarrow 3E$$

so that for any $x \in E$, x represents a satisfiable expression if and only if $f(x)$ does.

Let $$x = \bigwedge_{i=1}^{n} E_i$$

where each E_i is a disjunction of literals.

Define $$f(x) = \bigwedge_{i=1}^{n} F_i$$

where $F_i = E_i$ whenever E_i contains three or fewer literals, and if $E_i = \bigvee_{j=1}^{k} a_j$, with $k > z$,

$$F_i = (a_1 \vee a_2 \vee \alpha_1) \wedge (a_3 \vee \bar{\alpha}_1 \vee \alpha_2) \wedge (a_4 \vee \bar{\alpha}_2 \vee \alpha_3) \wedge .... \quad \wedge (a_{k-3} \vee \bar{\alpha}_{k-5} \vee \alpha_{k-4}) \wedge (a_{k-2} \vee \bar{\alpha}_{k-4} \vee \alpha_{k-3}) \wedge (a_{k-1} \vee a_k \vee \bar{\alpha}_{k-3}).$$

Here α_j's are new variable not occuring in x, and also that no α_j occur in more than one F_i

Suppose $t : E_i \rightarrow [T, F]$ is a truth assignment satisfying x, that is, satisfying each of the E_i's then we show the same assignment t, is also true for the extra variables α_j in F_i. Since t satisfies E_i, it must make one of the a_j's true. We now consider three cases.

(*i*) If t makes a_1 or a_2 true, then assigning the value false to every α_i makes F_i true, since every clause after the first term involves $\bar{\alpha}_i$.

(*ii*) If t makes a_{k-1} or a_k true, then assigning the value true to every α_i makes F_i true since every clause except the last involves an α_i.

(*iii*) For any m with $2 < m < k - 1$, all the clauses before the one containing a_m contain an α_l for some l with $1 \leq l \leq m - 2$; and all the clauses after this one contain an $\overline{\alpha}_l$ for some l with $m - 1 \le l \le k - 3$.

Therefore, if t makes a_m true, then letting α_l be true for $1 \le l \le m - 2$ and false for the remaining l's makes the expression to be satisfied.

Hence for any assignment satisfying x, the assignment together with some choices also satisfies $f(x)$.

Conversely, if t does not satisfy x, then t fails to satisfy some E_i and therefore makes all the aj's in E_i false. Hence for the assignment t, no assignment values to the new variables α_i make F_i be true. For the first clause of F_i to be true. α_1 must be true; for the second to be true, α_2 must be true; ... for the next-to-last to be true, α_{k-3} must be true; and the last clause is forced to be false. Therefore, if x is false, so is $f(x)$. Hence we can obtain a function $f_1 : \Sigma^* \to \Sigma^*$ such that for any x, $x \in L_{sat}$ if and only if $f(x) \in$ 3-satisfiable. Since the length of $f(x)$ is bounded by a polynomial function of $| x |$, f_1 is computable in polynomial time. Hence 3-satisfiable problem is NP-complete.

Another NP-complete problem that is reduced to other problems is the vertex cover problem.

Let $G = (V, E)$ be an undirected graph with V as the set of vertices and E as the set of edges. A subset $A \subseteq V$ is said to be a *vertex cover* of G if for every edge (v, w) in E, at least one of u or w is in A.

The *vertex cover* problem is this; given a graph G and an integer k, is there a vertex cover for G with k vertices ?

The *vertex cover* problem is represented as a language L_{VC} consisting of strings of the form: k in binary, followed by a marker, followed by the list of vertices, and a list of edges (v_i, v_j) in a coded form surrounded by parentheses.

4.6.7. Theorem

$_{VC}$, the vertex cover problem is NP-complete.

Proof. To show L_{VC} to be NP-complete by reducing 3-CNF satisfiability to L_{VC}. Let $F = F_1 \wedge F_2 \wedge \dots \wedge F_q$ be an expression in 3-CNF, where each F_i is a clause of the form $(\alpha_{i1} \vee \alpha_{i2} \vee \alpha_{i3})$, each α_{ij} is a literal. Now construct an undirected graph $G = (V, E)$ as follows.

The vertices of G are pairs of integers (i, j) $1 \le i \le q$, $1 \le j \le 3$. The vertex (i, j) represents the jth literal of the ith clause.'

The edges of G are represented by

(*i*) $[[i, j], [i, k]$, provided $j \ne k$,

(*ii*) $[[i, j], [k, l]]$ if $\alpha_{ij} = \urcorner\alpha_{kl}$, where $\urcorner\alpha_{kl}$ denotes the not of α_{kl}.

Now we show F is satisfiable if and only if G has a vertex cover with $2q$ vertices.

Assume F is satisfiable and fix an assignment satisfying F. Each clause must have a literal whose value is 1. Select one such literal for each clause. Delete the q vertices corresponding to these literals from V. The remaining vertices form a vertex cover having $2q$ vertices. Clearly for each i, only one vertex of the form (i, j) is missing from the cover, and hence each edge in (1) is incident upon atleast one vertex in the cover. Since edges in (2) are incident upon two vertices corresponding to some literal and its complement, and as we cannot delete both literal and its complement, one or the other of these vertices is in the cover. Thus there is a cover having $2q$ vertices.

Conversely, assume G has a vertex cover having $2q$ vertices. For each i, assign value 1 to the literal α_{ij} corresponding to the vertex (i, j) not in the cover. Note that for each i, the cover must contain all but one vertex of the form (i, j) and suppose two such vertices are not in the cover, then an edge $[(i, j), (i, k)]$ is not incident in any vertex in the cover. As two vertices not in the cover cannot correspond to a literal and its complement, an edge $[(i, j), (k, l)]$, provided $\alpha_{ij} = \neg\alpha_{kl}$, is not incident on any vertex of the cover. For this assignment F has value 1. Hence F is satisfiable. The reduction can be accomplished in log-space also. Hence L_{VC} is NP-complete.

Next we prove k-colorability problem is NP-complete.

A k- coloring of a graph G is an assignment to each vertex, one of the k colors so that no two adjacent vertices are colored with the same color.

k - colorability problem is : Given G and k, is there a k_0 coloring of G?

In order to show it is NP-complete, it is enough to show it is NP-hard.

4.6.8. Theorem

The k-colorability problem is NP-complete.

Proof. We show 3-satisfiable problem is polynomial time reducible to the k-colorability problem.

Let $x = A_1 \wedge A_2 \wedge \dots \wedge A_c$ be an ID of 3-satisfiability with the n-variables x_1, x_2, ... x_n where $n \geq 4$. Construct the ID (G_x, k_x) by letting $k_x = n + 1$ and define the graph $G_x = (V_x, E_x)$ as follows. There are $3n + c$ vertices:

$$V_x = \{x_1, x_2, \dots x_n, \overline{x}_1, \overline{x}_2, \dots, \overline{x}_n, y_1, y_2, \dots y_n, A_1, A_2, \dots, A_n\}$$

and 6 types of edges:

$$E_x = \{(x_i, \overline{x}_i) : 1 \leq i \leq n\} \cup \{(y_i, y_j) : i \neq j\} \cup \{(y_i, x_j) : i \neq j\} \cup \{(y_i, \overline{x}_j):$$

$i \neq j\} \cup \{(x_i, A_j) : x_i \notin A_j\} \cup \{(\overline{x}_i, A_j) : \overline{x}_i \notin A_j\}$

Suppose the graph is $(n + 1)$-colorable. As any two vertices are adjacent, no two of the y_i's can be colored with the same color. Hence there required n distinct colors. Suppose y_i's are colored with say 1, 2, ...,n. For any fixed i, consider the vertices x_i and $\overline{x}_i$.

Neither can be colored the same as y_j for any $j \neq i$, because they are both adjacent to every such y_j; and they cannot be colored the same, because they are adjacent to each other. The only possibility is that color i is used for one and color $n + 1$ for the $n + 1$.

Since A_j is adjacent to x_i and $\overline{x}_i$ one of them is colored $n + 1$, and A_j cannot be colored $n + 1$. The vertex A_j must be colored with some i for $1 \leq i \leq n$. Let z_j (either x_i or $\overline{x}_i$) be a literal appearing in A_j that is colored the same as A_j. Then no z_j is the negation of any other z_l, otherwise one should be colored $n + 1$. This means that there is a way of assigning truth values to the variables that makes every z_j true. The effect of this assignment is to satisfy each A_j, and if follows that x is satisfiable.

So color each y_i with color i. If x is satisfied by the assignment t, then each clause A_j contains a literal z_j that is true by using t. If z_j is either x_i or $\overline{x}_i$, color it with i and its negation with $n + 1$. After coloring x_i or $\overline{x}_i$, the remaining literals are colored.

For example, x_l is colored with l. If $x_l \notin A_j$, then A_j cannot be colored l because of x_l $(x_j \notin A_j)$, and A_j cannot be colored l because of x_l, as $\overline{x}_l$ is not true for the assignment t. Hence if x is satisfiable, then G_x is $(n + 1)$ Colorable. This construction can be carried out in polynomial time, and thus 3-satisfiable problem is polynomial-time reducible to the k-colorability problem.

4.6.9. Theorem

Integer linear programming is NP-hard.

Proof. We reduce 3-CNF satisfiability to integer linear programming.

Let $$F = A_1 \wedge A_2 \wedge \ldots \wedge A_q$$

be an expression in 3-CNF, and let $x_1, x_2, \ldots, x_n$ be the variables of F. The matrix A will have a column for each literal x_i or $\overline{x}_i$, $1 \leq i \leq n$. The inequality $Ax \geq b$ as a set of linear inequalities among the literals. For each i, $1 \leq i \leq n$, the inequalities.

$$x_i + \bar{x}_i \geq 1, \; x_i \geq 0$$

$$-x_i - \bar{x}_i \geq -1, \; \bar{x}_i \geq 0$$

which has the effect of saying one of x_i or $\bar{x}_i$ is 0 or 1 and vice versa respectively. For clause $\alpha_1 \vee \alpha_2 \vee \alpha_3$, we have the inequality.

$$\alpha_1 + \alpha_2 + \alpha_3 \geq 1$$

which gives that atleast one literal in each clause has value 1. It is obvious that A and b can be constructed in log-space and the inequlities are all satisfied if and only if E is satisfiable. Thus linear integer programming is NP-hard.

4.6.9. Theorem

NP is closed under complementation if and only if the complement of some NP-complete problem is in NP.

Proof. Let S be an NP complete problem, and suppose $\bar{S}$ be in NP. Since each $L \in$ NP is log-space reducible to S, each $\bar{L}$ is log-space reducible to $\bar{S}$. Thus $\bar{L}$ is in NP. Converse is obvious.

4.6.10. Lemma.

Let x and y be integers, with $0 \leq x, y < p$. Then

(*i*) $x + y \pmod p$ can be computed in time $O(\log p)$.

(*ii*) $xy \pmod p$ can be computed in time $O(\log^2 p)$

(*iii*) $x^y \pmod p$ can be computed in time $O(\log^3 p)$.

Proof. Since integer mod p requires only log p bits, the proof of (*i*) and (*ii*) follows. Compute x^y by repeated square to get $x^2, x^4, x^8, \ldots x^{(2)i}$ mod p, where $i \equiv [\log_2 y]$, then multiply the appropriate powers of x to get x^y. Hence we get (3).

4.6.11. Theorem

The set of primes is in NP.

Proof. If $p = 2$, then p is prime and even. By Fermat's theorem, for $p > 2$ is a prime if and only if there exists an x of order $p - 1$, that is, for some x, $1 < x < p$,

(1) $$x^{p-1} \equiv 1 \pmod p$$

(2) $$x^i \not\equiv 1 \bmod p, \text{ for } 1 \le i \le p-1.$$

Condition (1) is checked in $O(\log^3 p)$ steps. To check for (2), let $p-1$ can be factored as $p_1\ p_2, \ldots\ p_k$. Recorsively, check whether each p_j is prime. verify $p-1$ is the product of the p_j's. Finally verify $x^{\left(\frac{p-1}{p_j}\right)} \ne 1 \bmod p$, for $x^i \equiv 1 \bmod p$ for $1 \le i \le p-1$. Assume that the non-deterministic time to recognize that p is prime is bounded by $c \log^4 p$. We need to observe that

$$\sum_{j=1}^{k} c \log^4 p_j + \sum_{i=1}^{k} c_1 \log^3 p_i + c_1 \log^3 p \le c \log^4 p$$

for some sufficiently large constant c.

Next we show the Hamilton circuit problem is NP-complete.

The Hamilton circuit problem is : Given a graph G, does G have a path that visits each vertex exactly once and returns to its starting point. We represent these problem as languages by L_H by encoding graphs as in the vertex over problem.

4.6.12. Theorem

L_H for undirected graphs is NP-complete.

Proof.

Let $G = (V, E)$ be a directed graph. Construct an undirected graph G' with vertices v_0, v_1 and v_2 for each v in V, and edges

(1) (v_0, v_1) for each v in V

(2) (v_1, v_2) for each v in V

(3) (v_2, w_0) if an only if $v \to w$ is an arc in E.

Each vertex v in V has been expanded into three vertices. v_1 have only two edges, and since a Hamilton circuit must visit all vertices, the subscript of the vertices in any Hamilton circuit of G' must be in the order 0, 1, 2, ... or its reverse. The edges whose subscript goes from 2, 1, 0 correspond to a Hamilton circuit in G'.

Conversely, a Hamilton circuit in G may be converted to a Hamilton circuit in G' by replacing an edge $v \to w$ by the path from v_0 to v_1 to v_2 to w_0. Thus G' has a Hamilton circuit if and only if G has a Hamilton circuit. We can accomplish G' in log-space. Hence L_H is NP-complete.

4.13.13. Example

Consider the expression

$$F = (x_1 \vee x_2 \vee x_3) \wedge (\bar{x}_1 \vee x_2 \vee x_4) \wedge (\bar{x}_2 \vee x_3 \vee x_5) \wedge (\bar{x}_3 \vee \bar{x}_4 \vee \bar{x}_5).$$

Solution. The construction of L_{VC} yields the graph with $x_1 = 1$, $x_2 = 1$, $x_3 = 1$, $x_4 = 0$ satisfies F and corresponds to the vertex cover

[1, 2], [1, 3], [2, 1], [2, 3], [3, 1], [3, 3] [4, 1], [4, 3].

Double circle indicate vertices in set cover

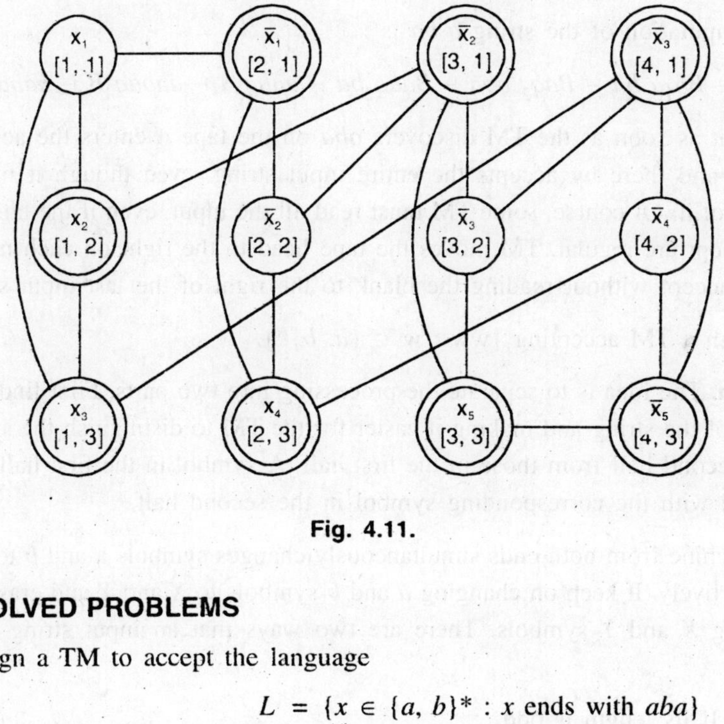

Fig. 4.11.

4.7. SOLVED PROBLEMS

1. Design a TM to accept the language

$$L = \{x \in \{a, b\}^* : x \text{ ends with } aba\}$$

Solution. Let $M = \{Q, \Sigma, \Gamma, q_0, \delta, B, F\}$ be a TM, where

$$Q = \{q_0, q_1, q_2, q_3, q_4, q_5\},$$

$$\Sigma = \{a, b\},$$

$$\Gamma = \{a, b, B\},$$

$$F = \{q_5\}$$

and δ is defined as:

$\delta\ (q_0, B) = (q_1, B, R)$ $\qquad\qquad$ $\delta(q_3, b) = (q_1, b, R)$

$\delta\ (q_1, b) = (q_1, b, R)$ $\delta(q_4, B) = (q_5, B, R)$

$\delta\ (q_1, a) = (q_2, a, R)$

$\delta\ (q_2, a) = (q_2, a, R)$

$\delta\ (q_2, b) = (q_3, b, R)$

$\delta\ (q_3, a) = (q_4, a, R)$

$\delta\ (q_4, b) = (q_3, b, R)$

$\delta\ (q_4, a) = (q_2, a, R).$

The computation of the string a^2ba is :

$q_0a^2ba \vdash Bq_1a^2ba \vdash Baq_2\ aba \vdash Baaq_2ba \vdash aabq_3a \vdash aabaq_4B \vdash aabaBq_5$

Note that as soon as the TM discovers *aba* on the tape it enters the accepting state q_5 and there by accepts the entire input string, even though it may not read all of it. Of course, some TM must read all the input, even if the languages they accept are regular. TM moves the tape head to the right on each move, it cannot accept without reading the blank to the right of the last input symbol.

2. Design a TM accepting $\{ww : w \in \{a, b\}^*\}$.

Solution. The idea is to separate the processing into two parts. First finding the middle of the string and making it easier for the TM to distinguish the symbols in the second half from those in the first half. A symbol in the first half has to matched with the corresponding symbol in the second half.

The machine from both ends simultaneously changes symbols a and *b* to *X* and *Y* respectively. It keep on changing *a* and *b* symbols to *X* and *Y* and erasing the matching *X* and *Y* symbols. There are two ways that an input string can be rejected.

(*i*) If its length is odd.

(*ii*) If the string has even length but a symbol in the first half fails to match the corresponding symbol in the second half.

Let $M = (Q, \Sigma, \Gamma, q_0, \delta, B, F)$ be the required TM with $Q = \{q_0, q_1, \ldots q_{10}\}$,

$\Sigma = \{a, b\}$,

$\Gamma = \{a, b, B\}$,

$F = \{q_{10}\}$, δ is given by table as follows.

States	a	b	B	X	Y
q_0	–	–	(q_1, B, R)	–	–
q_1	(q_2, X, R)	(q_2, Y, R)	(q_{10}, B, L)	(q_5, X, L)	(q_5, Y, L)
q_2	(q_2, a, R)	(q_2, b, R)	(q_3, B, L)	(q_2, X, L)	(q_2, Y, L)
q_3	(q_4, X, L)	(q_4, Y, L)	–	–	–
q_4	(q_4, a, L)	(q_4, b, L)	–	(q_1, X, R)	(q_4, Y, R)
q_5	–	–	(q_6, B, R)	(q_5, a, L)	(q_5, b, L)
q_6	(q_8, X, R)	(q_7, Y, R)	(q_{10}, B, H)	–	–
q_7	(q_7, a, R)	(q_7, b, R)	(q_7, B, R)	–	(q_9, B, L)
q_8	(q_8, a, R)	(q_8, b, R)	(q_8, B, R)	(q_9, B, L)	–
q_9	(q_9, a, L)	(q_9, b, L)	(q_9, B, L)	(q_6, X, R)	(q_6, B, R)

The computation of the string *abab*:

$$
\begin{aligned}
q_0\, Babab &\vdash Bq_1abab \vdash BXq_2bab \\
&\vdash BXbq_2ab \vdash BXbaq_2b \vdash BXbabq_2B \\
&\vdash BXbaq_3bB \vdash BXbq_4aY \vdash BXq_4baY \\
&\vdash Bq_4\, X\, baY \vdash BX\, q_1baY \vdash BXYq_2aY \\
&\vdash BXYaq_2Y \vdash BXYq_3aY \vdash BXq_4YXY \\
&\vdash BXYq_1XY \vdash BXq_5YXY \vdash Bq_5XbXY \\
&\vdash q_5BabXY \vdash Bq_6abXY \vdash BXq_8bXY \\
&\vdash BXbq_8XY \vdash BXq_9bBY \vdash Bq_9XbBY \\
&\vdash BXq_6bBY \vdash BXYq_7BY \vdash BXYBq_7Y \\
&\vdash BXYq_9B \vdash BXq_9Y \vdash BXYq_6B \\
&\vdash XYq_{10}B.
\end{aligned}
$$

Hence the string *abab* is accepted. We can prove that the string of the form *aba* is not accepted by the TM M.

3. Design a TM to compute n mod 2.

Solution. The numerical function that assigns to each natural number n, the remainder when n is divided by 2 can be computed by moving to the end of the input string, making a pass from right to left in which the 0's are countered and simultaneously erased, and either leaving a single 0 (if the original number was odd) or leaving nothing.

Let $$M = \{Q, \Sigma, \Gamma, q_0, \delta, B, F\}$$

be the required TM with $Q = \{q_0, q_1, q_2, q_3, q_4, q_5\}$,

$$\Sigma = \{0\},$$

$$\Gamma = \{0, B\},$$

$$F = \{q_5\}$$

and the transition function δ is defined as follows.

$$\delta(q_0, B) = (q_1, B, R)$$

$$\delta(q_1, 0) = (q_1, 0, R)$$

$$\delta(q_1, B) = (q_2, B, L)$$

$$\delta(q_2, 0) = (q_3, B, L)$$

$$\delta(q_3, 0) = (q_2, B, L)$$

$$\delta(q_3, B) = (q_4, B, R)$$

$$\delta(q_4, B) = (q_5, 0, L)$$

$$\delta(q_2, B) = (q_5, B, H)$$

For the string 0^6, the computation is:

$$q_0B0^6 \vdash Bq_10^6 \vdash^* B0^6q_1B \vdash B0^5q_20B$$

$$\vdash B0^4q_3\ 0BB \vdash B0^3q_20B \vdash B0^2q_30B$$

$$\vdash B0q_20B \vdash Bq_30B \vdash q_2B \vdash q_5B.$$

For the string $w = 0^3$, the computation is:

$$q_0B0^3 \vdash Bq_10^3 \vdash B0^3q_1B \vdash B0^2q_20B$$

$$\vdash B0q_30B \vdash Bq_20B \vdash q_3B \vdash Bq_4B \vdash q_5B0.$$

4. Design a TM to copy strings.

Solution. Let us contruct a TM that creates a copy of its input string, to the right of the input but with a blank separating the copy from the original.

If the initial configuration is q_0Bx where x is a string of non-blank symbols, then the final configuration should be $q_f\ Bx\ Bx$. The TM will examine the first symbol, copy it in the right place, examine the second, copy it and so on. The TM will keep track of its progress by changing the symbols it has copied to upper case. When the copying is complete, the upper case symbols will be changed back to the original.

Let $M = \{Q, \Sigma, \Gamma, q_0, \delta, B, F\}$ be the TM

where $Q = \{q_0, q_1, ..., q_9\}$,

$\Sigma = \{a, b\},$

$\Gamma = \{a, b, B, X, Y\}$

$F = \{q_9\}$ and δ is defined as follows:

States	a	b	B	X	Y
q_0	–	–	(q_1, B, R)	–	–
q_1	(q_2, X, R)	(q_7, Y, R)	(q_8, B, L)	–	–
q_2	(q_2, a, R)	(q_2, b, R)	(q_3, B, R)	–	–
q_3	(q_3, a, R)	(q_3, b, R)	(q_4, a, L)	–	–
q_4	(q_4, a, L)	(q_4, b, L)	(q_5, B, L)	–	–
q_5	(q_5, a, L)	(q_5, b, L)	–	(q_1, X, R)	(q_1, Y, R)
q_6	(q_6, a, R)	(q_6, b, R)	(q_4, b, L)	–	–
q_7	(q_7, a, R)	(q_7, b, R)	(q_6, B, R)	–	–
q_8	–	–	(q_9, B, H)	(q_8, a, L)	(q_8, b, L)

Let w $=a$. The computation of w is:

$$q_0Ba \vdash Bq_1a \vdash BXq_2B \vdash BXBq_3B \vdash BXq_4Ba$$
$$\vdash Bq_5XBa \vdash BXq_1Ba \vdash Bq_8XBa \vdash q_8BaBa$$
$$\vdash q_9aBa.$$

5. Design a Turing machine for deleting a symbol from a string.

Solution. Let $M = \{Q, \Sigma, \Gamma, q_0, \delta, B, F\}$ be a TM,

where $Q = \{q_0, q_1, q_2, q_3, q_4, q_5\},$

$\Sigma = \{a, b\},$

$\Gamma = \{a, b, B\},$

$\Gamma = \{q_5\},$

and δ is defined as follows.

States	a	b	B
q_0	(q_1, B, R)	(q_1, B, R)	(q_1, B, R)
q_1	(q_1, a, R)	(q_1, b, R)	(q_2, B, L)
q_2	(q_3, B, L)	(q_4, B, L)	(q_5, B, H)
q_3	(q_3, a, L) (q_3, b, L)	–	(q_5, a, H)
q_4	–	(q_3, a, L) (q_4, b, L)	(q_5, b, H)

Diagrammatic form

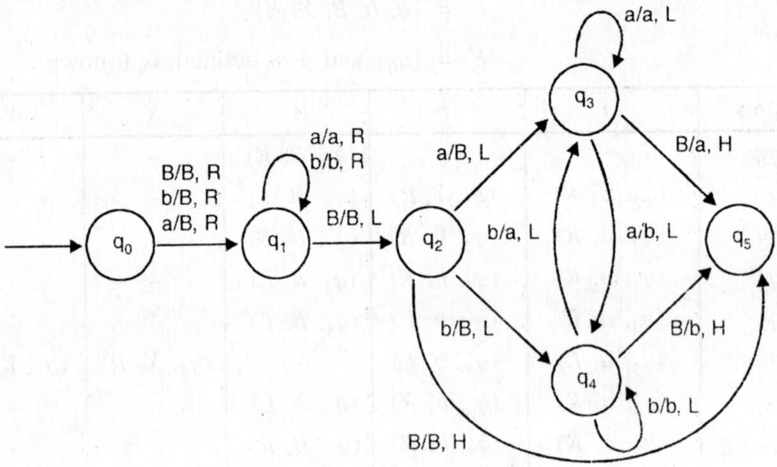

Fig. 4.12.

A TM delete a symbol from a string by changing the tape contents from $yqaz$ to $y\bar{q}\,z$ where $y \in \{\Sigma \cup \{B\})^*$, $a \in \Sigma \cup \{B\}$ and $z \in \Sigma^*$.

The TM starts by replacing the symbol to be deleted by a blank, so that it can be located easily later. It moves to the right end of the string z and makes a single pass from right to left, moving symbols one cell to the left as it goes, until it hits the blank.

The states q_3 and q_4 allow the machine to remember a symbol between the time it erases it and the time it writes it in the next cell to the left. Before it writes each symbol, it reads the symbol being written over, which determines the state it should go to next.

6. Design a TM to compute the function that reverse the input string. That is,

$$q_0 w \vdash^* q_f\, w^R$$

q_f a final state.

Solution. Let $\quad M = \{Q, \Sigma, \Gamma, \delta, q_0, B, F\}$ be the TM,

where $\quad Q = \{q_0, q_1, \ldots q_{10}\}$,

$\Sigma = \{a, b\}$,

$\Gamma = \{a, b, B, X, Y\}$,

$F = \{q_{10}\}$.

q_0 is the initial state. The state q_1 changes a and b into X and Y respectively and remembers it (by going to state q_2 in case of an 'a' and q_4 in the case of a 'b')

as it moves the tape head to the right. When the TM arrives at q_3 or q_5, if there is a lower case symbol on the right corresponding to the one on the left, the TM sees it, remembers it (by going to either q_6 or q_7) and changes it to the symbol it remembers from the left. For even length strings, the TM will return to q_1 and if there is no a or b change, then the machine move to q_8 and the final phase of processing. In the odd-length string the machine will move to either q_3 or q_5. Finally it moves back to the left to change all upper case symbols, X, Y, to a and b respectively.

Diagrammatic form

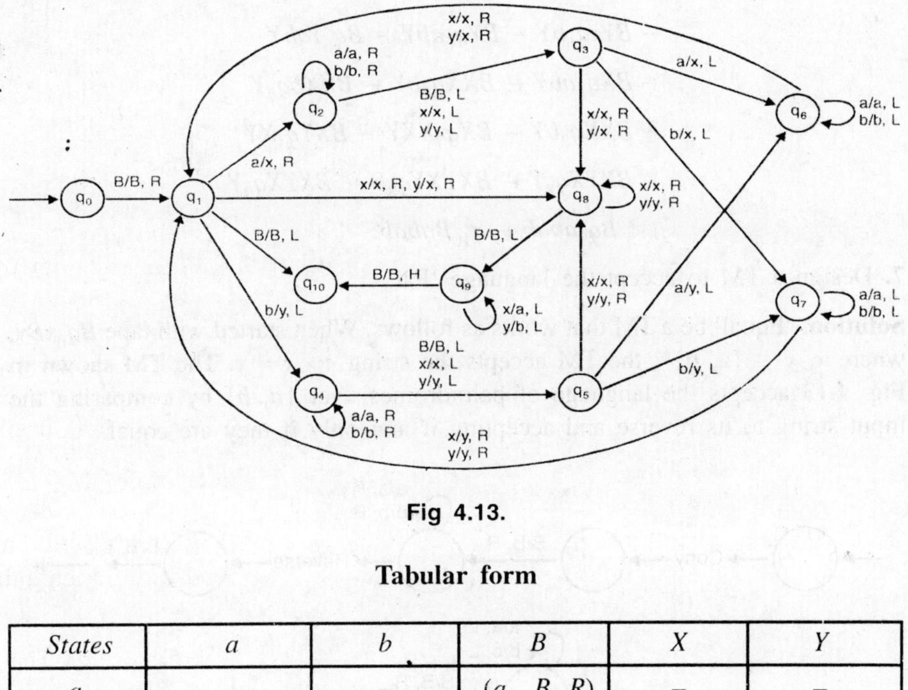

Fig 4.13.

Tabular form

States	a	b	B	X	Y
q_0	–	–	(q_1, B, R)	–	–
q_1	(q_2, X, R)	(q_4, Y, R)	(q_{10}, B, L)	(q_8, X, R)	(q_8, X, R)
q_2	(q_2, a, R)	(q_2, b, R)	(q_3, B, L)	(q_3, X, L)	(q_3, Y, L)
q_3	(q_6, X, L)	(q_7, X, L)	–	(q_8, X, R)	(q_8, X, R)
q_4	(q_4, a, R)	(q_4, b, R)	(q_5, B, L)	(q_5, X, L)	(q_5, Y, L)
q_5	(q_6, Y, L)	(q_7, Y, L)	–	(q_8, X, R)	(q_8, Y, R)
q_6	(q_6, a, L)	(q_6, b, L)	–	(q_1, X, R)	(q_1, X, R)
q_7	(q_7, a, L)	(q_7, b, L)	–	(q_1, Y, R)	(q_1, Y, R)
q_8	–	–	(q_9, B, L)	(q_8, X, R)	(q_8, Y, R)
q_9	–	–	(q_{10}, B, H)	(q_9, a, L)	(q_9, b, L).

Let w = *abb*, the computation is:

$$q_0Babb \vdash Bq_1abb \vdash BXq_2bb \vdash BXbq_2b \vdash BXbbq_2B$$
$$\vdash BXbq_3b \vdash BXq_7bX \vdash Bq_7XbX \vdash BYq_1bX$$
$$\vdash BYYq_4X \vdash BYq_5YX \vdash BYYq_8X \vdash BYYXq_8B$$
$$BYYq_9X \vdash BYq_9Ba \vdash Bq_9Yba \vdash q_9Bbba \vdash Bq_{10}bba.$$

For the string of even length w = *baba*, the computation is:

$$qBbaba \vdash Bq_1baba \vdash BYq_4aba \vdash BYaq_4ba$$
$$\vdash BYabq_4a \vdash BYabaq_4B \vdash BYabq_5a$$
$$\vdash BYaq_6bY \vdash BYq_6abY \vdash Bq_6YabY$$
$$\vdash BXq_1abY \vdash BXXq_2bY \vdash BXXbq_2Y$$
$$\vdash BXXq_3bY \vdash BXq_7XXY \vdash BXYq_1XY$$
$$\vdash BXYXq_8Y \vdash BXYXYq_8B \vdash BXYXq_9Y$$
$$\vdash^* Bq_9abab \vdash q_{10}Babab.$$

7. Design a TM to accept the language 'Pal'.

Solution. 'Equal' be a TM that works as follows. When started with tape Bq_0xBy, where $x, y \in \{a, b\}^*$, the TM accepts the string $\Leftrightarrow x = y$. The TM shown in Fig. 4.13 accepts the language of palindromes over $\{a, b\}$ by comparing the input string to its reverse and accepting if and only if they are equal.

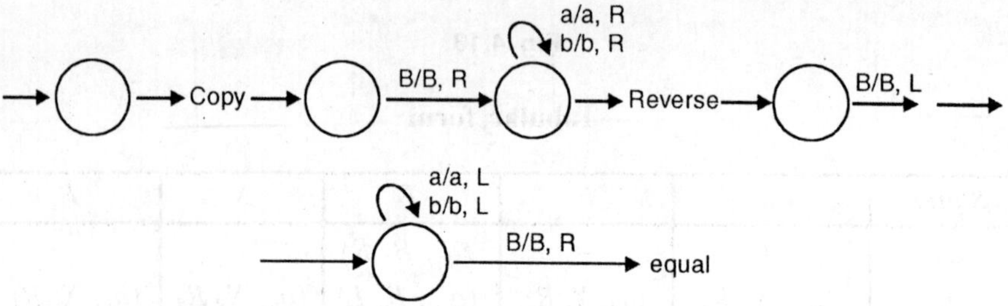

Fig. 4.13.

8. Design a TM to compute the input string 0011.

Solution. Let $M = \{Q, \Sigma, \Gamma, \delta, q_0, B, F\}$ be the TM with

$Q = \{q_1, q_2, q_3, q_4, q_5, q_6\}$,

$\Sigma = \{0, 1\}$,

$\Gamma = \{0, 1, B, X, Y\}$,

$F = \{q_6\}$, and the diagrammatic form for δ is given as

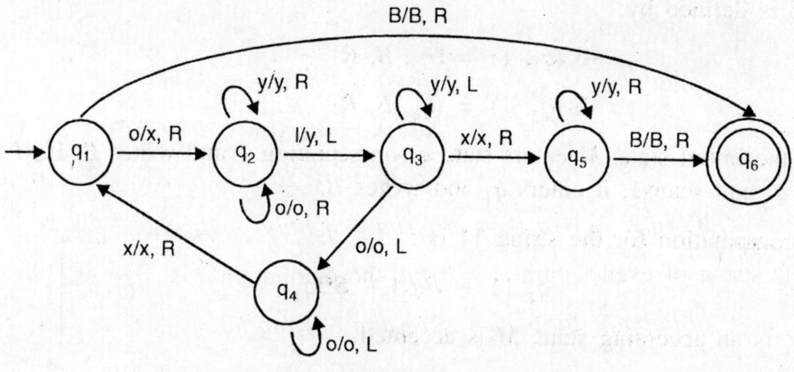

Fig. 4.14.

The computation of the string 0011 is :

$$q_1\ 0011 \vdash Xq_2011 \vdash X0q_211 \vdash Xq_30Y1 \vdash q_4X0Y1$$
$$\vdash Xq_1041 \vdash XXq_2Y1 \vdash XXYq_21 \vdash XXq_3YY$$
$$\vdash Xq_3XYY \vdash XXq_5YY \vdash XXYq_5Y \vdash XXYYq_6.$$

9. Consider the TM M described by the transition table 4.15. Describe the processing of (a) 011 (b) 001.

States	*0*	*1*	*B*	*X*	*Y*
q_1	$(q_2, X, R\}$	–	(q_5, b, R)	–	–
q_2	$(q_2, 0, R)$	(q_3, Y, L)	–	–	(q_2, Y, R)
q_3	$(q_4, 0, L)$	–	–	(q_5, X, R)	(q_3, Y, L)
q_4	$(q_4, 0, L)$	–	–	(q_1, X, R)	–
q_5	–	–	(q_6, b, R)	–	(q_5, Y, R)

(a) $$q_1011 \vdash Xq_211 \vdash q_3XY1 \vdash Xq_5Y1 \vdash XYq_51.$$

As $\delta(q_5, 1)$ is not defined, M halts, so the input string 011 is not accepted.

(b) $$q_1001 \vdash Xq_201 \vdash X0q_21 \vdash Xq_30Y$$
$$\vdash q_4X0Y \vdash Xq_10Y \vdash XXq_2Y \vdash XXYq_2B$$

M halts. As q_2 is not an accepting state, 001, is not accepted by M.

10. Design a TM to recognize all strings consisting of even number of 1's.

Solution. $M = (Q, \Sigma, \Gamma, \delta, q_1, B, F)$ be the TM,

with
$$Q = (q_1, q_2),$$
$$\Sigma = (1),$$
$$\Gamma = (1, B),$$
$$F = (q_2),$$

and δ is defined by:

$$\delta\ (q_1,\ 1) = (q_2,\ B,\ R)$$

$$\delta\ (q_2,\ 1) = (q_1,\ B,\ R)$$

q_1 is the initial state, M enters state q_2 on scanning 1 and writes B. If M is in state q_2 and scans1, it enters q_1 and writes B.

The computation for the string 11 is :

$$q_1\ 11 \vdash Bq_2 1 \vdash BBq_1.$$

As q_1 is an accepting state, M is accepted.

The computation for the string 111 is:

$$q_1 1111 \vdash Bq_2 1 \vdash BBq_1 1 \vdash BBBq_2.$$

As q_2 is non accepting state, m 111 is not accepted by M.

11. Design a TM M to recognize the language

$$\{1^n\ 2^n\ 3^n : n \geq 1\}.$$

Solution. Let $M = \{Q, \Sigma, \Gamma, \delta, q_1, B, F\}$ be a TM

with $Q = \{q_1, q_2, \ldots\ q_7\}$,

$\Sigma = \{1, 2, 3\}$,

$\Gamma = \{1, 2, 3, B\}$

q_1 is the initial state. The machine scans the left most 1, replaces 1 by B and changes the state to q_2 and moves to the right.

When scanning the leftmost 2, the machine replaces 2 by B and changes the state to q_3 and moves to the right. When scanning the leftmost 3, the machine replaces 3 by B and changes the state to q_4 and moves to the right.

After scanning the rightmost 3, it moves to the left to find the next leftmost 1. The process is continued until all 1, 2, 3 are replaced by B.

The transition table is given as follows:

States	*1*	2	3	B
q_1	(q_2, B, R)	–	–	(q_1, B, R)
q_2	$(q_2, 1, R)$	(q_3, B, R)	–	(q_2, B, R)
q_3	–	$(q_3, 2, R)$	(q_4, B, R)	(q_3, B, R)
q_4	–	–	$(q_5, 3, L)$	(q_7, B, L)
q_5	$(q_6, 1, L)$	$(q_5, 2, L)$	–	(q_5, B, L)
q_6	$(q_6, 1, L)$	–	–	(q_1, b, R)

The computation of 112233 is:

$$q_1 12233 \vdash Bq_2 12233 \vdash B1q_2 2233 \vdash B1Bq_3 233$$
$$\vdash B1B2q_3 33 \vdash B1B2bq_4 3 \vdash B1B2q_5 b3$$
$$\vdash B1Bq_5 2b3 \vdash B1q_5 B2B3 \vdash Bq_5 1B2B3$$
$$\vdash q_6 B1B2B3 \vdash Bq_1 1B2B3 \vdash BBq_2 B2B3$$
$$\vdash BBBq_2 2B3 \vdash BBBBq_3 B3 \vdash BBBBBq_3 B$$
$$\vdash BBBBBBq_4 B \vdash BBBBq_7 BB \vdash^* q_7 BBBBBB.$$

(2) Design a TM over $\{1, B\}$ which can compute concatenation function over $\Sigma = \{1\}$.

Solution. $M = (Q, \Sigma, \Gamma, \delta\ q_0, B, F)$ be a TM

with
$$Q = \{q_0, q_1, q_2, q_3, q_4\},$$
$$\Sigma = \{1\},$$
$$\Gamma = \{1, B\},$$
$$F = \{q_4\}$$

and δ is defined by:

States	*1*	*B*
q_0	$(q_0, 1, R)$	$(q_1, 1, R)$
q_1	$(q_1, 1, R)$	(q_2, B, L)
q_2	(q_3, B, L)	–
q_3	$(q_3, 1, L)$	(q_4, B, R)

Let $w_1 = 11$, $w_2 = 111$. Then

$$q_0 11\ B111 \vdash 1q_0 1B111 \vdash 11q_0 B111 \vdash 111q_1 111 \vdash 1111q_1 111$$
$$\vdash 11111q_1 1 \vdash 111111q_1 B \vdash 11111q_2 1B \vdash 1111q_3 1BB$$
$$\vdash 111q_3 1BB \vdash 11q_3 111BB$$
$$\vdash 1q_3 1111BB \vdash q_3 11111B \vdash q_3 B11111BB \vdash Bq_4 11111B.$$

13. Design a TM which, when given a tape which is completely blank except for a single 1 some where on it, find the 1, and halts.

Solution. This machine has two states q_0, q_1, In this case of blank squares on the tape, the machine replaces B by X on each square we examine. It moves left and right replacing blank by X and if it finds 1, then the machine halts.

States	B	X	1
q_0	(q_1, X, R)	(q_0, X, L)	$(q_2, 1, H)$
q_1	(q_0, X, L)	(q_1, X, R)	$(q_2, 1, H)$

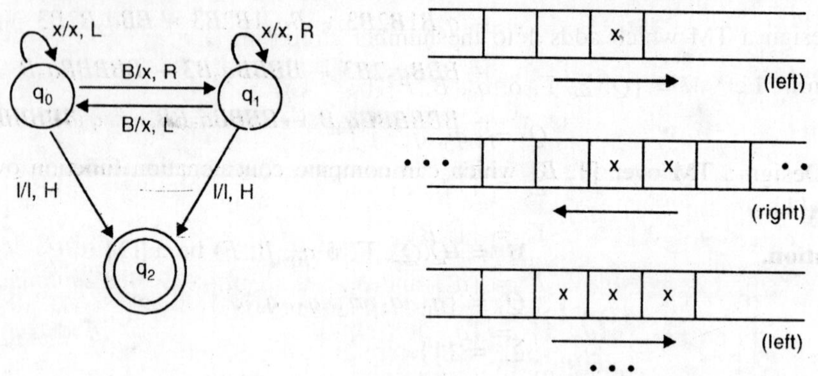

Fig. 4.15.

14. Design a TM which when started at the left most 1 on a tape which is blank except for a single string of consecutive 1's will double the length of the string, return to the leftmost 1, and halt.

Solution. We use two extra symbols. The symbol X will mark the location of 1 that has already been copied, and the symbol Y will mark the location of a copy of one of the original 1's.

First we will copy the leftmost 1 as in Fig. 4.16 (a).

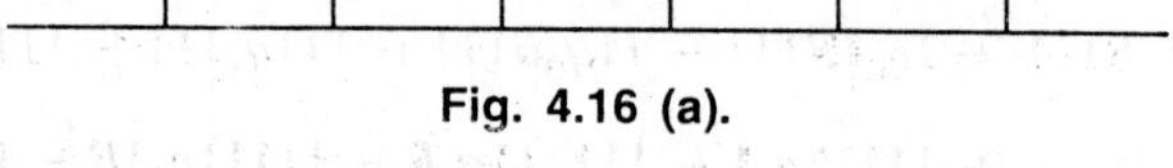

Fig. 4.16 (a).

The *copy* is placed in the first available blank square to the *left* of the original block of 1's. Then we will copy the second 1 (counting from the left), again using the first available blank square on the left as in Fig. 4.16(b).

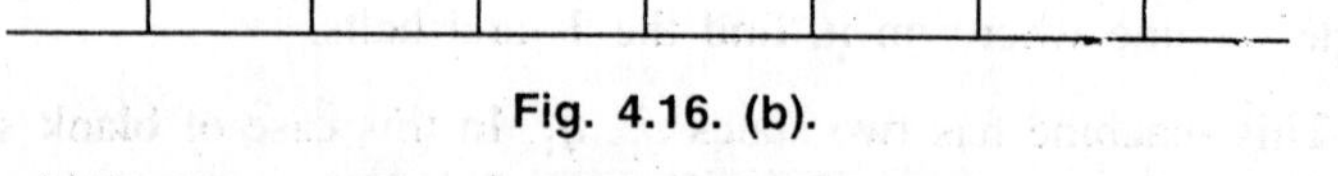

Fig. 4.16. (b).

We continue as shown, always marking with an X the first available 1 on the right, and placing a corresponding Y on the left until there are no more 1's on the tape. Finally we change the X's and Y's to 1's.

The action of δ is as follows :

States	1	X	Y	B
q_0	(q_1, X, L)	(q_0, X, R)	(q_0, Y, R)	(q_0, B, H)
q_1	–	(q_1, X, L)	(q_1, Y, L)	(q_0, Y, R)

15. Design a TM which adds 1 to the number stored on tape.

Solution. Let $M = \{Q, \Sigma, \Gamma, \delta, q_0, B, F\}$ be a TM

with
$$Q = \{q_0, q_1, q_2\},$$
$$\Sigma = \{1\},$$
$$\Gamma = \{1, B\}$$
$$F = \{q_2\} \text{ and } \delta \text{ is defined by:}$$
$$\delta\{q_0, 1\} = \{q_1, 1, L\}$$
$$\delta\{q_1, B\} = \{q_2, 1, H\}$$

The computation of the string 111 is:
$$q_0 111 \vdash q_1 B111 \vdash q_2 1111.$$

(q_2 is an accepting state)

16. Design a TM to accept the language
$$L = \{a^r b^s = r > 0, s > 0\}.$$

Solution. Let $M = \{Q, \Sigma, \Gamma, \delta, q_0, B, F\}$ be the TM

with
$$Q = \{q_0, q_1, q_2, q_3\},$$
$$\Sigma = \{a, b\},$$
$$\Gamma = \{a, b, B\},$$
$$F = \{q_3\},$$

and δ is defined as follows:

States	a	b	B
q_0	(q_1, a, R)	(q_4, b, R)	(q_4, B, R)
q_1	(q_1, a, R)	(q_2, b, R)	(q_4, B, R)
q_2	(q_4, a, R)	(q_2, b, R)	(q_3, B, R)

The computation of the string *abb* is:
$$q_0 abb \vdash aq_1 bb \vdash abq_2 b \vdash abbq_2 B \vdash abbq_3.$$

17. Design a TM 'M' which recoginizes the languages

$$L = \{ab\}^* = \{(ab)^m : m \geq 0\}.$$

Solution. Given an input w, M erases the first 'a' and last 'b' and again next 'a' and 'b' and so on. If all the letters are erased then M accepts w.

The construction of the transition table is:

States	*A*	*b*	*B*
q_0	(q_1, B, R)	(q_N, b, R)	(q_Y, B, R)
q_1	(q_1, a, R)	(q_2, b, R)	(q_N, B, R)
q_2	(q_N, a, R)	(q_2, b, R)	(q_3, B, L)
q_3	–	(q_4, B, L)	–
q_4	–	(q_5, b, L)	(q_y, B, L)
q_5	(q_6, a, L)	(q_5, b, L)	(q_N, B, L)
q_6	(q_6, a, L)	–	(q_0, B, R)

q_N denotes the non accepting state and q_Y denotes the accepting state.

For the input $w = (ab)^2$, the computation sequence is given by:

$$q_0abBab \vdash Bq_1b\ Bab \vdash Bbq_2Bab \vdash Bq_3bBab$$

$$\vdash q_4Bab \vdash q_4ab.$$

18. Let f be the function $f(n) = n - 1$, when $n > 0$ and $f(0) = 0$. Show that f is computable.

Solution. M erases one of the 0's in the input string 0^n when $n > 0$ and makes no change when $n = 0$.

Let $M = \{Q, \Sigma, \Gamma, q_0, \delta, B, F\}$ be the required TM

with $Q = \{q_0, q_1, q_Y\}$,

$\Sigma = \{0\}$,

$\Gamma = \{0, B\}$,

$F = \{q_y\}$.

and δ is defined by:

States	0	B
q_0	$\{q_1, B, R\}$	–
q_1	$(q_y, B, H\}$	$(q_Y, B, H\}$

Here q_0 erases the first 0 and moves to right. If there is only one 0, then M now scans a blank symbol B and halt.

19. Let $\Sigma = \{a, b\}$ and Let $L = \{ w \in \Sigma^* : w$ contains atleast one $a\}$.

Then L is accepted by the Turing machine $M = \{Q, \Sigma\ \Gamma, \delta\ q_0, B, F\}$

where

$$Q = \{q_0, h\}$$
$$\Gamma = \{a, b, B\},$$
$$F = \{h\}$$

and δ is given by the following table.

States	*a*	*b*	*B*
q_0	(h, a, H)	(q_0, b, R)	(q_0, B, R)

This machine when started in configuration $q_0\ B\ w\ B$ for some $w \in \Sigma^*$ simply scans right until an 'a' is encountered and then halts. If no 'a' is found, the machine does not halt.

20. Let f be the function $f(x, y) = y$. Show that f is computable.

Solution. We want to erase all the 0's in 0^x. This is accomplished by the action δ given as

$$\delta\ (q_0, 0) = (q_0, B, R)$$
$$\delta\ (q_0, 1) = (q_1, B, L)$$
$$\delta\ (q_1, B) = (q_2, B, H)$$

where q_2 is the accepting state. For example the computation of the string $0^x\ 1\ 0^y$ is

$$q_0\ 0^x\ 1\ 0^y \vdash^* BBBq_0\ 10^y \vdash Bq_1B0^y \vdash q_2B0^y.$$

21. Let f be the function $f(x, y) = x$. Show that f is computable.

Solution. Erase first 1 and then all 0's after B. The action of δ is defined as follows:

States	*0*	*1*	*B*
q_0	$(q_0, 0, R)$	(q_1, B, R)	–
q_1	(q_1, B, R)	–	(q_2, B, H).

The computation of the string $0^x\ 1\ 0^y$ is :

$$q_0\ 0^x\ 1\ 0^y \vdash^* 0^x\ q_0\ 10^y \vdash 0^x\ B\ q_1\ 0^y \vdash^* 0^x\ B\ Bq_2\ B$$
$$\vdash\ 0^xBq_2.$$

22. Let $\Sigma = \{a, b\}$. Find a TM M which recognizes the language

$$L = \{ab^n : n > 0\}.$$

Solution. Let $\qquad M = \{Q, \Sigma, \Gamma, \delta, q_0, B, F\}$ be the TM where $Q = \{q_1, q_2, q_N, q_Y\}$,

$$\Sigma = \{a, b\},$$

$$\Gamma = \{a, b, B\}$$

$$F = \{q_Y\}$$

and δ is defined as follows.

States	*a*	*b*	*B*
q_0	(q_1, a, R)	(q_N, b, R)	(q_N, B, R)
q_1	(q_N, a, R)	(q_2, b, R)	(q_N, B, R)
q_2	(q_N, a, R)	(q_2, b, R)	(q_4, B, R)

The computation sequence of the string *abbb* is:

$$q_0abbb \vdash aq_1bbb \vdash abq_2bb \vdash abbq_2b$$
$$\vdash abbbq_2B \vdash abbbq_YB.$$

23. Let $\Sigma = \{a, b\}$. Find a TM M which recognizes the finite languages $L = \{a, a^2\}$.

Solution. Let δ be defined by :

States	*a*	*b*	*B*
q_0	(q_1, a, R)	(q_N, b, R)	(q_N, B, R)
q_1	(q, a, R)	(q_N, b, R)	(q_Y, B, R)
q_2	(q_N, a, R)	(q_N, b, R)	(q_4, B, R)

Here q_Y denotes the accepting state and q_N denotes the rejecting state.

The computation of the string a^2 is: $q_0\, a^2 \vdash aq_1\, a \vdash aaq_2\, B \vdash aaq_YB.$

The computation of the string $a^3\, b$ is :

$$q_0\, a^3 \vdash a\, q_1\, a \vdash aa\, q_2\, a \vdash aaaq_Nb \vdash aaabq_N.$$

(rejection state)

24. Design a TM that takes a string of 0's and 1's and erases the right most symbol.

Solution. Let $M = \{Q, \Sigma, \Gamma, \delta, q_0, B, F\}$ be the TM with

$$Q = \{q_0, q_1, q_2, q_3, q_4\},$$

$$\Sigma = \{0, 1\},$$

$$\Gamma = \{0, 1, B\},$$

$F = \{q_4\}$ and δ is defined by the table as

States	1	0	B
q_0	$(q_1, 1, R)$	$(q_1, 0, R)$	–
q_1	$(q_1, 1, R)$	$(q_1, 0, R)$	(q_2, B, L)
q_2	(q_2, B, L)	(q_3, B, L)	–
q_3	$(q_3, 1, L)$	$(q_3, 0, L)$	(q_y, B, R)

The computation of the string 110 is :

$$q_0\,110 \vdash 1q_1 10 \vdash 11q_1 0 \vdash 110\; q_1\; B \vdash 11q_2\; 0\; B$$
$$\vdash 1\; q_3 1B \vdash q_3 11B \vdash q_3\; B11 \vdash Bq_4 11.$$

25. Design a TM that accept those strings beginning with a '1'.

Solution. Let $M = \{Q, \Sigma, \Gamma, q_0, \delta, B, F\}$ be the TM

where
$$Q = \{q_0, q_1, q_2\},$$
$$\Sigma = \{0, 1\},$$
$$\Gamma = \{0, 1, B\}$$
$$F = \{q_2\},$$

and δ is defined by:

$$\delta\,(q_0, 1) = (q_2, 1, H)$$
$$\delta\,(q_0, 0) = (q_1, 0, R)$$
$$\delta\,(q_1, 1) = (q_1, 0, R)$$
$$\delta\,(q_1, 0) = (q_1, 0, R)$$
$$\delta\,(q_1, B) = (q_1, 0, R)$$

The computation of the string 100 is:

$$q_0\;100 \vdash 1\;q_2\;00 \qquad \text{(Accepted)}$$

The computation of the string 001 is:

$$q_0 001 \vdash 0q_1 01 \vdash 00q_1 1 \vdash 000q_1 B \vdash 0000q_1$$

(Not accepted)

If the input string begins with a 1, M halts and accepts the string ; but if the string begins with *a,* 0, M creates on infinitely long string of 0's and does not halt.

26. Design a Turing machine to tests a string of parentheses to see if it balanced.

Solution. The machine keeps track of all the left parentheses that it has found and looks for right parentheses to form pairs of parentheses.

M searches for a right parentheses, if it found, then erases it and move left to find the left parentheses that it matches, and erases the matching parentheses. If all parentheses are erased, the machine halts in an accepting state. Here we use an extra symbol &

Let $M = \{Q, \Sigma, \Gamma, q_0, \delta, B, F\}$ be the TM with

$$Q = \{q_0, q_1, q_2, q_3\},$$

$$\Sigma = \{(\ ,\ )\},$$

$$\Gamma = \{(\ ,\ ),\ \&\ B\},$$

$$F = \{q_3\},$$

and δ is defined as follows :

States	(	)	&	*B*
q_0	(q_0, C, R)	$(q_1, \&, L)$	$(q_0, \&, R)$	(q_2, B, L)
q_1	$(q_0, \&, R)$	–	$(q_1, \&, L)$	–
q_2	–	–	(q_2, B, L)	(q_3, B, H)

$$q_0\ (\ )\ ((\ ))\ \vdash\ (q_0)\ ((\ ))\vdash q_1\ (\ \&\ ((\ )))$$

$$\vdash \&\ q_0\ \&\ ((\ ))\vdash \&\&\ q_0\ ((\ ))\vdash \&\&\ ((q_0))$$

$$\vdash \&\&\{q_1,(\&)\}\vdash \&\&(\&\ q_1\ \&)$$

$$\vdash \&\&(q_1\ \&\&)\vdash \&\&\ q_1\ (\&\&)$$

$$\vdash \&\&\&\ q_0\ \&\&\vdash \&\&\&\&\&\ q_0\ B$$

$$\vdash \&\&\&\&\ q_2\ \&\ B \vdash^* q_3\ B.$$

27. Consider the following machine

$$M = \{Q, \Sigma, \Gamma, \delta, q_0, B, F\}$$

where

$$Q = \{q_0, h\},$$

$$\Sigma = \{a, b\}$$

$$\Gamma = \{a, b, B\}$$

and δ is defined as :

$$\delta\{q_0, a\} = \{h, a, H\}$$

$$\delta\{q_0, b\} = \{q_0, b, R\}$$

Indicate how M processes the following strings and whether they are accepted.

(*i*) *abbbb*

(*ii*) *bbbba*

(*iii*) *bbbb.*

Solution.

(i) $q_0abbbb \vdash habbbb$ (halts)

(ii) $q_0bbbba \vdash bbbbq_0a \vdash bbbbah$ (halts with accepting)

(iii) $q_0\ bbbb \vdash bbbbq_0B$ (halts with rejecting)

28. $M = \{Q, \Sigma, \Gamma, \delta, q_0, B, F\}$ be a non-deterministic TM, with

$$Q = \{q_0, q_1, q_2, q_3, q_4, h\},$$

$$\Sigma = \{a, b\},$$

$$\Gamma = \{a, b, B\}$$

$$F = \{h\}$$

and δ is defined by

$$\delta(q_0, a) = \{(q_0, B, R), (q_1, B, R)\}$$

$$\delta(q_1, b) = \{(q_2, B, R)\}$$

$$\delta(q_2, b) = \{(q_2, B, R), (q_3, B, R)\}$$

$$\delta(q_3, a) = \{(q_4, B, R)\}$$

$$\delta(q_4, a) = \{(q_4, B, R)\}$$

$$\delta(q_4, B) = \{(h, B, H)\}$$

Then check whether the string *aabbbaa* is accepted by M or not.

Solution.

$$q_0\ aabbbaa \vdash Bq_0abbbaa$$
$$\vdash BBq_1bbbaa$$
$$\vdash BBq_2bb\ aa$$
$$\vdash Bq_2baa$$
$$\vdash BBq_3aa$$
$$\vdash BBBq_4a$$
$$\vdash BBBBq_4B$$
$$\vdash BBBBh.$$

Hence the machine accepts the string.

29. Let $\Sigma = \{a, b\}$ and let $f : \Sigma^* \to \Sigma^*$ be defined as follows. For any $w \in \Sigma^*$, define $f(w) = \overline{\omega}$, $\overline{\omega}$ is the result of replacing each occurrence of a in w by b and vice versa.

Solution. f is computed by a TM M which scans backward through its input, changing a's to b's and vice versa, until the blank marking the leftmost square is found. In order to leave the tape in the proper format, M must then return its head to the blank marking the right end of the input.

Let $M = \{Q, \Sigma, \Gamma, \delta, q_0, B, F\}$ be the TM

where $Q = \{q_0, q_1, q_2\}$,

$\Sigma = \{a, b\}$

$\Gamma = \{a, b, B\}$,

$F = \{q_2\}$

and δ is given by the following table.

States	Tape symbols		
	a	b	B
q_0	(q_1, b, R)	(q_1, a, R)	(q_1, B, L)
q_1	(q_0, b, R)	(q_0, a, R)	(q_2, B, H)

The computation of the string aab is

$$q_0aab \vdash bq_1ab \vdash bbq_0b \vdash bbaq_1B \vdash bbaq_2.$$

30. Design a TM that scans to the right until it find a non-blank cell, then copies the symbol in that cell on to the cell immediately to the left of where it was found.

Solution. Let $M = \{Q, \Sigma, \Gamma, \delta, q_0, B, F\}$ be the TM with

$Q = \{q_0, q_1, q_2\}$,

$\Sigma = \{a\}$,

$\Gamma = \{a, b\}$,

$F = \{q_2\}$

and δ is defined by:

$$\delta\,(q_0, B) = (q_0, B, R)$$

$$\delta\,(q_0, a) = (q_1, a, L)$$

$$\delta(q_1, B) = (q_2, a, H).$$

The computation of the string $BBBaBB$ is :

$$q_0\ BBB\ a\ BB \vdash^* BBBq_0aBB \vdash BBq_1BaBB \vdash BBq_2aaBB.$$

31. Let $U_i^m : N^m \to N$ defined by $U_i^m\,(a_1, a_2, \ldots a_m) = a_i$ be the projection function. Design a TM to compute U_i^m.

Solution. Let the input string be $0^{a1} x_1\ 0^{a2}\ x_2 \ldots 0^{am}\ x_m\ By$.

Let $M = \{Q, \Sigma, \Gamma, \delta, q_0, B, F\}$ be the TM with

$$Q = \{q_0, q_1, \ldots, q_8\},$$

$$\Sigma = \{0\},$$

$$\Gamma = \{B, 0, x_1, x_2, \ldots x_m', y\}$$

and δ is defined as follows:

$$\delta(q_0, z) = (q_0, z, R) \qquad \text{for all } z \in \Gamma - (x_i)$$

$$\delta(q_0, x_i) = (q_1, x_i, L)$$

$$\delta(q_1, 0) = (q_2, b, L)$$

$$\delta(q_1, b) = (q_8, b, L)$$

$$\delta(q_2, z) = (q_2, z, R) \qquad \text{for all } z \in \Gamma - (y)$$

$$\delta(q_2, y) = (q_3, 0, R)$$

$$\delta(q_3, B) = (q_4, y, R)$$

$$\delta(q_3, 0) = (q_3, 0, R)$$

$$\delta(q_4, z) = (q_4, z, L) \qquad \text{for all } z \in \Gamma - (x_i)$$

$$\delta(q_4, x_i) = (q_5, x_i, L)$$

$$\delta(q_5, 0) = (q_5, 0, L)$$

$$\delta(q_5, b) = (q_6, 0, R)$$

$$\delta(q_6, 0) = (q_7, 0, L)$$

$$\delta(q_7, 0) = (q_2, B, L)$$

$$\delta(q_6, x_i) = (q_6, x_i, L)$$

$$\delta(q_7, z) = (q_8, z, R) \qquad \text{for all } z \in \Gamma - (0)$$

For example, let us compute U_2^3 (1, 2, 1) :

$$q_0\ 0\ x_1\ 00\ x_2\ 0\ x_3 \text{ by} \vdash^* 0\ x_1\ 00 q_0\ x_2\ 0\ x_3 \text{ by}$$

$$\vdash 0x_1\ 0q_1\ 0x_2\ 0\ x_3 \text{ by}$$

$$\vdash 0x_1\ q_2 0\ bx_2\ 0x_3 \text{ by}$$

$$\vdash 0x_1\ 0q_2\ bx_2\ 0x_3 \text{ by}$$

$$\vdash^* 0x_1\ 0b\ x_2\ 0\ x_3\ bq_2 y$$

$$\vdash 0x_1\ 0bx_2\ 0x_3\ b\ 0q_3 B$$

$$\vdash 0x_1\ 0b\ x_20\ b0y\ q_4\ B$$
$$\vdash^* 0x_1\ 0bq_4\ x_2\ 0x_3\ b0y$$
$$\vdash 0x_1\ 0q_5\ \text{b}x_2\ 0x_3\ b0y$$
$$\vdash 0x_1\ 00q_6\ x_2\ 0x_3\ b0y$$
$$\vdash 0x_1\ 0q_6\ 0x_2\ 0x_3\ b0y$$
$$\vdash 0x_1\ q_7\ 00\ x_2\ 0x_3\ b0y$$
$$\vdash 0q_2x_1\ b0\ x_2\ 0x_3\ b0y$$
$$\vdash 0x_1\ q_2\ b0\ x_2\ 0x_3\ b0y$$

From the above derivation we see that

$$0x_1\ 00\ x_2\ 0x_3\ \text{by} \vdash^* 0x_1\ q_2b\ 0x_2\ 0x_3\ b0y$$

Repeating the above steps, we get

$$0x_1\ q_2b\ 0x_2\ 0x_3\ \text{b}0\text{y} \vdash^* 0x_1q_8\ 00x_2\ 0x_3\ b00y.$$

While computing U_i^m the head skips the portion of the input corresponding to aj, $j \neq i$, For every 0 in 0^{ai}, 0 is added to the left of y.

32. Construct a TM that can compute the zero function z.

Solution. The zero function z is defined as $z(a_1) = 0$ for all, $a_1 \geq 0$. Let the input string be $0^{a_1}\ x_1\ B_y$. We require the computed value $z(a_1)$, namely 0 to appear to the left of y, we require the machine to halt without changing the input.

Let $\quad M = \{Q, \Sigma, \Gamma, \delta, q_0, B, F)$ be the TM with

$$Q = \{q_0, q_1\},$$
$$\Sigma = \{0\},$$
$$\Gamma = \{B, 0, x_1, y\}$$

and δ is defined as follows.

$$\delta(q_0, B) = (q_0, B, R)$$
$$\delta(q_0, x_1) = (q_1, x_1, R)$$
$$\delta(q_0, 0) = (q_0, 0, R)$$

q_0 is used to move right until x_1 is encountered. If it finds x_1, then it enter the state q_1 with out altering the tape symbol. The computation is:

$$q_00^{a_1}x_1By \vdash^* 0^{a_1}q_0\ x_1By \vdash 0^{a_1}x_1q_1By$$

As there is no action of q_1 on B, M halts. By deleting q_1 in $0^{a_1}\ x_1q_1By$, we get $0^{a_1}\ x_1By$ yielding 0 (given by B).

33. Design a TM that can perform recursion.

Solution. Let $g(x_1, x_2, ..., x_m)$, $h(y_1, y_2, ..., y_{m+2})$ be computable functions. Let $f(x_1, x_2, ... x_{m+1})$ be defined by recursion as follows:

$$f(x_1, ..., x_m, 0) = g(x_1, x_2, ... x_m)$$

$$f(x_1, x_2, ..., x_m, y + 1) = h(x_1, x_2, ..., x_m, y; f(x_1, x_2, ..., x_m))$$

The computation of $f(a_1, a_1, ... a_m, c)$ is as follows:

Let the input be $0^{a_1} x_1 ..., 0^{a_m} x_m 0^c x_{m+1} By$.

Let M' be the TM which computes g. Let M simulates M'. If $c = 0$, the computed value $g(a_1, ... a_m) = f(a_1, a_1, ..., a_m, 0)$ is placed to the left of y. The head is placed to the right of x_m and M halts.

If $c \neq 0$, 0^c is replaced by B^c. The marker y is changed to x_{m+2} and By is added to the right of x_{m+2}. The head moves to the left of 0^{a_1}.

The M is allowed to compute $h(a_1, a_1, ..., a_m, 0, g(a_1, ..., a_m))$ which appear to the left of $x_1, x_2, ... x_m, x_{m+1}, x_{m+2}$, respectively. The computed value is $f(a_1, a_2, ..., a_m, 1), f(a_1, a_2, ..., a_m, 2) ... f(a_1, a_2, ..., a_m, c)$ and are computed successively by replacing the right most B and computing h for respective arguments. The computation stops with a terminal ID.

$$B0^{a_1} x_1 0^{a_2} x_2 ... q_f 0^c x_{n+1} 0^k y,$$

$k = f(a_1, a_2, ..., a_m, c)$, q_f is the final state.

33. Construct a TM that can perform minimisation.

Solution. $f(x_1, x_2, ..., x_m)$ is defined from $g(x_1, x_2, ..., x_m, y)$ by minimization, $f(x_1, x_2, ..., x_m)$ is the least of all k's such that $g(x_1, x_2, ..., x_m, k) = 0$. The problem reduces to computing $g(a_1, a_2, ..., a_m, k)$ for given arguments $a_1, a_2, ..., a_m$ and for values of k starting from 0. $f(a_1, a_2, ... a_m)$ is the first k for which $g(a_1, a_2, ..., a_m, k) = 0$. After computing $g(a_1, a_2, ..., a_m, y) = 0$. The TM '$M$' halts. If no y exists, then M never halts.

The construction of M is designed such away that it simulates the TM that computes $g(a_1, a_2, ..., a_m, k)$ for successive values of k. Once the computed value $g(a_1, a_2, ..., a_m, k) = 0$ for the first time, M erases 'By' and changes x_{m+1} to y. The head moves to the left of x_m and M halts.

34. Design a TM that can perform composition.

Solution. Let $f : N^k \to N$ and $g_1, g_2, ... g_k N^m \to N$ be computable functions and $h : N^m \to N$ is obtained from f and $g_1, g_2, ..., g_k$ by composition. To prove h is computable.

Let $M_f, M_1, M_2 ..., M_k$ be the TM's computing f and $g_1, g_2, ..., g_k$ respectively.

Let the tape content be $0^{a1}x_1$ ..., 0^{am} x_m.

The TM M_h which computes h, use this input k times, once for each of the M_i's. In order to do this, it makes an additional copy of the tape content each time before processing it. Let us denote by $X = (a_1, a_1, ..., a_m)$ and by 0^X = $0^{a1}x_1$ $0^{a2}x_2$ ..., 0^{am} x_m.

During the first iteration, M_h creates the tape content $x_1 0^X$ $x_2 0^X$ and executes M_1 to produce x_1 0^X $x_2 0^{g_1(X)}$. During the second iteration, it makes another copy of the input, to obtain $x_1 0^X$ $x_2 0^{g_1(X)}$ $x_3 0^X$, then executes M_2. After k iterations, the tape looks like

$$x_1 0^X x_2 0^{g_1(X)}\ x_3 0^{g_2(X)} \ldots\ x_k 0^{g_k(X)}.$$

M_h deletes the original input, so that the tape contains the input required for M_f as

$$x_2 0^{g_1(X)}\ x_3 0^{g_2(X)}\ \ldots x_k 0^{a_k(X)}.$$

The last step is to execute M_f, which produces the required output. F or any choice of X at which the composition is undefined, M_h fails to halt. Also during execution of M_i, if $g_i(X)$ is not defined then M_h fails to halt. Another restriction is during the execution of M_f if each $g_i(X)$ is defined but $f(g_1(X), ..., g_k(X))$ is not defined, then also M_h fails to halt.

35. Design a TM to compute $n!$.

Solution. Let $f(n) = n!$. Define f by recursion as follows:

$$f(0) = 1; f(n + 1) = (n + 1)! = (n + 1)n\,! = h(n, f(n))$$

where $h(x, y) = S(x)*\ y$, S is the successor function defined by $S(x) = x + 1$. The solution of this problem follows from problem 33.

36. Compute $Z(4)$ using the Turing machine constructed for computing the zero function.

Solution. Consider problem 32. Let the input string be $w = 0^4\ x_1\ By$. The computation of w is:

$$q_0 0^4\ x_1\ By \vdash^* 0^4 q_0\ x_1\ By \vdash 0^4\ x_1\ q_1\ By.$$

As B lies between x_1 and y, $z(4) = 0$ (given by B).

37. Let $\Sigma = \{a, b, c\}$. Let $M = \{Q, \Sigma, \Gamma, \delta, q_0, B, F\}$ be the TM illustrated in Fig. 4.17. Give the strings that are accepted by M.

Solution. $\Gamma = \{a, b, c, d, B\}$,

$$Q = \{q_0, q_1, q_2, q_3, q_4, h\}.$$

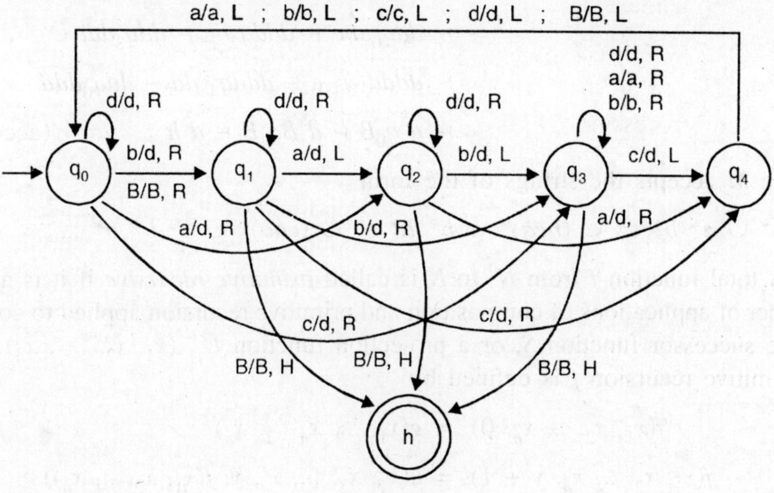

Fig. 4.17.

The computation of the strings

(*i*) *abcabc* (*ii*) $a^2\ b^2\ c^2$.

(*i*)

$$q_0\ abcabc \vdash dq_2bcabc \vdash q_3ddcabc \vdash ddq_3cabc$$
$$\vdash dq_4ddabc \vdash q_0dddabc \vdash dddq_0abc$$
$$\vdash ddddq_2bc \vdash dddq_3ddc \vdash d^5q_3c \vdash d^4q_4dd$$
$$\vdash d^3q_0d^3 \vdash d^6q_0B \vdash d^6Bq_1B \vdash d^6h.$$

(accepted by *M*)

(*ii*)

$$q_0a^2b^2c^2 \vdash dq_2ab^2c^2 \vdash ddq_4b^2c^2 \vdash dq_0db^2c^2$$
$$\vdash ddq_0b^2c^2 \vdash dddq_1bc^2 \vdash ddddq_3cc$$
$$\vdash dddq_4ddc \vdash ddq_0dddc \vdash dddddq_0c$$
$$\vdash d^6q_3B \vdash d^6h$$

(accepted by *M*).

(*iii*)

$$q_0a^3b^3c^3 \vdash dq_2a^2b^3c^3 \vdash ddq_4ab^3c^3 \vdash dq_0dab^3c^3$$
$$\vdash ddq_0ab^3c^3 \vdash dddq_2b^3c^3 \vdash dddq_3db^2c^3$$
$$\vdash d^4q_3b^2c^3 \vdash d^4b^2q_3ccc \vdash d^4bq_4bdcc$$
$$\vdash d^4q_0bbdcc \vdash d^4dq_1bdcc \vdash d^6q_3dcc$$
$$\vdash d^7q_3cc \vdash d^6q_4ddc \vdash d^5q_0d^3c$$
$$\vdash d^8q_0c \vdash d^9q_3B \vdash d^9h$$

(accepted).

(iv) $$q_0a^3bc \vdash dq_2a^2bc \vdash ddq_4abc \vdash dq_0dabc$$
$$\vdash ddq_0abc \vdash dddq_2bc \vdash ddq_3ddc$$
$$\vdash dddd\ q_3\ c \vdash dddq_4\ dd \vdash ddq_0ddd$$
$$\vdash d^5q_0B \vdash d^5Bq_1B \vdash d^5h \qquad \text{(accepted)}$$

Hence M accepts the strings of the form

$(abc)^* \cup a^*\ b^*\ c^* \cup (bca)^* \cup b^*\ a^*\ c^* \cup (cab)^* \cup c^*\ b^*\ a^* \ldots$.

38. A total function f from N^n to N is called *primitive recursive* if it is a finite number of applications of composition and primitive recursion applied to constant 0, the successor function S, or a projection function $U_i^n\ (x_1, x_2, \ldots, x_n) = x_i$. A primitive recursion f is defined by

$$f(x_1, x_2, \ldots x_n, 0) = g(x_1, \ldots, x_{n-1}, x_n)$$
$$f(x_1, x_2, \ldots x_n, y + 1) = h(x_1, x_2, \ldots, x_n, y, f(x_1, x_2, \ldots x_n))$$

where g and h are primitive recursive functions.

(*a*) Show that $f_1(x, y) = x + y$ is primitive recursive.

(*b*) Show that $f_2(x, y) = x * y$ is primitive recursive.

Solution.

(*a*) Let g be a function of single variable h be a function of three variables. Now

$$f_1(x, 0) = x + 0 = x = U_1^1(x) = g(x) \text{ (say)}$$

and
$$f_1(x, y + 1) = x + y + 1 = (x + y) + 1 = f_1(x, y) + 1$$
$$= S(f_1(x, y))$$
$$= S(U_3^3\ (x, y, f_1(x, y))$$
$$= h(x, y, f_1(x, y)).$$

As h is obtained from the initial functions U_3^3 and S by composition, and f_1 by recursion using g and h, f_1 is primitive recursive.

(*b*) Let $f_2\ (x, y) = x * y$. Now $f_2(x, 0) = x * 0 = 0$ and

$$f_2\ (x, y + 1) = x * (y + 1) = (x * y) + x = f_2(x, y) + x$$
$$= f_1\ \{f_2\ (x, y), x\}.$$

$$f_2(x, 0) = 0\ z(x) \qquad \text{[a constant function]}$$
$$f_2\ (x, y + 1) = f_1[f_2(x, y), x]$$
$$= f_1(U_3^3\ (x, y, f_2\ (x, y), U_1^3\ (x, y, f_2\ (x, y))$$

By taking $g = Z$, h defined by $h(x, y, z)$

$$= f_1\,(U_3^3\,(x, y, f_2\,(x, y), U_1^3\,(x, y, f_2(x, y))$$

We see that f_2 is defined by recursion. As g and h are primitive recursive, f_2 is primitive recursive.

39. A recursive function is a function defined by a finite set of rules that for various arguments specify the function in terms of variables, non-negative integer constants, the successor function, the function itself, or an expression built from these by composition of functions. For example, Ackermann's function A is defined by the rules

(1) $A(0, y) = y + 1 \qquad y \geq 0$

(2) $A(x, 0) = A(x - 1, 1), \qquad x > 0$

(3) $A(x, 0) = x + 2 \qquad$ for $x \geq 2$

(4) $A(x + 1, y + 1) = A(x, A(x + 1, y))$

(*a*) Evaluate $A\,(2, 1)$

(*b*) Evaluate $A\,(2, 2)$.

Solution.

(*a*) $A(2, 1) = A(1, A(2, 0))$

$A(2, 0) = A(1, 1)$

$A(1, 1) = A(0, A(1, 0))$

$A(1, 0) = A(0, 1) = 1 + 1 = 2$

Therefore $A(1, 1) = A(0, 2) = 2 + 1 = 3.$

Hence $A(2, 1) = A(1, 3).$

Now $A(1, 3) = A(0, A(1, 2))$

$A(1, 2) = A(0, A(1, 1))$

$= A(0, 3) = 4$

So $A(1, 3) = A(0, 4) = 5.$

Now $A(2, 1) = A(1, 3) = 5.$

(*b*) $A(2, 2) = A(1, 5) = A(0, A(1, 4))$

$A(1, 4) = A(0, A(1, 3)) = (0, 5) = 6.$

So $A\,(2, 2) = A(0, 6) = 7.$

40. Show that $f(x, y) = x^y$ is a primitive recursive function.

Solution. Note that $x^0 = 1$, for $x \neq 0$ and $x^0 = 0$ for $x = 0$.

Also $x^{y+1} = x^y * x$. Hence $f(x, y) = x^y$ is defined as

$$f(x, 0) = x^0 = \begin{cases} 0 \text{ for } x = 0 \\ 1 \text{ for } x \neq 0. \end{cases}$$

$$f(x, y + 1) = x^{y+1} = x^y * x = f(x, y) * x$$

$$= U^3_3(x, y, f(x, y)) * U^3_1(x, y, f(x, y))$$

since f is expressed as the known primitive recursive functions, f is a primitive recursive function.

41. Define by recursion the following.

(*i*) $n + m$

(*ii*) $n\ m$

(*iii*) $n \dot{-} m$

(*iv*) n !.

Solution.

(*i*) Let $f(n, m) = n + m$. Then

$$f(n, 0) = n + 0 = n = U^1_1(n)$$

$$f(n, m + 1) = n + m + 1 = (n + m) + 1 = f(n, m) + 1$$

$$S(U^3_3(n, m, f, (n, m))$$

(*ii*) Let $f(n, m) = nm$. Now

$$f(n, 0) = 0 = Z(n)$$

$$f(n, m + 1) = n(m + 1) = nm + n = f(n, m) + n$$

$$f(U^3_3(n, m, f(n, m)), U^3_1(n, m, f(n, m))$$

(*iii*) Note that $n \dot{-} m = 0 \quad n < n$

$n - m \quad n \leq m$

$$n \dot{-} m = \begin{cases} 0 & n < m \\ n - m & n \leq m \end{cases}$$

Let $f(n, m) = n \dot{-} m$. Now

$$f(n, 0) = 0 = Z(n)$$

$$f(n, m + 1) = n \dot{-} (m + 1) = P(n \dot{-} m)$$

where P is the predecessor function defined by

$$P(0) = 0$$

$$P(y + 1) = y = U_1^2 (y, P(y))$$

Hence the proper subtraction function $\dot{-}$ is defined in terms of constant function Z and predecessor function P.

(*iv*) Let $f(n) = n!$. Then it can be defined recursively as

$$f(0) = 0 = U(0)$$

$$f(n + 1) = (n + 1)\,! = (n + 1) * n! = (n + 1) * f(n)$$

$$= S(n) * U_1^1 (f(n))$$

where S is the successor function, Z is the constant function and U_1^1 is the projection function.

40. Check the function $f(x, y) = x + y$ is a total function or not.

Solution. Since the function is defined for all $x, y \in N$, f is a total function.

41. Check the function $f(x, y) = x - y$ is a total function or not.

Solution. Since the function is defined for those elements $x, y \in N$ such that $x \geq y$, the given function is not total. It is partial function.

42. Prove the Ackermann's function is not primitive recursive.

Solution. Before proving the problem, we first state a result.

Let f be any primitive recursive function. Then there exists some integer n such that

$$f(i) < A(n, i)$$

for all $\qquad i = n, n + 1, n + 2 ....$

Now we prove the problem. Let g be a function such that $g(i) = A(i, i)$ for all $i \in N$. If A is primitive recursive, then g is also primitive recursive. But according to the above result,

$$g(i) < A(n, i)$$

For all i. If we let $i = n$, then

$$g(n) = A(n, n) < A(n, n)$$

a contradiction. Hence A cannot be primitive recursive.

43. Define regular and partial recursive function.

Solution. Let $g(x_1, x_2, ... x_n, y)$ be a total function over N. g is said to be a *regular function* if there exists some natural numbers y_0 such that

$$g(x_1, x_2, ..., x_n, y_0) = 0$$

for all values of $x_1, x_2, ..., x_n \in N$.

A function $f(x_1, x_2, ..., x_n)$ over N is defined from a total function $g(x_1, x_2, ..., x_n, y)$ by *minimization* if

(*a*) $f(x_1, x_2, ..., x_n)$ is the least value of all y's such that $g(x_1, x_2, ..., x_n, y) = 0$ if it exists.

The least value is denoted by $\mu y\ ((g(x_1, x_2, ...\ x_n, y) = 0)$

(*b*) $f(x_1, x_2, ..., x_n)$ is undefined if there is no y such that

$$g(x_1, x_2, ...\ x_n, y) = 0$$

A function is said to be *partial recursive* if it can be obtained from the initial functions by a finite number of applications of composition, recursion and minimization.

44. Give one example for the following:

(*a*) regular function (*b*) not a regular function.

Solution. (*a*) Let $g(x, y) = \min(x, y)$. Then $g(x, 0) = 0$ for all $x \in N$.

Hence g is regular.

(*b*) Let $f(x, y) = | x - y |$. Since $f(x, y) = 0$ only when $x = y$, so we cannot find a fixed y such that $f(x, y) = 0$ for all $x \in N$. Hence f is not regular.

45. Prove that $f(x) = x/2$ is partial recursive over N.

Solution. Let $g(x, y) = | 2y - x |$. Note that $2y - x = 0$ only when x is even. Let $f_1(x) = \mu_y(| 2y - x | = 0)$.

The minimum value of y for which $2y - x = 0$ is $y = \frac{x}{2}$. When x is odd $f_1(x)$ is not defined. Hence f_1 is partial recursive. As $f(x) = \frac{x}{2} = f_1(x)$, f is a partial recursive function.

46. What are the initial functions over $\Sigma = \{a, b\}$.

Solution.

(*i*) For any $x \in \Sigma$, the 'nil' function is defined by $\text{nil}(x) = \varepsilon$ (empty string).

(*ii*) For any string $x \in \Sigma$, cons $a(x)$ denote the concatenation of the constant string a and x.

The initial functions over Σ is

$$\text{nil}(x) = \varepsilon$$

$$\text{cons } a(x) = ax$$

$$\text{cons } b(x) = bx.$$

For example
$$\text{cons } a(abab) = aabab$$

$$\text{cons } b(abab) = babab$$

$$\text{nil } (abab) = \varepsilon.$$

47. Show that the following functions are primitive recursive.

(*a*) constant functions *a* and *b* (*i.e.* $a(x) = a$, $b(x) = b$)

(*b*) Identity function

(*c*) Concatenation

(*d*) Transpose.

Solution.

(*a*) As $a(x) = \text{cons } a(\text{nil}(x))$, the function $a(x)$ is the composition of the initial function 'cons a' with the initial function 'nil' and hence is primitive recursive.

(*b*) Let 'Id' denote the identity function. Then

$$Id\ (\varepsilon) = \varepsilon$$

$$Id\ (ax) = \text{cons } a(x)$$

$$Id\ (bx) = \text{cons } b(x).$$

Id is defined by recursion using cons. *a* and cons *b*. Hence it is primitive recursive.

(*c*) The concatenation function is defined by

$$\text{con cat } (x_1, x_2) = x_1\ x_2$$

$$\text{con cat } (\varepsilon, x) = Id\ (x)$$

$$\text{con cat } (ax_1, x_2) = \text{cons } a(\text{concat } (x_1, x_2)$$

$$\text{con cat } (bx_1, x_2) = \text{cons } b(\text{concat } (x_1, x_2))$$

since concat. is defined by recursion using *Id*, cons *a* and cons *b*. Hence concats is primitive recursive.

(*d*) The transpose function can be defined by Trans $(x) = x^T$.

Then
$$\text{Trans } (\varepsilon) = \varepsilon$$

$$\text{Trans } (ax) = \text{concat } (\text{trans } (x), a\ (x_1))$$

$$\text{Trans } (bx) = \text{concat } (\text{trans } (x), b(x))$$

Hence Trans. is primitive recursive.

48. Show that a constant function over N *i.e.*, $f(n) = k$ for all $n \in N$, k is a fixed number, is primitive recursive.

Solution. Define f by $\quad f(0) = k, f(n + 1) = k = U_2^2\,(n, f(n)).$

Hence f is primitive recursive.

49. Show that the function $r(x, y)$ = the remainder obtained when x is divided by y, is primitive recursive.

Solution. Clearly $r(x, 0) = 0$. Also $r(x, y)$ increases by 1, when y is increased by 1 and $r(x, y) = 0$ when $y = x$. Using these observations we see that

$$r(x, y + 1) = S(r(x, y)) * sg(x \dot{-} S(r(x, y))$$

where 'sg' is the sign function, which is primitive recursive is given by

$$sg\ (0) = 0;$$

$$sg(y + 1) = 1.$$

Note that

$$sg(x \dot{-} S(r(x, y)) = sg \begin{cases} 0 & \text{for } x < S(r(x, y)) \\ x - S(f(x, y)), & x \geq S(r(x, y) \end{cases}$$

Hence r is primitive recursive.

50. Compute $S(3)$ using the Turing machine which computes S.

Solution. The problem is same as the computation derived from the TM that computes the function $f(x) = x + 1$. (Here substitute $x = 3$ in Exmple 4.2.2.)

EXERCISE

1. Consider the set of machine language instructions for a computer of your choice. Sketch how the various instructions in this set could be carried out by a turing machine.
2. Show that the language $L = \{a^n b^n c^n : n \geq 1\}$ is accepted by some linear bounded automaton.
3. Find a linear bounded automaton that accept the language $L = \{a^{n!} : n \geq 0\}$.
4. Find a Turing machine that recognizes the set of bit strings that have a 1 as their second bit, that is, the regular set $(0 \cup 1)\ 1\ (0 \cup 1)^*$.
5. Construct a TM that recognizes the set $\{0^{2n} 1^n : n \geq 0\}$.
6. Construct a TM that computes the function $f(n) = n - z$ if $n \geq 3$ and $f(n) = 0$, for $n = 0, 1, 2$, for all non-negative integers n.
7. Construct a Turing machine with tape symbols 0, 1 and B that replaces

the first 0 with a 1 and does not change any of the other symbols on the tape.

8. Construct a TM that recognizes the set of all bit strings that and with a 0.

9. Construct a TM that computes the function $f(n) = n(\text{mod } z)$.

10. Construct a TM that computes the function $f(n_1, n_2) = \min(n_1, n_2)$ for all non-negative integers n_1 and n_2.

11. Construct a TM that computes the function $f(n_1, n_2) = n_1 + n_2 + 1$ for all non negative integers n_1 and n_2.

12. Let $B(n)$ be the maximum number of 1S that a TM with n states with the alphabet $\{1, B\}$ may print on a tape that is initially blank. The problem of determining $B(n)$ for particular values of n is known as the busy beaver problem. This problem was first studied by Tibor Rado in 1962. Currently it is known that $B(2) = 4$, $B(3) = 6$, $B(4) = 13$, but $B(n)$ is not known for $n \geq 5$.

CHAPTER 5

Undecidability

A problem whose language is recursive is said to be decidable. otherwise, the problem is undecidable. That is, a problem is undecidable if there is no algorithm that takes as input an instance of the problem and determines whether the answer to that instance is "yes" or "no".

5.1 RECURSIVELY ENUMERABLE AND RECURSIVE

Here we will examine the languages associated with Turing machines and some of their restrictions. Because Turing Machines can perform any kind of algorithmic computation we expect to find that the family of languages associated with them is quite broad. It includes not only regular and context free languages, but also the various examples we have encountered that lie outside these families. The non-trivial question is whether there are any languages that are not accepted by some TM. We will answer this question first by showing that there are more languages than TMs, so that there must be some languages for which there are no TMs. We also eastablish relation between TM and certain types of grammars and to establish a connection between these grammars and regular and CFG.

There is an important distinction between languages for which there exists an accepting Turing Machine and languages for which there exists a membership algorithm. Because a TM does not necessarily halt on input that it does not accept, the first does not accept, the first does not imply the second.

5.1.1 Definition

A language is said to be recursively enumerable if there exists a TM that accepts it.

This definition implies only that there exists a TM M such that for every $w \in L$,

$$q_0 w \overset{*}{\underset{M}{\vdash}} x_1 q_f x_2,$$

with q_f a final state. The definition says nothing about what happens for w not in L; it may be that the machine halts in a non-final state or that it never halts and goes into an infinite loop. We can be more demanding and ask that the machine tell us whether or not any given input is in its language.

5.1.2. Definition

A language L on Σ is said to be recursive if there exists a TM M that accepts L and that halts on every w in Σ^+. In otherwords, a language is recursive if and only if there exists a membership algorithm for it.

5.1.3. Definition

A set is recursive if we have an algorithm to determine whether a given element belongs to X or not.

5.1.4. Definition

A recursively enumerable set is a set A for which we have a procedure to determine whether a given element belongs to X or not.

Note that a recursive set is recursively enumerable.

5.1.5. Definition

Let $L \subseteq \Sigma^*$ be a language. A Turing machine M with input symbol Σ is said to accept L if $L(M) = LM$ recognizes or decides L if M computes the characteristic function $\psi_L : \Sigma^* \to \{0, 1\}$. In otherwords, M recognizes L if M halts in state h_a (accepting state) for every string x in Σ^*, producing output 1 if $x \in L$ and output 0 otherwise.

A language L is recursively enumerable if there is a TM that accepts L, and recursive if there is a TM that recognizes L. We may called these languages as Turing acceptable and Turing decidable respectively.

5.1.6 Theorem

Every recursive language is recursively enumerable.

Proof. Let L be a recursive language. Then there is a Turing Machine M that determines membership in L. We first construct another Turing machine, say M_1, that generates all strings in Σ^+ in proper order, let us say w_1, w_2, ... As these strings are generated, they become the input to M, which is modified so that it writes strings on its tape only if they are in L.

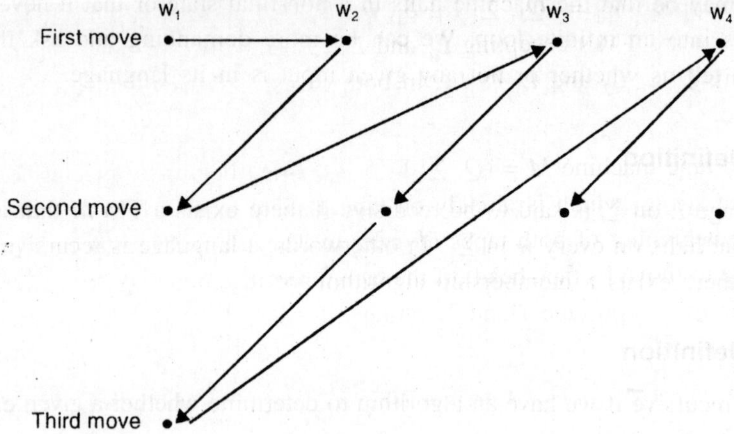

Fig. 5.0

We first let M_1 to generate w_1 and let M execute one move on it. Then we let M_1 generate w_2 and let M execute one move on w_2, followed by the second move on w_1. After this we generate w_3 and do one step on w_3, the second step on w_2, third step on w_1, and so on. The order of performance is given in Fig. 5.0. From this, it is clear that M will never get into an infite loop. Since any $w \in L$ is generated by M_1 and accepted by M in a finite number of steps, every string in L is finally proudced by M.

It is easy to see that every language for which an enumeration procedure exists is recursively enumerable. We simply compare the given input string aginst successive strings generated by the enumeration procedure. If $w \in L$, we will get a match, and the process can be terminated. Thus L is recursively enumerable.

Remark. There are recursively enumerable languages that are not recursive. We now state a theorem without proof.

5.1.7. Theorem

If L is accepted by a non-deterministic TM M, and every possible sequence of M causes to halt, then L is recursive.

Both the union and intersection operations preserve the property of recursive enumerability.

5.1.8. Theorem

If L_1 and L_2 are recursively enumerable languages over Σ, then $L_1 \cup L_2$ and $L_1 \cap L_2$ are also recursively enumerable.

Proof. Suppose $M_1 = (Q_1, \Sigma, \Gamma_1, \delta_1, q_1, B_1, F_1)$ and $M_2 = (Q_2, \Sigma, \Gamma_2, \delta_2, q_2, \delta_2, B_2, F_2)$ are TM's accepting L_1 and L_2 respectively. We now construct TMs accepting $L_1 \cup L_2$ and $L_1 \cap L_2$. In both cases, it is useful to use a two-tape machine.

The two tape machine $M = (Q, \Sigma, \Gamma, \delta, q_0, B, F)$ begins by placing a copy of the input string, which is already on tape 1, onto tape 2. It inserts the marker # at the beginning of both tapes in order to detect a crash resulting from T_1 or T_2 trying to move its tape head off the tape. From this point on, the simultaneous simulation of T_1 on tape 1 and T_2 on tape 2 is accomplished by allowing every possible move

$$\delta\ ((p_1, p_2)\ (a_1, a_2)) = ((q_1, q_2), (b_1, b_2), (D_1, D_2))$$

where, for both values of i,

$$\delta_i\ (p_i, a_i) = (q_i, b_i, D_i)$$

The possible outcomes of the simulation are:

1. Neither T_1 nor T_2 ever stops, in which case T never stops.
2. At least one of the two accepts, in which case T accepts.
3. One of the two rejects before either has accepted. If they both reject simultaneously T rejects. If one rejects, T abandons that simulation (*i.e.*, ignores that tape) and continues with the other. If the other halts, either by accepting or by rejecting, then T halts in the same way.

The construction causes M to accept if and only if atleast one of the two machines M_1 and M_2 accepts and we conclude that T accepts the language $L_1 \cup L_2$.

We can prove for $L_1 \cap L_2$ in the same way, except that this time T can reject if either T_1 or T_2 rejects, and it can accept only when T_1 and T_2 have both accepted.

5.1.9. Theorem

The complement of a recursive language is recursive.

Proof. Let L be a recursive language and M a Turing machine that halts on all inputs and accepts L. Construct M' from M so that if M enters a final state on input w, then M' halts without accepting. If M halts without accepting, M' enters a final state. Since one of these two events occurs M' is an algorithm. Clearly $L\ (M')$ is the complement of L and thus the complement of L is a recursive language. The following figure shows a construction of M' from M

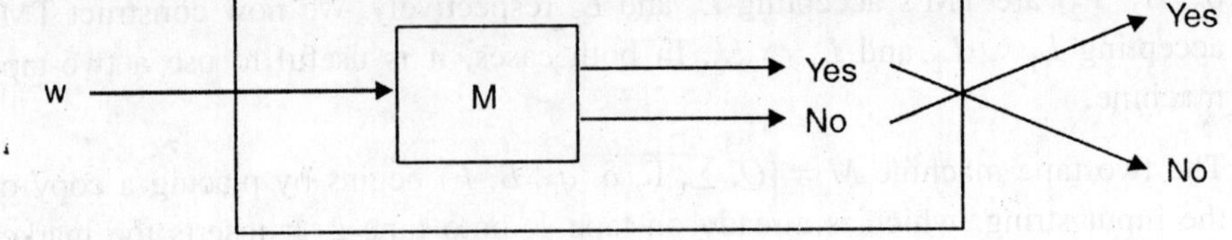

Figure 5.1.

5.1.10. Theorem

The union of two recursive language is recursive and the intersection of two recursive language is also recursive.

Proof. Let L_1 and L_2 be recursive languages accepted by algorithms M_1 and M_2. We construct M which first simulates M_1. If M_1 accepts, then M accepts. If M_1 rejects, then M simulates M_2 and accepts if and only if M_2 accepts. Since both M_1 and M_2 are algorithms, M is guaranteed to halt. Clearly M accepts $L_1 \cup L_2$. The two constructions for $L_1 \cup L_2$ are given below.

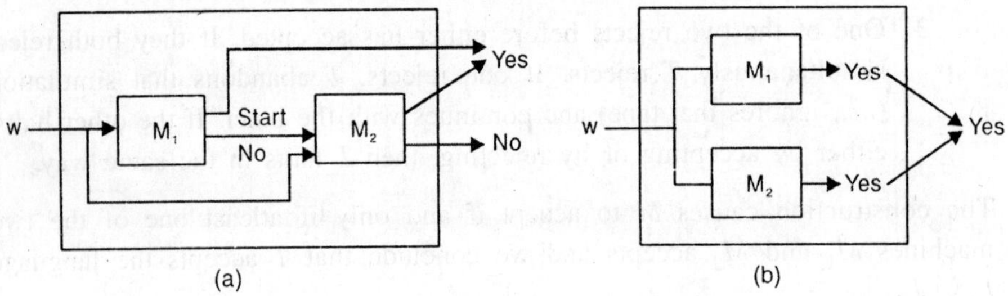

Fig. 5.2.

Proof for $L_1 \cap L_2$ is similar except that M accepts if and only if both M_1 and M_2 accepts.

5.1.11. Theorem

If both a language L and its complement L' are recursively enumerable then L is recursive.

Proof. Let M_1 and M_2 accept L and L' respectively construct M as in Figure 5.3 to simulate simultaneously M_1 and M_2.

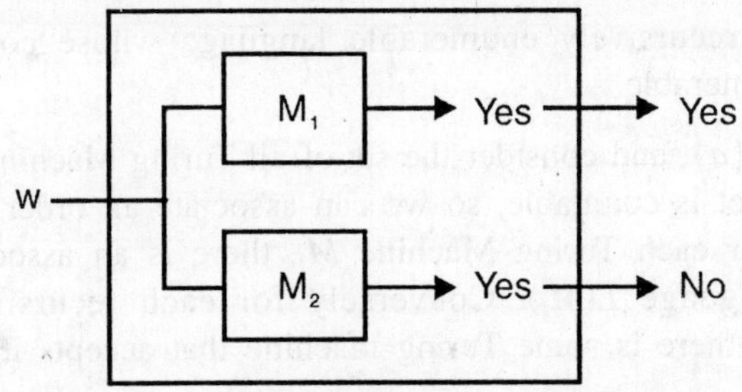

Fig. 5.3.

M accepts w if M_1 accepts w and rejects w if M_2 accepts w. Since w is in either L or L', we see that exactly one of M_1 or M_2 will accept. Thus M will always say either "yes" or "no" but will never say both. Note that there is no a prior limit on how long it may take before M_1 or M_2 accepts, but it is certain that one or the other will do. Since M is an algorithm that accepts L, it follows that L is recursive.

5.1.12. Corollary

If both a language L and its complement L' are recursively enumerable, then L' is recursive.

Proof. Follows from Theorem 5.1.11 and 5.1.9.

5.1.13. Corollary

If a language L is recursive, then L' is also recursive and consequently both are recursively enumerable.

Proof. Suppose L is recursive. Then there is a membership algorithm for L. This serves as a membership algorithm for L' by simply complementing its conclusion. Therefore L' is recursive. Now the result follows from 5.1.6.

5.1.14. Remark

5.1.9. and 5.1.11. have an important consequence. Let L and L' be a pair of complementary languages. Then either

1. both L and L' are recursive
2. neither L nor L' is recursively enumerable.
3. one of L and L' is recursively enumerable but not recursive, the other is not recursively enumerable.

5.1.15. Theorem

There exists a recursively enumerable language whose complement is not recursively enumerable.

Proof. Let $\Sigma = \{a\}$, and consider the set of all Turing Machines with this input alphabet. This set is countable, so we can associate an order $M_1, M_2, \ldots$, with its elements. For each Turing Machine M_i, there is an associated recursively enumerable language $L(M_i)$. Conversely for each recursively enumerable language on Σ, there is some Turing machine that accepts it.

We now consider a new language L defined as follows. For each $i \geq 1$, the string a_i is in L if and only if $a_i \in L(M_i)$. It is clear that the language L is well defined, since the element $a_i \in L(M_i)$, and hence $a_i \in L$, must either be true or false. Next, we consider the complement of L, $L' = \{a_i : a_i \notin L(M_i)\}$ ...(1)

which is also well defined but, as we will show, is not recursively enumerable.

We will show this by contradiction, starting from the assumption that L' is recursively enumerable. If this is so, then there must be some Turing Machine, say M_k such that

$$L' = L(M_k) \quad \text{...(2)}$$

Consider the string a_k. It is in L or in L' ? Suppose that $a_k \in L'$. By (2) this implies that

$$a_k \in L(M_k)$$

By (1), it follows that $a_k \notin L'$.

Conversely, if we assume that a_k is in L, then $a_k \notin L'$ and (2) implies that $a_k \notin L(M_k)$. But then from (1) we get that $a_k \in L'$. This is a contradiction. Hence L' is not recursively enumerable.

To prove that L is recursively enumerable

Give a_i, we first find i by counting the number of a's. We then use the enumeration procedure for Turing Machines to find M_i. Finally, we give its description along with a^i to a universal Turing Machine M_u that simulates the action of M on a_i. If a_i is in L, the computation carried out by M_u will finally halt. The combined effect of this is a Turing Machine that accepts every $a_i \in L$. Hence L is recursively enumerable.

5.1.16. Theorem

There exists a recursively enumerable language that is not recursive; that is the family of recursive languages is a proper subset of the family of recursively enumerable languages.

Proof. Consider the language L of 5.1.14. This language is recursively enumerable but its complement is not. By 5.1.13 L is not recursive. Hence the result.

5.2. ENUMERATING A LANGUAGE

We have seen that Turing machine can be viewed as language recognizers and as computers of functions on the non-negative integers. Turing machine can also be viewed as a generating device. Consider a multitape TM M that uses one tape as an output tape, on which a symbol, once written can never be changed, and whose tape head never moves left.

Suppose also that on the output tape, M writes strings over some alphabet Σ, separated by a marker symbol #. We can define

5.2.1. Definition

We can define $G(M)$, the language generated by M, to be the set of w in Σ^* such that w is finally printed between a pair of #'s on the output device.

Note that unless M runs forever, $G(M)$ is finite. Also we do not require that words be generated in any particular order or that any particular word be generated only once.

5.2.2. Canonical Order

Let Σ be an input set. We define a canonical order for Σ^* as follows. List words in order of size, with words of the same size in numerical order. That is let $\Sigma = \{x_0, x_1, ... x_{t-1}\}$, and imagine that x_i is the digit i in base t. Then the words of length n are the numbers 0 through $t^n - 1$ written in base t.

5.2.3. Example

If $\Sigma = \{a, b\}$, the canonical order is $\in$, a, b, aa, ab, ba, bb, aaa, aab, aba, ...

Note that the seemingly simpler order in which we generate the shortest representation of 0, 1, 2, ... in base k will not work as we never generate words like $a_0a_0a_1$, which have leading 0's.

Next consider generating pairs (i, j) such that each pair is generated after some finite amount of time. This task is not so easy as it seems. The naive approach, (1, 1) (1, 2), (1, 3), ... never generates any pairs with $i > 1$. Instead, we shall generate pairs in order of the sum $i + j$, and among pairs of equal sum, in order of increasing i. That is, we generate (1, 1), (1, 2), (2, 1), (1, 3), (2, 2), (3, 1),

(1, 4), ... The pair (i, j) is the $\{[(i + j - 1)(i + j - 2)]/2 + i\}$th pair generated. Thus this ordering has the desired property that there is a finite time at which any particular pair (i, j) is generated.

5.2.4. Theorem

A language L is recursively enumerable if and only if L can be enumerated by some Turing machine.

Proof. Suppose L is $G(M_1)$ for some TM M_1. Construct a TM M_2 with one or more tape than M_1. M_2 simulates M_1 using all but M_2's input tape. Whenever M_1 prints # on its output tape, M_2 compares its input with the word just generated. If they are the same, M_2 accepts, otherwise M_2 continues to simulate M. Clearly M_2 accepts an input x if and only if x is in $G(M_1)$. Thus $L(M_2) = G(M_1)$.

Conversely assume that L is recursively enumerable. We have to prove that $L(M_1) = G(M_2)$ M_2 simulates the pair generator. When (i, j) is generated M_2 produces the ith word w_i in canonical order and simulates M_1 on w_i for j steps. If M_1 accepts on the jth step (by considering initial ID as step 1), then M_2 generates w_i.

Surely M_2 generates no word not in L. If w is in L, let w be the ith word in canonical order for the alphabet of L and let M_1 accept w after exactly j moves. As it takes only a finite amount of time for M_2 to generate any particular word in canonical order or to simulate M_1 for any particular number of steps, we know that M_2 will finally produce the pair (i, j). At that stage, w will be generated by M_2. Thus $G(M_2) = L$.

5.2.5. Corollary

If L is recursively enumerable set, then there is a generator for L that enumerates each word in L exactly once.

Proof. M_2 described above has that property, since it generates w_i only when considering the pair (i, j), where j is exactly the number of steps taken by M_1 to accept w_i.

Now we will characterize recursive sets by generators.

5.2.6. Theorem

L is recursive if and only if L is generated in canonical order.

Proof. Only if part. Let $L = L(M_1) \subseteq \Sigma^*$, where M_1 halts on every input. Construct M_2 to generate L as follows. M_2 generates the words in Σ^*, one at a time, in canonical order. After generating some word w, M_2 simulates M_1 on w. If M_1 accepts w, M_2 generates w. Since M_1 is guranteed to halt, we know that

M_2 will finish processing each word after a finite time and will therefore finally consider each particular word in w^*. Clearly M_2 generates L in Cannonical order.

if part. When L is infinite, M_2 described above is a halting TM for L. Clearly, when L is finite, there is a finite automaton accepting L and thus L can be accepted by a TM that halts on all inputs. Note that in general we cannot exhibit a particular halting TM that accepts L, but the theorem merely states that one such TM exists.

5.3. MORE GENERAL GRAMMARS

In this section, we will see that a grammar of a type more general than a CFG is exactly what we need to generate the elements of a recursively enumerable language. We will also describe a slightly less general type of grammar, corresponding to languages that fall between context free and recursively enumerable.

5.3.1. Definition

An unrestricted or phrase structure grammar is defined by $G = (N, T, S, P)$ where

N, a finite non-empty set of non-terminals

T, a finite non-empty set of terminals with $N \cap T = \phi$, S a starting symbol and

P, a finite set of productions of the from $\alpha \to \beta$ where $\alpha \in (N \cup T)^+$ and $\beta \in (N \cup T)^*$.

That is a grammar with no restriction is called as *unrestricted grammar* or type-0 grammar.

5.3.2. Example

Consider the grammar $G = (N, T, S, P)$ where $N = \{S, A, B, C, D, E\}$

$$T = \{a, b\} \text{ and}$$

$$P = \{S \to ABC, AB \to aAD, AB \to bAE, DC \to BaC, EC \to Bbc, Da \to aD, Db \to bD, Ea \to aE, Eb \to bE, aB \to Ba, bB \to Bb, AB \to \lambda, C \to \lambda\}$$

Clearly G is an unrestricted grammar. It is easily seen that

$$L(G) = \{ww / w \in \{a, b\}^*\}$$

Now we will show that the languages generated by unrestricted grammars are precisely those accepted by Turing machines.

5.3.3. Theorem

For any unrestricted grammar $G = (N, T, S, P)$ there is a Turing machine $M = (Q, \Sigma, \Gamma, \delta, q_0\ B, F)$

with
$$L(M) = L(G).$$

Proof. The TM we construct to accept $L(G)$ will be the non-deterministic composite machine.

$$M = \text{Movepast Input} \rightarrow \text{Simulate} \rightarrow \text{Equal}$$

where the first component moves the tape head to the blank cell following the input string, the second simulates a derivation in G starting in the location and leaves the resulting string on the tape, and the third compares this result to the original input, accepting if and only if the two strings agree. If the input string x is in $L(G)$, the non-deterministic simulation can choose the sequence of moves that simulates the derivation of x, and the result will be that M accepts. The only way *simulate* can leave a string of terminal symbol on the tape is as a result of carrying out the steps of derivation; if $x \notin L(G)$, this component will either generate a string different from x or fail to complete a derivation at all, and M will fail to accept.

The *simulate* TM simulates a derivation in much the same way that a non-deterministic top-down PDA simulates a derivation in a CFG. In the case of the PDA, however, terminal symbols at the left of the current state are removed from the stack, and the production used in each step involves the leftmost variable. In the case of the TM, the current string remains on the tape in its entierty, and the production used in a step can involve a substring appearing anywhere within the current string. The tape alphabet of simulate will include all the symbols in $T \cup \Sigma$ and possibly others as well. The machine begins by moving one square to the right of where it starts and writing the start symbol S. Beginning at this point it enters a loop, which it may terminate after any number of iterations. At the beginning of each iteration, the portion of *simulate's* tape that it is using looks like $B\nu$, where ν is the current string in the simulated derivation. The next iteration corresponds to a particular production $\alpha \rightarrow \beta$ of G, selected non-deterministicaly. The steps in the iteration are attempting to find an occurrence of the string α; if one is found, replacing it by β ; and returning the tape head to the beginning of the resulting string. When *simulate* chooses to exit the loop, it returns the tape head to the leftmost square of its tape and halts normally.

Non-determinism is present in three places within *simulate*. Choosing a production to use in the next iteration of the loop, selecting an occurrence of the first symbol of α on the tape (which may or may not actually be the beginning of an occurrence of α), and deciding when to exit the loop. Incorrect choices at any of these three points may lead to a crash, or to a string left on the tape that still contains variables, or to a string in $L(G)$ that does not match the original input string to M. It should be clear, however that for any $x \in L(G)$, atleast one choice of moves will cause *simulate* to leave x on the tape, and that no strings other than elements of $L(G)$ can be the final output of *simulate.*

5.3.4. Theorem

For any recursively enumerable language $L \subseteq \Sigma^*$, there is an unrestricted grammar G generating L.

Proof. Let $M = (Q, \Sigma, \Gamma, \delta, q_0, B, F)$ be a TM accepting L. The grammar G that we construct will have three types of productions.

1. productions that can generate two copies of an arbitrary string in Σ^*, along with some symbols that act as markers to keep the two copies separate.
2. productions that can simulate a sequence of moves of M. During this portion of a derivation, one of the two copies of the original string is left unchanged; the other representing the input tape to M, is modified accordingly. (Since this second copy will contain tape symbols from T, all symbols in $\Gamma \cup \{B\} - \Sigma$ will be included as variables in the grammar.)
3. productions that can erase everything but the unmodified copy of the string provided that the simulated moves of M applied to the other copy causes M to accept.

The two copies of the original string $a_1\ a_2\ ...\ a_k$ will take the form.

$$(a_1 a_1)\ (a_2\ a_2)\ ...\ (a_k\ a_k)$$

The symbols "(" and ")" are used here as variables. The first symbol a of each pair (a, a) will stay the same, while the second can be modified during the simulation. When M begins, there is a blank in square 0 of the tape. In addition M can use some of the blank portion of the tape to the right of the string. This means that we actually need to begin with a string of the form.

$(BB)\ (a_1 a_1)\ (a_2 a_2)\ ...\ (a_k a_k)\ (BB)\ ...\ (B)$

If M accepts x by making moves that use n blank squares to the right of the input, the corresponding derivation of x in G will begin by placing atleast n copies of (BB) at the end of the string. (A derivation can begin by placing more than n copies of this substring at the end; it will simply be longer than necessary. It may be, however, that no sequence of steps starting with fewer copies of this substring allows x to be derived).

It is now clear how M's tape is represented in the simulation. In order to represent the complete TM configuration, we need a way of indicating both the state and the position of the tape head. We can do both by adding to set of variables the states of M, and letting such a variable appear in the string just before the symbol pair in the current position. Thus the current string when the simulation is about to begin is

q_0 (BB) $(a_1\ a_1)$ $(a_2\ a_2)$ ... $(a_k a_k)$ (BB) .... (BB)

If at some point during the processing M is in the configuration

$(q, b_0 b_1 \ldots b_{i-1}\ b_{i+1} \ldots b_m)$

the corresponding string in the derivation will be

(Bbo) $(a_1 b_1)$... $(a_{i-1}\ b_{i-1})$ $(a_i\ b_i)$ ... $(a_k\ b_k)$ (Bb_{k+1}) ... (Bb_m) (BB) ... (BB)

(This assumes that m is greater than k, the length of the original input string. In the other case the string will be slightly different.)

The productions that generate the starting string are these.

$$S \to S\ (BB)\ T$$

$$T \to T\ (\sigma\sigma) /\ q_0\ (BB)$$

where there is a production $B \to B\ (\sigma\sigma)$ for every symbol $\sigma \in \Sigma$. Corresponding to each Turing machine move.

$$\delta\ (p, a)\ =\ (q, b, R)$$

where $a, b \in \Gamma \cup \{\Delta\}$, we have productions

$$p\ (\sigma\ a) \to (\sigma\ b)\ q$$

One for each $\sigma \in \Sigma \cup \{\Delta\}$. Note that the symbol σ stays unchanged and the state variable has moved to the right of the symbol pair. For each move

$$\delta\ (p, a)\ =\ (q, b, s)$$

We have all the productions

$$p\ (\sigma\ a) \to q\ (\sigma\ b)$$

$(\sigma \in \Sigma \cup (\Delta\}$, and for each move

$$\delta\ (p, a)\ =\ (q, b, L)$$

We have the productions

$$(\sigma_1, \sigma_2)\ p\ (\sigma_3\ a) \to q\ (\sigma_1\ \sigma_2)\ (\sigma_3\ b)$$

One for every possible combination of $\sigma_1, \sigma_3 \in \Sigma \cup \{B\}$ and $\sigma_2 \in \Gamma \cup \{\Delta\}$. In all these cases, we ignore Turing machine moves that halt in the reject state; the symbol h_r is required in any productions.

If the sequence of moves of M leads to the accepting state h_a, and only in this case, the corresponding derivation produces a string with the symbol h_a in it.

The remaining productions allow us to erase from any string containing ha all the symbols in the second position of a pair, as well as the auxillary variables (that is $(C \geq B)$, and elements of $Q \cup \{h_a\}$), so as to leave only the terminal symbols of the input string accepted by M productions that accomplish this are

$$h_a (\sigma_1\sigma_2) \rightarrow h_a (\sigma_1 \sigma_2) h_a (\sigma_1 \in \Sigma \cup \{B\}, \sigma_2 \in \Gamma \cup \{B\})$$

$$(\sigma_1\sigma_2) h_a \rightarrow h_a (\sigma_1 \sigma_2) h_a (\sigma_1 \in \Sigma \cup \{B\}), \sigma_2 \in \Gamma \cup \{B\}$$

$$h_a (\sigma_1\sigma_2) \rightarrow \sigma_1 (\sigma_1 \in \Sigma, \sigma_2 \in \Gamma \cup \{\Delta\}$$

$$h_a (\Delta\sigma) \rightarrow \lambda (\sigma \in \Gamma \cup \{B\})$$

The productions in the first two lines simply propagate copies of h_a throughout the string, and those in the last two do the necessary erasing.

It is not hard to see that this grammar generates precisely the strings accepted by M, although we do not attempt a rigours proof.

5.4. CONTEXT SENSITIVE LANGUAGES

5.4.1. Definition

A grammar $G = (N, T, S, P)$ is called as a *context sensitive grammar* if every production has the form $\alpha \rightarrow \beta$ with $|\beta| \geq |\alpha|$.

A *Context Sensitive Language* (CSL) is a language that can be generated by such a grammar.

A language is context sensitive if and only if it can be generated by a grammar in which every production has the form

$$\alpha A \beta \rightarrow \alpha X \beta$$

where α, β and X are strings of variables and/or terminals, with X not null, and A is a variable. Such a production may allow A to be replaced by X, depending on the context.

5.4.2. Example

Consider the language

$L = \{a^n b^n c^n / n \geq 1\}$. We now construct a context sensitive grammar $G = (N, T, S, P)$

where $N = \{S, B, C\}$, $T = \{a, b, c\}$ and

$$P = \{S \rightarrow aSBc,\ S \rightarrow aBc,\ CB \rightarrow BC,$$
$$aB \rightarrow ab,\ bB \rightarrow bb,\ bC \rightarrow bc,$$
$$cC \rightarrow cc\}$$

It is easily seen that $L(G) = L$

Already we have proved that L is not context free [see 3.4.3 problem 1]. Hence L is a context sensitive language.

5.4.3. Definition

A Linear Bounded Automaton (LBA) is $M = (Q, \Sigma, \Gamma, \delta, q_0, B, F)$ that is the same as nondeterministic Turing machine except in the following respect. There are two extra tape symbols $<$ and $>$ assumed not to be elements of Γ. M begins in the configuration $(q_0, < x >)$, with its tape head scanning the symbol $<$ on cell 0 and the symbol $>$ in the first cell to the right of the input string x, in moving subsequently, M is not permitted to replace the symbols $<$ or $>$, or to move its head left from the square with $<$ or right from the square with $>$.

5.4.4. Theorem

If $L \subseteq \Sigma^*$ is a context sensitive language, there is a linear bounded automaton accepting L.

Proof. Suppose $G = (N, T, S, P)$ is a CSG generating L. In the proof of Theorem 5.3.3, the Turing machine used the portion of the tape to the right of the input for the simulated derivation. That option is not available to us here, but a satisfactory alternative is to convert the portion of the tape between $<$ and $>$ into two tracks, so that the second provides the necessary space. For this reason we let the tape alphabet of our machine M contain pairs (a, b), where $a, b \in \Sigma \cup V \cup \{B\}$, in addition to the elements of Σ. There may be other symbols needed as well.

The first action taken by M will be to convert the tape configuration

$< x_1\ x_2, \ldots\ x_n >$ to $< (x_1, B)\ (x_2, B) \ldots (x_n, B) >$

This step corresponds to the movepast input component of the TM in the proof of 5.3.3. Next, M places S in the second track of cell 1 and starts a loop exactly as before, except that the machine will reject if the string produced in the second track during any iteration has length greater than n. As before, M may exit the loop at any time. What it does, it rejects if the second track does not match the input in the first track. Since G is context sensitive, a string appearing in the derivation of $x \in L$ cannot be longer than x, so that if the LBA begins with input x there is a sequence of moves it can execute that will cause it to accept. If $x \notin L$, on the otherhand, M will either reject or loop forever, since no simulated derivation will be able to produce the string x.

Remark. The significant feature of an LBA is not that the tape head doesn't move past the input string at all, but that its motion is restricted to a portion of the tape bounded by some linear function of the input length.

5.4.5. Theorem

If there is a linear bounded automaton $M = (Q, \Sigma\ \Gamma, \delta, q_0, B, F)$ accepting the language $L \subseteq \Sigma^*$, then there is a context sensitive grammar generating $L - \{\lambda\}$.

Proof. We give only a sketch of the proof, which is similar to that of 5.3.4. As before, the grammar is constructed so that a derivation generates two copies of a string, simulates the action of M on one, and eliminates everything except the other from the string if and when the simulated moves of M lead to acceptance.

The grammar differs from the previous one in that more variables are needed and they are more complicated previously the variables included only S, T, left and right paranthesis, and one variable for each possible state of M. However, with these variables, productions such as $ha\ (\sigma_1\ \sigma_2) \rightarrow \sigma_1$ would violate the context sensitive condition. The way to salvage productions of this form is simply to interpret strings of the form $(\sigma_1\ \sigma_2)$ and $p\ (\sigma_1\ \sigma_2)$ as variables. This approach could have been used in the earlier proof as well and many of the productions would have been context sensitive as a result. The difference is that now we no longer need strings containing (BB) and productions like

$ha\ (B\sigma) \rightarrow \lambda$, because initially there are no blanks between the tape markers of M.

In addition, we must pay attention to the tape markers < and >; thus we may also have variables such as $(\sigma_1 < \sigma_2)$, $(\sigma_1\ \sigma_2 >)$, and $(\sigma_1 < \sigma_2 >)$ (as well as $p\ (\sigma_1 < \sigma_2)$ and so forth >, corresponding to points during the simulation when σ_2 is the leftmost, rightmost, and only symbol between the markers respectively. In each case, σ_1 represents the terminal symbol originally in that position and is not modified during the simulation. Finally, since M's tape head can move to the tape head can move to the tape cells containing the symbols < and >, we will also have variables of the form $q\ (\sigma_1 < \sigma_2)^L$, $q\ (\sigma_1\ \sigma_2 >)^R$, $q\ (\sigma_1\ \sigma_2)^L$ and $q\ (\sigma_1 < \sigma_2 >)^R$. The first one for example, signifies that M is in state q, its tape head is on the square containing <, and the next cell contains σ_2 now that originally contained σ_1.

The first step in a derivation is to produce a string of the form

$q_0\ (\sigma_1 < \sigma_1)L\ (\sigma_2\ \sigma_2) \ldots (\sigma_{n-1}\ \sigma_{n-1})\ (\sigma_n\ \sigma_n >)$ or $q_0\ (\sigma_1 < \sigma_1 >)^L$

Specifying productions that generate these strings is straightforward.

Because of the end markers, and because the states have been incorporated into the variables, there are more combinations to consider when describing the productions to be used in the LBA simulation. We give those corresponding to LBA moves in which the tape head moves right.

Corresponding to the move

$$\delta\ (p, a) = (q, b, R)$$

We have these productions

$$p\ (\sigma_1\ a)\ (\sigma_2\ \sigma_3) \to (\sigma_1\ b)\ q\ (\sigma_2\ \sigma_3)$$
$$p\ (\sigma_1 < a)\ (\sigma_1 \sigma_3) \to (\sigma_1 < b)\ q\ (\sigma_2\ \sigma_3)$$
$$p\ (\sigma_1 a)\ (\sigma_2\ \sigma_3 >) \to (\sigma_1\ b)\ q\ (\sigma_2\ \sigma_3 >)$$
$$p\ (\sigma_1 < a)\ (\sigma_2\ \sigma_3 >) \to (\sigma_1 < b)\ q\ (\sigma_2\ \sigma_3 >)$$
$$p\ (\sigma_1\ a >) \to q\ (\sigma_1\ b >)^R$$
$$p\ (\sigma_1 < a >) \to q\ (\sigma_1 < b >)^R$$

for every combination of σ_1, $\sigma_2 \in \Sigma$ and $\sigma_3 \in \Gamma \cup \{B\}$. Notice that in the first four of these, both sides of the production consist of two variables, and in the last two, both sides consist of one variable. Corresponding to the move

$$\delta\ (p, <) = (q, <, R)$$

we have the productions

$$p\ (\sigma_1 < \sigma_2)^L \to q\ (\sigma_1 < \sigma_2)$$
$$p\ (\sigma_1 < \sigma_2 >)^L \to q\ (\sigma_1 < \sigma_2 >)$$

for each $\sigma_1 \in \Sigma$ and $\sigma_2 \in \Gamma \cup \{B\}$.

As in the previous proof, we need a way to eliminate everything but the origional input once a variable of the form $ha\ (\sigma_1\ \sigma_2)$ or $ha\ (\sigma_1 < \sigma_2)$ etc., shows up in a derivation.

This time we can use productions such as

$$ha\ (\sigma_1\ \sigma_2)\ (\sigma_3\ \sigma_4) \to h_a\ (\sigma_1\ \sigma_2)\ h_a\ (\sigma_3\ \sigma_4)$$
$$(\sigma_1\ \sigma_2)\ h_a\ (\sigma_3\ \sigma_4) \to h_a\ (\sigma_1\ \sigma_2)\ h_a\ (\sigma_3\ \sigma_4)$$
$$h_a\ (\sigma_1\ \sigma_2) \to \sigma_1$$

and other comparable ones that include the symbols < and >. It is reasonably clear from the way we have defined variables that the grammar we and up with will be context sensitive. It is also possible to convince yourself that it generates precisely the non-null strings accepted by M.

5.4.6. Chomsky Hierarchy

The four classes of languages that we have studied regular, context free, context sensitive, and recursively enumerable are often referred to as the Chomsky Hierarchy. Chomsky himself designated the four type as type 3, type 2, type 1, and type 0, from most restrictive to most general. The hierarchy is given in the following table.

Type	*Languages (grammar)*	*Form of productions in grammar*	*Accepting device*
3	Regular	$A \to bC, A \to \beta$ $A, C \in N, b \in \Sigma$	Finite Automaton
2	Context free	$A \to \alpha$ $A \in N, \alpha \in (V \cup \Sigma)^*$	Pushdown Automaton
1	Context Sensitive	$\alpha \to \beta$ $\alpha, \beta, \in (N \cup \Sigma)^*$ $\mid \beta \mid \geq \mid \alpha \mid$ α contains a variable	Linear bounded automaton.
0	Recursively enumerable (unrestricted or pharse (structure))	$\alpha \to \beta$ $\alpha, \beta \in (V \cup \Sigma)^*$ α contains α variable	Turing Machine

Table 5.1. The Chomsky Hierarchy

Remark. We observe that for $1 \leq i \leq 3$, every language of type i is of type $i - 1$, except that a context free language is context sensitive only if it does not contain the null string. The following figure shows the relationship between the languages.

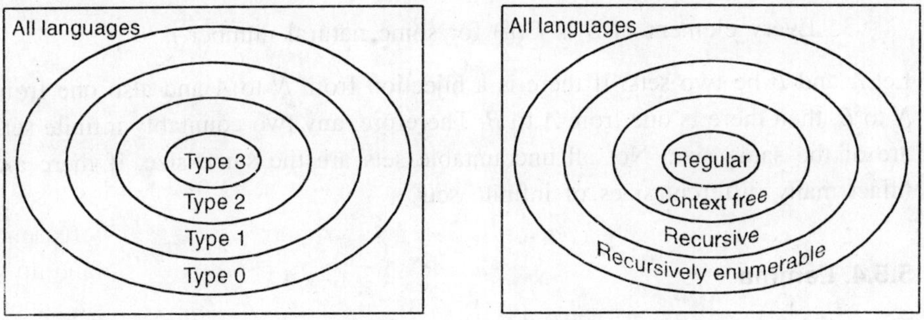

Fig. 5.4. Two ways of classifying Languages

5.5. NOT ALL LANGUAGES ARE RECURSIVELY ENUMERABLE

There are some languages which are not recursively enumerable. The set of languages is much bigger than the set of Turing machines, and one machine can accept only one language, therefore, there must be a language with no machine to accept it. Our first problem is to make sense of this idea, and to find a precise way to compare the size of two infinite sets. (It is easy to compare the size of two finite sets).

Now we recall few important results of Set Theory.

5.5.1. Lemma

Two sets are the same size if there is a bijection from one to the other.

5.5.2. Lemma

A set A is bigger than a set B if there is a bijection from a subset of A to B but no bijection from A to B.

5.5.3. Definition

A set S is countable infinite if there is a bijection from N to S, and countable (enumerable) if it is either countable infinite or finite. A set is uncountably infinite, or simply uncountable, if it is not countable.

A function $f : N \rightarrow S$ is a bijection means that

1. For every natural number n, $f(n) \in S$,
2. For any two different numbers m and n, $f(m) \neq f(n)$.
3. Every element of S is $f(n)$ for some natural number n.

Let A and B be two sets. If there is a bijection from N to A and also one from N to B, then there is one from A to B. Therefore, any two countably infinite sets are of the same size. Not all uncountable sets are the same size, if there are infact many different sizes of infinite sets.

5.5.4. Lemma

Every infinite set has a countably infinite subset.

Proof. We will show that if S is infinite, there is a bijection f from N to a subset of S. We will define f on one integer at a time as follows. Since S is infinite, there is atleast one element; choose one and call it $f(0)$. In general suppose that for some $n \geq 0, f(0), f(1) \ldots f(n)$ are distinct elements of S. Since S is infinite, there is an elements of S that is not one of these; choose any such element, and call it $f(n + 1)$. Therefore by the principle of mathematical induction, $f(n)$ can be defined for every $n \geq 0$.

5.5.5. Lemma

Every subset of a countable set is countable.

5.5.6. Example

1. The set N of natural numbers is countably infinite.
2. The set S = (0, 1/2, 1, 3/2, 2, 5/2, ...} is countably infinite.
3. The set Z of all integers is countable, because we can list the elements this way: $Z = \{0, -1, 1, -2, 2, ...\}$

5.5.7. Theorem

Suppose that for each integer $i \geq 0$, S_i is a countable set. Then the set $S = \bigcup_{i=0}^{\infty} S_i$ is countable.

Proof. If all the S_i's are empty, then S is empty and therefore countable. Otherwise we assume, by relabeling the sets if necessary, that $S_0 \neq \phi$. We describe a way of listing the elements of the union. Consider the two dimensional array in which the elements of S_i are listed in the ith row. Since S_i may be finite or infinite, these rows are likely to be of unequal length. Now consider the path shown in Figure. 5.5.

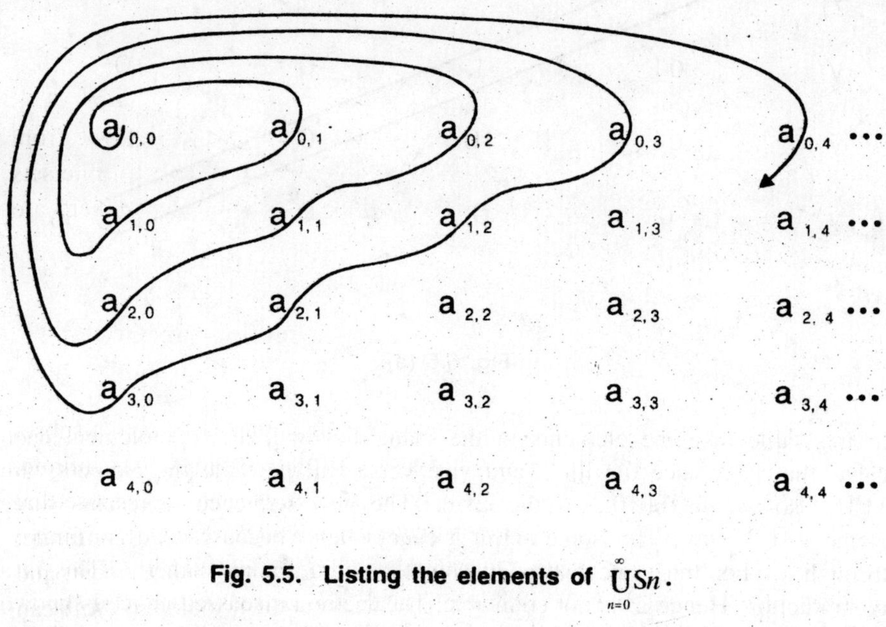

Fig. 5.5. Listing the elements of $\bigcup_{n=0}^{\infty} Sn$.

It is easy to convince yourself that this path will finally hit each element of S atleast once. It will hit an element more than once if that element belongs to S_i for more than one i. Suppose we define the function f by

$$f(n) = \begin{cases} a_0, \ 0 \text{ if } n = 0 \\ \text{the first element of } S - \{f(0), \ldots, f(n-1)\} \\ \text{on the path if } n > 0 \end{cases}$$

Then f is a bijection, either from $\{0, 1, \ldots, m\}$ to S or from N to S, depending on whether the set S is finite or infinite. Therefore, S is a countable set.

5.5.7. (a) Theorem

Let S be an infinite countable set. Then its power set 2^S is not countable.

Proof. Let $S = \{x_1, x_2, x_3, \ldots\}$. Then any element y of 2^S can be represented by a sequence of 0's and 1's with a 1 in position i if and only if x_i is in y. For example, the set $\{x_1, x_3, x_5\}$ is represented by 1010100..., while $\{x_2, x_4, x_6\}$ is represented by 010101... . Clearly any element of 2^S can be represented by such a sequence, and any such sequence represents a unique element of 2^S. Suppose that 2^S were countable, then its elements could be written in some order, say y_1, y_2,..., and we could enter these into a table as shown in Fig. 5.5(a).

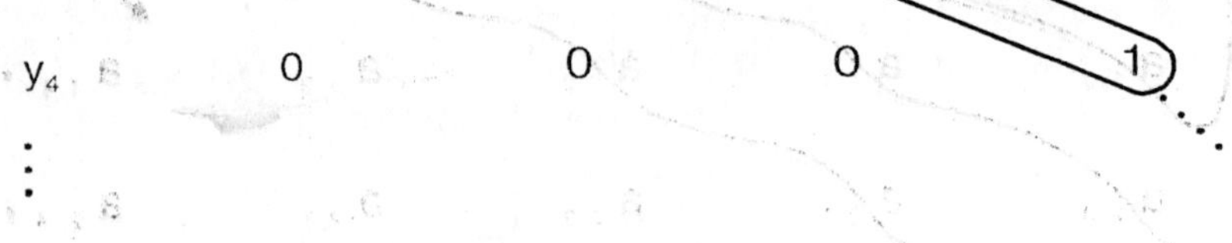

Fig. 5.5 (a).

In this table take the elements in the main diagonal, and complement each entry, that is replace 0 with 1 and vice versa. In the table the elements are 1101... so we get 0010... as the result. The new sequence represents some element of 2^S, say y_i for some i. But it cannot be y_1 because it differs from y_1 through x_1. For the same reason it cannot be t_2, t_3 or any other t_i. This is a contradiction. Hence 2^S is not countable. The method discussed above is known as diagonalization process.

5.5.8. Theorem

For any non empty Σ, there exist languages that are not recursively enumerable.

Proof. A language is a subset of Σ^*, and every such subset is a language. Therefore the set of all languages is exactly 2^{Σ^*}. Since Σ^* is infintie, 5.5.7 tells us that the set of all languages on ε is not countable. But the set of all Turing machines can be enumerated, so that set of all recursively enumerable languages is countable. Hence there must be some language on ε that are not recursively enumerable.

5.6. UNIVERSAL TURING MACHINE

Preceding discussion studies a Turing machine that execute a specific algorithm. If there is a Turing machine that computes one function, then for computing a different function or doing some calculation, there requires a different machine.

Turing describes a universal computing machine that works as follows. It is a machine M_u whose input consists essentially of a program and a data set for the program to process. The program takes the form of a string specifying some other (special purpose) TM M_1, and the data set is a second string z interpreted as input to M_1. In this section one such universal TM M_u will be discussed.

The first step is to encode both an arbitrary TM M_1 and an input string z over the alphabet $\{0, 1\}$. Let $M = (Q, \{0, 1\}, \{0, 1, B\}\ \delta, q_1, B, \{q_2\})$ be a TM with input alphabet $\{0, 1\}$ and the blank as the only additional tape symbol. We start by assigning positive integers to each state, each tape symbol, and each of the three directions L, R and H in the TM M_1 we want to encode.

The encoding function e to be one-to-one, so that a string of 0's and 1's encodes atmost one TM. Consider two TM's M_1 and M_2 that are identical except that the tape symbols of M_1 are a and b and those of M_2 are a and e. For two TM's to be different, the encodings of b and e should be different.

5.6.1. Definition. (The encoding function *e*)

Associate a code to each tape symbol (including B), to each state (including the accepting state q_a and rejecting state q_r) and to each of the three directions, in string of 0's. Let $s\ (a)$ be an encoding of a single symbol either a state or tape symbols or directions. Let

$$s\ (B) = 0$$

$$s\ (a_i) = 0^{i+1} \text{ (for each } a_i \in \Gamma)$$

$$s\ (q_a) = 0$$

$$s\ (q_r) = 00$$

$$s\ (q_i) = 0^{i+2} \text{ (for each } q_i \in Q)$$

$$s\ (L) = 00$$

$$s\ (R) = 000$$

$$s\ (H) = 0$$

Each move m of a TM described by the formula

$$\delta\ (p, a) = (q, b, D)$$

is encoded by the string.

$$e\ (m) = s\ (p) \mid s\ (a) \mid s\ (q) \mid s\ (b) \mid s\ (D) \mid$$

and for any TM M_1 with initial state q_1, M is encoded by the string.

$$e\ (M) = s\ (q_1) \mid e\ (m_1) \mid c\ (m_2) \mid \ldots \mid e\ (m_k) \mid$$

Where m_1, m_2, ..., m_k are the distinct moves of M arranged in some arbitrary order. Any string $z = z_1\ z_2 \ldots z_k$, where each $z_i \in \Gamma$ is encoded as $e\ (z) = \mid s\ (z_1) \mid s\ (z_2) \mid \ldots \mid s\ (z\ k) \mid$.

Note that the I at the beginning of the string $e\ (z)$ is included, so that in a composite string of the form $e\ (m)\ e\ (z)$, there will be no doubt as to where $e\ (M)$ stops. Also note that the encoding $s\ (a)$ of a single symbol $a \in \Gamma \cup Q$ is different from the encoding $e\ (a)$ of the one character string 'a'.

5.6.2. Example

Encode the following TM given in Fig 5.6.

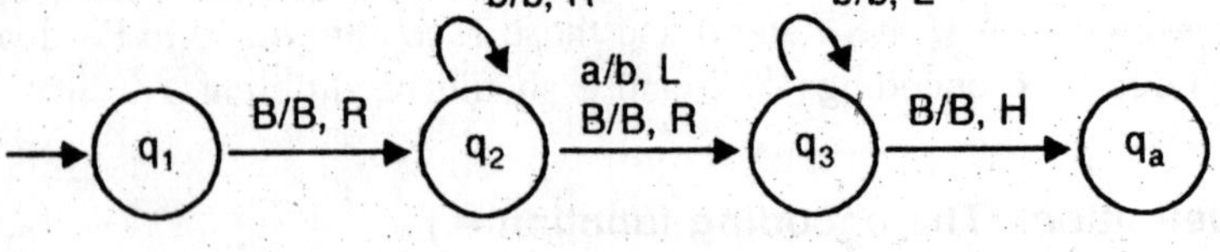

Fig. 5.6.

Solution. The TM transforms an input string of a's and b's by changing the left most a, if there is one, by b. Let us assume

$$s\ (B) = 0$$

$$s\ (a) = 00$$

$$s\ (b) = 000$$

$$s\,(q_i) = 0^{i+2} \text{ for } = 1, 2, 3$$

$s\,(q_1) = 0^3$, $s\,(q_2) = 0^4$, $s\,(q_3) = 0^5$, $s\,(q_4) = 0^6$

Encode the six moves in the order they appear, left-to-right move $\delta\,(q_1, B) = (q_2, B, R)$ is encoded by the string.

$$e\,(m_1) = s\,(q_1)\ 1\ s\,(B)\ 1\ s\,(q_2)\ 1\ s\,(B)\ 1\ s\,(R)\ 1$$
$$= 0^3\ 1\ 0\ 1\ 0^4\ 1\ 0\ 1\ 0^3.$$

Similarly the encoding of $\delta\,(q_2, b) = (q_2, b, R)$ is

$$e\,(m_2) = s\,(q_2)\ 1\ s\,(b)\ 1\ s\,(q_2)\ 1\ s\,(b)\ 1\ s\,(b)\ 1\ s\,(R)\ 1$$
$$= 0^4\ 1\ 0^3\ 1\ 0^4\ 1\ 0^3\ 1\ 0^3.1$$

The encoding of $\delta\,(q_2, a) = (q_3, b, L)$ is

$$e\,(m_3) = s\,(q_2)\ 1\ s\,(a)\ 1\ s\,(q_3)\ 1\ s\,(b)\ 1\ s\,(L)\ 1$$
$$= 0^4\ 1\ 00\ 1\ 0^5\ 1\ 000\ 1\ 00\ 1$$

The encoding of $\delta\,(q_2\,, B) = (q_3, B, L)$ is

$$e\,(m_4) = s\,(q_2)\ 1(s\,(B)\ 1\ s\,(q_3)\ 1\ s\,(B)\ 1\ s\,(L)\ 1$$
$$= 0^4\ 1\ 0\ 1\ 0^5\ 1\ 0\ 1\ 00\ 1$$

The encoding of $\delta\,(q_3, b) = (q_3\,, b, L)$ is

$$e\,(m_5) = s\,(q_3)\ 1\ s\,(b)\ 1\ s\,(q_3)\ 1\ s\,(b)\ 1\ s\,(L)\ 1$$
$$= 0^5\ 1\ 0^3\ 1\ 0^5\ 1\ 0^3\ 1\ 00\ 1$$

The encoding of $\delta\,(q_3, B) = (q_0\,; B, H)$ is

$$e\,(m_6 = s\,(q_3)\ 1\ s\,(B)\ 1\ s\,(q_a)\ 1\ s\,(B)\ 1\ s\,(H)\ 1$$
$$= 0^5\ 1\ 0\ 1\ 0^6\ 1\ 0\ 1\ 0\ 1$$

Therefore $e(M) = s\,(q_1)\ 1\ e\,(m_1)\ 1\ e\,(m_2\,)\ 1\ \ldots\ 1\ e\,(m_6)\ 1$

= 000 1 000 1 0 1 0000 1 0 1 000 1 1 0000 1 000 1 0000 1
000 1 0000 1 000 1 000 1 1 000 1 00 1 0000 1 0 1 00000
1 0 1 00 1 1 00000 1 000 1 00000 1 000 1 00000 1 000 1
00 1 1 00000 1 0 1 0 1 0 1 0 1 1. ... (5.1)

The first part of the string in this case 000 1 is to identify the initial state of the TM.

Note. The input to the universal TM M_U will consist of a string of the form $e(M)\ e(z)$ where M is a TM and z is a input string to M. In the above example, if the input string to M is baa, then the corresponding input string to M_U consists of the string e (m) followed by

$$e(baa) = s\ (b)\ 1\ s\ (a)\ 1\ (sca)\ 1$$
$$= 000\ 1\ 00\ 1\ 00\ 1$$

5.6.3. Definition (Universal language)

The language $L_U = \{e(M)\ e(w) = M \text{ accepts } w\}$ is called the **universal language.**

5.6.4. Theorem

L_U is recursively enumerable.

Proof. Proof of the theorem follows by the construction of M_U.

Like mulitape TM, universal TM M_U also contain three tapes. The first tape will serve as an input and output tape. It will initially contain the input string e (M) e (z). The second tape will be the working tape during the simulation of M, and the third tape will contain the encoded form of the current state of M.

As a first step, M_U move the string e (z) (except for the initial 1) from the end of tape 1 to tape 2, beginning in cell 3. Since M begins with its leftmost blank cell, M_U will write 01 (as s (B) = 0) in cells 1 and 2 of tape 2 ; cell 0 is left blank and the tape head is positioned on cell 1. The next step for M_U is to copy the encoded form of M's initial state from the beginning of tape 1 onto tape 3, beginning in cell 1, and to delete it from tape 1.

After these steps M_U is ready to simulate M (encoded on tape 1) on the input string (encoded on tape 2). As the simulation starts, the three tape heads are all in cell 1. The next move of M at any point is determined by M's state (encoded in tape 3) and the current symbol on M's tape, whose encoding starts in the current position on tape 2. In order to simulate this move M_U must search tape 1 for the 5-tuple (like coding of δ (q_1, B) = (q_2, B, R) of Example 5.6.2) whose first two parts match the state-input combination.

Once the appropriate 5-tuple is found the last three parts tell M_U how to simulate the move.

Before the search M_U's three tapes look like this:

B $\underline{0}$00 1 0 1 0000 1 0 1 000 1 1 0000 1 00 1 00000 1 0001 ... (encoded form of e (M) e (z))

B 0 1 $\underline{0}$0 1 00 1 000 1 B ... (Working tape)

B 0$\underline{0}$00 B ... (encoded form of current state)

Underlined symbol denotes where the finite control is pointing. The corresponding tape of M is $B\ a\ \underline{a}\ b\ B \ldots$

That is, the encoding of a and b are : $s(a) = 0^{1+1} = 00$; $s(b) = 0^{2+1} = 000$ and encoding of current state q_2 is $s(q_2) = 0^{2+2} = 0000$.

Decoding of input string in tape 2 is $BaabB$ and the current state in tape 3 is decoded as q_2.

After the search of tape 1, the tapes look like this:

$$B\ 0001010000101000110000100 1\underline{0}00001\ 0001 \ldots B\ 01\ 001\underline{0}010001\ B \ldots$$

$B\ \underline{0}000\ B$ ...The 5 tuple on tape 1 specifies that M's current symbol should be changed to b the head should be moved left, and the state should be changed to state q_3. (*i.e.*,$\delta(q_2, a) = (q_3, b, L)$).

After this changes, the position of the tapes are:

$$B\ \underline{0}0010100001010001100001001000001 \ldots$$

$$B01\underline{0}0100011\ B \ldots$$

$$B\underline{0}0000\ B \ldots .$$

(code of q_3)

Next M_U is ready to simulate the move

$$\delta(q_3, b) = (q_3, b, L) \text{ or}$$

$$\delta(q_3, B) = (q_4, B, H)$$

(See Example 5.6.2.). It is straight forward to check that M_U accepts the string $e(M)\ e(z)$ iff M accepts z. If M runs forever on z, then M_U will run forever on $e(M)\ e(z)$ and if M halts on z without accepting, M_U does so on $e(M)\ e(z)$.

5.6.5. Example

Let $M(\{q_1, q_2, q_3\}, \{0, 1\}, \{0, 1, B\}, \delta, q_1\ B, \{q_2\})$ has moves

$$\delta(q_1, 1) = (q_3, 0, R)$$

$$\delta(q_3, 0) = (q_1, 1, R)$$

$$\delta(q_3, B) = (q_3, 1, L)$$

The encoding of M and the string 1011 is:

$$e(M)\ 1011 = 0^3\ 1\ 0^3\ 111\ 0^5\ 101\ 0^3\ 1\ 0^5\ 1\ 0\ 1\ 0^3\ 11\ 0^3\ 10^5\ 1\ 0\ 1\ 0^3\ 111$$

$$0^3\,1\,0^5\,1\,0\,1\,0^5\,1\,1\,1\,0\,0\,1\,1\,0\,1\,1$$

Note that many different strings are also codes for M and the input string z.

5.6.6. Example

The language L_d obtained using the diagonal entries of the table (Fig. 5.7) is not recursively enumerable.

Table indicating acceptance of words by TM's

i \ j →	1	2	3	4	5	...
1	0	1	1	0	0	...
2	1	1	0	0	0	...
3	0	0	1	0	1	...
4	0	1	0	1	0	...
5	0	0	0	0	1	...
⋮	⋮	⋮	⋮	⋮	⋮	

Diagonal

Fig. 5.7.

Solution. Suppose we have a list of strings in $(0 + 1)^*$ in some canonical order. (See 5.2.2) Let w_i be the ith word and M_j be the TM whose code as in (5.1) is the integer j written in binary.

Imagine an infinite table depicted in Fig 5.7. tells for all i and j, whether w_i is in $L\,(M_j)$ or not. Fig 5.7. suggests that if (i, i) entry is 0, then $w_i \notin L\,(M_j)$ and if (i, i) entry is 1, then $w_i \in L\,(M_j)$.

Construct a language L_d by using the diagonal entries of the table to determine membership in L_d.

w_i is in L_d iff (i, i) entry is 0. Note that no TM accepts L_d. Suppose some TM, say M_j accepts L_d.

If $w_j \in L_d$, then (j, j) entry is 0, implying that $w_j \notin L\,(M_j)$. Otherhand, if $w_j \notin$

L_d, then (j, j) entry is 1, implying that $w_j \in L(M)$. In both cases we conclude that $L_d \neq L(M_j)$. As no TM accepts L_d, L_d is not recursively enumerable.

Note. Since L_d is not recursively enumerable, it is not recursive. Thus by Theorem 5.1.9, $\overline{L}_d$ is not recursive. Note that $\overline{L}_d = \{ w_i : M \text{ accepts } w_i\}$. We prove the universal language $L_U = \{ e(M)\, e(w): M \text{ accepts } w \}$ not to be recursive by reducing $\overline{L}_d$ to L_U. Hence L_U is an example of a language which is recursively enumerable but not recursive.

5.6.7. Theorem

L_U is not recursive.

Proof. Suppose A is an algorithm that recognizes L_U. Now we recognize $\overline{L}_d$ as follows.

Given a string $w \in (0 + 1)^*$, determine the value of i such that $w = w_i$. Integer i in binary is the code for some TM M_i. Now feed the code $e(M_i)\, e(w_i)$ to algorithm A and accept w if and only if M_i accepts w_i. The construction is shown in Fig. 5.8.

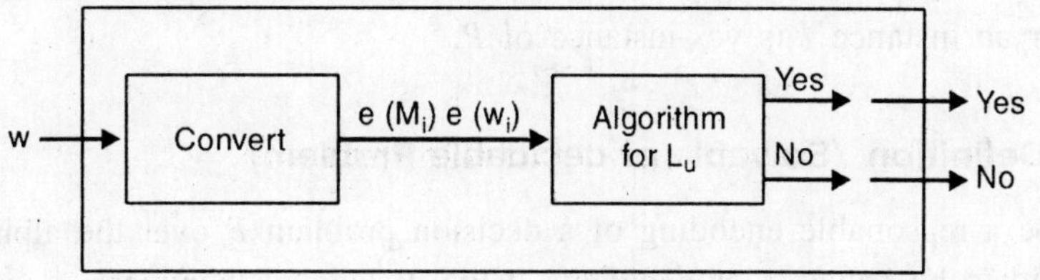

Fig. 5.8. Algorithm for $\overline{L}_d$

The constructed algorithm accepts w if and only if $w = w_i$ and $w_i \in L(M_i)$. Thus there is an algorithm for $\overline{L}_d$.

As no such algorithm exists, the Algorithm A for L_U exists, is false. Hence L_U is not recursive.

5.6.8. Example

The language $L = \{w \in \{0, 1\}^*\ w = :e(M)$, for some TM M and $w \notin L(M)\}$ is not recursively enumerable.

Solution. For any TM M, the string $w \in L$ if and only if $w \notin L(M)$. For M to accept L, it must be true that $e(M) \in L$ if and only if $e(M)$ is accepted by M. Therefore, no TM M can accept L, since M accepts this string by looping forever.

5.7. RICE'S THEOREM AND MORE UNDECIDABLE PROBLEMS

A problem that can be answered yes or no is said to be a *decision problem*. For example, (*i*) given a string *x* of *a's* and *b's* does *x* contain an occurrence of the substring *baa* ? or (*ii*) given a regular expression *r* and a string *x*, does *x* belong to the language corresponding to *r*.? The decision problem of this type consists of a set of specific 'instances' or specific cases in which we want to answer. An instance of (*i*) is a string *x* of *a's* and *b's* and the set of instances is the entire set $\{a, b\}^*$.

In order to solve a general decision problem *P*, we start by choosing an encoding function *e* so that we can represent instances *I* by strings *e* (*I*) over some alphabet Σ. Let us give the names *Y* (*P*) and *N* (*P*) to the set of strings representing Yes-instances and No-instances respectively. Then, if $E(P) = Y(P) \cup N(P)$, then E' (*P*) is the set of strings not representing instances.

Since encoding function *e* is one-to-one a string can represent at most one instance of *P*. So it must be possible to decode a string *e* (*I*) and get the original instance *I*. Finally there is an algorithm (means a TM) to decide whether a given string in Σ^* represents an instance of *P*. That is, *E* (*P*) is recursive.

If we start with the decision problem *P*, solving (or deciding) means answering whether an instance *I* is yes-instance of *P*.

5.7.1. Definition. (Solvable or decidable Problem)

Let *e* be a reasonable encoding of a decision problem *P* over the alphabet Σ, *P* is said to be *solvable* or *decidable* if the associated language.

$$L(P) = \{e(I) : I \text{ is a yes. Instance of } P\} \subseteq \Sigma^*$$

is a recursive language.

5.7.2. Theorem

The decision problem called **Accepting problem** defined by.

'Given a TM *M*, does *M* accept the string *e* (*M*)?, is undecidable.

Proof. In order to say the given problem is undecidable, it is enough to show the associated language is not recursive. Let

$$L_1 = \{w \in \Sigma^* : w = e(M) \text{ and } M \text{ accepts } e(M)\}$$

If L_1 is recursive, then so is $L_2 = \Sigma^* - L_1$, and this brings contradiction finally. For a string to be in L_2, either it is not the coding of a Turing machine or else it is the coding of a TM M which does not accept $e(M)$. Suppose L_2 is decided by a machine M_2. Now we determine whether $x = e(M_2) \in L_2$. If $x \in L_2$, then it follows that M_2 accepts x. Since x is the string representation of a Turing machine, the only way that x can be in L_2 is It x is $e(M)$ and M does not accept x. Thus if x is in L_1, then x is not in L_2. however, if x is not in L_2, then M_2 must reject x : but M_2 rejecting x means x is in L_2. The only conclusion to this contradiction is that L_2 is not recursive. If L_2 is not recursive, then L_1 is also not recursive.

5.7.3. Example

$$L_e = \{e(M) : M \text{ is a TM and } L(M) = \phi\}$$

is undecidable. That is the problem. *Accepts Nothing*: Given M, is $L(M) = \phi$ is undecidable.

Solution. We show L_e is not recursive. Suppose Le is recursive. Then there exists an algorithm A which accepts L_e. There is an algorithm B that, given $e(M)\,e(w)$, construct a TM M' that accepts ϕ if M does not accepts w and accepts the entire string in $(0 + 1)^*$ if M accepts w. The construction of M' is shown in Fig 5.9. M' ignores its input x and instead simulates M on input w, accepting if M accepts.

Note that M' is not B. B is like a compiler which takes $e(M)\,e(w)$ as 'source program' and produces M' as 'object program'. The construction of B is simple. It takes $e(M)\,e(w)$ and isolates w.

Let $w = a_1a_2 \ldots a_n$ be of length n. B creates $n + 3$ states $q_1, q_2, \ldots, q_{n+3}$ with moves

$$\delta(q_1, X) = (q_2, \$, R) \text{ for any } X$$

$$\delta(q_i, X) = (q_{i+1}, a_{i-1}, R) \text{ for every } X, 2 \le i \le n + 1$$

$$\delta(q_{n+2}, X) = (q_{n+2}, B, R) \text{ for } X \ne B$$

$$\delta(q_{n+2}, B) = (q_{n+3}, B, L)$$

$$\delta(q_{n+3}, X) = (q_{n+3}, X, L) \text{ for } X \ne \$$$

$$\delta(q_{n+3}, \$) = (q_{n+4}, \$, R)$$

Having produced the code for these moves, B then adds $n + 3$ to the indices of the states of M. The resulting TM has an extra tape symbol \$ and we can construct M' with tape alphabet $\{0, 1, B\}$ and the accepting state is q_4. For example q, $0001 \vdash \$q_2001 \vdash \$Bq_201 \vdash \$BBq_21 \vdash \$\,BBB\,q_2\,B \vdash \$\,BB\,q_3\,BB \vdash q_3\,\$\,BBBB \vdash \$\,q_4\,BBBB$.

The step completed the algorithm B and its output is the desired M' given in Fig. 5.9.

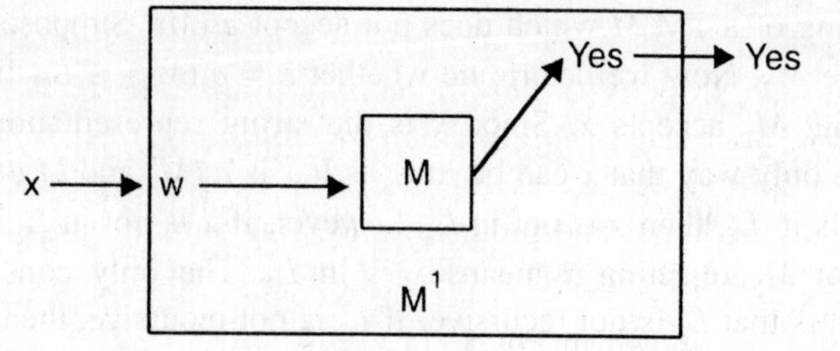

Fig. 5.9.

Now the construction of algorithm C for L_U is given in Fig. 5.10.

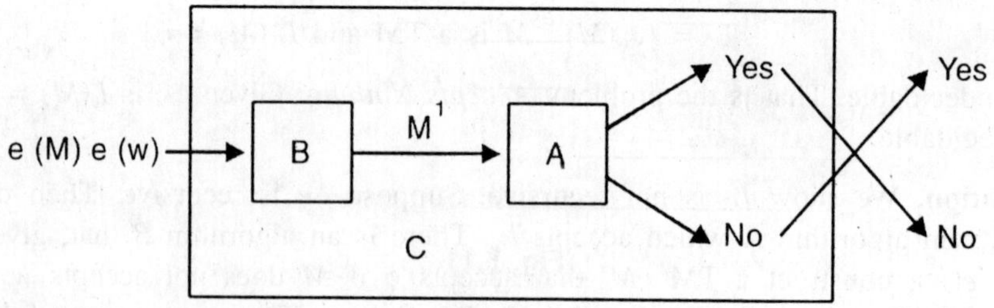

Fig. 5.10.

Algorithm for L_U assuming algorithm A exists

If M accepts w, then $L(M') \neq \phi$: so A says 'no' and C says 'Yes'.

If M does not accept w, then $L(M') = \phi$; so A says 'yes' and C says 'No'. As C does not exist by Theorem 5.6.7. A cannot exist. Thus L_e is not recursive.

Let ζ be a set of recursively enumerable languages each a subset of $(0 + 1)^*$. ζ is said to be a *property of the recursively enumerable languages.* A set L has property ζ if L is an element of ζ. For example.

(*i*) The property of being infinite is $\{L : L \text{ is infinite}\}$

(ii) They property of being trivial is $\{L : L = \phi\}$

(*iii*) $$L_\zeta = \{e(M) : L(M) \text{ is in } \zeta\}$$

The following theorem called as Rice's theorem discusses about the properties of the languages accepted by a TM, not the properties of a TM itself. For example, the question like. 'Does a TM have even number of states' is a decidable problem. But the problems like 'whether a TM always prints three consecutive 1's is an undecidable problem.

5.7.4. Rice's Theorem. (for recursive index sets)

Any non-trivial property ζ of the recursively enumerable languages is undecidable.

Proof. Assume that ϕ is not in ζ (otherwise consider ζ) since ζ is nontrivial, there exists L with property ζ. Let M_L be a TM accepting L. Suppose ζ were decidable. Then there exists an algorithm M_ζ accepting L_ζ. Using M_L and M_ζ, construct an algorithm for L_U as follows. First construct an algorithm A that takes $e(M)\ e(w)$ as input and produces $e(M')$ as output, where $L(M') \in \zeta$ if and only if M accepts w ($e(M)\ e(w) \in L_U$).

The design of M' is shown in Fig 5. 11.

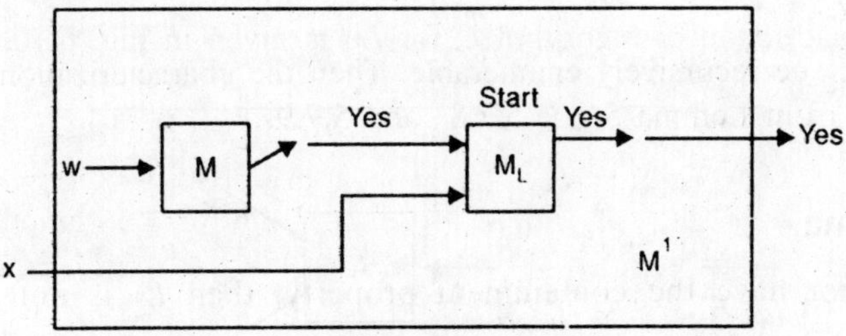

Fig. 5.11.

First M' ignores its input and simulates M on w. If M does not accept w, then M' does not accept x. If M accepts w, then M' simulates M_L on x, accepting x if and only if M_L accepts x. Thus M' either accepts ϕ or L depending on whether M accepts w.

We use hypothetical M_ζ to determine if $L(M')$ is in ζ. Since $L(M')$ is in ζ iff $e(M)\ e(w)$ is in L_U, we have an algorithm for recognizing L_U, a contradiction to the fact that L_U is recursive. Hence ζ is undecidable.

As a consequence of this theorem, we have the following corollary.

5.7.5. Corollary

The following properties of recursively enumerable sets are not decidable

(*i*) emptiness

(*ii*) finiteness

(*iii*) regularity

(*iv*) context freedom.

Rice's theorem is not applicable to problems like Accepts & Halts since the instance in both problems is a TM, not a pair (M, x).

5.7.6. Theorem (Rice Theorem for recursively enumerable Index sets)

L_ζ is recursively enumerable if and only if ζ satisfies the following three conditions:

(*i*) $L \in \zeta$ and $L \subseteq L'$ for some recursively enumerable L' then $L' \in \zeta$ (the containment property).

(*ii*) If L is an infinite language in ζ, then there is a finite subset of L in ζ.

(*iii*) The set of finite languages in ζ is *enumerable* in the sense that there is a TM that generates, the (possibly) infinite string $e\ (L_1)\ B\ e\ (L_2)\ B\ e\ (L_3)\ B\ ...\ B\ e\ (L_i)\ B...$, where $e\ (L_i)$ is the code for the *i*th finite language in ζ. The code for the finite languages $\{w_1,\ w_2,\ ...\ w_n\}$ is just $w_1,\ w_2,\ ..,\ w_n$.

Proof. Let L_ζ be recursively enumerable. Then the characterization of (*i*), (ii), (*iii*) follows from Lemma 5.7.7, 5.7.8 and 5.7.9.

5.7.7. Lemma

If ζ does not have the containment property, than L_ζ is not recursively enumerable.

Proof. Let $L_1 \in \zeta$ and $L_1 \subseteq L_2$ such that $L_2 \notin \zeta$. Let M_1 and M_2 be Turing machines that accept L_1 and L_2 respectively. Let M' be a TM that behaves as follows.

If M accepts w, then M_2 is started, and M' accepts x whenever x is in either L_1 or L_2.

If M does not accept w, then M_2 never starts, so M' accepts x if and only if x is in L_1. As $L_1 \subseteq L_2$,

$$L_1\ (M') = \begin{cases} L_2 \text{ if M accepts } \omega \\ L_1 \text{ if M does not accept } \omega \end{cases}$$

Thus $L\ (M')$ is in ζ if and only if M does not accept w.

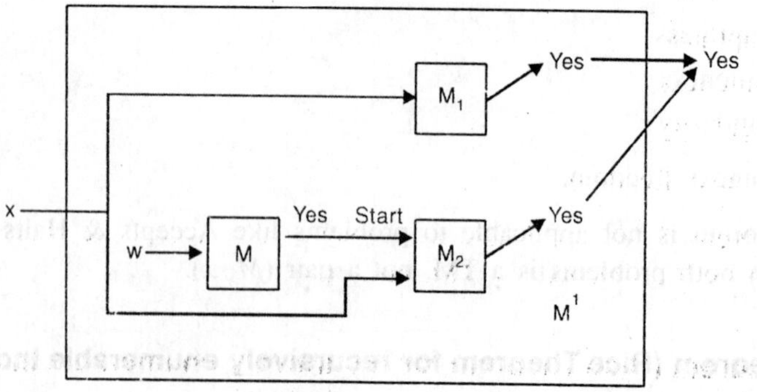

Fig. 5.12.

The TM M'

Construct algorithm A that takes as input $e\ (M)\ e\ (w)$ and produces as output TM M'. Use a TM M_ζ for L_ζ to accept $\overline{L}_U$ as shown in Fig. 5.12.

This TM accepts $e\ (M)\ e\ (w)$ if and only if M' accepts a language in ζ, or equivalently, if and only if M does not accept w. As such a TM does not exist, M_ζ cannot exists, so L_ζ is not recursively enumerable.

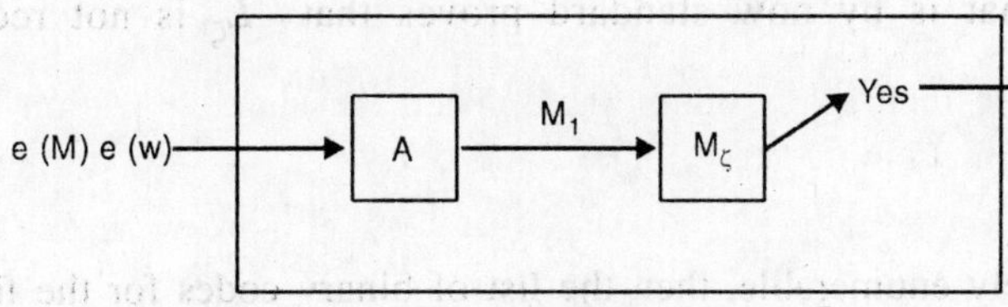

Hypothetical TM to accept $\overline{L}_U$

Fig. 5.13.

5.7.8. Lemma

Let L be an infinite language in ζ. If there is no finite subset of L in ζ, then L_ζ is not recursively enumerable.

Solution. Suppose L_ζ is recursively enumerable. Let L be an infinite language and let M_1, be a TM accepting L. Construct an algorithm A that takes $e\ (M)$ $e(w)$ as input and produces as output a TM M' that accepts L if w is not in L (M) and accepts some finite subset of L otherwise. That is,

$$L\ (M') = \begin{cases} \text{L if } w \notin \text{L (M)} \\ \text{k} \subseteq L\text{, where } \kappa \text{ is a finite subset of L, } \text{w} \in \text{L(M)} \end{cases}$$

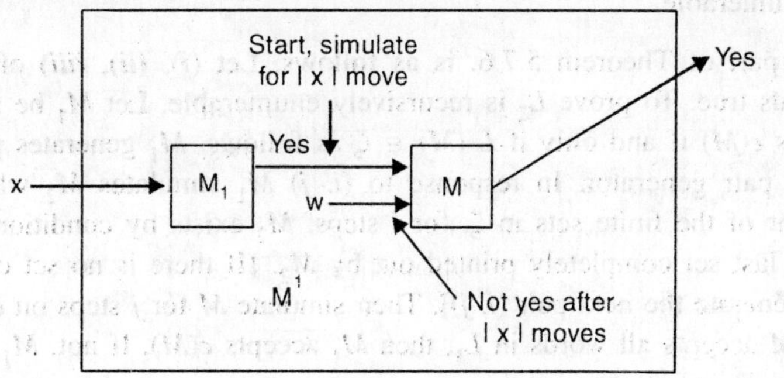

Construction of M^1

Fig. 5.14.

As shown in Fig. 5.13, M' simulates M_1 on its input x,. If M_1 accepts x, then M' simulates M on w for $|x|$ moves. If M fails to accept w after $|x|$ moves, then M' accepts x.

If $w \in L(M)$, then M accepts w after same number of moves, (say j). Then $L(M') = \{x : x \in L \text{ and } |x| < j\}$, which is a finite subset of L. If $w \notin L(M)$, then $L(M') = L$. Hence if M does not accept w $L(M') \in \zeta$, and if M accepts w, $L(M')$, being a finite subset of L, is not in ζ by the hypothesis of the lemma.

An argument that is by now standard proves that L_ζ is not recursively enumerable.

5.7.9. Lemma

If L_ζ is recursively enumerable, then the list of binary codes for the finite sets in ζ is enumerable.

Proof. Consider the pair generater (i, j), where i denotes the binary code of a finite set, assuming $s(,) = 0$; $s(0)\ i = 10$; $s(1) = 11$.

The generating pairs (i, j) are in the order of the sum $i + j$, and among pairs of equal sum, in the order of increasing i. That is like (0, 0), (0,1), (1, 0), (1, 1).... The pair (i, j) has the property that it is generated after some finite amount of time.

Construct a TM $M^{(i)}$ that accepts exactly the words in the finite language represented by i. Then simulate the enumerator for L_ζ for j steps. If it has printed $M^{(i)}$, then the code for the finite set represented by i, is printed; In any event, after the simulation, the finite control return back to the pair generator which generates the pair following (i, j). Since there is an one-to-one correspondence between the pair generator (i, j) and N the binary codes for the finite sets in ζ is countable (or enumerable). That is, the set of finite languages in ζ is enumerable.

Converse part of Theorem 5.7.6. is as follows. Let (*i*), (*ii*), (*iii*) of Theorem 5.7.6. holds true. To prove L_ζ is recursively enumerable. Let M_1 be a TM that recognizes $e(M)$ if and only if $L(M) \in \zeta$ as follows. M_1 generates pairs (i, j) using the pair generator. In response to (i, j) M_1 simulates M_2 which is an enumerator of the finite sets in ζ, for i steps. M_2 exists by condition (*iii*). Let L_1 be the last set completely printed out by M_2. [If there is no set completely printed, generate the next pair (i, j)]. Then simulate M for j steps on each word in L_1. If M accepts all words in L_1, then M_1 accepts $e(M)$. If not, M_1 generates the next (i, j) pair.

Use conditions (*i*) & (*ii*) to show $L(M_1) = L_\zeta$. Suppose L is in L_ζ, and let M be any TM with $L(M) = L$. By (*ii*) of Theorem 5.7.6:, there is a finite subset

L' of L which is in ζ. (Take $L' = L$, if L is finite). Let L' be generated after i steps of M_2, and let j be the maximum number of steps taken by M to accept a word in L' (if $L' = \phi$, then $j = 1$). Then, when M_1 generates (i, j), if not sooner, then M_1 with accept $e(M)$.
Conversely, suppose M_1 accepts $e(M)$. Then there is some (i, j) such that within j steps M accepts every word in some finite language L' such that M_2 generates L' with in its first steps. Then $L' \in \zeta$ and $L' \subseteq L(M)$. By (*i*) of Theorem 5.7.6, $L(M) \in \zeta$, so $e(M) \in L_\zeta$. Hence $L(M_1) = L_\zeta$.

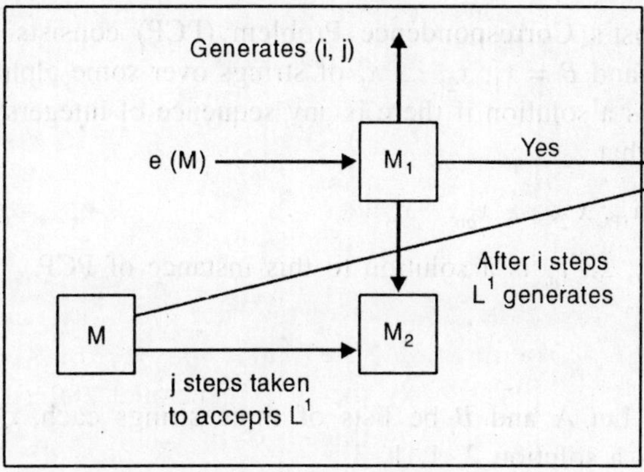

Fig. 5.15.

Construction of M_1.
The following corollaries are consequences of Theorem 5.7.6.

5.7.10. Corollary

The following properties of recursively enumerable sets are not recursively enumerable sets are not recursively enumerable

(*a*) $L = \phi$ (*b*) Σ^*

(*c*) L is recursive (*d*) L is not recursive

(*e*) L is a single ten set

(*f*) L is a regular set (*g*) $L - L_U \neq \phi$.

Proof. (*a*) Containment property described in Theorem 5.7.6. is violated.

(*b*) Condition (*ii*) of Theorem 5.7.6. is violated. For (*c*)-(*f*) containment property is violated.

(*g*) Condition (*iii*) of Theorem 5.7.6. is violated.

5.7.11. Corollary

The following properties of recursively enumerable sets are recursively enumerable.

(*a*) $L \neq \phi$ (*b*) L contains atleast 5 words (*c*)w is in L for some fixed word w. (*d*) $L \cap L_U \neq \phi$.

Proof is obvious.

5.7.12. POST'S CORRESPONDENCE PROBLEM

An instance of Post's Correspondence Problem (PCP) consists of two lists $A = w_1, w_2, ..., w_k$ and $B = x_1, x_2, ..., x_k$ of strings over some alphabet Σ. This instance of PCP has a solution if there is any sequence of integers $i_1, i_2, ..., i_m$, with $m \geq 1$, such that

$$w_1, w_{i2}, ..., w_{im} = x_{i1}, x_{i2}, ..., x_{im}.$$

The sequence $i_1, i_2, ..., i_m$ is a solution to this instance of PCP.

5.7.13. Example

Let $\Sigma = \{0, 1\}$. Let A and B be lists of three strings each, defined as in Fig. 5.16. PCP has a solution 2, 1, 1, 3.

	List A	*List B*
i	w_i	x_i
1	1	111
2	10111	10
3	10	0

An instance of PCP

Fig. 5.16.

Let $m = 4$, $i_1 = 2$, $i_2 = 1$, $i_3 = 1$, $i_4 = 3$. Now

$$w_2 w_1 w_1 w_3 = 101111110$$

$$x_2 x_1 x_1 x_3 = 101111110$$

Represent the string w_i on the top half and the string x_i on the bottom half as in Fig. 5.17.

10111	1	1	10
10	111	111	0

Fig. 5.17.

It is easy to verify the solution sequence beginning

10111	...
10	...

Fig. 5.18.

5.7.14. Example

Let $\Sigma = \{0, 1\}$. Let A and B be lists of three strings as shown in Fig. 5.19.

	List A	List B
i	w_i	x_i
1	10	101
2	011	11
3	101	011

Fig. 5.19.

Solution. Write the string from List A and the corresponding string from B which starts with the same symbol as in Fig. 5.20.

10	
101	

Fig. 5.20.

The next selection from A must begin with a 1 as in Fig. 5.21. The next selection from B must begin with 01.

10	101	
101	011	

Fig. 5.21.

Since the string from list B again exceeds the string from list A by single symbol 1, again select a string from beginning with 1 as in Fig. 5.22.

10	101	10
101	011	...

Fig. 5.22.

Continuing in this way, the sequence string B is always one character longer than A, this instance of PCP has no solution.

5.7.15. Modified Post's Correspondence Problem (MPCP)

Given Lists A and B of k strings each from Σ^*, $A = w_1, w_2, ..., w_k$ and $B = x_1, x_2, .., x_k$ does there exist a sequence of integers, $i_1, i_2, ... i_r$ such that

$$w_1, w_{i1}\ w_{i2} \ldots w_{ir} = x_1\ x_{i1}\ x_{i2} \ldots x_{ir}$$

The difference between the *M*PCP and PCP is that in the MPCP, a solution is required to start with the first string on each list.

5.7.16. Definition

If L_1 and L_2 are languages, over alphabets Σ_1 and Σ_2 respectively, then L_1 is said to be *reducible* to L_2, denoted $L_1 \leq L_2$, if there is a Turing-computable function $f : \Sigma_1^* \to \Sigma_2^*$ so that for any $x \in \Sigma_1^*$, $x \in L_1$ if and only if $f(x) \in L_2$.

5.7.17. Definition

Let P_1 and P_2 be decision problems. P_1 is said to be *reducible* to P_2 (written as $P_1 \leq P_2$) if there is an algorithmic procedure that allows to find an instance $F(I)$ of P_2 for every instance I of P_1, so that for every I, the answers for the two instances I and $F(I)$ are the same.

Let P_1 and P_2 be membership problems for two languages $L_1 \subseteq \Sigma_1^*$ and $L_2 \subseteq \Sigma_2^*$ respectively. In this case an instance of P_1 is a string $x \in \Sigma_1^*$ and an instance of P_2 is a string $y \in \Sigma_2^*$. Algorithmic procedure means finding a y for each x, that is computing a function from Σ_1^* to Σ_2^*.

If $L_1 \leq L_2$, then to solve the membership problem for L_2 is reduced to the problem of solving for L_1. For a string $x \in \Sigma_1^*$, in order to decide $x \in L_1$, it is enough to compute $f(x)$ and decide whether it is in L_2. The answers to the two questions are the same, because $x \in L_1$ if and only if $f(x) \in L_2$. More, generally, the statement $P_1 \leq P_2$ is equivalent to the statement $Y(P_1) \leq Y(P_2)$, where $Y(P_1)$ and $Y(P_2)$ are the corresponding languages of membership problems P_1 and P_2 respectively.

5.7.18. Definition

A *Valid Computation* of a TM $M = (Q, \Sigma, \Gamma, \delta, q_0, B, F)$ is a string of the form $w_1 \# w_2^{\#} \# w_3 \# w_4^{R} \# \ldots$ such that

(*i*) each w_i is an ID of M, a string in $\Gamma^*\ Q\ \Gamma^*$ not ending with B, (*ii*) w_1 is an initial ID, one of the form $q_0\, x$ for $x \in \Sigma^*$,

(*iii*) w_n is a final ID, that is, one in $\Gamma^*\, F\, \Gamma^*$,

(*iv*) $w_i \vdash_M w_{i+1}$ for $1 \le i < n$.

Assume that Q and Γ are disjoint and # is in neither Q nor Γ.

The set of invalid computations of a TM is the complement of the set of valid computations with respect to the alphabet $\Gamma \cup Q \cup \{\#\}$.

The notions of valid and invalid computations are useful in proving many properties of CFL'*s* to be undecidable. The reason is that the set of invalid computations is a CFL, and the set of valid computations is the intersection of two CFL's.

5.7.19. Lemma

The set of invalid computations of a TM

$M = (Q, \Sigma, \Gamma, \delta, q_0, B, F)$ is a CFL.

Solution. If a string w is an invalid computation, then one of the following condition is satisfied.

(1) w is not of the form $w_1 \# w_2^R \# w_3 \# \ldots$ where each w_i is an ID.

(2) w_1 is not an initial ID

(3) w_n is not an final ID

(4) $w_i \vdash_M w_{i+1}^R$ is false for some odd i.

(5) $w_i^R \vdash_M w_{i+1}$ is false for some even i.

The set of strings satisfying (1), (2), (3) is regular and there exists a FSA accepting the strings. The set of strings satisfying (4) and (5) are each CFL's.

A PDA P for (4) selects some w_i that is preceded by an even number of #'s and while reading w_i stores on its stack the ID z such that $w_i \vdash z$ with the right end of z at the top of the stack. After finding # on the input, P compares z with the following w_{i+1}. If $z \ne w_{i+1}$, the P scans its remaining input and accepts. Hence the set of invalid computations is the union of two CFL's and a regular set.

Hence it a CFL.

5.8. RECURSIVE FUNCTION THEORY PROOF OF PROPERTIES OF PROGRAMS

We know that the classes of all TM computable functions and recursive functions are equivalent. In this section, we shall study the relationship and applicability of the results of TM and recursive function theory to practical programming. Intuitively, it is clear that there does exist a close relationship since a computer program is nothing but an algorithm intended to control the behaviour of a machine and to perform certain desired actions on a set of input data, and the recursive function theory is at the very root of understanding and describing how such an algorithm is logically structured and can be constructed.

We shall first see how the construction of programs can be carried out by using a set of basic programs and a strategy set in a manner analogous to the construction of recursive functions. This directly takes us to the concept of structuring of algorithms and programs and also enables us to understand the theory of recursive functions in a practical rather than an abstract form.

5.8.1. Construction of Programs

We construct the programs by using an inductive definition. For this, we choose certain basic programs and a strategy set (consisting of concatenation, conditional branching, count loop, and while or repetition loop.)

Basic programs consists of the following

(*i*) Empty programs (that is, program with no operation on the data). This corresponds to the identity function.

(*ii*) Programs for the base functions ZERO, SUCC, SEL over numbers and programs for the base functions, ERASE, CONS, SEL over words.

Strategy Set. We can use strategy set to combine the basic programs and to construct composite programs.

(*i*) **Concatenation.** Given a program P_1 and another program P_2, the concatenation effectively results in a composition (fig. 5.23) of the functions computed by P_1 and P_2. Here if the initial values of $a_i = t_i$ $(1 \leq i \leq n)$, then their value before entering P_2 will be $f_i\ (t_1, t_2, ..., t_n)$. The value of a_i at the end is $r\ (x_1, ...\ x_n)$ which is the composition of the functions.

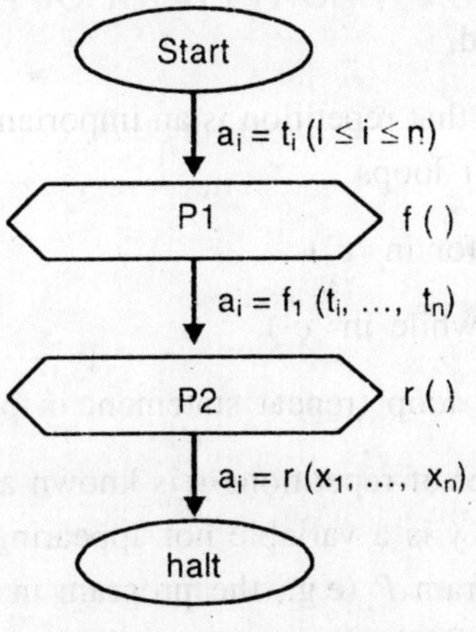

Fig. 5.23. Concatenation

(*ii*) **Conditional branching.** Given a program P_1 (Computing *a* function *g*) and another program P_2 (Computing a function *r*) the conditional branch picks one or the other programs according as a certain predicate *P* is true or false (Figure 5.24).

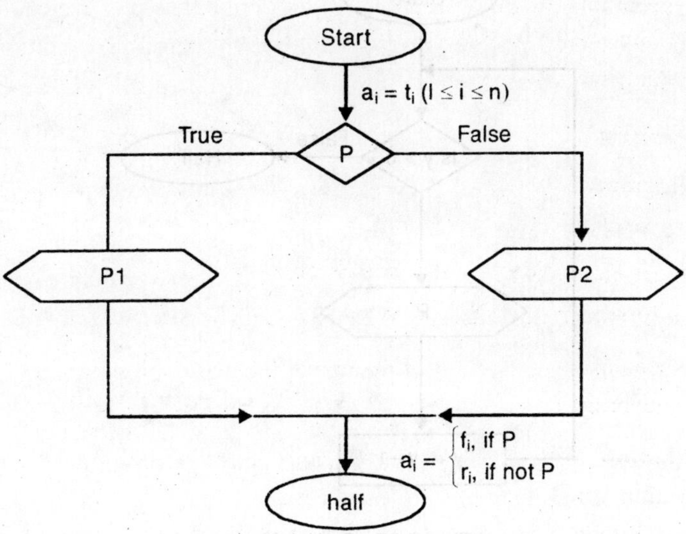

Fig. 5.24. Conditional branch

In the conditional branch, we find $a_i = f_i$ if *P* is true else $x_i = r_i$. Essentially, this means if *P* is true ($a_i = f_i$) else ($a_i = r_i$). That is, a conditional statement selects a single statement of its component statements for execution if a certain Boolean expression is true ; if the expression is false, then no statement or the statement following else is executed.

(*iii*) **Loops.** We know that repetition is an important step in algorithm. There are three types of loops.

(*a*) Count loop (for in '*c*').

(*b*) While loop (while in '*c*').

(*c*) Perform until loop (repeat statement in pascal).

Count loop. If the number of repetitions *y* is known already or a bound can be set to *y* and this number *y* is a variable not appearing on the left-hand side of any assignment is a program *P* (e.g., the program in Figure 5.25.) the loop is known as the count loop. Such a loop repeatedly executes the program *P* when a progression of values is assigned to a control variable in it. This control variable, the initial value, and the final value must not be altered by the repeated program *P*. Typical examples of count loop programs are evaluation of a polynomial of known degree and the primality test.

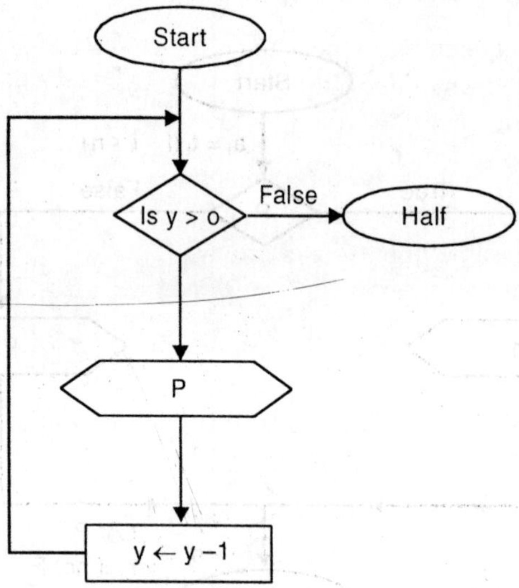

Fig. 5.25. Count loop.

While loop. In this loop (Figure 5.26), the expression controlling the repetition is a predicate which takes the value True (non-zero) or False (zero). The repeated execution will be carried out until the predicate becomes false. If the predicate is false at the beginning itself the statement will not be executed alteast once.

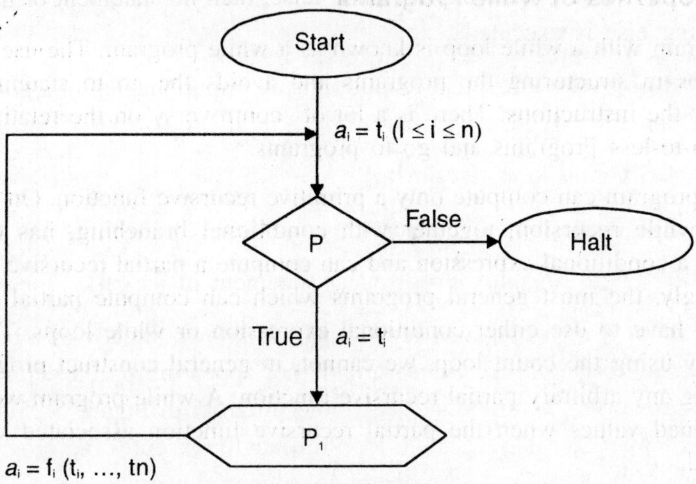

Fig. 5.26. While *P* do P_1.

Perform or repeat until loop. Here the statements P_1 between "repeat" and "until will be repeatedly executed till the expression becomes true. This is equivalent to saying that while not *P* do P_1.

The difference between the repeat until loop and while loop is that in repeat until loop (*i*) the termination condition is inverted and (*ii*) the repeatable statement is executed atleast once.

A program uses only the basic programs and the strategy set is called a normal form program. Also, if we define that two programs are equivalent if they terminate on the same inputs and produce the same outputs, then it can be shown that, for every program, there exists an equivalent program which is in normal form.

5.8.2. Properties of Count Programs

A count program is one which has a count loop. Since such a program uses the base functions, composition and predicates (such as $y > 0$) it can compute only the primitive recursive functions. Thus, the count program is closed under concatenation, conditional branching, and count loop construction.

Every count program is a while program. This is because a count loop construction is equivalent to a linear concatenation followed by a while construction. There are of course, while programs that are not count programs.

In summary, the count program (*i*) forms an interesting class of subsets of the while program (*ii*) computes a total function because it can compute only the primitive recursive functions.

5.8.3. Properties of While Programs

The program with a while loop is known as a while program. The use of while loop helps in structuring the programs and avoids the go to statements and labels for the instructions. There is a lot of controversy on the relative merits of the go-to-less programs and go to programs.

A count program can compute only a primitive recursive function. On the other hand, a while recursion, together with conditional branching, has the same power as a conditional expression and can compute a partial recursive function. Accordingly, the most general programs which can compute partial recursive functions have to use either conditional expression or while loops. Therefore, by merely using the count loop, we cannot, in general construct programs for computing any arbitrary partial recursive function. A while program would lead to undefined values when the partial recursive function associated with it is undefined.

5.8.4. Church's Thesis, Simple Programs, Snap Shots

A direct consequence of the recursive function theory and Me Carthy's formalism is that all computable functions are partial recursive and can be computed in a universal calculator provided with the following instructions.

(*i*) Add one to X and go to the next instruction.

(*ii*) If X is not zero, then subtract one from X and go to the instruction labelled A, B, ..., otherwise go to the next instruction.

(*iii*) Stop and print X.

In other words, every problem having an algorithmic solution can be solved by using a machine having the foregoing set of instructions. This is nothing but a restatement of Church's thesis. Thus, if we use the letters X, Y, Z with or without subscripts, as variables and A, B,C as the labels then the statements we can use to instruct a machine are of the form

$$< \text{variable} > \; = \; < \text{variable} > + 1$$

$$< \text{variable} > \; = \; < \text{variable} > - 1,$$

$$\text{to} < \text{label} > \text{if} \; < \text{variable} > \; = 0.$$

According, we can now define the following concepts.

5.8.5 Definition

A finite sequence of statements no two of which have the same label is called as a program.

5.8.6. Definition

A list of equations giving numerical values to each variable used in the program is called as a state of computation.

5.8.7. Definition

An ordered pair < statement of P, state of P > for a program is called a snap shot for P.

5.8.8. Definition

A snap shot $< S_1, Q_1 >$ is terminal for P if there is no snap shot $< S_2, Q_2 >$ such that $< S_1, Q_1 >$ yields $< S_2, Q_2 >$.

5.8.9. Definition

A computation for a program P is a finite sequence of snap shots

$< S_1, Q_1 >$ yields $< S_2, Q_2 >$ yields ... yields $< S_n, Q_n >$, where $< S_n, Q_n >$ is the terminal.

5.8.10. Definition

A program P is n-ary if it contains the n variables $X_1, X_2, ..., X_n$.

5.8.11. Definition

A state of an n-ary program is called on initial state if it has the form

$$X_1 = a_1, ..., X_n = a_n, Y = 0,$$

and all other variables are zero.

5.8.12. Definition

Let P be an n-ary program. We can then associate an n-ary function ψ with P as follows. We fix an initial snap shot which sets the input variable as

$$X_1 = a_1, ..., X_n = a_n.$$

This initial snap shot $< S_1, Q_1 >$ leads to a succession of snap shots of P. $< S_1, Q_1 >$ yields ... yields $< S_n, Q_n)...\}$.

If a terminal snap shot $< S_m, Q_m >$ is reached then $\psi_p (a_1, .., a_n)$ is defined and its value equals the value of the variable Y in the state Q_M. If a terminal snap shot is never reached, then ψ_p is undefined.

5.8.13. Example

A program to carry out proper subtraction is as follows :

$$
\begin{aligned}
&[C] \ \text{To } A \text{ if } X_2 \neq 0\\
&\quad\ \ Y = X_1\\
&\quad\ \ \text{To } E\\
&[A] \ \text{To } B \text{ if } X_1 \neq 0\\
&\quad\ \ \text{To } A\\
&[B] \ X_1 = X_1 - 1\\
&\quad\ \ X_2 = X - 1\\
&\quad\ \ \text{To } C\\
&[E] \ \text{print } Y \text{ and stop.}
\end{aligned}
$$

Here, $\psi_p\ (a_1, a_2) = a_1 - a_2$ if $a_1 \geq a_2$; ψ_p is undefined if $a_1 < a_2$, that is the terminal snap shot is never reached.

5.8.14. Definition

An n-ary function f is partially computable if there is a program P such that

$$f\ (a_1, a_2, ..., a_n) = \psi_p\ (a_1, ..., a_n)$$

where = means not only that the two functions have the same value when both are defined, but also that if one function is undefined, then so too is the other.

5.8.15. Definition. An n-ary function f is computable if f is partially computable and total.

The above concepts link up the concepts of recursive function theory and programmed machines.

5.9. SOLVED PROBLEMS

1. Find the language $L\ (G)$ over $\{a, b, c\}$ generated by the unrestricted grammar G with productions $S \rightarrow aSb$, $aS \rightarrow Aa$, $Aab \rightarrow c$

Solution. First we must apply the first production one or more items to obtain the word $w = a^n S b^n$ where $n > 0$. To eliminate S, we must apply the second production to obtain the word $w' = a^m\ Aabb^m$ where $m = n - 1 \geq 0$. Now we can only apply the third production to obtain the word $w^n = a^m c b^m$ where $m \geq 0$. Accordingly

$$L\ (G) = \{a^m c b^m \ ;\ m \text{ non-negative}\}$$

That is $L(G)$ consists of all words with the same non-negative number of a's and b's separated by a c.

2. Find the language $L(G)$ generated by the context sensitive grammar $G = (N, T, S, P)$ where $N = \{S, Z, A, B\}$, $T = \{a, b\}$ and

$$P = \{S \to aSA/aZA,\ Z \to bB/bZB,\ BA \to AB,\ AB \to Ab,\ bB \to bb,\ bA \to ba,\ aA \to aa\}.$$

Solution. When $n > 1$, $m > 1$

$S \overset{*}{\Rightarrow} a^{n-1} S A^{n-1}$ (applying $S \to aSA$ $(n-1)$ times)

$\Rightarrow a^n Z A^n$ (applying $S \to aZA$ once)

$\overset{*}{\Rightarrow} a^n b^{m-1} Z B^{m-1} A^n$ (applying $Z \to bZB(m-1)$ times)

$\Rightarrow a^n b^m B^m A^n$ (applying $Z \to bB$ once)

$\overset{*}{\Rightarrow} a^n b^m A^n B^m$ (applying $BA \to AB$ mn times)

$\Rightarrow a^n b^m A^n b B^{m-1}$ (applying $AB \to Ab$ once)

$\overset{*}{\Rightarrow} a^n b^m A^n b^m$ (applying $bB \to bb(m-1$ times)

$\Rightarrow a^n b^m a A^{n-1} b^m$ (applying $bA \to ba$ once)

$\Rightarrow a^n b^m a^n b^m$ (applying $aA \to aa$ $(n-1)$ times)

when $n = 1$, $m > 1$,

$S \Rightarrow aZA$ (applying $S \to aZA$ once)

$\overset{*}{\Rightarrow} ab^{m-1} ZB^{m-1} A$ (applying $Z \to bZB$ $(m-1)$ times)

$\Rightarrow ab^m B^m A$ (applying $Z \to bB$ once)

$\overset{*}{\Rightarrow} ab^m AB^m$ (applying $BA \to AB$ m times)

$\Rightarrow ab^m Ab B^{m-1}$ (applying $AB \to Ab$)

$\overset{*}{\Rightarrow} ab^m Ab^m$ (applying $bB \to bb(m-1)$ times)

$\Rightarrow ab^m ab^m$ (applying $bA \to ba$ once)

Similarly, when $n > 1$, $m = 1$, $S \overset{*}{\Rightarrow} a^n ba^n b$ and when $n = 1$, $m = 1$, $s \overset{*}{\Rightarrow} abab$.

3. Describe the language generated by the unrestricted grammar

$S \to LaR$, $L \to LD/\varepsilon$, $Da \to aaD$, $DR \to R$, $R \to \varepsilon$.

Solution. $S \Rightarrow LaR$ (applying $S \Rightarrow LaR$ once)

$\Rightarrow aR$ (applying $L \to \varepsilon$ once)

$\Rightarrow a$ (applying $R \to \varepsilon$ once)

That is $S \overset{*}{\Rightarrow} a$. Thus $a \in L(G)$.

$S \Rightarrow LaR$ (applying $S \to LaR$ once)

$\Rightarrow LDaR$ (applying $L \to LD$ once)

$\Rightarrow LaaDR$ (applying $Da \to aaD$ once)

$\Rightarrow LaaR$ (applying $DR \to R$ once)

$\Rightarrow Laa$ (applying $R \to \varepsilon$ once)

$\Rightarrow aa = a^2$ (applying $L \to \varepsilon$ once)

Thus $a^2 \in L(G)$.

$S \Rightarrow LaR$ (applying $S \to LaR$ once)

$\Rightarrow LDaR$ (applying $L \to LD$ once)

$\Rightarrow LDDaR$ (applying $L \to LD$ once)

$\overset{*}{\Rightarrow} LaaaaDDR$ (applying $Da \to aaD$ 3 times)

$\overset{*}{\Rightarrow} LaaaaR$ (applying $DR \to R$ 2 times)

$\Rightarrow aaaaR$ (applying $L \to \varepsilon$ once)

$\Rightarrow aaaa = a^4$ (applying $R \to \varepsilon$ once)

Thus $a^4 \in L(G)$.

$S \Rightarrow LaR$ (applying $S \to LaR$ once)

$\overset{*}{\Rightarrow} LD^n aR$ (applying $L \to LDn$ times)

$\overset{*}{\Rightarrow} La^{2^n} D^n R$ (applying $DR \to aa$D times 2^{n-1} times)

$\overset{*}{\Rightarrow} La^{2^n} R$ (applying $DR \to R$ n times)

$\Rightarrow a^{2^n} R$ (applying $L \to \varepsilon$ once)

$\Rightarrow a^{2^n}$ (applying $R \to \varepsilon$ once)

Thus $L(G) = \left\{a^{2^n} / n \geq 0\right\}$.

4. Describe the language generated by the unrestricted grammar with the given productions

$S \to LaR$, $L \to LD/LT/\varepsilon$, $Da \to aaD$, $Ta \to aaaT$, $DR \to R$, $TR \to R$, $R \to \varepsilon$.

Solution. Since we have only one *S*-production we have to apply $S \to LaR$ first. Since there are three *L*-productions then we can apply either $L \to LD$ or $L \to LT$. If we apply $L \to LD$ then it follows from problems that the productions $\{S \to LaR, L \to LD, L \to \varepsilon, Da \to aaD, DR \to R, R \to \varepsilon\}$ will generate the language

$$L_1 = \left\{a^{2^n} / n \geq 0\right\}.$$

If we apply $L \to LT$ we see that

$$S \Rightarrow LaR \Rightarrow a$$

$$\therefore \quad a \in L(G)$$

$S \Rightarrow LaR$ (applying $S \to LaR$ once)

$\Rightarrow LTaR$ (applying $L \to LT$ once)

$\Rightarrow LaaaTR$ (applying $Ta \to aaaT$ once)

$\Rightarrow aaaTR$ (applying $L \to \varepsilon$ once)

$\Rightarrow aaaR$ (applying $TR \to R$ once)

$\Rightarrow aaa = a^3$ (applying $R \to \varepsilon$ once)

Thus $a^3 \in L(G)$

$S \Rightarrow LaR$ (applying $S \to LaR$ once)

$\overset{*}{\Rightarrow} LTTaR$ (applying $L \to LT$ twice)

$\overset{*}{\Rightarrow} L a^9 TTR$ (applying $Ta \to aaaT$ thrice)

$\overset{*}{\Rightarrow} La^9 R$ (applying $TR \to R$ twice)

$\Rightarrow a^9 R$ (applying $L \to \varepsilon$ once)

$\Rightarrow a^9$ (applying $R \to \varepsilon$ once).

In general

$S \Rightarrow LaR$ (applying $S \to LaR$ once)

$\overset{*}{\Rightarrow} LT^n aR$ (applying $L \to LT$ n times)

$\overset{*}{\Rightarrow} L_{a^{3^n}} T^n R$ (applying $Ta \to aaaT$ several times)

$\overset{*}{\Rightarrow} L_{a^{3^n}} R$ (applying $TR \to R$ n times)

$\Rightarrow a^{3^n} R$ (applying $L \to \varepsilon$ once)

$\Rightarrow a^{3^n}$ (applying $R \to \varepsilon$ once).

Hence the productions

$\{S \to LaR, L \to LT/\text{l}, Ta \to aaaT, TR \to R, R \to \varepsilon\}$ generates

$$L_2 = \{a^{3^n} / n \geq 0\}$$

Thus $L(G) = L_1 \cup L_2$

$$= \{a^{2^n} / n \geq 0) \cup \{a^{3^n} / n \geq 0)$$

5. Describe the language generated by the unrestricted grammar with the productions $\{S \to ABCS/ABC, AB \to BA, AC \to CA, BC \to CB, BA \to AB, CA \to AC, CB \to BC, A \to a, B \to b, C \to c\}$

Solution. $S \Rightarrow ABC$ (applying $S \to ABC$)

$\overset{*}{\Rightarrow} abc$ (applying $A \to a$, $B \to b$, $C \to c$)

Thus $abc \in L(G)$.

$S \Rightarrow ABCS$ (applying $S \to ABCS$ once)

$\Rightarrow ABCABC$ (applying $S \to ABC$ once)

$\overset{*}{\Rightarrow} A^2B^2C^2$ (applying $CA \to AC$, $BA \to AB$, $CB \to BC$)

$\overset{*}{\Rightarrow} a^2b^2c^2$ (applying A $\to a$, $B \to b$, $C \to b$ twice).

In general $S \Rightarrow ABCS$ (applying $S \to ABCS$)

$\overset{*}{\Rightarrow} (ABC)^n$ (applying $S \to$ ABC $(n - 1)$ times)

$\overset{*}{\Rightarrow} A^nB^nC^n$ (applying $AB \to BA$, $AC \to CA$, $BC \to CB$, $BA \to AB$, $CA \to AC$, $CB \to BC$ several times)

$\overset{*}{\Rightarrow} a^n b^n c^n$ (applying $A \to a$, $B \to b$, $C \to c$ n times)

Thus $L(G) = \{a^n b^n c^n / n \geq 1\}$.

6. Find the language generated by the unrestricted grammar with productions

$\{S \to 0SAB, S \to \varepsilon, BA \to AB, 0A \to 01, 1A \to 11, 1B \to 12, 2B \to 22\}$

Solution. $S \Rightarrow \varepsilon \quad \therefore \quad \varepsilon \in L(G)$

$S \Rightarrow 0SAB$ (applying $S \to 0SAB$ once)

$\Rightarrow 0AB$ (applying $S \to \varepsilon$ once)

$\Rightarrow 01B$ (applying $0A \to 01$ once)

$\Rightarrow 012$ (applying $1B \to 12$ once)

$S \Rightarrow 0SAB$ (applying $S \to OSAB$ once)

$\Rightarrow 00SABAB$ (applying $S \to OSAB$ once)

$\Rightarrow 00ABAB$ (applying $S \to \varepsilon$ once)

$\Rightarrow 001BAB$ (applying $0A \to 01$ once)

$\Rightarrow 001ABB$ (applying $BA \to 13$ once)

$\Rightarrow 0011BB$ (applying $1A \to 11$ once)

$\Rightarrow 00112B$ (applying $1B \to 12$ once)

$\Rightarrow 001122$ (applying $2B \to 22$ once)

Thus $001122 \in L(G)$

In general $n > 2$

$S \overset{*}{\Rightarrow} 0^n S (AB)^n$ (applying $S \to OSAB$ n times)

$\overset{*}{\Rightarrow} 0^n (AB)^n$

$\Rightarrow 0^{n-1} 01 A^{n-1} B^n$ (applying $0A \to 01$ once)

$\overset{*}{\Rightarrow} 0^n 1^{n-1} AB^n$ (applying $BA \to AB$ nC_2 times)

$\Rightarrow 0^n 1^n B^n$ (applying $1A \to 11$ once)

$\Rightarrow 0^n 1^n 2 B^{n-1}$ (applying $1B \to 12$ once)

$\overset{*}{\Rightarrow} 0^n 1^n 2^n$ (applying $2B \to 22$ $(n-1)$ times)

Thus $L(G) = \{0^n 1^n 2^n / n \geq 0\}$

7. Prove that the language

$L = \{a^n b^n c^n / n \geq 1\}$ is recursive but not context free.

Solution. We describe the operation of a Turing machine which tests a string for membership in L.

1. Test the string to determine whether it is of the form $a^k b^l c^m$ without changing the string on the tape.
2. If the string has the proper format, rewind the tape, if it does not halt in a rejecting state.
3. For each 'a' found on the tape as the head scans to the right, replace it with a blank; locate one 'b' and one 'c' and replace them with blanks. Repeat this process for each a on the tape. If not enough b's are c's are found.
4. When no more a's can be found, test the tape to see whether it consists of entirely of blanks. If it does, accept the string. If the tape is not empty, halt in a rejecting state.

Hence L is recursive. For the proof of L is not context free see 3.4.3 problem 1.]

8. Let $G = (\{S, A, B\}, \{0, 1\}\ P, S)$ where P consists of $S \to 0AB0$, $A \to 1\ 0AB\ 1$, $B \to A01$, $0A \to 100$, $1B1 \to 0101$. Test whether $100110100011010 \in L(G)$.

Solution. We have to start with an S-production. At every stage we apply a suitable production which is likely to derive w.

Now
$$
\begin{aligned}
S &\Rightarrow 0AB0 && \text{(applying } S \to 0AB0 \text{ once)}\\
&\Rightarrow 100B0 && \text{(applying } 0A \to 100 \text{ once)}\\
&\Rightarrow 100A010 && \text{(applying } B \to A01 \text{ once)}\\
&\Rightarrow 10010AB1010 && \text{(applying } A \to 1\ 0AB\ 1 \text{ once)}\\
&\Rightarrow 1001100B1010 && \text{(applying } 0A \to 100 \text{ once)}\\
&\Rightarrow 1001100A011010 && \text{(applying } B \to A01 \text{ once)}\\
&\Rightarrow 100110100011010 && \text{(applying } 0A \to 11 \text{ once).}
\end{aligned}
$$

Thus $100110100011010 \in L(G)$.

9. Find the language generated by the unrestricted grammar given by the productions

$$S \to 0SBA/01A,\ AB \to BA,\ 1B \to 11,\ 1A \to 10,\ 0A \to 00.$$

Solution. $\quad S \Rightarrow 01A$

$$\Rightarrow 010$$

$\therefore \quad 010 \in L(G)$

$S \Rightarrow 0SBA$ (applying $S \to 0SBA$ once)

$\Rightarrow 001ABA$ (applying $S \to 01A$ once)

$\Rightarrow 001BAA$ (applying $AB \to BA$ once)

$\Rightarrow 0011AA$ (applying $1B \to 11$ once)

$\Rightarrow 00110A$ (applying $1A \to 10$ once)

$\Rightarrow 001100$ (applying $0A \to 00$ once)

Thus $001100 = 0^2 1^2 0^2 \in L(G)$.

$S \overset{*}{\Rightarrow} 00SBABA$ (applying $S \to 0SBA$ once)

$\Rightarrow 0001ABABA$ (applying $S \to 01A$ once)

$\Rightarrow 0001BAABA$ (applying $AB \to BA$ once)

$\Rightarrow 00011AABA$ (applying $1B \to 11$ once)

$\overset{*}{\Rightarrow} 00011BAAA$ (applying $AB \to BA$ once)

$\Rightarrow 000111AAA$ (applying $1B \to 11$ once)

$\Rightarrow 0001110AA$ (applying $1A \to 10$ once)

$\overset{*}{\Rightarrow} 000111000$ (applying $0A \to 00$ twice)

In general $S \overset{*}{\Rightarrow} 0^{n-1} S (BA)^{n-1}$ (applying $S \to 0SAB$ $(n-1)$ times)

$\Rightarrow 0^{n-1}\, 01\, A\, (BA)^{n-1}$ (applying $S \to 01A$ one time)

$\overset{*}{\Rightarrow} 0^n 1^n A^n$ (applying $AB \to BA$ several times and then $1B \to 11$ one time)

$\Rightarrow 0^n\, 1^n\, 0A^{n-1}$ (applying $1A \to 10$ one times)

$\overset{*}{\Rightarrow} 0^n 1^n 0^n$ (applying $0A \to 00$ $(n-1)$ times)

Thus $0^n 1^n 0^n \in L(G)$.

Hence $\{0^n 1^n 0^n / n \geq 1\} \subseteq L(G)$.

To prove that $L(G) \subseteq \{0^n 1^n 0^n / n \geq 1\}$, we proceed as follows. If we apply the production $S \to 01A$ first and then $1A \to 10$ we get 010.

Otherwise we have to apply $S \to 0SBA$ once or several times to get $0^{n-1} S (BA)^{n-1}$. To eliminate S we have to apply $S \to 01A$. Thus we arrive at the sentential form $0^n 1A (BA)^{n-1}$. To eliminate the variable B we have to apply $AB \to BA$ and $1B \to 11$ several times. Thus we get $0^n 1^n A^n$. Then we have to apply $1A \to 10$ one time and then $0A \to 00$ several times to get $0^n 1^n 0^n$. Thus

$$L(G) \subseteq \{0^n 1^n 0^n / n \geq 1\}$$

Thus $$L(G) = \{0^n 1^n 0^n / n \geq 1\}.$$

10. Prove that $\{a^{(n+1)^2} / n \geq 1\}$ is generated by the unrestricted grammar with productions $S \to a$, $S \to CD$, $C \to ACB$, $C \to AB$, $AB \to aBA$, $Aa \to aA$, $Ba \to aB$, $AD \to Da$, $BD \to Ea$, $BE \to Ea$, $E \to a$.

Solution. We prove

(a) $S \overset{*}{\Rightarrow} A^n B^n D$

(b) $A^n B^n D \overset{*}{\Rightarrow} a^{n^2} B^n A^n D$

(c) $B^n A^n D \Rightarrow a^{2n+1}$

(a) $S \Rightarrow CD$ (applying $S \to CD$ once)

$\overset{*}{\Rightarrow} A^{n-1} CB^{n-1} D$ (applying $C \to ACB$ $(n-1)$ times)

$\Rightarrow A^n B^n D$ (applying $C \to AB$ once)

(b) $A^n B^n D \Rightarrow A^{n-1}\, a\, BA\, B^{n-1} D$ (applying $AB \to aBA$ once)

$\Rightarrow A^{n-2}\, a\, ABAB^{n-1} D$ (applying $Aa \to aA$ once)

$\Rightarrow A^{n-2} a^2\, BA\, AB^{n-1} D$ (applying $AB \to aBA$ once)

$\Rightarrow A^{n-2} a^2\, BA\, a\, B\, AB^{n-2} D$ (applying $AB \to aBA$ once)

$\Rightarrow A^{n-2} a^2\, Ba\, ABAB^{n-2} D$ (applying $Aa \to aA$ once)

$\Rightarrow A^{n-2} a^3\, BA\, BAB^{n-2} D$ (applying $AB \to aB$ once)

$\Rightarrow A^{n-2} a^3\, Ba\, BAAB^{n-2} D$ (applying $AB \to aBA$ once)

$\overset{*}{\Rightarrow} a^4 A^{n-2} B^2 A^2 D^{n-2}$ (applying $Ba \to aB$ once and $Aa \to aA$ several times)

proceeding in a similar way we get

$$A^n B^n D \overset{*}{\Rightarrow} a^{n^2} B^n A^n D$$

Hence (b).

Finally $B^n A^n D \Rightarrow B^n A^{n-1} Da$ (applying $AD \to Da$ once)

$$\overset{*}{\Rightarrow} B^n\ Da^n \qquad \text{(applying } AD \to Da\ (n-1) \text{ times)}$$

$$\Rightarrow B^{n-1}\ E\ a^{n+1} \qquad \text{(applying } BD \to Ea \text{ once)}$$

$$\overset{*}{\Rightarrow} Ea^{2n} \qquad \text{(applying } BE \to Ea\ (n-1) \text{ times)}$$

$$\Rightarrow a^{2n+1} \qquad \text{(applying } E \to a \text{ once)}$$

Hence (*c*)

Now $\quad S \Rightarrow A^n B^n\ D \qquad$ (using (*a*))

$$\overset{*}{\Rightarrow} a^{n^2}\ B^n A^n D \qquad \text{(using } (b)\text{)}$$

$$\overset{*}{\Rightarrow} a^{n^2}\ a^{2n+1} \qquad \text{(using } (c)\text{)}$$

$$= a^{(n+1)^2}$$

Thus $\quad L\ (G) = \left\{a^{(n+1)^2} \,/\, n \ge 1\right\}.$

11. Prove that every context sensitive language is recursive.

Proof. Let $G = (N, T, S, P)$ and $w \in T^*$. We have to construct an algorithm to test whether $w \in L\ (G)$ or not. If $w = \varepsilon$, them $w \in L(G)$ iff $S \to \varepsilon$ is in P. As they are only finite number of productions in P, we have to test whether $S \to \varepsilon$ is in P or not.

Let $|\ w\ | = n \ge 1$. The algorithm is based on the construction of a sequence $\{W_i\}$ of subsets of $(N \cup T)^*$. W_i is simply the set of all sentential forms of length less than or equal to n derivable in atmost i steps. The construction is done recursively as follows.

(*i*) $W_0 = \{S\}$

(*ii*) $W_{i+1} = W_i \cup \{\beta \in (N \cup T)^*$ /there exists α in W_i such that $\alpha \Rightarrow \beta$ and $|\ \beta\ | \le n\}$. W_i's satisfy the following.

(*iii*) $W_i \subseteq W_{i+1}$ for all $i \ge 0$

(*iv*) There exists k such that $W_k = W_{k+1}$.

(*v*) If k is the smallest integer such that

$$W_k = W_{k+1}, \text{ then}$$

$$W_k = \{\alpha \in (N \cup T)^* \,/S \overset{*}{\Rightarrow} \alpha \text{ and } |\ \alpha\ | \le n\}.$$

Point (*iii*) follows form point (*ii*). To prove (*iv*), we consider the number N of strings over $N \cup T$ of length less than or equal to n. If $|\ N \cup T\ | = m$, then

$r = 1 + m + m^2 + ... + m^n$ since m^i is the number of strings of length i over $N \cup T$. That is $r = (m^{n+1} - 1) / (m - 1)$ and r is fixed as it depends only on n and m. As any string in W_i is of length atmost n, $| W_i | \leq r$. Therefore, $W_k = W_{k+1}$ for some $k \leq t$. This proves point (*iv*). Form (*ii*) it follows that $W_k = W_{k+1}$ implies

$$W_{k+1} = W_{k+2}$$

$$\{\alpha \in (N \cup T)^* / S \overset{*}{\Rightarrow} \alpha, | \alpha |, \leq n\} = W_1 \cup W_2 \cup ... \cup W_k \cup W_{k+1} ...$$

$$\vdots \qquad = W_1 \cup W_2 \cup ... \cup W_k$$

$$= W_k \text{ from } (iii).$$

This proves (*v*).

From (*v*) it follows that $w \in L(G)$ (*i.e.* $S \overset{*}{\Rightarrow} w$) if and only if $w \in W_k$. Also, $W_1, W_2, ..., W_k$ can be constructed in a finite number of steps. We give the required algorithm as follows.

Algorithm to test whether $w \in L(G)$.

1. Construct $W_1, W_2, ...$ using (*i*) and (*ii*). We terminate the construction when $W_{k+1} = W_k$ for the first time.
2. If $w \in W_k$ then $w \in L(G)$. Otherwise $w \notin L(G)$. (As $| W_k | \leq r$, testing whether w is in W_k requires atmost r steps)

12. Let Γ be the grammar $G = (N, T, S, P)$ where $N = \{S, A\}$, $T = \{0, 1, 2\}$ and $P = \{S \to 0SA2, S \to 012, 2A \to A2, 1A \to 11\}$

Test whether (*a*) $00112 \in L(G)$ and (*b*) $001122 \in L(G)$.

Solution.

(*a*) Construct the sets W_0, W_1, W_2 using the problem 11. Here $| w | = 5$.

$$W_0 = \{S\}$$

$$W_1 = \{012, S, 0SA2\}$$

$$W_2 = \{012, S, 0SA2\}$$

As $W_2 = W_1$, we terminate. (Although $0SA2 \Rightarrow 0012A2$, we cannot include $0012A2$ in W_1 as its length is > 5). $00112 \notin W_1$. Hence $00112 \notin L(G)$.

(*b*) To test whether $w = 001122 \in L(G)$. Here $| w | = 6$. We construct W_0, W_1, W_2 etc.

$$W_0 = \{S\}$$

$$W_1 = \{012, S, 0SA2\}$$

$$W_2 = \{012, S, 0SA2, 0012A2\}$$

$$W_3 = \{012, S, 0SA2, 0012A2, 001A22\}$$

$$W_4 = \{012, S, 0SA2, 0012A2, 001A22, 001122\}$$

$$W_5 = \{012, S, 0SA2, 0012A2, 001A22, 001122\}$$

As $W_5 = W_4$, we terminate. Then $001122 \in W_4$. Thus $001122 \in L(G)$.

13. Prove that there exists a recursive set which is not a context sensitive language over $\{0, 1\}$.

Solution. Let $T = \{0, 1\}$. We write the elements of T^* as a sequence (*i.e.* the elements of T^* are enumerated as the first element, second element etc.). For example one way of writing is ε, 0, 1, 00, 10, 11, 000, 001, 010, ... In this case 010 will be the 10th element.

As every grammar is defined in terms of finite alphabet set and a finite set of productions, we can also write all context sensitive grammars over T as a sequence, say G_1, G_2, ...

We define $X = \{w_i \in T^*/w_i \notin L(G_i)\}$. We can show that X is recursive. If $w \in T^*$ then we can find i such that $w = w_i$. This can be done in a finite number of steps (depending on $|w|$). For example, if $w = 01000$, then $w = w_{20}$. As G_{20} is context sensitive, we have an algorithm to test whether $w = w_{20} \in L(G_{20})$ by problem 11. Hence X is recursive.

We prove by contradiction that X is not a context sensitive language. If it is so, then $X = L(G_n)$ for some n. Consider w_n (the nth element in T^*). By definition of X, $w_n \in X$ implies $w_n \notin L(G_n)$. This contradicts $X = L(G_n)$. $w_n \notin X$ implies $w_n \in L(G_n)$ and once again, this contradicts $X = L(G_n)$. Thus $X \neq L(G_n)$ for any n *i.e.* X is not a context sensitive language.

14. Prove that the set $N \times N$ is countable where N is the set of all natural numbers.

Solution.

$$\begin{aligned} N \times N &= \{(x, y)/x, y \geq 0\} \\ &= \{(0, 0), (0, 1), (0, 2), \ldots\} \\ &\cup \{(1, 0), (1, 1), (1, 2), \ldots\} \\ &\cup \{(2, 0), (2, 1), (2, 2), \ldots\} \\ &\cup \ldots \\ &= \bigcup_{t=0}^{\infty} \{(t, y)/y \geq 0\} \\ &= \bigcup_{t=0}^{\infty} (\{t\} \times N) \end{aligned}$$

Since the function $f_t : N \to \{t\} \times N$ defined by $f_t\ (s) = (t, s)$ is a bijection each of the sets $\{t\} \times N$ is countable. (Note the t $\{t\} \times N$ is the set of elements in the tth row of Figure 5.4.). By 5.5.6. it follows that $N \times N$ is countable.

15. Prove that T^* = {set of all strings over a finite set T} is countable.

Solution. $$T^* = \bigcup_{r=0}^{\infty} T^r$$

where T^r is the set of strings over T of length r.

Since T^r is finite and therefore countable, it follows from 5.5.6 that T^* is countable. [For example when $T = \{0, 1\}$, one way of listing the elements of T^* is to use the canonical order :

$$\{0, 1\}^* = \{\varepsilon, 0, 1, 00, 01, 10, 11, 000, 001, ...\}].$$

16. Prove that any language over a finite set T is countable.

Solution. We know that a language L over T is a subset of T^*. Since every subset of a countable set is countable by problem 15 it follows that L is countable.

17. Prove that the set of all recursively enumerable languages is countable.

Solution. Let T be the set of all Turing machines and R be the set of all recursively enumberable languages. Here we are following our convention that all the states of a Turing machine are elements of the fixed set Q and all the tape symbols are elements of the set S. In particular, the recursively enumerable languages all involve alphabets that are subsets of S. Here we use the encoding function $e : T \to \{0, 1\}^*$.

The only property of e that we need here is that it is one-to-one and there a bijection from T to some subset of $\{0, 1\}^*$. Since $\{0, 1\}^*$ is countable and $T \subseteq \{0, 1\}^*$ we have T is countable.

A recursively enumerable language L can be accepted by some Turing machine. For each L, let t (L) be such a TM. The result is a function t from R to T, and since a Turing machine accepts precisely one language, t is one-to-one. Since T is countable, the same argument we used above shows that R is also countable.

18. Prove that $[0, 1) = \{x \in R\ /0 \le x < 1$ and R is the set of all real numbers $\}$ is uncountable.

Solution. We use the fact that real numbers in [0, 1) have infinite (possibly repeating) decimal expansions, with no digits before the decimal point. For example, $\frac{1}{2} = .5000\ ...$, $\frac{1}{3} = .333...$, $\frac{\pi}{3} = .7853981...$, and so on. It is not quite correct to say that every number in [0, 1) has exactly one such expansion, because a non-zero number whose expansion terminates (or ends in an infinite string of 0's) also has an expansion ending with infinitely many 9's ; for example, $\frac{1}{2}$ = 0.4999 ... . If we agree to disallow expansions that end with strings of 9's, then every number in [0, 1) has exactly one infinite decimal expansion, and every infinite decimal expansion represents a number in this interval.

Suppose that [0, 1) is countable, so that $[0, 1) = \{a_0, a_1, a_2,..\}$.

For each $i \geq 0$, suppose the decimal expansion of a_i is

$$a_i = a_{i;\,0}, a_{i;1}, a_{i;2} \dots$$

The contradiction is obtained by constructing a number $x \in [0, 1)$ that is not in the list. An easy way to guarantee that x is different from a_i for every i is to make the decimal expansion of x differ from that a_i the ith position. Therefore, we define

$$x_i = \begin{cases} a_{i,i+1} \ \textit{if}\ a_{i,i} < 8 \\ 7 \text{ if } a_{i,i} \geq 8 \end{cases}$$

and let x be the real numbers with decimal expansion. $x_0\ x_1\ x_2 \dots$. The two cases in the definition are to make sure that x_i's are single digits and not finally all 9's.

The diagonal aspect of the proof is that we have defined x_i in terms of the ith diagonal term of the infinite two-dimensional matrix

$$\begin{matrix} a_{0,0} & a_{0,1} & a_{0,2} & a_{0,3}\dots \\ a_{1,0} & a_{1,1} & a_{1,2} & a_{1,3}\dots \\ a_{2,0} & a_{2,1} & a_{2,2} & a_{2,3}\dots \\ a_{3,0} & a_{3,0} & a_{3,0} & a_{3,3}\dots \\ \dots \end{matrix}$$

(the diagonal terms are underlined). It is clear that for every $i \geq 0$, $x_i \neq a_{i,\,i}$ and therefore $x \neq a_i$. This is a contradiction, because $x \in [0, 1)$. Thus [0, 1) is uncountable.

19. Find an unrestricted grammar to generate the following language.

$$L = \{a^n\ b^n\ a^n\ b^n / n \geq 0).$$

Solution. Consider a unrestricted grammar

$$G = (N, T, S, P)$$

where $N = \{S, A, B, C, D\}$

$T = \{a, b\}$

and $P = \{S \to ABCD,\ AB \to aABb,\ A \to a,\ B \to b,\ CD \to aCDb,$
$C \to a,\ D \to b,\ S \to \varepsilon\}$

when $n = 0$

$$S \Rightarrow \varepsilon \quad \therefore \quad \varepsilon \in L(G)$$

when $n = 1$

$$\begin{aligned} S &\Rightarrow ABCD \\ &\Rightarrow aBCD && \text{(applying } A \to a \text{ once)} \\ &\Rightarrow abCD && \text{(applying } B \to b \text{ once)} \\ &\Rightarrow abaDC && \text{(applying } C \to a \text{ once)} \\ &\Rightarrow abab && \text{(applying } D \to a \text{ once)} \end{aligned}$$

Thus $abab \in L(G)$

When $n > 1$

$$\begin{aligned} S &\Rightarrow ABCD && \text{(applying } S \to ABCD \text{ once)} \\ &\Rightarrow aABbCD && \text{(applying } AB \to aABb \text{ once)} \\ &\overset{*}{\Rightarrow} a^{n-1} AB\, b^{n-1} CD && \text{(applying } AB \to aABb\ (n-2) \text{ times)} \\ &\Rightarrow a^n Bb^{n-1} CD && \text{(applying } A \to a \text{ once)} \\ &\Rightarrow a^n b^n CD && \text{(applying } B \to b \text{ once)} \\ &\overset{*}{\Rightarrow} a^n b^n a^{n-1} CD\, b^{n-1} && \text{(applying } CD \to a\, CDb\ (n-1) \text{ times)} \\ &\Rightarrow a^n b^n a^n Db^{n-1} && \text{(applying } C \to a \text{ once)} \\ &\Rightarrow a^n b^n a^n b^n && \text{(applying } D \to b \text{ once)} \end{aligned}$$

Thus $a^n b^n a^n b^n \in L(G)$

Hence G generates L.

20. For any languages $L_1 \subseteq \Sigma_1^*$, $L_2 \subseteq \Sigma_2^*$ with $L_1 \leq L_2$, if L_2 is recursive, then L_2 is recursive (or equivalently, if L_1 is not recursive, then L_2 is not). For any decision problems P_1 and P_2 with $P_1 \leq P_2$, if P_2 is solvable then P_1 is solvable. . (or, if P_1 is unsolvable, P_2 is unsolvable).

Solution. Suppose M_2 is a TM which decides the language L_2 and M_f be a TM that computes the function $f : \Sigma_1^* \to \Sigma_2^*$ involved in the reduction. Let M_1 be the composite $M_1 = M_f\, M_2$. On input $x \in \Sigma_1^*$, M_1 first computes $f(x)$, then halts with output 1 or 0, depending on whether $f(x)$ is in L_2 or not. The assumption that f is a reduction of L_1 or L_2 means that the output is 1 if $x \in L_1$ and 0 otherwise, and it follows that M_1 recognizes L_1.

The second part of the problem follows from the discussion after Definition 5.7.17.

21. Whether the decision problem, named *Accepts*.

Accepts : Given a TM M and a string w, is $w \in L(M)$? is undecidable.

Solution. An instance of *Accepts* consists of a Turing machine M and a string w. Using encoding function e represent it as the string $e(M)\, e(w)$.

Let $$L_U = \{e(M)\, e(w) : w \in L(M)\}.$$

To show *Accepts* is undecidable, it is enough to show L_U is not recursive. By Theorem 5.6.7. the result follows.

22. Whether the halting problem abbreviated as *Halts*

Halts: Given a TM M and a string w, does M halts on input w?

is undecidable.

Solution. Consider the corresponding language

$$H = \{e(M)\, e(w) : M \text{ halts on } w\}$$

is undecidable.

It is enough to show that 'Accepts' can be reduced to 'Halts', and from problems 20 and 21 it follows that 'Halts' is unsolvable.

For both problems, an instance is a pair consisting of a TM and a string. For an instance (M, w) of 'Accepts', construct an instance (M', w') of 'Halts', such that the answers are same in both cases. That is, M' halts on w' if and only if M accepts w. In other words, if M accepts w, M' must halts on w', and if M either rejects w or loops forever on w, M' must not halt on w'.

Let $w' = w$. Then M' can be obtained from M by changing move of the form $\delta(p, a) = (h_r, b, D)$ to $\delta(p, a) = (p, a, H)$, where h_r denotes the rejecting state. Other modification in machine M' is as follows. It begins to insert a new symbol say # in cell 0, moving everything else over one cell, and then move to state q_0 with the tape head in cell 1. Additional moves for M' is $\delta(q, \#) = (q, \# \ H)$ for all possible states q.

Besides these moves, M' also has all the moves as in M. The effect is that if M ever tries to moves its tape head off the tape, then M' enter an infinite loop with its tape head on cell 0.

This algorithm for obtaining M' from M gives the reduction, hence '*Halts*' is undecidable.

23. The language $E = \{ e(M) : M \text{ is a TM}\}$ is recursive.

Solution. A string x of 0's and 1's is in E if and only if it satisfies the following conditions:

(1) x corresponding to the regular expression $0000^*\, 1\, ((0^+\, 1)^5)^+$ so that the

substring following the first 1 can be viewed as a sequence of 5-tuples.

(2) For two distinct 5-tuples y and z in the string x, the first two of the five parts of y cannot be the same as the first two of the five parts of z (A deterministic TM cannot have two distinct moves for the same-symbol combination).

(3) None of the 5-tuples in x can have first part 0 or 00 (A TM cannot move from halt state)

(4) The last part of each 5-tuple must be 0, 00, or 000 (representing one of the three directions)

Any string satisfying these conditions represent a TM, whether or not it carries out a meaningful computation. There is an algorithm to take an arbitrary element of $\{0, 1\}^*$ and determine the truth or falsity of each condition, and it is possible to implement such an algorithm on a TM. Hence the language E is recursive.

24. The decision problem, named 'Accepts-B'

'Accepts-B' : Given a TM M, is M finally reach the accepting state, if it begins with a blank tape B.

is undecidable.

Solution. In order to show 'Accepts-B' is undecidable, it is enough to show 'Accepts' is reduced to 'Accepts-B' (*i.e.*, Accepts $\leq$ Accepts-B)

For both problems instance is a pair consisting of a TM and a string. Suppose (M, w) is a Yes-instance of 'Accepts' (*i.e.* M accepts w) if and only M' is an yes-instance of Accepts-B (*i.e.* M' accepts B).

M' starts with B, but create a tape with x on it by simply writing x. The computation it perform at that point will be exactly same as the computation performed by M on input x. In other words., M' is the composite write (x) M, where write (x) is the TM that halts with tape content B_{q_a} x when started with a blank. Write (x) assumes the tape is initially blank, and thus M' is likely to crash on any input other than B. Hence M' accepts B if and only if M accepts x.

The construction of M' in terms of M and x can be carried out algorithmicaly, it follows that 'Accepts-B' is undecidable.

25. Whether the decision problem,

'Accepts Something' : Given a TM M, is $L(M) \neq \phi$?

is undecidable.

Solution. To prove the result it enough to show **Accepts-*B*** can be reduced to **Accepts something**. For both problems , an instance is a Turing Machine. Start with a TM M and it is easy to construct a TM M' such that

M accepts B if and only if M' accepts atleast one string.

The computation of M' on any input is the one performed by M on B. M' simply erases its input first and then executes M; it is the composite machine M' = *Erase tape* $\rightarrow M$, where *Erase tape* erases its input string and leaves the tape head on cell 0. If M accepts B, then M' will eventually accepts, no matter what's its input is, and otherwise M, will never accepts. Since the function that takes M to M' is computable, the reduction follows.

26. Whether the decision problem.

Accepts everything : Given a TM M, with input alphabet Σ, is $L(M) = \Sigma^*$?

is undecidable.

Solution. The function constructed in the last problem is also a reduction of **Accepts-*B*** to **Accepts Every thing** because the machine M' accepts either everything (if T accepts B) or nothing. Hence **Accepts Everything** is undecidable.

27. Whether the decision problem

subset : Given two TMs M_1 and M_2, is $L(M_1) \subseteq L(M_2)$?

is undecidable.

Solution. An instance of *subset* is a pair (M_1, M_2) of Turing machines, and it is a yes-instance if $L(M_1) \subseteq L(M_2)$. The solution follows by showing Accepts *Everything* can be reduced to **subset.**

For that start with a TM M, and construct a pair (M_1, M_2) so that M accepts every string over its input alphabet if and only if $L(M_1) \subseteq L(M_2)$. The way to proceed here is to ignore everything but the set $A = L(M)$, and find other two B and C so that $A = \Sigma^*$ if and only if $B \subseteq C$. An appropriate choice is to let $B = \Sigma^*$ and $C = A$ (A subset of Σ^* is Σ^* if and only if it contains Σ^*). Therefore M' be the trivial TM with input alphabet Σ that immediately accepts, no matter what the input, so that $L(M_1) = \Sigma^*$ and let $M_2 = M$. This way of construction of (M_1, M_2) form M gives the reduction of **subset** from **Accepts Everything**.

28. The decision problem

Writes symbol Given a TM M, and a symbol 'a' in its tape alphabet, does M ever write 'a' if it is started with a blank tape ?

is undecidable.

Solution. To prove the undecidability of **write symbol,** it is enough to show *Accepts-B* is reduced to *writes Symbol.*

Starting with a TM M; an instance of *Accetps-B,* construct a pair (M', a) in such a way that M accetps B if and if M' eventually writes 'a' when started with a blank. The computation of M' is same as that of M, except that if M halts, M' writes a, and M' never writes a in any other situation. Precisely speaking, M' be a TM with the same input and tape alphabets as M except for one new tape symbol 'a' and the same transitions as M except the move.

$$\delta\ (p, \sigma) = (q_a, \tau, D)$$

of T becomes

$$\delta\ (p, \sigma) = (q_a, a\ , D)$$

Instead. Starting with input B, the two machines perform exactly the same computation until they accepts, and M' writes an 'a' if and only if this happens. Hence the reduction.

29. For any specific recursively enumerable language L_2, such that $L_2 = \{B\}$, the problem

Accepts (L_2): Given a TM M, is $L\ (M) = L_2$? is undecidable.

Solution. Because L_2 is a non-trivial property, by Rice's theorem the result follows.

30. Does the problem

Equivalent : Given TMs M_1 and M_2, is $L\ (M_1) = L\ (M_2)$?

undecidable?

Solution. The problem **Accepts (L_2)** is reducible to **Equivalent**, because if M_2 is a TM accepting L_2, then for any instance M of **Accepts (L_2)**, the pair (M, M_2) is an instance of **Equivalent** having the same answer. Hence **Equivalent** is undecidable.

31. The problem

'Given a TM M, does M make more than 50 moves on input B?

is decidable.

Solution. Given a TM M means given enough information to trace the processing of a fixed string for a certain fixed number of moves . So the given problem is decidable.

32. The decision problem

Writes Non blank : Given a TM M, does it ever write a non-blank symbol in its tape, when stated with a blank?

is decidable.

Solution. Given a TM M, construct a TM M' as follows. M' has the same tape alphabet as M except that it has one additional symbol #. The states of M_1 are the same as those of M. The transitions of M_1 are the same, except that for any transition of M in which a non-blank symbol is written, the corresponding transition of M_1 writes # and halts. Therefore starting with a blank symbol, M writes a non-blank symbol if and only if M_1 writes the symbol #. Hence **writes Non-blank** is solvable.

33. The decision problem

CFG Generates All: Given a context -free grammar (CFG) G with terminal alphabet Σ, is $L(G) = \Sigma^*$.

is undecidable.

Solution. Accepts Nothing (Given M is $L(M) = \phi$) is reducible to **CFG Generates All.** Starting with a TM M, there is an algorithm to construct a CFG G with terminal alphabet Σ_1, so that $L(G)$ is the complement C'_M of the set of valid computations of M. Saying that M accepts no string is equivalent to saying there are no valid computations of M or that C'_M contains every string over Σ_1. Therefore, M is a yes-instance of **Accepts Nothing** if an only if G is a yes-instance of **CFG Generates All**.

34. The problem

CFG Non-empty Intersection: Given two CFG*s* G_1 and G_2, is $L(G_1) \cap L(G_2)$ non empty?

is undecidable.

Solution. Accepts Something is reducible to **CFG Non-empty Intersection** For any TM M, the set C_M of valid computations of M can be expressed as $L(M_1) \cap L(M_2)$ for two CFG*s* G_1 and G_2 (Proof of this statement is left as an exercise). It is easy to construct an algorithm for the grammars G_1 and G_2 from M. Since M is an yes-instance of **Accepts something** if and only if the pair (G_1, G_2) is a yes-instance of **CFG Non-empty Intersection,** the first problem is reducible to the second and the second is therefore unsolvable.

35. Show that the language

$$L_r = \{e(M) : L(M) \text{ is recursive}\}$$

is not recursively enumerable.

Solution. Suppose L_r is recursively enumerable language. Let M_r be a TM accepting L_r. Now construct an algorithm A that takes $e(M)\ e(w)$ as input and produces as output a TM *M′*

such that

$$L(M') = \begin{cases} \phi \text{ if M does not accept } \omega \\ L_U \text{ if M accepts } \omega \end{cases}$$

Note that L_U is not recursive, so *M′* accepts a recursive language if and only if *M* does not accepts *w*. The construction of *M′* is shown in Fig. 5.27.

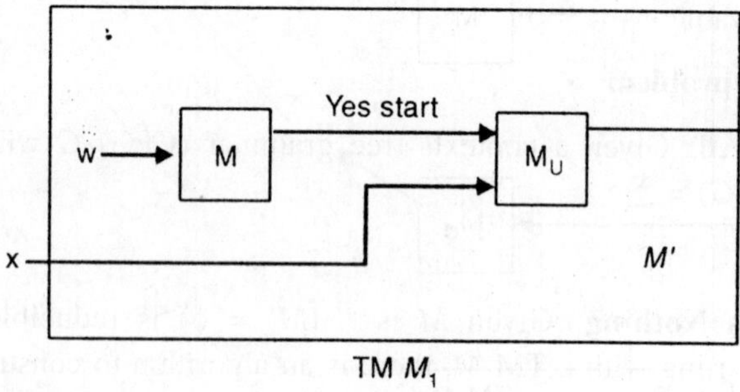

Fig. 5.27.

Given *A* and M_r, construct a TM accepting $\overline{L}_U$ as shown in Fig. 5.28.

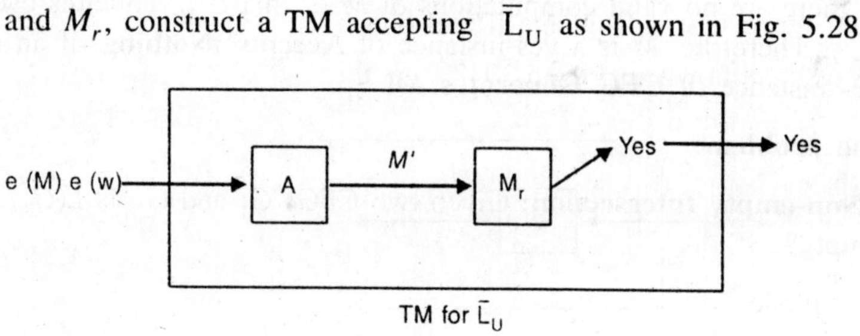

Fig. 5.28.

For an input *e*(*M*) *e*(*w*), the TM uses *A* to produce *M′*, uses M_r to determine if the set accepted by *M′* is recursive, and accetps if and only if *L* (*M′*) is recursive. But *L* (*M′*) is recursive if and only if *L* (*M′*) = φ which means *M* does not accept *w*. Thus the TM of Fig. 5.23. accepts *e* (*M*) *e* (*w*) if and only if *e* (*M*) *e* (*w*) is $\overline{L}_U$.

36. Show that the language

$$L_{nr} = \{e(M) : L(M) \text{ is not recursive}\}$$

is not recursively enumerable.

Solution. Suppose there is a TM M_{nr} accepting L_{nr}. Construct an algorithm *B* that takes *e* (*M*) *e* (*w*) as input and produces a TM *M′* such that

$$L(M') = \begin{cases} \Sigma^* \text{ if } M \text{ accepts } \omega \\ L_U \text{ if } M \text{ does not accept } \omega \end{cases}$$

The construction of *M'* is shown in Fig. 5.24.

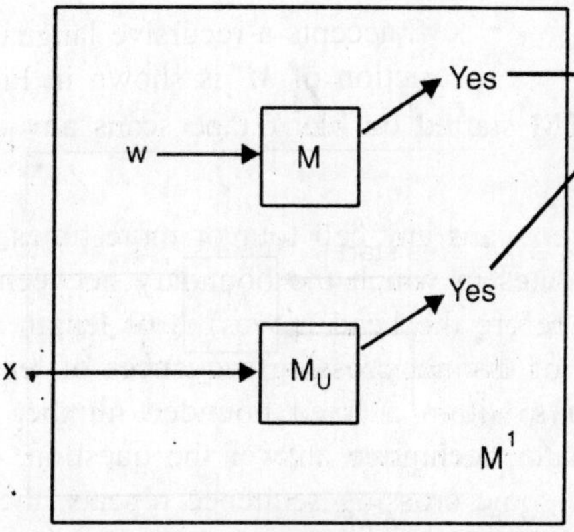

TM *M'*

Fig. 5.29.

M' accetps a recursive language if and only if *M* accepts *w*. Turing machine to accepts $\overline{L}_U$ is shown in Fig. 5.30.

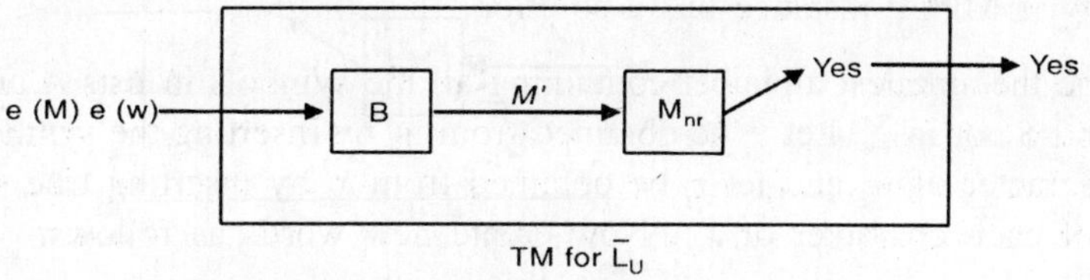

TM for $\overline{L}_U$

Fig. 5.30.

The TM of Fig. 5.30. accepts *e* (*M*) *e* (*w*) if and only if *L* (*M'*) is not recursive, or equivalently, if and only if *M* does not accepts *w*. That is, the TM Accepts *e*(*M*) *e*(*w*) if and only if *e*(*M*) *e*(*w*) is in $\overline{L}_U$. As no such TM exists, there does not exist any M_{nr} to accepts L_{nr}. Hence L_{nr} is not recursively enumerable.

37. Prove that "whether an arbitrary TM every prints three consecutive 1'*s* " is undecidable.

Solution. For each TM M_i construct a TM $\hat{M}_i$ which on blank tape simulates M_i on blank tape. However $\hat{M}_i$ uses 01 to encode a 0 and 10 to encode a 1. If

M_i's tape has a 0 in cell j, $\hat{M}_i$ has 01 in cells $2j - 1$ and $2j$. If M_i changes a symbol, $\hat{M}_i$ changes the corresponding 1 to 0, then the paired 0 to 1. Easily one can design $\hat{M}_i$ that never, has three consecutive 1's on its tape. $\hat{M}_i$ prints three consecutive 1's and halts iff M_i accepts ε. By Rice theorem, 'whether a TM accepts ε' is an undecidable problem as 'ε is in L'' is a non-trivial property. Hence the result follows.

38. The problem

Whether a single tape TM started on blank tape scans any cell four or more times is decidable.

Solution. If the TM never scans any cell four or more times, than every cross sequence (sequence of states in which the boundary between cells is crossed, assuming states change before the head moves) is of length atmost three. But there is a finite number of distinct crossing sequences of length three or less. Thus either the TM stays within a fixed bounded number of tape cells, in which case finite automaton technique answer the question, or some crossing sequence repeats. But if some crossing sequence repeats, then the TM moves right with some easily detectable pattern, and the question is decidable.

39. If PCP is decidable, then MPCP is decidable. That is MPCP reduces to PCP.

Solution. Let A = w_1 , w_2, ..., w_k and $B = x_1, x_2, ..., x_k$ be an instance of MPCP. Convert this instance of MPCP into an instance of PCP that has a solution if and only if MPCP instance has a solution.

Let Σ be the smallest alphabet containing all the symbols in lists A and B, and let $\not\subset$ and \$ not in Σ. Let y_i be obtained from w_i by inserting the symbol $\not\subset$ after each character of w_i and let z_i be obtained from x_i by inserting trhe symbol $\not\subset$ ahead of each character of x_i . Now create new words as follows:

$$y_0 = \not\subset y_1, \; z_0 = z_1$$

$$y_{k+1} = \$, \; z_{k+1} = \not\subset \$$$

Let $C = y_0, y_1, .., y_{k+1}$ and $D = z_0, z_1, ..., z_{k+1}$. For example, the list of C and D constructed form the lists of A and B of Example 5.7.13 are shown in table.

MPCP

	List A	List B
i	w_i	x_i
1	1	111
2	10111	10
3	10	0

PCP

	List C	List D
i	y_i	z_i
0	$\not\subset 1 \not\subset$	$\not\subset 1 \not\subset 1 \not\subset 1$
1	$1 \not\subset$	$\not\subset 1 \not\subset 1 \not\subset 1$
2	$1 \not\subset 0 \not\subset 1 \not\subset 1 \not\subset 1 \not\subset$	$\not\subset 1 \not\subset 0$
3	$1 \not\subset 0 \not\subset$	$\not\subset 0$
4	\$	$\not\subset \$$

In general the lists C and D represent an instance of PCP. This instance of PCP has a solution if and only if the instance of MPCP represented by lists A and B has a solution.

Note that if 1, i_1, i_2, ... i_r is a solution to MPCP with lists A and B, then 0, i_1, i_2, ..., i_r, $k + 1$ is a solution to PCP with lists C and D. Likewise, if i_1, i_2, ..., i_r is a solution to PCP with lists C and D, then $i_1 = 0$ and $i_r = k + 1$, since y_0 and z_0 are the only words with the same index that begin with the same symbol, and y_{k+1} and z_{k+1} are the only words with the same index that end with the same symbol. Let j be the smallest integer such that $i_j = k + 1$. Then i_1, i_2, ..., i_j is also a solution, since the symbol \$ occurs only as the lost symbol of y_{k+1} and z_{k+1}, and for no l, where $1 \leq l < j$,is $i_l = k + 1$. Clearly 1, i_2, i_3, ..., i_{j-1} is as solution to MPCP for lists A and B.

If there is an algorithm to decide PCP, there exists an algorithm to decide MPCP by converting any isntance of MPCP to PCP as above.

40. PCP is undecidable.

Solution. By the previous problem it is sufficient to show that if MPCP is decidable, then it is decidable that "whether a TM accepts a given w". That is, for each M and w, construct an instance of MPCP that has a solution if only if M accepts w.

An isntance of MPCP, if it has a solution, starts with # q_0w # $\alpha_1 q_1 \beta_1$ # $\alpha_2 q_2 \beta_2$ ... # $\alpha_k q_k \beta_k$ where strings between successive #'s are successive ID's in a computation of M with inptu w_1 and q_k is a final state. Assume there are no moves from a final state. The pairs of strings forming lists A and B of the instance of MPCP are as follows.

First pair is:

List A	List B
#	# q_0 w #

Group I.

List A	List B	
X	X	for each $X \in \Gamma$
#	#	

Group II. For each q in $Q - F$, p in Q, and X, Y and Z in Γ:

List A	List B	
$q\ X$	Yp	if $\delta\ (q, X) = (p, Y, R)$
$Zq\ X$	pZY	if $\delta\ (q, X) = (p, Y, L)$
q #	Yp#	if $\delta\ (q, B) = (p, Y, R)$
Zq #	pZY #	if $\delta\ (q, B, = (p, Y, L)$

Group III. For each q in F, X, Y in Γ

List A	List B
XqY	q
Xq	q
qY	q

Group IV

List A	List B	
q ##	#	for each q in F.

(x, y) is said to be a *partial solution* of MPCP with lists A and B if x is a prefix of y, and x and y are the concatenation of corresponding strings of lists A and B respectively.

If $xz = y$, then z is said to be the *remainder* of (x, y).

Claim: There is a parital solution (unique)

$(x, y) = (\# q_0w \# \alpha_1 q_1 \beta_1 \# ..., \# \alpha_{k-1} q_{k-1} \beta_{k-1} \#, \# q_0 w \# \alpha_1 q_1 \beta_1 \# ... \# \alpha_k q_k w_k \#)$

whose longer string is as long as $|y|$.

The above can be proved by induction on k.

If $k = 0$, the result is trivial, since the pair $(\#, \# q_0w\#)$ must be chosen first. Suppose the statement is true for some k and $q_k \notin F$. Then it is easy to show the statement for $k + 1$ is also true. The remainder of the pair (x, y) is $z = \alpha_k q_k \beta_k \#$. The next pairs must be chosen so that their strings from list A form z. Whatever symbols appear to the right and left of q_k, there is atmost one pair in Group II that enable the parital solution to be continued past q_k. This pair represents, the move of M from ID $\alpha_k q_k \beta_k$. The other symbols of z force choices from group I. No other choices will enable z to be composed of elements in list A.

Thus a new parital solution $(y, y \alpha_{k+1} q_{k+1} \beta_{k+1} \#)$ is obtained. It is straight forward to see that $\alpha_{k+1} q_{k+1} \beta_{k+1}$ is the one ID that M can reach on one move from $\alpha_k q_k \beta_k$. Also there is no other parital solution whose length of the second string equals $|y \alpha_{k+1} q_{k+1} \beta_{k+1} \#|$

If $q_k \in F$, then it is easy to find pairs from groups I and III which, when preceded by the partial solution (x, y) and followed by the pair in Group IV, provide a solution to MPCP with lists A and B.

Thus if M, started in ID q_0w, reaches an accepting state, the instance of MPCP with lists A and B has a solution. If M does not reach an accepting state, no paris of group III and IV are used. Therefore, there may be partial solutions, but the strings of B exceed the strings of A in length, so no solution is possible.

Hence the instance of MPCP has a solution if and only if M with input w halts in an accepting state. Since M and w are arbitrary, if there is an algorithm to solve MPCP, then there will be an algorithm to recognize L_U, contradicting that L_U is recursive. Hence MPCP is undecidable, which further implies PCP, is undecidable.

41. Let $M = (Q, \Sigma, \Gamma, B, \delta, q_1, F)$ be a TM with $Q = \{q_1, q_2, q_3\}$, $\Sigma = \{0, 1\}$, $\Gamma = \{0, 1, B\}$,

$F = \{q_3\}$ and δ be defined by:

States	*0*	*1*	*B*
q_1	$(q_2, 1, R)$	$(q_2, 0, L)$	$(q_2, 1, L)$
q_2,	$(q_3, 0, L)$	$(q_1, 0, R)$	$(q_2, 0, R)$

Let $w = 01$. Construct an instance of MPCP with lists A and B as follows.

First Pair:	*List A*	*List B*	
	#	$\# q_1 01 \#$	
Group I.	*List A*	*List B*	
	0	0	
	1	1	
	#	#	
Group II.	*List A*	*List B*	
	$q_1 0$	$1 q_2$	from $\delta(q_1, 0) = (q_2, 1, R)$
	$0 q_1 1$	$q_2 00$	from $\delta(q_1, 1) = (q_2, 0, L)$
	$1 q_1 1$	$q_2 10$	
	$0 q_1 \#$	$q_2 01$	from $\delta(q_1, B) = (q_2, 1, L)$
	$1 q_1 \#$	$q_2 11\#$	
	$0 q_2 0$	$q_3 00$	from $\delta(q_2, 0) = (q_3, 0, L)$
	$1 q_2 0$	$q_3 10$	
	$q_2 1$	$0 q_1$	from $\delta(q_2, 1) = (q_1, 0, R)$
	$q_2 \#$	$0 q_2 \#$	from $\delta(q_2, B) = (q_2, 0, R)$
Group III.	*List A*	*List B*	
	$0 q_3 0$	q_3	
	$0 q_3 1$	q_3	
	$1 q_3 0$	q_3	
	$1 q_3 1$	q_3	
	$0 q_3$	q_3	
	$1 q_3$	q_3	
	$q_3 0$	q_3	
	$q_3 1$	q_3.	

Group IV. *List A* *List B*

q_3 ## #

For the input $w = 01$, the computation is

$$q_1\, 01 \vdash 1q_2\, 1 \vdash 10q_1\, B \vdash 1q_2\, 01 \vdash q_3\, 101$$

Hence the ID's are

$q_1 01$, $1q_2 1$, $10q_1 B$, $1q_2\, 01$, $q_3\, 101$.

For the MPCP constructed as above, the next task is to check whether there is a solution.

The first pair gives a parital soltuion (# , #, $q_1$01 #). That is

#
$q_1 0_1$

Fig. 5.31 (a).

Since the length of second string is longer, next choose the pair ($q_1$0, 1q_2) (see (Fig, 5.31 (*b*))

#	$q_1$0
# q_1 01 #	1q_2

Fig. 5.31 (b).

The resulting partial solution is (# q_1 0, # $q_1$01, 01 # q_2)

(That is, Fig 5.31(*c*))

#$q_1$0
q_1 01 # 1 q_2

Fig. 5.31 (c).

The remainder is 1 # 1q_2. The next pair chosen must be (1, 1). In this case the partial solution is (see Fig. 5.31 (*e*)).

# q_1 0	1
# q_1 01 # 1q_2 1	1

Fig. 5.31 (d).

$q_1$01
$q_1$01 # 1q_2 1

Fig. 5.31 (e).

The next wo choices are (#, #) and (1, 1). The partial solution becomes (# $q_1$01 # 1, # q_1 01 # 1q_2 1 # 1). The remainder now is q_2 1 # 1 (see Fig. 5.31 (*f*)).

q_1 01 # 1
q_1 01 # 1 q_2 1 # 1

Fig. 5.31 (f).

Constinuing in this way, one can obtain a partial solution, where the length of second string is 14, is (x, x_0 q_1 # 1), where x = # q_1 01 # 1 q_2 1 # 1.

The next choice is (0, 0) or (0q_1 #, q_2 01 #)

x	0
x 0q_1 # 1	0

or

x	q_1 #
x 0 q_1 # 1	q_2 01 #

Fig. 5.31 (g). **Fig. 5.31 (h).**

By Fig. 5.31. (*g*), the resulting parital solution is (x0, x0q_1 # 10). The remainder is now q_1 # 10. There is no string in list A starting with q_1 #, it is not possible to make another partial solution. Hence this cannot lead to a solution. By Fig. 5.31 (*h*), the resulting parital solution is (x0q_1#, x0q_1 #1$q_2$01 #). The remainder is now 1 q_2 01 #. The next possible pair is (1q_2 0, q_3 10)

x 0 q_1 #	1$q_2$0
x0q_1 # 1 q_2 01 #	q_3 10

Fig. 5.31. (i).

By Fig. 5.31. (*i*), the resulting partial solution is (x 0 q_1 # 1q_2, x 0 q_1 #1q_2 01 #). Continning in this way, the final parital solution obtained is of the form (y, y1 # q_3 10), where y = # $q_1$01 # 1$q_2$1 # 10 q_1 # 1$q_2$0. Since q_3 is a final stage, use pairs in Groups I, III, IV to find a solution to the instance of MPCP.

The choice of pairs is

(1, 1), (#, #) , ($q_3$1, q_3) , (0, 0) , (1, 1), (# , #) ($q_3$0, q_3), (1, 1), (#, #), (q_3 1, q_3), (#, #) (q_3 ##, #).

Thus the shortest word that can be composed of strings from lists A and B starting with pair 1 is

q_1 01 # q_2 1 # 10 q_1 # 1 q_2 01 # q_3 101 # q_3 01 # q_3 1 # q_3

42. The problem 'whether an orbitrary CFG is ambiguous is undecidable.

Solution. Let $A = w_1, w_2, ..., w_n$; $B = x_1, x_2, ..., x_n$ be two lists of strings over a finite alphabet Σ. Let a_1, a_2 , ..., a_n be new symbols. Let

$$L_A = \{w_{i_1} w_{i_2} \ldots w_{i_m} a_{i_m} a_{i_{m-1}} \ldots a_{i_1} : m \geq 1\}$$

$$L_B = \{x_{i_1} x_{i_2} \ldots x_{i_m} a_{i_m} a_{i_{m-1}} \ldots a_{i_1} : m \geq 1\}$$

Let G be the CFG such that $G = (\{S_1, S_2, S_3\}, \Sigma \cup \{a_1, a_2, \ldots, a_n\} P, S)$ where contains the productions $S \to S_A$, $S \to S_B$

and
$$S_A \to w_i S_A a_i, S_A \to w_i a_i,$$

$$S_B \to x_i S_A a_i, S_B \to x_i a_i, \text{ for all } i, 1 \leq i \leq n.$$

If the instance (A, B) of PCP has a soluton, say $i_1, i_2, \ldots, i_m$, then

$$x_{i_1} x_{i_2} \ldots x_{i_m} a_{i_m} a_{i_{m-1}} \ldots a_{i_1} = w_{i_1} w_{i_2} \ldots w_{i_m} a_{i_m} a_{i_{m-1}} \ldots a_{i_1}$$

This string has a leftmost derivation beginning with $S \to S_A$ and another beginning with $S \to S_B$. Hence G is ambiguous.

Conversely, suppose G is ambiguous. since the a' dictate the productions used, it is easy to see that there is only one left most derviation from S_A as well as from S_B. Thus it must be that some word has left most derivations from both S_A and S_B. If this is a word $y\, a_{i_m} a_{i_{m-1}} \ldots a_{i_1}$, $y \in \Sigma^*$, then $i_1, i_2, \ldots i_m$ is a solution of PCP.

Thus G is ambiguous if and only if the instance (A, B) of PCP has a soluton. Thus if there it an algorithm for ambiguity problem for CFG's then there exists an algorithm for PCP. As PCP is undecidable, (no algorithm exists for PCP), the ambiguity problem for CFG's is undecidable.

43. For any arbitrary CFG G, whether

$$L(G) = \Sigma^*$$

is undecidable.

Solution. For a TM M, CFG G can be constructed with terminal alphabet Σ such that

$$L(G) = \Sigma^* \Leftrightarrow L(M) = \phi.$$

That is, by Lemma 5.7.19. There is a CFG G that generates the invalid computations of M. Thus if for arbitrary G, $L(G) = \Sigma^*$ were decidable, then $L(M) = \phi$ is decidable for arbitrary M. Hence a contradiction.

44. Let G_1 and G_2 be arbitrary CFG's and R be an arbitrary regular set. Then the following are undecidable problems.

(1) $L(G_1) = L(G_2)$

(2) $L(G_2) \subseteq L(G_1)$

(3) $L(G_1) = R$

(4) $R \subseteq L(G_1)$

Solution. Fix G_2 to be a grammar generating Σ^*, where Σ is the terminal alphabet of G_1. Then (1) and (2) are equivalent to $L(G_1) = \Sigma^*$.

Fix $R = \Sigma^*$, (3) and (4) are equivalent to $L(G_1) = \Sigma^*$. By previous problem each of these problems is undecidable.

45. It is undecidable for arbitrary CFG's G_1 and G_2 whether (*a*) $\overline{L(G_1)}$ is a CFL (*b*) $L(G_1) \cap L(G_2)$ is a CFL.

Solution.

(*a*) Given an arbitrary TM *M*, modify without changing, the set accepted, so that *M* makes atleast two moves on every input. Construct CFG *G* generating the invalid computations. $\overline{L(G)}$ is a CFL if and only if *M* accepts a finite set.

(*b*) Proceed as in (*a*), but construct CFG's G_1 and G_2 such that $L(G_1) \cap L(G_2)$ is the set of valid computations of *M*.

46. Prove that any language generated by an unrestricted grammar is recursively enumerable.

Solution. The grammar in effect defines a procedure for enumerating all strings in the language systematically. For example, we can list all *w* in *L* such that

$$S \to w,$$

that is *w* is derived in one step. Since the set of the productions of the grammar is finite, there will be a finite number of such strings. Next we list all *w* in *L* that can be derived in two steps.

$$S \to y \to w,$$

and so on. We can simulate these derivations on a Turing Machine and therefore, have an enumeration procedure for the language. Hence it is recursively enumerable.

EXERCISES

1. Which of the following properties of recursively enumerable sets are themselves recursively enumerable.

(*a*) *L* contains atleast two strings

(*b*) *L* is infinite

(*c*) $L = L^R$

2. Show that it is undecidable whether a TM halts on all inputs.

3. Show that for CFL L, it is undecidable whether $L = L^R$?

4. Show that the following properties of linear languages are undecidable. Here use the fact that every regular set is a linear language.

   (*a*) L is a regualr set

   (*b*) $\overline{L}$ is a CFL

   (*c*) L has no ambiguous linear CFG.

5. Show that for CFL L, it is undecidable whether $L = L^R$.

6. Show that PCP is decidable for words over a one-symbol alphabet.

7. Show that the problem *subset* can be reduced to the problem *Equivalent.*

8. Show that the special case of PCP in which the alphabet has only two symbols is still undecidable.

9. Is the decision problem : Given a CFG G, and a string x, is $L(G) = \{x\}$? Solvable or unsolvable ? Give reason for your answer.

10. For each decision problem given, determine whether it is solvable or unsolvable, and prove your answer

    (*a*) Given a TM M, does it accept the string $\wedge$ in an even number of moves?

    (*b*) Given a TM M and a string w, does M reject input w?

    (*c*) Given a TM M and a string w, does M loop forever on input w?

11. Is the following statement true or false ? If $L_1, L_2, \ldots$ are any recursively enumerable subset of Σ^*, then $\bigcup_{i=1}^{\infty} L_i$ is recursively enumerable. Give reasons for your answer.

12. Suppose $L_1, L_2, \ldots, L_k$ form a partition of Σ^*; in otherwords, their union is Σ^* and any two are disjoint. Show that if each L_i is recursively enumerable then each L_i is recursive.

13. Suppose $L \subseteq \Sigma^*$. Show that L is recursively enumerable if and only if there is a computable parital function form Σ^* to Σ^* that is defined precisely at the pionts of L.

14. Describe algorithms to enumerate these sets. (you do not need to discuss the mechanics of constructing Turing machine to execute algorithms.)

    (*a*) The set of all pairs (n, m) for which n and m are relatively prime positive integers.

(*b*) The set of all strings over {0, 1} that contain a non-null substring of the form *www*.

(*c*) $\{n \in N \,/$ for some positive integers x, y and z such that $x^n + y^n = z^n\}$

15. Prove that if $f : N \to N$ is computable and strictly increasing then the range of f is recursive.

16. Describe the language generated by the unrestricted grammar with the given productions

$S \to LA^*R$, $A \to a$, $L \to LI$, $IA \to AI$, $I^* \to A^*IJ$, $IR \to A^*R$, $JA \to AJ$, $J^* \to {}^*J$, $JR \to AR$, $LA \to EA$, $EA \to AE$, $E^* \to E$, $ER \to \varepsilon$.

17. Consider the unrestricted grammar with the following productions $S \to TD_1D_2$, $T \to ABCT/\varepsilon$, $AB \to BA$, $BA \to AB$, $CA \to AC$, $CB \to BC$, $CD_1 \to D_1C$, $CD_2 \to D_2a$, $BD_1 \to D_1b$, $A \to a$, $D_1 \to \varepsilon$, $D_2 \to \varepsilon$.

(*a*) Describe the language generated by this grammar

(*b*) Find a single production that could be substituted for $BD_1 \to D_1b$ so that the resulting language would be $\{xa^n \,/ n \geq 0,\ |x| = 2^n$, and $n_a(x) = n_b(x) = n\}$.

18. Find unrestricted grammars to generate each of the following languages

(*a*) $\{a^n x\, b^n \,/ n \geq 0,\ x \in \{a, b\}^*,\ |x| = n\}$

(*b*) $\{www \,/ w \in \{a, b)^*\}$

(*c*) $\{ww^R w / w \in \{a, b\}^*\}$

19. Find a context sensitive grammar generating the language

$\{ww/w \in \{a, b\}^+\}$

20. Prove that any subset of a countable set is countable.

21. Show that if S is uncountable and T is countable then $S - T$ is uncountable.

22. Show that, if a language is not recursively enumerable its complement cannot be recursive.

23. Prove that the complement of a context free language must be recursive.

24. Let L_1 be recursive and L_2 recursively enumerable. Show that $L_2 - L_1$ is necessarily recursively enumerable.

25. If L is recursive, is it necessarily true that L^+ is also recursive.

CHAPTER 6

Closure Properties of Regular Sets and Context Free Languages

In this chapter we will study some of the topics which are not covered in the previous chapter. We recall that any set represented by a regular expression is called a regular set. In chapter we established the equivalence between regular expressions and finite state automata. In this chapter we establish the relation between regular sets and FA. Enumeration properties of the CFL are also included.

6.1. CLOSURE PROPERTIES OF REGULAR SETS

If a class of languages is closed under a particular operation we call that fact a closure property of the class of languages.

In this section we discuss the closure properties of regular sets under (*a*) set union (*b*) concatenation (*c*) closure (*d*) complementation (*e*) intersection (*f*) transpose (*g*) substitution (*h*) homomorphism.

6.1.1. Theorem

The regular sets are closed under union, concatenation and Kleene closure.

Proof. Let L_1 and L_2 be regular sets such that

$$L_1 = T(A_1) \text{ and } ' = T(A_2) \text{ where}$$

$$A_1 = (Q_1, \Sigma, \delta_1, q_1, F_1) \text{ and } A_2 = (Q_2, \Sigma_2, \delta_2, q_2, F_2)$$

we shall assume that $Q_1 \cap Q_2 = \phi$.

(i) **Union.** Let $A = (Q, \Sigma, \delta, q_0, F)$ where

$$Q = Q_1 \cup Q_2 \cup \{q_0\},\ q_0 \notin Q_1 \cup Q_2$$

is the start state, $\Sigma = \Sigma_1 \cup \Sigma_2$, $F = F_1 \cup F_2$ and δ is defined as follows:

$$\delta(q_0, \lambda) = \{q_1, q_2\}$$

If $q \in \delta_1(p, a)$ then $q \in \delta(p, a)$

If $q \in \delta_2(p, a)$ then $q \in \delta(p, a)$

It is clear that $T(A) = L_1 \cup L_2$.

(ii) **Concatenation :** Let $A = (Q, \Sigma, \delta, q_0, F)$ where

$$Q = Q_1 \cup Q_2, \Sigma = \Sigma_1 \cup \Sigma_2, q_0 = q_1, F = F_2 \text{ and}$$

δ is defined as follows:

$$\delta(q, a) = \{\delta_1 (q, a) \text{ for each } q \text{ in } Q_1 - F_1,$$

$$\delta(q, a) = \{\delta_1 (q, a)\ \delta_2(q_2, a)\} \text{ for each } q \text{ in } F_1,$$

and $\delta(q, a) = \{\delta_2(q, a) \text{ for each } q \text{ in } k_2.$

A word w is in $L_1\ L_2$ iff $w = w_1\ w_2$ where $w_1 \in L_1$ and $w_2 \in L_2$. This is equivalent to $\delta_1(q_1, w_1)$ being in F_1 and $\delta_2\ (q_2, w_2)$ being in F_2 which is equivalent to $w_1\ w_2$ being in $T(A)$. Thus $L_1\ L_2 = T(A)$.

(*iii*) **Star:** Let $L = T(A)$ be a regular set where

$$A = \{Q, \Sigma, \delta, q_0, F).$$

Let, $B = (Q, \Sigma, \delta', q_0, F)$

where δ' is defined as follows:

$$\delta'\ (q, a) = \{\delta(q, a)\} \text{ if } q \text{ is in } K - F \text{ and}$$

$$\delta'\ (q, a) = \{\delta(q, a), \delta(q_0, a)\} \text{ if } q \text{ is in } F$$

It is easy to see that $L^* = T(B)$. If λ is in L, then it is accepted by B. Otherwise, we can modify B to accept λ.

6.1.2. Theorem

The class of regular sets is closed under complementation. That is if X is a regular set and $X \subseteq \Sigma^*$, then $\Sigma^* - L$ is a regular set.

Proof. Let X be $X(M)$ for DFA $M = (Q, \Sigma_1, \delta, q_0, F)$ and let $X \subseteq \Sigma^*$. First we assume $\Sigma_1 = \Sigma$, for if there are symbols in Σ_1 not in Σ, we may delete all transitions of M on symbols not in Σ. The fact that $X \subseteq \Sigma^*$ assumes us that we shall not thereby change the language of M. If there are symbols in Σ not in Σ_1 then none of these symbols appear in words of X. We may therefore introduce a dead state d into M with $(d, a) = d$ for all a in Σ and $\delta(q, a) = d$ for all q in Q and a in $\Sigma - \Sigma_1$. Now to accept $\Sigma^* - X$, complement the final states of M. That is, let $M' = (Q, \Sigma, \delta, q_0, Q - F)$.

Then M' accepts a word w if and only if $\delta(q_0, w)$ is in $Q - F$, that is, w is in $\Sigma^* - X$. Note that it is essential to the proof that M is deterministic and without λ moves.

6.1.3. Theorem

If X and Y are regular sets over Σ, then $X \cap Y$ is also regular over Σ.

Proof. $X \cap Y = \overline{\overline{X} \cup \overline{Y}}$ by Demorgon's law where—denotes complementation with respect to an alphabet including the alphabets of X and Y. Closure under intersection then follows from closure under union and complementation.

6.1.4. Theorem

If L is regular then L^R is also regular.

Proof. As L is regular, we can construct a FA

$$M = (Q, \Sigma, \delta, q_0, F) \text{ such that } T(M) = L.$$

We can construct a transition system (or transition diagram or transistion graph) M' by starting with the state diagram of M, and reversing the direction of the directed edges. The set of initial states of M' is defined as the set F, and q_0 defined as the (only) final state of M' is $M' = (Q, \Sigma, \delta', F, \{q_0\})$.

If $w \in T(M)$, we have a path from q_0, to some final state in F with path value w. By reversing the edges, we get a pair in M' from some final state in F to q_0. Its path value is w^R. So $w^R \in T(M')$. In a similar way, we can see that if $w_1 \in T(M')$, then $w_1\ R \in T\ (M)$. Thus from the state diagram it is easy to see that $T(M') = T(M)R$. We can prove that $w \in T(M)$ iff $w^R \in T(M')$ by induction on $|\ w\ |$. So $T(M)^R = T(M')$. Since $T(M')$ is regular it follows that $T(M)^R$ is regular.

6.1.5. Theorem

The class of regular sets is closed under substitution.

Proof. Let $R \subseteq \Sigma^*$ be a regular set and for each a in Σ let $Ra \subseteq \Delta^*$ be a regular set. Let $f: \Sigma \to \Delta^*$ be the substitution defined by $f(a) = Ra$. Select regular expressions denoting R and each Ra. Replace each occurrence of the symbol a in the regular expression for R by the regular expression for Ra. To prove that the resulting regular expression denotes $f(R)$, observe that the substitution of a union, product or closure is the union, product, or closure of the substitution.

[Thus for example, $f(L_1 \cup L_2) = f(L_1) \cup f(L_2)$].

A simple induction on the number of operators in the regular expression completes the proof.

6.1.6. Example

Let $f(0) = a$ and $f(1) = b^*$. That is $f(0)$ is the language $\{a\}$ and $f(1)$ is the language of all strings of b's. Then $f(01\ 0)$ is the regular set ab^*a. If L is the language $0^*\ (0 + 1)\ 1^*$, then $f(L)$ is $a^*\ (a + b^*)\ (b^*)^* = a^*\ b^*$.

6.1.7. Theorem

The class of regular sets is closed under homomorphisms and inverse homomorphisms.

Proof. Closure under homomorphisms follows immediately from closure under substitution, since every homomorphism is a substitution in which $h(a)$ has one member.

To show closure under inverse homomorphism, let $M = (Q, \Sigma, \delta, q_0, F)$ be a DFA accepting L, and let h be a homomorphism from Δ to Σ^*. We construct a DFA M' that accepts $h(L)$ by reading symbol a in Δ and simulating M on $h(a)$. Formally, let $M' = (Q, \Delta, \delta', q_0, F)$ and define $\delta'(q, a)$ for q in Q and a in Δ to be $\delta(q, h(a))$. Note that $h(a)$ may be a long string or λ but δ is defined on all strings by extension. It is easy to show by induction on $| x |$ that $\delta'(q_0, x) = \delta(q_0, h(x))$. Therefore M' accepts x if and only if M accepts $h(x)$. That is $L(M') = h^{-1}\ (L(M))$.

6.1.8. Definition

Let L_1 and L_2 be two languages. The quotient of L_1 and L_2 denoted by L_1/L_2 is defined as $L_1/L_2 = \{x/$ there exists y in L_2 such that xy is in $L_1\}$.

6.1.9. Theorem

The class of regular sets is closed under quotient with arbitrary sets.

Proof. Let $M = (Q, \Sigma, \delta, q_0, F)$ be a finite automation accepting some regular set R, and let L be an arbitrary language. The quotient R/L is accepted by a finite automation $M' = (Q, \Sigma, \delta, q_0, F')$ which behaves like M except that the final states of M' are all states q of M such that there axists y in L for which $\delta(q, y)$ is in F. Then $\delta(q_0, x)$ is in F' if and only if there exists y such that $\delta(q_0, xy)$ is in F. Thus M' accepts R/L.

6.2. REGULAR, RIGHT LINEAR AND LEFT LINEAR GRAMMARS

6.2.1. Definition

A Grammar $G = (N, T, S, P)$ is said to be *right-linear* if all productions are of the form

$$A \to xB,$$

$$A \to x,$$

where $A, B \in N$ and $x \in T^*$

In otherwords, in any productions, the left hand string is always a single nonterminal and the right hand string is either a terminal or terminal follows by a nonterminal.

A grammar is said to be *left-linear* if all products are of the form

$$A \to Bx,$$

or $$A \to x$$

A *regular grammar* is one that is either right-linear or left linear.

6.2.2. Problem

Construct a right linear grammar for the language $L(G) = \{a^n ba^m / n, m \geq 1\}$.

Solution. Construct $G = (N, T, S, P)$ where

$N = \{S, A, B, C\}$, $T = \{a, b\}$ and

$P = \{S \to aS, S \to aB, B \to bC, C \to aC, C \to a\}$

For $a^2 ba^3$: $S \Rightarrow a\underline{S} \Rightarrow aa\underline{B} \Rightarrow aabC$

$\Rightarrow aaba\underline{C} \Rightarrow aabaa\underline{C} \Rightarrow aabaaa = a^2\ b\ a^3$

Clearly this grammar $G = (N, T, S, P)$ is a regular grammar and the language

$L(G) = \{a^n\ b\ a^m / \ n, m \geq 1\}$ is a regular language.

6.3. EQUIVALENCE BETWEEN REGULAR LINEAR GRAMMAR AND FINITE AUTOMATA

6.3.1. Theorem

(Construction of a regular grammar generating $T(M)$ for a given DFA M). If M is a finite automata, then a regular grammar G can be constructed such that $L(G) = T(M)$.

Proof. We take M to be a NFA. Let $M = (Q, \Sigma, \delta, q_0, F)$. Define a regular grammar

$G = (N, T, S, P)$ where

$N = Q$, $T = \Sigma$, $S = q_0$ and

$P = \{A \to aB / \ \delta(A, a) = B\} \cap \{A \to a / \delta(A, a) = B$, where $B \in F\}$.

(We add the rule $S \to \varepsilon$ if $q_0 \in F$). We can easily see that the set accepted by M is equal to $L(G)$.

6.3.2. Theorem

(Construction of a Finite automata for a regular grammar). Every regular set is accepted by a finite state automata.

Proof. Let $L(G)$ be a regular language generated by a regular grammar $G = (N, T, S, P)$. We shall define a finite state automata M to accept $L(G)$. Without loss of generality, assume that there is no rule of the form $A \to B$, where $A, B \in N$ in G.

Let $M = (Q, \Sigma, \delta, q_0, F)$ where Q is a finite non-empty set of states and $F \subseteq Q$ is the set of final states.

Define $Q = N \cup \{q\}, q \notin N, q_0 = S,$

$F = \{q\} \cup \{A/A \in N$ and $A \to \lambda$ is in $P\}$ and δ as follows :

If $A \to aB$ is a rule in P, $\delta(A, a)$ contains B.

If $A \to a$ is a rule in P, $\delta(A, a)$ contains q.

We can show that corresponding to a derviation of a word w in G, there is a sequence of moves of M which accepts w. Conversely, corresponding to a sequence of moves of M which accepts w, there is a derivation of w in G. Hence $L(G) = T(M)$ (Here M is a NFA).

6.4. INTERCONVERSION

The construction for conversion of non-deterministic systems to deterministic systems we are going to give is similar to the construction of a DFA equivalent to a NFA and involves three steps.

Step 1. Convert the given transition system into state transition table where each state corresponds to a row and each input symbol corresponds to a column.

Step 2. Construct the successor table which lists subsets of states reachable from the set of initial states.

Step 3. The transition graph given by the successor table is the required deterministic system. The final states contain some final state of NDFA. If possible reduce the number of states.

Remark. We note that the above construction is similar to one for automata except for the initial step. In the earlier method for automata, we started with $[q_0]$. Here we start with the set of all initial states. The other steps are similar.

6.5. ENUMERATING PROPERTIES OF CFL

Chapter 3 established the relation between the language generated by context free grammars and the languages accepted by pushdown automata. These characterizations enrich our understanding of the context free languages, since they provide two different methods for comprehending context freeness. The context free language can in principle be described in either way ; the representation are inter-convertible. In this section we will see some of the properties of context-free languages. Three kinds of properties are considered.

1. Closure properties.
2. Periodicity properties.
3. Algorithmic properties.

1. Closure Properties.

These properties are included in Chapter 2. Closure properties can be used to prove that certain language are not context free.

2. Periodicity properties.

Infinite context free languages display periodicity of a some what subtler form than do regular languages. We have already seen that derivations can be represented in the form a derivation tree or parse tree. A path in a parse tree is a sequence of distinct nodes, each connected to the previous one by a line segment; the first node is the root and the last node is a leaf. The length of a path is the number of line segments, which is one less than the number of nodes. The height of a parse tree is the length of the longest path.

In this section we give some periodicity properties of CFL.

6.5.1. Theorem

(Pumping lemma for CFL). See 3.4.2.

6.5.2. Theorem

The context free languages are not closed under intersection or complementation.

Proof. Clearly $\{a^n\ b^n\ c^m : m, n \geq 0\}$ and $\{a^m\ b^n\ c^n : m, n \geq 0\}$ are context free. The intersection of these two CFL's is the language $\{a^n\ b^n\ c^n : n \geq 0\}$ which is not context free. [See 3.4.3 problem 1]. And if the context free languages were closed under complementation, they would be closed under intersection, since

$$L_1 \cap L_2 = \Sigma^* - ((\Sigma^* - L_1) \cup (\Sigma^* - L_2)).$$

6.5.3. Remark

Unfortunately, there are very simple non-context free languages which cannot be shown not to be context free by a direct application of the pumping Lemma. One example is

$\{a^m b^n$: either $m > n$ or m is a prime number and $n \geq m\}$.

The difficulty is that the pumping lemma does not restrict where within a string the pumping is to be done. There are various ways of tightening the pumping theorem, but we instead establish a related result of some what different type. Let $\Sigma = \{a_1, ..., a_n\}$ be an alphabet. Define $\psi_\Sigma : \Sigma^* \to N^n$ by $\psi_\Sigma(w) = (m_1, ..., m_n)$, where for $i = 1, ..., n$, m_i is the number of occourences of a_i in w. Thus if $\Sigma = \{a_1, a_2\}$ then $\psi_\Sigma(a_1\ a_2\ a_2\ a_1\ a_2) = (2, 3)$ (where Σ is fixed, we omit the subscript on ψ). We shall show that only certain sets of n-tuples of natural numbers can arise as $\psi[L]$, where L is a context-free language.

Let B and P be finite subsets of N^n. Then define $L(B, P) = \{b + p_1 + p_2 + ... + p_k ; b \in B, k \geq 0, p_1, ..., p_k \in P\}$.

Here addition of n-tuples is done componentwise :

$$(a_1, ..., a_n) + (b_1, ..., b_n) = (a_1 + b_1, ..., a_n + b_n).$$

For example , if $n = 2$

$$B = \{(0, 0)\} \text{ and } P = \{(0, 1), (1, 1)\} \text{ then}$$

$$L(B, P) = \{(m, n) : n \geq m\}.$$

Any set $L(B, P)$, where B and P are finite subsets of N^n is said to be linear. A semi-linear set is a finite union of linear sets.

Now we will state a theorem without proof.

6.5.4. Theorem(Parikh's Theorem)

If L is context free, then $\psi(L)$ is semi-linear.

6.5.5. Theorem

Every context free language over a one symbol alphabet is regular.

Proof. If $L \subseteq \{a\}^*$ is context free, then

$\psi\{L\} = \{n : a^n \in L\}$ is semi-linear. But if S is a semi-linear subset of N, then $\{a^n : n \in S\}$ is regular. Since for $L \subseteq \{a\}^*$,

$L = \{a^n : n \in \psi[L]\}$, it follows that $L \subseteq \{a\}^*$ is regular if it is context free.

3. Algorithmic properties

Although we have studied context-free languages in some detail, there are a number of simple natural questions we have not addressed. When confronted with a context-free grammar and a string, how can one tell if the string is in the language generated by that grammar ? Convert the grammar into an equivalent pushdown automaton, one might argue, and then simply run the automaton on the given input. Unfornuately, this approach does not work atleast directly, a pushdown automaton may compute for a long time without reading any input, and how are we to know when we have let it run long enough to be sure it will not eventually accept ? Instead we can approach this problem through an analysis of parse trees.

Problem

1. Give an example to prove that the class of regular sets is closed under homomorphism and inverse homomorphism.

Solution. Let $h(0) = aa$ and $h(1) = aba$. Then

$h(010) = aaabaaa$. If L_1 is $(01)^*$, then $h(L_1)$ is $(aaaba)^*$. Let $L_2 = (ab + ba)^*$ a. Then $h^{-1}(L_2)$. Consists only of the string 1. Here we observe that a string in L_2 that begins with b cannot be $h(x)$ for any string in L_2 that begins with b cannot be $h(x)$ for any string x of 0's and 1's, since $h(0)$ and $h(1)$ each begin with an a. Thus if $h^{-1}(w)$ is non-empty and w is in L_2, then w begins with a . Now either $w = a$, in which case $h^{-1}(w)$ is empty, or w is abw' for some w' in $(ab + ba)^*$ a. We conclude that every word in $h^{-1}(w)$ begins with a 1, and since $h(1) = aba$, w' must begin with a. If $w' = a$, we have $w = aba$ and $h^{-1}(w) = \{1\}$. However, if $w' \neq a$, then $w' = abw''$ and hence $w = ababw^{2''}$. But no string x in $(0 + 1)^*$ has $h(x)$ beginning $abab$. Consequently we conclude that $h^{-1}(w)$ is empty in this case. Thus the only string in L_2 which has an inverse image under h is aba, and therefore $h^{-1}(L_2) = \{1\}$.

Observe that $h(h^{-1}L_2) = \{aba\} \neq L_2$. One the other hand, it is easily shown that $h(h^{-1}(L)) \subseteq L$ and $h^{-1}(h(L)) \subseteq L$ for any language L.

2. Prove that $\{a^n\ ba^n/n \geq 1\}$ is not regular by using closure properties of regular sets.

Solution. We know that $(0^n\ 1^n/n \geq 1\}$ is not regular.

If we had an FA M accepting $\{a^n\ ba^n/n \geq 1\}$ we could accept $\{0^n\ 1^n/n \geq 1\}$ by simulating M on input a for each 0. When the first 1 is seen, simulate M on ba and thereafter simulate M on a for each 1 seen. However to be rigourous it is necessary to formally prove that $\{a^n\ b\ a^n/\ n \geq 1\}$ is not regular. This is done by showing that $\{a^n\ ba^n\ /\ n \geq 1\}$ can be converted to $\{0^n\ 1^n/n \geq 1\}$ by use of operations that preserve regularity. Thus $\{a^n\ ba^n\ /\ n \geq 1\}$ cannot be regular.

$$h_1(a) = a, h_2(c) = 0$$

$$h_1(b) = ba, h_2(b) = 1$$

$$h_1(c) = a, h_2(c) = 1$$

Then $h_2(h_1^{-1}(\{a^n ba^n / n \geq 1\}) \cap a^* b^* c^*) = \{0^n 1^n / n \geq 1\}$ ...(i)

That is, $h_1^{-1}(\{a^n ba^n / n \geq 1\})$ consists of all strings in $(a + c)^* b (a + c)^*$ such that the number of symbols preceeding the b is one greater than the number of symbols following the b. Thus

$h_1^{-1}(\{a^n ba^n / n \geq 1\} \cap a^* bc^* = \{a^n bc^{n-1} / n \geq 1\}$

(1)then follows immediately by applying homomorphism h_2.

If $\{a^n ba^n / n \geq 1\}$ were regular, then since hormomorphisms, inverse homomorphism and intersection with a regular set all preserve the property of being regular, it would follow that $\{0^n 1^n / n \geq 1\}$ is regular, it would follow that $\{0^n 1^n / n \geq 1\}$ is regular, a contradiction.

3. Give an example to prove that the class of regular sets in closed under quotient with arbitrary sets.

Solution. Let L be 0* 10* and L_2 be 10*1. Then L_1/L_2 is empty. Since every y in L_2 has two ones and every string xy which is in L_1 can have only one 1, there is no x such that xy is in L_1 and y is in L_2.

Let L_3 be 0*1. Then L_1/L_3 is 0*, since for any x in 0* we may choose y = 1. Clearly xy is in L_1 = 0* 10* and y is in L_3 = 0* 1. Since words in L_1 and L_3 each have one 1, it is not possible that words not in 0* are in L_1/L_3. As another example, L_2/L_3 = 10*, since for each x in 10* we may again choose y = 1 from L_3 and xy will be in L_2 = 10*1. If xy is in L_2 and y is in L_3 then evidently, x is in 10*.

4. Consider the FA M given by the following figure. What is $T(M)$? Show that $T(M)^R$ is regular.

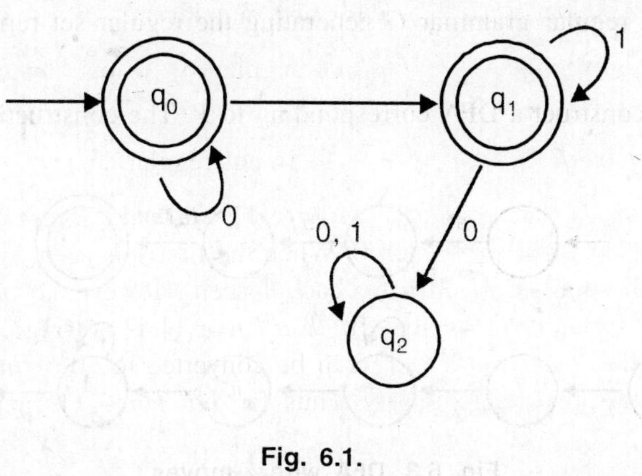

Fig. 6.1.

Solution. As elements of $T(M)$ are given by path values of paths from q_0 to itself or from q_0 to q_1.

As arrows do not come into q_0, paths from q_0 to itself are self loops repeated any number of items. The corresponding path values are 0^i, $i \geq 1$. As no arrow comes from q_2 to q_0 or q_1, the paths from q_0 to q_1 are of the form $q_0 \ldots \rightarrow q_0$ $q_1 \ldots \rightarrow q_1$. The corresponding path values are $0^i 1^i$, where $i \geq 0$ and $j \geq 1$. As the intial state q_0 is also a final state, $\lambda \in T(M)$.

Thus $T(M)$ is $\{0^i 1^j / i, j \geq 0\}$

Hence $\qquad T(M)^R = \{1^j 0^i / i, j \geq 0\}$

The transition system M' is constructed as follows:

(*i*) The initial states of M' are q_0 and q_1.
(*ii*) The (only) final state on M' is q_0.
(*iii*) The direction of the directed edges is reversed M' is given in Fig. 6.2.

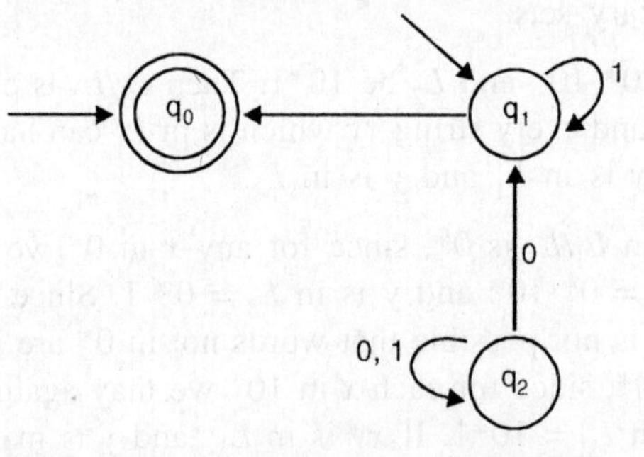

Fig. 6.2.

From (*i*) – (*iii*) it follows that $T(M') = T(M)^R$.

Hence $T(M)^R$ is regular.

5. Construct a regular grammar G generating the regular set represented by $P = a^*b\ (a + b)^*$.

Solution. We construct a DFA corresponding to P. The construction is given in Fig. 6.3.

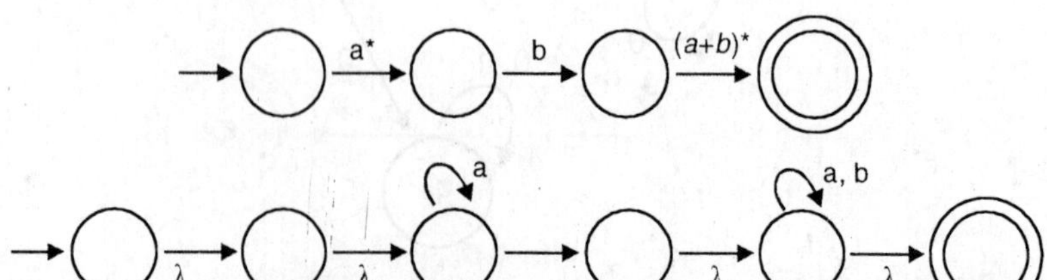

Fig. 6.3. DFA with λ-moves.

$$h_1(b) = ba, h_2(b) = 1$$

$$h_1(c) = a, h_2(c) = 1$$

Then $h_2(h_1^{-1}(\{a^n\ ba^n / n \geq 1\}) \cap a^*\ b^*\ c^*) = \{0^n\ 1^n\ /\ n \geq 1\}$ ...(*i*)

That is, $h_1^{-1}(\{a^n\ ba^n\ /\ n \geq 1\})$ consists of all strings in $(a + c)^*\ b\ (a + c)^*$ such that the number of symbols preceeding the b is one greater than the number of symbols following the b. Thus

$$h_1^{-1}(\{a^n\ ba^n\ /\ n \geq 1\} \cap a^*\ bc^* = \{a^n\ bc^{n-1}\ /\ n \geq 1\}$$

(1)then follows immediately by applying homomorphism h_2.

If $\{a^n\ ba^n/n \geq 1\}$ were regular, then since hormomorphisms, inverse homomorphism and intersection with a regular set all preserve the property of being regular, it would follow that $\{0^n\ 1^n\ /\ n \geq 1\}$ is regular, it would follow that $\{0^n\ 1^n\ /\ n \geq 1\}$ is regular, a contradiction.

3. Give an example to prove that the class of regular sets in closed under quotient with arbitrary sets.

Solution. Let L be $0^*\ 10^*$ and L_2 be 10^*1. Then L_1/L_2 is empty. Since every y in L_2 has two ones and every string xy which is in L_1 can have only one 1, there is no x such that xy is in L_1 and y is in L_2.

Let L_3 be 0^*1. Then L_1/L_3 is 0^*, since for any x in 0^* we may choose y = 1. Clearly xy is in $L_1 = 0^*\ 10^*$ and y is in $L_3 = 0^*\ 1$. Since words in L_1 and L_3 each have one 1, it is not possible that words not in 0^* are in L_1/L_3. As another example, $L_2/L_3 = 10^*$, since for each x in 10^* we may again choose y = 1 from L_3 and xy will be in $L_2 = 10^*1$. If xy is in L_2 and y is in L_3 then evidently, x is in 10^*.

4. Consider the FA M given by the following figure. What is $T(M)$? Show that $T(M)^R$ is regular.

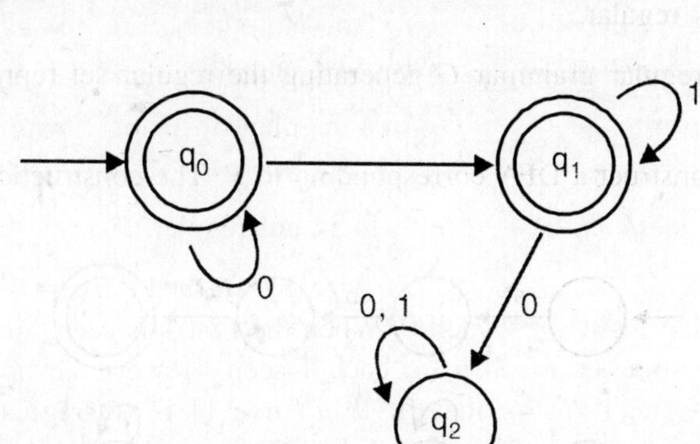

Fig. 6.1.

Solution. As elements of $T(M)$ are given by path values of paths from q_0 to itself or from q_0 to q_1.

As arrows do not come into q_0, paths from q_0 to itself are self loops repeated any number of items. The corresponding path values are 0^i, $i \geq 1$. As no arrow comes from q_2 to q_0 or q_1, the paths from q_0 to q_1 are of the form $q_0 \ldots \rightarrow q_0$ $q_1 \ldots \rightarrow q_1$. The corresponding path values are $0^i 1^i$, where $i \geq 0$ and $j \geq 1$. As the intial state q_0 is also a final state, $\lambda \in T(M)$.

Thus $T(M)$ is $\{0^i\ 1^j\ /\ i, j \geq 0\}$

Hence $\qquad T(M)^R = \{1^j\ 0^i\ /\ i, j \geq 0\}$

The transition system M' is constructed as follows:

(*i*) The initial states of M' are q_0 and q_1.
(*ii*) The (only) final state on M' is q_0.
(*iii*) The direction of the directed edges is reversed M' is given in Fig. 6.2.

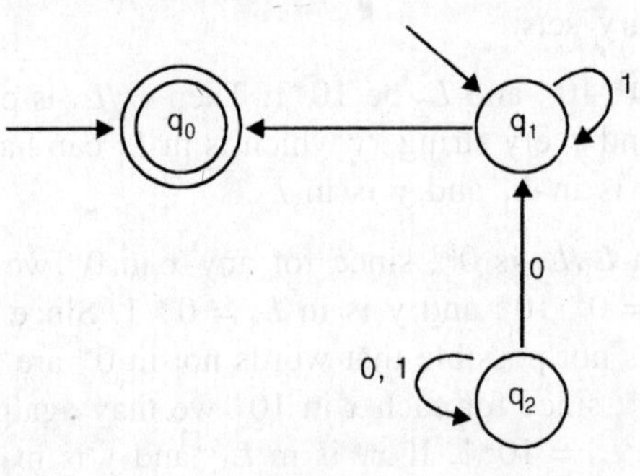

Fig. 6.2.

From (*i*) – (*iii*) it follows that $T(M') = T(M)^R$.

Hence $T(M)^R$ is regular.

5. Construct a regular grammar G generating the regular set represented by $P = a^*b\ (a + b)^*$.

Solution. We construct a DFA corresponding to P. The construction is given in Fig. 6.3.

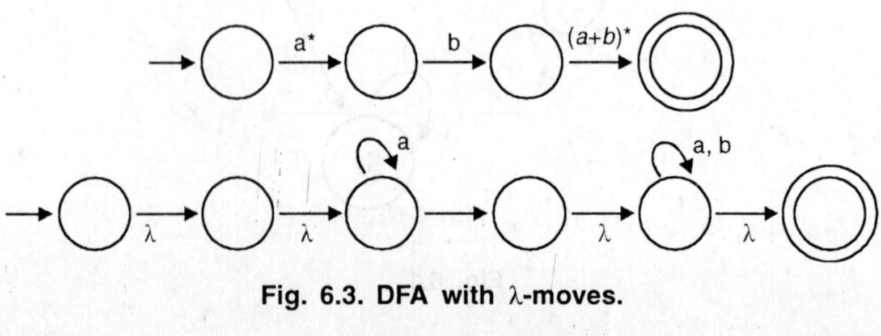

Fig. 6.3. DFA with λ-moves.

After eliminating λ-moves, we get the DFA straightaway as shown in Fig. 6.4.

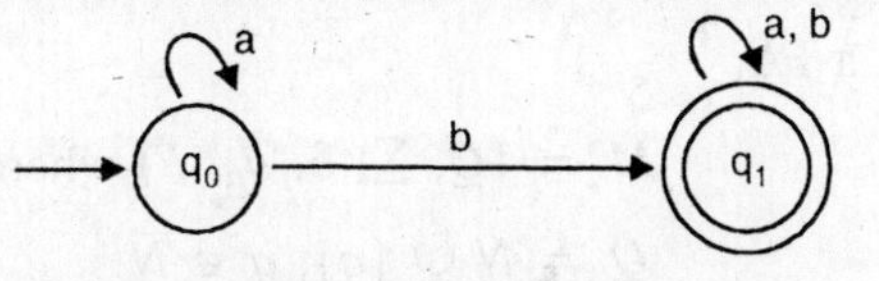

Fig. 6.4. DFA without λ-moves.

Lete $G = (\{X_0, X_1\}, \{a, b\}, P, X_0)$, where P is given by $X_0 \rightarrow aX_0$, $X_0 \rightarrow bX_1$, $X_0 \rightarrow b$, $X_1 \rightarrow bX_1$, $X_1 \rightarrow bX_1$, $X_1 \rightarrow a$, $X_1 \rightarrow b$.

G is the required regular grammar.

6. For the grammar $G = (\{S, A\}, \{a, b\}, P, S)$ where P consists of $S \rightarrow aB$, $B \rightarrow bB$, $B \rightarrow a$, $B \rightarrow bS$. Construct a transition system M accepting $L(G)$.

Solution. Let $M = (\{q_0, q_1, q_f\}, \{a, b\}, \delta, q_0 \{q_f\})$,

where q_0 and q_1 correspond to S and A, respectively and q_f is the new (final) state introduced $S \rightarrow aB$ induces a transition from q_0 to q_1 with label a. Similarly, $B \rightarrow bB$ and $B \rightarrow bS$ induce transitions from q_1 to q_1 with label b and from q_1 to q_0 with label b, respectively. $B \rightarrow a$ induces a transition from q_1 to q_f with label a. M is given in Fig. 6.5.

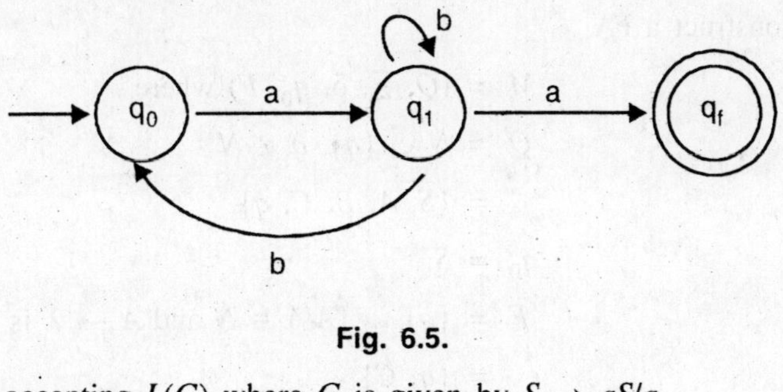

Fig. 6.5.

7. Find M accepting $L(G)$ where G is given by $S \rightarrow aS/a$.

Solution. Let q_0 correspond to S and q_f which is the new (final) state. M is given in Fig. 6.6.

Symbolically $$M = (\{q_0, q_f\}, \{a\}, \delta, q_0, \{q_f\}).$$

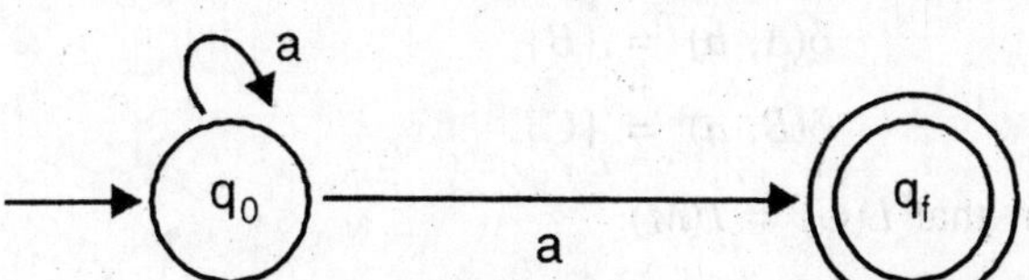

Fig. 6.6.

8. Construct a finite automaton recognizing $L(G)$, where G is the grammar $S \to aS/bA/b$ and $A \to aA/bS/a$.

Solution. Construct a FA,

$$M = \{Q, \Sigma, \delta, q_0, F) \text{ where}$$

$$Q = N \cup \{q\}, q \notin N$$

$$= \{S, A, q\}, q_0 = S$$

$$F = \{q\} \cup \{A/A \in N \text{ and } A \to \lambda \text{ is in } P\}$$

$$= \{q\} \cup \phi = \{q\}$$

and δ is defined as follows:

$$\delta(S, a) = \{S\}$$

$$\delta(S, b) = \{A, q\}$$

$$\delta(A, a\} = \{A, q\}$$

$$\delta\{A, b\} = \{S\}.$$

It is easily seen that $L(G) = T(M)$.

9. Construct a deterministic finite automaton equivalent to the grammar.

$$S \to aS/bS/aA,\ A \to bB,\ B \to aC,\ C \to \lambda.$$

Solution. Construct a FA

$$M = (Q, \Sigma, \delta, q_0, F) \text{ where}$$

$$Q = N \cup \{q\}, q \notin N$$

$$= \{S, A, B, C, q\}$$

$$q_0 = S.$$

$$F = \{q\} \cup \{A/A \in N \text{ and } A \to \lambda \text{ is in } P\}$$

$$= \{q, C\}$$

and δ is defined as follows:

$$\delta(S, a) = \{S, A\}$$

$$\delta(S, b) = \{S\}$$

$$\delta(A, b) = \{B\}$$

$$\delta(B, a) = \{C\}.$$

It is easily seen that $L(G) = T(M)$.

10. Find a regular grammar accepting the set recognized by the FA M represented by the diagram.

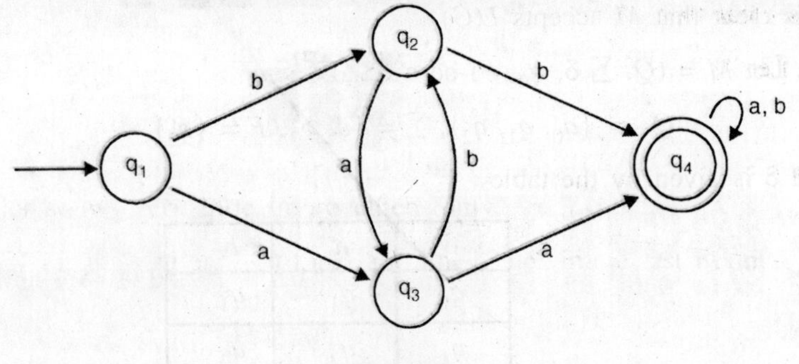

Fig. 6.7.

Solution. Construct a regular grammar

$G = (N, T, S, P)$ where

$N = Q = \{q_1, q_2, q_3, q_4\}$

$T = \Sigma = \{a, b\}$

$S = q_1$ and

$P = \{q_1 \to aq_3,\ q_1 \to bq_2,\ q_2 \to aq_3,$
$q_2 \to bq_4,\ q_3 \to aq_4,\ q_3 \to bq_2,$
$q_4 \to aq_4,\ q_4 \to bq_4,\ q_2 \to b,$
$q_3 \to a,\ q_4 \to a,\ q_4 \to b\}.$

It is easily that $L(G) = T(M)$.

11. Construct a FA recognizing $L(G)$, where G is the regular grammar given by $S \to aA$, $A \to bS$, $A \to b$.

Solution. The given regular grammar is

$G = (N, T, S, P)$ where $N = \{S, A\}$, $T = \{a, b\}$
and P is given by $S \to aA$, $A \to bS$, $A \to b$.

Construct a FA, $M = (Q, \Sigma, \delta, q_0, F)$ where

$Q = N \cup \{q\} = \{S, A, q\}$

$q_0 = S$

$F = \{q\} \cup \{A/A \in N \text{ and } A \to \lambda \text{ is in } p\}$

$= \{q\}$

and δ is given by

$\delta\{q_0, a\} = A,\ \delta(A, a) = \phi,\ \delta(q, a) = \phi,$

$\delta(q_0, b) = \phi,\ \delta(A, b) = \{q_0, q_1\},\ \delta\{q, b\} = \phi.$

It is clear that M accepts $L(G)$.

12. Let $M = (Q, \Sigma\ \delta, q_0, F)$ be a FSA where

$$Q = \{q_0, q_1, q_2\}, \Sigma = \{a, b\}, F = \{q_2\}$$

and δ is given by the table

δ	a	b
q_0	q_1	q_1
q_1	q_2	q_2
q_2	q_0	q_0

Solution. Construct $G = (N, T, S, P)$ where

$$N = \{q_0, q_1, q_2\}, T = \{a, b\}, S = q_0 \text{ and } P$$

consists of the rules:

$q_0 \to aq_1, q_1 \to aq_2, q_2 \to aq_0, q_0 \to bq_1$

$q_1 \to bq_2, q_2 \to bq_0, q_1 \to a, q_1 \to b.$

It is clear that $L(G)$ equals the set accepted by M.

13. *P.T.* the language.

$$L = \{ww/w \text{ is in } (a + b)^*\} \text{ is not context free.}$$

Solution. $L = \{ww/w$ is in $(a + b)^*\}$. That is L consists of all words whose first and last halves are the same. Suppose L were context free. Then $L_1 = L \cap a^+ b^+ a^+ b^+$ would also be a CFL (Since the inter-section of a regular set and a CFL is a CFL). But $L_1 = \{a^i b^i a^i b^j / i \geq 1\ j \geq 1\}$. But L_1 is not context free [See chapter 3, exercise 6(*d*)]. This is a contradiction. Hence L is a CFL.

14. Construct a left linear grammar for the language $L(G) = \{a^n ba^m / n \geq 1\}$.

Solution. Construct $G = (N, T, S, P)$ where

$$N = \{S, A, B, C\}, T = \{a, b\} \text{ and}$$

$$P = \{S \to Sa, S \to Ba, B \to Cb, C \to Ca, C \to a\}$$

For a^2ba^3 $S \Rightarrow Sa \Rightarrow Saa \Rightarrow Baaa \Rightarrow Cbaaa \Rightarrow Cabaaa \Rightarrow aabaaa = a^2ba^3$

Clearly the grammar G is a regular grammar and the language $L(G) = \{a^n ba^m / n, m \geq 1\}$ is a regular language.

EXERCISES

1. Is the class of regular sets closed under infinite union ?
2. What is the relationship between the class of regular sets and the least class of languages closed under union, intersection, and complement containing all finite sets.
3. Give a finite automaton construction to prove that the class of regular sets is closed under substitution.
4. It is class of regular sets closed under inverse sub-stitution ?
5. Let h be the homomorphism $h(a) = 01$, $h(b) = 0$.
   (*a*) Find $h^{-1}(L_1)$, where $L_1 = (10 + 1)^*$.
   (*b*) Find $h(L_2)$, where $L_2 = (a + b)^*$.
   (c) Find $h^{-1}(L_3)$, where L_3 is the set of all string of 0's and 1's with an equal number of 0's and 1's.
6. Construct a FA equivalent to the regular grammar given by
   (*i*) $S \to bS$, $S \to aA$, $A \to bA$, $A \to b$
   (*ii*) $S \to bS$, $S \to aA$, $A \to aS$, $A \to bA$, $A \to a$, $S \to b$.
7. Suppose that L is context-free and R is regular. Is $L - R$ necessarily context-free ? What about $R - L$? Justify your answers.
8. Show that the class of deterministic context free language is not closed under homomorphism.
9. Construct a regular grammar equivalent to the following FA.

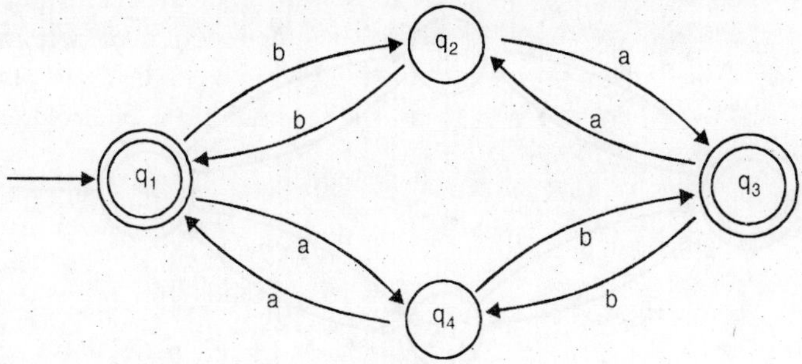

Fig. 6.8.